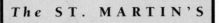
W9-BVF-673

The ST. MARTIN'S

HANDBOOK

for CANADIANS

The ST. MARTIN'S

HANDBOOK

for CANADIANS

Andrea Lunsford
OHIO STATE UNIVERSITY

Robert Connors
UNIVERSITY OF NEW HAMPSHIRE

Judy Z. Segal
UNIVERSITY OF BRITISH COLUMBIA

*with a new section for multilingual
writers by*

Franklin Horowitz
TEACHERS COLLEGE, COLUMBIA UNIVERSITY

SECOND EDITION

Nelson Canada
I(T)P An International Thomson Publishing Company

Toronto • Albany • Bonn • Boston • Cincinnati • Detroit • London • Madrid • Melbourne
Mexico City • New York • Pacific Grove • Paris • San Francisco • Singapore • Tokyo • Washington

I(T)P ™
International Thomson Publishing
The ITP logo is a trademark under licence

© Nelson Canada
A division of Thomson Canada Limited, 1995

Published in 1995 by
Nelson Canada
A division of Thomson Canada Limited
1120 Birchmount Road, Scarborough, Ontario M1K 5G4

Original U.S. edition published by St. Martin's Press (second edition copyright 1992).

COVER AND INTERIOR DESIGN: Teri McMahon

Canadian Cataloguing in Publication Data

Lunsford, Andrea A., 1942–
    The St. Martin's handbook for Canadians

2nd ed.
Includes index.
ISBN 0-17-604213-X

1. English language – Grammar – 1950–   – Handbooks, manuals, etc. 2. English language – Rhetoric – Handbooks, manuals, etc. 3. Report writing – Handbooks, manuals, etc. I. Connors, Robert J., 1951–   . II. Segal, Judith Zelda, date. III. Title.

PE1112.L85 1995   428.2   C94-932282–2

ACQUISITIONS EDITOR	Andrew Livingston
PRODUCTION EDITOR	Bob Kohlmeier
DEVELOPMENTAL EDITOR	Joanne Scattolon
ART DIRECTOR	Liz Harasymczuk
SENIOR PRODUCTION COORDINATOR	Sheryl Emery
COMPOSITION ANALYST	Nelson Gonzalez
INPUT OPERATORS	Elaine Andrews and Michelle Volk

Printed and bound in Canada
1 2 3 4 (BG) 98 97 96 95

Contents

Part One:
Working with the Writing Process

Part Two:
Writing Essays

Part Three:
Doing Research and Using Sources

Part Four:
Making Sentence-Level Choices: Grammar

Part Five:
Making Sentence-Level Choices: Conventions

Part Six:
Making Sentence-Level Choices: Style

Part Seven:
Selecting Effective Words

Part Eight:
Using Conventional Punctuation

Part Nine:
Using Conventional Mechanics

Part Ten:
For Multilingual Writers: Understanding the Nuances of English

Preface

When I set out to revise *The St. Martin's Handbook for Canadians,* I thought I was undertaking a relatively small job. The book already had the features I thought were important in a handbook: it treated issues of composing before issues of mechanics; it attended to writers' choices, not just their errors; it walked students through the complex process of composing in a realistic way; it suggested many opportunities for collaboration among students; it used excellent Canadian writing samples, including several essays by Canadian students; it drew from nonliterary as well as literary sources; and, while attending well to the "English" essay, it was useful for writing in a variety of disciplines. Finally, the book was, as my students have said, "user friendly."

However, there was a lot of work still to do. In revising *The St. Martin's Handbook for Canadians,* I relied on two major resources. The first was the second edition of Andrea Lunsford and Robert Connors's *The St. Martin's Handbook.* The second was my students. From Lunsford and Connors, I borrowed a lot of new material, leading to a new first chapter on producing a writing inventory and a great deal of updated material—on the research process, on writing in the disciplines, on inclusive language, and on other topics too numerous to mention. From Lunsford and Connors as well, I borrowed an *approach* to revision: there is nothing in the first edition of a text that can't be changed. Following is just a partial list of additional changes to *The St. Martin's Handbook for Canadians:*

- My own prose has been pared down considerably. (Was I being paid by the word for the first edition?)

- Advice on composing with a computer is more fully integrated into the writing process chapters.

- The research chapters provide more guidance for students using on-line catalogues and computer databases.

- Students are given additional practical advice on writing in the disciplines and writing essay examinations.

- Four sample essays have been replaced and two have been added; both new essays direct students' attention to matters of style.

- A new section, written by Franklin Horowitz of Teachers College, Columbia University, has been added for students of English as a Second Languge.

My students were helpful in a variety of ways: they helped me "field-test" the first edition of the book to discover what worked and what didn't work so well; they offered new essays for me to include as writing samples; and they participated in revision workshops with me, directly suggesting ways to improve the text (there's nothing like a student saying, "No one would read this introduction; it's too long" to make an author think again about what she's written).

My students also kept me thinking about the concerns of students in Canada. That is, while many writing textbooks and handbooks seem to construct a universe in which all students are middle-class young people who hang out at the soda shoppe (or cappuccino bar) and wash the Chevy (or the Miata) on the weekends, this handbook is meant to live in the real world. I have tried, even in sample sentences, to acknowledge students' real lives, making the culture of the handbook more welcoming to students— and including them more directly in the project of the book.

As a result of what turned out to be quite a lot of revision work, the second edition of *The St. Martin's Handbook for Canadians* contains much more useful material yet is only a little longer than the first edition. Accomplishing this seeming paradox was no mean feat, and I am indebted to many people for their help. I thank Andrea Lunsford and Robert Connors for once again producing the best American handbook on the market. For their reviews of the manuscript, I thank Peter Allen, Innis College, University of Toronto; Arnold Keller, University of Victoria; Larry N. McKill, University of Alberta; Kate Murton, University of Ottawa; Audrey Neufeldt, University of Victoria; and Pat Rogin, Durham College. I thank Lara Dal Monte, Sherry Devins, Twila Krown, Roger Millette, and Andrea Williams for permitting me to include their essays—and the many other students who would have permitted me to include theirs. Thanks to Andrew Livingston and Joanne Scattolon at Nelson Canada for their support throughout the project, and to Cy Strom for his amazing copy edit near the end of it. Special thanks to Andrea Williams and Vivian Stieda, my research assistants, on whom I relied for so much. I close with a list of the students of my Advanced Composition class (1993–94), who took the revision of my work as seriously as they had learned to take the revision of their own. I am very grateful for their help.

Natasha Alimohamed

Nancy Au

Lara Dal Monte

Sherry Devins

Kayo Kakiuchi

Dawn Lessoway

Gabriella Licsko

Shane Lutness

Tamara Malloff

Lesley Matthews

Michael Mityok

Diane Nishikihama

Gwen Oger

Nicole Porter

Jaida Ranson

Tim Rutledge

Aaron Scally

Kirsten Skarsgard

Ai Tang

Catherine Yamomoto

Judy Z. Segal
University of British Columbia, 1994

Introduction: Taking a Writing Inventory

The word *inventory* comes from a Latin work meaning "find," and in reference to writing, taking inventory carries the familiar meaning of taking stock. But taking inventory also carries another sense of "find," one we more often associate with the words *invent* and *invention*. In this sense, taking inventory means discovering new things about your writing and thus producing improvements in it that will, in turn, become part of the stock of your inventory.

This dual sense of what it means to take inventory runs throughout *The St. Martin's Handbook for Canadians*, asking you to look closely and analytically at your own writing—and helping you to produce stronger and stronger pieces of new writing, which can then serve as material for further analysis. This chapter aims to get you started on a full inventory of your writing by asking you to identify a representative sample of your written work and then to analyze its features.

How might you identify those features of your writing most important for an inventory? In an analysis of a representative sample taken from 20 000 first- and second-year college and university student essays, we found that the features that readers most often comment on fall into three categories:

1. Broad content issues

2. Organization and presentation

3. Surface errors

You can benefit from organizing an inventory of your own writing according to these three major categories. Following are some guidelines for doing so.

Taking a writing inventory

1. If you are using this chapter in a writing course, assemble copies of the first two or three pieces of writing you do, making sure to select pieces to which either your instructor or other students have responded.

2. Read through this writing, adding your own comments about its strengths and weaknesses.

3. Examine the instructor and peer comments very carefully, and compare them with your own comments.

4. Group all the comments into the categories discussed in this chapter—broad content issues, organization and presentation, and surface errors.

5. Make an inventory of your own strengths and weaknesses in each category.

6. Identify the appropriate sections of this book for more detailed help in areas where you need it.

7. Make up a priority list of three or four particular problems you have identified, and write out a plan for eliminating them.

8. Note at least two strengths you want to build on in your writing.

Keeping a writing log

One very good way to keep track of your writing strengths and weaknesses is to establish a **writing log**, a notebook or folder in which you can record observations and comments about your writing—from instructors, other students, or yourself. This book will offer you frequent opportunities to make entries in a writing log. As you take inventory of some of your writing, you will be gathering information about how readers respond to various features of it—broad content issues, organization and presentation, and surface errors. This information can serve as the data for an opening entry in your writing log. Here is an example:

	Strengths	Weaknesses
Broad content issues	lots of good examples	ideas not in logical order
Organization, presentation	great title! (Everyone loved it.)	Paragraphs too short to make my points (Two are only one sentence long.)

	Strengths	Weaknesses
Surface errors	semicolons used correctly—I was worried about this!	one unintentional sentence fragment *Its/it's* mistake(!) (See punctuation chapter.)

Assessing broad content issues

Writing is a complex task that calls on you to attend carefully to several big questions: what is the purpose of your writing? what points does it make? does it fully develop, support, or prove those points? to whom is it addressed? does this writing reflect your full powers as a writer? Answering such questions as part of your writing inventory is important, for readers expect your purpose to be clear, your points to be fully established, and so on.

Our research indicates that readers comment most often on the following broad content issues in student writing:

1. Use of supporting evidence
2. Use of sources
3. Achievement of purpose
4. Attention to audience
5. Overall impression

Use of supporting evidence

According to Aristotle's *Rhetoric*, an effective speaker needs to do two basic things: make a claim and prove it. Readers, too, expect that a piece of writing will make one or more points clearly and illustrate or support those points with ample evidence—good reasons, examples, or other details. Effective use of such evidence helps readers understand a point, makes abstract concepts concrete, and offers "proof" that what you are saying is sensible and worthy of attention and assent. In fact, the use of evidence is what readers in our research commented on *most often*, accounting for 56 percent of all comments we analyzed. These readers tended to make statements like these: "This point is underdeveloped" or "I like the way you back up this claim."

For more discussion of the use of good reasons, see 5c; of examples and details, see 5d–f. For more on providing such support in paragraphs, see 6d.

Use of sources

One special kind of supporting evidence for your points comes from source materials. Choosing possible sources, evaluating them, and using the results of your research effectively in your writing not only supports your claim but also builds your credibility as a writer. It also demonstrates that you understand what others have to say about a topic and that you are fully informed about varying perspectives on the topic. But finding enough sources, judging their usefulness, and deciding when to quote, when to summarize, and when to paraphrase—and then doing so accurately and working the results smoothly into your own writing—is a skill that takes considerable practice. You can begin developing that skill now by taking a close look at how well you use sources in your writing. The readers whose responses we studied commented regularly on such use of sources. Here are some of their remarks: "Only two sources? You need several more"; "This quotation beautifully sums up your argument"; "Why do you quote at such length here— why not paraphrase?" For more discussion on choosing, reading, and evaluating sources, see 11a–b; on quoting, paraphrasing, and summarizing, see 11c; and on incorporating source materials in your text, see 11d.

Achievement of purpose

Purposes for writing vary widely. In college and university writing, your primary purpose will often be directly related to the assignment you receive. As a result, you need to pay careful attention to what an assignment asks you to do, noting particularly any key terms in the assignment, such as "analyze," "argue," "define," or "summarize." Such words are important in meeting the requirements of the assignment, staying on the subject, and thus achieving your purpose.

Readers' responses can often reveal how well you have achieved your primary purpose. Here are two comments responding to purpose: "Why are you telling us all this?"; "What is the issue here, and what is your stand on it?" For guidelines on considering purposes, see 2c.

Attention to audience

All writing is written to be read, if only by the writer. Most college writing is addressed to instructors and other students, though you may sometimes write to another audience—a political figure, a prospective employer, a campus administrator. The most effective writing is that which is sensitive to readers' backgrounds, values, and needs. Such writing, for example, takes time to define terms readers may not know, to provide necessary background information, and to consider readers' perspectives on and feelings about a topic. On the subject of audience, readers have made comments like these: "Careful you don't talk down to your readers," and "You've left me behind here. I can't follow."

For guidelines on considering your audience, see 2e.

Overall impression

When friends or instructors read your writing, they may give you information about the overall impression it makes. As a writer, you will do well to note such responses carefully, and try to pin them down. Setting up a conference with the instructor is one way to explore these general responses. Before doing so, however, carry out your own analysis of the comments, and then find out what your instructor thinks.

In the essays we examined, readers tended to give their overall impression most often in a note at the very beginning or the very end of an essay, saying things like the following: "Your grasp of the material here is truly impressive," or "What happened here? I can't understand your point in this essay."

For more specific ways of assessing the overall impression your writing creates, see the exercises entitled *Taking Inventory* that conclude most of the chapters of this book.

Exercise I.1

Begin your writing inventory be recording the results of a careful look at broad content issues in at least one piece of your own writing. (1) First, list all comments your instructors and classmates have made about your use of supporting evidence, use of sources, achievement of purpose, attention to audience, and overall progress. If you find other large-scale issues referred to, include them in your list. (2) Then, look over your writing with your own critical eye, using the guidelines in this introduction to evaluate your handling of broad content elements. (3) After examining the lists, summarize your major areas of strength and those areas in which you need to improve. (4) If you are keeping a writing log, enter this inventory there.

Assessing organization and presentation

The most important or brilliant points in the world will have little effect on readers if they are presented in a way that makes them hard to recognize, read, or follow. Indeed, research for this book confirms that readers depend on writers to organize and present their material—sections, paragraphs, sentences, arguments, details, source citations—in ways that provide aids to understanding. After use of supporting evidence, the features of student writing most often commented on had to do with organization. In addition to clear and logical organization of information, readers appreciate careful formatting and documentation of sources. Because organization and presentation of writing give important signals to your readers, they are well worth including in your writing inventory. Here are those features most often commented on in the student writing we examined:

1. Overall organization
2. Sentence structure and style
3. Paragraph structure
4. Format
5. Documentation

Overall organization

Readers expect a writer to provide organizational patterns and signals that will help them follow the thread of what the writer is trying to say. Sometimes such organizational cues are simple. If you are giving directions, for example, you might give chronological cues (first you do A, then B, and so on), and if you are describing a place, you might give spatial cues (at the north end is A, in the centre is B, and so on). But complex issues often call for complex organizational patterns, and you might find yourself needing to signal readers that you are moving from a problem to several possible solutions, for example, or that you are moving through a series of comparisons and contrasts. Our readers responded, for example, in these ways to organizational features: "I'm confused here—what does this point have to do with the one before it?"; "How did we get here? You need a transition"; "I'm lost: this sentence seems totally out of place."

For more discussion of overall organization, see 4e and 5g. For more on organizational methods of development, see 3e; on transitional signals that aid organization, see 6c; and on ways of linking paragraphs, see 6f.

Sentence structure and style

If you have never taken a close look at how your sentences work (or don't work) to help organize your writing and guide readers, a little time and effort now will provide an overview. How long do your sentences tend to be? Do you use strings of short sentences that make the reader work to fill in the connections between them? Do any long sentences confuse the reader or wander off the topic? How do your sentences open? How do you link them logically? Answering these questions provides additional data for your writing inventory. Here are some comments the readers in our research made about sentences: "Combine your sentences to make the logical connection explicit here"; "This sentence goes on forever—how about dividing it up?; "Your use of questions helps clarify this complex issue."

For detailed discussion of sentence types, see 14d; of sentence effectiveness, see Chapter 25; and of sentence variation, see Chapter 28.

Paragraph structure

Just as overall organization can help readers follow the thread of thought in a piece of writing, so too can paragraph structure. You may tend to paragraph by feel, so to speak, without spending much time thinking about structure. In fact, the time to examine your paragraphs should generally be *after* you have completed a draft. Since paragraphs play such a major role in making your writing coherent and clear, however, you can profit by examining them carefully now. Begin by studying any readers' comments that refer to your paragraphs. You might find comments like these: "The sentences in this paragraph don't follow a logical order" or "Why the one- and two-sentence paragraphs? Elaborate!"

For guidelines on checking paragraphs, see 6g. For detailed information on paragraph development in general, see Chapter 6.

Format

Readers depend on the format of a piece of writing to make reading as pleasant and efficient as possible. Therefore, you need to pay very close attention to how your materials are physically presented and to the visual effect they create. Because format guidelines vary widely from discipline to discipline, even from assignment to assignment, part of your job as a writer is always to make certain you know what format is most appropriate for a particular course or assignment.

In the research conducted for this book, readers made comments like these: "Your headings and subheadings helped me follow this report"; "You need a title, one that really works to get across your meaning"; "This tiny single-spaced type is almost impossible to read."

Documentation

Any writing that uses source materials requires careful documentation—parenthetical citations, endnotes, footnotes, lists of works cited, bibliographies—to guide readers to your sources and let them know you have carried out accurate research. While very few writers, even strong writers, carry all the documentation guidelines around in their heads, they do know where to look to find them. Here are two readers' comments that focus on documentation: "Footnote numbers should come at the *end* of quotations"; "I can't tell where this quotation ends."

For more information on documenting sources, see Chapter 13.

Exercise I.2

Continue your writing inventory by analyzing the five features of organization and presentation described above in at least one piece of your writing. (1) Chart your instructor's comments, and consider asking a classmate whose opinions you value to comment on your use of these features. (2) Then, add your own observations about your use of these features. (3) On the basis of these analyses, summarize what you take to be your major areas of strength as well as those areas in which you need to improve. (4) If you are keeping a writing log, enter the results of your analysis there.

Learning from your surface errors

Readers may notice your handling of broad content issues and your organization and presentation either because these provide stepping-stones for following your meaning or because they create stumbling blocks to such understanding. However, your spelling, grammar, punctuation, word choice, and other small-scale matters will seldom draw attention or comment unless they look wrong. (Indeed, absence of error is seldom in itself remarkable. No one ever said, for example, "Wow, that was a great novel; there were no mistakes in it at all.")

What can we tell you about the kinds of surface errors you are likely to find in your writing and the response they elicit from readers? Our study of student writing reveals, first of all, that—even with word processors and spell checkers—spelling errors are *by far the most common*, by a factor of more than three to one. (A list of the words most often misspelled can be found in Chapter 33.) Second, readers are not disturbed by all surface errors, nor do instructors always mark all of them. In fact, whether your instructor comments on an error in any particular assignment will depend on his or her judgment about how serious and distracting it is and what you should be dealing with at the time. Finally, not all surface errors are even consistently viewed as errors. In fact, some of the patterns identified in our research are considered errors by some instructors but stylistic options by others.

While many people may tend to think of "correctness" as absolute, based on hard and fast, unchanging "rules," instructors and students know better. We know that there are "rules," all right, but that the rules change all the time. Our own research points to some fairly recent shifts. In the late 19th century, for instance, instructors at Harvard said that the most serious writing problem their students had was an inability to distinguish between the proper uses of *shall* and *will*. Similarly, split infinitives seemed to many instructors of the 1950s a very serious problem, but at least since the starship *Enterprise* set out "to boldly go" where no one had gone before, split infinitives have wrinkled fewer brows.

These examples of shifting standards do not mean that there is no such thing as "correctness" in writing—only that *correctness always depends on some context*. Correctness is not so much a question of absolute right or wrong as it is a question of the way the choices a writer makes are perceived by readers.

This book assumes that you want to understand and control not only the broad content issues and organizational features of writing but the surface conventions of academic writing as well. Since you already know the vast majority of these conventions, the most efficient way to proceed is to focus on those that are still unfamiliar or puzzling. Achieving this practical focus means identifying, analyzing, and overcoming patterns of surface error in your writing.

Statistically, the following errors are the ones most likely to cause you trouble. A brief explanation and examples of each one are given in this chapter, and each error pattern is cross-referenced to at least one place elsewhere in this book where you can find more detail or additional examples.

Missing comma after an introductory element

When a sentence opens with an introductory word, phrase, or clause, readers usually need a small pause between the introductory element and the main part of the sentence. Such a pause is most often signalled by a comma.

INTRODUCTORY WORD

Frankly, we were baffled by the committee's decision.

INTRODUCTORY PHRASE

To tell the truth, I never have liked the Expos.

INTRODUCTORY CLAUSE

Though I gave detailed advice for revising, his draft did not improve.

Short introductory elements do not always need a comma. The test is whether the element seems to need a pause after it. The following sentence, for example, would at first be misunderstood if it did not have a comma—readers would think the introductory phrase was *In German nouns,* rather than *In German.* The best advice is that you will rarely be wrong to add a comma after an introductory element.

In German, nouns are always capitalized.

For more on commas and introductory elements, see 14c, 28b, and 34a.

2

Vague pronoun reference

A pronoun like *he, she, it, they, this, that,* or *which* should refer clearly to a specific word (or words) elsewhere in the sentence or in a previous sentence. When readers cannot tell for sure whom or what the pronoun refers to, the reference is said to be vague. There are two common kinds of vague pronoun reference. The first occurs when there is more than one word that the pronoun might refer to; the second, when the reference is to a word that is implied but not explicitly stated.

POSSIBLE REFERENCE TO MORE THAN ONE WORD

Before Mary Grace physically and verbally assaulted Mrs. Turpin, *the latter* ~~she~~ was a judgmental woman who created her own ranking system of people and used it to justify her self-proclaimed superiority.

REFERENCE IMPLIED BUT NOT STATED

The Hudson's Bay Company force seized the Nor'Westers' post in response to the earlier attack. This *seizure of the post* intensified the conflict.

They believe that a zygote, an egg at the moment of fertilization, is as deserving of protection as the born human being, but *such an assertion* ~~it~~ cannot be proven scientifically.

For guidelines on checking for vague pronoun reference, see 19c. For more on pronoun reference, see Chapter 19.

3

Missing comma in a compound sentence

A compound sentence is made up of two (or more) parts that could each function as an independent sentence. If there are only two parts, they may be linked by either a semicolon or a coordinating conjunction (*and, but, so, yet, nor, or, for*). When a conjunction is used, a comma should usually be placed before it to indicate a pause between the two thoughts.

The words "I do" may sound simple, but they mean a complex commitment for life.

We wish dreamily upon a star, and then we look down to see that we have stepped in the mud.

In *very* short sentences, this use of the comma is optional if the sentence can be easily understood without it. Still, the best advice is to use the comma before the coordinating conjunction because it will always be correct.

Meredith wore jeans, and her feet were bare.

For further discussion and examples, see 14d1 and 34b.

4

Wrong word

"Wrong word" errors range from simple lack of proofreading, like using *should* for *would*, to mistakes in basic word meaning, like using *prevaricate* when you mean *procrastinate*, to mistakes in shades of meaning, like using *sedate* when you mean *sedentary*.

A knowledge of computers is ~~inherent~~ **assumed** in his office.

Paradise Lost contains many ~~illusions~~ **allusions** to classical mythology.

For additional, more detailed information about choosing the right word for your meaning, see Chapter 30.

Missing comma(s) with a nonrestrictive element

A nonrestrictive element is a word, phrase, or clause that gives additional information about the preceding part of the sentence but does not restrict or limit the meaning of that part. A nonrestrictive element is not essential to the sentence; it can be deleted without changing the sentence's basic meaning. As an indication that it is not essential, it is always set off from the rest of the sentence with a comma before it and, if it is in the middle of the sentence, after it as well.

> The bottom of the pond was covered with soft brown clay, a natural base for
>
> a good swimming hole.

> Marina, who was the president of the club, was first to speak.

For additional explanation, see 34c.

Wrong preposition

Many words in English are regularly used with a particular preposition to express a particular meaning; for example, throwing a ball *to* someone is different form throwing a ball *at* someone. Using the wrong preposition in such expressions is a common error.

Finally, she refused to comply ~~to~~ *with* school regulations.

In his moral blindness Gloucester is similar ~~with~~ *to* Lear.

Natalie is absolutely enamoured ~~with~~ *of* her new computer.

For additional information about choosing the correct preposition, see 14b6.

7

Comma splice

A comma splice occurs when two (or sometimes more) clauses that could each stand alone as a sentence are written with only a comma between them. Such clauses must be either clearly separated by a punctuation mark stronger than a comma—a period or semicolon—or clearly connected with a word like *and* or *although*, or else the ideas they state should be combined into one clause.

      for

I was strongly attracted to her, she had special qualities.

    Having

~~They always had~~ roast beef for Thanksgiving, ~~this~~ was a family tradition.

8

Missing or misplaced possessive apostrophe

To show that one thing belongs to another, either an apostrophe and an *-s* or an apostrophe alone is added to the word representing the thing that possesses the other. An apostrophe and *-s* are used for singular nouns (words that refer to one thing, such as *leader* or *Calgary*); for indefinite pronouns (words like *anybody, everyone, nobody, somebody*); and for plural nouns (words referring to more than one thing) that do not end in *-s*, such as *men* and *women*. For plural nouns ending in *-s*, such as *creatures* or *fathers*, only the apostrophe is used.

       child's

Overambitious parents can be very harmful to a ~~childs~~ well-being.

    Laus'

We met at a party at the ~~Laus~~ summer home.

    For discussion and guidelines on checking for possessive apostrophes, see 37a.

9

Unnecessary shift in tense

An unnecessary shift in tense occurs when the verbs in a sentence or passage shift for no reason from one time period to another, such as from past to present or from present to future. Such tense shifts confuse the reader, who must guess which tense is the right one.

Each team of detectives is assigned to three or four cases at a time. They ~~will~~ investigate only those leads that seem most promising.

In the film, C.S. Lewis is in love with an American woman who ~~died~~ *dies* of cancer.

For more on using verb tenses in sequences, see 16g.

Unnecessary shift in pronoun

An unnecessary pronoun shift occurs when a writer who has been using one kind of pronoun to refer to someone or something shifts to another for no reason. The most common shift in pronoun is from *one* to *you* or *I*. This shift often results from an attempt at a more formal level of diction, which is hard to maintain when it is not completely natural.

When one first sees a painting by Georgia O'Keeffe, ~~you are~~ *one is* impressed by a sense of power and stillness.

If we had known about the ozone layer, ~~you~~ *we* could have banned aerosol sprays years ago.

For more on unnecessary pronoun shifts, see 20d.

Sentence fragment

A sentence fragment is a part of a sentence that is written as if it were a whole sentence, with a capital letter at the beginning and a period, question mark, or exclamation point at the end. A fragment lacks one or both of the two essential parts of a sentence, a subject and a complete verb, or else it begins with a subordinating word, which means that it depends for its meaning on another sentence.

LACKING SUBJECT

Marie Antoinette spent huge sums of money on herself and her favourites.

Her extravagance helped

~~Helped~~ bring on the French Revolution.

LACKING COMPLETE VERB

was

The old aluminum boat sitting on its trailer.

BEGINNING WITH SUBORDINATING WORD

, where

We returned to the restaurant, ~~Where~~ we waited for our friends.

For additional, more detailed information on sentence fragments, see Chapter 22.

Wrong tense

Errors that are marked as being the wrong tense include using a verb that does not indicate clearly that the action or condition it expresses is (or was or will be) completed, and using a verb that does not indicate clearly that an action is (or was or will be) continuing.

had

Ian was shocked to learn that Joe died only the day before.

were buying

By the 1970s, many North Americans ~~bought~~ smaller cars.

For additional, more detailed information about verb tenses and forms, see 14b1, Chapter 16, and Chapter 17.

Lack of agreement between subject and verb

A subject and verb must agree, or match. In many cases, the verb must take a different form depending on whether the subject is singular (one) or plural (more than one): *The old <u>man is</u> angry and <u>stamps</u> into the house* but *The old* *men are* angry and *stamp* into the house. Lack of agreement between the subject and verb often results from particular kinds of subjects and sentence constructions.

When other words come between subject and verb, a writer may mistake the noun nearest the verb for the verb's real subject. In the following sentence, for example, the subject is the singular *part,* not the plural *goals.*

A central part of my life goals ~~have~~ *has* been to go to law school.

Other problems can arise from subjects made up of two or more parts joined by *and* or *or;* subjects like *committee* or *jury,* which can take either singular or plural verb forms depending on whether they are treated as a unit or as a group of individuals; and subjects like *mathematics* and *measles,* which look plural but are singular in meaning.

My brother and his friend Larry commute/ every day from St. John's.

The committee ~~was~~ *were* taking all the responsibility themselves.

Measles ~~have~~ *has* become much less common in Canada.

Pronoun subjects can cause problems as well. Most indefinite pronouns, like *each, either, neither,* or *one,* take singular verb forms. The relative pronouns *who, which,* or *that* take verbs that agree with the word the pronoun refers to.

Each of the items in these designs ~~coordinate~~ *coordinates* with the others.

Johnson was one of the athletes who ~~was~~ *were* disqualified.

Finally, some problems occur when writers make the verb agree with a word that follows or precedes it rather than with the grammatical subject.

Behind the curtains ~~stand~~ *stands* an elderly man producing the wizard's effects.

For additional, more detailed information about subject-verb agreement, see Chapter 17.

14

Missing comma in a series

A series consists of three or more parallel words, phrases, or clauses that appear consecutively in a sentence. Traditionally, all the items in a series are separated by commas. Many books, newspapers, and magazines do not use a comma before the *and* or *or* that appears between the last two items, and some instructors do not require it. Check your instructor's preference, and be consistent in either using or omitting this comma.

Sharks eat mostly squid **,** shrimp **,** crabs **,** and other fish.

You must learn to talk to the earth **,** smell it **,** squeeze it in your hands.

For more on parallel structures in a series, see 27a, or on using commas in a series, see 34d.

Lack of agreement between pronoun and antecedent

Most pronouns (words like *I, it, you, him, her, this, themselves, someone, who, which*) are used to replace another word (or words), so that it does not have to be repeated. The word that the pronoun replaces or stands for is called its antecedent. Pronouns must agree with, or match, their antecedents in gender—for example, using *he* and *him* to replace *Jean Chrétien* and *she* and *her* to replace *Queen Elizabeth*. They must also agree with their antecedents in referring to either one person or thing (singular) or more than one (plural)—for example, using *it* to replace *a book* and *they* and *them* to replace *fifteen books*.

Most people have few problems with pronoun-antecedent agreement except with certain kinds of antecedents. These include words like *each, either, neither,* and *one,* which are singular and take singular pronouns; antecedents made up of two or more parts joined by *or* or *nor*; and antecedents like *audience* or *team,* which can be either singular or plural depending on whether they are considered a single unit or a group of individuals.

Every one of the puppies thrived in ~~their~~ *its* new home.

Neither Jane nor Susan felt that they ~~had~~ *she* been treated fairly.

The team frequently changed ~~its~~ *their* positions to get varied experience.

The other main kind of antecedent that causes problems is a singular antecedent (such as *each* or *an employee*) that could be either male or female. Rather than use masculine pronouns (*he, him,* and so on) with such an antecedent, a traditional rule that excludes or ignores females, a writer should use *he or she, him or her,* and so on, or else rewrite the sentence to make the antecedent and pronoun plural or to eliminate the pronoun.

Every student must provide his **or her** own uniform.

All students Every student must provide his own **their** uniform **uniforms.**

Every student must provide his **a** own uniform.

For additional, more detailed information about pronoun-antecedent agreement, see Chapters 17 and 19.

Unnecessary comma(s) with a restrictive element

A restrictive element is a word, phrase, or clause that restricts or limits the meaning of the preceding part of the sentence; it is essential to the meaning of what precedes it and cannot be left out without changing the sentence's basic meaning. Because of this close relationship, it is *not* set off from the rest of the sentence with a comma or commas.

Several groups/opposed to the use of animals for cosmetics testing,/picketed the laboratory.

The chair cannot be re-elected/once he or she has served two consecutive terms.

Shakespeare's tragedy/*Othello*/deals with the dangers of jealousy.

In the last example above, the appositive is essential to the meaning of the sentence because Shakespeare wrote more than one tragedy.

For additional, more detailed information about restrictive phrases and clauses, see 34c and 34i1.

Fused sentence

Fused sentences (sometimes called run-on sentences) are created when two or more groups of words that could each be written as an independent sentence are written without any punctuation between them. Such groups of words must be either divided into separate sentences, by using periods and capital letters, or joined in a way that shows their relationship, by adding words and punctuation or by rewriting completely.

The current was swift ~~he~~ . He could not swim to shore.

Klee's paintings seem simple , but they are very sophisticated.

She doubted the value of meditation ; nevertheless she decided to try it once.

For more detailed information about ways to revise fused sentences, see Chapter 21.

Misplaced or dangling modifier

A misplaced modifier is a word, phrase, or clause that is not placed close enough to the word it describes or is related to. As a result, it seems to modify some other word, phrase, or clause, and readers can be confused or puzzled.

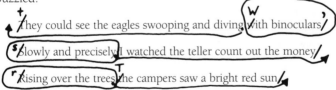

They could see the eagles swooping and diving with binoculars.

Slowly and precisely I watched the teller count out the money.

Rising over the trees the campers saw a bright red sun.

A dangling modifier is a word, phrase, or elliptical clause (a clause from which words have been left out) that is not clearly related to any other word in the sentence. The word that it modifies exists in the writer's mind, but not on paper in the sentence. Such a modifier is called "dangling" because it hangs precariously from the beginning or end of the sentence, attached to nothing very solid.

one sees
Looking down the stretch of sandy beach, people ~~are~~ lying face down trying

to get a tan.

a ~~As~~ a male college student, *M*any people are surprised that I want to attend

the Take Back the Night rally.

For additional, more detailed information on misplaced and dangling modifiers, see 23a and 23c.

Its / It's confusion

The word *its,* spelled without an apostrophe, is the possessive form of *it,* meaning "of it" or "belonging to it." The word *it's,* spelled with an apostrophe, is a shortened form of *it is* or *it has.* Even though with nouns an apostrophe often indicates a possessive form, the possessive form of a pronoun in this case is the one *without* the apostrophe.

The car is lying on it side in the ditch.

Its a white 1986 Buick.

For more on *its* and *it's,* see 33b, 37a, and 37b.

Exercise I.3

Take time now to continue your writing inventory by analyzing the surface errors as well as "surface strengths" in at least one piece of your writing. (1) Go through your writing, noting down every instance in which your instructor or classmates have marked an error or made a comment in such areas as spelling, grammar, punctuation, and other issues like those discussed in the section above. (2) Then go through once more, using the guidelines on common errors in this introduction, to add your own observations about strengths and areas that need improvement. (3) Finally, compile a list of both strengths and weaknesses, and decide which areas you plan to work on first. (4) If you are keeping a writing log, enter the results of your writing inventory there.

PART ONE

Working with the Writing Process

Understanding the Writing Process

Considering Purpose and Audience

Exploring, Planning, Drafting

Revising and Editing

1

Understanding the Writing Process

The writing process you really want to understand is your own. How do you go about preparing a piece of writing—from the time you get the assignment to the time you, drained and hopeful, hand the final version to your instructor? Do you plan what you want to say before you start composing on paper or do you use writing as a way of working out what you want to say? Do you write out whole drafts before you even think about revising or do you revise as you draft? Is composing a solitary process for you or do you talk over your ideas with other people and share your drafts with them? Do you work at a computer? Do you tend to read in your topic before you write anything? Most important, whatever your answers to these questions, does your writing process work for you? If it does not, you can change it—and probably improve both your essays and your mood while you work on them.

The next several sections discuss the writing process and the related processes of reading and collaboration. The chapters that follow suggest a number of process variations for you to try.

Considering the recursive parts of the writing process

The mental processes that actually accompany the writing process are tremendously complex. They are, moreover, so subtle and so lightning-fast that we are only now beginning to learn how they all interact. But we *do* know that writers always set and shift and reset a series of goals as they write. These goals range from those as large as "try to make the reader laugh here" or "explain that concept" to ones as small as "use a semicolon instead of a period here to make this section less choppy." Researchers often describe the process of writing as seamless and **recursive**, meaning that its goals or parts are constantly flowing into and influencing one another, without any clear break between them. The shifting set of goals may focus one moment on deciding how to organize a paragraph and the next moment on using knowledge gained from that decision to revise the wording of a sentence. Repetitive, erratic, and often messy, writing does not proceed in nice, neat steps: first an idea; then a plan; then an introduction, body, and conclusion. In fact, these "steps" often take place simultaneously, in a kind of spiralling sequence, with various activities taking place throughout the process of writing. A writer may get an idea for a conclusion while drafting the introduction, or may plan one paragraph while revising the previous one.

In any case, writers seldom pay conscious attention to these constantly shifting goals and recursive patterns. As you become more practised as a writer, more and more of the goal-juggling you do will become automatic.

Although the following sections discuss exploring and planning, drafting, and revising and editing in that order, remember that in the process of writing these activities are always interwoven.

1. Considering purpose and audience

In most of your college work, the writing process will begin with an assignment for a course—and you will do well to begin by thinking carefully about the assignment itself, making sure you understand what it is asking you to do and, if necessary, clarifying it with your instructor.

As you think about the assignment, you will want to decide what major purposes you hope to accomplish in the piece of writing—for example, to persuade your readers of the worth of a particular interpretation or to win their support for a particular course of action. And because specific purposes can be fulfilled only in relation to specific readers, you will want to think carefully about the audience to whom your piece of writing is directed. (Purpose and audience are examined in detail in Chapter 2.)

2. Exploring

Writing that is worth reading usually starts with a nagging question or puzzle or idea that calls for some exploration—thinking about what you already know, coming up with a working thesis, and gathering information, if necessary. Although this exploring continues throughout the writing process, it is often the way a writer begins.

Depending on the writing task, exploring can last a few minutes or several weeks. If you have to write a one-page essay in class about a member of your family, you will probably jot down a few notes and then quickly start drafting. If, on the other hand, you have six weeks to prepare a fifteen-page paper on the factors leading to the defeat of Kim Campbell in the 1993 federal election, you will need to do some research and explore the topic thoroughly before deciding exactly what you want to say. (Strategies for exploring a topic are presented in Chapter 3.)

3. Planning

Exploring is closely connected to planning, which involves deciding how to organize your writing. Sometimes a possible organizational plan will occur to you at an early stage and help shape your thesis and direct any research you need to do. More often, perhaps, a plan will grow out of the thesis or your search for information. However your plan develops and however tentative it is, it will act as a guide as you produce a first draft. Your thesis and organization may well shift as you draft, but just having them there will help you keep on course, or at least remember where you are headed. (Organizing and planning are discussed in Chapter 3.)

4. Drafting

As much as anything, drafting continues a process of exploration. The great British writer E.M. Forster once wrote, "How can I know what I think until I see what I say?" Indeed, some kinds of understanding come only from trying to express your ideas for others—in writing. No matter how thoroughly you explore your topic while planning, you will discover more about the topic while drafting your essay. Sometimes these new insights will cause you to turn back—to change your organizational plan, to bring in more information, to approach the subject from a new angle, or to rethink your appeal to your audience. Drafting, then, is *not* merely "putting your ideas down on paper."

Because writing out the actual draft is just one part of a complex recursive activity, many experienced writers report that they rarely try to make their writing come out perfectly the first time. Rather, they view drafting as just that—the process of working out a *first draft,* during which they explore thoughts and try out arguments and examples. The goal of drafting is not to produce a final copy, or even a version good enough to show anyone else. Smooth sentences, the ideal word choice, and the right punctuation can come later; in your first draft, just get your thoughts down, and keep drafting until you run out of ideas to explore. (See Chapter 3 for more on drafting.)

5. Revising

With your first draft, you have a version of your essay before you. The rest of your work will be devoted to making sure it says what you want it to say. Doing so requires careful rereading and analysis of the draft with an eye toward establishing a systematic plan for revising.

Re-vision means literally "seeing again." It means looking at a draft with a critical eye—seeing it anew and deciding if it accomplishes your original goals. You may have assumed before now that revising is simply a matter of correcting misspellings, inserting missing commas, and typing up the result. Although such tasks are important, true revision is something more. It means examining the draft to reassess the main ideas, the organization, the structure of paragraphs, the variety of sentences, the choice of words, the attitudes shown toward the topic and the audience, and the thoroughness with which the topic is developed. It means polishing to achieve smooth phrasing and memorable prose. It may mean writing new sentences, moving paragraphs, eliminating whole sections, doing additional research, or even choosing a new topic and starting all over again. In fact, because it can be extensive, revising often closely resembles drafting. (Revision is discussed in Chapter 4.)

6. Editing and proofreading

The tasks of editing and proofreading begin once revision is complete. Editing involves making what you have written ready for the world, which means making it meet those conventions of written form known as "correctness." Sentence structure, spelling, mechanics, punctuation—all must meet conventional standards. Even editing may lead you to reconsider an idea, a paragraph, a transition, or an organizational pattern—and you may find yourself planning or drafting once again. When all editing is complete and you have produced a final manuscript, you then must proofread to catch and correct any typographical errors. (See Chapter 4.)

7. Taking inventory of your own writing

To get started on thinking about and evaluating your own writing process, answer the following questions. If you are keeping a writing log, record your answers there.

Examining your own process of writing

1. How do you typically go about preparing for a writing assignment? Describe the steps you take, including rereading the assignment, asking questions about it, talking to instructors or friends, jotting down ideas,

gathering information, and so on. How far in advance of the due date do you usually begin working on the assignment?

2. When and where do your best ideas often come to you?

3. Where do you usually do your writing? Describe this place. Is it a good place to write? Why, or why not?

4. When you write, are you usually physically alone? Is there usually music, conversation, or other noise in the background?

5. What materials do you use? pen or pencil, note pad, loose-leaf paper, index cards, typewriter, computer? What do you find most (and least) helpful or appealing about these materials?

6. What audience do most assignments ask you to address? the instructor? classmates? a wider audience? How much thought do you typically give to the audience as you work on the assignment?

7. What strategies do you typically use to explore a topic?

8. How do you typically go about writing a first draft? Do you finish it in one sitting, or do you prefer to take breaks?

9. How do you typically go about revising, and what does your revising include? Do you write out complete revised drafts or simply insert, delete, or move material in the previous draft? How many drafts or stages of revision do you usually go through before the final version? Why? What are the things you think about most as you revise?

10. If you "get stuck" while writing, what do you usually do to get moving again?

11. What would you say is most efficient and effective about your writing process? What is most enjoyable? What is least efficient and effective about your writing process? What is least enjoyable?

12. What specific steps could you take to improve your writing process?

Reading with an eye for writing

Reading is closely related to writing, if only because writers need to be able to read their own work with a careful eye. Indeed, one good way to improve your writing is by paying close attention to what you read, taking tips from writers you especially admire. In the words of William Faulkner, "Read, read, read. Read everything—trash, classics, good and bad, and see how they do it." Throughout this handbook, we will be examining the work of well-known writers to "see how they do it," to see what they do with the strategies and structures you yourself will be practising.

In addition, most chapters include exercises asking you to read a passage with an eye for some element in the writing: adjectives, subordination, dashes, and so on. These exercises are designed to help you learn to use these elements in your own work—and they can lead you to insights about how you can make your own writing more accurate and powerful.

For examining your own reading process

The writer Anatole Broyard once cautioned readers about the perils of "just walking through" a book.* A good reader, he suggested, "stomps around" in a book—underlining passages, scribbling in the margin, noting any questions or comments.

How would you describe yourself as a reader—avid? hurried? meticulous? relaxed? what else? Do you annotate the text as you read, or are you careful never to write in a book? What role does reading play in your life as a student and as a writer?

Benefiting from collaboration

Philosopher Hannah Arendt once remarked that "for excellence, the presence of others is always required." Nowhere is Arendt's observation more accurate than in college and university communities. Your coursework will call on you to read, write, and research a vast amount of material. But you will not—or need not—do all that reading, writing, and researching alone. Far from it. Instead, you can be part of a broad conversation that includes all the texts you read; all the writing you produce; all the discussions you have with teachers, friends, family members, and classmates; all the observations and interviews you conduct. It is this conversation we have in mind when we stress the importance of collaboration to you as a student seeking to achieve excellence in your studies and throughout your life.

Collaboration can play an important part in all the writing you do: first if you talk with others about your topic and your plans for approaching it,

---

*Anatole Broyard, "The Pride of Reading Is Eternal Vigilance," *New York Times Book Review,* 10 Apr. 1988, pp. 11–12.

and then if you seek responses to your draft and gather suggestions for improving it. In much the same way, reading can be done "with others": first by entering into mental conversation with the author, and then by comparing your understanding of the text with that of other readers and using points of agreement or disagreement as the basis for further analysis.

For this term at least, the most immediate and valuable of your collaborators may be the members of the class in which you are using this book. Indeed, you can learn a great deal by listening carefully not only to your instructor but to all of your classmates. You can profit even more by talking over issues with them, by comparing notes and ideas with them, and by using them as a first and very important audience for your writing; for they will inevitably offer you new perspectives, new ways of seeing and knowing. Here are some tips for working in a group.

Establishing a study group

1. Set up a group with an odd number of members, such as three or five.

2. Trade phone numbers and schedules, and set a regular meeting time.

3. Set an agenda for each meeting. If, for instance, you want to work on introductions to an essay, agree to bring several versions for each member of the group to evaluate. If you intend to read and critique entire drafts, make arrangements to distribute copies to each member ahead of time.

4. Use the group to work through difficult readings, assignments, or problems. If an assignment is long, have each member take one section to explain, illustrate, and "teach" to the others. If you as a group cannot understand or solve something, seek out an instructor for help.

5. Give every member an opportunity to contribute.

6. Listen carefully to what each person says. If discussion lags or if disagreements arise, try paraphrasing what each person has said to see if all members are hearing the same things.

7. Establish regular times to assess how effective the group is, making individual notes on the following questions: What has the group accomplished so far? What has it been most helpful with? What has it been least helpful with? What have I contributed to it? What has each of the others contributed? How can we make the group more effective?

2

Considering Purpose and Audience

As a careful and effective writer, you will want to understand as much as possible about your purposes for writing and about those readers you're addressing. This chapter will get you started thinking about these crucial elements in any writing process.

2a

Deciding to write

In a general sense, of course, the decision to write is often made for you: you must take an essay examination at 10 a.m.; the editor of your newspaper sets a specific deadline; an instructor announces that an essay will be due next Tuesday. But even in such situations, consciously *deciding to write* is an important step to take. Experienced writers report that making up their minds to begin a writing task represents a big step toward actually getting the job done.

Experienced writers also tell us that when a topic is not assigned but left open, the best way to choose one is often to let the topic choose you. That is to say, those subjects that compel you—that puzzle, intrigue, or even irritate you—are likely to engage your interest and hence encourage your best writing. Even with assigned topics, you can often look for some aspect of the topic that is particularly compelling. Once you start to *wonder* about a topic, you are at the point of having something to write about.

It makes sense, then, to broaden your definition of writing to include your earliest thoughts on a topic and to move deliberately from those early thoughts to begin writing. The decision to begin working toward a draft represents an important point in the writing process.

Understanding writing assignments

Most on-the-job writing addresses specific purposes, audiences, and topics: a group of chemists produces a report on food additives for the federal government; an editorial assistant composes a memo for an editor summarizing the problems in a new manuscript; a team of psychologists prepares scripts for videos intended to help corporations deal with employee alcoholism. These writers all have one thing in common: specific goals. They know exactly why and for whom they are writing.

Academic writing assignments, in contrast, may seem to appear out of the blue, with no specific purposes, audiences, or topics. In extreme cases, a writing assignment may be only one word long, as in a theatre examination that consisted of the single word "Tragedy!" At the opposite extreme come assignments in the form of fully developed cases, often favoured in business, commerce, and engineering courses.

In between the one-word assignment and the fully developed case lies a wide spectrum of assignments and topics. You may get assignments that specify purpose but not audience—to write an essay arguing for or against capital punishment, for example. Or you may be given an organizational pattern to use—to compare and contrast, for example—but no topic. Because each assignment is different, and because comprehending a topic is crucial to your success in responding to it, you should always make sure you understand the assignment as fully as possible. Consider the following questions as you analyze any assignment:

- *What, exactly, does this assignment ask you to do?* Look for words like *analyze, classify, compare, contrast, describe, discuss, define, explain,* and *survey.* These are key terms, and you should be sure you understand what task they set. Remember that these words may differ in meaning among disciplines—*analyze* might mean one thing in literature and something rather different in biology.

- *What knowledge or information do you need to fulfil this assignment?* Do you need to do any research?

- *How can you limit—or broaden—the topic or assignment to make it more interesting?* Is there any particular aspect of the topic in which you have special interest or knowledge? Be sure to check with your instructor if you wish to redefine the assignment in any way.

- *What are the assignment's specific requirements?* Consider length, format, organization, and deadline. If this information was not given to you, you should ask for it.

- *What is your purpose as a writer in this assignment?* Do you need to demonstrate knowledge of a certain body of material, or do you mainly need to show the ability to express certain ideas clearly? See 2c for a discussion of ways to assess purpose.

- *Who is the audience for this piece of writing?* Does the writing task tell you to assume a particular readership besides your instructor? See 2e for a discussion of ways to assess your audience.

Once you can answer these questions, you will have gone a good way toward exploring an assignment and making it one you can accomplish.

Exercise 2.1

The following assignment was given recently to an introductory psychology class: *Discuss in an essay the contributions of Jung and Freud to modern clinical psychology.* Discuss with another student what you would need to know about the assignment in order to respond successfully. Then, using the set of questions in 2b, analyze this assignment.

2c

Deciding on purposes

The writing of essays, reports, and other papers almost always involves dual or multiple purposes. On one level, you are writing to establish your credibility with your instructor, to demonstrate that you are a careful thinker and effective writer. Fulfilling this purpose means considering your instructor's expectations very carefully, a concern addressed in detail in 2e. But good writing also accomplishes some other, more individual purpose that the writer has in mind. In fact, the best writing you do will be writing that in some way achieves a goal or goals of your own, that says as clearly and forcefully as possible what you think about a topic of importance to you, and what you have to say to readers about this topic. For example, if you are writing an essay about abortion, your purposes might be to share your knowledge of the topic with your readers, to persuade them to support or oppose current abortion legislation, or even to clarify in your own mind the medical information about abortion or the moral debate over it. If you are writing a profile of an eccentric friend you might be trying to amuse your readers at the same time that you are paying tribute to someone who is important to you.

In ancient Rome, the great orator Cicero noted that a good speech generally fulfilled one of three major purposes: to delight, to teach, or to move. Although the world has changed a great deal in the two thousand years since Cicero, our purposes when we communicate with one another remain pretty much the same: we seek to *entertain* (delight), to *inform and explain* (teach), and to *persuade or convince* (move). Most of the writing you do in college or university will address one or some combination of these purposes, and it is thus important for you to be able to recognize the overriding purpose of any piece of writing. If, for example, your sociology professor asks you to explain Canada's immigration policy (primary purpose: to explain) and you respond by writing an impassioned plea for increased openness to refugee claimants (primary purpose: to persuade), you are not complying with the purpose of the assignment.

For most of your writing, you should think in terms of purposes rather than one single purpose. Specifically, you should consider **purpose** in terms of the *assignment*, in terms of the *instructor's expectations*, and in terms of *your own goals*.

The assignment

Is the primary purpose of the assignment to entertain, to explain, to persuade—or some other stated purpose? What does the primary purpose suggest about the best ways to achieve it? If you are unsure of the primary purpose, have you talked with your instructor or other classmates about it? Are there any secondary purposes to keep in mind?

The instructor's expectations

What are the instructor's purposes in giving this assignment—to make sure you have read certain materials? to determine whether you understand certain materials? to evaluate your thinking and writing abilities? to determine whether you can evaluate certain materials critically? What can you include in your essay to fulfil these purposes?

Your own goals

What are your purposes in carrying out this assignment—to respond to the topic adequately and accurately? to meet the instructor's expectations? to learn as much as possible about a new topic? to communicate your ideas as clearly and forcefully as possible? What can you include in your essay in order to achieve these goals?

Exercise 2.2

Working with a small group, choose one of the following assignments and describe its various purposes. One group member should take notes and prepare to report to the rest of the class.

1. Discuss the controversies surrounding some aspect of the Royal Commission report on reproductive technologies.

2. Write about a person who has been important in your life, and describe why he or she has affected you strongly.

3. Support or attack Canadian policy on peacekeeping.

4. Analyze the use of headlines in a group of twenty advertisements.

5. Discuss the effect of some recent invention on everyday life.

2d

Considering your rhetorical stance

"Where do you stand on that?" is a question often asked, particularly of those running for office or already occupying positions of authority. As writers, we must ask the question of ourselves as well. "Where you stand" on your topic, your **rhetorical stance**, is important to your writing; and an understanding of this stance is closely related to an understanding of your purposes for writing and of your intended audience. Thinking about your stance will help you examine the feelings you have on any topic and thus help you address the topic fully. And knowing your own stance well will help you see in what way the stance might differ from those positions held by members of your audience.

A student writing a proposal for increased disability services, for instance, knew that her stance on this topic was profoundly influenced by the fact that she had a brother with Down's syndrome. She knew, therefore, that she brought to this topic an intense interest that she couldn't count on in her audience. She would need to work hard, then, on finding ways to get her audience to understand—and share—her stance.

These questions will help you consider your own rhetorical stance:

- What is your overall attitude toward the topic? approval? dislike? curiosity? indifference? How strong are your feelings?

- How much do you know about the topic? What questions do you have about it?

- What interests you *most* about the topic? Why?
- What interests you *least* about it? Why?
- What seems important (or unimportant) about the topic?
- What preconceptions, if any, do you have about it?
- What do you expect to conclude about the topic?

2e

Considering audiences

Although you may sometimes write only to yourself (as in diaries or personal journals, for example), most of your college or university writing will be addressed to others. An important part of your writing process, therefore, involves thinking about your **audience**.

For much of your academic writing, an instructor may serve as the primary audience. You may, however, sometimes find yourself writing for others: lab reports addressed to your class, business proposals addressed to a hypothetical manager, or, in one Canadian history class, a letter to a 17-year-old living in the year 1914. Every writer can benefit from thinking carefully about who the audience is, what the audience already knows or thinks, and what the audience needs and expects to find out. The following questions will help you begin to think about the audience for your writing:

- What group of people do you most want to reach? your boss? other students? scientists? people already sympathetic to your views? people unsympathetic to your views? potential voters? members of a group you belong to—or don't belong to?

- How much do you know about your intended audience? In what ways may its members differ from you? from one another? Think in terms of level of education, geographical region, age, sex, occupation, social class, ethnic and cultural heritage, politics, religion, marital status, sexual orientation, and so on.

- What assumptions do you make about your audience? What might its members value? Think in terms of qualities such as brevity, originality, conformity, honesty, security, adventure, wit, seriousness, thrift, generosity, and so on. What goals and aspirations do they have?

- What is your audience's stance on your topic? What are the audience members likely to know about it? What preconceived views might they have?

- What do you need to be sensitive to in your audience's background?
- What is your relationship to the audience? Is it student to instructor? friend to friend? subordinate to superior? superior to subordinate? citizen to community? something else?
- What is your attitude toward the audience? friendly? hostile? neutral? admiring? impatient?
- What attitudes will the audience expect you to hold? What attitudes might disturb or offend its members?
- What kind(s) of response(s) do you want to evoke?

1. Addressing specific audiences

Thinking systematically about your audience will help you decide what sort of organizational plan to follow, what information to include or to exclude, and even what specific words to choose. If you are writing an article for a magazine for nurses about a new drug prescribed to prevent patients from developing infections from intravenous feeding tubes, you will not need to give much information about how such tubes work or to define many terms. But if you are writing about the same topic in a pamphlet given to patients when they check into the hospital, you will have to give a great deal of background information and define (or avoid) any technical terms.

Exercise 2.3

In order to experiment with the way considerations of appropriateness for a particular audience affect what you write, describe the last cultural or social event you especially enjoyed to three different audiences: first to your best friend, then to a parent or other older relative, then to a group of high-school students attending an open house at your college or university. Then discuss with another student the differences in content, organization, and wording that the differences in audience led you to make.

2. Appealing to your whole audience

Writers must attend carefully to the ways in which their writing can make readers feel part of an audience or can leave them out. Look at the following sentence, for example:

> As every schoolchild knows, the world is losing its rain forests at the rate of one acre per second.

The writer here gives a clear message about who is and who is not part of her audience. Those who do not know what "every schoolchild knows" are excluded by this writing. In order to make your readers feel they are really a part of your audience, you should be careful *not* to assume that your audience thinks as you do or knows what you know.

Exercise 2.4

Reading with an eye for purpose and audience

Advertisements provide good examples of writing that is tailored carefully for specific audiences. Find two ads for the same product that appeal to different audiences. You might compare ads in a men's magazine with those in a women's magazine to see what differences there are in the message and photography. Or you could look at products that seem to appeal to men (Irish Spring soap perhaps) next to those that are marketed to women (such as Dove soap). What conclusions can you draw about ways of appealing to specific audiences?

Exercise 2.5

Taking inventory: purpose and audience

Consider something you have written or are working on right now.

1. Can you state its purpose(s) clearly and succinctly? If not, what can you do to clarify its purpose(s)?

2. What other purposes for this piece of writing can you imagine? How would fulfilling some other purpose change the writing?

3. Can you tell from reading the text who the intended audience is? If so, what in your text clearly aims to relate to that audience? If not, what can you add that will help you appeal to this audience?

4. What other audiences can you imagine? How would the writing change if you were to address some different audience?

If you are keeping a writing log, enter any conclusions you can make about purpose and audience in your own writing.

3

Exploring, Planning, Drafting

Lewis Thomas, a leading American essayist, began writing essays when he was invited to contribute a monthly column for the *New England Journal of Medicine*. A scientist and medical doctor, Thomas at first tried various methods of planning and organizing his columns, including meticulous outlines. Nothing seemed to work. After producing several of what Thomas himself considered "dreadful" essays, therefore, he shook off all attempts at detailed planning and plunged right in, thinking about and developing his ideas by simply writing as fast as he could.

Like Thomas, you may do best by diving right into your writing projects, exploring your topics as you draft. Or you may work more effectively by doing extensive exploration and producing detailed blueprints before you ever begin drafting. This chapter takes a look at several ways of exploring, planning, and drafting.

Exploring a topic

The point is so simple that we often forget it: we write best about topics we know well. One of the most important parts of the entire writing process, therefore, is exploring your topic, surveying what you know about it, and then determining what you need to find out.

You may already have a good system for exploring topics you wish to write about. If so, use it and share it with friends and members of your class. If you have no particular personal system, however, this chapter provides a brief description of strategies designed to help you explore a topic. These strategies can be very useful in getting you started in your thinking about a topic and in helping you determine what you already know–and indeed in helping you solve problems that crop up later in the writing of an essay. The strategies include brainstorming, freewriting, looping, clustering, and questioning.

1. Brainstorming

Used widely in business, industry, and engineering, **brainstorming** involves tossing out ideas—often with several other people—in order to find new or fresh ways to approach a topic. You can adapt brainstorming to writing, however, by quickly writing down everything that occurs to you about a topic. All you need is a pen or pencil and a blank sheet of paper with which to carry out the following steps:

1. Give yourself a time limit—five or ten minutes, perhaps—and write down in list form *every* word or phrase that comes into your mind about your topic. Just put down key words and phrases, not sentences. No one has to understand the list but you. Don't worry about whether something will be useful or not. Just get it *all* down.

2. If nothing much seems to occur to you, try "thinking the opposite." If you are trying, for instance, to think of reasons to reduce tuition at your college and are coming up blank, try concentrating on reasons to *increase* tuition. Once you start generating ideas in one direction, you can move back to exploring the other side of the topic.

3. When the time is up, stop and read over your list. If anything else comes to you, add it to the list. Then reread the list, looking for patterns, clusters of interesting ideas, or one central idea.

2. Freewriting

Freewriting is a method of exploring a topic by writing about it—or whatever else it brings to mind—for a period of time *without stopping*. Here is the way to do it:

1. Set a time limit of no more than ten minutes. Begin by thinking about your topic, and then simply let your mind wander and write down everything that occurs to you, in complete sentences as much as possible. Don't stop for anything; if necessary, write "I can't think of what to write next" over and over until something else occurs to you.

2. When the time is up, stop and look at what you've written. You are sure to find much that is unusable, irrelevant, or nonsensical. But you may also find important insights and ideas that you didn't even know you had.

3. Looping

Looping is a form of directed freewriting that narrows or focuses a topic in five-minute stages, or "loops." As in freewriting, you first write whatever comes to mind about your topic, basically following the free flow of your thoughts. Then you follow the central thread of those thoughts wherever it leads you. Here is how to do looping:

1. With your topic in mind, spend five minutes freewriting *without stopping*. This is your first loop.

2. Look back at what you have written. Find the strongest or most intriguing thought. This is your "centre of gravity," which you should summarize in a single sentence; it will become the starting point of your next loop.

3. Starting with the summary sentence from your first loop, spend another five minutes freewriting. This second loop circles around the centre of gravity in the first loop, just as the first loop circled around your topic. Look for a centre of gravity within this second piece of freewriting, which will form the basis of a third loop.

4. Keep this process going until you have discovered a clear angle on your topic or something about it you can pursue in a full-length essay.

4. Clustering

Clustering is a way of generating ideas using a visual scheme or chart. It is especially useful for understanding the relationships among the parts of a broad topic or for developing subtopics. Clustering is done as follows:

1. Write down your topic in the middle of a blank piece of paper, and circle it.

2. Write down what you see as the main parts of the topic in a ring around the topic circle. Circle each one and draw a line from it to the topic in the centre.

3. Think of any ideas, examples, facts, or other details relating to each main part. Write each of these down near the appropriate part, circle it, and draw a line from it to the part.

4. Repeat this process with each new circle until you can't think of any more details to add. Some of these trails may lead to dead ends, but you will end up with various trains of thought to follow and many useful connections among ideas.

5. Questioning

The strategies presented thus far for exploring topics are all informal and based on free association of ideas. But there are more formal and structured ways of approaching topics that involve **asking**—and answering—particular **questions**. The following are several widely used sets of questions designed to help you generate ideas about your topic.

Questions to describe a topic

Originally developed by Aristotle, these questions can help you explore any topic by carefully and systematically describing it:

1. *What is it?* What are its characteristics, dimensions, features, and parts? What does it look like?

2. *What caused it?* What changes occurred to create your topic? How is it changing? How will it change? What part of a changing process is your topic? What may it lead to in the future?

3. *What is it like or unlike?* What features differentiate your topic from others? What analogies does your topic support?

4. *What is it part of?* What larger system is your topic a part of? How is your topic related to this larger system?

5. *What do people say about it?* What reaction does your topic arouse in people? What about the topic causes those reactions?

Questions to explain a topic

This is the well-known question set of *who, what, when, where, why,* and *how.* Widely used in news reporting, these questions are especially useful to help you explain a topic:

1. *Who* is doing it?
2. *What* is at issue?
3. *When* does it begin? *When* does it end?
4. *Where* is it taking place?
5. *Why* does it occur?
6. *How* is it done?

Questions to persuade

When your purpose is to persuade or convince, answering the following questions developed by the philosopher Stephen Toulmin can help you think analytically about your topic:

1. What CLAIM are you making about your topic?
2. What GOOD REASONS support your claim about the topic?
3. What UNDERLYING ASSUMPTIONS support the reasons for your claim?
4. What BACKUP EVIDENCE do you have or can you find to add further support to your claim?
5. What REFUTATIONS can be made against your claim?
6. In what ways is or should your claim be QUALIFIED?

Systematically using any of these strategies will be helpful, for doing so will get you thinking seriously about your topic—and putting your thoughts on paper. So don't be discouraged if your first attempts at looping or answering questions about a topic fail to produce timeless prose or revolutionary ideas. Be persistent, and these exploratory systems should begin to show results.

3b

Using a computer for exploring and planning

Some specially designed planning programs for word processors can help you with preliminary writing tasks by asking a series of questions and recording your responses. After the questioning session, you can print your answers and use them to guide your composing.

If you do not have access to a planning program, you can use a word processor to explore your topic as you would on paper, a technique that is especially helpful if you are accustomed to writing on a keyboard. You can key in notes, freewrite, make lists, write a series of loops, answer questions, and store all of these ideas in safe, yet easily accessible files on your data disk.

1. Looking at one student's exploratory work

Given the essay topics listed in Exercise 2.2, University of Waterloo student Andrea Imada chose to write on the effect of a recent invention on everyday life. The topic gave her fairly little direction—its key term was "discuss"—and this freedom of exploration appealed to her. She quickly chose television as her "recent invention," and identified her stance as basically in favour of the technology, but a little cynical about it and a little suspicious of its possibilities. She knew, since her main audience was her teacher, that she needed to make a logical argument and that she needed to be able to support her views with solid evidence. She identified as a further audi-ence—beyond her instructor—a group of fairly knowledgeable adults more or less represented by her instructor. She knew her first challenge would be to articulate a clearer purpose, and she began by brainstorming. Here are her brainstorming notes:

Communication	– local, global	news
Everyday life	– ideas	sitcoms
	information	drama
	entertainment	soaps
	violence	movies
	values	newsmagazines
	fantasy	cartoons
Technology		adventure
American culture/Canadian culture		documentaries
multicultural channel		educational
Newsworld		specialized
TVOntario		
Canadian content		

Brainstorming helped Andrea to get an idea of what she might have to say about television and its effect on everyday life. In order to find out whether she really knew enough to write an essay on the subject, she then decided to try one of the questioning techniques for further exploration.

1. What is television? It's a box filled with electrical wires, tubes, and other mysterious connections. It has dials, knobs, and a screen. Your turn it on, and a picture, a moving picture that is "real," appears. And sound comes from the TV speaker.

2. What caused television? Maybe movies and newsreels "caused" televi-sion. Years of technology, though, went into the creation of television. At first, it was black and white TV, then colour TV, now TV in stereo and high-resolution big screens. Television keeps changing and we keep changing with it. (What causes what?)

3. What is television like or unlike? It's like movies, only smaller. It's like photographs that move added to sound. It's like looking through a win-dow and seeing things within a frame. Only the picture keeps chang-ing. It's almost like being there, and it makes the world smaller, puts it at your fingertips.

4. What is it part of? It's part of a technological, electronic, cultural revo-lution. It's part of a communications system that includes radio, tele-

phones, computers, and everyday conversations. It's part of a fantasy world that acts out scenes; it's part of the "real" world, where scenes, events, and people are played back. It makes it hard to tell fantasy from reality sometimes.

5. What do people say about television? They say it's informative. They say it's violent. They say it's misleading. They say it's stupid. They say they can't stop watching it. They say a lot of different things.

Exercise 3.1

Choose a topic that interests you, and explore it by using two of the strategies described above. When you have generated some material, compare your results with those of other members of the class to see how effective or helpful each of the systems was. If you have trouble choosing a topic, use one of the working theses in Exercise 3.2

3c

Establishing a working thesis

A **thesis** states the main idea of your essay. Most kinds of academic writing contain a thesis statement, often near the beginning of the essay, which functions as a promise to the readers, letting them know what will be discussed. Though you will probably not have a finished thesis when you begin to write, you should establish a tentative **working thesis** early on in your writing process. The word *working* is important here, as the working thesis may well be modified, clarified, or otherwise changed as you write. In spite of the fact that it will probably change, a working thesis is important for three main reasons: (1) it directs your thinking, research, and investigation and thus keeps you on track; (2) it helps you to focus on a particular point about the topic; (3) it provides concrete questions to ask about purpose and audience.

A working thesis should have two parts: a topic part and a comment part. The **topic** part states the topic, while the **comment** part makes an important point about the topic. Here are some examples.

```
┌────────── Topic ──────────┐ ┌────────── Comment ──────────┐
Recent studies of depression suggest that it is much more closely
────────────────────────────────────────────────────────────┐
related to physiology than scientists had previously thought.
```

┌──────── Topic ────────┐┌──────── Comment ────────┐
The current Canadian fishery crisis can be traced to three major causes.

A successful working thesis has three characteristics. It is potentially *interesting* to your intended audience. In its language, it is as *specific* as possible; and it limits and focuses a topic enough to make it *manageable*. You can evaluate a working thesis by checking it against each of these criteria. For example:

Preliminary working thesis

Theories of global warming are being debated around the globe.

INTEREST   The topic itself holds interest, but it seems to have no real comment attached to it. The thesis merely states a bare fact, and there seems no place to go from here except to more bare facts.

SPECIFICITY   The thesis is fairly clear, but not very specific. Who is debating the theories? What are the larger implications of the debate? What does the writer think of the theories or the debate?

MANAGEABILITY   The thesis is not manageable: approaching it adequately would require research in many countries and in many languages.

ASSESSMENT   The thesis is very general and needs to be narrowed before it will be useful. This preliminary thesis can be narrowed into the following working thesis:

Working thesis

Some scientists have challenged the notion of global warming and claimed that it is more propaganda than science.

Throughout this chapter and the next, we continue to follow the writing process of Andrea Imada as she works her way through one writing assignment. For her essay on a "recent invention," she produced the following preliminary working thesis:

    Television has revolutionized the way we communicate.

When Andrea subjected this working thesis to the tests of interest, specificity, and manageability, she found that her thesis was deficient in both manageability and specificity. It contained only a statement of fact and did not make any arguable comment on the topic. After considering the problem, Andrea did some freewriting, and arrived at the following working thesis:

> Television has revolutionized mass communication by bringing about a rise in consumer demands for an accessible, multi-focused, and instant vehicle for communication.

Exercise 3.2

Choose one of the following preliminary working theses, and, after specifying an audience, evaluate the thesis in terms of interest, specificity, and manageability. Revise it as necessary to meet these criteria. Compare your results with those of other students who have chosen the same preliminary thesis.

1. Drug abuse presents Canadians with a big problem.
2. Advertisements directed at children should be abolished.
3. Othello is a complex character whose greatest strength is, ironically, also his greatest weakness.
4. Beauty pageants degrade women.
5. White-collar crime poses greater danger to the economy than street crime.

Exercise 3.3

Using the topic of the assignment you chose in Exercise 2.2 write a preliminary working thesis. Evaluate it in terms of interest, specificity, and manageability, and then revise it as necessary to create a satisfactory working thesis.

3d

Gathering information

Many of your writing assignments will call for some research. Your instructor may specify that you research your topic and cite your sources, or you may find that you do not know enough about your topic without doing some research. Not all of your assignments requiring research will be described by your instructor as "research assignments." In any case, you may need to do research at various stages of the writing process—early on to help you define your topic, or at a later point to find examples in support of your thesis—but usually you will want to consider what additional information you might need once you have defined a working thesis.

Research itself can take many forms. In Chapter 4, for instance, we shall see how Andrea Imada spent time talking to other people to discover their attitudes toward television.

Detailed discussion of how to conduct both library and field research is given in Chapter 10.

3e

Organizing information

Exploring a topic and gathering information will provide essential data for an essay, but the data are *raw* until they are organized. Even as you are finding information, therefore, you should be thinking about how you will group or organize that information in your writing in a way that will make it accessible and persuasive to your readers.

The way you group your information will ultimately depend on your topic, purpose, and audience. In general, however, writers tend to group information according to these three principles: **space** (*where* bits of information occur); **time** (*when* bits of information occur); and **logic** (*how* bits of information are related).

1. Organizing information spatially

If the information you have gathered is *descriptive*, you may choose to organize it spatially (see 3a for questions that help you describe a topic). Using **spatial organization** allows the reader to "see" your information, to fix it in space. A report on the library's accessibility to students in wheelchairs, for example, might well group information spatially. In describing the spaces in the library that are most often used and evaluating their accessibility to a student in a wheelchair, the writer would most certainly present information one room or area at a time. (See 6c for examples of information organized spatially.)

2. Organizing information chronologically

Chronological organization is the basic method used in stories, cookbooks, and instructions for assembling or using various products. All of these kinds of writing group information according to when it occurs in some process or sequence of events. Reports of laboratory studies and certain kinds of experiments also use chronological ordering of information.

A student studying the availability of motorcycle parking in a campus lot ordered some of her information chronologically to show the times when motorcycles entered and exited the parking lot and thus to identify peak periods of demand for parking spaces. This student chose to present this information in narrative (story) form, using chronological order to build tension as the minutes tick by and the lot gets more and more crowded, the drivers more and more frustrated. She could have altered the narrative order, however, and told the story backward (using a kind of flashback technique). If you choose to use a narrative or story form for presenting information, you will probably use chronological order, but reversing that order—or starting "in the middle" and then going back to the beginning—can be effective in organizing data as well.

Chronological order is especially useful in **explaining a process**, step by step. A biology report, for instance, might include a description of a frog's process of circulation. An essay for an anthropology class might include an explanation of the rituals of initiation in a particular culture. If you decide to organize information about a process in chronological order, you can test whether your explanation is clear and precise by asking a fellow student to read the explanation and report how easy (or hard) it is to follow the steps of the process. See 6c for examples of information organized chronologically.

3. Organizing information logically

In much of the writing you do in college or university you will find it appropriate to organize information according to some set of logical relationships. The most commonly used **logical patterns** include *illustration, definition, division/classification, comparison/contrast, cause-effect,* and *problem-solution.* (See 6c for examples of information organized logically.)

Illustrating points

Often, much of the information you gather will serve as examples to **illustrate a point**. An essay discussing how one scientist influenced another might cite a number of examples from the two scientists' publications. An appeal for donating money to an environmental group might be organized around a series of examples of how such money will be used. If you use illustration in writing intended to persuade or convince, arrange the examples in order of increasing importance, for maximum effect.

Defining terms

Many topics can be developed by **definition**: saying what something is—and is not—and perhaps identifying the characteristics that distinguish it from things that are similar or in the same general category. A magazine article about poverty in Canada, for example, would have to define very carefully what it meant by poverty—what level of personal income, household assets, or other measure defined a person, family, or household as poor. A student essay about Hassidism for a religion class might develop the topic by explaining what characteristics separate Hassidism from other forms of Judaism.

Dividing and classifying

Division means breaking a single item into its parts; **classification** means grouping many separate items according to their similarities. Dividing a topic involves beginning with one object or idea and discussing each of its components separately. An essay about the state of the armed forces in Canada, for instance, might be organized by dividing the military into its different branches—army, air force, and so on—and then discussing the current state of each branch. Classifying involves putting items or pieces of information into categories. A writer discussing the student organizations on a college or university campus would probably call on classification as a way of organizing the information, classifying students' groups into service, academic, and social groups, for example. If you have been reading histories of the 18th century in preparation for an essay on women's roles in that time, and you have accumulated dozens of pages of notes in the process, you could begin to organize your information by classifying it: information related to women's education, women's occupations, women's legal status, and so on.

Comparing and contrasting

Comparison focuses on the similarities between two things while **contrast** highlights their differences, but the two are often used together. Asked to read two chapters in an introductory philosophy text, one on Plato and the other on Aristotle, to analyze the information presented and to write a brief response, a student might well use an organizational framework based on comparison and contrast. The student could then organize the response in one of two ways: by presenting all the information on Plato in one section and all on Aristotle in another (*block comparison*) or by alternating between Plato and Aristotle, looking at particular characteristics of each (*alternating comparison*).

Analyzing causes and effects

Cause-effect analysis either examines why something happens or happened by looking at its causes, or looks at a set of conditions and explains what effects result or are likely to result from them. An environmental-impact study of the probable consequences of building a proposed dam, for instance, suggests moving from causes to effects. On the other hand, a newspaper article on racial tension in Canadian public schools might well be organized by focusing on the effects of the tension and then tracing those effects back to their causes.

Considering problems and solutions

Moving from a **problem** or set of problems to a **solution** or solutions presents a natural and straightforward way of organizing certain kinds of information. The student studying motorcycle parking, in fact, decided to structure the overall organization of her data in just this way: she identified a problem (the need for more parking) and then offered two possible solutions to the problem. Many assignments in engineering, business, and economics call for a similar organizational strategy. One economics professor recently asked students to gather information on the latest slide in the stock market and to use that information to give advice to investors who lost money. The information that students gathered first defined the problem the investors faced and then formed the basis for potential solutions.

Exercise 3.4

Using the topic you chose in Exercise 2.2, identify the most effective means of organizing your information. Explain to another student why you chose this particular method (or these methods) of organization.

3f

Writing out a plan

Information that is well organized often suggests a plan for a draft. Our student who wrote about some possible solutions to the motorcycle parking problem on campus organized all her data and developed the following rough plan. Notice that her plan calls for several organizational strategies within an overall problem-solution framework:

INTRODUCTION
give background to problem (use *chronological order*)
give overview of problem (use *division*)
state purpose—to offer solutions

BODY

present proof of problem in detail (use *illustration*)
present two possible solutions (use *comparison*)

CONCLUSION

recommend that first solution be scrapped for reasons of (a) cost
(b) space (c) relative disadvantages

recommend that second solution be adopted and summarize benefits
of doing so

While an informal plan worked well for this writer, you may wish to prepare a more formal outline. Whatever form your organizational plan takes, however, you may want or need to change it as you begin drafting. Writing has a way of stimulating thought, and you may find yourself getting new ideas in the process of drafting. Or you may find that you need to go back and re-examine some information or gather more information.

Andrea Imada, whom we last saw exploring her topic and organizing the information she generated, worked with an informal outline. Outlining before writing is sometimes difficult, but Andrea was able to generate the following outline on the basis of her exploratory work for her essay on television.

```
    I  Introduction
       personal examples - TV 15 years ago
                         - TV today

   II  Life without television
       past vs. present - sources of news
                        - sources of entertainment
                          (examples)

  III  Life with television today
       Accessibility - all ages
                     - all groups (e.g., hearing-impaired
                       people, busy people)
       Expanded programming - number of channels
                            - specialty channels
       Speed - seeing things as they happen
             - consumer demands for everything in an
               instant (an "instant" society)
```

```
IV Television in the future
   More expansion in technology and programming
```

This informal outline shows elements of chronological order, description, division, and comparison and contrast. Andrea considers the development of television from past to future (temporal order); provides personal examples of the changing face of television (description); focuses on types of programs (division); and compares life without television to life with television and early television to current television (comparison and contrast).

Using a computer for organizing and outlining

Outlining is an important step in organizing an essay, but it is sometimes difficult to do on paper. By its very nature, planning is a dynamic process that changes as your ideas mature; often, however, as soon as you write an outline, it seems fixed and hard to change. For this reason, many writers find it convenient to outline with the help of a computer, since they can rearrange headings and subheadings freely.

1. Using outlining programs

Several commercial outlining or "idea-processing" programs can help you create a short, simple outline and gradually expand it into a full, multi-level sentence outline. You can experiment with your ideas, expanding a section of the outline by filling in more sublevels; or you can condense a section by removing various levels from the screen until you wish to call them up again. Some word-processing programs also have this capability.

2. Outlining with a word processor

If you do not have access to an outlining program, you can use word-processing software in much the same way, although it is less flexible. Start by making a list of the main topics you want to cover in your essay, and number them with roman numerals (I, II, III, and so on). Add subtopics as they occur to you, labelling subheadings with letters, the next level down with numbers, and so on (see 12b). Then use the **block insert** and **move** commands to add, reorganize, or renumber subheadings. With these functions, you can easily move, add, or delete topics, and consider various arrangements of topics.

Exercise 3.5

Write an informal outline for an essay supporting the working thesis you developed in Exercise 3.3.

Producing a draft

Most of us are in some sense "producing a draft" the moment we begin thinking about a topic. One writer reports that his best ideas for opening essays almost always come to him in the shower, another that she "practises" writing versions of paragraphs or sentences in her head while driving to and from work. At some point, however, we commit our thoughts to paper, sitting down with pen, typewriter, or computer to produce a draft.

No matter how good your planning, investigating, and organizing have been, chances are that you will want and need to alter some things as you draft. This fact of life leads to a first principle of successful drafting: be flexible. If you see that your rough plan is not working as you begin drafting, do no hesitate to alter it. If some information now seems irrelevant leave it out, even if you went to great lengths to obtain it. (One of the advantages of drafting on a computer is that the technology makes it easy to store—in a file of "outtakes"—the wonderful paragraphs you couldn't quite fit into the essay at hand.)

Through the entire drafting process, you may need to go back to some point you have already been through: you may learn that you need to do more research, or that your whole thesis must be reshaped, or that your topic is too broad and should be narrowed. It's best to approach writing as a learning process and not expect it to be otherwise.

Definite principles of drafting are hard to come by, because we actually know very little about how writers produce drafts. Nevertheless, you can profit by learning as much as possible about what kind of situation is likely to help you produce your best writing. *Where* and *when* are you most comfortable and productive? *What conditions* do you prefer—complete quiet? music? Do you have any *rituals* that help—exercising beforehand? making a pot of coffee?

Once you have learned as much as you can about the atmosphere most conducive to your best writing, make every effort to do your drafting in that atmosphere. A few other practical tips about the drafting process may be helpful to you:

- *Have all your information close at hand and arranged according to your organizational plan.* Stopping to search for a piece of information can break your concentration or distract you.

- *Try to write in bursts of at least twenty to thirty minutes.* Writing can provide its own momentum, and once you get going the task becomes easier.

- *Don't let small questions bog you down.* As you write, questions will come up that need to be answered, but unless they are major ones, just put a note in the margin and move on.

- *Stop writing at a place where you know exactly what will come next.* Doing this will help you get started easily when you return to the draft.

- *Remember that a first draft need not be perfect.* In order to keep moving and get a draft done, you often must sacrifice some fine points of writing at this stage. Concentrate on getting your ideas down on paper, and don't worry about anything else.

3i

Drafting on a computer

Drafting on a computer makes it especially easy to make changes—so easy, in fact, that you may be tempted to spend too much time correcting errors during your early drafting. Because the text that appears on the screen and on the printout is neat and clean, mistakes are not hidden as in the congenial messiness of a handwritten draft and tend to stand out more glaringly than they would in handwriting. Try not to interrupt your momentum and train of thought, however, by pausing frequently to correct mistakes. Concentrate first on setting down all your ideas, and second on revising and editing.

Once you become comfortable, drafting on a computer is so fast that you may find your eyes and mind getting tired. Many writers find that frequent short breaks help them work more efficiently at the computer.

Saving your text

Just as you can walk away from your handwritten or typewritten draft, you can let your word-processed draft rest while you relax and revise a bit in your head. But before you step away from the computer or turn the machine off, remember to *save* your draft, using the **save** command. In fact, it is a good idea to save your text after every few new paragraphs. Similarly, you should make a **backup copy** of material on your hard disk on a floppy disk after each session at the computer. These are ways to protect the product of hours of work.

It is also a good idea to print out your work at the end of each session. By looking over a printout of what you have written so far, you may discover the next point you should discuss or a different organization—ideas that didn't occur to you when you were looking at one page at a time on the screen. When you return to the computer you can incorporate these ideas and have all your changes in one place rather than on numerous handwritten inserts.

Andrea likes to draft on a computer because she enjoys the sense of the fluidity of her draft that she gets from the screen. Here is the first draft of her essay.

Changing Channels

It's Wednesday afternoon, 1974. I'm watching cartoons on television after school. My dad comes in and tells me to switch the station: he wants to watch the news. I think to myself. I don't understand why everyone always wants to watch the news. But I reluctantly get up and turn the channel dial. The dial clicks into place as I turn it. Channel 11 ... channel 10 ... channel 9 ... channel 8 ... the news. I go and sit beside my dad on the couch. "Don't worry," he says, "one day you'll want to watch the news too."

It's Wednesday night after class, 1989. I walk into the house that I share with three other students and throw my knapsack on the couch. One of my roommates says, "hi," and continues pushing the channel button on the television remote control. I can barely see the movement of her finger as she presses the button. Thirty different images flicker on the screen as she forays through thirty different channels. Flick ... The Sports Network. Flick ... MuchMusic. Flick ... weather. We settle on "The Nature of Things." In this episode, David Suzuki explores the problem of acid rain. My friend begins taking notes; she's writing a paper on the topic for next week.

These two examples illustrate some similarities and differences between television fifteen years ago and television today. Technology has improved, programming has expanded, and the popularity of television has remained steadfast. The profound effect television has had on the way our society communicates, though, is more telling than its popularity. Television has dramatically altered our means of mass communication and consequently, has impacted on our lifestyles.

It's difficult for many of us to imagine what it would be like without television. Before television, radio, newspapers, magazines, and the grapevine were the main sources of news and information. And movies, theatre, community events, games, reading, and the radio were the major sources of entertainment. Television has had a marked influence on our communication channels. Now, when we want the most up-to-date news on the election returns, we turn on the television. Many people who were once avid movie-goers now turn down an offer to go see a film on the big screen and say, "I'll wait for it to come out on video."

Television has expanded enormously over the past decades since the first prototype was plugged in. A glance at the listings in the local TV guide reveals 25 regular channels and 11 "specialty" channels. A closer look at the listings reveals a myriad of programs for almost every interest and age group.

In sheer numbers, television is accessible to more people than most forms of communication. Television can captivate pre-schoolers with moving images on the screen, even if they do not fully understand the narration. In contrast, a radio broadcast does not have the same captivating power because the visual element is missing, and the language is too complex for youngsters. Closed-captioning has made television programs accessible to people with hearing impairments. For those who don't have the time to read the newspaper, television offers short summaries of information that deliver the essence of international, national, and local news.

The popularity of television has resulted in the expansion in programming. Television viewers are no longer content with a selection of five or ten channels. Now, Canadian airwaves boast more than thirty channels offering a variety of programs that suit almost every taste, interest, and preference. Specialty channels have emerged which cater to consumer interests. Fifteen years ago, more than ten channels seemed luxuriant. Today, access to over three times that number is commonplace.

Television has had irreversible impacts on our society and our speed of processing information. We now expect to see events "as they happen." Television's ability to pass on information quickly has contributed to demands for "instant" products. "Instant" television is now a part of our society. We have come to expect the convenience of instant food, instant banking, and instant communication. Fast electronic transmission has fostered our expectations of a fast-paced society, where line-ups are short, and information is always "at our fingertips."

Consumer demands have propelled television to become a news, information, and entertainment industry which is continually expanding in both technology and content. In a few years, high resolution television on big screens will likely be in every home, and shopping television will become more popular. Both innovations reflect demands in the quality and convenience in our methods of communication. Television has revolutionized mass communication by bringing about a rise in consumer demands for an accessible, multi-focused, and instant vehicle for communication.

Exercise 3.6

Write a draft of an essay from the rough plan you worked on in Exercise 3.5.

Reflecting on your writing process

Finishing a draft provides a good opportunity to sit back, relax, and reflect a bit on your drafting, and to make an entry in your writing log if you are keeping one (see the Introduction, p. I-2). With the experience of writing still fresh in your mind, you can note down what went well, what gave you problems and why, what you would like to change or improve. When

Andrea Imada reflected on her writing process, she noted that freewriting was more useful for exploring her topic than was brainstorming or the posing of questions. She noted too that conversations with friends were particularly helpful for generating material for her essay. She thought that a real strength of her essay was its organization (you will see in Chapter 4 that the students who read her draft did not agree), and that a real weakness was her conclusion. She wrote in her log, "As is usual for me, the conclusion is weak, but I ran out of steam thinking about it."

Here are some questions for reflecting on your own writing process:

1. How did you arrive at your specific topic?
2. When did you first begin to think about the assignment?
3. What type of exploring or planning did you do?
4. How long did it take to complete your draft (including time spent gathering information)?
5. Where did you write your draft? (Briefly describe the setting.)
6. How did awareness of your particular audience help to shape your draft?
7. What have your learned from your draft about your own rhetorical stance on the topic?
8. What do you see as the major strengths of your draft?
9. What do you see as the major weaknesses of your draft?
10. What would you like to change about your drafting process?

Taking inventory: your own writing process

Using the questions above, reflect on the process you went through as you prepared for and wrote the draft of the essay you've been working on. Make your answers an entry in your writing log, if you are keeping one.

4

Revising and Editing

If you have analyzed your own process of writing, you probably know when you tend to revise and when you tend to revise extensively. Perhaps you also know what kinds of revisions you typically make. And a careful look at any essay you have submitted to an instructor will reveal how well you edited the paper. You may, however, have thought of revising and editing as one and the same thing; after all, both involve changes in a draft. The distinction between the process of revising and editing, however, is one that will be useful as you become a more powerful and efficient writer.

Revising involves re-envisioning your draft—taking a fresh look at how clearly your thesis is stated and how persuasively it is developed, how logical your organization is, how varied your sentences are, how appropriate and memorable your choice of words is. In each case, you are rethinking your aims and methods in terms of your original purpose and audience, and of all you have learned during work on the essay. Revising may call for changes both large and small. You may need to reshape sentences, rethink sections, gather more information to support a point, perhaps even do some further exploratory writing.

Editing, on the other hand, involves fine-tuning your prose, attending to details of grammar, punctuation, and spelling. As you edit, you work toward making your essay ready for an audience. This chapter will explore the processes of revising and editing, and provide you with a systematic plan for making the best use of these processes in your own writing.

4a

Getting distance before revising

The ancient Roman poet Horace advised aspiring writers to get distance from their work by putting it away for nine years. While this is not quite realistic advice for students (in fact, putting your work away for nine hours will sometimes be impossible), the fact is that the more time and distance you give yourself between the writing of a draft and its final revision, the more objectivity you will gain and the more options you will have as a writer.

Rereading your draft

You can best begin revising by finding a quiet and comfortable place to reread your draft carefully. For this reading, don't worry about small details. Instead, concentrate on your meaning and how clearly you have expressed it. If you see places where meaning seems unclear, note them in the margin. Reading your draft aloud can help you identify what needs to be revised.

After rereading, quickly note the main purpose of the essay and decide whether it matches your original purpose. At this point, you may want to go back to your original assignment to see exactly what it asks you to do. If the assignment asks you to "prove" something, make sure you have done so. If you intended to propose a solution to a problem, make sure you have not simply analyzed the problem instead.

At this time, think as well about how appropriate the essay is for your audience. Is the language formal or informal enough for the audience? Will the audience be interested and be able to follow your discussion? What objections might the audience raise?

Exercise 4.1

Take twenty to thirty minutes to look critically at the draft you prepared in Exercise 3.6, rereading it carefully, checking how well the purpose is accomplished, and considering how appropriate the draft is for the audience. Then write a paragraph that describes how you would go about revising it.

Getting critical responses to your draft

Rereading and reviewing purpose and audience will allow you to take a good, critical look at your draft. In addition to your own critical response to your writing, however, you may want to get responses from friends or classmates. Although you may trust your friends or colleagues to do a thorough job for you, remember that they probably don't want to hurt your feelings by criticizing your writing. You can help by convincing them that constructive criticism is what you need, and that trying to protect you by not mentioning problems does you no good.

But even honestly critical readers need to know where to focus their responses. In some cases, you may get exactly the advice you need by asking a quick, direct question: "What do you see as my thesis?" Be sure to pose questions that require more than yes/no answers. Ask readers to tell you in detail what they see, and then compare their reading with what you see. Merely asking "Is my thesis clear?" will not elicit nearly as much as asking "Would you paraphrase my thesis so I can see if it's clear?"

Following are some questions for evaluating a draft. They can be used to respond to someone else's draft or one of your own. When you ask someone to evaluate your draft, be sure that the person knows your assignment, intended audiences, and major purposes.

Reviewing a draft

1. *Assignment:* Does the draft carry out the assignment? What could the writer do to better fulfil the assignment?

2. *Title and introduction:* Does the title tell the reader what the draft is about? Does it catch the reader's interest? What does the opening accomplish? How does it catch the reader's attention? How else might the writer begin?

3. *Thesis and purpose:* Paraphrase the thesis as a promise: "In this paper, I will ..." Does the draft fulfil that promise? Why or why not? Does it fulfil the writer's major purpose?

4. *Audience:* How does the draft capture the interest of the intended audience?

5. *Rhetorical stance:* Where does the author stand on the issues involved in the topic? Is the writer an advocate or a critic?

6. *Supporting points:* List the main points made in the draft, in order of presentation. Then number them in order of interest to you, noting particularly parts that were *not* interesting to you or material that seemed unnecessary or added on for no reason. Review the main points one by one. Do any need to be explained more fully or less fully? Should any be eliminated? Are any confusing or boring to you? Do any make you want to know more?

7. *Organization:* What kind of overall organizational plan is used—spatial, chronological, or logical? Are the points presented in the most useful

order? What, if anything, might be moved, deleted, or added? Can you suggest ways to make connections between paragraphs clearer and easier to follow?

8. *Paragraphs:* Which paragraphs are clearest and most interesting to read, and why? Which ones are well developed, and how are they developed? Which paragraphs need further development? What kinds of information seem to be missing?

9. *Sentences:* Number each sentence. Then reread the draft, and choose the three to five sentences you consider the most interesting or the best written—stylistically effective, entertaining, or memorable for some other reason. Then choose the three to five sentences you see as weakest, whether boring, bland, or simply uninspired. Are sentences varied in length, in structure, and in their openings?

10. *Words:* Mark words that are particularly effective—those that draw vivid pictures or provoke strong responses. Then mark words that are confusing or unclear. Do any words need to be defined? Are verbs active and vivid?

11. *Tone:* How does the writer come across in the draft—as serious, humorous, satiric, persuasive, passionately committed, highly objective? Mark specific places in the draft where the writer's voice comes through most clearly. Is the tone appropriate to the topic and the audience? Is the tone consistent throughout the essay? If not, is there a reason for varying the tone?

12. *Conclusion:* Does the essay conclude in a memorable way, or does it seem to end abruptly or trail off into vagueness? If you like the conclusion, tell why. How else might the essay end?

13. *Final thoughts:* What are the main strengths and weaknesses in the draft? What surprised you—and why? What was the single most important thing said?

Two student responses to Andrea Imada's draft

RESPONSE ONE

1. *Assignment:* You're talking about the effect of television, but somehow not on everyday life, exactly.

2. *Title and introduction:* I like your title. And I think your opening is great—not a standard intro, but better. You set up the

compare/contrast idea right away. It makes me want to keep read-ing. I liked that you even contrasted the clicking sound of the dial in 1974 and the touch of the remote in 1989.

3. *Thesis and purpose:* Your essay describes how "technology has improved, programming has expanded, and the popularity of television has remained steadfast." But if you really want to talk about the effect of TV on everyday life, maybe you should expand on "television has dramatically altered our means of mass com-munication and consequently has impacted on our lifestyles."

4. *Audience:* Seems like this could be written for any of us in the class.

5. *Rhetorical stance:* I'm getting the impression you feel pretty critical of television and even of us, its slaves.

6. *Supporting points:* (1) News sources and entertainment sources not what they used to be; (2) Many more programs are available now and TV is more accessible now; (3) Programming has expanded. You don't seem to start to get into impact until the second to last paragraph, so ...

7. *Organization:* May need some work. The supporting points for your thesis statement (if it's the one on the impact of TV) don't come up till the end of the essay. To support what I think is your thesis, you say (1) we expect to "see" events; (2) we expect instant everything; (3) we expect access to everything. Maybe you should say more about these things earlier.

8. *Paragraphs:* Your paragraphs are developed really well. I liked all of them. I don't always see how they're connected, though.

9. *Sentences:* These are my favourite sentences: "My dad comes in ..." in the first paragraph; "My friend begins ..." in the second; the pair of sentences starting "Fifteen years ago" in the third to last paragraph. You're really good at balance and create great effects with semicolons. These sentences could be better: the first one—because there are 52 Wednesdays in 1974; the first sentence in paragraph 4, "It's difficult for many of us to imagine what it would be like without television"—too many "it"s.

10. *Words:* I liked "instant" because it captures just the right idea and "knapsack" because it's so specific. I also thought using "flick" and "flicker" in the second paragraph was really nice. I didn't like "impacted" where "impact" is used as a verb or "luxuriant" which doesn't sound right or "narration" in paragraph 6 because the sound on TV is not necessarily narration.

11. *Tone:* You come across sounding confident, which makes you very credible. And I think the connection to the audience is good because you seem to think well of the audience. You're sharing your insights with us.

12. *Conclusion:* This tries to tie together strands in your essay that aren't that easy to tie together. It seems, actually, sort of vague to me.

RESPONSE TWO

1. *Assignment:* Yes, I think you carry out the assignment.

2. *Title and introduction:* Your title is catchy but not very descriptive, so it doesn't give me an idea of what to expect from your essay. Your introduction really draws me in—though I'm not sure it tells me what to expect either. The emphasis on the news makes me expect that in your second paragraph, you will be the one wanting to watch the news (as your father predicted), but that's not what happens.

3. *Thesis and purpose:* Three possibilities for your thesis: (1) Television today is different from 15 years ago; (2) Television has a profound effect on how our society communicates; (3) Television has dramatically altered our means of mass communication and has thus had an impact on our lifestyles.

4. *Audience:* I feel like you're talking to me, so I suppose that's good. On the other hand, I already know some of what you're telling me. Is that a problem?

5. *Rhetorical stance:* You seem to have strong opinions and to be in favour only of the best television has to offer.

6. *Supporting points:* (1) Before TV, things were different: TV has replaced other sources of information and entertainment; (2) TV has expanded—number of channels, types of programs; (3) TV is accessible to more people and more kinds of people; (4) TV has expanded (repeat of 2 in more detail); (5) TV has created (?) a consumer demand for "instant" everything.

7. *Organization:* Your organization plan seems to be a list. I can't find another pattern. You state your thesis in paragraph 3, and I expect you to develop it. But in P4, you're talking about life without television. P5 makes the same points as P7 and could be eliminated.

8. *Paragraphs:* I like your first two paragraphs because they use specific detail and I can "see" what's going on. P6 needs to be more specific. You have a good point about accessibility, but you use the word to mean a lot of different things.

9. *Sentences:* I like the pace of the last sentence in P8. Sometimes your sentences say basically the same thing in a slightly revised way. P7, for example, would be better if you eliminated repetition.

10. *Words:* I like the use of "flicker" and "flick" in P2, and in P6 the word "captivate" really captures the sense you're after. I'm confused by the shifting meanings of "communication" and "accessible," and I have problems with "forays," "impacted," and "luxuriant," which don't work for me in the contexts you've used them in.

11. *Tone:* I like the opening paragraphs where you seem to talk to me directly. You give up this immediacy of voice, though.

12. *Conclusion:* Maybe you shouldn't introduce new terms like "high resolution" and "shopping by television," which you don't have time to deal with.

As these responses demonstrate, different readers react in different ways to the same piece of writing. They do not always agree on what is strong or weak, effective or ineffective; they may or may not agree on what the thesis is. In addition, you may find that you simply do not agree with their advice. As the author, the authority on what you want to say, you must decide what advice to follow and how best to do so. In examining responses to your writing, you can often proceed efficiently by looking first for areas of agreement ("everyone was confused by this sentence—I'd better review it") or strong disagreement ("one person said my conclusion was 'perfect' and someone else said it 'didn't conclude'—better look carefully at that paragraph again").

On the basis of broad areas of agreement in the responses she received, Andrea decided on the following changes: (1) to develop her thesis about TV as an "accessible, multi-focused, and instant vehicle for communication" more directly and with fewer digressions; (2) to describe television less and concentrate on its effects more; (3) to say less about TV of the past and TV of the future.

Andrea also had some response from her instructor, who asked two questions: (1) Can you revise your opening paragraphs to support your thesis more clearly? I'm not sure of the connection between these paragraphs and the rest of your essay; (2) Is the main purpose of your essay to describe changes in TV or to argue the point that we communicate differently now because of TV? Andrea was certain that support of her thesis and organization were the two main areas she needed to work on.

Exercise 4.2

Using the questions listed in 4c as a guide, analyze the draft you wrote in Exercise 3.6.

4d

Evaluating the thesis and its support

Once you have studied the response to your essay and considered advice from all sources available to you, reread your essay once more, paying special attention to your thesis and its support. Check to make sure your thesis sentence contains a clear statement of the *topic* that the essay will discuss and a *comment* explaining what is particularly significant or noteworthy about the topic. As you continue to read, ask yourself how each sentence and paragraph relates to or supports the thesis. Such careful rereading can help to eliminate irrelevant sections or details and to identify sections needing further explanatory details or examples. If some points need more support, look back at your exploratory work and at suggestions from those who responded to your essay. If necessary, take time to gather more information and to do further exploration of ideas.

Exercise 4.3

After rereading the draft you wrote in Exercise 3.6, evaluate the revised working thesis you produced in Exercise 3.3, and then evaluate its support in the draft. Identify points that need further support, and list those things you must do to provide that support.

4e

Analyzing organization

One good way to check the organization of a draft is by outlining it. You may have written an outline *before* the draft, but your organization may well have changed as your drafted. Drawing up an outline *after* the draft is finished allows you to evaluate the organizational plan as it actually exists in the draft. After numbering paragraphs in the draft, read through each one, jotting down its main idea or topic in a sentence or phrase. Then examine your list, and ask yourself the following questions:

- What organizational strategies are used? spatial? chronological? logical? Are they used effectively?
- Do the main points clearly relate to the thesis and to one another?
- Can you identify and confusing leaps from point to point?
- Can you identify clear links between paragraphs and ideas? Do any others need to be added?
- Have any points been left out?
- Are any of the ones included irrelevant?

Andrea briefly outlined her draft in the following way:

1. Television then
2. Television now
3. Television has changed the way we communicate
4. Television and video vs. newspapers, radio, and movies
5. Expansion in programming
6. Accessibility to various groups
7. Expansion in programming (again)
8. Television and the instant society
9. The future of television and statement of thesis: "television has revolutionized mass communication by bringing about a rise in consumer demand for an accessible, multi-focused, and instant vehicle for communication."

Andrea's outline helped her locate some of the problems in the organization of her draft. She noticed that each paragraph dealt with some aspect of television, but that these aspects of television were not very well tied together— or shown in any clear way to support her thesis. She decided to concentrate especially on opening and closing sentences of her paragraphs, paying special attention to transitions.

Look, for example, at her revision to the opening of paragraph 4:

~~It's difficult for many of us to image what it would be like without television.~~ Before television, radio, newspapers, magazines, and the grapevine were the main sources of news and information. And movies, theatre, community events, games, reading, and the radio were the major sources of entertainment. Television has had a marked influence on our communication channels. Now when we want the most up-to-date news on the election returns, we turn on the television ...

Exercise 4.4

On the basis of Andrea's list of paragraph points, evaluate the organization of the rest of her first draft (in 3i). Begin by answering the questions given in 4e.

Reconsidering the title, introduction, and conclusion

First and last impressions count. In fact, readers remember the first and last parts of sentences—and of essays—better than anything else. For this reason, it is wise to pay careful attention to three important elements in an essay: the title, the introduction, and the conclusion.

1. The title

A good **title** gives readers information, draws them into the essay, and even gives an indication of the writer's view of the topic. It is an important device for defining what the essay will be. Andrea's original title, "Changing Channels," was catchy but did not suggest to readers what her essay was about. Andrea decided to add more information to her title, and changed it to "Changing Channels: Television's Influence on Mass Communication."

2. The introduction

A good **introduction** accomplishes two important tasks: first, it draws readers into the essay, and, second, it clearly states the topic and makes some comment on it. It contains, in other words, a strong lead, or a "hook," and often an explicit thesis as well. The most common kind of introduction opens with a general statement about the topic and then goes into more detail, leading up to a statement of the specific thesis at the end. A writer can also introduce an essay effectively with an *intriguing quotation,* an *anecdote,* a *question,* or a *strong opinion.* (See 6e for a fuller discussion and examples of various kinds of introductions.)

Both students who read Andrea's draft found Andrea's unusual opening appealing, and Andrea herself liked it. She decided to keep it, despite the fact that one student found it a little confusing and her teacher raised some question about its relationship to the rest of the essay.

Andrea tried, however, to respond to those comments by drawing the opening into the rest of the essay with changes to the third paragraph:

> Television has emerged from the realm of simple news and
> ^ ~~These two examples illustrate some of the similari-~~
> entertainment to become the central fixture in
> ~~ties and differences between television fifteen years~~
> the majority of Canadian homes.
> ~~ago and television today. Technology has improved, pro-~~
>
> ~~gramming has expanded, and the popularity of television~~
>
> ~~has remained steadfast.~~ The profound effect television
>
> has had on the way our society communicates, though, is
>
> more telling than its popularity....

3. The conclusion

Like introductions, **conclusions** present special challenges to a writer. If a good introduction captures readers' attention, sets the scene, and signals what is to come, a good conclusion leaves readers satisfied that a full discussion has taken place. Often a conclusion will begin with a restatement of the thesis and then end with more general statements that grow out of it; this pattern reverses the common general-to-specific pattern of the introduction. Writers can also draw on a number of other ways to conclude effectively, including, for example, a *provocative question,* a *quotation,* a *vivid image,* a *call for action,* or a *warning.* (See 6e for a fuller discussion and examples of various kinds of conclusions.)

Andrea's conclusion restated her thesis, but was unsatisfying because it introduced new material—about the nature of television in the future—that she was not able to explore. She decided to delete her specific comments about television in the future, and move from her statement of thesis to another general statement. She revised her conclusion substantially and ended it with this statement:

> It's a revolution that will inevitably continue, if our society continues to expect more innovation from television.

Exercise 4.5

Review Andrea's draft in 3i, and compose an alternative conclusion. Then write a paragraph commenting on the strengths and weaknesses of the conclusion she actually used.

Examining paragraphs, sentences, words, and tone

In addition to the large-scale task of examining the logic, organization, and development of their essays, effective writers look closely at the smaller elements: paragraphs, sentences, and words. Many writers, in fact, look forward to this part of revising because its results can often be very dramatic. Turning a bland, forgettable sentence into a memorable one—or finding exactly the right word to express a thought—can yield great satisfaction and confidence.

1. Examining paragraphs

Paragraphing serves the reader by visually breaking up long expanses of writing and by signalling a shift in topic or focus. Readers expect a paragraph to develop an idea or topic, a process that almost always demands several sentences or more (see 6a). The following guidelines can help you evaluate your paragraphs as you revise:

1. Look for the topic or main point of each paragraph, whether it is stated or merely implied. Then check to see that every sentence serves to expand or support the topic.

2. Check to see how each paragraph is organized—spatially, chronologically, or by some logical relationship such as cause-effect or comparison-contrast. Then determine whether the organization is appropriate to the topic of the paragraph and if it is used fully to develop the paragraph. (See 6c and 6d.)

3. Count the number of sentences in each paragraph, noting those paragraphs that have only a few. Do these paragraphs sufficiently develop their topics?

In preparing her outline following the draft of her essay, Andrea noted (as one of the students who read her essay had noted) that paragraphs 5 and 7 both covered the topic of expansion of television programming, and were separated by a discussion of accessibility of programming to particular groups (paragraph 6). She decided to consolidate the discussion of expansion of programming, though she still handled the topic in two paragraphs. The first developed the topic sentence, *"The growth of the television audience has also prompted greater variety and diversity in programming"*; the second developed the topic sentence, *"Viewers believe television should allow them to witness more events, give them access to more variety, and let them enjoy flexibility in their viewing hours."*

Exercise 4.6

Choose two other paragraphs in Andrea's draft in 3i, and evaluate them using the guidelines listed above. Write a brief paragraph in which you suggest ways to improve the development or organization of these paragraphs.

2. Examining sentences

You can add interest—and even elegance—to your sentences by looking closely at their length, structure, and opening patterns, and revising with these features in mind.

Varying sentence length

Too many short sentences, especially one after another, can sound like an elementary-school textbook, while a steady stream of long sentences may bore or confuse readers. So, most writers aim for variety of length, breaking up a series of fairly long sentences with a very brief one, for example.

In looking at the paragraph just before her concluding paragraph, Andrea found most of its sentences fairly short: fourteen, nine, fourteen, nine, fifteen, and twenty-two words. In revising, she decided to expand some of her sentences by adding more detail and making them more precise. She tried to combine two short sentences (the third and the fourth) to create one longer one, but found she then risked the monotony of too many *long* sentences. This is what she finally produced:

Television has had irreversible ~~impacts~~ effect on our society and ~~our~~ the speed ~~of~~ with which we processing information. We now expect to see events "as they happen." Television's ability to ~~pass on~~ transmit whether it's testimony at a murder trial, election returns, or the sold-out hockey game. information so quickly has contributed to demands for "instant" ~~products~~ goods and services. We have come to expect

the convenience of instant food, instant banking, and instant communication. Fast electronic
transmission has fostered our expectations of a
fast-paced society, where line-ups are short and
information is always "at our fingertips."

Varying sentence structure

The simple sentence is the most common kind of sentence in modern English, but using all simple sentences can sound very dull. On the other hand, constant use of compound sentences may result in a singsong or repetitive rhythm, while long strings of complex sentences may sound, well, overly complex. The best rule is to strive to vary your sentences; see 28c for advice on ways to do so.

One of the strengths of Andrea's writing is the control she has over sentence structure. Look at her sixth paragraph, for example. She begins with a simple sentence, expanded with various kinds of phrases. The second sentence is complex; the third is compound-complex; the fourth is simple; and the fifth sentence is complex with two dependent clauses.

Varying sentence openings

If anyone has ever noted that your writing seemed "choppy," the cause of the problem may have been unvaried sentence openings. Most sentences in English follow subject-predicate order and hence open with the subject of an independent clause (like the sentence you are reading now). But opening too many sentences in a row this way results in a jerky, abrupt, or "choppy" rhythm. You can vary sentence openings by beginning with a dependent clause, a phrase, or a subordinating conjunction. (See 28b for more information on ways of opening sentences.)

Leaving aside her two opening paragraphs, Andrea found she could improve the flow of some of her writing by varying sentence openings. She further revised her third paragraph, as follows, to shift one of her sentences out of subject-predicate order.

Television has emerged from the realm of simple news
and entertainment to become the central fixture in the
More telling than its popularity, though, is
majority of Canadian homes. ʌThe profound effect television has had on the way our society communicates. though,
is more telling than its popularity....

Note: As you go over the sentences of your draft, look especially carefully at the ones beginning with *it is, there is,* or *there are.* In some cases, such as the first sentence of Andrea's draft (*It's Wednesday afternoon, 1974*), which helps to set the scene for her essay, these constructions are perfectly good ways to start a sentence. But they can easily be overused or misused. A more subtle problem with these openings, however, is that they may be used to avoid taking responsibility for a statement. Look at the following two sentences:

> It is necessary to raise student fees.
>
> The university must raise student fees.

The first sentence avoids responsibility by beginning with the weak *It is*— and fails to tell us *who says* it is necessary.

Many writers use *it is, there is,* and *there are* openings not to avoid responsibility but just because they are easy ways of getting a sentence going. But they are often unnecessary, and using them gives the important opening spot of a sentence to a vague, weak word (*it* or *there*) and the most overused verb in the English language (*be*). Usually a sentence will be much stronger if it is rewritten to begin another way. Andrea decided to change the first sentence of her fourth paragraph this way:

Many of us cannot imagine what life
~~It's difficult for many of us to imagine what it~~ would
be like without television.

But you'll note when you look at her next draft that she finally decided to delete the sentence completely.

Exercise 4.7

Choose a paragraph of your own writing, and analyze it for variety of sentence length, sentence structure, and sentence openings. Then write a revised version of your paragraph.

3. Examining words

To an even greater extent than their paragraphs or sentences, writers' word choice, or diction, creates a sense of their personal voice in a piece of writing. As a result, writers often study their diction very carefully, making sure they get the most mileage out of each word. Because word choice is highly individual, general guidelines are hard to define. Nevertheless, the following questions should help you become aware of the kinds of words you most typically use.

1. Are the nouns primarily abstract and general or concrete and specific? Too many abstract and general nouns can create boring prose. To say

that you bought a new car is much less memorable or interesting than to say you bought a new convertible or a new Porsche. (See Chapter 30.)

2. Are there too many nouns in relation to the number of verbs? The *effect* of the *overuse* of *nouns* in *writing* is the *placing* of too much *strain* on the inadequate *number* of *verbs* and the resultant *prevention* of *movement* of the *thought*. In the preceding sentence, one tiny form of the verb *be* (*is*) has to drag along the entire weight of all those nouns. The result is a heavy, boring sentence. Why not say instead, *Overusing nouns places a big strain on a few verbs and consequently slows down the prose?*

3. How many verbs are forms of *be?* If *be* verbs account for any more than about a third of your total verbs, you are probably overusing them. (See Chapter 16.)

4. Are verbs *active* whenever possible? Passive verbs are harder to read and remember than active ones. *The student's question was answered* is not as easy to understand or remember as *Professor Corbett answered the student's question.* The passive voice has many uses (see Chapter 16), but in general your writing will be stronger—more lively and energetic—if you use active verbs.

4. Examining tone

Word choice is closely related to **tone**, the attitude toward the topic and the audience that the writer's language conveys. In examining the tone of your draft, you need to consider the nature of the topic, your own attitude toward it, and the attitude of your intended audience. Check the use of slang, jargon, and emotional language and the level of formality to see whether they create the tone you want to achieve (humorous, serious, impassioned, and so on) and whether that tone is an appropriate one given your audience and topic. You may even discover from your tone that your own attitude toward the topic is not what you originally thought.

Exercise 4.8

Turn to 3i, reread Andrea's draft, and describe the tone you think she achieves. Does the tone seem appropriate to her "interested, fairly well educated" audience? What changes in wording would you recommend and why? Revise the essay to create what you consider an appropriate tone.

4h

Editing

Because readers expect, even demand, a final copy that is clean and correct in every way, and because you want to make the best possible impression on your readers, you need to make time for thorough and careful **editing**. You can make editing somewhat systematic by keeping a personal checklist of editing problems. All writers have personal trouble spots, problems that come up again and again in their writing. Paying attention to the *patterns* of editing problems you find in your writing can help you overcome errors.

After identifying any typical trouble spots in your writing and getting advice on editing from this handbook, organize the information you have gathered in a systematic way. To begin, list all the errors or corrections marked on the last piece of writing you did. Then note the context of the sentence in which each error appeared. Finally, try to derive a guideline that will tell you what to look for to spot future errors of the same kind. You can broaden these guidelines as you begin to find patterns of errors, and you can then add to your system every time you write and edit a draft. Here is an example of such a checklist:

MARKED ERRORS	IN CONTEXT	LOOK FOR
wrong preposition	*to* for *on*	*to*
spelling	*to* for *too*	*to* before adjectives, adverbs
fragment	starts with *when*	sentences beginning with *when*
spelling	*a lot*	*alot*
missing comma	after *however*	sentences opening with *however*
missing apostrophe	*Michael's*	all names
missing apostrophe	*company's*	all possessive nouns
tense shift	*think* for *thought*	use of present tense
fragment	starts with *while*	sentences beginning with *while*
spelling	*sacrifice*	*sacrafice*
comma	after *for example*	*for example*

This writer has begun to identify patterns, like her tendency to write sentence fragments beginning with subordinating conjunctions (*when* and *while*), her trouble with apostrophes in possessives (*company's* and *Michael's*), and her tendency to skip commas after introductory elements. Some sorts of errors, such as the use of wrong words or misspellings, may seem so unsystematic that you may not be able to identify patterns in an editing checklist. (If spelling presents a special problem for you, keeping a separate spelling checklist as explained in Chapter 33 can help, or you may have a program that checks spelling as part of a word-processing package.) But keeping an editing checklist will gradually allow you to identify most of the error patterns that trouble you.

Exercise 4.9

Using several essays you have written, establish your own editing checklist based on the one shown in this section.

4i

Proofreading the final draft

Your final draft, of course, should be error-free, so you must **proofread** it to correct any typographical errors or other slips, such as inconsistencies in spelling and punctuation. To proofread most effectively, read through the copy *aloud*, making sure that punctuation marks are used correctly and consistently and that all sentences are complete and no words are left out. Then you might go through again, this time reading *backward* so that you can focus on each individual word and its spelling.

4j

Using a computer for revising, editing, and proofreading

If you have access to a computer, you will probably want to take advantage of it as you revise, edit, and proofread. A computer's word-processing program allows you to move sentences, paragraphs, and even whole sections of your essay around easily, so that you can experiment with various possibilities. You can also use a word-processing program to identify misspelled words and various other problems.

1. Revising on a computer

Some of the basic word-processing functions are especially helpful for revision: inserting, deleting, and moving. These functions allow you to reshape your text any number of times until you are completely satisfied with it.

Inserting text

The **insert** function found in word-processing programs allows you to supply details, supporting evidence, transitional words and sentences, and other material without retyping the entire draft. With this function, added copy merely pushes apart the words and sentences around it, making a place for itself automatically.

Deleting text

When you **delete** text, the rest of the document closes around it so that only the desired copy remains. In some programs, the text is not truly erased, but rather relocated into a temporary memory, from which it can be restored on command. If yours does not have this feature, be sure that you really do not want the text you are deleting. If you are at all unsure about whether you want to delete the text permanently, you may want to move the text temporarily.

Moving text

The **move** function permits you to move a block of text—a sentence, a paragraph, or an entire page—from one place in the essay to another. Because the original order is easily restored, this feature enables you to experiment with the organization of your draft without any retyping. You can even save the rearranged version under a new file name, print both the new file and the original one, and compare them to see which is more effective.

Revising from hard copy

While some writers find it useful to make revisions directly on the screen (not only near the end of the writing process, but all the way through it), many like to print out a hard copy and then revise on paper. Some will triple-space these draft versions of the essay or print them on the left half of the page only (where technology permits), so they can pen in changes easily. This system seems to work very well, with the writer then returning to the computer to enter changes and print the next version, which itself may be revised. The biggest problem here is the use of a great deal of paper.

If you are producing hard copies of drafts, it is a good idea to use the "draft mode" of print if your printer offers one. Letter-quality print, and certainly laser print, can impart an illusory sense of completeness to a draft long before the writing is finished.

Getting responses to your draft

Another advantage to printing out your early drafts is that you can easily print out several copies, distribute them to some of your classmates, and receive a number of responses at the same time.

2. Editing and proofreading on a computer

Once you have revised your draft and are ready to edit and proofread, the speed and thoroughness with which computers operate can be a great advantage to you, especially through the tasks performed by the **search** and **search and replace** commands. In addition, a spell checker can ease your task of proofreading for misspelled words.

Searching text

The **search** command enables you to identify a character or string of characters, such as a mark of punctuation, a word, or several words. The program then scans the entire text, stopping every time it finds the designated characters, which you can then change or correct. For example, if you tend to place a comma before the word *and,* even when one is not called for, you can execute the search command and enter *and.* The screen will highlight each place *and* appears. You can then check to see if it follows a comma, and then decide whether the use is correct.

Replacing text

The **search and replace** command not only locates a character or string, but also replaces it automatically with another. If you find, for instance, that you have been writing *affect* for *effect,* you can use the search and replace command to find every occurrence of the word *affect* and check to see whether it should really be *effect.* If you want to make the change, a keystroke will allow the computer to replace *affect* with *effect.* With search and replace you can also save time by abbreviating a long title or a phrase that occurs repeatedly in your paper: key in the abbreviation while drafting; after finishing the draft, use the search and replace command to find the abbreviation and replace it with the full word or phrase.

Using a spell checker

Spell checkers may be an integral part of your word-processing software; if not, they are available as separate add-on programs. Both work similarly: the program examines all the words in the text and tries to match each one against a word in its memory. If it cannot find a match, the program alerts you to the problem and you must examine the word yourself. Some spell checkers work as you type: the computer beeps if you type a word it does not recognize. Others you must institute yourself after you have finished typing. A good spell checker not only has a large standard dictionary of words, which you can add to, but also helps you correct errors by displaying a choice of words similar to the one it cannot match.

No matter how sophisticated the spell checker may be, the full responsibility of correction rests on you. If the program finds a word it cannot match in its memory, there may be several reasons. The word may in fact be misspelled, or it may not be in the program's dictionary. Many errors do not show up in a spell checker because the word, though incorrect in context, is nevertheless a recognizable English word: you may have used a permissible variant spelling, for example, *civilise* instead of *civilize*. The program also cannot tell that you meant to use *their* instead of *there, thorough* instead of *through*, or *either* instead of *ether*. Spell checkers can alert you to some misspellings and typographical mistakes, but only your own vigilance can produce an error-free paper.

Editing from hard copy

Even after using a spell checker and editing and proofreading on the screen, you should print out your essay and proofread hard copy meticulously. You may overlook errors on the screen (and so may your spell checker) that you may catch on hard copy. Furthermore, you can share your hard copy with classmates and have them check it over also. Once you have found and marked all errors and changes on the printed copy, correct them on the screen; then you can print a final copy.

Using a text-analysis program

Text-analysis programs are designed to identify a variety of patterns in sentences. Some programs look for punctuation errors; others look at sentence length; and some even attempt to identify wordy or vague sentences. Some point out a variety of grammatical errors.

The program creates a file of comments on your document. Depending on the capabilities of your particular program, it will isolate long sentences, too frequent use of the verb *be* and other weak constructions, and so on.

Text-analysis software is limited, however, in its usefulness: its judgments are relatively simplistic and may even be wrong; it is not sophisticated enough to judge shades of meaning, tone, the effect of a passage on its intended audience, or other stylistic considerations. If you experiment with a text-analysis program, act on its comments only when your own judgment tells you that they are valid.

You have already seen a number of the revisions Andrea made in her draft. Following is the edited and proofread version she handed in to her instructor.

Changing Channels: Television's Influence on Mass Communication

It's Wednesday afternoon, 1974. I'm watching cartoons on television after school. My dad comes in and tells me to switch the station: he wants to watch the news. I think to myself, I don't understand why everyone always wants to watch the news. But I reluctantly get up and turn the channel dial. The dial clicks into place as I turn it. Channel 11 ... channel 10 ... channel 9 ... channel 8 ... the news. I go and sit beside my dad on the couch. "Don't worry," he says, "one day you'll want to watch the news too."

It's Wednesday night after class, 1989. I walk into the house that I share with three other students and throw my knapsack on the couch. One of my roommates says "Hi," and continues pushing the channel button on the television remote control. I can barely see the movement of her finger as she presses the button. Thirty different images flicker on the screen as she forays through thirty different channels. Flick ... The Sports Network. Flick ... MuchMusic. Flick ... weather. We settle on "The Nature of Things." In this episode, David Suzuki explores the problem of acid rain. My friend begins taking notes; she's writing a paper on the topic for next week.

Television has emerged from the realm of simple news and entertainment to become the central fixture in the majority of Canadian homes. More telling than its popularity, though, is the profound effect television has had on the way our society communicates. With an expanding audience and diversified programming, television has become the dominant means of mass communication and has helped fuel our fast-paced lifestyle.

Television has had a marked influence on our access to communication ranging from news and information to entertainment. Before television, radio, newspapers, magazines, and the grapevine were the main sources of news and information. And movies, theatre, community events, games, reading, and the radio were major sources of entertainment. Now, when we want the most up-to-date news on election returns, we don't run to the corner store and pick up a newspaper; we turn on the television. Many people who were once avid movie-goers now turn down an offer to go see a film on the big screen and say, "I'll wait for it to come out on video."

In sheer numbers of users, television reaches more people than most other forms of communication. Television can captivate pre-schoolers with moving images on the screen, even if they do not fully understand the meaning. With the advent of closed-captioning, television programs are now available to people with hearing impairments. And for those who can't read the newspaper because of illiteracy or time constraints, television offers news, information, and entertainment without the need for reading. The near-universal accessibility of television, coupled with its convenience and availability, has transformed it into a predominant vehicle for all types of communication in our society.

The growth of the television audience has also prompted greater variety and diversity in programming. Television has expanded enormously over the past decades since the first prototype was plugged in. A glance at the listing in the local TV guide reveals twenty-five regular channels and eleven "specialty" channels. A closer look at the listings reveals a myriad of programs for almost every interest and age group: drama, comedy, news, movies, adventure, cartoons, documentaries, sports, talk shows, legislative debates, weather. Specialty channels have emerged to cater to specific consumer interests: The Sports Network, Newsworld, Youth TV, MuchMusic; seven others exist in Canada.

Fifteen years ago, more than ten channels certainly seemed ample. Today, access to over three times that number is commonplace. As a result, programming that reflects our social interests and preferences has become more readily available to television viewers. In turn, viewers, as consumers, have begun to demand more from television. Viewers believe television should allow them to witness more events, give them access to more variety, and let them enjoy flexibility in their viewing hours.

Television has also had an irreversible effect on the speed with which we process information. We now expect to see events "as they happen," whether it's testimony at a murder trial, election returns, or the sold-out hockey game. Television's ability to transmit information so quickly has contributed to consumer demands for "instant" goods and services. We have come to expect the convenience of instant food, instant banking, and instant communication. In our society, where time is at a premium, television has promoted and reinforced this attitude. Fast electronic transmission has fostered our expectations of a fast-paced society, where line-ups are short and information is always "at our fingertips."

Television is a communication device which is continually expanding its audience, its programming, and its technology. With these expansions, television has revolutionized mass communication by bringing about a rise in demands for an accessible, multi-focused, and instant vehicle for communication. It's a revolution that will inevitably continue, if our society continues to expect more innovation from television.

Exercise 4.10

Using the guidelines presented in this chapter, revise, edit, and proofread the draft you wrote in Exercise 3.6.

Taking inventory: your own revising process

While your revising, editing, and proofreading are still fresh in your mind, answer the following questions. Make your answers an entry in your writing log if you are keeping one.

1. How did you first begin revising?

2. What kinds of comments on or responses to your draft did you have? How helpful were they and why?

3. How long did the revising process take? How many drafts did you produce?

4. What kinds of changes did you tend to make—in organization, paragraph development, sentence structure, wording, adding or deleting information?

5. What gave you the most trouble as you were revising?

6. What pleased you most?

7. What would you most like to change about your process of revising, and how do you plan to go about doing so?

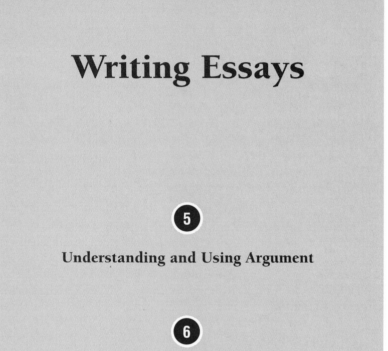

5

Understanding and Using Argument

Some 2400 years ago, Aristotle noted that we need to understand rhetoric (the art of language use) in order to create meaning, to express meaning clearly, and to defend ourselves against others who would use language to manipulate us. Those needs are no less pressing today as we approach the 21st century than they were for Aristotle and the Greeks in the 4th century B.C.E. In fact, written language surrounds us more than ever before, and this language—advertisements, news stories, memos, reports—not only competes for our attention but argues for our agreement.

Even supposedly abstract and uncontroversial subjects like mathematics depend to a large extent on successful **argument**: language whose purpose is to persuade. As two professors point out in a recent book, the common idea that mathematics represents an absolute, abstract level of truth is in fact a myth. "Mathematics in real life is a form of social interaction," the authors note, in which "proving" anything involves a mixture "of calculations and casual comments, of convincing argument and appeals to the imagination."* Since argument so pervades our lives, we need to understand and be able to use the strategies of effective argument. In this chapter, you will practise these "survival arts" of recognizing, understanding, and using written arguments.

---

* Philip J. Davis and Reuben Hersh, *Descartes' Dream: The World According to Mathematics* (Boston: Houghton Mifflin, 1988).

5a

Recognizing argument

In a way, all language use is argumentative, not in the sense of being combative, but in the sense of being persuasive. Even when you greet someone warmly, you wish to convince the person that you are genuinely glad to see him or her, that you value the person's presence. In this sense we are immersed in argument the way we are immersed in air: advertisements argue that we should buy their products; clothing argues that we should admire or respect the people inside; our friends argue—through their actions, their language, even their personal style—that we should accept and value them. Even the apparently objective reporting of newspapers and television has strong argumentative overtones: by putting a particular story on the front page, for example, a paper "argues" that this subject is more important than others, or by using emotional language and focusing on certain details in reporting an event, a newscaster tries to persuade us to view the event in a particular way. What one reporter might call *public assistance*, for example, another might call *welfare,* and yet another, the *dole.* We could legitimately find an argumentative "edge," therefore, wherever we find meaning in language.

As we saw in the last two chapters, for example, Andrea Imada's primary purpose in her essay "Changing Channels" is to explain changes in the uses and effects of television. Yet her essay clearly has an argumentative purpose as well: to persuade readers to see television as she sees it—critically. In Andrea's essay, then, explanation plays a major role and argument a secondary one. This chapter, in contrast, will look at writing whose *primary purpose* is argument, and specifically at ways to provide convincing support for a claim.

Of course, argument is not necessary in *every* case. If everyone can agree on the truth of a statement, no argument is needed. For instance, saying that personal ownership of computers in North America has increased in the last twenty years makes a factual statement that should not produce an argument. On the other hand, saying that computers pose dangers to mental health presents an arguable assertion that must be convincingly supported before it can be accepted.

In many important areas of our lives, widespread factual agreement seldom exists. Is nuclear power generation necessary? Should governments lower taxes on cigarettes? Should we take one job or another, live in one location or another, marry one person or another, or marry at all? Should we risk job security by protesting a policy we feel to be unethical? Is a new building an architectural masterpiece or an eyesore? Such arguable questions are often at the centre of our lives, and in most instances they fall into that area where absolute knowledge or truth is simply unavailable. To acknowledge that we can seldom find *absolute* answers to moral, political, and artistic questions, however, is not to say that we cannot move toward agreement on such questions by thinking clearly about them. In fact, this is precisely the way most human knowledge is gained: through the process of moving toward agreement through discourse.

In much of your academic work, you will be asked to participate in this process by taking a position and arguing for that position—whether to analyze a trend or explain a historical event or prove a mathematical equation. Such work will usually require you to make an arguable statement, to make a claim based on the statement, and finally to present *good reasons* in support of the claim.

The first step in the process of argument is to make a statement about a topic and then to check that the statement can, in fact, be argued. An arguable statement should have three characteristics:

- It should attempt to convince readers of something, change their minds about something, or urge them to do something.

- It should address a problem for which no easy solution exists or ask a question to which no absolute answers exist.

- It should present a position that readers could disagree with realistically.

Exercise 5.1

Using the three guidelines above, decide which of the following statements are arguable and which are not.

1. *Schindler's List* was the best movie of 1993.

2. The climate of the earth is gradually getting warmer.

3. The provinces must reduce health-care spending in order to balance their budgets.

4. Shakespeare died in 1616.

5. Marlowe really wrote the plays of Shakespeare.

6. Water boils at 100 degrees Celsius.

7. Van Gogh's paintings are the work of a madman.

8. The incidence of lung cancer has risen in the last ten years.

9. Campus day-care is primarily for the use of students.

10. Reduced speed limits contribute to lower accident rates.

Formulating an argumentative thesis

Once you have an arguable statement, you need to **make a claim** about the statement, one you will then work to persuade readers to accept. Your claim becomes the working thesis for your argument. For example, look at the following statement:

> The use of pesticides endangers the lives of farm workers.

Because some people defend the widespread use of pesticides, the statement is apparently arguable—it aims to convince, it addresses an issue with no easy answer, and it can be disagreed with. Although it does make a kind of claim—that pesticides threaten lives—the claim is just a factual statement about *what is*. To develop a claim that can become the working thesis for an argument, you usually need to direct this kind of statement toward some action; that is, your claim needs to move from *what is* to *what ought to be:*

STATEMENT ABOUT WHAT IS

Pesticides endanger the lives of farm workers.

CLAIM ABOUT WHAT OUGHT TO BE

Because pesticides endanger the lives of farm workers, their use should be banned.

This claim becomes your argumentative thesis. Like any working thesis, this one contains two elements: a topic (the statement about what is) and a comment (the claim about what ought to be). See 3c for more discussion of how to formulate a thesis.

TOPIC
Because pesticides endanger the lives of farm workers,

COMMENT
their use should be banned.

In some fields, such as literature or history, you will usually be making a claim that urges readers not to take action but to interpret something in a certain way. In this case, the claim about what ought to be will usually be implied rather than stated directly. For example, a history essay that makes the claim that moral opposition to oppression was the major underlying cause of the rise of the Parti Québécois is in effect arguing that readers should view the rise of the PQ in this light rather than as an economically or politically motivated process. Even scientific writers try to persuade an audience to view matters in a particular way—to view the molecular composition of a substance using a particular model, to account for an environmental effect using a particular theory, to explain an experimental outcome using a particular set of principles.

Exercise 5.2

Using two arguable statements from Exercise 5.1 or two that you create, work with another student to formulate two working argumentative theses, identifying the topic and the comment for each one.

Formulating good reasons

In his *Rhetoric*, Aristotle discusses the various ways one can argue a point. Torture, he notes, makes for a very convincing argument, but not one that reasonable people would resort to. Today we still rely on the three types of good reasons named by Aristotle—those that establish credibility, those that appeal to logic, and those that appeal to emotion.

Establishing credibility

To make your argument convincing, you must first gain the respect and trust of your readers, or **establish your credibility** with them. Your character is embodied in your essay, and the way this character is perceived by others largely influences how effective your arguments will be. The ancient Greeks called the character of the speaker *ethos* and placed great value on its role in persuasion. The little boy who cried "Wolf!" when there really was no wolf approaching was very quickly mistrusted by his townspeople. His was essentially a problem of *ethos*.

In general, writers can establish credibility in three ways: (1) by being knowledgeable about the topic at hand; (2) by establishing common ground with the audience, in the form of respect for their points of view and concern for their welfare; and (3) by demonstrating fairness and even-handedness.

1. Demonstrating knowledge

A writer can establish credibility first by establishing his or her credentials. You can, for instance, show that you have some personal experience with your subject. In addition, showing that you have studied a subject, done research on it, and thought about it carefully will itself be persuasive.

To determine whether you can present yourself effectively as one knowledgeable enough to argue an issue, you might consider the following questions:

- Can you provide information from *several* sources to support your claim?

- What are the sources of your information?

- How reliable are your sources?

- Do any sources contradict each other? If so, can you account for or resolve the contradictions?

- If you have personal experience relating to the issue, is this experience directly applicable to your claim?

These questions will help you to assess your own credibility in making a claim, and they may help you to see what other work you need to do to establish your credibility. They may well tell you that you must do more research, check sources, try to resolve contradictions, refocus your working thesis, or even change your topic.

The key point is this: arguments that establish credibility can *at the same time* be arguments that appeal to logic. By showing yourself to be knowledgeable (and, of course, you would not simply *tell* people that you were), you serve your persuasive purpose in a variety of ways. Keep in mind too that writing style—as well as grammar and even spelling—affects your credibility.

2. Establishing common ground

Many arguments between people or groups are doomed to end without resolution because the two sides occupy no common ground, no starting point of agreement. Such has often been the case, for example, in the abortion debate. The lack of common ground also dooms other arguments. If you and your roommate cannot seem to agree on how often to clean the apartment, for instance, your difficulty may well be that your definition of a clean apartment conflicts radically with your roommate's. You may find, in fact, that you will not be able to resolve the issue until you can establish a common definition on which to base the argument.

Common ground is just as important in written arguments as it is in public or personal disputes. Because topics and writers and audiences are so individual and varied, no absolute guidelines exist for a writer to establish common ground with an audience. Following are some questions, however, that can help you find common ground in presenting an argument:

- What are the differing perspectives on this issue?

- What are those aspects of the issue on which all sides agree?

- How can you express such areas of agreement clearly to all sides?

- How can you discover—and consider—opinions on this issue that differ from your own?

If you can establish common ground on an issue, you will have taken a giant step toward demonstrating good will toward your readers. We are inclined, after all, to listen with most interest and attention to those we believe to have our best interests at heart.

3. Demonstrating fairness

In arguing a position, writers must demonstrate fairness toward opposing arguments. Audiences tend to find more credible those writers who seem to represent fairly their opponents' views than those who seem not to have considered these views or who dismiss them. It is important, therefore, to establish yourself as open-minded and even-handed. Doing so often requires a genuine attempt to see things from another point of view—specifically, if possible, from your reader's point of view. Following are some questions that can help you discover ways of doing so:

- Can you show that you are taking into account all points of view? How?

- Can you demonstrate that you understand and sympathize with other points of view? How?

- What can you do to show that you have considered evidence carefully, even that which does not support your position?

- How can you demonstrate that you are open to other arguments, that you are not blindly advocating your claim?

4. Recognizing ethical fallacies

Some arguments focus not on establishing the credibility of the writer but on destroying the credibility of an opponent. In some cases such attacks are justified: if a political candidate has acted in unethical ways in law school, for example, that information is a legitimate argument against the candidate's election. Other times, however, someone may attack a person's character in order to avoid dealing with the issue at hand. Such unjustified attacks are called **ethical fallacies**. They take two main forms: *ad hominem* charges and guilt by association.

Ad hominem (Latin for "to the man") **charges** directly attack someone's character rather than focus on the issue under discussion, suggesting that because something is "wrong" with this person, then whatever he or she says must also be wrong.

> Molly Yard is just a hysterical feminist. We shouldn't listen to her views on abortion. [These "character" terms are used to distract the audience from the issue at hand.]

Guilt by association attacks someone's credibility by linking that person with a person or activity the audience considers suspicious or untrustworthy.

> Mr. Fleming does not deserve re-election as an MP. One of his staff assistants turned out to be involved with drugs. [Is there any evidence that Mr. Fleming knew about the drug involvement?]

Exercise 5.3

An advertisement for Greenpeace, an environmental group, appears on page 72. Study it carefully, and then list the ways in which the copywriters demonstrate knowledge, establish common ground, and demonstrate fairness. Do you think they succeed or fail in establishing credibility?

Exercise 5.4

Using a working argumentative thesis you drafted in Exercise 5.2, discuss with another student how you would go about establishing your credibility in arguing that thesis. Be sure to get some response to your strategy.

IF YOU KNEW HOW MANY DOLPHINS DIED TO MAKE THIS TUNA SANDWICH, YOU'D LOSE YOUR LUNCH.

Tuna fishermen have killed 6,500,000 dolphins over the last thirty years.

They didn't kill these dolphins for food. Or for use in any product. They killed them out of pure, blind greed. Then they tossed their bodies back into the sea.

It's just these dolphins' bad luck that schools of tuna often swim below dolphin herds. And in the 50's, fishermen began using "purse seine" nets to catch tuna more efficiently.

After a long chase, huge nets are set around dolphin herds to catch the tuna beneath. The nets are then drawn closed.

Exhausted and entangled in the nets, many dolphins suffocate. Others are crushed to death.

The Marine Mammal Protection Act of 1972 has helped. But not enough. Over 100,000 dolphins are still being murdered by tuna fishermen every single year.

Please donate your time or money to Greenpeace so we can continue our efforts to save the dolphins.

And if you must eat tuna, buy only albacore or chunk white tuna which isn't caught "on dolphins."

Better yet, don't buy any tuna at all. It will only leave a bad taste in your mouth.

GREENPEACE

Used by permission of Greenpeace, 185 Spadina Avenue, Toronto, Ontario

Appealing to logic

While the character we present in writing always exerts a strong appeal (or lack of appeal) in an argument, our credibility alone cannot and should not carry the full burden of convincing a reader. Indeed, we are inclined to view the **logic of the argument**—the reasoning behind it—as more important than the character of the person presenting the case. In truth, the two are usually inseparable and thus of equal importance. Nevertheless, strong logical support characterizes most good arguments. This section will examine the most effective means of providing logical support for a written argument: examples and precedents, testimony and authority, and causes and effects.

1. Providing examples and precedents

A well-conceived **example** can be extremely valuable in arguing a point. Examples are used most often to support generalizations or to bring abstractions to life. For instance, a *Newsweek* review of the movie *Star Trek IV* made the general statement that the movie contained "nutty throwaway lines that take a minute to sink in" and then illustrated the generalization with this example:

> When the crew, flying the Klingon warship they inherited … , land in Golden Gate Park, they fan out to different corners of the city … Kirk's parting command, spoken like a PTA mother at the county fair: "Everybody remember where we parked."

The generalization would have meant little without the example to bring it to life.

Examples can also help us understand abstractions. "Famine," for instance, may be difficult for us to think about in the abstract—but a graphic description of a drought-stricken community, its riverbed cracked dry, its people listless, emaciated, and with stomachs bloated by hunger, speaks directly to our understanding.

Precedents are particular kinds of examples taken from the past. The most common use of precedent occurs in law, where an attorney may argue a case by citing the precedent of past decisions. A judge may be asked to rule that a defendant was negligent, for example, because the Supreme Court upheld a ruling of negligence in an almost identical case ten years earlier.

Precedent appears in everyday arguments as well. For example, if as part of a report on campus safety, you back up your request for increased lighting in the library parking garage by pointing out that the university has increased lighting in four similar garages in the past year, you are arguing on the basis of precedent.

In research-based writing, you must list your sources for examples and precedents that are not based on your own knowledge (see 11d, 12d, and 12g).

2. Citing authority and testimony

Another way to support an argument logically is to cite **authority**. In recent years, for example, the use of authority has figured prominently in the antismoking movement. Some people will remember, for instance, the dramatic impact of the U.S. surgeon general's 1963 announcement that smoking is hazardous to health. The Canadian government followed suit with a variety of messages on cigarette packages, such as this one: "Warning: Health and Welfare Canada advises that danger to health increases with amount smoked—avoid inhaling." When these messages started to appear, many people quit smoking, largely convinced by the authorities offering the evidence.

As with other such strategies for building support for an argumentative claim, citing authorities demands careful consideration. Following are some questions you might consider to be sure that you are using authorities effectively:

- Is the authority timely? (To argue that Canada should pursue a foreign policy because it is one supported by John Diefenbaker will probably fail because Diefenbaker's times were so radically different from ours.)

- Is the authority qualified to judge the topic at hand? (To cite a chemist in an essay on linguistics is not likely to strengthen your argument.)

- Is the authority likely to be known and respected by readers? (To cite an unfamiliar authority without some identification would lessen the impact of the evidence given.)

Authorities are commonly cited in research-based writing (treated in Part Three), which relies on the findings of other people. In addition, you can cite authorities in answering essay examination questions (treated in Chapter 8) or in an assignment that asks you to review the literature in any field (treated in Chapter 7).

Testimony—the evidence an authority presents in support of a claim—is a feature of much contemporary argument. Most familiar are the testimonials found in advertisements—a television personality giving testimony for dog food, or a star athlete speaking for breakfast cereal. In fact, we are so inundated with the use of testimonials in television advertising that we may be inclined to think of them only in terms of *misuse*. But if the testimony is timely, accurate, representative, and provided by a respected authority, then it, like authority itself, can add powerful support to an argument. In an essay for a literature class, for example, you might argue that a new edition of a literary work will open up many new areas of interpretation. You could strengthen this argument by adding a quotation from the author's biographer noting that the new edition carries out the author's intentions much more closely then the previous edition did.

In research-based writing you should list sources for authority and testimony that are not based on your own knowledge (see 11d, 12d, and 12g).

3. Establishing causes and effects

Showing that one event is the cause—or the effect—of another can sometimes help to support an argument. To take an everyday example, suppose you are trying to explain, in a petition to change your grade in a course, why you were unable to take the final examination. In such a case you would most naturally try to trace the **causes** of your failure to appear—the death of your grandmother followed by the theft of your car, perhaps—so that the committee reading the petition would change your grade. We tend not to think of such analysis as a form of argument, but in many ways it is: in identifying the causes of a situation, you are implicitly arguing that the **effect**—your not taking the examination—should be given new consideration.

Tracing causes often lays the groundwork for an argument, particularly if the effect of the causes is one we would like to change. Recent figures, for example, indicate that the number of high-school dropouts is rising. If we can identify and understand the causes of this increased dropout rate—for example, a decline in reading skills—we may be able to make an argument for programs aimed at reversing the trend by affecting the causes in some way—such as hiring more teachers to provide remedial reading instruction.

In academic writing, you may often be asked to show causes and effects. In an environmental studies class, for example, a student may argue that a federal law regulating smokestack emissions from utility plants is needed because (1) acid rain originates from emissions at utility plants, (2) acid rain kills trees and other vegetation, and (3) unless checked, acid rain will destroy most forests by 2020. In this case, the first point is that the emissions cause acid rain; the second is that acid rain causes destruction of forests. The third point ties the previous points together to provide an overall argument from effect: "unless X, then Y."

In fact, a cause-effect relationship is often extremely difficult to establish. Scientists and politicians continue to disagree, for example, over the extent to which acid rain is responsible for the so-called dieback of many forests. In spite of the difficulty, though, if we can show that X definitely causes Y, we will have a powerful argument at our disposal. That is why so much effort has gone into establishing a definite link between smoking and cancer and between certain dietary habits and heart disease; if the causal link can be established, it will argue most forcefully that we should alter our behaviour in certain ways.

4. Using inductive and deductive reasoning

Traditionally, logical arguments are classified as using either inductive or deductive reasoning, which almost always work together. **Inductive**

reasoning, most simply, is the process of making a generalization based on a number of specific instances: if you find you are ill on ten occasions after eating seafood, you will be likely to draw the inductive generalization that seafood makes you ill. It may not be an absolute certainty that the seafood was the culprit, but the *probability* lies in that direction.

We all use such inductive reasoning for simple everyday discussions, but induction can be quite complex, as demonstrated by medical response to the sudden outbreak of an apparently new illness in the mid-1970s. This illness, later named Legionnaires' disease, resulted in many deaths. Medical researchers used a painstaking and time-consuming process of inductive elimination, examining every case in great detail to determine what the patients had in common, before they were able to generalize accurately about the cause of the disease.

Deductive reasoning, most simply, reaches a conclusion by assuming a general principle (known as a **major premise**) and then applying that principle to a specific case (the **minor premise**). In practice, this general principle is usually derived from induction. The inductive generalization "seafood makes me ill," for instance, could serve as the major premise for a deductive argument: "Since all seafood makes me ill, the plate of it just put before me is certain to make me ill." Here, of course, inductive and deductive reasoning would be working together to protect you from the likely effect of this plate of seafood.

The fictional detective Sherlock Holmes was famous for using deductive reasoning to solve his cases. Beginning, for instance, with the major premise "watchdogs always bark at strangers," Holmes applied that premise to the case of a stolen racehorse and reasoned that since the watchdog did not bark when the horse was stolen, the thief was not a stranger but someone the dog knew.

Deductive arguments like these have traditionally been analyzed as **syllogisms**, three-part statements containing a major premise, a minor premise, and a conclusion:

MAJOR PREMISE   All people die.

MINOR PREMISE   I am a person.

CONCLUSION   I will die.

Syllogisms may work for technical logical purposes, but rarely do they prove useful in the kind of arguments you are likely to write. They are simply too rigid and absolute to serve in arguments about questions that have no absolute answers, and they often lack any appeal to an audience. From

Aristotle came a less rigid alternative, the **enthymeme**, which calls on the audience to supply part of the argument. For example:

> This bridge is carrying twice as much traffic as it was built for, so we need to build a new bridge or restrict traffic on this one.

You can analyze this enthymeme by restating it in the form of two premises and a conclusion:

MAJOR PREMISE   Bridges should carry only the amount of traffic they were built for.

MINOR PREMISE   This bridge is carrying twice as much traffic as it was built for.

CONCLUSION   We need to build a new bridge or restrict traffic on this one.

Note that the major premise is one the writer can count on an audience agreeing to, or supplying: safety and common sense demand that bridges carry only the amount of traffic they are built for. By thus inspiring audience "participation," an enthymeme actually gets the audience to *contribute* to the argument.

Whether it is expressed as a syllogism or an enthymeme, however, a deductive conclusion is only as strong as the premises upon which it is based. The citizen who argues that "Edmunds is a crook who shouldn't be elected to public office" is arguing deductively, based on an implied major premise: "No crook should be elected to public office." In this case, most people would agree with this major premise. But the issue in this argument rests on the minor premise—that Edmunds is a crook. Only if that premise can be proven satisfactorily are we likely to accept the deductive conclusion that Edmunds shouldn't be elected to office.

While we may well agree with some unstated major premises (such as that no crook should be elected), at other times the unstated premise may be more problematic. The person who says, "Don't bother to ask for Jack's help with physics—he's a jock" is arguing deductively on the basis of an implied major premise: "Jocks don't know anything about physics." Careful listeners should demand proof of this premise. Because bigoted or prejudiced statements often rest on such irresponsible reasoning, writers should be particularly alert to it.

5. Recognizing logical fallacies

Logical fallacies are errors in reasoning. Though they cannot stand up to analysis, they are often hard to spot as errors. Indeed, such reasoning can often convince uncritical audiences. Sharp readers will detect fallacious appeals, however—and may even reject an otherwise worthy argument that relies on them. Your time will be well spent, therefore, in learning to recognize—and to avoid—these fallacies. Common logical fallacies include begging the question, *post hoc, non sequitur*, either/or, hasty generalizations, and oversimplification.

Begging the question treats a question as if it has already been answered.

> The United States was right to defend democracy in Nicaragua by supporting the freedom fighters in their struggle with tyranny. [By calling the Nicaraguan rebels freedom fighters and the government a tyranny, this writer begs the question of whether U.S. aid to the rebels actually helped to defend democracy.]

Note that "begging the question" denotes a specific kind of logical fallacy, and should *not* be used (as it often is used) to suggest the need to ask a particular question, as in "The change in legislation begs the question of who will benefit from the change."

The *post hoc* **fallacy**, from the Latin *post hoc ergo propter hoc, which* means "after this, therefore because of this," assumes that just because Event B happened *after* Event A, it must have been *caused* by Event A.

> Ever since the Liberals came to power, we've had problems with the deficit. [A causal relation is implied, but did the Liberals create the deficit problem or did they inherit it?]

A *non sequitur* (Latin for "it does not follow") attempts to tie together two or more logically unrelated ideas as if they *were* related.

> If we can send a spacecraft to Mars, then we can discover a cure for cancer. [These are both scientific goals, but do they have anything else in common? What does achieving one have to do with achieving the other?]

The **either/or fallacy** asserts that a complex situation can have only two possible outcomes, one of which is necessary or preferable.

> If we do not build the new aqueduct system this year, residents of the area will be forced to move because of lack of water. [What is the evidence for this claim? Do no other alternatives exist?]

A **hasty generalization** bases a conclusion on too little evidence or on bad or misunderstood evidence.

> I couldn't understand the lecture today, so I'm sure this course will be impos-

sible. [How can the writer be so sure of this conclusion based on only *one* piece of evidence?]

Oversimplification of the relation between causes and effects is another fallacy based on careless reasoning.

If we prohibit the sale of alcohol, we will get rid of the problem of drunk driving. [This oversimplifies the relation between laws and human behaviour.]

Exercise 5.5

The following brief article from *Newsweek* raises some provocative questions about causes and effects, and in doing so it uses example and authority. Read the article, and assess it in terms of the questions that follow.

Mom always told you chicken noodle soup could cure a cold. But could it prevent a disabling disease like Alzheimer's? That's what researchers are asking about a new chicken soup under development by Thomas J. Lipton Co. Inc. The still-to-be-named soup is enriched with purified lecithin, a nutrient undergoing testing as an Alzheimer's treatment. In accordance with Food and Drug Administration regulations, Lipton stops short of attaching medical claims to its new product. But the company may introduce it simply as "chicken soup with lecithin" sometime next year.

The soup is the brainchild of MIT Prof. Richard Wurtman and Harvard neurologist John Growden. Wurtman and Growden approached Lipton after discovering that purified lecithin could affect the chemistry of the brain. The purified lecithin, which is more concentrated than that sold in health-food stores, raises blood levels of choline, which, in turn, may aid memory.

Whether the new soup could benefit the general population is still unclear. But Wurtman and Growden are studying the product's effect on memory and fatigue. Says Lipton spokesman Larry Hicks, "The market may be much larger than we now know."

1. What is the cause-effect argument?
2. Is the link between cause and effect fully established?
3. What evidence would be required to establish that link more fully?
4. Does the use of authority or testimony help establish the link? Why, or why not?
5. What example is used in the introduction—and is it effective in illustrating the point?
6. Can you identify any logical fallacies?

Exercise 5.6

Analyze the advertisement in Exercise 5.3 for the use of examples and precedents; authority and testimony; causes and effects; induction and deduction; and logical fallacies.

Exercise 5.7

Using a working argumentative thesis that you created in Exercise 5.2, discuss with another student the logical appeals you would use to support your thesis.

Appealing to emotion

Most successful arguments appeal to our hearts as well as to our minds. Good writers, therefore, supplement appeals to logic and reason with those designed to **enlist the emotional support** of their readers. This principle was vividly demonstrated several years ago when North Americans began hearing about a famine in Africa. Facts and figures (logical appeals) did indeed convince many people that the famine was both real and serious. What brought an outpouring of aid, however, were not the facts and figures but the arresting photographs of children, at once skeletal and bloated, dying of starvation. In this case, the emotional appeal of those photographs spoke more powerfully than did the logical statistics. Writers can gain similarly powerful effects through the use of description, concrete language, and figurative language.

1. Using description

Vivid **description** provides one of the most effective means of appealing emotions. Travel articles and advertisements draw heavily on this principle: think of all the descriptions of sunny beaches that appear in newspapers during the dreary winter months. Description can work just as effectively in your written arguments. Using strong, descriptive details can bring a moving immediacy to any argument.

The student described in Chapter 3 who was at work on a proposal to make the library more accessible to students in wheelchairs had amassed plenty of facts and figures, including diagrams and maps, illustrating the problem. But her first draft seemed dry and lifeless in spite of all her information. She decided, therefore, to ask a friend who used a wheelchair to accompany her to the library—and she revised her proposal to open with a detailed description of that visit and the many frustrations her friend encountered.

Keep in mind that to say an argument is emotional is not to say it is *illogical*. Emotional reasons can be good reasons, and they are best used to support other good reasons.

2. Using concrete language

Concrete language stands at the heart of effective description and hence helps to build emotional appeal. The student urging improved wheelchair access to the library, for instance, could have said simply that her friend "had trouble entering the library." Such a general statement, however, has little impact; it does not allow readers to imagine themselves in a similar position. The revised version, full of concrete description, does so: *Maria inched her heavy wheelchair up the narrow, steep entrance ramp, her arms straining to pull up the last twenty feet, her face pinched with the sheer effort of getting into Main Library.* (Concrete language is discussed in greater detail in 30d.)

3. Using figurative language

Figurative language, or figures of speech, can also help to paint a detailed and vivid picture. Figurative language does so by making striking comparisons between something you are writing about and something else that is easier for a reader to visualize, identify with, or understand. Figures of speech include metaphors, similes, and analogies. **Metaphors** compare two things directly: *Richard the Lion-Hearted; old age is the evening of life.* **Similes** make comparisons using *like* or *as: Richard is as brave as a lion; old age is like the evening of life.* **Analogies** are extended metaphors or similes that compare an unfamiliar concept or process to a more familiar one to help the reader understand the unfamiliar concept:

> The most instructive way I know to express this cosmic chronology is to imagine the fifteen-billion-year lifetime of the universe (or at least its present incarnation since the Big Bang) compressed into the span of a single year. Then every billion years of Earth history would correspond to about twenty-four days of our cosmic year, and one second of that year to 475 real revolutions of the Earth about the sun.
>
> — CARL SAGAN, "The Cosmic Calendar"

Metaphors, similes, and analogies can all make an abstract or otherwise difficult concept understandable in terms of more concrete, everyday experience. James Watson and Francis Crick, who won the Nobel Prize for their work on the structure of DNA, used the metaphor of a zipper to describe how two strands of molecules could separate during cell division. In the same way, a student arguing for a more streamlined course registration process may find good use for an analogy, saying that the current process makes students feel like laboratory rats in a maze. This analogy, which suggests manipulation, helpless victims, and a clinical coldness, creates a vivid description and hence adds emotional appeal to the argument. For an analogy to work effectively, however, it must be supported by additional evidence: the student would have to show that the current registration process has a number of similarities to a laboratory maze, such as uncaring officials overseeing the process and confused students wandering through complex bureaucratic channels and into dead ends.

4. Shaping your appeal to your audience

As with appeals to credibility and to logic, appealing to emotions is effective only insofar as it moves your particular audience. Of course, you must always evaluate such appeals, being sensitive to your audience. You can't predict absolutely any audience's emotional response, but you can consider your topic and assess its probable emotional effects.

A student arguing for increased lighting in campus parking garages, for instance, might consider the emotions such a discussion will potentially raise (fear of attackers, anger at being subjected to such danger, pity for victims of such attacks), decide which emotions would be most appropriately appealed to, and then look for descriptive and figurative language to carry out such an appeal.

In a leaflet to be distributed on campus, for example, the student might describe the scene in a dimly lit garage as a student parks her car and then has to walk to an exit alone through shadowy corridors and staircases. Parking in the garage might be compared to venturing into a jungle with dangerous animals lurking behind every tree.

In a proposal to the university administration, on the other hand, the student might describe past attacks on students in campus parking garages and the negative publicity and criticism these provoked among students, parents, alumni, and other groups. For the administration, the student might compare the lighting in the garages to gambling, arguing that the university is taking a significant chance with the current lighting conditions and that increased lighting would lower the odds against future attacks.

5. Recognizing emotional fallacies

Appeals to the emotions of an audience constitute a valid and necessary part of argument. Unfair or overblown emotional appeals, however, attempt to overcome the reasonable judgment of readers. The most common kinds of these **emotional fallacies** include bandwagon appeal, flattery, in-crowd appeal, veiled threats, and false analogies.

Bandwagon appeal suggests that a great movement is under way and that the reader will be a fool or a traitor not to join it.

> Voters are flocking to candidate Smith by the millions, so you'd better cast your vote the right way. [Why should you jump on this bandwagon? Where is the evidence to support this claim?]

Flattery tries to persuade readers to do something by suggesting that they are thoughtful, intelligent, or perceptive enough to agree with the writer.

> We know you have the taste to recognize that an investment in an ArtForm ring will pay off in the future. [*How* will it pay off?]

In-crowd appeal, a special kind of flattery, invites readers to identify with an admired and select group.

> Want to know a secret that more and more of Vancouver's successful young professionals are finding out about? It's Coquitlam Cottage, the condominiums that combine the best of the old with the best of the new. [Who are these "successful young professionals?" Will you become one by moving to Coquitlam Cottage?]

Veiled threats try to frighten readers into agreement by hinting that otherwise they will suffer adverse consequences.

> If the airline does not get an immediate 15 percent fare increase, its services to you, its customers, will be seriously affected. [What is the evidence for this claim? Is such an effect on services legal or likely?]

False analogies make misleading comparisons between two situations that are *not* alike in most or important respects.

> Anglophones should restrict language rights for francophones in Ontario as francophones have restricted language rights for anglophones in Quebec. [Is there any point of analogy except that both are cases of majority/minority relationships?]

Exercise 5.8

Following is the text of a letter written by a concerned parent to a school principal. Read it carefully, locate its emotional appeals, and consider their possible effectiveness.

I am writing because my husband and I—and several other parents we've spoken to—are extremely concerned about the presence of the goal post that stands at the foot of the toboggan run in the school playground. This post, which I understand has no real function in winter games in any case, simply stands there posing a threat to our children, who come on every imaginable sliding device at great speeds down the hill.

Last winter, I frequently watched children using the toboggan run with their various mats and tubs and saw many of them, my own daughter included, narrowly escape collision with this post. I have heard from the children that there *have* been some collisions, but no one has been seriously hurt. Yet.

I petition you now to take that post down *before* there is a serious accident. We've all heard too many closing-the-barn-door stories to ignore our obligation to get rid of certain obvious dangers before it is too late for one child.

I urge you to act immediately, as the snow has come and the toboggans will follow.

Exercise 5.9

Using a working argumentative thesis you formulated in Exercise 5.2, discuss with another student the emotional appeals most appropriate to your topic and audience. Then spend ten to fifteen minutes brainstorming together looking for descriptive and figurative language to carry out the appeals.

5g

Organizing an argument

Once you have assembled good reasons in support of an argumentative thesis, you must organize your material in order to present the argument convincingly. While there is no ideal or universally favoured organizational framework for an argumentative essay, you may find the classical five-part system useful to try. This five-part pattern was often followed by ancient Greek and Roman orators. The speaker began with an *introduction,* which stated the thesis, then gave the *background* information. Next came the different *lines of argument,* and then the *refutation of opposing arguments.* A *conclusion* both summed up the argument and made an emotional appeal to the audience. You can adapt this format to written arguments as follows:

ORGANIZING AN ARGUMENT

1. *Introduction*
   gains readers' attention and interest
   establishes your qualifications to write about your topic
   establishes common ground with readers
   demonstrates fairness
   states or implies your thesis

2. *Background*
   presents any necessary background information

3. *Lines of argument*
   present good reasons (including logical and emotional appeals) in support of
       your thesis
   generally present reasons in order of importance
   demonstrate ways your argument is in readers' best interest

4. *Refutation of opposing arguments*
   considers opposing points of view
   notes both advantages and disadvantages of opposing views

5. *Conclusion*
   summarizes the argument
   elaborates on the implication of your thesis
   makes clear what you want readers to think or do
   makes a strong ethical or emotional appeal

The following essay by University of British Columbia student Sherry Devins analyzes the persuasive strategies used in a magazine advertisement for Old Spice Antiperspirant. The essay is of interest now for two reasons: not only is the essay a perceptive analysis of persuasive structures, it is also itself a persuasive piece of writing. In the process of analysis, Sherry tries to get us to see the ad the way she sees it. She makes an argument: the Old Spice ad is based on the claim that a woman's "No" means "Yes" when the man in question is wearing Old Spice antiperspirant—and this claim is both absurd and irresponsible.

Because its primary purpose is analytical, Sherry's essay does not conform to a classical structure for argumentation (it does not, for example, include a section for refutation of opposing arguments). In the exercises following the essay, you will be asked to consider, among other things, the effectiveness of her organization.

Old Spice: I Smell a Rat
By Sherry Devins

Aftershave, older men, and the fresh smell of the sea: Old Spice acquired a prestigious reputation based on the union of these three elements. It was a successful union. For many people the name Old Spice became synonymous with Dad — the older, solid, respectable man. Recently, Old Spice has begun targeting young, single men. In order to engage this new audience, the company has revamped its advertising strategy. The strategy involves divorcing Old Spice from the older product, aftershave, and pitching a newer product, antiperspirant. The advertisement for "New Old Spice Antiperspirant" is artfully arranged and strategically styled; however, its logical, ethical, and emotional appeals are based on an implicit argument that is fallacious, unethical, and contemptible.

The advertisement's arrangement attracts attention and builds an implicit argument with a word and a picture. At the top, a single word "NO" stands out in large, bold print. Directly beneath "NO" is a large picture of a man, handsome of course, and a woman, beautiful of course. The man is above; the woman is below. His arms are stretched out above her and his body towers over her. His body language signifies that he is in "control," cutting off attempts at escape from his advances. His smiling eyes and mouth indicate that he is enjoying himself. While the body language of the man is unequivocal, the body language of the woman is ambiguous. The position of her arms, raised against the man's chest, suggest that she is protesting the man's advances. However, her nose and forehead touch his in apparent intimacy, and her mouth and eyes indicate that she is enjoying herself too. A picture can speak a thousand words. This picture speaks only three: an explicit "NO," an implicit "no," and implicit, antithetical "yes." The arrangement of word and picture begins to develop an implicit argument: women may mean "yes" when they say "no" to a man's advances. This specious argument is no doubt meant to grab the audience's attention. It certainly grabbed mine.

Although the man and woman dominate the picture, it contains one other item. Behind the woman, tiny and relatively obscure, is a container of Old Spice Antiperspirant. Its presence subtly links the man, the woman, and the antiperspirant. The clever arrangement of the picture augments the implicit argument made by the more obvious images of the man and the woman with the less obvious image of the antiperspirant. Together, the implied deductive conclusion is this: a woman's "no" to your advances will really mean "yes" if you are wearing Old Spice Antiperspirant. By linking the man, the woman, and the antiperspirant, the picture also introduces two subjects intended to evoke emotional and ethical appeals in young, single men: perspiration and women. The appeal is developed further by the style of the small print under the picture.

The large, highlighted word "sweat" below the picture combines with the larger, highlighted word "NO" above the picture, to complete a phrase: "NO sweat." Because most people have been conditioned to view sweat as a malodorous bodily fluid, most young men believe it can sabotage their attempts at wooing women. Based on this emotional argument, the phrase "NO sweat" is used to enlist emotional support from the advertisement's young audience.

The word "sweat" is also used to construct an ethical appeal. The word is repeated in a later sentence: "New Old Spice Antiperspirant helps stop the sweat that causes odour." Although the type of odour produced by sweat is unspecified, the coarse word "sweat," rather than the more polite word "perspiration," is repeatedly used. The creators of this advertisement imply that, like many young men, they view sweat and the odour produced by it as offensive. With young men's best interests at heart, they offer a solution to the problem: Old Spice. If one ignores the fact that sweating is not a noxious problem but a natural process that the body uses to cool itself, and that this process is essential for our health, the creators' argument from ethos may seem sincere.

The creators of the advertisement attempt to augment

their arguments from ethos and pathos by cultivating an informal tone with "locker-room" phrases. The expression "no sweat" is a double entendre. Used figuratively, it encourages action by implying that something is easy to accomplish. Two phrases follow the expression "NO sweat": "Go all out. We'll keep up." The style of these three phrases imitates that of a sports coach giving a pep talk to the team before they tackle the opposition. In this sporty manner, the creators reassure young men that if they stop the sweat that causes odour – a concept that appeals to most young men – by wearing Old Spice Antiperspirant, the game of wooing a protesting woman – a concept that is perhaps equally appealing although ethically questionable – will end in victory.

What is the proof behind this claim? This question is asked and answered in the text: "The proof? You're looking at her." The use of the pronoun "her" directs the audience's attention neither to the man nor the antiperspirant, but back to the woman's "yes." In the next sentence the word "proof" is repeated in larger, bolder print: "For great odor protection, now you've got proof not promises." The highlighted word "proof" combines with the highlighted word "sweat" to form the phrase "sweat proof." This phrase directs the audience's attention to the man, who is obviously sweat proof, and to the container of Old Spice Antiperspirant, which is the reason the man is sweat proof. Once again, the style and arrangement of the advertisement link the man, the woman, and the antiperspirant. However, the advertisement's style and arrangement cannot conceal the flaws in logical, ethical, an emotional appeals.

The advertisement's argument from logos is clearly fallacious. Perhaps unbeknownst to its creators, the highlighted words "NO" and "proof" can also be linked to form the phrase "NO proof," which is, in my opinion, an accurate verdict on the argument. While Old Spice Antiperspirant may help stop the sweat that causes odour, the advertisement gives no logical proof for this claim.

The advertisement's arguments from ethos and pathos are also flawed. Anyone in the 1990s who encourages

young men to believe that if they wear a particular
brand of deodorant, they can pursue a woman despite her
apparent protestations, is frighteningly amoral and
unethical. The excuse of she said "no," but she really
meant "yes" is often used by men who rape women to justify a behaviour that is not justifiable. Furthermore,
while the subjects of sweat and the pursuit of women may
be emotionally appealing to young men, the emotion
aroused by this advertisement, because of its inappropriate message, should be anger rather than desire. This
advertisement, and the argument behind it, reek of logical, ethical, and emotional offences. It has tainted
the reputation of Old Spice. I no longer smell the fresh
sea; I smell a rat.

Exercise 5.10

Using the questions for revision listed in Chapter 4, consider what commentary
you might provide for Sherry Devins if you were working with her in a peer writing group. Attend especially to her own use of the range of persuasive strategies
and to the organization of her essay.

Exercise 5.11

Draft an essay concerning the thesis you formulated and worked to support in earlier parts of this chapter. Collaborate with another student to consider ways to
strengthen the argument.

Taking inventory: your own arguments

When you have completed a draft of an essay and have received some response to
it, try to answer the following questions in a further attempt to judge its effectiveness. These analytical questions can be applied to many pieces of persuasive
writing.

INTRODUCTION

- What, specifically, have I done to gain the audience's attention and interest?
- How have I established my qualifications to write about this topic?
- What have I done to establish common ground with my readers?
- How have I shown fairness to opposing viewpoints?
- How have I made known my thesis?

BACKGROUND

- What background have I presented?

LINES OF ARGUMENT

- What good reasons have I presented to support my thesis?
- How have I shown that my claim is in the readers' best interest?

REFUTATION OF OPPOSING ARGUMENTS

- How have I dealt with opposing points of view and noted their advantages as well as disadvantages?

CONCLUSION

- How have I summarized my argument?
- How have I elaborated on any implications of my claim?
- What action have I called for from readers? What kind of ethical or emotional appeal have I ended with?

6

Constructing Paragraphs

Long before the age of the printing press, sections of text were set off from one another by marks in the margin. In Greek, *para graphos* means "mark beside," and these marks looked like this: ¶. With the invention of movable type, printers had to fit lines of type into frames; because they could no longer use the margins easily, they began marking a paragraph by indenting its first line, as we still do today. The old name stuck, however, and so we call these units *paragraphs*.

Most simply, a **paragraph** is a group of sentences or a single sentence set off as a unit. Usually the sentences in a paragraph are related in some way because they all revolve around one main idea. When a new idea comes up, a new paragraph begins. Within this broad general guideline, however, paragraph structure is highly flexible, allowing writers to create many varied individual effects.

Paragraphing for readers

Readers come to any piece of writing with certain conventional expectations. In terms of paragraphs, readers usually have the following expectations:

- That the beginnings and ends of paragraphs contain important guiding information
- That the opening sentence provides direction and lets readers know what the paragraph is about
- That the middle of the paragraph develops what the paragraph is about
- That the end of the paragraph sums up the paragraph's contents, bringing the discussion of an idea to a close in anticipation of the paragraph that follows

- That the paragraph "makes sense" as a whole, its words and sentences clearly related

- That the paragraph relates in some clear way to the paragraphs around it

In general, readers like to know where they are and where they are going. First and last sentences of paragraphs can be especially important in providing a sense of purpose and direction to readers, since these sentences can perform a variety of functions, and more than one function at a time: stating main points, connecting these points to the thesis of the essay, and providing transitions between one main point and another.

Exercise 6.1

The following passage consists of a series of paragraphs, run together, from a book on "the myth of scientific objectivity" by University of Toronto professor Beth Savan. Read the passage carefully, and decide how you would divide it into paragraphs. Bring your paragraphed passage to class for discussion and comparison with those of your classmates.

We're all getting used to hearing two scientists give opposing answers to the same question, but it's still a very uncomfortable experience. It confuses and disturbs us to see two experts, examining the same problems with the same data, come up with contrary conclusions. Not only does such a situation make it much more difficult to resolve the important controversies the scientists are commenting on, but the scientists' contradictions also challenge the popular and rather comforting image of the scientist as selfless truth-seeker. They suggest that scientific information is equivocal—that its meaning may, like beauty, lie in the eye of the beholder. If so, scientists are not simply discovering external facts but rather are, in a sense, manufacturing knowledge from their personal templates. The individual choices scientists make so limit their conclusions that two investigators can set out on the same research trail and arrive at entirely different destinations. If, meanwhile, we are seeking clarity and certitude in scientific results, we cannot help but be concerned when we find that the same basic research problem or set of data has spawned more than one answer to the question that matters to us. Science and scientists have traditionally been held in high esteem, even revered. Earlier in this century, the public had unbounded faith in the power of science to explain mysteries and solve practical problems. As Richard Gregaroy, former editor of the journal *Nature,* put it: "My grandfather preached the gospel of Christ, my father preached the gospel of socialism, I preach the gospel of science."

— BETH SAVAN, *Science Under Siege*

6a

Constructing unified, coherent, and well-developed paragraphs

Let us look now at the specific elements that make up a well-written paragraph—one that makes a point in a way that is easy for readers to understand and follow. Consider the following paragraph by Denis W. Johnston:

> Without question, the most important new Canadian playwright to emerge in the latter half of the 1980s has been Tomson Highway. In less than three years, and with only two major plays, Highway has joined a select group of playwrights whose new plays, sight unseen, are treated as significant cultural events by Canadian critics, scholars, and audiences. The two plays, *The Rez Sisters* and *Dry Lips Oughta Move to Kapuskasing*, both won the coveted Dora Mavor Moore award for the best new play produced in Toronto, the former for the 1986–87 season and the latter for 1988–89. Tomson Highway says his ambition in life, and therefore presumably in his plays, is "to make 'the rez' cool, to show and celebrate what funky folk Canada's Indian people really are." In this, *The Rez Sisters* and *Dry Lips Oughta Move to Kapuskasing* have been wildly successful, attracting enthusiastic audiences, both white and Native, far beyond the real-life reserve where *The Rez Sisters* was conceived and first performed.
>
> — DENIS W. JOHNSTON, "Lines and Circles:
> The 'Rez' Plays of Tomson Highway"

This paragraph begins with a general statement of the main idea: that Tomson Highway is an important new Canadian playwright. All the other sentences support and deepen this main claim, while the last sentence, in addition, points the way to the next paragraph in which the more specific discussion of Highway and the "Rez" plays begins. This example demonstrates the three qualities found in most successful paragraphs: **unity**, **coherence**, and **development**. It focuses on one main idea (unity); its parts are clearly related (coherence); and its main idea is supported with specifics (development).

6b

Making paragraphs unified: focusing on one main idea

To be readable and effective, paragraphs generally focus on one main idea. One good way to achieve such paragraph **unity** is to state the main idea clearly in one sentence and relate all the other sentences in the paragraph to that idea. The sentence that presents the main idea is called the **topic sentence**. Like the thesis for an entire essay, the topic sentence of a paragraph includes a topic and some comment on that topic.

1. Positioning a topic sentence

While a topic sentence usually appears at the beginning of a paragraph, it may appear anywhere in the paragraph—or it may not appear at all, but rather be implied.

At the beginning of a paragraph

It is a good idea to open with the topic sentence when you want readers to see your point immediately. Such a strategy can be particularly useful in essay examinations (Chapter 8) or in argumentative essays (Chapter 5). The author of the following paragraph opens with a clear topic sentence from which subsequent sentences follow:

> *Although the current Canadian health care system is complex, at its core it is a government-run, nonprofit insurance plan that uses public funds to pay for a private, comprehensive system.* Patients have free choice of physicians who are paid by separate medical insurance plans on a fee-for-service basis. The federal government sponsors and administers the cost-sharing program with the provinces; in some provinces, the public is charged minimal premiums as subscribers to the services. The medical profession remains independent and self-regulating, and doctors are given the choice of opting in or out of the plan, according to their interests. Hospitals are not government owned, but locally controlled, nonprofit organizations.
>
> – RALPH NADER, *Canada Firsts*

At the end of a paragraph

When specific details lead up to a generalization, putting the topic sentence at the end of the paragraph makes good sense. In the following paragraph, the last sentence is a general statement that sums up and accounts for the specifics that have preceded it.

During the visit, Dee takes the pictures, every one of them, including the one of the house that she used to live in and hate. She takes the churn top and dasher, both whittled out of a tree by one of Mama's uncles. She tries to take Grandma Dee's quilts. Mama and Maggie use these inherited items every day, not only appreciating their heritage but living it too. *Dee, on the other hand, wants these items only for decorative use, thus forsaking and ignoring their real heritage.*

Implied but not stated in the paragraph

Occasionally, a topic will be so obvious or so clearly implied that no topic sentence is necessary at all. Here is an example of such a paragraph, from an essay about cocktail parties and cocktail party conversations.

Going back into the house, I listened in on a group of men: I've always thought of Highway 7 as the square route … When the postal strike ends, how will people be able to tell? … I've at last figured it out, Doris Day is her own grandmother … I know beer's the drink of moderation, that's why I hate it … When your plane lands in Toronto, you have to set your watch back thirty years … Liquor at the C.N.E.? It's enough to make Judge Robb turn over in his grave … I'm still looking for a woman who measures down to my standards … I didn't mind Marge's boozing and infidelity; what drove me out was that she never changed the blade after shaving her legs with my razor.

– RICHARD NEEDHAM, "A Sound of Deviltry by Night"

Here the implied topic sentence might be stated as *at cocktail parties inane remarks pass for clever conversation.*

Exercise 6.2

Choose an essay you have written, and identify the topic sentence of each paragraph, noting where in the paragraph each topic sentence appears and whether any is implied rather than stated. Experiment with one paragraph, positioning its topic sentence in at least two different places. If you have any implied topic sentences, try stating them explicitly. Is the paragraph then easier to read?

2. Relating each sentence to the main idea

Whether the main idea of a paragraph appears in the topic sentence or is only implied, writing unified paragraphs demands that you make sure each sentence relates or contributes to the main idea. Look, for example, at the following paragraph, which opens an essay about the image of women in magazines in the 1920s.

The 1920s was an ambiguous decade, a decade of change and contradiction. In many respects it was a very conservative period, when Canadians clung to traditional values and institutions for stability and security. At the same time, however, Canadians in the twenties were fully conscious that the past was irretrievable. They were aware that society was in a state of flux, and that they were living in the first years of a new era. Simultaneously they looked both back and ahead.

> — MARY VIPOND, "The Image of Women in Mass Circulation
> Magazines in the 1920s"

The author announces her topic (the 1920s as a decade of change and contradiction) in sentence one. The next three sentences relate to the topic by discussing how the 1920s was a time of conservatism as well as flux. The last sentence then ties the paragraph together by rephrasing the topic sentence. Each sentence clearly relates to the topic, and the paragraph as a whole is unified.

Exercise 6.3

Working with another student, return to a piece of writing you have completed recently and examine the second, third, and fourth paragraphs. Does each have a topic sentence or strongly imply one? Do all the other sentences in the paragraph focus on its main idea? Would you now revise any of these paragraphs—and if so, how?

6c

Making paragraphs coherent: fitting details together

A paragraph is **coherent** if its details fit together clearly in a way that readers can easily follow. You can achieve paragraph coherence in three ways: by organizing ideas; by repeating key terms or phrases; and by using parallel structures, pronouns, and transitions.

1. Organizing ideas

Clear organization of ideas goes a long way toward creating coherence. The following discussion will review the most often used means of organizing a paragraph: spatial order, chronological order, and logical order.

Using spatial order

Paragraphs organized in **spatial order** take a "tour" of an object, person, or place, beginning at one point and moving, say, from near to far, left to right, north to south. Especially useful in **descriptive** paragraphs, spatial order allows a writer to direct readers' attention in an orderly way to various elements of something in physical space. A topic sentence is frequently unnecessary in a paragraph using spatial order, but it can be useful to set the scene or tell the reader what is going to be described. Note the movement from ceiling to walls to floor in the following paragraph.

The professor's voice began to fade in the background as my eyes wandered around the classroom in the old administration building. The water-stained ceiling was cracked and peeling, and the splitting wooden beams played host to a variety of lead pipes and coils. My eyes followed these pipes down the walls and around corners, until eventually I saw the electrical outlets. I thought it was strange that they were exposed, and not built in, until I realized that there was probably no electricity when the building had been built. Below the outlets the sunshine was falling in bright rays across the hardwood floor, and I noticed how smoothly it was worn. Time had certainly taken its toll on this building.

Using chronological order

Paragraphs organized in **chronological order** arrange a series of events according to time, putting earliest events first, followed in sequence by later events, one at a time. Chronological order is used frequently in **narrative** paragraphs, which basically tell a story. Rarely do they require a topic sentence, because the main idea is obvious in the action. The following paragraph used careful chronology to tell a story and also to build suspense: we want to know what the last event in the sequence will be. The words expressing time help build this suspense: *all of a sudden, three months, a year later,* and so on.

The experience of Lloyd S., a Calgary businessperson, is one of the most convincing cases for taking vitamins. For his first forty years, Lloyd was healthy and robust. He owned a thriving nursery and loved to hike, fish, and camp. All of a sudden, he started feeling fatigued. A loss of appetite and weight soon followed, and in three months he was transformed from a ruddy, muscular man into a pallid, emaciated one. Lloyd had cancer of the pancreas. After he was given a prognosis of six months to live, his family and friends were devastated, but Lloyd was a fighter. When the conventional treatments of drugs and chemotherapy did not help, he turned to a holistic approach, which emphasized a change in diet and lifestyle—and large doses of vitamins. After a series of blood tests to discover every possible nutritional deficiency, Lloyd was given concentrated vitamin and mineral supplements to ensure maximum cell efficiency and growth so that his body could attempt to heal itself. At the end of six months, Lloyd not only was alive but also showed improvement. A year later he was free of cancer and began the long battle to regain his original vitality. Coincidence? Perhaps. To Lloyd and me, however, his recovery became a powerful demonstration of how the world's most intricate machine, the human body, performs—if only we supply it with the needed nutrients.

Chronological order is also commonly used in **explaining a process**. Paragraphs that explain how something happens or how something is done proceed in chronological order: first one step, then the next, then the next. You are already familiar with process as a means of organizing information. After all, every set of directions, every recipe, every user's manual presents a series of steps that make up a process someone wants to learn or to follow. In academic writing, you will probably use process paragraphs less often to tell readers how to do something than to explain to them how a process occurs in general—for example, how a bill becomes law in the British Parliament or how aerosol sprays destroy the ozone layer of the atmosphere.

Using logical order

Paragraphs organized in **logical order** arrange details to reflect certain logical relationships. Explanations and examples of some of these relationships—illustration, definition, division/classification, comparison/contrast, cause-effect, and problem-solution—are given in 6d. Two other logical patterns commonly used in paragraphs are *general-to-specific* and *specific-to-general*.

Paragraphs organized in **general-to-specific** pattern usually open with a topic sentence presenting a general or abstract idea, followed by a number of more specific points designed to substantiate or prove or elaborate on the generalization. The following paragraph uses general-to-specific organization:

> We have surely all cheated at least one time in our lives. GENERAL
> People cheat in dozens of ways, ranging from small-scale TOPIC
> things like writing notes on their hands for tests to the monu-
> mental deception of having an affair. We cheat when we pass
> the speed limit. Powerful families and corporations cheat their SPECIFICS
> way out of legal binds with the help of highly paid lawyers.
> Businesspeople record activities, such as dining out, as busi-
> ness-related so they will not have to pay for the expense per-
> sonally. Dieters are always cheating, and if we really think
> about it, people cheat when they use makeup or fashion to
> cover up or disguise features they find unattractive. Even my

grandmother cheats by taking short cuts in her prescribed daily walks.

Paragraphs can also follow a **specific-to-general** organization, first providing a series of specific examples or details and then tying them together with a general conclusion. The following paragraph uses a specific-to-general pattern:

> When you work for ten hours at hard labour, whether you are seventeen or fifty-seven, there is precious little time or energy for anything else. We rose at six, performed our swift ablutions, wolfed an enormous breakfast, and headed off for the job which had to begin at seven. At noon we started back up the valley slopes through the mud to the messhall, wolfed another vast meal, and finished it just in time to head back once more. At six we were finished, in more ways than one. I have seen men so tired they could not eat the last meal of the day which was always consumed in silence and at top speed. (It was said that any man who stumbled on the messhall steps on the way in found himself trampled by the rush coming out.) When this was over, large numbers of men of varying ages simply lay down on their bunks, utterly fagged out, and slept. There was nothing else to do anyway: no library, no recreation hall, no lounge, no radio or films—nothing but a roadhouse five miles distant where you could buy bootleg rum. Civilization was represented by Dawson, forty miles away; we never visited it. We were like men in a prison camp, except that we worked much harder.
>
> — PIERRE BERTON, "The Dirtiest Job in the World"

SPECIFIC DETAILS

GENERAL TOPIC

Exercise 6.4

Choose one of the following topic sentences or create one of your own, and try writing two different paragraphs on the topic, using a different organizational pattern for each. Then discuss with another student why you used the organizational patterns you did. Which seems more effective and coherent, and why?

1. Explaining _____ to my parents was the hardest thing I've ever done.
2. People who are extremely vain about their looks often go to ridiculous lengths to keep up their appearance.
3. My classes this term can, with understatement, be described as demanding.
4. Many people share one basic fear: public speaking.

2. Repeating key words and phrases

A major means of building coherence in paragraphs is through **repetition**. Weaving in repeated references to key words and phrases not only links sentences but also alerts readers to the importance the words or phrases hold in the larger piece of writing. Notice how the repetition of the key words *textbooks, tuition, cost, pay,* and *army* helps hold the following paragraph together.

> "Thirty-nine fifty for one *textbook!* You've got to be kidding," I mumbled as I dragged myself slowly toward the checkout stand. I did not know how I was going to *pay* for *tuition*, housing, phone bills, and groceries if all my *textbooks cost* me that much. "I might as well as well join the *army*," I thought. At least it would *pay* my *tuition* and give me *army* rations. Right now, *army* chow sounded considerably better than boiled pages from a psychology text. I stood there full of resentment; I had no intention of spending all my hard-earned money on *textbooks*. Yet I had no choice. This was a book I had to have, whatever the *cost*.

Notice also that the cluster of terms related to money helps make the paragraph hang together: *pay, cost, spending, hard-earned money, cost.* Such repetition helps us follow the logic of a paragraph and understand the point the writer is making.

Exercise 6.5

Read the following paragraph. Then identify the places where the author repeats key words and phrases, and explain how this strategy brings coherence to the paragraph.

> Nobody knows, of course, how many megatons would be exploded in a real nuclear war. There are some who think that a nuclear war can be "contained," bottled up before it runs away to involve many of the world's arsenals. But a number of detailed analyses, war games run by the U.S. Department of Defense and official Soviet pronouncements, all indicate that this containment may be too much to hope for: Once the bombs begin exploding, communications failures, disorganization, fear, the necessity of making in minutes decisions affecting the fates of millions and the immense psychological burden of knowing that your own loved ones may already have been destroyed are likely to result in a nuclear paroxysm. Many investigations, including a number of studies for the U.S. government, envision the explosion of 5000 to 10,000 megatons—the detonation of tens of thousands of nuclear weapons that now sit quietly, inconspicuously, in missile silos, submarines and long-range bombers, faithful servants, awaiting orders.
>
> – CARL SAGAN, "The Nuclear Winter"

3. Using parallel structures

Parallel structures—structures that are grammatically similar—provide another effective way of bringing coherence to a paragraph. Parallel structures emphasize the connection between related ideas or events in different sentences, as in the following paragraph.

> William Faulkner's "Barn Burning" tells the story of a young boy trapped in a no-win situation. If he betrays his father, he loses his family. If he betrays justice, he becomes a fugitive. In trying to free himself from his trap, he does both.

In this paragraph, the writer skilfully uses the parallel structures *if he X, he Y,* in order to give the effect of a "no-win situation." At the end of the paragraph, we are prepared for the last sentence in the parallel sequence: *In doing X, he Y.* As readers, we feel pulled along by the force of the parallel structures in the paragraph.

Exercise 6.6

Read the following paragraph and identify every use of repetition and parallel structures. In a brief paragraph of your own, explain how their use helps build coherence in this paragraph.

> I would like to go back to school so that I can become economically independent, support myself, and, if need be, support those dependent upon me. I want a wife who will work and send me to school. And while I am going to school I want a wife to take care of my children. I want a wife to keep track of the children's doctor and dentist appointments. And to keep track of mine, too. I want a wife to make sure my children eat properly and are kept clean. I want a wife who will wash the children's clothes and keep them mended. I want a wife who is a good nurturant attendant to my children, who arranges for their schooling, makes sure that they have an adequate social life with their peers, takes them to the park, the zoo, etc. I want a wife who takes care of the children when they are sick, a wife who arranges to be around when the children need special care, because, of course, I cannot miss classes at school. My wife must arrange to lose time at work and not lose the job. It may mean a small cut in my wife's income from time to time, but I guess I can tolerate that. Needless to say, my wife will arrange and pay for the care of the children while my wife is working.
>
> – JUDY BRADY, "I Want a Wife"

4. Using pronouns

Writers also achieve coherence in a paragraph through the use of **pronouns**. Because pronouns usually refer back to nouns or other pronouns, they act as natural coherence devices, leading readers naturally from sentence to sentence. The following paragraph, from an essay on old age, uses pronouns effectively in linking sentences to one another. Note how much slower and more awkward the paragraph would be if each pronoun were replaced with the noun it stands for. Also note that the writer uses the name when he first introduces each new artist—and then uses pronouns thereafter to refer to that person. (Italics added for emphasis.)

> For such [old] persons, every new infirmity is an enemy to be outwitted, an obstacle to be overcome by force of will. *They* enjoy each little victory over *themselves*, and sometimes *they* win a major success. Renoir was one of *them*. *He* continued painting, and magnificently, for years after *he* was crippled by arthritis; the brush had to be strapped to *his* arm. "You don't need your hand to paint," *he* said. Goya was another of the unvanquished. At 72 *he* retired as an official painter of the Spanish court and decided to work only for *himself*. *His* later years were those of the famous "black paintings" in which *he* let *his* imagination run (and also of the lithographs, then a new technique). At 78 *he* escaped a reign of terror in Spain by fleeing to Bordeaux. *He* was deaf and *his* eyes were failing; in order to work *he* had to wear several pairs of spectacles, one over another, and then use a magnifying glass; but *he* was producing splendid work in a totally new style. At 80 *he* drew an ancient man propped on two sticks, with a mass of white hair and beard hiding *his* face and with the inscription "*I* am still learning."
>
> – MALCOLM COWLEY, *The View from 80*

Exercise 6.7
_____

Choose three paragraphs from a piece of writing you have done recently and analyze them for pronoun use. How do the pronouns bring coherence to the paragraphs? Is it clear what noun or pronoun each of the pronouns refers back to? Can you see ways of using pronouns to improve the coherence of these paragraphs?

---

5. Using transitional devices

Transitions are words and phrases that help bring coherence to a paragraph by signalling the exact relationships between sentences. In acting as signposts from one idea to the next, transitional expressions such as *after all, for example, indeed, so,* and *thus* help readers follow the progression of a paragraph. *Finally* indicates that a last point is at hand; *likewise*, that a similar point is about to be made, and so on.

> In "The Fly," Katherine Mansfield tries to show us the "real" personality of "the boss" beneath his exterior. The fly *in the story's title* helps her to portray this real self. *In the course of the story*, the boss goes through a range of emotions and feelings. *At the end*, he *finally* expresses these feelings on a small but determined fly, whom the reader realizes he unconsciously relates to his son. *To accomplish her goal*, the author basically splits up the story into three parts, with the boss's emotions and actions changing quite measurably *throughout*. *First* with Old Woodifield, *then* with himself, and *last* with the fly, we see the boss's manipulativeness. *With each part*, our understanding of him as a hard and cruel man grows.

Note how the writer carefully leads us through the points of her paragraph. Most of the transitional devices here point to movement in time, helping us follow the chronology of the story being discussed: *in the course of the story; at the end; finally; throughout; first; then; last.*

It is important to note that transitions can only clarify connections between thoughts; they cannot *create* them. If you open a sentence with *therefore*, for example, be sure that the thought expressed by the rest of the sentence really follows logically from the previous sentences.

The following list contains commonly used transitional devices, grouped by the functions they perform.

TO SIGNAL SEQUENCE

again, also, and, and then, besides, finally, first … second … third, furthermore, last, moreover, next, still, too

TO SIGNAL TIME

after a bit, after a few days, after a while, afterward, as long as, as soon as, at last, at length, at that time, before, earlier, immediately, in the meantime, in the past, lately, later, meanwhile, now, presently, shortly, simultaneously, since, so far, soon, then, thereafter, until, when

TO SIGNAL COMPARISON

again, also, in the same way, likewise, once more, similarly

TO SIGNAL CONTRAST

although, but, despite, even though, however, in contrast, in spite of, instead, nevertheless, nonetheless, notwithstanding, on the contrary, on the one hand … on the other hand …, regardless, still, though, yet

104 6c ¶ CONSTRUCTING PARAGRAPHS

TO SIGNAL EXAMPLES

after all, even, for example, for instance, indeed, in fact, of course, specifically, such as, the following example . . ., to illustrate

TO SIGNAL CAUSE AND EFFECT

accordingly, as a result, because, consequently, for this purpose, hence, so, then, therefore, thereupon, thus, to this end

TO SIGNAL PLACE

above, adjacent to, below, beyond, closer to, elsewhere, far, farther on, here, near, nearby, opposite to, there, to the left, to the right

TO SIGNAL CONCESSION

although it is true that, granted that, I admit that, it may appear that, naturally, of course

TO SIGNAL SUMMARY, REPETITION, OR CONCLUSION

all in all, as a result, as has been noted, as I have said, as we have seen, in any event, in conclusion, in other words, in short, on the whole, therefore, to conclude, to summarize, to sum up

For a discussion of using transitional devices to link separate paragraphs together, see 6f.

Exercise 6.8

For the following paragraph, identify each of the devices—repetition of key words or phrases, parallel structures, pronouns, and transitional expressions—that make the paragraph coherent.

> All we have to do is, each for himself, to keep down dissensions which can only weaken, impoverish and keep back the country; each for himself do all he can to increase its wealth, its strength and its reputation; each for himself—you, and you, gentlemen, all of us—to welcome every talent, to hail every invention, to cherish every gem of art, to foster every gleam of authorship, to honour every acquirement and every gift, to lift ourselves to the level of our destinies, to rise above all low limitations and narrow circumscriptions, to cultivate that true catholicity of spirit which embraces all creeds, all classes and all races, in order to make of our boundless province, so rich in known and unknown resources, a great new Northern nation.
>
> – THOMAS D'ARCY MCGEE, speech in Quebec City, 1862

6d

Developing paragraphs fully: providing details

In addition to being unified and coherent, a paragraph must hold readers' interest and explore its topic fully, using whatever details, evidence, and examples are necessary. Without such **development**, a paragraph may seem lifeless and abstract.

Most good essay writing does two things: it presents generalized ideas and explanations, and it backs up these generalities with specifics. This balance, the shifting between general and specific, is especially important at the paragraph level. Almost every paragraph can be improved by making sure that its general ideas rest on enough specific detail. You can, of course, add too many details, pushing examples at the reader when no more are needed. For every writer who has to chop back jungles of detail, however, there are five whose greatest task is to irrigate deserts of generality.

1. Using logical patterns of development

The **logical patterns** presented in 3e for organizing essays or sections of essays can also serve as a means of developing paragraphs. These patterns include illustrating, defining, dividing and classifying, comparing and contrasting, exploring causes and effects, and considering problems and solutions or questions and answers.

Illustrating a point

Illustrating a point is one of the most useful ways of developing the main idea of a paragraph. You can **illustrate a point** with examples or with reasons.

The following paragraphs use **concrete examples** to illustrate a point. The first offers one extended example, while the second offers a series of examples.

A SINGLE EXAMPLE

The Indians made names for us children in their teasing way. Because our very busy mother kept my hair cut short, like my brothers', they called me Short Furred One, pointing to their hair and making the sign for short, the right hand with fingers pressed close together, held upward, back out, at the height intended. With me this was about two feet tall, the Indians laughing gently at my abashed face. I am told that I was given a pair of small moccasins that first time, to clear up my unhappiness at being picked out from the dusk behind the fire and my two unhappy shortcomings made conspicuous.

– MARI SANDOZ, "The Go-Along Ones"

SEVERAL EXAMPLES

Now it happens that when a Native of a tribe makes anything, he includes his personality and traditional beliefs, and when the article is completed he talks to it as if it were a human being. If it is a bow and arrow, it must be accurate in what it is destined to do. If it is a mask, it, like a person, demands to be fed; if it is not fed it can be treacherous. The Indian dolls have their own ways. The large iron kettle has a history of centuries past: Hiawatha saw his sinful ways in the reflections of the kettle; human beings have boiled in the same kettle and could do so again. The proud Indian's personality is entombed in the Indian Head mug. The other objects follow his advice because he has the head of wisdom.

– ALMA GREENE, *Tales of the Mohawks*

At times illustrating a point involves providing not examples but **good reasons** for believing the main idea of the paragraph to be true (see 5c). The following paragraph opens with a generalization in the topic sentence and then offers reasons to support generalization:

The influence of gender on peer and family relationships is rooted in our socialization into feminine and masculine patterns of behavior and is maintained by social arrangements that favor these patterns. Girls learn at an early age that intimate, self-disclosing friendships are rewarding and socially approved. Boys learn equally early that too much intimacy with another male is often regarded with suspicion in a society influenced by competitive and homophobic attitudes. The narrow emphasis on sexuality in male–female relationships makes it unlikely that cross-sex friendships will develop, and the separation of males and females into different kinds of jobs and even different domestic roles contributes further to this situation

– HILARY LIPS, *Sex and Gender: An Introduction*

Defining

You will sometimes have occasion to develop an entire paragraph by **defining** a word or concept. Some college and university courses, particularly ones that deal with difficult abstractions, require writing that calls for this strategy. A philosophy exam, for instance, might require you to define words such as *truth* or *validity*. In the following paragraph, Tom Wolfe defines *pornoviolence*, a word he has coined, by contrasting it first with "accumulated slayings and bone crushings" and then with violence seen from the point of view of "the hero."

It is not the accumulated slayings and bone crushings that make [this TV show into] pornoviolence, however. What makes pornoviolence is that in almost every case the camera angle, therefore the viewer, is with the gun, the fist, the rock. The pornography of violence has no point of view in the old sense that novels do. You do not live the action through the hero's eyes. You live with the aggressor, whoever he may be. One moment you are the hero. The next you are the villain. No matter whose side you may be on consciously, you are in fact with the muscle, and it is you who disintegrate all comers, villains, lawmen, women, anybody. On the rare occasions in which the gun is emptied into the camera—i.e., into your face—the effect is so startling that the pornography of violence all but loses its fantasy charm. There are not nearly so many masochists as sadists among those little devils whispering into one's ears.

— TOM WOLFE, "Pornoviolence"

Dividing and classifying

Dividing breaks a single item into parts. **Classifying**, which is actually a form of dividing, groups many separate items according to their similarities. You could, for instance, develop a paragraph evaluating a history course by dividing the course into several segments—textbooks, lectures, assignments—and examining each one in turn. Or you could use classification in developing a paragraph giving an overview of history courses at your college or university, grouping the courses in a number of ways—by the time periods or geographic areas covered, by the kinds of assignments demanded, by the numbers of students enrolled, or by some other criterion.

Dividing:

We all listen to music according to our separate capacities. But, for the sake of analysis, the whole listening process may become clearer if we break it up into its component parts, so to speak. In a certain sense we all listen to music on three separate planes. For lack of a better terminology, one might name these: (1) the sensuous plane, (2) the expressive plane, (3) the sheerly musical plane. The only advantage to be gained from the mechanically splitting up the listening process into these hypothetical planes is the clearer view to be had of the way in which we listen.

— AARON COPLAND, *What to Listen for in Music*

Classifying:

Two types of people are seduced by fad diets. Those who have always been overweight turn to fad diets out of despair; they have tried everything, and yet nothing seems to work. The second group who succumb are those who appear perfectly healthy but are baited with slogans such as "look good, feel good." These slogans prompt self-questioning and insecurity—do I *really* look good and feel good?—and as a direct result, many of these people also fall prey to fad diets. With both types of people, however, the problems surrounding fad diets are numerous and dangerous. In fact, these diets provide neither intelligent nor effective answers to weight control.

Comparing and contrasting

You can develop some paragraphs easily and effectively by comparing and/or contrasting various aspects of the topic or by comparing and/or contrasting the topic to something else. **Comparing** things highlights their similarities; **contrasting**, their differences. Whether used alone or together, comparing and contrasting bring the topic at hand more clearly into focus (we can better understand an unknown, for example, by comparing it to something we know well) or help us evaluate the items compared and/or contrasted.

You can structure comparison/contrast paragraphs in two basic ways: by first presenting all the information about one item, then presenting all the information about the other item (block method); or by alternating between the two items, focusing in turn on particular characteristics of each (alternating method).

> Trudeau had been educated by the Jesuits, had devoted years to political theory, and had worked as a professor of constitutional law. His training, therefore, had left him susceptible to ruthless Cartesian logic, grand plans, great codes, big ideas, and a second-hand understanding of the practical world. Turner had been educated by Oblate fathers (a down-to-earth missionary order ready to adapt to any circumstance) and had spent the first eight years of his career practising commercial and tax law in the courts of Montreal. Moreover, his liberalism wasn't a late-blooming, ideological overlay on his native political culture, as was Trudeau's. Turner had learned it at his mother's breast.
>
> – RON GRAHAM, *One-Eyed Kings*

Alternating method:

> Ever since his election as Tory chief in 1976, at the age of thirty-six, Clark had suffered in comparison to Pierre Trudeau. Trudeau was what Canadians wished to be—suave, intellectual, worldly, independent, and spontaneous. Clark was what Canadians feared they were—earnest, nice, honest, predictable, and rather dull. As a young man Trudeau had wandered the earth from adventure to adventure; as a young man Clark had cut short a visit to Europe to return to write pamphlets for the Diefenbaker government. Of course, many people hated Trudeau and loved Clark for the same reasons. "Joe" was one of them, ordinary but trustworthy, sympathetic and

decent, neither a threat nor an arrogant sophisticate, a dedicated and open-minded human being with his own brand of complexity and courage. Old ladies smiled on his small-town politeness and veterans admired his clean-cut perseverance. However, many more Canadians reacted against this fumbly, pompous reflection of themselves. Joe Clark just wasn't good enough to make them greater.

— RON GRAHAM, *One-Eyed Kings*

Exploring causes and effects

Certain topics will require you to consider the process of **cause and effect**, and you can often develop paragraphs by detailing the causes of something or the effects that something leads to. The following paragraph discusses the effects of television on the North American family:

Television's contribution to family life has been an equivocal one. For while it has, indeed, kept the members of the family from dispersing, it has not served to bring them *together.* By its domination of the time families spend together, it destroys the special quality that distinguishes one family from another, a quality that depends to a great extent on what a family *does*, what special rituals, games, recurrent jokes, familiar songs, and shared activities it accumulates.

— MARIE WINN, *The Plug-in Drug: Television, Children, and the Family*

Considering problems and solutions

Paragraphs developed by the **problem-solution pattern** open with a statement of a problem, usually the topic sentence, and then offer a solution in the sentences that follow, as in this paragraph:

All over the country, textbook choice committees face the same challenge: choosing textbooks that are factually accurate, of high intellectual quality, and acceptable to various "watchdog" committees. Such a choice is very difficult for nonspecialists. To aid these committees in deciding what textbooks to adopt, I would like to see the formation of an academic journal devoted entirely to reviewing new texts. The most efficient way to accomplish this goal would probably be to have a journal covering each field of study, since it would be inefficient to review English and physics texts in the same journal. The new texts would be scrutinized carefully by scholars in the respective fields and would be judged for their intellectual quality. In this way, the textbook choice committees would have a guide to aid them in selecting texts that are of certified intellectual value.

PROBLEM

SOLUTION

Considering questions and answers

In the **question-answer pattern**, the first sentence poses a question, and the rest of the paragraph provides the answer. Beginning with a question provides a means of getting readers' attention—and focusing that attention—as it does in the following paragraph from a student essay on preventing the birth of unwanted puppies:

> Whose fault is it that these puppies are born? Humane Society officials and veterinarians confirm that the vast majority of unwanted dogs are the result of pet owners simply not engaging in family planning for their pets. In other words, many so-called animal lovers don't bother getting their pets neutered, even though they have no intention of selectively breeding them. They seem to think, "it won't happen to my dog ... and if, by chance, it does, I can always get rid of the pups."

Exercise 6.9

Choose two of the following topics or two others that interest you, and brainstorm or freewrite about each one for ten minutes (see 3a). Then discuss with another student which method(s) of development would be most appropriate for each topic.

1. The most intriguing place you've visited
2. The best job you've ever had
3. Sinéad O'Connor's image and Madonna's image
4. Why the environment is an important issue (or set of issues) for you
5. The pleasure a hobby has given you

Exercise 6.10

Refer to the essay you drafted in Exercise 5.11, and study the ways you have developed each paragraph. For one of those paragraphs, write a brief evaluation of its development, including recommendations for expanding and/or improving the development. You may want to discuss the paragraph development with collaborating students.

2. Determining paragraph length

While numerical information might seem helpful at first, saying that the average paragraph has so many words or sentences is like saying the average family has 2.3 members and owns 1.8 cars. The numbers themselves mean very little. In general, a paragraph should be long enough to develop an idea, create an effect, and advance the piece of writing it is a part of. Fulfilling these aims will sometimes call for long paragraphs and sometimes for short ones. That is, paragraph length should be determined by the author's purpose, not by a set of hard and fast rules.

Notice how the following passage, the last three paragraphs of an essay on women and science, uses a very short paragraph as well as a fairly long one.

> Science is undeniably hard. Often, it can seem quite boring. It is unfortunately too often presented as laws to be memorized instead of mysteries to be explored. It is too often kept a secret that science, like art, takes a well developed esthetic sense. Women aren't the only ones who say, "I hate science." That's why everyone who goes into science needs a little help from friends. For the past ten years, I have been getting more than a little help from a friend who is a physicist. But my stepdaughter—who earned the highest grades ever recorded in her California high school on the math Scholastic Aptitude Test—flunked calculus in her first year at Harvard. When my friend the physicist heard about it, he said, "Harvard should be ashamed of itself." What he meant was that she needed that little extra encouragement that makes all the difference. Instead, she got that little extra discouragement that makes all the difference. "In the first place, all the math teachers are men," she explained. "In the second place, when I met a boy I liked and told him I was taking chemistry, he immediately said: 'Oh, you're one of those science types.' In the third place, it's just a kind of social thing. The math clubs are full of boys and you don't feel comfortable joining."
>
> In other words, she was made to feel unnecessary, and out of place.
>
> A few months ago, I accompanied a male colleague from the science museum where I sometimes work to a lunch of the history of science faculty at the University of California. I was the only woman there, and my presence for the most part was obviously and rudely ignored. I was so surprised and hurt by this that I made an extra effort to speak knowledgeably and well. At the end of the lunch, one of the professors turned to me in all seriousness and said: "Well, K.C., what do the women think of Carl Sagan?" I replied that I had no idea what "the women" thought about anything. But now I know what I should have said: I should have told him that his comment was unnecessary, injurious and out of place.
>
> – K.C. COLE, "Women and Physics"

Cole uses the long paragraph to build up our frustrations as we learn about why science is so "hard" for her stepdaughter. The short, one-sentence paragraph then emphasizes the point made by the long paragraph, how out of place the stepdaughter was made to feel. With the final paragraph, the author turns the tables, ending with the assertion that it is really the male comment that is "out of place."

The absence of firm guidelines for paragraphing does not imply an absence of reader expectations about paragraph length. A paragraph that goes on for twenty or thirty sentences will likely strain the reader's interest (and send him or her looking for indications of paragraph unity); a series of one-sentence paragraphs may strain the reader's patience, because such a series could mean that no idea is being developed in a satisfying way.

While paragraphs that are very short can often be developed more fully, paragraphs that are very long may be harder to revise. It can be helpful to keep in mind that a single idea need not always be developed in a single paragraph. If, for example, you are writing an essay elaborating three reasons for supporting a particular political candidate, you should not feel compelled to devote just one paragraph (possibly a very *long* paragraph) to each reason regardless of its complexity. With good transitions and a good overall organization, you can devote more than one paragraph to each component of your essay without violating principles of unity, coherence, and development.

Exercise 6.11

Examine the paragraph breaks in an essay you have written recently. Explain to another student why you decided on each of the breaks. Would you change any of them now? If so, how and why?

Composing special-purpose paragraphs

In addition to those that make up the main body of an essay, some paragraphs serve more specialized functions. These include opening paragraphs, concluding paragraphs, transitional paragraphs, and dialogue paragraphs.

1. Introducing an essay

Even a good piece of writing may remain unread if it has a weak opening paragraph. In addition to announcing your topic (usually in a thesis statement), therefore, an introductory paragraph must engage the readers' interest and focus their attention on what is to come next. At their best, introductory paragraphs work like the title sequences in a film, carefully setting the scene and establishing themes the movie will explore. Because of the introduction's importance, writers often leave the *final* drafting of it until last, realizing that the focus of the introduction may change over the process of writing.

One common kind of opening paragraph follows a general-to-specific pattern, ending with the thesis. In such an introduction, the writer opens with a general statement and then gets more and more specific, concluding with the most specific sentence in the paragraph—the thesis. The following paragraph illustrates such an opening:

> Despite the best intentions of many Canadians, real environmental improvement seems a long way away. The Canadian government has allocated billions of dollars in subsidies to fossil-fuel megaprojects; it has cut back Via Rail, with no immediate plans to replace it with another mass transportation system; and Canada has done nothing to honour the resolution taken at the Toronto conference of 1988 to reduce production of chlorofluorocarbons by 20 percent by 2004. Real improvement will come only with massive changes in the way Canadians live—changes that will affect every facet of our lives.

(margin notes: GENERAL STATEMENT / MOVE TO SPECIFICITY / THESIS)

In this paragraph, the opening sentence introduces a general subject, the environment; the next very long sentence focuses more specifically on matters concerning the environment; and the last sentence presents the thesis that the rest of the essay will develop. Other ways of opening an essay include quotations, anecdotes, questions, or strong statements.

Opening with a quotation

"Go back to hell where you came from, you old wart hog," says Mary Grace, an unattractive girl from a Massachusetts college, to Mrs. Ruby Turpin, a hypocritical southern woman, in Flannery O'Connor's "Revelation." Mary Grace's words sting poor Mrs. Turpin, who is not used to taking criticism from anyone. Mary Grace's message is that Mrs. Turpin is not better than the people she thinks badly of, and her attack causes Mrs. Turpin to stop and scowl, in a moment of uncharacteristic self-doubt.

Opening with an anecdote

"Your daughter is absolutely beautiful!" the woman gushed to my father. A friend of his from work, she had heard much about my sister Tracy and me but had never met us before. I could tell that she was one of those blunt elderly ladies, the type that pinches cheeks, because as soon as she finished appraising my sister, she turned to me with a judgmental look in her eye. Her face said it all. Beady brown eyes traveling slowly from my head to my toes, she sized me up and said rather condescendingly, "Oh, and she must be the smart one." I stared down at my toes as I rocked nervously back and forth. Then, looking at my sister, I realized for the first time that she was very pretty and I was, well, the smart one.

– JENNIFER GERKIN, "The Smart One"

Opening with a question

Why is the Canadian population terrified of turning to nuclear power as a future source of energy? People are misinformed, or not informed at all, about its benefits and safety. If Canadians would take time to learn about what nuclear power offers, then their apprehension and fear might be transformed into hope.

Opening with a strong statement

The products that we rely on as part of everyday life—Crest toothpaste, Ivory soap, and Mr. Clean, just to name a few—are responsible for over 55,000 animals deaths every *day* in North America. The reason is toxicity testing and the majority of consumers are, as I was, unaware of the amount of testing done on animals for grooming and household care products. The fact is that we have been betrayed by the companies that we trust to get us through everyday life.

Although this section has spoken of single opening *paragraphs*, keep in mind that an essay introduction may be more than one paragraph long, especially if the subject matter is complex. Keep in mind too that a good introduction will introduce not only your topic or a set of issues, but also your essay. While statements of your essay's purpose and direction need not be explicit (e.g., "The purpose of this essay is ..."), it does seem to be the case that most readers like to know, as they get into an essay, where they are going—and why they are making the trip.

Exercise 6.12

Refer once more to the essay you drafted in Exercise 5.11. Examine your introduction carefully, and then write an alternative introduction. Finally, write a paragraph stating which introduction is more effective and why.

2. Concluding an essay

A good conclusion wraps up an essay in a meaningful and memorable way. If a strong opening paragraph whets readers' appetites or arouses their curiosity, a strong concluding paragraph satisfies them that the job the essay set out to do is indeed completed, that their expectations have been met.

One common strategy for concluding an essay makes use of the specific-to-general pattern, often beginning with a restatement of the thesis, and moving to several more general statements, almost in a reverse of the general-to-specific opening. The concluding paragraph of Evelyn Fox Keller's epilogue to one of her books moves in such a way, opening with a general statement, specifying it, and then ending with a much more general statement:

> To know the history of science is to recognize the mortality of any claim to universal truth. Every past vision of scientific truth, every model of natural phenomena, has proved in time to be more limited than its adherents claimed. The survival of productive difference in science requires that we put all claims for intellectual hegemony in their proper place—that we understand that such claims are, by their very nature, political rather than scientific.
>
> — EVELYN FOX KELLER, *Reflections on Gender and Science*

Other effective strategies for concluding an essay include questions, quotations, vivid images, calls for action, and warnings.

Concluding with a question

> All so-called "permanent" antifreeze is basically the same. It is made from a liquid known as ethylene glycol, which has two amazing properties: It has a lower freezing point than water, and a higher boiling point than water. It does not break down (lose its properties), nor will it boil away. And every permanent antifreeze starts with it as a base. Also, just about every antifreeze has now got antileak ingredients, as well as antirust and anticorrosion ingredients. Now, let's suppose that, in formulating the product, one of the companies comes up with a solution that is pink in color, as opposed to all the others, which are blue. Presto—an exclusivity claim. "Nothing else looks like it, nothing else performs like it." Or how about, "Look at ours, and look at anyone else's. You can see the difference our exclusive formula makes." Granted, I'm exaggerating. But did I prove a point?
>
> — PAUL STEVENS, "Weasel Words: God's Little Helpers"

Concluding with a quotation

> Despite the celebrity that accrued to her and the air of awesomeness with which she was surrounded in her later years, Miss Keller retained an unaffected personality, certain of her optimistic attitude toward life was justified. "I believe that all through these dark and silent years God has been using

my life for a purpose I do not know," she said. "But one day I shall understand and then I will be satisfied."

— ALDEN WHITMAN, "Helen Keller: June 27, 1880–June 1, 1968"

Concluding with a vivid image

It is, in any case, finally you that I end up having to trust not to laugh,
not to snicker. Even as you regard me in these lines, I try to imagine your face
as you read. You who read "Aria," especially those of you with your theme-
divining yellow felt pen poised in your hand, you for whom this essay is yet
another "assignment," please do not forget that it is my life I am handing you
in these pages—memories that are as personal for me as family photographs
in an old cigar box.

— RICHARD RODRIGUEZ, from a postscript to "Aria: A Memoir of a
Bilingual Childhood"

Concluding with a strong call for action

It is now almost 40 years since the invention of nuclear weapons. We
have not yet experienced a global thermonuclear war—although on more
than one occasion we have come tremulously close. I do not think our luck
can hold forever. Men and machines are fallible, as recent events remind us.
Fools and madmen do exist, and sometimes rise to power. Concentrating
always on the near future, we have ignored the long-term consequences of
our actions. We have placed our civilization and our species in jeopardy.

Fortunately, it is not yet too late. We can safeguard the planetary civilization and the human family if we so choose. There is no more important
or more urgent issue.

— CARL SAGAN, "The Nuclear Winter"

Concluding with a warning

Because propaganda is so effective, it is important to track it down and
understand how it is used. We may eventually agree with what the propa-
gandist says because all propaganda isn't necessarily bad; some advertising,
for instance, urges us not to drive drunk, to have regular dental checkups, to
contribute to the United Way. Even so, we must be aware that propaganda is
being used. Otherwise, we will have consented to handing over our inde-
pendence, our decision-making ability, and our brains.

— ANN MCCLINTOCK, "Propaganda Techniques in Today's Advertising"

The concluding paragraph provides the last opportunity for you to impress
the message of an essay on your readers' minds and to create effects you
desire. As such, it is well worth your time and effort.

Choose a piece of writing you have done recently, and examine the conclusion carefully. Then write at least one new conclusion, striving for the maximum effect on readers. Finally, discuss with another student the techniques you used in your revision.

3. Using transitional paragraphs

On some occasions, you may need to call your readers' attention very powerfully to a major transition between ideas. To do so, consider using an entire short paragraph to signal that transition, as in the following example from an essay on "television addiction." The opening paragraphs of the essay characterize addiction in general, concluding with the paragraph about its destructive elements. The one-sentence paragraph that follows arrests our attention, announcing that these general characteristics will now be related to television viewing.

> Finally a serious addiction is distinguished from a harmless pursuit of pleasure by its distinctly destructive elements. A heroin addict, for instance, leads a damaged life: his increasing need for heroin in increasing doses prevents him from working, from maintaining relationships, from developing in human ways. Similarly an alcoholic's life is narrowed and dehumanized by his dependence on alcohol.
>
> Let us consider television viewing in the light of the conditions that define serious addictions.
>
> — MARIE WINN, *The Plug-in Drug: Television, Children, and the Family*

4. Using paragraphs to signal dialogue

Paragraphs of dialogue can bring added life to almost any sort of writing. The traditional way to set up dialogue in written form is simple: simply start a new paragraph each time the speaker changes, no matter how short each bit of conversation is. This example of a piece of writing incorporating dialogue is from the Montreal author Josh Freed:

> THE PARIS-TRAINED WAITER: Brought up in the trenches of Montmartre, this waiter can walk by you a dozen times and never even see you—although you are a foot away, waving both arms and shouting for a fork, a menu, a meal—along with everyone else in the room.
>
> When he finally decides to visit the table you quickly realize you are too ignorant to eat there. The look on his face tells you that the wine you have ordered is mouthwash and your entrée of melon is supposed to be dessert.
>
> Recently, I asked a waiter at a bistro what "Poulet Julienne" was.

"Obviously sir," he said icily, "it is chicken ... prepared in the style Julienne."

– JOSH FREED, *Sign Language and Other Tales of Montreal Wildlife*

Exercise 6.14

Go through some of your favourite books, articles, or essays to find an opening or concluding paragraph that you consider particularly effective. Try to analyze what makes the paragraph so effective. Then, choosing a topic of great interest to you, try to write an opening or concluding paragraph imitating the paragraph you admire—the structure of its sentences, the pattern of its development, its use of particular devices such as quotations, questions, and so on. Then compare the two paragraphs, and decide how effective your own is.

6f

Linking paragraphs

The same methods that can be used to link sentences and create coherent paragraphs can be used to link paragraphs themselves so that an essay as a whole flows smoothly and coherently. Some reference to the previous paragraph, either explicitly stated or merely implied, should occur in each paragraph after the introduction of an essay. As in linking sentences, you can create this reference by repeating or paraphrasing key words and terms and by using parallel structures, pronouns, and transitional expressions.

Repeating key words

. . . In fact, human offspring remain *dependent on their parents* longer than the young of any other species.

Children are *dependent on their parents* or other adults not only for their physical survival but also for their initiation into the uniquely human knowledge that is collectively called culture . . .

Using parallel structure

. . . The student, in this case, is seen as part of an institution and part of a partnership. *Every student needs* a teacher.

Every student also needs a job . . .

Using pronouns

Singer's tale is of a pathetic Polish Jew, Gimpel, who because of *his* strong faith believes everything *he* is told. At the beginning of the tale, we learn that Gimpel has had a gruesomely cruel life. *He* is an orphan, and all *his* life *he* has been teased and tormented for believing everything *he* hears.

Even the most ridiculous and far-fetched tales take *him* in. For example, when *he* is told that the messiah has come and *his* parents have risen from the dead, *he* goes out to search for *them!* In *his* seemingly foolish search, *he* is berated by the townsfolk.

Using other transitional devices

. . . Authority accrues to the medical author not only as individual speaker but also as the voice of medicine which speaks through him or her. *This appeal of medical ethos may carry a journal article even when* scientific logos is weak . . .

Exercise 6.15

Look at the essay you drafted in Exercise 3.6, or the one you drafted in Exercise 5.11, and identify the ways your paragraphs are linked together. Identify each use of repetition, parallel structures, pronouns, and transitional expressions, and then evaluate how effectively you have joined paragraphs.

6g

Checking paragraphs

Here is a checklist you can use to evaluate—and to improve—your paragraphing:

1. What is the topic sentence of each paragraph? (Is it stated or implied?) Where in the paragraph does it fall? Should it come at some other point? Would any paragraph be improved by deleting or adding a topic sentence?

2. Which sentences, if any, do not relate in some way to the topic sentence? Is there any way to justify their inclusion?

3. What is the most general sentence in each paragraph? If it is not the topic sentence, should it remain or be omitted?

4. Is each paragraph organized in a way that is easy for readers to follow? By what means are sentences linked in each paragraph? Do any more links need to be added? Do any of the transitional expressions try to create links that do not really exist between ideas?

5. How completely does each paragraph develop its topic sentence? What methods of development are used, and are they effective? What other methods might be used? Does the paragraph need more material?

6. How long is each paragraph? Are paragraphs varied in length? Does any paragraph seem too long or too short? Is there anything that might be given strong emphasis by a one-sentence paragraph?

7. By what means are the paragraphs linked together? Do any more links need to be added? Do any of the transitional expressions try to create links that do not really exist between ideas?

8. How does the introductory paragraph catch the interest of readers? How exactly does it open—with a quotation? an anecdote? a question? a strong statement? How else might it open?

9. How does the last paragraph draw the essay to a conclusion? What lasting impression will it leave with readers? How exactly does it close— with a question? a quotation? a vivid image? a warning or call for action? How else might this essay conclude?

Reading with an eye for paragraphs

Think of a writer you admire, and read something she or he has written. Find one or two paragraphs that impress you in some way, and analyze them using the above questions.

Taking inventory: paragraphs

Examine one or two paragraphs you have written, using the above questions to evaluate their unity, coherence, and development. Identify the topic of each paragraph, the topic sentence (if one is explicitly stated), any methods of development, and any means used to create coherence. Decide whether each paragraph is successful as a paragraph, and discuss your reasons with another student. Finally, choose one paragraph and revise it.

Writing in Different Disciplines

Rhetorician Kenneth Burke describes the way people become active participants in the "conversation" of humankind in the following way. Imagine, he says, that you enter a crowded room in which everyone is engaged in talking and gesturing. You know no one there and cannot catch much of what is being said. Slowly you move from group to group, listening, and finally you take a chance and "put in your oar": you interject a brief statement into the conversation. Others listen to you and respond—and slowly, you come to participate in, rather than observe, the conversation.

Entering an academic discipline or a profession is much like entering into such a conversation. At first, you feel like an outsider; perhaps you do not catch much of what you hear or read. But slowly, you come to participate. Trying to enter the conversation may be difficult at first, but new vocabulary and conventions gradually become familiar and participating in the conversation seems natural.

The purpose of this chapter is to help you become aware of elements of the writing conventions of different disciplines in order to facilitate your entry into these disciplinary conversations. While a range of writing types may coexist within a particular discipline, it is possible to make some useful generalizations about disciplinary conventions. In fact, you may already be aware of some of the features of writing in different disciplines, perhaps noticing that professors of sociology, for example, have different expectations of student essays than do professors of history or biology.

As you learn to analyze the writing of different disciplines, it is helpful to keep in mind the principles of persuasion discussed in Chapter 5, for academic and professional writing is by nature persuasive. Although persuasive strategies may be more subtle and harder to locate in a scientific article than in an essay on abortion or an advertisement for antiperspirant, persuasive strategies are at work in all kinds of disciplinary writing. Think, for example, of the persuasive power of statistics in social science or the persuasive force of an author's credentials in medicine.

This chapter will help you analyze writing assignments in different disciplines and identify conventional features of academic and professional writing.

Analyzing academic assignments and expectations

Assignments vary widely from course to course and even from instructor to instructor. You may be asked to prepare one-sentence answers to study questions in history or business, detailed laboratory reports in biology, or case studies in psychology. Thus the directions this section offers can only be general, based on experience and on discussions with instructors in many disciplines.

When you receive an assignment in *any* discipline, your first job is to make sure you understand what that assignment is asking you to do. Some assignments may be as vague as "Write a five-page essay on one aspect of World War II." Others, like this psychology assignment, will be fairly specific: "For your first research assignment, you are to collect, summarize, and interpret data drawn from a sample of letters to the editor published in two newspapers, one in a small rural community, and one in an urban community, over a period of three months. Organize your research report into four sections: problem, methods, results, and discussion." In any case, you must begin by analyzing the assignment. Answering the following questions can help you to do so.

Questions for analyzing an assignment

1. *What is the purpose of the assignment?* Does it serve an informal purpose—as a basis for class discussion or as a way to brainstorm about a topic? Or is the purpose more formal—a way to demonstrate your understanding of certain material and your competence as a writer?

2. *What is the assignment asking you to do?* Are you to summarize, explain, evaluate, interpret, illustrate, define? If the assignment asks you to do more than one of these things, does it specify the order in which you are to do them?

3. *Do you need to ask for clarification of any terms?* Students responding to

the psychology assignment might well ask the instructor, for instance, to discuss the meaning of "collect" or "interpret" and perhaps to give examples. Or they might want further clarification of the term "urban community" or the size of a suitable "sample."

4. *What do you need to know or find out to do the assignment?* Students doing the psychology assignment need to develop a procedure—a way to analyze or categorize the letters to the editor. Furthermore, they need to know how to carry out simple statistical analyses of the data.

5. *Do you understand the instructor's expectations regarding background reading and preparation, method of organization and development, and format and length?* The psychology assignment mentions no background reading, but in this field an adequate statement of a problem usually requires setting that problem in the context of other research. A student might well ask how extensive this part of the report is to be.

6. *Can you find an example of an effective response to a similar assignment?* If you can, or if the instructor will provide one, you can analyze its parts and use it as a model for developing your own response.

7. *Does your understanding of the assignment agree with that of other students?* Talking over an assignment with classmates is one good way to test your understanding.

Exercise 7.1

Here is an assignment from a communications course. Read it carefully, and then, working with another student, use the list of seven questions in 7a to analyze the assignment.

Assignment: Distribute a questionnaire to twenty people (ten male, ten female) asking these four questions: (1) What do you expect to say and do when you meet a stranger? (2) What don't you expect to say and do when you meet a stranger? (3) What do you expect to say and do when you meet a very close friend? (4) What don't you expect to say and do when you met a very close friend? When you have collected your twenty questionnaires, read through your results and answer the following questions:

1. What, if any, descriptions were common to all respondents' answers?

2. What similarities and differences were found between the male and female responses?

3. What similarities and differences were found between the responses to the stranger and to the very close friend situations?

4. What factors (such as environment, time, status, gender, and so on) do you believe have an impact on these responses? How do the factors affect the responses?

5. Discuss your findings, using concepts and theories explained in your text.

Understanding disciplinary vocabularies

Studying the vocabulary of a discipline is the first step in joining the conversation of that discipline. Determine how much of what you are hearing and reading depends on specialized or technical vocabulary. Try highlighting key terms in your reading or your notes to help you distinguish the specialized vocabulary of the field from the larger discussion. If you find little specialized vocabulary, try to learn the new terms quickly by reading your textbook carefully, by asking questions of the instructor and other students, and by looking up a few key words or phrases.

If you find a great deal of specialized vocabulary, however, you may want to familiarize yourself with it somewhat methodically. Any of the following procedures may prove helpful:

- Keep a reading log, listing unfamiliar or confusing words *in context*. To locate definitions or explanations, review past reading or check the terms in your textbook's glossary or index.

- Review your class notes each day after class. Underline important terms, review their definitions, and identify anything that is unclear. Use your textbook or ask questions to clarify anything confusing before the class moves on to a new topic.

- Check to see if your textbook has a glossary of terms or sets off definitions in italics or boldface type. If so, study pertinent sections carefully to master the terms.

- Try to start using or working with key concepts. Even if they are not yet entirely clear to you, working with them will help you to formulate questions that will assist you in understanding them. For example, in a statistics class, try to work out (in words) how to do an analysis of covariance, step by step, even if you are not sure you could come up with your own precise definition of the term. Or in a biology class, try charting the circulation of the blood even if you do not understand the whole process.

- Find the standard dictionaries or handbooks of terms for your field. Students beginning the study of literature, for instance, can turn to several guides such as *A Dictionary of Literary, Dramatic, and Cinematic Terms*. Those entering the discipline of sociology may refer to the *Dictionary of the Social Sciences*, while students beginning statistical analysis may turn to *Statistics Without Tears*. Ask your instructor or a librarian for help finding the standard references in your field.

Whatever your techniques for learning a field's specialized vocabulary, begin to use the new terms whenever you can—in class, in discussion with instructors and other students, and in your assignments. This ability to *use* what you learn in speaking and writing is crucial to your full understanding of and participation in the discipline.

Exercise 7.2

Here are the opening paragraphs of *General Chemistry*, a textbook by John B. Russell. Read through the passage, and then analyze it by answering the questions that follow the passage about the special vocabulary in the passage:

> At one time it was easy to define chemistry. The traditional definition goes something like this: Chemistry is the study of the nature, properties, and composition of matter, and how these undergo changes. That served as a perfectly adequate definition as late as the 1930s, when natural science (the systematic knowledge of nature) seemed quite clearly divisible into the physical and biological sciences, with the former being comprised of physics, chemistry, geology, and astronomy and the latter consisting of botany and zoology. This classification is still used, but the emergence of important fields of study such as oceanography, paleobotany, meteorology, and biochemistry, for example, have made it increasingly clear that the dividing lines between the sciences are no longer at all sharp. Chemistry, for instance, now overlaps so much with geology (thus we have *geochemistry*), astronomy (*astrochemistry*), and physics (*physical chemistry*) that it is probably impossible to devise a really good modern definition of chemistry, except, perhaps, to fall back on the operational definition: chemistry is what chemists do. (And that chemists do is what this book is all about!) . . .
>
> To make a very long story short, copper and bronze gave way to iron and steel, the latter being an iron-carbon alloy. Metals were very important in early civilization and the practice of metallurgy provided a wealth of chemical information. Egyptians, for example, learned how to obtain many different metals from their ores, and according to some experts the word *chemistry* is derived from an ancient word *khemeia*, which may refer to the Egyptians' name for their own country, *Kham*. However, some experts believe *chemistry* came from the Greek word *chyma*, which means "to melt or cast a metal" . . .

It was not until around 600 B.C. that the beginnings of chemical theory emerged. Thales, a Greek philosopher, proposed that all chemical change was merely a change in the aspect of one fundamental material or *element*. Later, Empedocles, who lived about 450 B.C. proposed that there were four elements: earth, air, fire, and water . . .

1. What terms are defined? Highlight or circle each one, and underline each definition.

2. What techniques or methods are used to point out or emphasize key terms? Note an example of each.

3. What techniques or methods are used to present definitions of key terms? Note an example of each.

4. How many different ways is *chemistry* defined? What is the function or purpose of each definition?

5. Which terms seem most important? Why do you think so?

6. After reading the passage, which of the special vocabulary here is clear to you, and which needs further definition?

Identifying the style of a discipline

Getting familiar with technical vocabulary is one important way of initiating yourself into a discipline or field of study. Another method is to identify stylistic features of the writing in that field. You will begin to assimilate these features automatically if you immerse yourself in reading and thinking about the field. To speed up this process, however, study some representative pieces of writing in the field. Consider them with the following questions in mind:

- In general, how long are the sentences? How long are the paragraphs?

- Are verbs generally active or passive—and why? Do active or passive verbs seem to be part of a characteristic manner of speaking used by writers and researchers in the field?

- How would you describe the overall *tone* of the writing? Is it very formal, somewhat formal, informal?

- Do the writers use first person (*I*) or prefer terms such as *one* or *the investigator*? What is the effect of this stylistic choice?

- Does the writing use visual elements such as graphs, tables, charts, or maps? How are these integrated into the text?

- What bibliographical styles (such as MLA, APA, note, or number style) are used? (See Chapter 13 for illustrations of several styles.)

Exercise 7.3

The following passage comes from the opening of *The Social Construction of Reality*, by sociologists Peter L. Berger and Thomas Luckmann. Read the passage carefully and answer the questions that follow it. You might work on this with another student or in a small group.

The term "sociology of knowledge" (*Wissenssoziologie*) was coined by Max Scheler. The time was the 1920s, the place was Germany, and Scheler was a philosopher. These three facts are quite important for an understanding of the genesis and further development of the new discipline. The sociology of knowledge originated in a particular situation of German intellectual history and in a philosophical context. While the new discipline was subsequently introduced into the sociological context proper, particularly in the English-speaking world, it continued to be marked by the problems of the particular intellectual situation from which it arose. As a result the sociology of knowledge remained a peripheral concern among sociologists at large, who did not share the particular problems that troubled German thinkers in the 1920s. This was especially true of American sociologists, who have in the main looked upon the discipline as a marginal specialty with a persistent European flavor. More importantly, however, the continuing linkage of the sociology of knowledge with its original constellation of problems has been a theoretical weakness even where there has been an interest in the discipline. To wit, the sociology of knowledge has been looked upon, by its protagonists and by the more or less indifferent sociological public at large, as a sort of sociological gloss on the history of ideas. This has resulted in considerable myopia regarding the potential theoretical significance of the sociology of knowledge.

There have been different definitions of the nature and scope of the sociology of knowledge. Indeed, it might almost be said that the history of the subdiscipline thus far has been the history of its various definitions. Nevertheless, there has been general agreement to the effect that the sociology of knowledge is concerned with the relationship between human thought and the social context within which it arises. It may thus be said that the sociology of knowledge constitutes the sociological focus of a much more general problem, that of the existential determination (*Seinsgebundenheit*) of thought as such. Although here the social factor is concentrated upon, the theoretical difficulties are similar to those that have arisen when other factors (such as the historical, the psychological or the biological) have been proposed as determinative of human thought. In all these cases the general problem has been the extent to which thought reflects or is independent of the proposed determinative factors . . .

Neither the general problem nor its narrower focus is new. An awareness of the social foundations of values and world views can be found in antiquity. At least as far back as the Enlightenment this awareness crystallized into a major theme of modern Western thought. It would thus be possible to make a good case for a number of "genealogies" for the central problem of the sociology of knowledge. It may even be said that the problem is contained *in nuce* in Pascal's famous statement that what is truth on one side of the Pyrenees is error on the other. Yet the immediate intellectual antecedents of the sociology of knowledge are three developments in nineteenth-century German thought—the Marxian, the Nietzschean, and the historicist.

1. How long are the sentences and paragraphs?
2. Are the verbs mainly active or passive?
3. What is the overall tone?
4. Do the writers refer to themselves? In what way? What effect do such references have on tone?

Understanding the use of evidence in different disciplines

"Good reasons" form the core of any writing that argues a point, for they provide the *evidence* for the argument. Chapter 5 explains how to formulate good reasons. However, what is acceptable and persuasive evidence in one discipline may be less so in another. Observable, quantifiable data may constitute the very best evidence in, say, experimental psychology, but the same kind of data may be less appropriate—or even impossible to come by—in a historical study. As you grow familiar with any area of study, you will gather a sense of what it takes to prove a point in that field. You can speed up this process or make it more efficient, however, by doing some investigating and questioning of your own. As you read your textbook and other assigned materials, make a point of noticing the use of evidence. The following questions are designed to help you do so:

- How do writers in the field use precedent and authority? What or who counts as an authority in this field? How are the credentials of an authority established?

- What use is made of empirical data (things that can be observed and measured)? What kinds of data are used? How are such data gathered and presented?

- How are statistics used? How is numerical information used and presented? Are tables, charts, or graphs common? How much weight do they seem to carry?

- How is logical reasoning used? How are definition, cause and effect, analogies, and examples used in this discipline?

- How does the field use primary and secondary sources? What are the primary materials—the firsthand sources of information—in this field? What are the secondary materials—the sources of information derived from others? How is each type of source likely to be presented?

- How are quotations used and integrated into the text?

In addition to carrying out your own informal investigation of the evidence used in your discipline, you may well want to raise this issue in class. Ask your instructor how you can best go about making a case in that field.

Exercise 7.4

Do some reading in books and journals associated with your prospective major or a discipline or particular interest to you, using the questions above to study the use of evidence in that discipline. If you are keeping a writing log, make an entry in it summarizing what you have learned.

7e

Using conventional patterns and formats

You can gather all the evidence in the world and still fail to produce effective writing in your discipline if you do not know the field's conventions, the generally accepted format for organizing and presenting evidence. Again, these formats vary widely from discipline to discipline and may even vary within the discipline, but patterns do emerge. In fact, disciplines may share similar conventions for similar types of studies. The typical laboratory report, for instance, follows a fairly standard organizational framework whether it is in botany, chemistry, or parasitology. A case study in sociology or education or anthropology likewise follows a typical organizational plan. And many disciplines share a conventional format for problem-solution reports: statement of problem, background for the problem's formulation, review of the literature on the subject, findings and possible solution, conclusions, and recommendations.

Your job in any discipline is to discover its conventional formats and organizing principles so that you can practise using them. This task is easy enough to begin. Ask your instructor to recommend some excellent examples of the kind of writing you will do in the course. Then analyze these examples in terms of format and organization. You might also look at major scholarly journals in your field, checking to see what types of formats seem most common and how each is organized. Study these examples, keeping in mind the following questions about organization and format:

- What types of essays or reports are common in this field? What is the purpose of each type?

- What can a reader expect to find in each type of essay or report? What does each type assume about its readers?

- How is a particular type of essay or report organized? What are its main parts? Are they labelled with conventional headings? What logic underlies this sequence of parts?

- How does a particular type of essay or report show the connections among ideas? What assumptions of the discipline does it take for granted? What points does its organization emphasize?

The following sections illustrate three general patterns common in research essays: surveying literature, reporting experimental or field research, and interpreting sources.

1. Surveying literature in the social sciences

An introductory psychology class was given the assignment to write a brief literature review related to one aspect of child development, summarizing three journal articles addressing the topic, and drawing some conclusions based on their findings. Following are the notes Laura Brannon made analyzing first the assignment and then the vocabulary, style, evidence, and organizational pattern appropriate for the field of psychology. These notes correspond to the questions for analysis presented in 7a–7e.

ANALYZING THE ASSIGNMENT AND THE EXPECTATIONS

1. The purpose is for me to familiarize myself with some aspect of child development and see several viewpoints in the field.

2. Assignment says to summarize three journal articles. Then evaluate and interpret their findings.

3. "Literature review" is defined in the assignment.

4. The articles I plan to review focus on a particular study, so I need to be able to see the strengths and weaknesses of each study. (I also must be able to understand their use of statistics to be able to evaluate the data and then must be able to draw conclusions based on this evaluation.)

5. No specific format is specified.

6. By examining previous responses to similar assignments, I can determine an acceptable format—will ask professor for some.

ANALYZING THE SPECIALIZED VOCABULARY

1. Articles will have technical vocabulary from psychology and statistics.

2. I will need to know terms such as *variables, inter-rater agreement,* and so on to understand reading.

3. Terms showing reliability of research need to be mentioned in my summary.

ANALYZING THE STYLE

1. Sentences and paragraphs tend to be short.

2. Many passive verbs are used, especially in the sections presenting data (resembles newspaper style).

3. Overall tone is very formal (although can be slightly less so in the introduction).

4. First person is used very little.

5. Visual elements are used when necessary to clarify the findings. They are first mentioned in text (e.g., *see Table 1*) and then table follows (i.e., at end of paragraph).

6. Professor says journals use APA style; must check out exactly what this means.

ANALYZING THE USE OF EVIDENCE

1. Psychology relies heavily on previous related findings. Credentials are often based on data alone. Statistically significant findings are very important.

2. Experimental data are very important. Experiments are devised to control for all variables other than the one being manipulated. (If extraneous variables are not controlled, the data will probably be rejected as worthless.)

3. Statistics are very important—results must be within the 0.05 level of significance (only a 5 percent possibility that the results were caused by chance). Probabilities must be presented with results, but tables and graphs are used as necessary.

4. Cause-to-effect logic is very important. Frequently, generalizations are made concerning the "real" world, based on current research findings.

5. All three articles report on primary research.

6. Quotations are used to help make a point.

ANALYZING CONVENTIONAL PATTERNS

1. In a literature survey, the three articles can be discussed in separate sections. Label each one with a heading. Change to new section for each article discussed, and introduction to each.

2. Arrange articles in chronological order.

3. Summarize each article and include quotations as appropriate to make my main points clear.

4. End with my conclusions about what articles show and about what may happen in the future.

After browsing through her textbook and thinking about the assignment, Laura Brannon decided to focus on child abuse. A trip to the library turned up many articles on this subject, and she chose three. She summarized the three articles, worked through a draft, and analyzed it, following revision guidelines (see Chapter 4). Here are the opening and closing sections of Laura Brannon's essay, a literature survey reviewing three articles and drawing conclusions about what they show and mean.

Note that she first presents the subject of her literature review and acknowledges the complexity of the issue—child abuse—as a means of leading into the three articles she intends to survey. She then summarizes the first article, giving pertinent information about the subjects of the study, the size of the study, and the methods used, before presenting significant results and reporting on shortcomings noted by the authors. Her summaries of the two other articles have been omitted in the excerpt printed here.

In her conclusion, Laura moves on to offer her own interpretation of the significance of the three articles and draws out the implications of these studies for those who seek to prevent child abuse. Note that her citations and references follow APA style guidelines throughout (see Chapter 13).

Early Detection of Child Abuse

There is no simple one-word answer to the question of what causes child abuse. The abuse of children results from a complex interaction among parent, child, and environmental factors. This complexity does not necessarily mean, however, that potential victims and abusers cannot be identified before serious damage is done. Researchers have examined methods of detecting potential or actual child abuse.

Prediction of Child Abuse: Interviews

In a study by Altemeier, O'Connor, Vietze, Sandler, and Sherrod (1984), 1,400 women between nine and forty weeks pregnant were interviewed to test their abusive tendencies. Four researchers were present (with an inter-rater agreement of 90 percent or better). The Maternal History Interview included questions about the mother's own childhood, self-image, support from others, parenting philosophy, attitudes toward pregnancy, and health-related problems (including substance abuse). Maternal and paternal stresses during the preceding year were measured with a modified Life Stress Inventory. Any information not included in the standard interview but felt by the researchers to make the mother a high risk for abuse of her child — for example, being overtly untruthful — was also recorded. When the infants were twenty-one to forty-eight months old, the Juvenile Court and the Department of Human Services were checked for reports of their abuse or neglect.

Although the interview predicted abuse (p < .0001), its ability to predict decreased with time; for example, although "six of seven families reported for abuse within the first nine months following the interview were high risk, ... after 24 months only one of seven had been assigned to this group" (Altemeier et al., p. 395). The researchers point out some shortcomings of their study, particularly the high rate of false positives. (Only 6 percent of the high-risk population was reported for abuse, 22 percent if failure to thrive and neglect were included.) Although many incidents of abuse may go unreported (which could account for some of the false positives), this false-positive percentage should be reduced. Also, it would be preferable if the role of subjective judgments in the method for prediction could be reduced as well.

[Brannon's review of two additional studies follows.]

<u>Conclusions</u>

Overall, the findings of these studies seem to indicate that tests can be devised to predict potential child abusers. The study by Murphy, Orkow, and Nicola (1985), which relies less on subjective judgments, has a significantly lower false positive rate than the earlier study by Altemeier and associates (1984). Therefore, although such tests have not yet been perfected, they appear to be improving.

The two studies tried to integrate the complex relationships between child, parent, and environmental factors that are involved in child abuse. Ideally, if potential abusers could be identified early enough, they could undergo treatment even before the child is born. Of course, a parent could not be separated from a child on the basis of one test, and therefore, the results should remain confidential to avoid any potential for abuse of the test itself.

Whereas the tests look carefully at the parent's situation, the injury variables analyzed in the Johnson and Showers study (1985) focus attention on the child. If teachers or other people notice that children have frequent injuries (especially with the locations, types, and causes associated with different ages and races), abuse can be detected early and perhaps stopped.

References

Altemeier, W. A., O'Connor, S., Vietze, P., Sandler, H., & Sherrod, K. (1984). Prediction of child abuse: A prospective study of feasibility. Child Abuse and Neglect: The International Journal, 8, 393-400.

Johnson, C. F., & Showers, J. (1985). Injury variables in child abuse. Child Abuse and Neglect: The International Journal, 9, 207-215.

Murphy, S., Orkow, B., & Nicola, R. (1985). Prenatal prediction of child abuse and neglect: A prospective study. Child Abuse and Neglect: The International Journal, 9, 225-235.

2. Reporting research in the natural sciences

An introductory biology class was asked to write a report analyzing a genetic question about a particular species of crayfish: when a female heterozygous for red claws was mated with a male with black claws, the resulting offspring included 154 red claws, 235 black claws, and 43 blue claws. Students were asked to explain the results by constructing hypotheses and evaluating them through the use of the Chi-square test. They were to include in their explanation an elaboration on gene expression, and to refer to at least two scientific journals.

Julie Slater's response to this assignment follows. Note that her report uses the format recommended by her instructor: the Introduction explains the principles on which the experiment was conducted; the Methods and Materials section offers a brief description of the experiment; and the Results section explains what the experiment produced. In the Summary section, Julie presents the crosses she made in determining the male genotype and explains what factors her procedures could not take into account. Note that she uses the number style of documentation common to scientific writing (see Chapter 13).

Determining the Genotype of One Parent —
When the Other Is Known — By Evaluation
of the Offspring Frequencies

INTRODUCTION

The purpose of this experiment was to determine the genotype of a male crayfish with black claws that was mated with a red-clawed female known to be heterozygous for claw colour. This determination was made by evaluating the frequencies of three different claw colours observed in the offspring. Hypotheses involving Mendelian principles of genetics and various possible hybrid crosses were proposed and either proven false or recognized as probable by meeting the given stipulations of a black mated to a heterozygous red and the offspring frequencies.

METHODS AND MATERIALS

Two crayfish of a particular species complex were mated. The female, known to be heterozygous for the phenotype of red claws, was mated with a male that expressed black claws. The offspring were grouped according to claw colour and counted. The data were analyzed statistically using a Chi-square test.

RESULTS

In the 432 offspring produced, three phenotypes were noted: 235 crayfish with black claws, 154 with red, and 43 with blue. The observed ratio was 5.4 : 3.6 : 1.

DISCUSSION

The ratio results, which were derived directly from the counting of colour patterns, can be accounted for by only one type of mating. Other possibilities were evaluated, but only one passes the specificities of known female genotype along with the ratio results.

A monohybrid cross with one parent heterozygous for red claws and one homozygous for black produces a ratio of 1:1, which is not in accordance with the three different phenotypes expressed in the offspring. (See Figure 1.) Crossing two heterozygous parents would produce a phenotypic ratio of 3:1. (See Figure 2.) This again does not fit the observed ratio of the crayfish offspring, and it also contradicts the condition that one parent is heterozygous for red claws while the other shows black.

Because neither of the monohybrid crosses accounts for the observed ratio of the offspring, the next probable way to account for the male's genotype was dihybrid cross. A dihybrid cross involving two parents heterozygous for both gene pairs would produce a phenotypic ratio of 9:3:3:1. (See Figure 3.) However, such parents would themselves express the same claw colour; in addition, only three different phenotypes were observed in the resulting offspring.

If the parent with red claws is heterozygous on both gene pairs and the one with black claws is homozygous recessive on the first gene pair and heterozygous on the second pair, the expected phenotypic ratio of the offspring would be 1:3:3:1 (See Figure 4.) This cross again produces too many phenotypes for the observed ratio. If, however, epistasis were involved in this cross, the expected ratio would be 4:3:1. (See Figure 5.) Epistasis occurs when a phenotype does not appear because one gene pair hides the effect of the other. In this cross, epistasis was hypothesized to function as follows. If one gene pair includes a dominant gene and the other is homozygous recessive, a black phenotype will be produced. To produce a red-clawed offspring, it is necessary to have a dominant gene on each gene pair. And for the blue phenotype to occur, both gene pairs must be homozygous recessive. The observed ratio approaches the ratio expected under these conditions. To further support this hypothesis, a Chi-square test was performed. The Chi-square value was 4.31 with two degrees of freedom. This value had a significance level between .2 and .1. For all these reasons, the hypothesis was accepted.

Even though a Mendelian dihybrid cross was found to be an acceptable hypothesis for the ratio observed in the offspring, the pigmentations on body surfaces cannot be explained solely by such a cross. There is substantial evidence that the genetic characteristic of colouring in other animals is governed by at least three to five loci

(2). (As defined by Gardner (3), a locus is "a fixed position on a chromosome occupied by a given gene or one of its alleles.")

According to Crow (4), it is also possible during meiosis for genes to subvert the process of equal selection by "cheating" so that their own survival is more likely. This cheating, which was shown in experiments with <u>Drosophila</u> eye pigmentations, throws off the frequencies of the offspring phenotypes and thereby produces more difficult stipulations that have to be met and explained using Mendelian standards.

In addition to these possibilities, the frequencies of the offspring phenotypes can also be affected by the process assumed by the central dogma. (See Figure 6.) This dogma is the idea that information coded in the sequence of base pairs in DNA is passed on to new molecules of DNA, which transcribes codes for the production of mRNA, which then translates, by means of RNA, the information that will be coded into protein (5). At any stage of this process where information is passed on, there can be some form of interference that would prevent the achievement of the expected outcome. There could also be environmental factors that could possibly alter the phenotypes.

SUMMARY

The genotype of the male crayfish was determined as rrBb. This determination was made by using a dihybrid cross of RrBb x rrBb, where epistasis was taken into account, with an expected ratio of 4:3:1. It does not take into account the possibility that the offspring frequencies have been altered by interference during gene replication, transcription, or translation. Other knowledge that should be considered is the evidence that colouring of body surfaces is governed by at least three to five loci and that genes can actually "cheat" to ensure self-survival. Each of these possibilities could create a result that would require further extensive study into the chromosomal makeup of the species. Despite these possibilities, however, the genotype of the male was proposed and accepted as rrBb.

MONOHYBRID CROSSES
    Figure 1
        Rr × rr →   1 Rr red
        f, red m, black   1 rr black
        f=female, m=male
    Figure 2
        Rr × Rr → 3R_?
        f,?m,? 1rr?

DIHYBRID CROSSES
    Figure 3
        RrBb × RrBb → 9/16 R_B_?
        f,?   m,?   3/16 R_bb?
                      3/16 rrB_?
                      1/16 rrbb?
    Figure 4
        RrBb × rrBb → 3/8 R_B_ red
        f,red m,black 1/8 R_bb?
                       3/8 rrB_ black
                       1/8 rrbb?
    Figure 5 (involving epistasis)
        RrBb × rrBb → 3/8 R_B_ red
        f,red m,black 1/8 R_bb black
                       3/8 rrB_ black
                       1/8 rrbb blue

CENTRAL DOGMA
    Figure 6
    replication

                    DNA →   mRNA → Protein
                    transcription translation
                            involving
                              tRNA

LITERATURE CITED
1. Strickberger, Monroe W. 1968. Genetics. New York:
Macmillan.
2. Branda, R. F., and J. W. Eaton. 1978. Skin color and
nutrient photolysis: An evolutionary hypothesis. Sci.
pp. 625-626.
3. Gardner, Eldon J. 1965. Principles of genetics. New
York: Wiley.

4. Crow, James F. 1979. Genes that violate Mendel's rules. <u>Sci. Amer.</u>: pp. 134–146.
5. Purves, William K., and G. H. Orians. 1987. Life: The science of biology. Sunderland: Sinauer Associates Inc.

Exercise 7.5

1. On the basis of the paper about the crayfish genotype, make a list of the characteristics of a research report in biology. Your list will constitute an initial set of criteria that you could use in writing a report of your own.

2. Based on this paper, what can you surmise about the expectations, vocabulary, style, evidence, and conventional patterns or formats of this field?

3. Can you identify strategies of persuasion at work in this piece of scientific writing?

3. Writing the interpretive essay in the humanities

As a reader of literature, you are not a neutral observer—an empty cup into which the "meaning" of a literary work is poured. If such were the case, literary works would have exactly the same meanings for all of us, and reading would be not nearly so interesting.

Your reading is based to some extent on your personal history and knowledge, and your reasons for reading. Likewise, your writing about literature is based to some extent on your critical stance. What perspective do you bring to the work? How do you approach the text you are writing about? What theory informs your reading? In literary studies today, critical stances vary widely, and you may encounter, among courses and professors, a number of different ones.

In general, student writers tend to adopt one of three stances to literature: a *text-based stance* that builds an argument by focusing on specific features of the literary text in question; a *context-based stance* that builds an argument by focusing on the context in which a literary text exists; a *reader-based stance* that focuses on the response of a particular reader to the text and an interpretation that grows out of his or her personal response; or some combination of these approaches.

Students in a literature class on the 18th-century novel were asked to choose and write about a particular theme as it is elaborated in two novels. University of Toronto student Andrew Wu wrote the following text-based essay in response. Note that he often cites the novels in question, making the texts themselves illustrate his thesis that, in both novels, "clothes and nakedness underscore the discrepancy between appearance and reality, thereby exposing societal hypocrisy in a way that is at once critical and comical." Andrew uses the MLA documentation style (see Chapter 13).

Clothes and Nakedness in Don Quixote
and Joseph Andrews

Clothes and Nakedness function in several important ways in <u>Don Quixote</u> and <u>Joseph Andrews</u>. In both novels, clothes and nakedness underscore the discrepancy between appearance and reality, thereby exposing societal hypocrisy in a way that is at once critical and comical.

Don Quixote's first mad act is to outfit himself in a makeshift suit of armour in an attempt to resemble his vision of knight-errant (31). His clothes contribute to the humour of his madness as he is described travelling the countryside wearing a barber's basin on his head, which he mistakes for "Mambrino's helmet" (163). Don Quixote is further deluded when he imagines the clothes of the Asturian maid to be those of a beautiful princess: "Then he felt her shift and, although it was of sackcloth, it seemed to him of the finest, most delicate satin" (122). Through Don Quixote's random substitution of reality for fancy, we see the absurdity of romantic conventions as well as the potential self-delusion in a naive reading of fictional material.

Similarly, in <u>Joseph Andrews</u>, Fielding uses the leitmotif of clothes to critique the hypocrisy of a society that ranks people "High" or "Low" according to fashion, rather than physical or moral qualities (140-141). The interpolated stories depict fashionable men as being unreliable and lacking in substance: Leonora in <u>Joseph Andrews</u> and Leandra in <u>Don Quixote</u> are both jilted by men who initially charm them with their external finery. Both Bellarmine and Vincente de la Roca hold an exotic appeal for the young women, since they have acquired their clothes abroad. Bellarmine boasts to Leonora of his French wardrobe, and complains of the ineptitude of English tailors: "I would see the dirty island at the bottom of the Sea, rather than wear a single rag of English work about me" (99). In addition, the squire who tries to rape Fanny also follows the French way of fashion. Thus, obsession with clothing and pretension to foreign fashion are associated with perfidy.

Wilson's rakish youth is further testimony to the common and skewed perception of a gentleman as being someone who is well-dressed. While he appeared to be a gentleman, in his conduct he led a life of debauchery. Ironically, his excessive lifestyle is brought to an end when he is thrown in jail for failing to pay his tailor. Significantly, the reformed Wilson is described in his new state as "a plain kind of a Man" (173). Thus, greater vanity is associated with weaker moral character and his transformation into a virtuous man is reflected in his humble appearance.

Conversely, the steadfast and virtuous Joseph wears extremely modest clothes and is not perceived as a gentleman until he is dressed in one of Mr. Booby's suits: ". . . whoever hath seen him in his new Clothes, must confess he looks as much like a Gentleman as anybody," Mrs. Slipslop proudly pronounces (267). Fielding ironically refers to Joseph from the moment he dons the suit, as "Mr. Andrews" (264).

In both novels, clothing is closely tied to identity and much of the comedy springs from confusion surrounding these two elements. For example, the priest and barber fool Don Quixote with their flimsy disguises; Parson Adams is mistakenly chided for "robbing in the dress of a clergyman" (131). Thus, although clothing has its darker meaning in <u>Joseph Andrews</u>, it also provides humour in both novels.

Nakedness in <u>Joseph Andrews</u>, although humorous in the case of Parson Adams, equally exposes hypocrisy and underscores power relationships. For example, when Joseph rebuffs Lady Booby's sexual advances, she has him "stripped and turned away" (42). When Joseph leaves her house and is robbed, beaten, and left naked by the side of the road, his vulnerable state serves to illuminate the callousness of the "High People" who refuse to offer him clothing. Tellingly, it is the lowly Postillion who finally offers Joseph a garment. Furthermore, in this "naked" state, the prudery and vanity of the gentry are shown when the lady travelling in the coach that discovers Joseph's half-dead body protests that they leave him where he is because he is naked, while the men are busily trying to be witty at Joseph's expense.

Fielding also uses nakedness to illustrate the arrogant and ignorant attitudes of the upper class. When Adams tries to explain to Peter Pounce that "Hunger and Thirst, Cold and Nakedness" are genuine social problems (245), the wealthy miser Pounce argues that they are "Evils introduced by Luxury and Custom" (245). His words are highly ironic given the fact that through Joseph's recent experience we are made aware of the difficulty of survival without the accoutrements of wealth.

In both Don Quixote and Joseph Andrews nakedness, in the sense of an absence of artifice or ornamentation, is depicted as a noble quality. For example, when Fanny and Joseph are married, they refuse all finery, as their union is a spiritual and physical one, rather than a material one. Hers is an inner beauty that requires no adornment, so that when she undresses, it is a "discovery" or revealing of her true nature, as opposed to a removal of ornaments (311). Similarly, in Don Quixote, the natural beauty of the shepherdesses is exalted above the artificial enhancements of the Court ladies (86). This same passage harks back to the imaginary time when truth and sincerity triumphed over fraud and deceit so that these beautiful maidens could roam the countryside without risk. Thus in both Joseph Andrews and Don Quixote, natural beauty, and the absence of artifice, is idealized.

In short, clothes and nakedness signify the gap between reality and appearance, and nature and culture, thereby exposing the underlying values of society. In the case of Don Quixote, this discrepancy exposes the hollow cult of romanticism, while in Joseph Andrews the hypocrisy of society itself is revealed.

Works Cited

Fielding, Henry. Joseph Andrews and Shamela. London: Oxford University Press, 1966.

Cervantes, Miguel. The Adventures of Don Quixote. Trans. J. M. Cohen. London: Penguin, 1950.

Taking inventory: writing in a discipline

Choose a piece of writing you have produced for a particular discipline—an essay on literature, a laboratory report, a review of the literature in the discipline, or any other assignment. Examine it closely for its use of that discipline's vocabulary, style, methods of proof, and conventional format. How comfortable are you in writing a piece of this kind? In what ways are you using the conventions of the discipline easily and well? What conventions of the discipline give you difficulty, and why? If you are keeping a writing log, make an entry in it on what you need to know about writing effectively in that discipline. Use this entry as the basis for interviewing an instructor in that field.

8

Writing Essay Examinations

Writing an effective essay examination requires two important abilities: recalling information and organizing the information in order to draw relevant conclusions from it. These conclusions form the thesis of the essay while the information serves as support. While this process sounds simple, writing an effective essay examination under pressure in limited time is sometimes a daunting task. This chapter suggests ways to turn this task into a manageable one.

8a

Preparing for essay examinations

As you have probably discovered, essay exams are least daunting when you have prepared for them throughout the term by taking careful notes on lectures and assigned readings—and perhaps by discussing course material with other students.

A useful strategy for staying in control of course material is to outline a lecture or reading assignment, list its main points, define its key terms, and briefly summarize its argument or main points. A particularly effective method is to divide your notes into two categories. In a notebook, label the left-hand pages "Summaries and Quotations." Label the right-hand pages "Questions and Comments." Then as you read your text or other assigned material, use the left-hand page to record brief summaries of the major points made, the support offered for each point, and noteworthy quotations. On the right-hand page, record questions that your reading has not answered, ideas that are unclear or puzzling to you, and your own evaluative comments. This form of note-taking encourages active reading and, combined with careful class notes, will do much to prepare you for the essay examination. Here is an entry from a student's notebook, written in response to Chapter 5 of this book.

Summaries and Quotations	Questions and Comments
- rhetoric — art of language (Aristotle) - all language is argumentative — purpose is to persuade	Maybe all language *is* persuasive, but if I greet people warmly, I don't *consciously* try to persuade them that I'm glad to see them. I just respond naturally (unless they're having an insecure day).
- to identify an *argument*, ask: 1. Does it try to persuade me? 2. Does it deal with a problem without a clear-cut answer? 3. Could I actually disagree with it?	Of all the statements that can be debated, I think the less absolute the possible answers, the more important the question (such as nuclear disarmament) and the harder to solve (otherwise the answer would be obvious — no problem).

Writing can also help you organize and consolidate course material in the days before an examination. Some students find that they learn a great deal, for example, by compiling a comprehensive set of notes, then reducing the notes through a process of summary, then reducing them further, and further, until perhaps a sheet of key words suggests a whole body of course material. In addition, your can prepare for an essay examination by writing out answers to questions you think may appear on the examination (or questions that have appeared on your instructor's previous exams, to which you might have access). Last-minute cramming, sometimes effective for short-answer and multiple-choice exams, is considerably less effective for essay exams. Another hint: you might try writing for ten or fifteen minutes just before you go into an examination in order to get your thinking/writing muscles warmed up.

8b

Doing preliminary work in an essay examination

Before you begin composing exam answers, you should do a number of things. First, read exam instructions very carefully, perhaps underlining key words. You would be amazed at the number of times students respond, for example, to three questions when they were required to respond to four, or respond to all parts of a question when they needed to respond to only two parts of it. Reading instructions carefully is important for other reasons as well. Instructors may specify, for example, that they do not want material from one section repeated in another or that they want all answers informed by examples. If you keep in mind your audience—say, a professor who has read sixty other exam papers before reading yours, perhaps late at night with her marks due the next day—you'll remember how important it is to follow instructions closely. Second, you should establish (if you have a choice) which questions you are going to answer, note their mark values, and then budget your time accordingly, taking, for example, twice as much time on a 50-mark question as on a 25-mark one. Third, once you have read through all the exam questions, you might dispel some of your anxiety by jotting down some notes in response to each one you plan to answer. This procedure is useful because it keeps you from trying to remember what you wanted to say in response to question 6, for example, as you are working on question 1. The procedure also calms you because it reassures you at each point in the examination that you will probably survive the whole thing. Fourth, you should *analyze* exam questions carefully; and finally, you should *outline* exam answers. These last two steps are described in the following sections.

8c

Analyzing essay examination questions

Read the question over carefully several times, and *analyze* what it asks you to do. Most essay examination questions contain two kinds of terms, **strategy** terms that describe your task in writing the essay and **content** terms that define the scope and limit of the topic.

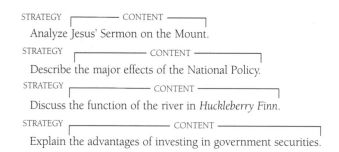

STRATEGY ┌──── CONTENT ────┐
Analyze Jesus' Sermon on the Mount.

STRATEGY ┌──────── CONTENT ────────┐
Describe the major effects of the National Policy.

STRATEGY ┌──────── CONTENT ────────┐
Discuss the function of the river in *Huckleberry Finn*.

STRATEGY ┌──────── CONTENT ────────┐
Explain the advantages of investing in government securities.

Words like *analyze, describe, discuss,* and *explain* tell what logical strategy to use and often help set the form of your essay answer. Since not all terms mean the same thing in every discipline, be sure you understand *exactly* what the term means in context of the material covered on the examination. In general, however, the most commonly used strategy terms have standard meanings.

ANALYZE   Divide an event, idea, or theory into its component elements, and examine each one in turn: *Analyze Pierre Elliott Trudeau's notion of a "just society."*

COMPARE AND/OR CONTRAST   Demonstrate similarities or dissimilarities between two or more events or topics: *Compare the portrayal of women in* The Great Gatsby *with that in* Pride and Prejudice.

DEFINE   Identify and state the essential traits or characteristics of something, differentiating it clearly from other things: *Define Hegelian dialectic.*

DESCRIBE   Tell about an event, person, or process in detail, creating a clear and vivid image of it: *Describe the dress of a medieval knight.*

EVALUATE   Assess the value or significance of the topic: *Evaluate the contribution of Québécois musicians to the development of a Canadian musical tradition.*

EXPLAIN   Make a topic as clear and understandable as possible by offering reasons, examples, and so on: *Explain the functioning of the circulatory system.*

SUMMARIZE   State the major points concisely and comprehensively: *Summarize the major arguments against using animals in laboratory research.*

Strategy terms give you important clues for the thesis of your essay answer. Sometimes, strategy terms are not explicitly stated in an essay question. In these cases, you need to infer a strategy from the content terms. For example, a question that mentions two groups working toward the same goal may imply comparision and contrast, or a question referring to events in a given time period may imply summary.

   An important rule to keep in mind is to answer the question as it has been asked. Do not use every question, regardless of wording, as an opportunity to "dump" everything you know on a topic. Many well-prepared students have done poorly on examinations (or perhaps received "B" grades instead of "A" ones) because they have just written everything they could think of in connection with an examination question instead of actually answering it.

Outlining your examination essay

Begin by deciding which major points you need to make and in what order to present them. Then jot down support or evidence for each point. Craft a clear, succinct *thesis* that satisfies the strategy term of the exam question. Although in most writing situations you start from a working thesis in outlining your topic, when writing under pressure you will probably find it easier and more efficient to outline your ideas and craft your thesis from your outline. Suppose you were asked to define the major components of personality, according to Freud. This is a clear question and, assuming that you have read the material and studied your notes, you should be able to make a brief outline as a framework for your answer.

> Id
> basic definition—what it *is* and *is not*
> major characteristics of
> functions of
>
> Ego
> basic definition—what it *is* and *is not*
> major characteristics of
> functions of
>
> Superego
> basic definition—what it *is* and *is not*
> major characteristics of
> functions of

From this outline, you can develop a thesis:

> According to Freud, the human personality consists of three major and interlocking elements: the id, the ego, and the superego.

Drafting your answer

Your goal in producing an essay examination answer is twofold: to demonstrate that you have understood the course material and to communicate your ideas and information clearly, directly, and logically. During the drafting stage, follow your outline as closely as you can. Once you depart from it, you will lose time and perhaps have trouble returning to the main discussion. As a general rule, develop each major point into at least one paragraph. And make clear the connections among your main points by using transitions: "*The last element of the human personality, according to Freud, is the superego.*"

Besides referring to your outline for guidance, pause and read what you have written before going on to a new point. This kind of rereading may remind you of other ideas while you still have time to include them; it should also help you establish a clear connection with whatever follows.

Revising and editing your answer

Like an essay, an examination essay will likely require some revision. Although it is probably too optimistic to expect that you will have time for a proper revision, you will certainly benefit from leaving five to ten minutes at the end of the exam in order to read through your answers with the following questions in mind. Sometimes even small revisions—if they serve the purpose of clarification or correction—will make a big difference.

- Is the thesis clearly stated? Does it answer the question?
- Are all the major points covered?
- Are the major points adequately developed and supported?
- Is each sentence complete?
- Are spelling, punctuation, and syntax correct?
- Is the handwriting legible?

The more familiar you become with the process of taking an essay exam, the better your answers will be.

8g

Considering a sample essay answer

In a final examination for an English course on the history and theory of rhetoric, students were given two kinds of questions in an examination consisting of two parts of equal mark value. In the first part of the examination, a list of eight names and terms was accompanied by these instructions (some key words were already underlined):

> Identify and explain <u>five</u> of the following names or terms and discuss the <u>significance</u> of each to the history of rhetorical theory. Be <u>specific</u>; use <u>examples</u> whenever possible; demonstrate familiarity with the assigned <u>primary texts</u> where you can.

In the second part of the examination, students were given three essay questions and were instructed to choose one for response.

Student Andrea Williams spent the first fifteen minutes of the three-hour exam reading the exam, choosing questions, and jotting down notes. She then spent an hour and fifteen minutes on the first part (fifteen minutes per item), leaving an hour and fifteen minutes for the larger essay question. She had decided as soon as she saw it that this question was the most intriguing: "What effect has science had on rhetoric? Comment also on the effect rhetoric has had on science. Use examples whenever possible."

In analyzing the essay question, Andrea had little trouble recognizing that her professor was after a *cause-and-effect* essay that focused primarily on the effect of science on rhetoric and secondarily on the effect of rhetoric on science. She also knew of her professor's preference for very specific responses, accompanied by a lot of examples. She prepared this outline:

<u>FX of science on rhetoric</u>
Rhetorical invention: Bacon and the syllogism
                          Descartes "   "   "
Style: virtue of plain style—e.g. Sprat
Genre: the scientific article as persuasive genre—e.g. Pons and Fleishman
Following science, a limited function for rhetoric as revealing truth

<u>FX of rhetoric on science</u>
Paradigm shifts as rhetorical (Kuhn)
Recognition of value-ladenness of science—e.g. Martin

<u>Conclusion</u>
Rhetoric uses scientific appeals; science is public discourse

She then crafted the following thesis:

> Just as science has had a tremendous impact on rhetoric since the seventeenth century, so has rhetoric had an impact on science, especially in the twentieth century.

This is Andrea's examination essay:

Just as science has had a tremendous impact on rhetoric since the seventeenth century, so has rhetoric had an impact on science, particularly in the twentieth century. While to some rhetoric and science make strange bedfellows, they have been and continue to be inextricably linked.

The beginning of this relationship can be traced to Francis Bacon. Bacon's inductive method revolutionized rhetorical invention. Since classical times, deductive reasoning in the form of the syllogism was the method of invention. Bacon's scientific experiments turned this method of invention on its head, replacing the syllogism that had been arrived at through common consent with scientific investigation and discovery. Thus, rather than moving from general or universal theories to particular claims, Bacon's induction worked from particulars to general statements. (The syllogism does not get reinstated until the eighteenth century, when theorists acknowledge its usefulness in detecting invalid reasoning.) Furthermore, Bacon argues that rhetoric's value lies not in discovering truth, for truth can be arrived at only through scientific investigation, but in presenting truth to an audience.

Descartes' scientific Rationalism also affected the course of rhetoric. Unlike Bacon, Descartes used deductive reasoning, but based only on premises already proven to be true (e.g., "I think, therefore I am"). Descartes discounts rhetoric as a means of arriving at truth; argument may convince or persuade, but it does not discover truth. Thus Descartes further devalues rhetoric, restricting its domain to stylistics. Thus, the "doubting game," whereby propositions are disbelieved until proven true, cripples rhetoric by relegating it to the realm of moral reasoning.

From the seventeenth century on, science also had the effect of turning stylistic plainness into a virtue, whereas formerly plainness was a rhetorical choice rather than a singular virtue. The emergence of science as the new God coincides with a new emphasis on perspicuity that condemns "specious tropes and figures" (Thomas Sprat, The History of the Royal Society, 1667).

The values of scientific investigation also affected rhetorical genres. Scientific experiments, once witnessed by members of the scientific community whose testimonials lent credibility to scientific claims, are converted into written documents. While published reports of experiments claim to be objective accounts or explanations of what happened in the laboratory, they nonetheless constitute a persuasive genre. However, it is not until many years later that scientists admit to "authoring" their experiments, and even now, of course, some do not. Furthermore, the potential for experiments to be replicated becomes a key persuasive value and remains so today. (The controversy surrounding the Pons and Fleishman cold fusion experiments is a case in point. Because of the difficulty other established scientists have had in replicating their experiment, and because, in addition, the two circumvented rigorous scientific publication, Pons and Fleishman were dismissed as quacks.)

Since invention becomes restricted to science and logic in the eighteenth century, the domain of rhetoric also becomes restricted. While arguments were sought through a process of invention in Ancient Greece and Rome, rhetoric is now the managing of ordering of pre-existing truths. According to Whately (1828), rhetoric's function is to put truth in a better light.

It is not until the twentieth century that the reductive effect of science is challenged. Rhetoricians such as Richard Weaver blame science for the separation between reason and passion in rhetoric since the eighteenth century. Weaver claims that this division has turned us into thinking or reason machines. Instead, Weaver proposes an acknowledgment of all language as persuasive (or "sermonic," as he says). However, while Weaver expands the realm of rhetoric to include the social sciences, he himself stops at the physical sciences.

In his landmark work, The Structure of Scientific Revolutions (1962), Thomas Kuhn outlines a theory of scientific change involving "paradigm shifts." Within a given paradigm all "facts" cohere around accepted theories. When enough scientific discoveries are made that challenge the existing "paradigm," a shift occurs that forces scientists to consider previous experiments and data in a new light. Thus, Kuhn shows how inductive reasoning is always based on particular premises, for we are always operating within a given paradigm — and how scientists must persuade other scientists to adopt new paradigms.

Rhetoricians have joined Kuhn in exposing science as a value-laden enterprise. Chaim Perelman's and Lucie Olbrechts-Tyteca's assertion that fact-status is connected to majority belief is one step closer to the view of contemporary rhetoricians that the realm of the probable is infinitely expandable. Anthropologist Emily Martin, for example, has shown how scientific discussion of the "passive egg" and the "aggressive sperm" is overlaid with cultural values. Such challenges to the neutrality of science have not been readily accepted by scientists themselves, most of whom prefer to see their own research as neutral.

In conclusion, the twentieth century has seen the relationship between rhetoric and science become a more mutual one. Science has posed important challenges to rhetoric and, while debasing it, science has also been influenced by rhetoric. While the notion of science as rhetorical is still abhorrent to many scientists, interdisciplinary studies have exposed the values inherent in both scientific research and discourse. At the same time, scientific ethos remains extremely effective among the general public (as is evident in the many commercial endorsements by medical doctors and other scientists). Our vocabulary concerning environmental and health issues, and the importance we assign scientific reasoning and evidence, attests to the way that science has become what rhetoric has always been: the stuff of public discourse.

As you can see, Andrea had a great deal to say in this examination answer. Her biggest challenge was organizing her material and using it to argue a thesis. Her outline was indispensable. Andrea responded fully and accurately enough in the allotted time to receive a mark of A+ for this essay.

8h

Analyzing and evaluating your answer

Although you will not have time to analyze your answers during an examination, you can improve your essay examination abilities by analyzing your own answers later.

When her professor returned her exam, Andrea went through her answer sentence by sentence to see if she could learn anything from it that might be of use in future examinations.

Thesis: My thesis was clear. Sticking to the question helped focus my essay and prevented me from merely summarizing the material.

Major points: Closely following my outline was really helpful, although I could have clarified certain points more (my explanation of Kuhn could have been more clear, I think). The fact that we were instructed to use lots of examples was good, because the examples actually helped me think through my general points.

Organization: Next time, I will leave myself more time to write a conclusion. Mine was pretty rushed. I also think I could have used more transitional sentences at the beginning of paragraphs to let my reader know I was staying on track and keeping my thesis in mind.

Grammar and punctuation: Overall, I'm pleased with what I wrote—but I've got some tense shifts (past to present to past) that should have been taken care of. Tense is something I'll attend to on my next exam.

Taking inventory: your own essay answers

Choose at least two of your recent answers to essay examination questions. Review each question, and then read your answer carefully. How could you improve the organization, content, and accuracy of your answer? Make an entry in your writing log, if you are keeping one, noting any new strategies you can use for improving your essay exam answers.

9

Becoming a Researcher

Research essays and reports are not generically different from other types of college and university writing. The English word *research* derives from the French *chercher*, to search, and from the Latin *circare*, to circle around, explore. Searching, circling around, and exploring are activities that can be important to any writing that you do. This chapter, which focuses on research, will guide you through investigative processes you can use in many types of writing, and will help you especially prepare essays and reports that *require* research.

Work in many professions—engineering, news reporting, law, medicine, law enforcement—relies heavily on research. But this process of investigating sources, compiling data, and drawing conclusions based on what we find pervades our personal lives as well as our work. We find something out, and then we act on it. This chapter thus rests on the assumption that we are all researchers. From this basic assumption come four important premises:

1. You already know how to do research.

You act as a researcher whenever you investigate something—whether a college, a course, a computer, or a car—by reading up on it, discussing its features with your friends, or by checking to see what your choices are and what is available.

In addition, you already possess many essential research skills. You know how to combine experience, observation, and new information when you try to solve a problem, answer a question, make a decision, or analyze a situation. You know how to seek out pieces of information, evaluate their usefulness, fit them all together, and then use them to draw conclusions. These are the very skills you will build on as you become more familiar with academic research.

2. Research is always driven by a purpose.

There is no doubt that when you do the kind of research just described, you do not simply accumulate and record your findings; rather, you use these findings for some purpose. Such is also the case with academic research. All researchers seek out facts and opinions for a reason—wanting to make a discovery; hoping to answer a question, solve a problem, or prove something; wishing to teach or to correct an error or to advocate a position. Research is not an end in itself. Instead it is a process or method, used in many situations and fields, for systematically discovering, testing, and sharing new ideas.

3. Your purpose influences the research you do, which in turn refines your purpose.

When you begin any research, it is impossible to know exactly what you will find out. You begin with a question you want to answer or a general idea that you want to explore, but you may find that your specific purpose shifts as you learn more about your subject. The evidence you have gathered, for example, may prove so startling that it calls for you to persuade—to advocate a solution to a problem—when you originally had meant only to explain the problem. In turn, as you refine your purpose, that purpose will help guide you in choosing additional sources and organizing material.

4. Research rarely progresses in a neat line from start to finish.

You begin with a question that may or may not be explorable or supportable. Then you do some background research and perhaps some writing. Your initial investigation, however, may lead you to start all over again—or to modify your idea and then to refer to other, more specific, sources. This additional research focuses your idea even more, leading you to more and more specific sources. Writing is an important part of this investigative process, for it forces you to sharpen your ideas and perhaps to turn back to your sources for more information. Wherever the process of research takes you, however, your overriding goal remains the same: to develop a strong critical understanding of the information you are gathering.

Understanding and choosing a research topic

In college and university, most research you do responds to a writing assignment. Before you do anything else, therefore, be sure that you understand the requirements and limits of the assignment.

1. Analyzing a research assignment

Begin your research by paying close attention to the exact wording of the assignment. Consider any requirements for purpose, audience, scope of research, length, and deadline. These factors will be especially important to consider carefully if you are asked to select a topic of your own. When you have a topic, consider your rhetorical stance—your perspective on the topic. Then, try to rough out a schedule for research (see the example on page 162). Many students report that it is very helpful for instructors to set a number of due dates—for outlines, draft introductions, drafts, and so on. However, since most instructors do not break down assignments in this way, you should try to take the initiative to do so yourself.

Identifying the purpose

Read through the assignment for **cue words**, such as *describe, survey, analyze, explain, classify, compare,* or *contrast,* that specify the pattern the instructor expects the essay to follow. What do such words mean in this particular field or discipline? What do these meanings suggest about the purpose(s) of the assignment? Keeping these meanings in mind as you begin researching will help you identify sources that fulfil that purpose. (See 2c for a discussion of ways to assess purpose.)

Identifying the audience

Find out if your assignment specifies an audience other than the instructor. Then consider what they and your instructor will expect you to provide, by answering the following questions.

- Who will be interested in the information you gather, and why?
- What do you know about their backgrounds?
- What will they want to know?
- What will they already know?
- What response do you want to elicit from them?

- What assumptions might they hold about the topic?
- What kinds of evidence will you need to present to convince them?
- What will your instructor expect in a strong essay on this topic?

(See 2e for additional questions to consider about your audience.)

Considering your rhetorical stance

When you have at least a broad topic, think about your own attitude toward it, your rhetorical stance. Are you primarily just curious about it? Do you approve of it? dislike it? find it bewildering? Monitoring where you stand on the topic will help you understand your purpose, your audience, and your relationship to your sources. (See 2d.)

Gauging the scope of research

Next consider any information about the kind of research you will need to do. Does the assignment specify anything about how many or what kind of library sources you can or should use? Does it require or suggest any field research—interviewing, surveying, or observing? If your assignment includes such requirements, keep them in mind as you plan your research.

Noting the length

Does your assignment specify the length of the final draft? The amount of research and writing time you must budget for a five- to seven-page essay differs markedly from that needed for one of fifteen to twenty pages. And whatever your preliminary estimate, you may need more time if materials are not readily available or if you discover after a first draft that you need to do more research.

Working toward the deadline

What is your deadline for the completed project? Are any preliminary materials—a working bibliography, a research thesis, an outline, or a first draft—due before this date?

Keeping a research log

You might want to set up a **research log** for keeping track of your work. If you already keep a writing log, you might set off a special section of it for your research project. Use the log to jot down thoughts about your topic, lists of things to do, ideas about possible sources or connections between information, or to use it to keep track of library materials you need to get (or return). Such notes may help you proceed more efficiently and give you a sense of the progress—or the need for progress—in your research.

Scheduling a research project
Following is an example of a research schedule:

Assignment date _____	Try to complete by

Analyze assignment; decide on primary
    purpose and audience; choose topic if necessary.   _____
Arrange library tour; develop search strategy.   _____
Do background reading; narrow topic if necessary.   _____
Decide on research question, tentative hypothesis.   _____
Start working bibliography; track down sources.   _____
Develop working thesis and rough outline.   _____
If necessary, conduct interviews or observations,
    or distribute and collect questionnaires.   _____
Send for needed materials by mail.   _____
Read and evaluate sources; take notes.   _____
Draft explicit thesis and outline.   _____
Prepare first draft.   _____
Obtain and evaluate critical responses.   _____
Do more research if necessary.   _____
Revise draft.   _____
Prepare list of works cited.   _____
Edit revised draft; use spell checker, if available.   _____
Prepare final draft.   _____
Do final proofreading.   _____

Final draft due _____

2. Choosing your own topic

If your assignment does not specify a topic, you can begin framing one by considering what subjects puzzle you, challenge you, engage your curiosity in some way. Remember to keep in mind your instructor's specifications about purpose, audience, scope, length, and deadline, and ask yourself the following questions:

- What subjects do you know something about?

- What subjects might you like to become an expert on?

- What subjects evoke a strong reaction from you—intense curiosity, puzzlement, or scepticism?

In addition, skim through your textbooks or class notes, or perhaps current magazines or journals, looking for a topic or question that intrigues you. Conversations with classmates might be especially productive. In addition, you may find the exploratory techniques presented in Chapter 3—

brainstorming, freewriting, questioning, and so on—helpful for discovering a topic. In fact, if your instructor has suggested a broad topic, you may find these techniques helpful as you try to decide what aspect of the topic to investigate.

Getting response to your topic

As soon as you come up with a topic, draft several sentences that describe it. Then try to get some response to it from your instructor or from other students. You might ask them the following questions:

- Would you be interested in reading about this topic?
- Is the topic manageable?
- Can you suggest and interesting angles or approaches?
- Can you suggest any good sources of information?

9b

Narrowing and focusing a topic

Any topic you choose to research must be manageable—must suit the purpose, audience, scope, length, and time limits for your assignment. Making a topic manageable often requires "narrowing" it, but narrowing is not always sufficient in itself. "The City of Toronto" may be too general a topic, but "Public Transportation in Toronto" will probably not be any easier to manage. Rather than simply narrowing a broad subject to a smaller one, it may be more useful to *focus* on a specific aspect, on a particular slant, looking for a governing question to guide your research.

Asking a research question and developing a hypothesis

The result of this focusing process is a **research question** that can be answered or considered through research. The research question may be tentatively answered by a **hypothesis**, a statement of what you anticipate your research might show. Thus you can begin your research by trying to answer this question, eventually trying to prove, disprove, or illustrate your hypothesis. (If your research question has an obvious answer or requires technical knowledge beyond your grasp, refocus your question.)

Like a working thesis (see 3c), a hypothesis must be not only manageable, but interesting and specific. In addition, it must be arguable, a debatable proposition that can be proved or disproved by research evidence (see 5b). For example, a statement like this one cannot be disproved: "Joe Clark's

Conservative government was defeated by a vote of nonconfidence after only six months in power." No one would argue against this fact, and its statement is not a hypothesis. On the other hand this statement is debatable: "The fall of Clark's Conservative government in December 1982 was due to his failure to acknowledge the limits imposed on a minority government." Such a statement would have to be proved or disproved; thus, it is a hypothesis.

In most cases, you will want to explore your topic by doing background reading and making notes before formulating a research question or developing a hypothesis. In moving from a general topic to a useful hypothesis, you progress from subject to issue to research question and eventually to hypothesis. In other words, from a large field of knowledge or interest, you narrow down to one single manageable issue within the field. You then raise a question about that issue and put forward a possible answer, your hypothesis. Throughout this process, you will profit by *writing*. The following examples outline two students' movements from general subject to hypothesis:

SUBJECT	The city of Toronto
ISSUE	The public transportation system
RESEARCH QUESTION	Is it a world-class system or are there major flaws?
HYPOTHESIS	Toronto's public transit system seriously adds to the city's unemployment and social welfare problem because it denies safe access to disabled persons.

SUBJECT	Shelley's poetry
ISSUE	My responses to the poem "The Sensitive Plant"
RESEARCH QUESTION	What accounts for the fact that I seem to read this poem in two conflicting ways?
HYPOTHESIS	Shelley's "The Sensitive Plant" resists easy reading or set interpretation.

Each of these student writers focuses on an issue about which a research question can be asked. The hypothesis that tentatively answers each question is precise enough to be supported or challenged by a manageable amount of research.

9c

Investigating what you know about your topic

Once you have narrowed and focused a topic, you need to marshal everything you already know about it. In practice, this step calls for what computer scientists would call a "data dump." Here are some methods for getting all your knowledge down on paper:

Brainstorming

Take five minutes to list everything you can think of concerning your hypothesis. You may find it helpful to work with one or two other students.

Freewriting in favour of your hypothesis

For five minutes, write in support of your hypothesis. As in freewriting, do not stop writing for any reason; write for the full five minutes. No one will see this writing; its purpose is simply to provoke you to recall and write down what you already know and think about a topic.

Freewriting against your hypothesis

For five minutes, write down every argument you can think of that someone opposed to your hypothesis would make. Simply attack your hypothesis in every way you can, even in ways that might seem improbable.

Freewriting on your audience

Write for five minutes about your audience, including your instructor. Write about what they need or want to know in order to accept your hypothesis. What do they currently believe about your topic? What sorts of evidence will convince them to believe your hypothesis? What sort of sources will they respect?

Tapping your memory for sources

List, in the form of short notes, everything you can remember about *where* you learned about the topic you are writing on: books, magazines, courses, conversations, television. Much of what you know may seem to you "common knowledge," but common knowledge comes from somewhere, and "somewhere" can serve as a starting point for investigation.

Moving from hypothesis to working thesis

As you gather information and begin reading sources (see Chapters 10 and 11), your research question is likely to be refined and your hypothesis to change. Only after you have explored it, tested it, and sharpened it through your reading and writing does the hypothesis become a **working thesis.**

The hypothesis illustrated in 9b, for instance, might be focused further, or even completely changed, once research begins. The first writer might be able to discover very little about access for the disabled in general but so much about problems of older people using public transportation that she decides to stick to that focus. The second writer might find in his research a critical reading of the Shelley poem that resolves his conflicting readings. In consequence, he would have to change the whole thrust of his discussion.

In doing your own research, you may find that your interest shifts, that a whole line of inquiry is unproductive, that a journal you need to complete an argument is not available, or that your hypothesis is simply wrong. In each case, the process of research pushes you to know more about your hypothesis, to make it more focused and precise, to become an expert on your topic. In short, you are becoming a researcher.

Taking inventory: research

If you have done research for an essay before, now is a good time to go back and evaluate the work you did both as a researcher and as a writer in the light of the principles developed in this chapter. What was the purpose of that research? What kinds of sources did you use? Did you have any audience other than your instructor? How was your topic focused? What were you most pleased with about your research, and about your essay? What were you least pleased with? What advice would you give yourself if you were to revise that essay?

10

Conducting Research

Different topics, questions, and hypotheses will call for different approaches to research. This chapter explores two kinds of research: *field* research and *library* research.

Using both primary and secondary sources

Primary sources are the basic sources of raw information. Primary sources you produce include laboratory experiments you conduct, notes you take in the field, and surveys or interviews you conduct. Also considered primary sources are objects or artworks you examine, literary works you read, and performances you attend. Other primary sources include diaries, letters, first-hand accounts of events by eyewitnesses, contemporary news reports, historical documents, and raw data from experiments conducted by others.

Secondary sources consist of oral and written accounts produced by others. Secondary sources include reports and analyses by scholars, experts, and researchers of other people's laboratory work, field experiences, surveys, and so forth. Secondary sources also include various sorts of critical writing, such as biographies and reviews.

Sometimes, what constitutes a primary or secondary source depends on your purpose or your field of study. A critic's evaluation of a painting, for instance, serves as a secondary work if you are writing an essay on that painting, but as a primary work if you are conducting a study of that critic's writings.

Most research writing depends on both primary and secondary sources. The primary sources ground the project in facts from first-hand accounts and your own discoveries, while the secondary sources provide background for your investigation and support for your conclusions. Literary research, for instance, is very likely to combine primary and secondary sources: your major primary source is the text of the work you are examining, and secondary sources are biographies, analyses of the text, and other works of criticism.

Some research projects, such as background survey or a review of the literature on a given topic, may require no primary sources at all. Secondary sources, on the other hand, are necessary for most research projects; even a report of a laboratory experiment is sometimes prefaced by a discussion of what other researchers have done previously. Research very often builds on secondary sources in this way. You read to find out what is known or not known about a problem; you formulate a question based on what needs to be found out; then you devise a research method to answer that question.

Collecting data in the field

For many research projects, you will need to collect data "in the field"— whether that field is your own home, a laboratory, or the local shopping mall. When you gather information in the field, you are the primary reporter. You must discover where you can find relevant information, decide on the best ways to gather it, and find the best people to inform you about it. Three useful techniques for field research are observing, interviewing, and surveying.

1. Observing

Much professional writing depends on careful direct observation: a doctor's diagnostic notes, a reporter's news article, a social worker's case study. Observing can also provide rich information for your research writing. Sometimes called naturalistic research, **observation** calls on you to look at phenomena without trying to alter them in any way, keeping yourself out of the picture as much as possible. You can observe anything in this way, from the use of bicycle paths on campus to the kinds of products advertised during Saturday morning television shows to the growth of chicks in an agriculture lab.

Careful observation can supply support for a hypothesis or working thesis. For example, one student decided to write a proposal to try to persuade the traffic and parking division of her university to provide more motorcycle parking space in her residence parking lot. Because she wanted to show the need for such space, she set aside an eight-hour period to sit in the lot, recording the number of cars and motorcycles unable to find space.

When she found that the ratio of motorcycles to cars was roughly three to one, direct observation paved the way for her request by helping to demonstrate a need.

Observation is also useful for finding out what people are actually doing as opposed to what they think or say they are doing. The university may think that few students use the library on Sunday, but observation over a few weeks may reveal that Sunday is actually a higher use day than Saturday. The head of campus food services may believe that most students eat two eggs for breakfast, but observation of people eating may reveal that most of them throw away at least one egg.

Preparing for observation

Before you go out into the field to observe, decide exactly what you are trying to find out and try to anticipate what you are likely to see. Then, consider how "objective" you are likely to be. Will you be able to observe phenomena without altering them in some way? Does your hypothesis bias you and threaten to colour your observation? Discuss potential problems with other students and with your instructor.

A checklist for conducting observation

- Determine the purpose of the observation, and review your research question and hypothesis to see that they relate.
- Set a definite period of time for the observation.
- If necessary, make an appointment.
- Develop a system for recording information. (The student studying motorcycle parking, for instance, used lined paper with three vertical columns to tabulate cars, motorcycles, and times.)
- Take materials for keeping notes.
- Consider using a camera, tape recorder, or videocassette recorder.
- Assume the role of reporter, using the questions in Chapter 3 (who, what, when, where, why, and how) to note down what you see and hear.
- Remember to keep an open mind and to pay attention even to observations that seem to *contradict* your hypothesis.

2. Interviewing

Sometimes you will need information that is best sought by **interviewing**, or asking direct questions, of other people. If you can talk with an expert, in person or on the telephone, you might get information you could not get through any other kind of research. In addition to getting "expert opinion," you might ask for first-hand accounts, for biographical information, or for suggestions of other places to look or people to consult.

Finding people to interview

How do you go about identifying people to interview? Check first to see whether your research thus far names any people you might contact directly. Next, take a few minutes to brainstorm for names. In addition to authorities on your topic, consider people in your community who might be knowledgeable—lawyers, librarians, local government officials, alumni of your college.

Once you identify people you would like to talk with, write or telephone to see whether an interview might be arranged.

Composing questions

To prepare useful questions, you need to know your topic well and to know a fair amount about your interviewee. Try to learn as much as you can about his or her experience and opinions. You will probably want to ask several kinds of questions. **Factual questions** ask for specific answers, ones that do not invite expansion or opinion.

> How many schools in this district offer heritage language programs?
> What is the rate of absenteeism among your employees?
> How many other companies in Canada manufacture fibreglass canoes?

In contrast, **open-ended questions** ask the interviewee to think out loud, to go in directions that interest him or her, and to give additional details or anecdotes.

> How would you characterize the atmosphere at the leadership convention?
> What are the most difficult adjustments you have had to make since arriving in Canada five years ago?
> What is the future for literary magazines in Canada?

Avoid questions that may (1) insult the interviewee—"Why did you drop out of high school?" (2) invite the interviewee to ramble on—"What do you think of youth today?" (3) elicit short yes/no answers—"Should the new expressway be built?" (Instead, ask questions that require answers with support: "What other ways can traffic be handled?")

A checklist for planning an interview

- Determine your exact purpose, and check it with your research question and hypothesis to be sure they all relate.

- Set up the interview well in advance, specifying the amount of time it will take and asking permission to tape if you wish to do so.

- Prepare a written list of questions you can use to structure the interview. Brainstorming or freewriting techniques can help you to come up with questions.

- If possible, try out your questions on one or two people to determine how clear and precise they are.

- Check out all equipment beforehand. Record the subject, date, time, and place of interview at the beginning of all tapes.

- Be familiar with the operation of all your equipment.

- Make sure you have all the supplies you need—enough paper, pens, tapes, and so on.

Conducting an interview

Be prompt, and dress appropriately for meetings. If you bring a tape recorder, ask the interviewee again for permission to record your conversation. Even if you use a recorder, bring a notebook with your questions, and write down the answers and any other notes you wish to make. Do not feel bound to the exact structure of your prepared questions, as long as the interview proceeds in a direction that seems fruitful. Be flexible. Note the time, and be careful not to take up more time than you said you would. End the interview with a thank you—and follow up with a letter thanking the person for taking time to meet with you.

3. Surveying opinion

Surveys can take the form of interviews but more often they depend on **questionnaires**. For an introductory language course, for instance, one student decided to investigate the variety of terms used to refer to grandparents. To gather this information, she prepared a simple questionnaire and distributed it to the members of five sections of the linguistics class she was taking.

The student investigating campus parking for motorcycles surveyed people living in her residence, asking how many owned motorcycles and how many of them had difficulty finding parking spaces. She sent questionnaires to everyone in the residence, although such extensive surveying is often unwieldy and even unnecessary. What you need is a representative sample of people, enough so that your survey accurately reflects opinion within the group you are discussing. And you need a large enough sample so that you are not drawing conclusions or making generalizations based on too little data or too small a population.

Questions should be clear and easy to understand and should be designed so that you will be able to analyze the answers easily. For example, questions that ask respondents to say yes or no or to rank something on a five-point scale of most to least desirable are easy to tabulate.

A checklist for designing a questionnaire

1. Write out your purpose and review your research question and hypothesis to determine the kinds of questions to ask.
2. Determine the audience for your questionnaire, and figure out how you will reach them.
3. Using brainstorming, freewriting, or another strategy from 3a, draft some potential questions.
4. Check each question to see that it calls for short, specific answers.
5. Test the questions on three or four people—including your instructor, if possible. Note which questions are hard to answer and why, and how much time the answers require.
6. If the questionnaire is to be mailed, draft a cover letter explaining its purpose and asking the respondent to complete it. Provide an addressed, stamped envelope.
7. Be sure to state a deadline as well as a place for returning the form.
8. Consider adding a question that asks for any other comments.
9. Type the questionnaire so that it is easy to follow, leaving adequate space for all answers.
10. Proofread your questionnaire.

Exploring library resources

Libraries provide two necessary kinds of information: general background, which gives you an overview of your topic and places your research question in context, and particular support, which helps answer your research question and develop your hypothesis.

1. Beginning your library research

Start by reviewing your research question, hypothesis, and knowledge you already have about your topic (see 9b and c). Where did that knowledge come from? Do you own any books about your topic? Have you recently read any magazine articles about it? Do your textbooks help? By jotting down these and any other sources of information you can think of, you will begin creating a working bibliography.

Next, turn to other people who may be able to help you. Perhaps a classmate has done a project on a similar topic, or perhaps your instructor can point you in a useful direction. Library staff can usually help as well. If your instructor has not arranged a library orientation tour for your class, find out about regularly scheduled tours, go along, and ask about your topic.

Developing a research strategy

At this point, you are ready to begin your library research. The chart that follows will help you explore library resources in a systematic way, describing where to look to find various categories of information.

WHERE TO FIND GENERAL BACKGROUND MATERIAL

- Guides to reference books
- Encyclopedias
- Biographical dictionaries and indexes
- Sources for current events
- Maps and atlases
- Bibliographies

WHERE TO FIND SPECIFIC INFORMATION IN PERIODICALS

- Periodical indexes
- Abstracts and citation indexes
- Computer databases

WHERE TO FIND SPECIFIC INFORMATION IN BOOKS

- Library catalogue

WHERE TO FIND MATERIALS NOT AVAILABLE IN YOUR LIBRARY

- Interlibrary loan

Identifying key words

Looking through online catalogues, card catalogues, indexes, or databases will go more efficiently if you have identified **key words** to look for—

synonyms for your topic, broader terms that would include it, or appropriate subtopics. Information on ice cream, for instance, might appear under the headings of frozen desserts, dairy products, or sherbet.

A good place to check for key words is the *Library of Congress Subject Headings,* which lists the headings under which books are catalogued in most libraries. As you search a particular print index or computer database, check its list of key words, or **descriptors**, because many indexes and databases use terms peculiar to their systems. Also check the glossary and index of appropriate textbooks.

Finding Sources

Where to start? You may decide to begin with an overview, looking first at an encyclopedia, for example. This approach may be especially useful if you need a better focus on a research question or want to check for basic bibliographies. On the other hand, you may already have ideas about where to begin and prefer to go right to the library catalogue and periodical indexes. Before you plunge in, however, ask yourself a few questions.

- *How much time do you have to spend?* If you have only two weeks to do your research, you will want to be selective. If you have several months, however, you can follow a broader course, perhaps even consulting materials beyond those available in your library.

- *How current do your sources need to be?* If you must investigate the very latest findings in a field, you will want to check periodicals. On the other hand, if you want broader, more detailed coverage and background information, you will look more to books.

- *Do you need to consult sources contemporary with an event or a person's life?* If your research deals with a specific time period, you may need to examine newspapers, magazines, and books written during that period.

- *What kinds of sources do you need to consult?* Check your assignment to see if you are required to consult different kinds of sources. If you need to use primary sources, find out if they are readily available or if you will need to make special arrangements. If you need to locate nonprint sources or items in special collections, find out where they are kept in the library and if you need special permission to access them.

- *How many sources should you consult?* You can expect to look over many more sources than you actually end up using. Your best guideline is to make sure you have enough sources to support your hypothesis or to prove your thesis. Check to see if your assignment specifies a minimum or maximum number of sources.

Consulting the library staff

Your most valuable source at the library is the highly trained staff, especially the reference librarians. To get the most helpful advice from them, pose *specific* questions: not "Where can I find information about computers?" but "Where can I find information on the history of computers?" The more precise your question, the more useful an answer you will get.

If you find yourself unable to ask clear and precise questions, you probably need to do some general background research into your topic. Then work again on narrowing and focusing, defining a clearer issue, asking a more specific research question, and finding a sharper hypothesis.

2. Selecting reference books

Your library's reference collection includes two broad types of reference materials: those that are general in scope and those that deal with specific disciplines. Guides to reference books can help you identify the ones that suit your purpose. Your research question can then help you choose the best sources to use. Among the types most often consulted are encyclopedias, biographical dictionaries, sources for current events, and book indexes. A great deal of reference material is available on CD-ROM (see 10c3) as well as in bound volumes. Keep in mind that, at this stage of your research, a reference librarian can be extremely helpful.

Guides to reference books

The following guides group reference books by subject fields. Because these guides list other reference books—not actual sources—a few minutes with them can be a shortcut to the books that match your interests and purposes.

Guide to Reference Materials for Canadian Libraries, 8th ed., 1992. Edited by Kirsti Nilsen with Alanna Kalnay. This guide lists general reference books as well as those in specialized areas, including humanities, social sciences, and technology.

Canadian Reference Sources: A Selective Guide, 2nd ed., 1981. Edited by Dorothy E. Ryder. This annotated guide lists reference materials published before 1981. It is divided into five sections: General Reference, History and Allied Subjects, Humanities, Science, and Social Sciences.

Guide to Reference Books, 10th ed., 1986. Edited by Eugene P. Sheehy. This book supplies annotated lists of general reference works and specialized bibliographies and is divided into five sections: General

Reference; Humanities; Social and Behavioral Sciences; History and Area Studies; and Science, Technology, and Medicine.

Walford's Guide to Reference Material. This book consists of three volumes: Volume 1—Science and Technology (now in its sixth edition); Volume 2—Social and Historical Sciences, Philosophy, and Religion (4th edition); and Volume 3—Generalia, Language and Literature, and the Arts (4th ed.). The sixth edition includes books and periodicals as well as microforms and online and CD-ROM sources.

Encyclopedias

For general background on a subject, **encyclopedias** are a good place to begin, particularly because many include bibliographies that could lead you to valuable sources. Though some encyclopedias do provide in-depth information, more often they serve as a place to start, not as a major source of information.

GENERAL ENCYCLOPEDIAS

Encyclopaedia Britannica, 16th ed., 32 volumes. The *Britannica* has a two-part structure; the *Micropaedia*, which contains general knowledge and short entries; and the *Macropaedia*, which contains longer entries that treat selected important subjects in depth. For fine essays on subjects in the classics and humanities, see if your library has the famous eleventh edition of the *Britannica*, published in 1911 and considered by many to be the most thoughtful and scholarly encyclopedia ever produced.

Collier's Encyclopedia, 24 volumes. *Collier's* presents many topics and illustrations chosen to meet the needs of current student research.

Encyclopedia Canadiana, 10 volumes. The *Canadiana* coverage of Canadian people, places, and institutions is more comprehensive than that of any other work.

The Canadian Encyclopedia, 2nd ed., 4 volumes. Editor-in-Chief, James H. Marsh. This 1988 encyclopedia presents information about Canada's culture, politics, history, geography, flora and fauna, as well as biographies of notable Canadians.

Encyclopedia Americana, 30 volumes. The *Americana* pays particular attention to American public figures, institutions, and places.

SPECIALIZED ENCYCLOPEDIAS

Compared with general encyclopedias, **specialized encyclopedias** usually provide more detailed articles by authorities in the field as well as more extensive bibliographies for beginning research. These volumes are often located in the reference area or reading room for the particular discipline. Here are just a few examples:

Encyclopedia of Anthropology
Encyclopedia of Banking and Finance
Encyclopedia of Bioethics
Encyclopedia of Chemistry
Encyclopedia of Computer Science and Technology
Encyclopedia of Crime and Justice
Encyclopedia of Earth Sciences
Encyclopedia of Educational Research
Encyclopedia of Management
Encyclopedia of Music in Canada
Encyclopedia of Newfoundland and Labrador
Encyclopedia of Ontario
Encyclopedia of Philosophy
Encyclopedia of Physical Education, Fitness and Sports
Encyclopedia of Physics
Encyclopedia of Psychology
Encyclopedia of Religion and Ethics
Encyclopedia of Social Work
Encyclopedia of World Art
International Encyclopedia of the Social Sciences
McGraw-Hill Encyclopedia of Environmental Science
McGraw-Hill Encyclopedia of Science and Technology
McGraw-Hill Encyclopedia of World Drama
New Illustrated Encyclopedia of World History

Biographical dictionaries and indexes

The lives and historical settings of famous people are the topics of **biographical dictionaries** and **indexes**. Before you use these sources, consider whether you need a volume covering people who are living or people who are dead. If the latter, decide if you want a current volume covering deceased people or an older volume covering living people that was published during the person's lifetime. Here are a few examples of biographical reference works; many others, particularly volumes specialized by geographic area or field, are available.

Biography Index, 1946–. This quarterly index lists biographical material found in current books and over 1500 periodicals.

Dictionary of National Biography, 1882–1900 plus supplements. The *DNB* covers deceased notables from Great Britain and its colonies (excluding the postcolonial United States).

Dictionary of Canadian Biography. This reference is similar to the *DNB*. Each volume covers a specific time period; the whole work, when finished, will cover the years from 1000 to 1900. Entries are indexed by geography, profession, and other designations.

The Macmillan Dictionary of Canadian Biography. This work includes brief articles on Canadians deceased before 1976.

Dictionary of American Biography, 1928–1937 plus supplements. Usually called the *DAB*, these volumes contain biographies of over 15 000 deceased Americans from all areas of public life since colonial days. The entries include bibliographies of sources.

Current Biography, 1940–. This monthly publication carries informative articles on men and women in current events. It includes photographs and useful short biographies.

The Canadian Who's Who. Published annually since 1979, and every three years before that. Contains short biographies of famous Canadians from all walks of life.

Who's Who in Canada. Biennial; includes many portraits.

Who's Who on America, 1899–. Published every other year, this is the standard biographical reference for information about famous living Americans. Notable Americans no longer living are included in *Who Was Who in America*, covering 1607 to the present. Similarly specialized reference works include *Who's Who of American Women, Who's Who in Government*, and so on.

Who's Who, 1849–. Published annually, this reference supplies brief biographical listings for well-known British people. *Who Was Who*, with volumes covering about a decade each, lists British notables who died between 1897 and the present.

International Who's Who, 1935–. Published annually, this source contains biographies of persons of international status.

Sources for current events and statistics

Almanacs, yearbooks, gazetters, directories, and other sources provide information on current events and **statistical** and **geographical data**.

In general, statistics are found in the government publications section of the library, while almanacs and other reference works are shelved in the reference section of the library or library division. In addition to the following works, some of the general encyclopedias listed earlier in this section publish an annual yearbook surveying events and developments of the preceding year in various fields.

Canadian Almanac and Directory, 1847–. Canada's oldest almanac contains directory information for institutions, education, government, and some businesses; it also contains an almanac, statistics, and a legal directory.

Canada Yearbook and *Canada Handbook.* Annual statistical yearbooks published by the federal government. They offer statistics and general information in economic, social, political, and cultural areas. The *Handbook* is a condensed version of the *Yearbook.*

Canadian Annual Review of Politics and Public Affairs. This book reviews political and public affairs issues and events of the year in a series of essays. The most recent years contain essays from both federal and provincial perspectives.

Editorial Research Reports. Each of the weekly reports in this series consists of a twenty-page survey of a current issue and includes a current bibliography.

Facts on File. This weekly publication summarizes and indexes facts about American current events, making topical information easy to find.

World Almanac and Book of Facts. This annual publication presents data and statistics on business, education, sports, government, population, and many other topics.

Maps and atlases

Atlases contain physical maps of all parts of the world as well as maps showing population, food distribution, mineral concentrations, temperature and rainfall, political borders, and more. In large libraries, maps and atlases are generally filed in their own division or section. However, some gazeteers are filed in the reference section of each division, and maps and atlases are sometimes found with statistical materials. A reference librarian can direct you to the appropriate location

Hammond Medallion World Atlas
National Geographic Atlas of the World
The New International World Atlas

Bibliographies

Other useful sources located in the reference room are bibliographies or indexes to books, which can be helpful for quickly locating complete information on a book when you know only one piece of it—the author's last name, perhaps, or the title. They can also be valuable for alerting you to other works by a particular author or on a particular subject. Bibliographies can lead you to current sources or retrospective books.

CURRENT

Books in Print. Annual. Lists by author, subject, and title all books distributed in the United States and Canada that are currently in print.

Canadian Books in Print. Annual. Lists by author, subject, and title all books currently distributed in Canada (that is, by Canadian publishers or by publishers with Canadian subsidiaries).

Cumulative Book Index. Monthly. Lists by author, subject, and title books in English distributed in the United States and Canada as well as internationally.

Paperbound Books in Print. Semiannual. Lists by author, subject, and title all paperbacks distributed in the United States and Canada that are currently in print.

RETROSPECTIVE

Canadiana. The National Library of Canada's retrospective list of books published or printed in Canada, written by Canadians or about Canada.

National Union Catalogue. Bibliographic descriptions of all the books held by the Library of Congress in Washington, D.C., and other North American libraries. Includes also pamphlets, music scores, atlases, and serials.

General Catalogue of Printed Books. Bibliographic descriptions of holdings of the British Museum.

3. Using periodical indexes and computer databases

Because periodicals—journals, magazines, and newspapers—are published frequently and more quickly than books, they can lend an immediacy to your research that books cannot. In addition, while an entire book may not be devoted to your specific topic, a number of articles may be. You can locate articles in periodicals by searching periodical indexes and computer databases.

Once you have located articles to examine, check your library's **serials catalogue** or **serials list**, usually kept in the periodicals reading room. This catalogue names all the periodicals available in the library and notes their form—original publications, bound volumes, microform. As you search indexes, check the serials catalogue often to make sure you aren't noting down periodicals that aren't available in your library or through interlibrary loan.

Periodical indexes

Periodical indexes are guides to articles published in periodicals. Each index covers a specific group of periodicals, usually identified at the beginning of the index or volume. In addition to printed indexes, your library may own microform indexes that cover many of the same entries. Microform indexes cover only the past three or four years, however, so if you are searching for earlier material, check printed indexes. Microforms are rolls of film (microfilm) or sheets (microfiche) that must be read on motorized projection machines. Ask the librarian for help in locating the microforms and using the machines.

Many libraries also offer access to the online and CD-ROM computer database versions of many periodical indexes. These databases and their use are discussed in the next section. Those indexes discussed here that are available in computer databases are so noted. Check with a reference librarian to see what databases are available at your library.

General indexes for periodicals—usually located in the periodicals reading room—list articles from current general-interest magazines, newspapers, or a combination of these. General indexes will usually provide current sources on your topic, though these may not treat the topic in sufficient depth for your purposes.

Canadian Periodical Index. A good place to begin for any topic of general or popular interest in Canada. It indexes over 375 periodicals—both popular magazines and scholarly journals—and includes such specialized topics as book reviews, short stories, and poetry. While most of the entries are in English, the index does include French-language publications. Entries are arranged by author and subject, with cross-references leading to related topics. Here is a typical *CPI* entry, covering items under the subject heading, "Politicians."

POLITICIANS

    Battling the odds: six Liberals [Sheila Copps; Donald Johnston; Clifford Lincoln; Dennis Mills; John Nunziata; Thomas Wappel] with hope . . . Paul Kaihla. il. *Maclean's* 103 no 6 (F 5 '90): p28–9

    Brain's trust behind Jean Chrétien. Peter C. Newman. *Maclean's* 103 no 4 (Ja 22 '90): p29

    Hot welcome for a home-comer: barbs fly as Fisheries Minister Siddon visits the west coasts. Tim Gallagher. port. *B.C. Report* 1 no 20 (Ja 22 '90): p11

    'Little guy' to beat: Jean Chrétien returns for his second run at the Liberal leadership. Ross Laver. il port. *Maclean's* 103 no 6 (F 5 '90): cover, 22–5

    Trade, investment endeavours top priority for [minister John] Ciaccia. Richard Conrad. port. *This Week in Business* 3 no 2 (Ja 27 '90): p1,5

    See also

    Women in politics

Quebec (Province)

Victor again: Pierre Sévigny has conquered the anger, bitterness and private pain of political humiliation. Johan Sarrazin. port. *Montreal* 19 no 1 (Ja-F '90): p18–19

United States

Busting the mayor . . . Marion Barry is arrested in a cocaine charge. Tom Morganthau. il port. *Newsweek* 115 no 5 (Ja 29 '90): cover, 24–8

Capital scandal: Washington's mayor [Marion Barry] faces a cocaine charge. Hilary Mackenzie. port. *Maclean's* 103 no 5 (Ja 29 '90): p30–1

Model and the mayor: how a mystery woman brought down [Washington DC mayor Marion] Barry. Mark Miller. il. *Newsweek* 115 no 6 (F5 '90): p21

Readers' Guide to Periodical Literature. This index covers around 170 general-interest and popular magazines.

Canadian News Index. This index lists articles from seven major Canadian daily newspapers.

The New York Times Index. This work dates back to 1851. For many of the articles, short summaries are also included.

Many disciplines have **specialized indexes** to help researchers find information in great depth. In general, such indexes list articles in scholarly journals for that discipline, but they may include other publications as well. Many indexes available also in computer databases (online or CD-ROM) have two titles: one for the print volume and one for the database. For example, the medical periodical index, called *Index Medicus* in print, is CD-ROM: MEDLINE.

Applied Science and Technology Index
Art Index
Canadian Education Index
Cumulative Index to Nursing and Allied Health Literature
Humanities Index
Index to Canadian Legal Periodical Literature
Index to Legal Periodicals (CD-ROM:LEXIX)
MLA Bibliography of Books and Articles in the Modern Languages and Literature
Social Sciences Index

Abstracts and citation indexes

Abstracts are specialized indexes that also briefly summarize entries, thus helping you better judge an item's potential usefulness. **Citation indexes** list sources cited in an article as well as information about the article. They list the author cited in the *author* volumes and who cited the author in the *citation* volumes.

Biological Abstracts (BIOSIS)
Dissertation Abstracts International
Historical Abstracts
Psychological Abstracts (CD-ROM: PsycLIT)
Science Citation Index (CD-ROM: SciSearch)
Social Sciences Citation Index (CD-ROM: Social SciSearch)

Searching computer databases

Your college or university library may subscribe to **online databases** that are accessed through a computer network, and may own **CD-ROM (compact disk read-only memory)** indexes and readers. Computer databases are specialized electronic indexes listing thousands of books and articles.

Check to see which CD-ROM indexes your library has. Many libraries offer introductory sessions on how to use the CD-ROM. Because libraries may have only one copy of each, you may have to book a time to use a particular index. In any case, you may have to book terminal time. In general, you pay nothing for the use of CD-ROM; you may pay only to print the results of your search.

You will find that CD-ROM indexes are more versatile than print ones. For instance, with a print index, your search is limited to title, author, and subject, while with CD-ROM (or online indexes), you can also do keyword searches. Furthermore, because electronic indexes are regularly updated and expanded, one search covers all the years of the index; rather than looking up each year separately in the bound indexes, you need only search the electronic index once.

You may be able to access a database on CD-ROM yourself, but you will probably need a librarian to conduct an *online* search for you. To use a database, you provide a list of authors, titles, or other keywords, and the computer searches the database for references to them and prints out a list of every reference it finds. Because you may be charged for access time and printing for an online search or given a time limit for using a terminal and CD-ROM database, you may want to ask a librarian about available services and any costs before deciding to consult a database.

Sometimes the keywords you use to conduct a database search will be authors or titles, but more often they will be subject headings. Computer databases contain so much information that your most difficult task will usually be choosing keywords precise enough to cut down the number of items you have to consider. Most databases include a thesaurus of keywords, or descriptors, that can help you.

You might, for instance, type the keyword "bulimia" into the database PsycLIT, and the computer would tell you that it could show you 1365 items. How do you know which to consult? You must narrow the search by using more keywords, usually by using *and* between them. Depending on the way your thesis is developing, you might try "bulimia and treatments" (47 items), "bulimia and treatments and group therapy" (14 items), or "bulimia and agoraphobia" (5 items). The narrower you can make your search, the more specific the sources you find will be.

After you have narrowed your search to a reasonable number of items, look at the references to them on the screen and choose which ones you wish to print out. Using the printouts, you will be able to read the abstract attached to each reference and determine whether you need to find the actual article for further information.

4. Using the library catalogue

A library catalogue lists all the library's materials, or holdings. The traditional format for the library catalogue is the **card catalogue**. Today, however, many libraries have a **microfiche catalogue** and most have transferred (or are in the process of transferring) holdings to a **circulation computer** or online catalogue, which allows users to search for material on public terminals. (If you have a modem in your home computer system, you may be able to access your library's online catalogue from home.) Many libraries with circulation computers maintain card catalogues as well—especially for the older materials.

In whatever form, library catalogues follow a standard organization. Each holding in the library is identified by three kinds of entries: one headed by author, one by title, and one or (usually) more subject. If you look up a book under one of these headings and don't find it, try the others.

When you use a computer terminal, you usually have additional approaches to a library's catalogue. You can still search by author, title, or subject; you may also be able to search by call number or by the number assigned to a book by its publisher.

An online catalogue saves you time, simply because it lets you do your search while sitting in one place. It also makes it possible for you to see many entries at the same time. For example, if you type in the subject "Nuclear Energy," the computer will be likely to present you with an alphabetized list like the following subheadings that appear under that subject:

NUCLEAR ENERGY
NUCLEAR ENERGY—ABSTRACTS
NUCLEAR ENERGY—ADDRESSES, ESSAYS, LECTURES
NUCLEAR ENERGY AND METEOROLOGY
NUCLEAR ENERGY—AUSTRIA—PUBLIC OPINION
NUCLEAR ENERGY—AWARDS
NUCLEAR ENERGY—BIBLIOGRAPHY
NUCLEAR ENERGY—BIOGRAPHY
NUCLEAR ENERGY—CANADA

If you now select the heading "Nuclear Energy—Canada," the computer will present you with a list of items available, arranged by author:

NUCLEAR ENERGY—CANADA
1. Canadian Nuclear Association. Proceedings of the annual
2. Carpenter, Jean-Marc. Face au nucléaire

3. Peat, F. David. Nuclear book
4. Rosenblum, Simon. Non-nuclear way:
5. Rubin, Norman. What keeps us from freezing in the

If you now select item 5, the computer will display something like this:

Rubin, Norman

What keeps us from freezing in the dark: a breakdown of Canada's secondary energy consumption by fuel type.

Location	MICFIC	MFCL	STATUS
ARTS		2718	in library
		no. 81-0357	

The entire search is likely to take no longer than two minutes to complete.

Identifying subjects

Subjects in the library catalogue are usually identified and arranged according to the system presented in *Library of Congress Subject Headings(LCSH)*. This three-volume reference may be kept at the reference desk or near the catalogue so that you can check the exact wording of subject headings and define key terms of interest to you. The LCSH can be useful because it identifies headings that might not readily occur to you. For most headings, you'll find other subjects that are treated under that heading (identified by *UF*, "use for"), broader headings that include the subject (*BT*, "broader topic"), and narrower headings that might be relevant (*NT*, "narrower topic"). These abbreviations are new to the most recent edition of LCSH and replace a system that used *sa* ("see also") and *xx* ("broader topic"), and listed subdivisions without labels.

Searching only subject entries is likely to be inefficient, however, because the headings are so broad. If the best Library of Congress heading you can identify does not match your particular needs or is so broad that it lists many books but only a few that will be useful to you, use other leads. Look to bibliographies, book indexes, reference books, periodical indexes, and notes in other publications to identify potentially useful authors and titles. Such leads are likely to be much more specific and helpful.

Locating library material

Besides identifying a book's author, title, subject, and publication information, each catalogue entry also lists a **call number**—the book's identification number. Once you have written down the complete call number, if you are using an online catalogue, check to see if the book is available. If it is in, look for a library map or shelving plan to tell you which section or floor houses your book. When you find the area where your book is shelved, take the time to browse through the books shelved around it. Very often you will find the immediate area a more important treasure trove than any bibliography or index.

If your book is out or not on the shelf, ask about it at the circulation desk. If someone has checked it out, you may be able to find out when it is due. Very often a library will recall a book when another user needs it. Allow for the time required for the library to notify the user to return the book and then to notify you that it is available. Your deadline will determine whether it is realistic to request a recall.

5. Using other library resources

In addition to books and periodicals, libraries hold other useful materials that might be appropriate for your research. For example:

- *Vertical file.* Pamphlets and brochures from government and private agencies, usually kept in file cabinets.

- *Special collections.* Manuscripts, rare books, local literature and memorabilia.

- *Audio collections.* Records, audiocassettes, and compact disks of all kinds of music, readings, and speeches.

- *Video collections.* Slides, filmstrips, and videocassettes.

- *Art collections.* Drawings, paintings, engravings, and photographs.

- *Interlibrary loans.* Many libraries will borrow books from another library for you: be aware that interlibrary loans often take some time and may involve some cost to you.

Taking inventory: your research

Return to the inventory you completed at the end of Chapter 9. Add to that inventory by examining the ways in which you conducted research: What use did you make of primary and secondary sources? What field and library work did you carry out? What was most satisfying to you about the process of conducting research? What was most disappointing or irritating? What sources were most (and least) useful? How might you conduct research more efficiently in the future? If you are keeping a writing log, or a research log as part of your writing log, record your answers there.

11

Evaluating and Using Source Materials

All research builds on the astute, judicious, and sometimes inspired use of sources—research work done by others. As Isaac Newton noted, those researchers who see the farthest do so because they stand "on the shoulders of giants." As a reader, you will want to make the most of your sources, using the insights you have gained from them in creating powerful prose of your own. This chapter will guide you in considering your use of sources in research.

11a

Choosing sources

One of your goals as a researcher is to learn to recognize which sources will be most useful to you, which ones will allow you to see the farthest. The following sections will provide some guidance to help you make such judgments.

1. Assessing the usefulness of a source

Several characteristics of a book or article can help you assess its usefulness.

- *Relevance.* Is the source closely related to your research question?
- *Author's credentials and stance.* Is the author an expert on the topic? Where does the author stand on the issues involved—and does this stance support or challenge your own views?
- *Date of publication.* How current is the material? Recent sources are often more useful than older ones, particularly in the sciences. However, the most authoritative works are often older ones.

- *Level of specialization.* Does the source provide a general or specialized view? General sources may be helpful as you begin your research, but you may then need the authority or up-to-dateness of more specialized sources. Extremely specialized works, on the other hand, may be too hard to understand.

- *Publication background.* If a book was published not by a commercial publishing house or academic press but by a corporation, government agency, or interest group, what is the publisher's position on the topic? What kind of periodical published an article? popular? academic? alternative?

- *Intended audience.* For what audience was the source written? general readers? specialists? advocates of something? opponents of something? a particular group?

- *Cross-referencing.* Is the source cited in other works?

- *Length.* Is the source long enough to provide adequate detail?

- *Availability.* Do you have access to the source?

You can determine many of these characteristics just by quickly looking at the parts of a source that are listed below. If you then want to explore the source more thoroughly, these elements can also help you decide how to do so most efficiently.

- *Title and subtitle.* If you are investigating coeducation in the 19th century and find a book called *Women in Education*, the subtitle *The Challenge of the 1970s* will tell you that you probably do not need to examine the book.

- *Copyright page.* In a book, this page will show you when the book was originally published, whether it is a revised edition, and who published it.

- *Abstract.* Abstracts are concise summaries of articles or books. They routinely precede articles in some journals and are included in certain periodical or bibliographical guides. Abstracts can help you decide whether to read the entire work.

- *Table of contents.* Part and chapter titles can often give you a good idea of what a book contains. Try to determine whether the chapter topics seem *specific* enough to be useful to you. In a periodical, the table of contents often includes brief descriptions of articles and can also give you a general impression of the periodical if it is unfamiliar to you.

- *Preface or foreword.* Very often these preliminary pages of a book specify in detail the writer's purposes, range of interests, intended audience, topic restrictions, research limitations, and thesis.

- *Subheadings.* Subheadings in the text can give you an idea of how much detail is given on a topic and whether that detail would be helpful to you.

- *Conclusion or afterword.* Some books and articles end with a summary of the contents and a statement of significance that could help you decide how appropriate that source is for your project.

- *Note on the author.* Check the dustcover of a book, the first and last few pages of a book or article, or an article itself for author information.

- *Index.* Check the index for words and topics key to your project; then see whether they seem to have much importance in the book. Are the listings for your key terms many or few?

- *Bibliography and/or footnotes.* List of references, usually at the end of a book or article, show how carefully a writer has investigated the subject. In addition, they may help you find other sources.

Reading sources

Research calls for active, aggressive reading. "Active" readers take up conversation with the books they read, responding to the text with questions and comments. The more attentively you read, and the more you respond to what you read, the better your research will be. This section will help you become an active, questioning reader.

1. Building a working bibliography

One of the basic requirements of reading for research is the creation of a working bibliography—a list of books, articles, and other sources that seem likely to address your research question. The emphasis here is on *working*—for this list will continue to evolve as you go along.

Before you begin a working bibliography, check your assignment or ask your instructor to determine what system you are required to follow for documenting the sources you use (see Chapter 13). If you familiarize yourself with the system now and follow it carefully, you will have, in the proper format, all the information necessary to prepare your final list of sources cited.

Keeping a working bibliography

1. Decide on a format: use index cards (one for each source), a notebook, or a computer file. If you use cards or notebook pages, record information on one side only so that you can arrange entries alphabetically when preparing the list of sources cited. Many word-processing programs will sort the entries for you. Whatever system you use, follow it consistently and completely.

2. For each book, record the following:
   - Call number or other location information
   - Author and/or editor
   - Title and subtitle, if any
   - Publisher's name and location
   - Year of publication
   - Other information—translator, volume number, edition, etc.
   - Inclusive page numbers for chapters or short works consulted within the book

3. For each article, list the following:
   - Author and/or editor
   - Article title and subtitle, if any
   - Periodical name, volume number, and date
   - Inclusive page numbers for the article

4. For entries from bibliographic or periodical indexes, list the name of the index in case you need to check the information again, and add the call number or other location information when you find the source in your library catalogue.

5. For entries from database searches, use printouts. You will need to convert the entries of any sources you use to the correct documentation style, but the printout can save you the time of copying the information by hand.

6. For nonprint sources, list the information required by the documentation system you are using and note where you found the information.

7. When you examine the actual sources, check the accuracy of your information by consulting the title and copyright pages of a book and the table of contents and first page of an article in a journal or magazine.

Here are examples of bibliography cards for a book and a magazine article. They use the MLA documentation style (see Chapter 13).

QL 84.24
R66X
1986
EMS

    Roots, Clive: <u>Endangered Species:</u>
<u>Canada's Disappearing Wildlife.</u>
Toronto: Fitzhenry and Whiteside,
1986.

Wake, Winifred. "Species in
danger: waterfront property
is costly for piping plovers."
<u>Nature Canada</u> Winter 1990:
53.

Exercise 11.1

If you have been making a working bibliography during your current research, take time now to check your entries for accuracy and completeness of information. If you have not yet made any entries, do so now.

2. Reading your sources with a critical eye

Researchers read with a strong sense of purpose: How does this source relate to my research goals? Does it support my ideas, develop them further, or challenge them? Because of time constraints and the wealth of material available on most topics, you probably will not have time to read completely through all of your potential material. Thus, reading with a critical eye can make your research process more efficient. The following considerations can guide your critical reading:

Reading with your research question in mind

A good way of focusing your attention on the information most necessary to your research is to read with your research question in mind. Use the index and the table of contents to zero in on the parts of books that will help you answer your research question. Consider the following questions as you read:

- How does this material address your research question?
- In what ways does it provide support for your hypothesis?
- How might particular quotations help support your thesis?
- Does the source include counterarguments to your hypothesis that you will need to answer? If so, what answers can you provide?

Identifying the author's stance and tone

Every author holds opinions that affect his or her discussion of an issue, opinions that you as a reader must try to recognize and understand. Even the most seemingly factual report, like an encyclopedia article, is necessarily filled with judgments, often unstated. Read with an eye for the author's overall rhetorical stance, or perspective on the topic, as well as for facts and explicit opinions. This stance is related to the author's tone, the way his or her attitude toward both topic and audience is conveyed in the writing. Alertness to perspective and tone will help you more fully understand a source and, as a result, better decide how (or whether) to use it. The following questions can help you with your reading:

- What is the author's stance or perspective? Is he or she an enthusiastic advocate of something, a strong opponent, a sceptical critic, an amused onlooker, a confident specialist in the field?
- Are there any clues to why the author takes this stance?
- How does this stance affect the author's presentation?
- If the author has a professional affiliation, how might the affiliation affect his or her stance?
- In what ways do you share—or not share—the author's stance?
- What is the author's tone? Is it cautious, angry, flippant, serious, impassioned? What words express this tone?

Assessing the author's argument and evidence

Just as every author has a point of view, every piece of writing has what may be called an argument, a position it takes. Even a report of scientific data implicitly "argues" that we should accept it as reliably gathered and reported. As you read, then, try to identify the author's argument, for it is his or her main point. Then, try to decide *why* the author holds this view. Considering the following questions, as you read can help you to recognize—and assess—the points being argued in your sources:

- What is the author's main point?
- How much and what kind of evidence supports that point?
- How persuasive do you find the evidence?
- Can you offer any counterarguments or refutations to the evidence?
- Can you detect any questionable logic or fallacious thinking? (See 5e.)

Questioning your sources

Because all sources make an explicit or implicit argument, they often disagree with one another. Disagreements among sources arise sometimes from differences about facts, sometimes from differences about how to interpret facts. For instance, if an authoritative source says that the chances of a nuclear power plant melting down are 1 in 100 000, two different commentators could interpret that statistic very differently. A critic of nuclear power could argue that nuclear accidents are so terrible that this is too great a chance to take, while a supporter of nuclear power could argue that such a small chance is essentially no chance at all.

The point is that all knowledge must be interpreted by people. You must build your own informed opinion by seeking out and assessing many viewpoints as you read. Not all disputes can be solved by appealing to "neutral facts," because there *are* no neutral facts in the world of meanings. You must examine all works critically, using them not as unquestioned authorities but as contributions to your own interpretation.

Taking notes

After you have decided that a source is useful, you will need to take careful notes on it. Doing so most efficiently calls for approaching a source with some general questions in mind. What do you expect to learn about the topic? What can the source help you demonstrate? To what part of your research is the source most relevant?

Note-taking methods vary greatly from one researcher to another. Whatever method you adopt, however, your goals will include (1) getting down enough information to help you recall the major points of the source; (2) getting down the information in the form in which you are most likely to want to incorporate it into your essay, and (3) getting down all the information you will need to cite the source accurately. Taking careful and complete notes will not only help you digest the source information as you read but will also help you incorporate the material into your essay without inadvertently plagiarizing the source. These are steps to effective note-taking:

1. Using index cards, notebook pages, or a computer file, list the author's name and a shortened form of the title of the source. Your working bibliography entry for the source (see 11b) should contain full publication information, so you need not repeat it in your notes.

2. Record exact page references. If the note refers to more than one page, indicate page breaks so that if you decide to use only part of the note, you will know which page to cite.

3. Label each note with a subject heading.

4. Identify the note as a quotation, a paraphrase, a summary, a combination of these forms, or some other form—such as your own critical comment—to avoid any confusion later. Mark quotations accurately with quotation marks, and paraphrase and summarize entirely in your own words to be sure you do not inadvertently plagiarize the source. (See 11d.)

5. Read over each completed note carefully to recheck quotations, statistics, and specific facts for accuracy.

Most of your notes will take the form of direct quotation, paraphrase, or summary. Deciding what material to include in your notes and whether to quote, paraphrase, or summarize it is an outgrowth of reading with a critical eye. You may use some sources for background information and others as support for your thesis, and these different purposes may guide you to take one kind of note rather than another—summarizing background information, for example, but quoting statements that support your views. Likewise, as you read, you will want to evaluate the usefulness of the source to your project and begin to assign the role a particular source will play in your paper.

1. Quoting

Quoting involves noting down a source's *exact words*. As a general rule, use direct quotations when the quotation is so memorable or expresses a point so perfectly that you cannot improve or shorten it without destroying the meaning you need. Because they represent a source's words exactly, direct quotations give special weight to their author's opinion. Quotations from those directly involved in an issue (crime victims, political leaders) are effective in social science essays; quotations from primary sources (literary works, diaries) are especially important in humanities essays.

In any research essay, quotations from reliable and respected authorities can help establish your credibility as a researcher by showing that you have sought out experts in the field. In addition, well-chosen quotations can broaden the appeal of your final essay by drawing on emotion as well as logic, appealing both to the reader's mind and heart. A student writing a research essay on the ethical issues involved in bullfighting, for example, might introduce an argument demonstrating that bullfighting is not a real sport by quoting Ernest Hemingway's striking comment that "the formal bull-fight is a tragedy, not a sport, and the bull is certain to be killed." (See 5e and 5f for more on logical and emotional appeals.)

In beginning research on traditional distinctions between *mind* and *brain*, a student writer came across the following sentences. The first could easily be paraphrased; the second, however, seemed particularly memorable, so the student recorded it exactly.

ORIGINAL SOURCE

Mind is nothing more than a term we employ to describe some of the functions of the brain.

And further brain research isn't going to define further the matter of "mind" any more than turning over all the turf in Ireland is likely to turn up a colony of leprechauns.

— RICHARD RESNICK, *The Brain*

Following are steps for quoting accurately.

- Copy quotations *carefully*, with punctuation, capitalization, and spelling exactly as in the original.

- Use brackets if you introduce words of your own into the quotation or make changes in it, and use ellipses if you omit material (see 39b and 39f). Remember to use the brackets and ellipses if you incorporate the quotation into your essay.

- Enclose the quotation in quotation marks; don't rely on your memory to distinguish your own words from those of the source.

- Record the author, shortened title, and page number(s) on which the quotation appeared.
- Make sure you have a corresponding working bibliography entry with complete source information (see 11b).
- Label the note with a subject heading.

Resnick, The Brain, p.343

"And [more] brain research isn't going to define... 'mind' any more than turning over all the turf in Ireland is likely to turn up a colony of leprechauns."

---

2. Paraphrasing

A **paraphrase** accurately states all the relevant information from a passage *in your own words and phrasing*, without any additional comments or elaborations. A paraphrase is useful when the main points of the passage, their order, and at least some details are important but—unlike passages worth quoting—their particular wording is not. Unlike a summary, a paraphrase always restates *all* the main points of the passage in the same order and in about the same number of words.

Paraphrasing material helps you digest a passage, because chances are you can't restate the passage in your own words unless you grasp its full meaning. When you incorporate an accurate paraphrase into your essay, you show readers your understanding of that source.

In order to paraphrase without plagiarizing inadvertently, *use your own words and sentence structures*; do not simply substitute synonyms, and do not imitate the author's style. If you wish to cite some of the author's words within the paraphrase, enclose them in quotation marks. A good way of assuring your originality is to paraphrase without looking at the source. When you have finished, turn back to the source and check to see that the paraphrase accurately presents the author's meaning and that it uses your own words and phrasing.

Writing acceptable paraphrases

Looking at the following examples of paraphrases that resemble the original too closely will help you understand how to write acceptable paraphrases. Be aware that even for acceptable paraphrases you must include a citation in your essay identifying the source of the information.

ORIGINAL

But Frida's outlook was vastly different from that of the Surrealists. Her art was not the product of a disillusioned European culture searching for an escape from the limits of logic by plumbing the subconscious. Instead, her fantasy was a product of the temperament, life, and place; it was a way of coming to terms with reality, not of passing beyond reality into another realm.

— HAYDEN HERRERA, *Frida: A Biography of Frida Kahlo* (258)

UNACCEPTABLE PARAPHRASE: USING THE AUTHOR'S WORDS

As Herrera explains, Frida's vision *differed vastly from* the Surrealists' outlook, which grew out of a *disillusioned European culture* hoping to *escape* the confines of *logic*. Her fantasy was due to her own personality and life, including her Mexican roots, and she used it to *come to terms with reality* rather than to move *beyond reality* (258).

Because the italicized language is either borrowed from the original without quotation marks or changed only superficially, this paraphrase plagiarizes.

UNACCEPTABLE PARAPHRASE: USING THE AUTHOR'S SENTENCE STRUCTURES

As Herrera explains, Frida's vision was completely unlike the vision of the Surrealists. Her paintings were not the result of a disenchanted European civilization looking for a release from the confines of logical thinking by probing beneath the conscious mind. Rather, her dream was the result of her personality, situation, and location; it was a means of dealing with the real world, not of moving past it to a new dimension (258).

While this paraphrase does not rely on the words of the original, it does follow the sentence structures too closely. Substituting synonyms for the major words in a paraphrase is not enough to avoid plagiarism. The paraphrase must represent your own understanding of the material, and thus must show your own thought patterns.

Now look at two examples of paraphrases of the same passage that express the author's ideas accurately and acceptably, the first completely in the writer's own words and the second including quotations from the original.

ACCEPTABLE PARAPHRASE: IN THE WRITER'S OWN WORDS

As Herrera explains, Frida's surrealistic vision was unlike that of the European Surrealists. While their art grew out of their disenchantment with their society and their desire to explore the subconscious mind as a refuge from rational thinking, Frida's vision was an outgrowth of her own personality and life experiences in Mexico. She used her surrealistic images to understand better her actual life, not to create a dreamworld (258).

ACCEPTABLE PARAPHRASE: QUOTING SOME OF THE AUTHOR'S WORDS

As Herrera explains, Frida's surrealistic vision was unlike that of the European Surrealists. While their art grew out of their "disillusioned European culture" and their desire "for an escape from the limits of logic" through an exploration of the subconscious, Frida's dream was an outgrowth of her own personality and life experiences in Mexico. She used her surrealistic images to understand better her actual life, not to "[pass] beyond reality into another realm" (258).

Notice that in the last sentence of the second paraphrase, *passing* needed to be changed to *pass* for the quotation to fit smoothly into the sentence. This change is indicated by using brackets (see 39b). Following are steps for paraphrasing accurately:

- Include all main points and any important details from the original, in the same order in which they were presented.

- State the meaning in your own words and sentence structures. If you want to include especially memorable language from the original, enclose it in quotation marks.

- Leave out your own comments, elaborations, or reactions.

- Record the author, shortened title, and the page number(s) on which the original material appeared.

- Make sure you have a corresponding working bibliography entry.

- Label the note with a subject heading, and identify it as paraphrase to avoid confusion with a summary.

- Recheck the paraphrase against the original to be sure that the words and sentence structures are your own and that they express the author's meaning accurately.

Exercise 11.2

Choose an important passage from one of the sources you listed in the working bibliography in Exercise 11.1 and paraphrase it following the guidelines above.

3. Summarizing

A **summary** is a significantly shortened version of a passage, a section, or even a whole chapter or work that *captures main ideas in your own words.* Unlike paraphrasing, a summary uses just enough information to record the main points or the points you wish to emphasize. You needn't include all the author's points or any details, but be sure not to distort his or her meaning. The length of a summary depends on how long the original is and how much information you will need to use. Your goal is to keep the summary as brief as possible, capturing only the gist of the original.

For a short passage, try reading the passage carefully and without looking at the text, writing a one- or two-sentence summary. For a long passage or an entire chapter, skim the headings and topic sentences and make notes of each before writing your summary in a paragraph or two. For a whole book, you may want to refer to the preface and introduction as well as chapter titles, headings, and topic sentences—and your summary may take a page or more. Following are the steps for summarizing accurately:

- Include just enough information to recount the main points you wish to cite. A summary is usually much shorter than the original.

- Use your own words. If you want to include language from the original, enclose it in quotation marks.

- Record the author, shortened title, and page number(s) on which the original material appeared.

- Make sure you have a corresponding working bibliography entry.

- Label the note with a subject heading, and identify it as a summary to avoid confusion with a paraphrase.

- Recheck any material you plan to use against the original to be sure you have captured the author's meaning and that your words are entirely your own.

Exercise 11.3

Choose a section from a source you listed in the working bibliography in Exercise 11.1 and write a summary of it, emphasizing the main ideas in your own words.

4. Photocopying source material

Nearly all libraries provide photocopying machines that you can use to copy pages or even whole articles or chapters. You can then annotate the photocopies with thoughts and questions, highlight interesting quotations, and call out key terms. Try not to rely on photocopying too heavily, however. Remember that you still need to read the material carefully, and resist the temptation to treat photocopied material as notes, an error that could lead to inadvertent plagiarizing as well as to wasting time looking for information you only vaguely remember having read. If you have read and taken careful notes on your sources rather than relying primarily on photocopies, your drafting will be more efficient.

If you do photocopy material, write out on the photocopy all the information you need to cite the material in your list of sources cited. (And check that page numbers are clearly legible on copies.)

The Canadian Copyright Act places restrictions on your right to copy material, and prevents you, for example, from making multiple copies of an article for distribution. Section 27 (2) (a) of the act, however, does provide that "any fair dealing with any work for the purposes of private study, research, criticism, review, or newspaper summary" does *not* constitute an infringement of copyright. "Fair dealing" implies that copying does not affect the potential market for sale of the work in question, causes no injury to the value of the copyright, and is not significant in quantity.

11d

Recognizing plagiarism, acknowledging sources

Whatever research we do is influenced and affected by everything we have already read and experienced. If you try, for instance, to trace the origins of every idea you have had just *today,* you will quickly see the extent to which we are all indebted to others as the sources of information.

Giving full acknowledgment to those sources presents a challenge, but doing so is important for several reasons. First, acknowledging your sources allows you to thank those whose work you have built on and thus to avoid plagiarism. Second, it helps readers by placing your research into a context of other thinking and research; it shows in what ways your research is part of a larger conversation and lets readers know where they can find more information. Finally, acknowledging your sources helps you critically examine your own research and thinking. How timely and reliable are those sources? Have you used them accurately?

Acknowledging sources fully and generously, then, provides a means of establishing your *ethos*, or credibility, as a researcher. Failure to credit sources breaks trust both with the research "conversation" and with readers; as a sign of dishonesty, it can easily destroy the credibility of both researcher and research.

1. Recognizing plagiarism

Plagiarism, the use of someone else's words or ideas as your own without crediting the original writer, can result in serious consequences. At some colleges, students who plagiarize fail the course automatically; at others, they are expelled. Outside academic life, eminent political, business, and scientific leaders have been stripped of candidacies, positions, and awards following charges of plagiarism.

You are probably already aware of cases of deliberate plagiarism— handing in a paper that a friend wrote for a similar course, copying passages directly from source materials. In addition, however, you need to know about unintended plagiarism—a quotation accidentally used without quotation marks, a paraphrase that too closely resembles the original, background details gleaned from a source but used without acknowledgment in the mistaken belief that none was necessary. By understanding what material you must document, taking systematic, accurate notes, and giving full credit to sources in both parenthetical citations and your list of sources cited, you can avoid unintended plagiarism. Doing so for every idea you build on, however, is an impossible task. In practical terms, where do you draw the line?

2. Knowing which material requires acknowledgment

Some of the information you use does not need to be credited to another source because it is well known or because you gathered the data yourself. The following lists should help you discern which materials you need to credit and which ones you can use without credit.

Materials not requiring acknowledgment

Common knowledge. If most readers like yourself would be likely to know something, you need not provide a citation for it. You do not need to credit a source for a statement that Audrey McLaughlin was the first female leader of a federal political party, for example. If, on the other hand, you were to name the delegates who supported her at the leadership convention, you should cite the source for that information.

Facts available in a wide variety of sources. If a number of encyclopedias, almanacs, or textbooks include the information, you need not cite a specific source. For instance, you would not need to cite a source for the fact that Prime Minister St. Laurent approved a Royal Commission on the Arts in Canada in 1949. You would, however, need to credit a source that suggested that most Canadians had no interest in the arts.

Your own findings from field research. If you conduct field research—observation, interviews, surveys—and produce results, simply announce those results as your own.

Materials requiring acknowledgment

Direct quotations. Whenever you use another person's words directly, credit the source. (If two quotations from the same source appear close together and separate parenthetical citations would be awkward, use only one citation, placed *after* the second quotation.) Even if you are quoting in the middle of a paraphrase whose source you intend to acknowledge, set off in quotation marks and *separately* acknowledge the direct use of the author's words.

Assertions that are arguable or facts that are not widely known. If your readers would be unlikely to know a fact, or if an author presents an assertion that may or may not be true, cite the source. To claim, for instance, that Switzerland is amassing an offensive nuclear arsenal would demand citing a source, because Switzerland has long been an officially neutral state. If you are not sure whether a fact is familiar to your readers or a statement is debatable, cite a source.

Judgments, opinions, and claims of others. Whenever you summarize or paraphrase anyone else's opinion, give the source for that summary or paraphrase. Even though the wording may be completely your own, you need to give credit for the idea.

Statistics, charts, tables, and graphs from any source. Credit all graphic material, even if you yourself create the graph from data in another source.

Information or help provided by friends, instructors, or others. A conference with an instructor may give you just the idea you need to clinch an argument. Give credit. Friends may help you conduct surveys, refine questionnaires, or think through a major problem. Credit them too.

11e

Interpreting sources

Your task as a reader is to identify and understand sources and sets of data as completely as possible. As a writer, your aim must be to present data and sources *to other readers* so that they can most readily understand the point you are making. Doing so calls for careful thinking on your part, as you work to interpret sources.

Turning data into information

Computer scientists sometimes distinguish between **data**—bits of facts or strings of statements—and **information**—the meaning attached to the data. As a researcher, you will gather a great deal of data, probably more than you need or can use. But those data become information only when their meaning is made clear. You may have gathered two dozen facts about a particular city's finances, for example, but together they form a rather random list of facts. Turning them into information calls for pointing out their significance or meaning—that, for instance, the city is on the brink of bankruptcy.

Synthesizing data and drawing inferences

You can begin turning data into information by **synthesizing**—grouping similar pieces of data together; looking for patterns or trends, identifying the gist, or main point, of the data. Most often, finding the gist of a source or set of data will call for drawing **inferences**—conclusions that are not explicitly stated but that follow logically from the data given. For example, you may have data indicating severe drought in the Prairie provinces. Other data report very low levels of crop production in those provinces. From these data, you draw the inference that farmers on the prairies face financial crisis. As a researcher, you have turned data into information.

Recording your thoughts and ideas

Perhaps the most exciting part of research occurs when the materials you are reading spark something in your mind and new ideas take hold. As you read, your mind is busy processing all the materials you are discovering with those you have previously discovered, seeking connections and similarities, making distinctions, synthesizing in the ways discussed above. As you work, ideas will occur to you that will become part of your position or argument. *Don't let them get away.* Jot down the ideas that come to you as you read, perhaps in a special section of your writing log if you are keeping one. Do not worry about whether an idea is true or right or even useful—just get it down and think about it later. Some ideas may be thrown away because they do not suit the final shape your essay takes, but others will be likely to *provide* that final shape.

Disagreements among sources can provide particularly fruitful areas to consider and may provoke you to new insights all your own. Consequently, you need to pay close attention to the arguments put forth by all your sources—those you agree with as well as those you disagree with. Jot down your thoughts as you read—agreements, questions, comments, reactions.

Taking inventory: your use of sources

Along with another student, select two or three paragraphs from a book or article of source material. On your own, write a paraphrase of the original, using the guidelines on page 199. Then summarize the same material, using the guidelines for preparing summaries (page 200). Once you have finished, compare your paraphrase and summary to those of the other student working on the same paragraphs. Are your efforts similar? Discuss any differences you discover, and revise if necessary.

12

Organizing, Drafting, and Revising a Research Essay

While you may continue to pursue a research question for a long time, there comes a time to draw the strands of research together and to articulate your conclusions in writing. This chapter will help you at that point.

The processes of research and writing are intimately linked. While you are conducting research, you will also be coming up with ideas, considering organizational possibilities, and recognizing connections among your materials, making notes and perhaps attempting partial drafts as you work. From these thoughts you will eventually choose the final form in which to cast your own conclusions.

You will probably do most of your final organizing and drafting when your research is largely complete and you have most of the facts, evidence, quotations, and other data you think you need. Ideally, for college and university research essays, the process of drafting a final version should begin at least two weeks before the deadline, in order to allow for response to the draft, for further research, and for revision.

12a

Refining your plans

Throughout your research, you have been generating notes that answer your research question and reflect on your hypothesis. Your growing understanding of the subject, in turn, has no doubt led you to gather other information, which may have altered your original question. This somewhat circular process, which may best be described as a research spiral, is at the heart of all research-based writing.

You should by now have a fair number of notes containing facts, opinions, paraphrases, summaries, quotations, and other material. You probably also have thoughts about the connections among the many pieces of information you found. And you should have some sense of whether your hypothesis has been established sufficiently to serve as the thesis of an essay. At this point, you should reconsider your purpose, your audience, and your thesis.

1. Reconsidering purpose, audience, and thesis

Given what you now know about your research question, consider questions such as the following:

1. What is your central purpose? What other purposes, if any, do you have?

2. What stance do you take toward your topic? Are you an advocate, a critic, a reporter? (See 2d.)

3. Are you addressing an audience other than your instructor?

4. How much about your research question does your audience know already? How much background will they need to be given?

5. What sorts of supporting information are they likely to find convincing—examples? precedents? quotations from authorities? (See 5e.)

6. What tone will most appeal to them and help them understand your points? Should you present yourself as a colleague, an expert, or a student?

7. How can you establish common ground with them and show consideration of points of view other than your own? (See 5d and Chapter 2.)

8. What is your thesis trying to establish? How likely is your audience to accept it?

2. Developing an explicit thesis

A useful means of relating your purpose, thesis, and audience before you begin a full draft is to write out an **explicit thesis statement.** Such a statement forces you to articulate all your major lines of argument and to see how well those arguments carry out your purpose and appeal to your audience. At the drafting stage, your explicit thesis statement might take the following form:

> In this essay, I plan to (explain, argue, demonstrate, analyze, and so on) for an audience of _____
> that _____
> because (or if) (1) _____, (2) _____,
> (3) _____.

You will not be importing this explicit thesis statement into the paper itself, although you may want to compose a *version* of it later on for inclusion.

3. Testing your thesis

Writing out an explicit thesis will often confirm the research you have been doing and support your hypothesis. Sometimes, however, it may reveal that your hypothesis is invalid, inadequately supported, or insufficiently focused. In such cases, you must rethink your original research question, perhaps do further research, and work toward a revised hypothesis and eventually a revised thesis. To test your explicit thesis at this point, consider the following list of questions:

1. How can you state the topic of your thesis or your comment about the topic more precisely or more clearly? (See 3c for more information about topic and comment.)

2. In what ways will your thesis interest and appeal to your audience? What can you do to make that interest grow? (See 5f.)

3. How could the wording of your thesis be more specific? Could you use more concrete nouns (see 30d) or stronger verbs (see 29a)? Should you add qualifying adjectives or adverbs (see Chapter 18)?

4. Is your thesis going to be manageable, given your limits of time and knowledge? What might you do to make it more manageable?

5. What research evidence do you have to support each aspect of your thesis? What additional evidence do you need?

Organizing information

Experienced writers differ considerably in the ways they go about the task of organizing information, and you will want to experiment until you find an organizational method that works well for you. This section will review two common planning strategies: grouping material by subject headings and outlining.

1. Grouping notes by subject headings

During your research, you have been taking notes and keeping lists of ideas. To organize these materials using a grouping strategy, examine them for connections, finding what might be presented with what, which notes will be more useful and which less useful, which ideas lend support to the thesis and which should be put aside. Brainstorm about your research question one last time, and add the resulting notes to your other materials, looking to see if they fit with any of the materials you already have.

If you have been keeping notes on cards, you can arrange the cards in stacks by subject headings, putting the ones with your main topics in the centre and arranging any related cards around them. If you have been taking notes in a notebook, you can cut the pages apart and group the slips of paper. (You can use photocopies if you don't want to damage your notebook.) If your notes are in a computer file, see if your program can sort them by subject headings or search for particular headings.

Grouping your notes in this way will help you to identify your major ideas and to see whether you have covered all the necessary areas. It will help you see whether you have too many ideas to manage—or whether you need to do more research in some area. Most important, it will allow you to see how the many small pieces of your research fit together and result in the larger structure of a complete essay.

2. Outlining

Writers use outlines in various ways. Some group their notes, draft, and then outline the draft to study its tentative structure. Others develop a working outline from their notes, listing the major points in a tentative order with support for each major point. Such a working outline may see you through the rest of the process, or you may decide to revise it as you go along. Still other writers prefer to plot out their organization early on and do so in a formal outline.

A formal outline allows you to see before drafting exactly how all the main parts of your essay will fit together—how your ideas relate, how abstract your ideas are, what the overall structure of your argument will be. However, many people find a full formal outline hard to write before they have considered their material in some less formal way, perhaps through the process of drafting itself. That is why you may decide to make a rough outline *before* a normal outline.

Most formal outlines follow a conventional format of numbered and lettered headings and subheadings using Roman numerals, capital letters, Arabic numbers, and lower-case letters to show the levels of importance of the various ideas and their relationships. Each new level is indented to show its subordination to the preceding level. Following is a model of a typical formal outline:

Thesis statement
I. First main topic
  A. First subordinate idea
    1. First supporting idea
    2. Second supporting idea
    3. Third supporting idea
  B. Second subordinate idea
    1. First supporting idea
    2. Second supporting idea

II. Second main topic
  A. First subordinate idea
    1. First supporting idea
    2. Second supporting idea
  B. Second subordinate idea
    1. First supporting idea
    2. Second supporting idea
      a. First supporting detail
      b. Second supporting detail

Each level contains at least two parts, so there is no A without a B, no 1 without a 2. Comparable items are placed on the same level—all capital letters, for instance, or all Arabic numbers. Each level develops the idea before it—1 and 2 under A, for example, include the points that develop, explain, or demonstrate. Headings are stated in parallel form—either all sentences, or all topics that are grammatically parallel.

Remember, finally, that any outline is at best a means to an end, not an end in itself. New ideas will almost surely occur as you write, and you should not feel bound to the ideas in your outline. Though an outline serves, on one level, as a plan for your essay, it can also serve to stimulate altogether new thoughts and plans, ones you should feel free to consider and pursue. (See 3e and 3f for more on outlining.)

12c

Drafting your essay

When you are ready to draft your essay, set yourself a deadline and structure all your tasks with that deadline in mind. Gather your notes, outline, and any sources you may need to consult. Most writers find that some sustained work (perhaps two or three hours) at this point pays off. Begin drafting where you feel most confident. If you have a good idea for an introduction, begin there. If you are not sure exactly what you want to do in the introduction but do know how you want to approach some particular point, begin with that and return to the introduction later. The most important thing is to get started.

The drafting process itself varies considerably among researchers. Some writers try to make the first draft as perfect as possible, working meticulously paragraph by paragraph. Others draft as fast as they can, getting all their material down in whatever form and smoothing it out later. Some follow an outline from start to finish; others draft sections separately and arrange them later. Your writing process is your own, and no one else can tell you what works best for you. (For more on outlining, see 3g and 3h.)

1. Drafting your introduction

The introduction to a research essay plays a special role, for it must provide the context for what is to come. Like any introduction, it should draw readers into the essay, but also it needs to provide them with any background they will need to understand the discussion. You can find general advice on writing introductions in 4f and 6c. When drafting an introduction for a research essay, keep in mind that you'll need to introduce not only your thesis but also your paper. Your readers will want to know the purpose of your essay and, perhaps, how it will proceed. Think of the function of your introduction as being to supply your readers with everything you think they will need to know in order to read your essay well. You may, for example, want to forecast the main point of your essay in order to help readers get their bearings.

2. Drafting your conclusion

A good conclusion to a research essay informs readers of what they have learned. Its job is not to persuade (the body of your essay should already have done that), but it *can* leave the reader with a memorable phrase or example that will in fact contribute to the overall effectiveness of your argument. General advice on writing conclusions can be found in 4f and 6c. When drafting a conclusion for a research essay, you might consider a specific-to-general pattern, operating with a restatement of your thesis and then expanding to some more general conclusion to remind readers of the significance of your discussion. You might try to end with something that will have a lasting impact—a provocative question, a vivid image, an apt quotation, or even a call for action.

Incorporating source materials

Once you are at the point of drafting your essay, you must focus on the task of weaving your source materials into your writing. The challenge is to use your sources and yet remain the author of your essay—to quote, to paraphrase, and summarize other voices while at the same time remaining the single dominant voice in your essay. Some students have difficulty avoiding the "collage" essay—a pasting together of bits of source material—but if you have taken notes and recorded quotations carefully, and if you keep your thesis firmly in mind, you should have little trouble integrating material *purposefully* and maintaining your own authorial voice.

You tentatively decided to quote, paraphrase, or summarize material when you read your sources critically and took notes (see Chapter 11). As you choose which sources to use in your essay and how to use them, however, you may want to re-evaluate those decisions, perhaps deciding to summarize material you had paraphrased, or to use direct quotation only infrequently. Of course, you must document any source material you include *in any form* with a parenthetical citation (see Chapter 13) and an entry in your list of sources.

1. Using direct quotations

Your essay must be your own work, and you should depend on other people's words as little as possible, limiting quotations to those *necessary* to your argument or *memorable* for your readers. Reasons to use direct quotations include the following:

- To incorporate a statement expressed so effectively by the author that it cannot be paraphrased without altering meaning

- To contribute to your own credibility as a writer by quoting an authority on your topic

- To allow an author to defend his or her position in his or her own words

- To use a striking quotation for effect

Once you have decided to use a quotation, you need to consider how to work it into your text.

Enclosing brief quotations within your text

Quotations of no more than four lines (MLA style) or no more than forty words (APA style) should be worked into your text, enclosed by quotation marks. For example:

> In Miss Eckhart, Wetly recognizes a character who shares with her "the love of her art and the love of giving it, the desire to give it until there is no more left" (10).

> The Canadian electorate demonstrates a great deal of apathy. According to Clotfelter and Prysby, however, many Canadians exercise their right to vote because they feel "a sense of civic duty" (29).

Notice that both of the preceding examples alert readers to the quotations by using **signal phrases** that include the author's name. When you cite a quotation in this way, you need put only the page number in the parentheses.

When you introduce a quotation without mentioning the author's name, place the name in the parentheses before the page number. Be sure, however, that you always distinguish for your readers where someone else's words begin. For example, look at this passage from Barbara Godard:

> This is a one-room school that goes only to Grade 6. But it is different from the residential school which offers the higher grades in that, as his cousin Joe says, kids there were "beat up for talking Indian" (Armstrong 17).

These are but two ways of introducing a quotation. Both the MLA and the APA styles dictate conventions for what should appear in parenthetical citations in what circumstances and how it should be punctuated. See Chapter 13 for guidelines.

Setting off long quotations

Quotations longer than four lines (MLA style) or forty words (APA style) should be set off from the regular text. Begin such a quotation on a new line, and indent each line of it ten spaces (MLA) or five spaces (APA) from the left margin. This indentation sets off the quotation clearly so that quotation marks are unnecessary. Type the quotation to the regular right margin, and double-space it like regular text. Long quotations are usually introduced by a signal phrase or a sentence followed by a colon.

> A good seating arrangement can prevent problems; however, "withitness," as defined by Woolfolk, works even better:
>
> > Withitness is the ability to communicate to students that you are aware of what is happening in the classroom, that you "don't miss anything."

> With-it teachers seem to have "eyes in the back of their heads." They avoid becoming too absorbed with a few students, since this allows the rest of the class to wander. (359)

This technique works, however, only if students actually believe that their teacher will know everything that goes on.

Although long quotations are often necessary in research essays, use them cautiously. Too many of them may suggest to your readers that you did not rely on your own thinking in writing the essay. In addition, long quotations can make an essay seem choppy, and they can distract attention from your analysis of the material. If you think you may be overusing them, substitute paraphrases or summaries for some of them.

Integrating quotations into your text

Quotations have to be carefully integrated into your text so that they link smoothly and clearly with the surrounding sentences. In most cases, you need to use a signal phrase to provide such a link. For example:

WITHOUT A SIGNAL PHRASE

> In *Death of a Salesman*, Willy Loman dreams the wrong dreams and idealizes the wrong ideals. "He has lived on his smile and on his hopes, survived from sale to sale, been sustained by the illusion that he has countless friends in his territory, that everything will be all right ..." (Brown 97).

It is possible to figure out the connection between the quotation and text, but see how the following revision uses a signal phrase to make the link far easier to recognize. Note also the slightly awkward shift in verb tenses from text to quotation, which is smoothed out in the revision.

WITH A SIGNAL PHRASE

> In *Death of a Salesman*, Willy Loman dreams the wrong dreams and idealizes the wrong ideals. His misguided perceptions are well captured by Brown: "He has lived on his smile and on his hopes, survived from sale to sale, been sustained by the illusion that he has countless friends in his territory, that everything will be all right ..." (97).

Introducing a quotation with the author's name and a **signal verb** is a clear and simple way of integrating it into your text. Remember, however, that the verb must be appropriate to the idea you are expressing.

> As Eudora Welty notes, "Learning stamps you with its moments. Childhood's learning," she continues, "is made up of moments. It isn't steady. It's a pulse." (9)

In this example, two signal verbs—*notes* and *continues*—integrate the quotations appropriately for the sense of the sentence.

Indicating changes with brackets and ellipses

Sometimes, for the sake of clarity or length, you will wish to alter a direct quotation in some way—to make a verb tense fit smoothly in your text, to replace a pronoun with a noun, to eliminate unnecessary detail. Enclose any changed or added words with brackets, and indicate any deletions with three ellipsis points.

> Charles M. Anderson argues for a revised medical rhetoric, or rather "a balanced dynamic between the two [rhetorics] that at once allows the physician to have the benefits of medical science and to use those benefits in a humane manner" (18–19).

> Sociologist Aaron Cicourel explains that medical diagnosis is a process by which physicians "convert the often unidiomatic and sometimes ambiguous language ... of patients into unambiguous declarative knowledge using a systematic notation system" (94).

Be especially careful that any changes you make in a quotation do not alter its essential meaning. In addition, use these marks sparingly, for too many brackets and ellipsis points make for difficult reading. (For more information on brackets and ellipses, see 39b and 39f.)

2. Using paraphrases and summaries

When you want to use ideas from sources but have no need to quote their exact words, use paraphrases or summaries. Reasons for using paraphrases and summaries include the following:

- To present background information and other facts that your readers may not know
- To explain various positions on your topic

Integrating paraphrases and summaries

As with quotations, you need to introduce paraphrases and summaries clearly, usually by using a signal phrase that includes the name of the author of the material. Using the author's name also helps lend authority to the material. Sometimes, in fact, you will want to highlight the source even more prominently. Notice in the following example how the writer focuses on one authority, first introducing her by name and title and then both quoting and summarizing her work.

On the other hand, some observers of the battle of the sexes are trying to arrange cease-fires. Professor of linguistic Deborah Tannen says that she offers her book *That's Not What I Meant!* to "women and men everywhere who are trying their best to talk to each other" (19). Tannen goes on to illustrate how communication between women and men breaks down and then to suggest that a full awareness of "genderlects" can improve relationships (297).

In the following example, on the other hand, the writer focuses more on the information paraphrased, identifying the authors only parenthetically.

Three areas of established differences in cognitive abilities are recognized by the majority of researchers: verbal ability, mathematical ability, and spatial ability (Block 517). As shown by current research, a specific cognitive sex difference exists in verbal ability; in general, females are superior to males in this area starting in early childhood (Weitz 99).

Remember that indicating the sources of paraphrases and summaries is important. Even unintentional failure to cite sources for materials that are not in quotation marks but that you could not have known or arrived at by yourself constitutes plagiarism. Make certain that you record the sources of general background information as well as specific quotations, facts, viewpoints, and so forth. If your notes are incomplete or your source is unclear, locate and reread the original to clarify the information. If you are unable to do so, you would be wise to leave out the material rather than risk plagiarism.

Incorporating quotations, paraphrases, and summaries

1. In general, use signal phrases or other clues to indicate where the cited material begins.

2. Identify quotations by enclosing ones of up to four lines (MLA style) or forty words (APA style) in quotation marks and setting off longer ones.

3. Check that you reproduced the wording, spelling, punctuation, and capitalization of quotations accurately and that you indicated changes by brackets and ellipses. If your notes are unclear, look again at the original.

4. Document every quotation, paraphrase, and summary with a citation in your text and a corresponding entry in your list of sources cited. If you use some of the author's words within a paraphrase or summary, enclose them in quotation marks, and give a separate citation for them after the closing quotation mark.

3. Checking for excessive citations

Exactly how much citation of sources belongs in your essay has to depend on your purpose, your audience, and the section of your essay. In general, however, your essay should not give the impression of being a collage of quotations, paraphrases, and summaries from other people. If it does, you will have merely accumulated data; you won't have actually presented information in your own way (see 11b2). You need a rhetorical stance, a perspective that represents you as the author. If you are over-quoting and over-citing, your own voice will disappear. The following passage illustrates this problem:

> One opinion is that " 'wildlife conservation' in its fullest and deepest meaning as 'preservation' simply does not exist" (Livingston 21). However, "wildlife preservation is a good thing," and "there is a rational argument for wildlife preservation," although "whatever that argument is, we have not yet used it effectively" (23). Livingston suggests that if we examine some basic conservation ideas more carefully, we will see that they "are not wildlife issues; they are people issues" (24).

Most readers would think that the source, Livingston, was much too prominent here. If this passage were a background discussion or a literature survey, with each source different, such a large number of citations might be acceptable. But all these citations are from the same source, and readers are likely to conclude that the source is primary and the author only secondary.

12e

Reviewing your draft

Because a research essay involves a complex mix of your thoughts and materials from outside sources, it calls for an especially careful review before you begin revising. As with most kinds of writing, however, taking a break after drafting a research essay is important. Get away from the draft and try to put it out of your mind. Stay away from it for as long as you can, so that when you reread it you can bring a fresh eye to the task.

When you return to the draft, read it straight through without stopping. Then, read it again slowly, reconsidering four things: purpose, audience, thesis, and support. You might find that outlining your draft helps you to analyze it at this point (see 3e).

- From your reading of your draft, what do you now see as its *purpose?* How does this compare with your original purpose? Does the draft do what your assignment requires?

- What *audience* does your essay address?
- What is your *stance* toward the topic?
- What is your *thesis*? Is it clearly stated?
- What *evidence* supports your thesis? Is the evidence thorough and compelling?

Answer these questions as best you can, since they are the starting point for revision. Next, you need a closer reading of your essay. At this point, you might benefit from the comments of other readers. Consider asking friends or classmates to read your draft and respond to the questions for reviewing a draft in 4c. You can also use these questions yourself as you analyze your own essay in greater detail.

You may also get helpful advice if you ask questions specific to your essay. If you are unsure about whether to include a particular point, how to use a certain quotation, or where to add more examples, ask readers specifically what they think you should do. (For more on getting critical responses to a draft, see 4c).

Revising and editing your draft

Using any responses you have gathered and your own analysis of your draft, turn now to your final revision. It is advisable, at this stage, to work in several steps.

- *Considering any responses.* Have readers identified any problems you need to solve? If so, do they make any specific suggestions about ways to revise? Have they identified any strengths that might suggest ways of revising? For example, if they showed great interest in one point but no interest at all in another point, consider expanding the first and deleting the second.

- *Reconsidering your original purpose, audience, and stance.* From the above analysis, do you feel confident that you have achieved your purpose? If not, what is missing? Have you made your strongest possible appeal to your readers? How have you established common ground with them? How have you satisfied any special concerns they may have? Has your rhetorical stance toward your topic changed in any way? If so, what effect has that change had on your essay?

- *Gathering any additional material.* If you need to strengthen any points, go back to your notes to see if you have the necessary materials. If not, consider whether you need to do any more research. If you failed to consider adequately any opposing viewpoints, for instance, you may need to find more material.

- *Deciding on any changes you need to make.* Figure out everything you have to do to perfect your draft, and write it out. With your deadline firmly in mind, plan your revision.

- *Rewriting your draft.* Do the major work first—changes in content, added examples or evidence, paragraph-level concerns. Then turn to sentence-level work, and finally to individual words. Revise for clarity and to sharpen the dominant impression of the essay as a whole.

- *Reconsidering your title, introduction, and conclusion.* In the light of your re-evaluation and revision of your draft, reread these important parts to see whether they still serve their purpose. Does the introduction accurately predict and the conclusion accurately restate what the body of the final essay discusses? If not, do you need to forecast your main points in the introduction or to summarize them in the conclusion? Does your introduction capture readers' attention? Does your conclusion help them see the significance of your argument? Is your title specific enough to let your readers know about your research question and engaging enough to make then want to read *your* answer to it?

- *Checking your documentation.* Have you included a citation in your text for every quotation, paraphrase, and summary you incorporated, following consistently the required style? (See Chapter 13.)

- *Editing your draft.* Now is the time to attend carefully to any remaining problems in grammar, usage, spelling, punctuation, and mechanics. If you are writing on a computer, take the time to use the spell checker. Check for any patterns you have identified as problems in your own writing. It may be fruitful as well to turn back to Taking a Writing Inventory (the introductory chapter) and to consult the editing checklist in 4h.

Preparing your lists of works cited or references

Once you have a final draft with your source materials in place, prepare your list of works cited (MLA) or references (APA). Follow the guidelines for your required style carefully, creating an entry for each source used in your essay. Double-check your draft against your list of sources cited to see that you have listed every source mentioned in the parenthetical citations and that you have not listed any sources not cited in your essay. (See Chapter 13 for guidelines.)

Preparing and proofreading your final copy

Your final rough draft may end up looking very rough indeed, filled with cross-outs, additions in the margins, circles, and arrows. So your next task is to create a final, carefully typed, painstakingly prepared clean copy. This is the version of the paper that you will submit, the one that will represent all your work and effort.

Proofreading is a time for celebration. At this point, you are making your research essay as perfect as possible, your very best effort. Many writers look forward to this final reading, often taking time to read through once backward in order to catch every word-level typographical error.

Taking inventory: your research essay

Pause now to reflect on the research essay you have written. How did you go about organizing your information? What would you do to improve this process? What problems did you encounter during drafting? How did you solve these problems? How many quotations did you use, and how did you integrate them into your text? When and why did you use summaries and paraphrases? What did you learn from revising? Record your findings in your writing or research log, if you keep one.

Reading with an eye for research

The following research essay was written by University of British Columbia student Roger Millette. Read the essay carefully and answer the following questions about it:

1. Is the reader given enough information in the first few paragraphs to read the paper well? Can you think of other possible introductions to such an essay?

2. Did you find the topic headings helpful to you as a reader? Comment on their advantages and disadvantages.

3. What functions do quotation, paraphrase, and summary perform in the essay? Comment, in particular, on each of Roger's uses of direct quotation.

4. Did you agree with Roger's decisions about what needed to be documented and what might reasonably fall under the heading "fact available in a wide variety of sources"?

5. What techniques does Roger use to retain his own voice in the essay even though he uses a great deal of source material?

6. Did you find Roger a credible author? How was his credibility "argued"?

The Search for Extraterrestrial Intelligence:
Pitfalls and Possibilities

TITLE PAGE

by Roger Millette

English 303
Professor Segal
1 April 1993

The Search for Extraterrestrial Intelligence:
Pitfalls and Possibilities

Many years ago, humans actually believed the earth was at the centre of the universe. As they became wiser, humans believed the earth rotated around the sun, which of course was at the centre of the universe. Since that time, through vast amounts of study, astronomers have discovered that we are not at, or near, the centre of the universe, and probably do not really mean much in the overall scheme of things. In fact, in the universe, the earth is about as important as a grain of sand in the Sahara Desert. Although our views of the structure of the universe have altered over time, one thing has not changed: our curiosity about our place in the universe. It is this curiosity that has caused astronomers to wonder whether we are alone in the universe.

STAGE SET FOR THIS QUESTION

The question is puzzling to be sure, and unfortunately, it has no definite answer. If you ask the scientists heading the Search for Extraterrestrial Intelligence, known as SETI, they will probably say, "We're working on it." With problems such as the enormous distances involved from one star system to another and the current limitations of human technology, the outlook for success is not good. Will radio transmission or satellite technology be enough to establish contact with aliens beings, or must the human race advance further in order to have some opportunity for success?

THESIS QUESTION STATED

The greatest problem that scientists encounter during their SETI is the overall size of the universe and the distances involved from one star to another. For example, five of the seven stars in the Big Dipper are part of a star cluster 75 light years away (Dickinson 14). This means that their light travelling at roughly 300,000 kilometres per second takes a human lifetime to reach Earth. In our own galaxy, the Milky Way, light travels for 7,000 years before it

FIRST MAIN POINT: SIZE AND DISTANCE POSE GREAT PROBLEMS

PARENTHETICAL
CITATION USED

reaches us from the next spiral arm, beyond the one that we occupy (Dickinson 14). The light from the closest galaxy to the Milky Way, Andromeda, takes over two million years to travel the enormous distance to Earth. Unfortunately for the SETI scientists, Andromeda is the nearest of billions of galaxies similar to the Milky Way. Scientists today are receiving light images from

SUPERSCRIPT
NUMBER
INDICATES
BIBLIOGRAPHIC
NOTE

galaxies so far away that what is being observed actually occurred 12 billion years ago.[1]

Fortunately for SETI scientists, there are over 200 billion stars in our own galaxy to be explored before they even think about assessing others. But even in our own galaxy, distance is an extremely limiting factor. Consider the fact that it would require light 80,000 years to travel from one end of the galaxy to the other. Since light speed is the fastest thing known to humans (there is presently no warp speed, con-

EXAMPLES
AND DETAILS
PROVIDED

trary to what is seen on Star Trek), scientists' major problem is time. If humans sent a radio message to one of the star systems in the Big Dipper, and the message was received and replied to, the whole process would take 150 years to be completed. This means that scientists must narrow their search significantly.

In order for the process to be completed in a reasonable time frame, the majority of SETI researchers have narrowed the search to 1,000 stars within a light year radius from Earth. This means that the process of sending and receiving a reply by radio will occur within a two hundred year period. However, this process severely limits the chance for success in SETI. This limitation means that within our galaxy alone roughly 199,999,999,000 solar systems are being ignored. Also, of the one thousand nearest stars to us, many have to be severely questioned as to whether they could support life, within their solar systems. Alpha Centauri, for example, the closest star system to Earth, has almost no chance for supporting life, because it is a triple star system. In this particular case, three stars are held within one light year of each other by gravitational pull. If there were a planet orbiting one of the stars, the resulting fluctuations in surface temperature from the other two stars would make the planet inhospitable to life (Dickinson 68).

Other stars, such as Betelgeuse in the constellation of Orion, are over 10,000 times as luminous and 500 times the diameter of our own Sun. These stars, called supergiants, have a much shorter and more volatile existence than our own Sun, living approximately eleven million years and ending in an enormous explosion called a supernova. Since it took at least 3.5 billion years for life to progress to the point that it is at on Earth, the chances for intelligent life on a planet orbiting a supergiant are remote at best.

Probabilities that Extraterrestrial Life Exists

HEADING USED FOR TOPIC SHIFT

"[I]n the observable universe, there are as many as 1,000,000,000,000,000,000,000 (a billion trillion) stars; this one consideration alone makes it almost certain that extraterrestrial intelligence exists" (Asimov 223f).

Among scientific researchers involved in SETI there is almost unanimous agreement that extraterrestrial intelligence exists in the universe. Even using our own galaxy, with its 200 billion stars, it is difficult to imagine that extraterrestrial intelligence is not relatively nearby. This belief is supported by the widely accepted cosmological principle, which states that "except for some local peculiarities, no part of our universe is unique or privileged, and that therefore our own solar system is not a special, but rather a quite typical case" (Schenkel 151). The cosmological principle is supported by the well-known astronomer Dr. Carl Sagan, who suggests that

SIGNAL PHRASE USED FOR NAMING WELL-KNOWN SOURCE

BLOCK QUOTA-
TION USED FOR
MORE THAN
4 LINES
(INDENTED 10
SPACES)

> the laws of nature are the same every-
> where. Not only do the same chemical ele-
> ments exist everywhere in the universe
> . . . distant galaxies revolving around one
> another follow the same laws of gravita-
> tional physics as govern the motions of
> an apple falling to Earth, or Voyager on
> its way to the stars. (296)

The only reasonable conclusion that can be drawn
from these assertions is that the evolution of
intelligent life on Earth could not have been
some random event, but rather this event is
occurring all over the universe. This means that
"given a suitable and sufficiently enduring environment, life is a normal, natural consequence of
the long-term application of the basic physical
and chemical processes of the universe"
(Billingham 392).

In order for communication to occur with
other life forms throughout the universe, humans
must have a working hypothesis of how rare
extraterrestrial civilizations and intelligence
are. The importance of this is fairly straightforward. If these civilizations are abundant,
then contact with them would occur quite easily.
On the other hand, if extraterrestrial intelligence is rare, then present technology levels
will not be sufficient to find them.

Estimates of the abundance of extraterrestrial life have ranged from the overly optimistic
to the incredibly pessimistic. Isaac Asimov has
optimistically concluded that 390 million technological civilizations have come to fruition
within the life span of our galaxy and that
530,000 currently exist (91). This means that the
average separation between civilizations is
about 650 light years; any attempt at radio contact and reply with these civilizations would
take about 1,300 years.

A few scientists belonging to the school of
pessimism conclude that the emergence of life is

EACH POSITION
ASSOCIATED
WITH AN
EXPERT; MANY
RENDERED
IN APT
QUOTATIONS

a much more rare phenomenon than is widely accepted. They base their beliefs on the fact that no advanced civilizations have detected and made themselves known to us. One of their chief proponents, Frank J. Tipler, concludes that "our technological civilization is the only civilization which has ever existed in the whole of galactic history" (5–6). There is no evidence to dispute this belief, but I tend to think that these are the same egocentric scientists who would have thought the Earth to be the centre of the universe centuries ago. In my opinion, the most convincing argument falls somewhere between the optimistic and the pessimistic views.

One of the main advocates of this mid-range point of view is Michael D. Papagiannis. He bases his argument on the fact that it took about 3.5 billion years of evolution for intelligence and technology to develop on Earth. Papagiannis suggests that "the painfully slow evolution to high intelligence represents the bottleneck of the whole [evolutionary] process" (82). By conforming to this long time variable, Papagiannis has come to the arbitrary figure of about 1,000 civilizations throughout the history of our galaxy. This would mean that the nearest extraterrestrial intelligence to Earth would be well over 1,000 light years away (82).

This brings up an important point that has been made by the Russian astronomer Nikolai S. Kardashev. He is convinced that "extraterrestrial civilizations have not yet been found, because in effect they have not yet been searched for" (497). In other words, the sum of all current human technology does not have the capacity to search effectively for extraterrestrial civilizations. Certainly, humans have the ability to make some response to an extraterrestrial hailing, but not to initiate first contact with a civilization 1,000 light years away.

RESPONSE TO RESEARCH QUESTION IS FORMING

Human Attempts at SETI

Although life on the planet Earth has existed in some form for over 3 billion years, the attempts to contact life forms on other planets is a relatively new phenomenon. The search has essentially been restricted to the twentieth century and in particular the last thirty years of that century. Before this time, interstellar communication was technologically unfeasible, and therefore totally impossible from a human standpoint. However, by the last half of the twentieth century this was all about to change.

The most technologically unfeasible attempt at extraterrestrial contact has to do with the Voyager space probes. Following their exit of the solar system in 1990, these two probes are currently on an unchartered trip through space. They contain a video recorder with diagrammed directions on how to use it, and include a videotaped message by President Jimmy Carter and directions about the Earth's position in the galaxy. Currently these two probes are travelling at the amazing speed of 30 km/sec, or 108,000 kph. At this rate of speed they should arrive in another solar system in about 800 years (Jones 36). Fortunately for humans, there is a considerably faster way to achieve interstellar communication: by radio.

SPECIFIC INFORMATION SUPPORTED BY DOCUMENTATION   In 1960, from the National Radio Astronomy Observatory, the astronomer Frank Drake launched Project Ozma. Over a period of 200 hours, he attempted to detect interstellar radio signals from Tau Ceti and Epsilon Eridani, two stars approximately 11 light years away. The observation was performed on a one-channel receiver using the 21 centimetre wavelength of hydrogen (Schenkel 140). This particular wavelength was used then, and is still used today, because it provides the least intergalactic background noise. Predictably, this first search failed, as have many subsequent attempts, because the sample of stars was extremely small, as was the amount of time utilized. Another mitigating factor is that there are thousands of transmission wavelengths which extraterrestrials could be utilizing. Mr. Drake did not receive any radio transmissions from those stars in 1960, and neither did he receive a reply from his message sent in 1982. Similar searches since 1960 have targeted a significantly larger number of stars, but have also met with similar failure.

Arecibo, Puerto Rico, is the site of the largest astronomical radio telescope in the world. Twenty acres of aluminum panels form a 1,000 foot wide reflector dish, while 500 feet above, a 600 ton platform, filled with radio receivers, is suspended by cables (David 26). At about three o'clock on October 12, 1992, humans began the most comprehensive search for extraterrestrial intelligence ever attempted. The project will receive ten million dollars a year until the end of the century, as part of the overall NASA program. Its mission is to scan 1,000 stars, similar in type and spectrum to our own Sun, within a 100 light year radius of Earth. As in the Drake experiment, the radio channels being utilized are in the low end of the microwave spectrum, in order to suffer the least amount of intergalactic interference (David 27).

Even after thirty years, the amount of work done on communicating with extraterrestrial intelligence has been infinitesimal. This becomes evident when one hears John Billingham, NASA's chief of the SETI program, say of Arecibo, "we have only been operating for a few minutes, but we have already exceeded the sum of all previous SETI searches ..." (David 27). What this essentially means is that even Arecibo, with its 10 million dollar annual budget (and 23 million dollar overhaul in 1995), is still a learning experience for the scientists involved. For this reason, and the relatively small number of stel-

lar systems targeted, I would suggest that the
chances for success are only slightly larger than
Drake's initial study in 1960.

At this point in time there are considerable
difficulties inherent in the use of radio technology. First, radio transmissions must be
incredibly powerful in order to be heard above
the background radiation in the galaxy. Second,
signals must be sent directly from point A to
point B in order to be detected (a difficult
proposition considering that humans have yet to
be able to pinpoint any other planets in the universe, other than in our own solar system.[2]

Another important point to remember is this:

> [E]arthlings have [broadcast] their exis-
> tence for about 60 years through radio,
> television, radar and other electronic
> transmissions that escape into space.
> These all flood out from our planet at the
> speed of light and now form an expanding
> bubble 60 light years in radius.
> (Dickinson 126)

BLOCK
QUOTATION
INTRODUCED
BY FULL
CLAUSE AND
COLON

So even with this obvious beacon in space, either
extraterrestrial intelligence does not exist
within 60 light years, or does not reply, or is
not listening.

It is entirely possible that no extraterrestrial intelligence exists within a 60 light year
radius of Earth (a relatively tiny distance cos-
mically speaking). However, there is also no reason to believe that a technologically advanced
civilization even uses radio transmissions as a
form of communication. Humans only began using
the technology 60 years ago and already we are
moving to the use of satellite dishes, fibre
optics, and cable television, which allow considerably less leakage into space. Therefore, the
possibility certainly exists that intelligent
extraterrestrials use a more contained and efficient form of communication (Dickinson 125). This
brings me to the most plausible possibility; that

is, if communication with extraterrestrials occurs, it will be initiated by a more technologically advanced species than humans are currently.

ESSAY CONTINUES TO FOCUS ITS RESPONSE TO THE RESEARCH QUESTION

Will First Contact Be Made by Extraterrestrials?

The evidence that technologically superior beings exist within the universe is supported mainly be observing our own solar system and galaxy. The Sun and, in turn, the Earth are situated in one of the outer arms of the Milky Way. Star birth occurs most abundantly at the outer edges of galaxies, where gas and dust particles are abundant and therefore can gravitationally collapse and coaelsce into stars.[3] Scientists have estimated with a high degree of certainty that the Sun and its nine planets formed about 4.6 billion years ago. This is about one-third of the estimated life span of the universe. However, in the spiral arm of the galaxy just inside of ours, stars of similar type and spectrum with our Sun and roughly 7-9 billion years old. This one consideration alone presents an amazing hypothesis for the existence of vastly superior technological beings.

As stated earlier, life began on the planet Earth approximately 3.5 billion years ago. However, humans did not emerge until about the last 1 million years of this time span. Using the scope of Carl Sagan's "Cosmic Calendar," with the Big Bang beginning the universe on January 1 at midnight, the Sun did not appear until September, and humans did not appear until the last minute of December 31 (Sagan 56). Now consider, that of the million years that humans have been on the planet Earth, it is only within the last 150 years that the first combustion engine was built. Since that time human technology has increased exponentially. Humans are now travelling to the moon and back and sending satellites to the four corners of our solar system and beyond. Remember, this incredible technological leap has occurred in the last 150 years.

If a planet existed similar to Earth, next to a star similar to our Sun (not an odd occurrence considering the abundance of stars) within the inside spiral arm of the galaxy, that planet's inhabitants would have gone through the 150 years of the industrial and technological revolution approximately 3 billion years ago. As the astronomer Schenkel suggests, "if our scientific and technological progress, attained in a ludicrously short period of time, has been so impressive, just what will the science and technology of a civilization look like that has . . . a technical age of millions of years!" (173). If one assesses the reign of another earthly species, the dinosaurs, it becomes quite evident that human domination of this planet could last at least hundreds of millions of years. If this is the case, then we have achieved less than 0.2 percent of our technological capabilities. Surely, if other civilizations are further along in their technological enlightenment than we are, then the chances that they will contact us are much greater than the chances of us contacting them.

ESSAY MOVES TO ITS CONCLUSION

Throughout history humans have always been a rather egocentric species. Perhaps this is because we are at the highest level of technological intelligence on our planet. However, when it comes to astronomy and technological abilities, humans have always been humbled by the fact that we are usually wrong. Scientific progress since the sixteenth century has allowed humans to realize that we are on only one planet in a solar system not unlike hundreds of millions of others in the galaxy. Furthermore, we have become aware that our galaxy is only one among billions of galaxies in the observable universe.

Each step in the progression of our astronomical knowledge has been a lesson in modesty. The most logical continuation of this knowledge would be to find out that we are only one of millions of planets like the Earth, and that the galaxy is covered with innumerable life forms. Unfortunately, humans have not demonstrated the technological abilities to contact distant life forms, although some of those life forms may have the technological capabilities of contacting us. It is useless for me to speculate upon what those technological capabilities may be, but at the rate that humans are progressing perhaps in 50 years we may have a better idea. For the time being we must be content with the knowledge that if any extraterrestrials are trying to contact us by radio, the scientists at Arecibo will be listening.

Notes

[1] For a comprehensive look at the ability to see the past through the light images from distant galaxies, see Phillips.

[2] For information on the difficulties with planet detection and the most likely stellar candidates for planetary orbits, see Bruning.

[3] Star information is one of the most vital elements to the continual evolution of the universe. William J. Kaufmann provides a detailed analysis of star birth and death in his book Universe.

Works Cited

Asimov, Isaac. Interstellar Contact. Chicago: Regnery, 1974.

Billingham, John. Life in the Universe. New York: Pergamon, 1982.

Bruning, David. "Desperately Seeking Jupiters." Astronomy 20.7 (1992): 36–41.

David, Leonard. "The Search Begins." Final Frontier 6.1 (1993): 24–29, 53–54.

Dickinson, Terence. The Universe . . . and Beyond. Toronto: Camden House, 1992.

Jones, Brian. Exploring the Planets. London: Trodd, 1991.

Kardashev, Nikolai S. "On the Inevitability and Possible Structures of Supercivilizations."

ENDNOTES PROVIDE ADDITIONAL INFORMATION AND INDICATE OTHER SOURCES, KEYED TO THE LIST OF WORKS CITED

ENTRIES ARRANGED IN ALPHABETICAL ORDER BY AUTHORS' LAST NAMES

ALL LINES AFTER THE FIRST ARE INDENTED 5 SPACES

The Search for Extraterrestrial Life: Recent
Developments: Proceedings of the Inter-
national Astronomical Union Held at Boston
University. Ed. Michael D. Papagiannis.
Boston: Reidel, 1985. 497–504.

Kaufmann, William J. Universe. New York: W. H.
Freeman, 1988.

Papagiannis, Michael D. "Colonies in the Asteroid
Belt, or a Missing Term in the Drake
Equation." Extraterrestrials — Where Are
They? Eds. M. H. Hart and Ben Zuckerman, New
York: Pergamon, 1982. 77–86.

Phillips, Stephen. "Counting to the Edge of the
Universe." Astronomy 21.4 (1993): 38–43.

Sagan, Carl. Cosmos. New York: Random House,
1980.

Schenkel, Peter. ETI: A Challenge for Change. New
York: Vantage, 1988.

Tipler, Frank J. "The Most Advanced Civilization
in the Galaxy Is Ours." Mercury Jan.-Feb.
1982: 5–6.

13

Documenting Sources

Documentation styles vary among disciplines, with one format favoured in the humanities, for instance, another in the social sciences, and another in engineering, but they all require the same basic information. Thus you will want to use the conventions of documentation appropriate to a particular course and field. Correct use of punctuation and format are central to consistency, demonstrate that you have taken pains to follow the conventions of your discipline, and protect you from plagiarizing because of omitted source information (see 11d).

The widely used citation styles presented here have in common two central objectives: to let your readers know what sources you used in your writing, and to help them find the sources, should they wish to. To accomplish these objectives, each style uses specific citations in the text that indicate that source information is being used and corresponding entries in the list of sources cited following the text of the essay that give all the information readers need to find a source.

The **Modern Language Association (MLA) style** is widely used in literature and languages as well as other fields. Revised in 1984, MLA style calls for noting brief references to sources in parentheses in the text of an essay and appending an alphabetical list of sources, called *Works Cited*, at the end.

Used in many journals in the field of psychology, the **American Psychological Association (APA) style** is widely followed throughout the social sciences. Like MLA style, APA parenthetical citations within the text direct readers to a list of sources. In APA style, this list is titled *References*.

Various versions of the **number style**, whose parenthetical citations identify each work by a number assigned to it in the list of sources (usually titled *Literature Cited*) document work in many scientific papers and journals. Finally, history and some other humanities disciplines still prefer the traditional **note-and-bibliography (Old MLA) style.** This style uses note numbers in the text, keyed to a numerical list of *Notes;* an alphabetically arrange *Bibliography* lists the same sources at the end. Examples of documentation forms, parenthetical citations, and note forms in each of these styles appear in this chapter.

Modern Language Association style

The MLA style uses parenthetical citations of sources within the text and a list of these sources at the end of the text. This section discusses the basic format for MLA style and shows examples of parenthetical citations and bibliographic forms for various kinds of source materials. For further reference, consult:

> Gibaldi, Joseph, and Walter S. Achtert. *MLA Handbook for Writers of Research Papers.* 3rd ed. New York: Mod. Lang. Assoc., 1988.

1. MLA format for parenthetical citations

MLA style uses **parenthetical citations** in the text of an essay to document every quotation, paraphrase, summary, or other material from a source. Parenthetical citations correspond to full-information bibliographic entries in an alphabetical list of works cited at the end of the text. Usually the author's name is mentioned in a signal phrase that introduces the material, and the page number of the original source is given in parentheses after the material. Be sure to use an author's full name the first time you cite him or her. For later citations, use the author's last name. In general, make your parenthetical citations as short as possible, but include enough information for your readers to locate the material in your Works Cited list.

Place a parenthetical citation as near to the material as is possible without disrupting the flow of the sentence, usually before the punctuation mark at the end of the phrase that contains the material. Place any punctuation mark *after* the closing parenthesis. If your citation refers to a quotation, place it *after* the closing quotation mark but *before* any punctuation mark. For long quotations typed as block, place the parenthetical citation two spaces after the final punctuation mark. Here are examples of the various ways to cite sources.

Author named in a signal phrase

Ordinarily, use the author's name in a signal phrase to introduce the material, and simply cite the page number(s) in parentheses.

> Herrera indicates that Kahlo believed in a "vitalistic form of pantheism" (328).

Author named in a citation

When you do not name the author in the text, include the author's last name before the page number(s) in the parenthetical citation, with no comma between them.

> In places, de Beauvoir "sees Marxists as believing in subjectivity as much as existentialists do" (Whitmarsh 63).

Two or three authors

Use all the authors' last names in a signal phrase or parenthetical citation.

> Gortner, Hebrun, and Nicolson maintain that "opinion leaders" influence other people in an organization because they are respected, not because they hold high positions (175).

Four or more authors

Use the first author's name and *et al.* ("and others") or name all the authors in a signal phrase or parenthetical citation.

> Similarly, as Belenky et al. assert, examining the lives of women expands our understanding of human development (7).

Unknown author

Use the title, if brief, or a shortened version in a signal phrase or parenthetical citation.

> "Hype," by one analysis, is "an artificially engendered atmosphere of hysteria" ("Today's Marketplace" 51).

Author of two or more works

For a work by an author of two or more works in your *Works Cited* list, include a shortened version of the title in a signal phrase or parenthetical citation.

> Gardner presents readers with their own silliness through his description of a "pointless, ridiculous mon-ster, crouched in the shadows, stinking of dead men, murdered children, and martyred cows" (<u>Grendel</u> 2).

Two or more authors with the same surname

If your *Works Cited* list includes works by different authors with the same surname, always include the author's first name in signal phrases or parenthetical citations for those works.

Children will learn to write if they are allowed to choose their own subjects, James Britton asserts, citing the Schools Council study of the 1960s (37–42).

Multivolume work

Name the author in a signal phrase or parenthetical citation. Note the volume number and page number(s), with a colon and one space between them, in the parentheses.

Modernist writers prized experimentation and gradually even sought to blur the line between poetry and prose, according to Forster (3: 150).

If you name only one volume of the work in the Works Cited, you need include only the page number in the parenthetical citation.

Literary work

For literary works available in many editions, cite the page number(s) from the edition you used, followed by a semicolon and such information as part or chapter in a novel (*175; ch. 4*) or act and/or scene in a play (*37; sc. 1*). For poems, cite only the line number(s), using the word *line(s)* in the first reference to alert readers that the numbers do not refer to pages (*lines 33–34*). For verse plays, give only the act, scene, and line numbers, separated by periods.

As <u>Macbeth</u> begins, the witches greet Banquo as "Lesser than Macbeth, and greater" (1.3.65).

Bible

Identify biblical quotations by chapter and verse. For books whose names are longer than five letters, use an abbreviation in a parenthetical citation (*Gen.* for *Genesis; Matt.* for *Matthew*). Spell out all books named in your text. If you use the King James Version, you do not need to include a *Works Cited* entry. If you use any other version, treat it as you would a book in the *Works Cited* list (see 13a3).

Indirect source

Use the abbreviation *qtd. in* to indicate that you are quoting from an indirect source—that is, someone else's report of a conversation, statement, interview, letter, or the like.

> As Arthur Miller says, "When somebody is destroyed everybody finally contributes to it, but in Willy's case, the end product would be virtually the same" (qtd. in Martin and Meyer 375).

Two or more sources in the same citation

If you refer to more than one source in parentheses, include the information for each of them, separated by semicolons.

> Recently, however, some economists have recommended that <u>employment</u> be redefined to include unpaid domestic labor (Clark 148; Nevins 39).

Entire work or one-page article

To cite a whole work rather than a specific passage, or a one-page article, include the reference in the text without any page numbers or parentheses.

> Thomas Hardy's tragic vision is given full vent in his <u>Jude the Obscure</u>, a bleaker novel than <u>The Return of the Native</u>.

Nonprint source

Give enough information in a signal phrase or parenthetical citation for readers to locate the source in the *Works Cited* list. Usually, use the name or title under which you listed the source.

> Kahlo is seated with a Judas doll, identified in the film <u>Portrait of an Artist: Frida Kahlo</u> as a papier-mâché doll stuffed with firecrackers to be exploded on the day before Easter.

2. MLA format for explanatory and bibliographic notes

MLA style allows **explanatory notes** for information or commentary that would not readily fit into the text but is needed for clarification or further explanation. In addition, MLA style permits **bibliographic notes** for citing several sources for one point and for offering information about or evaluation of a source. Superscript numbers are used in the text to refer readers to the notes, which may appear as endnotes (typed under the heading *Notes* on a separate page after the text but before the *Works Cited*) or as footnotes at the bottom of the page (typed four lines below the last text line). For example:

Superscript number in text

Stewart emphasizes the existence of social contracts in Hawthorne's life so that the audience will accept a different Hawthorne, one more attuned to modern times than the figure in Woodberry.[3]

Note

[3] Woodberry does, however, show that Hawthorne <u>was</u> often an unsociable individual. He emphasizes the seclusion of Hawthorne's mother, who separated herself from her family after the death of her husband, often even taking meals alone (28). Woodberry seems to imply that Mrs. Hawthorne's isolation rubbed off onto her son.

3. MLA format for a list of works cited

A list of *Works Cited* is an alphabetical list of the sources actually cited in your essay. (If your instructor asks that you list everything you have read as background, call the list *Works Consulted*.) Start your list on a separate page after the text of your essay and any notes. Number the page as you did those in your text. Type the heading *Works Cited*, neither underlined nor in quotation marks, centred one inch from the top of the page. Double-space and begin your first entry. Start each entry flush with the left margin; indent any subsequent line of the entry five spaces. Double-space the entire list.

List your sources alphabetically by authors' last names. If a source is by an unknown author, alphabetize it by the first major word of the title after any initial *A, An,* or *The.*

On the following pages, you will find sample entries that follow the MLA specifications for various kinds of sources.

Books and pamphlets
The basic entry for a book includes the following elements:

1. *Author.* List the author by last name first followed by a comma and the first name.
2. *Title.* Underline the title and any subtitle and capitalize all major words (see 40c for more on capitalizing titles).

3. *Publication information.* Give the city of publication (and country, state, or province if the city is unfamiliar), and add a colon, a space, and a shortened version of the publisher's name—dropping *Press, Publishers, Inc.,* and so on (*St. Martin's* for *St. Martin's Press, Inc.*), using only the first surname (*Harcourt* for *Harcourt Brace Jovanovich*), and abbreviating *University Press* (*Oxford UP* for *Oxford University Press*)—a comma, and the year of publication.

These elements are separated from one another by a period and two spaces, and the entry ends with a period. Here is an example of a basic entry for a book:

author, last name first | two spaces | title, underlined | one space after colon | subtitle

Secord, James A.   Controversy in Victorian Geology: The Cambrian-

double space →
indent 5 spaces →   Silurian Dispute.   Princeton: Princeton UP, 1986.   publisher's city and name

A book written by one author

Coupland, Douglas, <u>Generation X: Tales for an Accel-
        erated Culture</u> New York: St. Martin's, 1991.

A book written by two or three authors
List the first author last name first; then list the other author or authors in regular order, with commas between the names.

Markusen, James R., and James R. Melvin. <u>The Theory of
        International Trade and Its Canadian Applications</u>.
        Toronto: Butterworths, 1984.

A book written by more than three authors
Name the first author listed on the book's title page, follow it with a comma, and then add the abbreviation *et al.* ("and others").

Cheng, Maisy, et al. <u>The Every Secondary Student Survey:
        Fall 1987</u>. Toronto: Board of Education 1989.

A book written by a group
Use the name of a group or organization listed on the title page as the author in place of individual authors.

Economic Council of Canada. <u>A Framework for Financial
        Regulation</u>. Ottawa: ECC, 1987.

A book prepared by an editor

If a work was prepared by an editor, list this person as you would an author and add a comma and the abbreviation *ed.* (for *editor*).

> New, W. H., ed. <u>Native Writers and Canadian Writing</u>. Vancouver: University of British Columbia, 1990.

If a book has both an author and an editor, your entry should show whose work you cite. If you cite the author's work, name the author first. Then add the editor's name, with the abbreviation *Ed.*, after the title. If you cite the editor's work, such as the variations in the edition or the commentary, name the editor first, followed by *ed.* After the title, add the author's name, introduced with *By.*

A book prepared by a translator

When a book has an author and a translator, your entry should show whose work you cite. If you cite the author's work—the text itself—begin with the author's name with *Trans.* (for *translator*).

> Jansson, Sven B. F. <u>The Runes of Sweden</u>. Trans. Peter G. Foote. Stockholm: Norstedt Forlag, 1962.

A second work by the same author

If you cite more than one work by a particular author, arrange the entries alphabetically by title. After the first entry, begin with three hyphens followed by a period instead of the author's name.

> Booth, Wayne C. <u>Modern Dogma and the Rhetoric of Assent</u>. Notre Dame: Notre Dame UP, 1974.
>
> ---.The Company We Keep: An Ethics of Fiction. Berkeley and Los Angeles: University of California Press, 1988.

A republication

If you cite a modern edition of an older book, a paperback edition, or other republication, add the original publication date, with a period, right after the title. Then give the publication details for the edition you used.

> Scott, Walter. <u>Kenilworth</u>. 1821. New York: Dodd, 1956.

A particular edition

If a book is identified on its title page as a particular edition, add this information, in abbreviated form, after the title.

```
Stockwood, David. Civil Litigation. 2nd ed. Toronto:
    Carswell, 1986.
```

A work in two or more volumes

If a work has more than one volume, note the number of volumes in the complete work before the publication information, if you used more than one volume. If the volumes were published over several years, give the inclusive dates.

```
Braudel, Fernand. The Mediterranean and the Mediter-
    ranean World in the Age of Phillip II. Trans. Siân
    Reynolds. 2 vols. New York: Harper, 1972-73.
```

If you used only one volume, cite only that volume before the publication information; then give the number of volumes at the end of the entry. (Then, because the volume is specified, your text citation needs only the page number.)

```
Stevenson, Ian. Cases of the Reincarnation Type. Vol. 3.
    Charlottesville: UP of Virginia, 1980. 4 vols.
```

A book that is part of a series

If a book is part of a series (as noted on the title page or the page before), add the series name and any number after the title.

```
Bloom, Harold, ed. Ralph Waldo Emerson. Modern Critical
    Views. New York: Chelsea, 1985.
```

An item in an anthology or collection

If you cite a selection in an anthology, name the author of the selection. Then list the selection's title, set off by quotation marks (or by underlining if the selection first appeared as a book), the anthology's title, underlined, and the name of any editor. Finally, note the inclusive pages of the selection, followed by a period.

```
McLaren, Christie. "Suitcase Lady." The Act of Writing.
    Ed. Ronald Conrad. Toronto: McGraw-Hill Ryerson,
    1987. 90-2.
```

An article in an encyclopedia

List the author of the article, often identified by initials corresponding to full names in a list of contributors. If no author is identified, begin with the title. For a well-known encyclopedia, just note any edition number and date. If the encyclopedia entries are arranged in alphabetical order, no volume or page numbers are needed.

```
Schrodt, Barbara. "Bobsledding." The Canadian Encyclo-
     pedia. 2nd ed. 1988.
```

A preface, introduction, foreword, or afterword

List the author of the item, then its title, set off only by an initial capital letter, and a period. After the title of the work in which the item appears, introduce the name of the author of the complete work with *By.* (If the same person wrote both, just the last name is needed here.) List the item's page numbers at the end of the entry.

```
Duffin, Jacalyn. Introduction. Langstaff: A Nineteenth-
     Century Medical Life. By Duffin. Toronto:
     University of Toronto Press, 1993. 3-7.
```

A government document

List government documents as you would books, beginning with the author, if identified, and giving the name of the government agency after the title. If no author is given, first list the government and then the department or agency.

```
Saskatchewan. Dept. of Agriculture. Services and Programs
     for Rural Saskatchewan 1979-80. Saskatoon, 1979.
```

An unpublished dissertation

Set off the title of an unpublished dissertation with quotation marks. Add the identification *Diss.*, the name of the school at which the study was done, a comma, and the date.

```
Werder, Carmen. "Expressed Silence: A Study of the
     Metaphorics of Word in Selected Nineteenth-Century
     American Texts." Diss. University of British
     Columbia, 1994.
```

Periodicals

The basic entry for a periodical includes the following elements:

1. *Author.* List the author by last name first, followed by a comma and the first name.

2. *Article title.* Enclose the title and any subtitle in quotation marks and capitalize all major words. (See 40c for more on capitalizing titles.)

3. *Publication information.* Give the periodical title (excluding an initial *A, An,* or *The*), underlined and with all major words capitalized; the volume number and issue number, if appropriate; and the date of

publication. For journals, list the year in parentheses followed by a colon, a space, and the inclusive page numbers. For magazines and newspapers, list the month (abbreviated, except for May, June, and July) or the day and month before the year, and do not use parentheses. Do not use *p.*, or *pp.* before the inclusive page numbers. For inclusive page numbers, note all digits for numbers 1 to 99 and note only the last two digits and any others that change for numbers above 99 (24–27, 134–45).

These elements are separated from one another by a period and two spaces, and the entry ends with a period. Here is an example of a basic for an article journal.

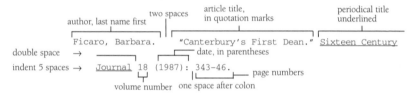

An article in a scholarly periodical that numbers pages consecutively within a volume

If a periodical continues page numbering from one issue to the next within the annual volume, follow the title of the publication with the volume number in arabic numerals.

    Pelz, David M., and Richard G. Haddad. "Radiologic
        Investigation of Low Back Pain." CMAJ 140 (1989):
        289-95.

An article in a scholarly periodical that numbers pages separately within each issue

If a periodical numbers pages in each issue separately, include the volume number and the issue number, separated by a period.

    Loffy, John. "The Politics at Modernism's Funeral."
        Canadian Journal of Political and Social Theory 6.3
        (1987): 89-96.

An article in a monthly or weekly periodical

For a monthly or bimonthly periodical, abbreviate the month (except May, June, or July), and put the date after the periodical's title.

    Said, Edward. "Through Gringo Eyes." Harper's Apr. 1988:
        70-72.

For a weekly or biweekly periodical, note the day, the month, the year.

```
Dixon, Michael. "Manager Switches Closely Linked to
     Corporate Success." Financial Post 5 June, 1989: 18.
```

An article in a newspaper
List the author, article title, and then the newspaper's title (dropping any initial *A, An,* or *The)* as it appears on the front page. Follow it with the city or place in square brackets if this information is not part of the title. Give the exact date of the issue, followed by a colon and the page number. If the page number does not include the section (such as B4 or C1), follow the date with a comma, the section (with *sec.*) followed by a colon, and the page number.

```
Howlett, Karen. "Spectre of Bankruptcy Looms over
     Quintette." Globe and Mail 16 June 1990, sec. B:1.
```

An editorial or letter in a periodical
Identify an editorial or letter by adding the word *Editorial* or *Letter* after the title.

```
Doyle, Kevin. "Dangerous Times." Editorial. Maclean's 26
     Feb. 1990: 2.

Stewart, Francis. Letter. Economist 19-25 Mar. 1988: 4.
```

A review in a periodical
Give the author's name, if identified, and the title, if the review has one. If not, begin the entry with the phrase *Rev. of* (with just a capital *R)* and the name of the work being reviewed. After this title, add a comma, *by,* and the work's author.

```
Block, J. H. "Debatable Conclusions about Sex
     Differences." Rev. of The Psychology of Sex
     Differences, by E. E. Maccoby and C. N. Jacklin.
     Contemporary Psychology Aug. 1976: 517-22.
```

An article whose author is not identified
Begin with the article title, dropping any initial *A, An,* or *The,* and place it in alphabetical order. The article below begins on page 20 and continues on pages 23 and 24. To show that the pages are not consecutive, note only the first page number followed by a plus sign.

```
"The Odds of March." Time 15 Apr. 1985: 20+.
```

Other Sources

The examples below show how to treat the main types of entries for other sources of information.

An interview

List first the person who has been interviewed. Then list the title, if the interview has one, in quotation marks (or underline if it is the complete work). If it does not have a title, use the word *Interview*. If the interview comes from a source, identify the source. If you were the interviewer, identify the type as *Telephone Interview* or *Personal Interview* and note the date.

> Beatty, Perrin. Interview. <u>Morningside</u>. CBC Radio. 29 June 1990.
>
> Luger, Moberley. Personal Interview. 5 July 1994.

A letter

If you cite a published letter, enter it like a selection from a book. Note the letter's date and any number used in the source after the title of the letter.

> Frost, Robert. "Letter to Editor of the <u>Independent</u>." 28 Mar. 1894. <u>Selected Letters of Robert Frost</u>. Ed. Lawrance Thompson. New York: Holt, 1964. 19.

Follow the form below if you cite a letter sent to you.

> Diaz, Gloria. Letter to the author. 12 Feb. 1989.

A computer software program

List the writer of the program if identified. Then add the title of the software, underlined, followed by the words *Computer Software*. Next identify the company that distributes the software, and the date. Note the computer type, memory required, operating system, format, and any other details.

> <u>Nota Bene</u>. Vers. 3.0. Computer Software. Dragonfly Software, 1988. MS-DOS 2.0, 512 KB, disk.

A film or videotape

For a film, a videotape, or a slide program, include the film's title, underlined; director; the company distributing the film; and the date. Other contributors, such as writers or actors, may follow the director's name. If you are interested in one person's work, such as the director's, list that person's name first.

Not a Love Story: A Film About Pornography. Dir. Bonnie
    Sherr Klein. National Film Board. 1986.

A television or radio program

Begin the entry with the title of the program, underlined. Add other
details (such as narrator, director, writer, and principal actors) after the title
as necessary. Then identify the network, the local station and city, and the
date. If you are interested in the work of a particular person, begin the entry
with that person's name. If you cite a particular episode, begin with the
episode's title in quotation marks.

Degrassi Junior High. Dir. Linda Schuyler and Kit Hood.
    With Bill Parrott and Neil Hope. CBC. CBLT,
    Toronto. 25 June 1990.

A recording

Your research interest determines whether the name of the composer,
artist, or conductor precedes the title of the album or tape, which is underlined, or the name of the composition recorded, which is not underlined.
Then add the names of any other pertinent people. End with the name of
the manufacturer, the catalogue number, and the date, all separated by
commas.

Cockburn, Bruce. Dart to the Heart. True North, TNK 82,
    1993.

Grieg, Edvard. Concerto in A Minor, op. 16. Perf. Van
    Cliburn. Cond. Eugene Ormandy. Philadelphia Orch.
    RCA, Red Seal LSC 3065, 1969.

An artistic work

List the artist, and then give the work's title, underlined. Add the name
of the museum or other location, and identify the city.

Munch, Edvard. The Cry. Museum of Fine Arts, Boston.

A performance

List the title or the name of someone involved if that person's work is
your particular interest. Add other appropriate details (such as the composer, writer, director). Then identify where and when the performance
took place.

No Make-up. Vancouver Youth Theatre. Dir. Judith Hogan.
    Frederick Wood Theatre, Vancouver. 3 Dec. 1993.

American Psychological Association style

The APA style cites sources parenthetically in the text and then lists these references in full-information bibliographic entries at the end of the paper. This section discusses the basic format for APA style and shows examples of parenthetical citations and bibliographic forms for various kinds of sources. For further reference, consult the following:

> American Psychological Association. *Publication Manual of the American Psychological Association.* 3rd ed. Washington: Amer. Psych. Assoc., 1983.

1. APA format for parenthetical citations

In APA-style parenthetical citations, the author's name is generally used in a signal phrase to introduce the cited material, and the date in parentheses immediately follows the author's name. For a quotation, the page number, preceded by *p.*, appears in parentheses after the quotation. Following are examples of ways to cite various kinds of sources.

Author named in a signal phrase

Key (1983) argues that the placement of women in print advertisements is subliminally important.

As Briggs (1970) observes, parents play an important role in building their children's self-esteem because "children value themselves to the degree that they have been valued" (p. 14).

Author named in a parenthetical citation
When you do not name the author in your text, give the name and the date, separated by a comma, in parentheses at the end of the cited material.

One study has found that only 68% of letters received by editors were actually published (Renfro, 1979).

Two Authors
Use both names in all citations. Join the names with *and* in a signal phrase, but use an ampersand (&) instead in a parenthetical reference.

Murphy and Orkow (1985) reached somewhat different conclusions by designing a study that was less dependent on subjective judgment than were previous studies.

A recent study that was less dependent on subjective judgment resulted in somewhat different conclusions than had previous studies (Murphy & Orkow 1985).

Three to five authors
List all the authors' names in a signal phrase or parenthetical citation for the first reference.

Belenky, Clinchy, Goldberger, and Tarule (1986) suggest that many women rely on observing and listening to others as ways of learning about themselves.

In any subsequent references, use just the first author's name plus *et al.* ("and others"). Note that all the authors' names should appear in the entry in the list of *References*.

From this experience, observe Belenky et al. (1986), women learn to listen to themselves think, a step toward self-expression.

Six or more authors
Use the first author's name and *et al.* ("and others") in every citation, including the first. Note that all the authors' names should appear in the entry in the list of *References*.

As Mueller et al. (1980) demonstrated, television holds the potential for distorting and manipulating consumers as free-willed decision makers.

Unknown author
Use the title or the first few words of it in a signal phrase or parenthetical citation.

The school profiles for the region substantiate this trend (<u>Guide to Secondary Schools</u>, 1983).

Two or more authors with the same surname
If your list of references includes works by different authors with the same surname, include the author's first or first two initial(s) in each citation.

G. Jones (1984) conducted the groundbreaking study of retroviruses.

Two or more sources in the same parenthetical citation

If you cite more than one source in the parentheses, list all the sources in the order in which they appear in the list of *References*. That is, list works by different authors in alphabetical order (separated by semicolons) and works by the same author in chronological order (separated by commas).

```
(Chodorow, 1978; Gilligan, 1982)
(Gilligan 1977, 1982)
```

Specific parts of a source

Use abbreviations (*chap., sec.,* and so on) in the parenthetical citation to name the part you are citing.

```
Montgomery (1988, chap. 9) argues that his research
yielded the opposite results.
```

Personal communication

Cite any personal letters, telephone conversations, or interviews in your text with the person's name, the identification *personal communication*, and the date. Because your readers would not be able to recover these sources, you do not need to include them in your list of *References*.

```
J. L. Morin (personal communication, October 14, 1990)
supported the claims made in her recent article with new
evidence.
```

2. APA format for content notes

APA style allows content notes for information you wish to include to expand or supplement your text. Notes are indicated in the text by superscript numerals in consecutive order throughout the text, and the notes themselves are typed on a separate page after the last page of the text, under the headings *Footnotes*, centred at the top of the page. Double-space all entries. Indent the first line of each note five spaces, but begin subsequent lines at the left margin.

Superscript in text

```
The age of the children involved was an important fac-
tor in the selection of items for the questionnaire.[1]
```

Footnote

```
[1] Marjorie Youngston Forman and William Cole of the
Child Study Team provided great assistance in identi-
fying appropriate items.
```

3. APA format for a list of references

The alphabetical list of the sources actually cited in your essay is called **References**. (If your instructor asks that you list everything you have read as background, call the list *Bibliography*.) Start your list on a separate page *after* the text of your essay and any notes, but *before* any appendices that explain your research procedures or results. Number the page as you did those in your text. Type the heading *References*, neither underlined nor in quotation marks, centred one and one-half inches (about 4 centimetres) from the top of the page. Double-space and begin your first entry. Start each entry flush with the left margin; indent any subsequent lines of the entry three spaces. Double-space the entire list.

List your sources alphabetically by authors' last names. If a source is by an unknown author, alphabetize it by the first major word of the title after any initial *A, An,* or *The.*

The APA style specifies treatment and placement of four basic elements—author, publication date, title, and publication information—as follows. These elements are separated from one another by a period and two spaces, and the entry ends with a period.

1. *Author.* List all authors last name first, and use only initials for first and middle names. Separate multiple authors with commas, and use an ampersand before the last author.

2. *Publication date.* Enclose the date in parentheses. Use only the year for books and journals; use the year, a comma, and the month or month and day for magazines. Do not abbreviate the month.

3. *Title.* Underline titles and subtitles of books and periodicals, but do not enclose titles of articles in quotation marks. For books and articles, capitalize only the first word of the title and subtitle and any proper nouns or proper adjectives. Capitalize all major words in a periodical title. (See 40c for information on capitalization.)

4. *Publication information.* For a book, list the city of publication (and the country, state, or province if the city is unfamiliar), a colon and the publisher's name, dropping any *Inc., Co.,* or *Publishers.* For a periodical, follow the periodical title with a comma, the volume number (underlined), the issue number (if appropriate) in parentheses, a comma, and the inclusive page numbers of the article. For newspapers and magazines, include the abbreviations *p.* ("page") or *pp.* ("pages").

Consult the various sample entries below for information on where in an entry you should place other information. Here are examples of basic book and periodical entries.

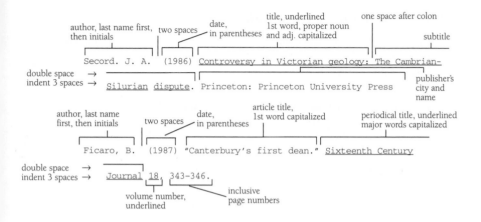

Books and pamphlets

A book written by one author

Griffiths, F. (1987). <u>The politics of the Northwest Passage</u>. Montreal: McGill-Queen's University Press.

A book written by two or more authors

Stirling, D., & Woodford, J. (1975). <u>Where to go bird-watching in Canada</u>. Surrey, B.C.: Hancock House.

A book written by a group

Canadian Institute of Chartered Accountants. (1973). <u>Financial reporting for life insurance companies</u>. Toronto: CICA.

A book prepared by an editor

Leyton, E. (Ed.). (1986). <u>Hunting humans: The rise of the modern mass murderer</u>. Toronto: McClelland & Stewart.

A second work by the same author

Rutherford, E. (1988). <u>Dance for cats</u>. Charlottetown: Ragweed.

Rutherford, E. (1988). <u>Yoga for cats</u>. Charlottetown: Ragweed.

An item in an anthology or collection

Tremblay, M. (1986). The thimble. In W. H. New (Ed.).
Canadian short fiction: From myth to modern. (pp.
499-500). Scarborough: Prentice-Hall.

A government document

Statistics Canada. (1989). Atlas of cancer mortality in
British Columbia 1956-1983. Ottawa.

Periodicals

An article in a scholarly periodical that numbers pages consecutively within a volume

Tiessen, H. F. (1988). Mother tongue as shibboleth in
the literature of Canadian Mennonites. Studies in
Canadian Literature, 23, 34-35.

An article in a scholarly periodical that numbers pages separately within each issue

Maienza, J. G. (1986). The superintendency: Characteristics of access for men and women. Educational
Administration Quarterly, 22(4), 59-79.

An article in a monthly or weekly periodical

Steinhart, J. (1990, Feb.). RDBMs: What's the state of
the art? Canadian Datasystems, pp. 32-35.

An article in a newspaper

Drohan, M. (1990, June 15). Personal bankruptcies jump
32 per cent. Globe and Mail, p. A1.

A letter to a periodical

Burney, P. S. (1985, May). Cryptographic message sending [Letter to the editor]. Byte: The Small Systems
Journal, p. 14.

An article whose author is not identified

What sort of person reads creative computing? (1985,
August). Creative Computing, pp. 8, 10.

Other sources

An interview

Kort, M. (1988, February). Ms. conversation [Interview
    with Martina Navratilova & Billie Jean King]. <u>Ms.</u>,
    pp. 58-62.

A computer software program

<u>SuperCalc3 Release 2.1</u> (1985). [Computer program]. San
    Jose, CA: Computer Associates, Micro Products
    Division.

13c

Number style

Number-style documentation is used in many of the natural sciences. In this
style, each parenthetical citation is a number that corresponds to a full citation in a list of sources, usually called *Literature Cited*. The *Literature Cited*
entries are made up of author, title, and publication information.
Requirements for arranging and punctuating these three elements vary
greatly among disciplines, so be sure to ask your instructor which style you
should follow. Some common style manuals include the following:

> American Chemical Society. *Handbook for Authors of Papers in the American
> Chemical Society Publications.* Washington: American Chemical Soc., 1978.

> American Institute of Physics. *Style Manual for Guidance in the Preparation of
> Papers.* 3rd ed. New York: American Inst. of Physics, 1978.

> Council of Biology Editors. *CBE Style Manual: A Guide for Authors, Editors, and
> Publishers in the Biological Sciences.* 5th ed., rev. and exp. Bethesda, MD:
> CBE, 1983.

The following discussion pertains to the style advocated by the Council of
Biology Editors (CBE). In CBE style, the *Literature Cited* list includes only
works actually cited in the essay. The list is arranged either alphabetically by
authors' last names, with each entry assigned a number in sequence, or in
the order in which the sources are cited in the text.

Citations in the text are identified by a number in parentheses following any quotation, paraphrase, summary, or other reference from a source.
Each number corresponds to a *Literature Cited* entry. If a citation refers to a

specific page, it includes the entry number, a comma, the abbreviation *p.*, and the page number (*1, p. 245*). Here are a sample text reference and two literature-cited entries, one for a book and one for a periodical, that conform to CBE style.

Text reference

```
First, Freidson argues, the doctor is in the autonomous
position of having a monopoly on the applied uses of
medical scientific knowledge (1).
```

Literature cited

```
1.  Freidson, E. Profession of medicine. New York: Dodd-
    Mead; 1972.

2.  Finkel, M. J. Drugs of limited commercial value. New
    Engl. J. Med. 302:643-44; 1980.
```

Note-and-bibliography style

The note-and-bibliography style was the standard format preferred by the Modern Language Association (MLA) until 1984 and thus is sometimes referred to as Old MLA style. This style is still used in some fields, particularly in the humanities.

1. Note-and-bibliography format for bibliography entries

The format for entries in the *Bibliography* is the same as the current MLA format for entries in a *Works Cited* list. The *Bibliography* appears on a separate page at the end of the essay, after the list of *Notes*.

2. Note-and-bibliography format for notes

The note-and-bibliography style uses superscript numbers ([1]) to mark citations in the text. Citations are numbered sequentially throughout the text and correspond to notes that contain complete publication information about the sources cited.

In the text, the superscript number for each note is placed near the cited material—at the end of the quotation, sentence, clause, or phrase. The number is typed after any punctuation, and no space is left between it and the preceding letter or punctuation mark.

> As Glueck says, "Most addicts have had dealings with some type of crime before they became acquainted with narcotics."[5]

Notes can be footnotes (typed at the bottom of the page on which the citation appears in the text) or endnotes (typed on a separate page under the heading *Notes*). The first line of each note is indented five spaces and begins with a superscript number and one space before the first word of the entry. All remaining lines of the entry are typed flush with the left margin. A note usually begins with the author's name, in normal order, followed by a comma, the title of the source, the publication information in parentheses, and the page number(s). The first note for a source gives full information about it. Subsequent notes use a shortened reference, usually the author's name and the page number(s).

Examples of some variations in first notes are shown below.

Books and pamphlets

A book written by one author

[1]Timothy Findley, The Telling of Lies: A Mystery (New York: Viking, 1986) 61.

A book by more than one author

[2]James R. Markusen and James R. Melvin, The Theory of International Trade and Its Canadian Applications (Toronto: Butterworths, 1984) 101.

A book written by a group

[3]Economic Council of Canada, A Framework for Financial Regulation (Ottawa: ECC, 1987) 40.

A book prepared by an editor

[4]Rick Linden, ed., Criminology: A Canadian Perspective (Toronto: Holt, 1987) xxi–xxv.

A book prepared by a translator

[5]Sven B. F. Jansson, The Runes of Sweden, trans. Peter G. Foote (Stockholm: Norstedt Forlag, 1962) 38.

A republication

[6]Walter Scott, <u>Kenilworth</u> (1821; New York: Dodd, 1956) 85–86.

A particular edition

[7]Alfred A. Kelly, Winifred A. Harbison, and Herman Belz, <u>The American Constitution: Its Origins and Development</u>, 6th ed. (New York: Norton, 1983) 187.

A work in two or more volumes

[8]Fernand Braudel, <u>The Mediterranean and the Mediterranean World in the Age of Phillip II</u>, trans. Siân Reynolds, vol. 1 (New York: Harper, 1972–73) 345.

An item in an anthology or collection

[9]Christie McLaren, "Suitcase Lady," <u>The Act of Writing</u> ed. Ronald Conrad (Toronto: McGraw-Hill Ryerson, 1987) 90.

An article in an encyclopedia

[10]"Traqair, Sir John Stewart," <u>Encyclopaedia Britannica</u>, 11th ed.

Periodicals

An article in a scholarly periodical that numbers pages consecutively within a volume

[11]Margot Norris, "Narration under a Blindfold: Reading Joyce's 'Clay'," <u>PMLA</u> 102 (1987): 206.

An article in a scholarly periodical that numbers pages separately within each issue

[12]John Loffy, "The Politics at Modernism's Funeral," <u>Canadian Journal of Political and Social Theory</u> 6.3 (1987): 88.

An article in a monthly or weekly periodical

[13]Edward Said, "Through Gringo Eyes," <u>Harper's</u> Apr. 1988: 71.

An article in a newspaper

[14]Karen Howlett, "Spectre of Bankruptcy Looms over Quintette," <u>Globe and Mail</u> 16 June 1990: B1.

An editorial in a periodical

[15]Kevin Doyle, "Dangerous Times," <u>Maclean's</u> 26 Feb. 1990: 2.

A review in a periodical

[16]J. H. Block, "Debatable Conclusions about Sex Differences," rev. of <u>The Psychology of Sex Differences</u>, by E. E. Maccoby and C. N. Jacklin, <u>Contemporary Psychology</u> Aug. 1976: 517.

An article whose author is not identified

[17]"Lovely Luna Moth," <u>Ranger Rick</u> Sept. 1989: 2.

Other sources

An interview

[18]Perrin Beatty, interview, <u>Morningside</u>, CBC Radio, 29 June 1990.

[19]Larry Berkson, personal interview, 16 May 1988.

A letter

[20]Robert Frost, "Letter to the Editor of the <u>Independent</u>," 28 Mar. 1894, <u>Selected Letters of Robert Frost</u>, ed. Lawrance Thompson (New York: Holt, 1964) 19.

A speech or lecture

[21]Virginia F. Stern, "Sir Stephen Powle as Adventurer in the Virginia Company of London," Seminar on the Renaissance, Columbia University, New York, 15 Oct. 1985.

A computer software program

[22]<u>Nota Bene</u>, vers. 3.0., computer software, Dragonfly Software, 1988 (MS-DOS 2.0, 512KB, disk).

A film or videotape

[23]Not a Love Story: A Film about Pornography, dir. Bonnie Sherr Klein, National Film Board, 1986.

A television or radio program

[24]<u>Degrassi Junior High</u>, dir. Linda Schuyler and Kit Hood, with Bill Parrott and Neil Hope, CBC, CBLT, Toronto, 25 June 1990.

A performance

[25]<u>Mud Pack Madness</u>, by Dawn and Marshall French, dir. Leo Burns, Kitchener Public Library, Kitchener, 11 May 1989.

Subsequent notes to the same source

After you have given the full information for a source in a note, you can use a shortened form, usually the author's name and the page number, in subsequent notes. If you use two works by the same author, add a comma and a short version of the title after the author's name so that a reader will know which source you are citing.

[26]Findley 82.

[27]Findley, <u>Lies</u> 37.

If you need to cite a particular source repeatedly, such as one literary work, mention in your first reference that subsequent references to the work will be found in the text. Then, for subsequent references, simply note the page, line, or act, scene, and line numbers in parentheses after your quotations or references.

[1]Kenneth Roberts, <u>Lydia Bailey</u> (New York: Doubleday, 1947) 14. All subsequent references to this work will appear in the text.

13e

Using common abbreviations

Many research essays and scholarly works use abbreviations, some of them Latin. The use of such abbreviations is somewhat discouraged today, but you may come across them in sources you consult. In your own papers, you should use only those abbreviations that are part of your citation style—unless your instructor specifies that you use others. Here is a list of the most commonly used abbreviations.

anon.	anonymous
bk., bks.	book, books
c., ca.	around a given date (*circa*)
cf.	compare (*confer*)
ch., chs.	chapter, chapters
col., cols.	column, columns
ed., eds	edition(s) or editor(s)
e.g.	for example (*exempli gratia*)
et al.	and others (*et alli*)
etc.	and so on (*et cetera*)
ff.	and the following pages
ibid.	in the same place (*ibidem*)
i.e.	that is (*id est*)
illus.	illustrated by or illustrations
l., ll.	line, lines
loc. cit.	in the same place cited (*loco citato*)
ms., mss.	manuscript, manuscripts
n., nn.	note, notes
n.d.	no publication date
no.	number
n.p.	no place or no publisher
n. pag.	no pagination
op. cit.	in the work cited (*opere citato*)
p., pp.	page, pages
q.v.	which see (*quod vide*)
rev.	revision, revised by, review
rpt.	reprint, reprinted
sec.	section
supp., supps.	supplement, supplements
trans.	translated by, translator
viz.	namely or that is (*videlicet*)

Taking inventory: documentation

Take time to look carefully at the parenthetical citations and/or notes and list of works cited (or references or bibliography) you have prepared for a research essay. Using the guidelines in this chapter, check each citation, note, and entry, noting (1) any whose form is incorrect, and (2) any source you are still unsure of how best to document. If you are keeping a writing log or a research log, enter your findings there. Check with your instructor on puzzling matters of documentation.

Making Sentence-Level Choices: Grammar

Constructing Grammatical Sentences

Understanding Pronoun Case

Using Verbs

Maintaining Agreement

Using Adjectives and Adverbs

14

Constructing Grammatical Sentences

All speakers learn the grammar of their language naturally as they learn to speak. This intuitive grasp of grammar allows us to say, "The bright red cardinal surprised me" rather than "Cardinal bright the surprised me red"—without even thinking about it. This ability to make meaningful sentences comes, in fact, very early to each of us and accounts for the fact that young children often produce sophisticated sentences out of the blue, without having to study or "learn" a system by which to produce them.

If we learn the basic grammar of language as we learn to speak, then why bother to study it? In the first place, though all speakers know the *basic* grammatical "rules," these rules can generate a very broad range of sentences, some of which will be much more effective than others. As someone who uses written language, you want not simply to write, but to write skilfully and effectively, and understanding grammatical structures can help you do so.

Furthermore, because language is so closely related to thought, studying our language patterns—our grammar—can give us insight into our own ways of thinking. If in some important sense we *are* what we say (and write), then examining the principles through which we express our meanings can help us understand ourselves as well as others.

In the context of this chapter, *grammar* is defined as the patterns into which words can be arranged to convey meanings.

Understanding the basic grammar of sentences

Put most simply, a **sentence** is a grammatically complete group of words that expresses a thought. To be grammatically complete, a group of words must contain two major structural components—a subject and a predicate. The **subject** identifies what the sentence is about, and the **predicate** asserts or asks something about the subject, or it tells the subject to do something.

SUBJECT	PREDICATE
We	sat down,
I	never eat blueberries.
Sam	is always unkind to strangers.
(You)	Clean your room.
The students at this university	seem especially motivated.
Puff, the magic dragon,	lived by the sea.

Some very brief sentences have one-word subjects and predicates (for example, *Time passes*) or even a one-word predicate with an implied or "understood" subject (for example, *Stop!*). Most sentences, however, contain additional words that expand the basic subject and predicate. In the last of the examples above, for instance, the subject might have been simply *Puff;* the words *the magic dragon* merely say more about the subject. Similarly, the predicate of that sentence could grammatically be *lived;* the words *by the sea* expand the predicate by telling us where Puff lived. No matter how many words a sentence contains, however, it can always be divided into two basic parts: a subject and a predicate.

Exercise 14.1

The following sentences are taken from the entry on the Canadian National Railways in Ralph Nader's *Canada Firsts.* Identify the subject and predicate in each sentence, underlining the subject once and the predicate twice. (Note: Answers to even-numbered items in this and many of the following exercises appear at the end of this book.)

EXAMPLE
The Canadian National Railways was created in 1919 as a Crown (government) Corporation.

1. Over the next four years the company took over five financially troubled railway systems.

2. On October 4, 1922 the separate lines were consolidated into one system with a new board of directors, with Sir Henry Thornton as president, forming the new transcontinental Canadian National Railways.

3. The company (now called CN Rail) is Canada's largest railroad and the longest railway system in North America, controlling 31 050 (50 000 kilometres) of track in Canada and the United States.

4. The company is one of the world's major transportation and communication systems.

Recognizing the parts of speech

If the basic parts of sentences are subjects and predicates, the central elements of subjects and predicates are nouns and verbs. For example:

```
 ┌ SUBJECT ┐ ┌──────── PREDICATE ────────┐
 |   NOUN VERB                            |
 The little girl ran quickly down the path.
```

Nouns and verbs are two of the eight **parts of speech**, one set of grammatical categories into which words may be classified. The other six parts of speech are pronouns, adjectives, adverbs, prepositions, conjunctions, and interjections. Many English words can function as more than one part of speech. Take the word *book*, for instance: when you *book a plane flight*, it is a verb; when you *take a good book to the beach*, it is a noun; and when you *have book knowledge*, it is an adjective.

The system of categorizing words by part of speech comes to English from Latin, where it was first set forth by the Roman grammarian Donatus in the 4th century C.E. The differences between Latin and English are many, of course, and the parts of speech system is in certain ways not as precise for English as it is for Latin. Many grammarians argue that students of English grammar should focus less on the parts of speech and more on the parts of a sentence. Even so, the parts of speech remain an important part of our grammatical vocabulary, and all dictionaries use them to label their entries. In this chapter we will see how the various parts of speech are used in sentences.

1. Recognizing verbs

The word *verb* comes from the Latin *verbum*, which simply means "word." As this history indicates, **verbs** are among the most important words, for they move the meaning of sentences along by showing action (*glance, jump*), occurrence (*become, happen*), or a state of being (*be, live*).

Verbs change form to show *time, person,* and *number.*

TIME	we *work*, we *worked*
PERSON	I *work*, she *works*
NUMBER	one person *works*, two people *work*

See Chapter 17 for a discussion of how verbs change form to show person and number. **Auxiliary verbs** (also known as **helping verbs**) combine with other verbs (often called **main verbs**) to create *verb phrases*. Auxiliaries include the forms of *be, do,* and *have,* which are also used as main verbs, and the words *can, could, may, might, must, shall, should, will,* and *would.*

> I *must get* some sleep tonight!
> You *can find* Professor Kinder during his office hours.

Chapter 16 provides a complete discussion of the forms and functions of verbs.

Exercise 14.2

Identify and underline the verbs in each of the following sentences.

EXAMPLE
Magda <u>should do</u> fine in Saturday's tennis match.

1. Her future does look bright.
2. The ice cream ran all over the table and the floor.
3. Over the next few days, I tapped about seventy maple trees.
4. One person can collect sap, a second might run the evaporator, and a third should finish the syrup.
5. A trip to the Yukon would be great.
6. On a crisp morning in early spring, a man walked alone through the forest.
7. The deer population rose drastically in the early 20th century, after the disappearance of the cougar and the wolf.
8. The bookcase will extend from floor to ceiling.
9. One Saturday morning my mother, an orthopedic surgeon, took my brother and me to the hospital.
10. The kitchen smelled like old fish.

2. Recognizing nouns

The word *noun* comes from the Latin *nomen*, which means "name." That is what **nouns** do: they name things. Nouns can name persons (*aviator, chef*), places (*lake, library*), things (*truck, suitcase*), or concepts (*happiness, balance*). **Proper nouns** name specific persons, places, things, or concepts: *Nitya, Dartmouth, Petro-Canada, Buddhism.* Proper nouns are capitalized. (See 40b for an explanation of which nouns are considered proper nouns.) **Collective nouns** name groups: *team, flock, navy.* (See 17d for more information about collective nouns.)

Most nouns can be changed from **singular** (one) to **plural** (more than one) by adding *-s* or *-es: tantrum, tantrums; box, boxes.* Some nouns, however, have irregular plural forms: *woman, women; alumnus, alumni; mouse, mice.* (See 33 for more information about forming plurals.) **Mass nouns** cannot be made plural because they name something that cannot easily be counted: *dust, peace, tranquillity, milk.*

Nouns can also take a **possessive** form to show ownership. You form the possessive by adding *-'s* to a singular noun and just an apostrophe to a plural noun: *the horse's owner, the boys' department.* (See 37a for more information about forming possessives.)

Nouns are often preceded by one of the **articles** *a, an,* or *the: a rocket, an astronaut, the launch.* Articles are also known as **noun markers** or **determiners.**

3. Recognizing pronouns

Pronouns function as nouns in sentences and often take the place of specific nouns, serving as short forms so that we do not have to repeat a noun that has already been mentioned. A specific noun that a pronoun replaces or refers to is called the **antecedent** of the pronoun. (See Chapters 17 and 19 for more about pronouns and antecedents.) In the following example, the antecedent of the pronoun *it* is *bus.*

The *bus* was already late, but *it* stopped for Charlotte.

You are already familiar with pronouns; we could scarcely speak or write without them. (The preceding sentence, for instance, includes the pronouns *you, we,* and *them.*) You may not, however, be familiar with all the categories of pronouns, which include the following:

Personal pronouns refer to specific persons or things.

PERSONAL   I, you, he, she, it, we, they
PRONOUNS

After the children ate, *they* went outside to play.

Each personal pronoun has several different forms (for example, *I, me, my, mine*) depending on how it functions in a sentence. (See Chapter 15 for a discussion of these forms and how to use them.)

Reflexive pronouns refer back to the subject of the sentence or clause in which they appear. They end in *-self* or *-selves.*

REFLEXIVE   myself, yourself, himself, herself, itself, oneself,
PRONOUNS   ourselves, yourselves, themselves

The seals sunned *themselves* on the warm rocks.

Intensive pronouns have the same form as reflexive pronouns. They are used to emphasize their antecedents.

She decided to paint the apartment *herself.*

Indefinitive pronouns do not refer to specific nouns, although they may refer to identifiable persons or things. They express the idea of "all," "some," "any," or "none." Indefinite pronouns are one of the largest categories of pronouns; the following list does not include all of them.

INDEFINITE   all, anybody, both, each, everything, few, most,
PRONOUNS   none, one, some, somebody

Somebody screamed when the lights went out.

Demonstrative pronouns identify or point to specific nouns.

DEMONSTRATIVE   this, that, these, those
PRONOUNS

These are Peter's books.

Interrogative pronouns are used to ask questions.

INTERROGATIVE   who, which, what
PRONOUNS

Who is teaching composition this term?

Relative pronouns introduce dependent clauses and "relate" the dependent clause to the rest of the sentence (see 14c4).

RELATIVE   who, which, that, what, whoever, whichever,
PRONOUNS

Margaret owns the car *that* is parked by the corner.

The interrogative pronoun *who* and the relative pronouns *who* and *whoever* have different forms depending on how they are used in a sentence. (See Chapter 15.)

Demonstrative pronouns, the possessive forms of personal pronouns, and some indefinite, interrogative, and relative pronouns can be used as adjectives. (See 14b4 for further discussion of pronouns used as adjectives.)

Reciprocal pronouns refer to the individual parts of a plural antecedent.

> RECIPROCAL   each other, one another
> PRONOUNS

The children began to quarrel with *one another* over their toys.

4. Recognizing adjectives

Adjectives modify (limit the meaning of) nouns or pronouns, usually by describing, identifying, or quantifying those words.

> The *red* Corvette ran off the road. [describes]
> It was *red*. [describes]
> *That* Corvette needs to be repaired. [identifies]
> We saw *several* Corvettes race by. [quantifies]

Most adjectives, like *red* in the examples above, are used to describe. In addition to their basic form, most descriptive adjectives have other forms that are used to make comparisons: *small, smaller, smallest; foolish, more foolish, most foolish, less foolish, least foolish.*

> This year's attendance was *smaller* than last year's.
> This year's attendance was the *smallest* in ten years.

Many of the pronouns introduced in 14b3 can also be used as adjectives to identify or quantify.

> *Those* are my favourite dogs. [pronoun]
> *Those* dogs should be on a leash. [adjective]

Kinds of pronouns that can be used as adjectives include personal (*her* idea), interrogative (*which* model should we buy?), relative (we're not sure *which* model we should buy), demonstrative (*this* book), and indefinite (*many* moons). Other kinds of adjectives that identify or quantify are articles (*a*, *an*, *the*) and numbers (*three*, *sixty-fifth*, *five thousand*).

Proper adjectives are adjectives that are formed from or related to proper nouns (*French*, *Freudian*). Proper adjectives are capitalized. (See 40b for more information about proper adjectives.)

Chapter 18 provides a complete discussion of the forms and functions of adjectives.

5. Recognizing adverbs

Adverbs modify verbs, adjectives, other adverbs, or entire clauses. You can recognize many adverbs by their -*ly* ending, though some adverbs do not have such an ending (*always*, *never*, *very*, *well*) and some words that end in -*ly* are not adverbs but adjectives (*friendly*, *lovely*, *likely*). Among the most common adverbs is *not*.

> Virginia and Kim *recently* visited Banff. [modifies the verb *visited*]
>
> They had an *unexpectedly* exciting trip. [modifies the adjective *exciting*]
>
> They *very* soon fell under the spell of the Rockies. [modifies the adverb *soon*]
>
> *Frankly*, they would have liked to stay another month. [modifies the independent clause that makes up the rest of the sentence]

Adverbs often answer one of the following questions: *how? when? where? why? to what extent?* In the first example sentence above, for instance, *recently* answers the question *when?* In the third sentence, *very* answers the question *to what extent?*

Many adverbs, like many adjectives, have different forms that are used in making comparisons: *forcefully, more forcefully, most forcefully, less forcefully, least forcefully.*

> That leadership candidate spoke *more forcefully* than her opponent.
>
> Of all the candidates, she speaks the *most forcefully.*

Conjunctive adverbs modify an entire clause and express the connection in meaning between that clause and the preceding clause (or sentence). Examples of conjunctive adverbs include *however, furthermore, therefore*, and *likewise*. (See 14b7 for more information about conjunctive adverbs.)

The most movable of all parts of speech, adverbs can often be placed in different positions in a sentence without changing or disrupting the meaning of the sentence. Notice in the following examples how placement creates only slight differences in emphasis:

> *Quickly* Charles ran for the door.

> Charles *quickly* ran for the door.
>
> Charles ran for the door *quickly.*

Chapter 18 provides a complete discussion of the forms and function of adverbs.

Exercise 14.3

Choose three paragraphs from a favourite piece of writing. Identify all the adjectives and adverbs you can find, and note the purpose each one serves.

6. Recognizing prepositions

Prepositions are important structural words that express relationships—in space, time, or other senses—between nouns or pronouns and other words in a sentence.

> We did not want to leave *during* the game.
>
> Careful writers read their own pages *with* infinite care.
>
> Drive *across* the bridge, go *down* the avenue *past* three stoplights, and then turn left *before* the gas station.

Here is a list of some common prepositions:

about	behind	from	over
above	below	in	past
across	beneath	inside	regarding
after	beside	into	since
against	between	like	through
along	beyond	near	toward
among	by	of	under
around	down	off	until
as	during	on	up
at	except	onto	with
before	for	out	without

In addition to the words in this list, some prepositions, called **compound prepositions**, are made up of more than one word: *according to, because of, by way of, due to, except for, in addition to, in front of, in place of, in spite of, instead of, next to, out of, with regard to.*

If you are ever in doubt about which preposition to use (for example, whether to write *agree to* or *agree with*), consult your dictionary. Your library may also have Frederich Wood's *English Prepositional Idioms*, a dictionary devoted entirely to prepositions.

A *prepositional phrase* is made of a preposition together with the noun or pronoun it connects to the rest of the sentence. For more information about prepositional phrases, see 14c3.

Exercise 14.4

Identify and underline the prepositions in each of the following sentences.

EXAMPLE
<u>In</u> the centre <u>of</u> the cabin stood an old wood-burning stove.

1. A gust of wind blew through the window, upsetting the vase on the table.
2. She ran swiftly through the brush, across the beach, and into the sea.
3. A few minutes past noon the police arrived at the scene.
4. Far from sight, beyond the horizon, our ship heads toward the open sea.
5. The book, by Anne Morrow Lindbergh, describes the flight the Lindberghs made to the Orient by way of the Great Circle Route.

7. Recognizing conjunctions

Conjunctions connect other words or groups of words to one another. There are four kinds of conjunctions: coordinating conjunctions, correlative conjunctions, subordinating conjunctions, and conjunctive adverbs.

Coordinating conjunctions (*and, but, or, nor, for, so, yet*) join equivalent structures—two or more nouns, pronouns, verbs, adjectives, adverbs, prepositions, conjunctions, phrases, or clauses.

Marika plays violin *and* viola.

Moberley's performances are comedic *but* moving.

Please print *or* type the information on the application form.

Her work demanded much time, *yet* she was able to join the team.

Nor, for, and *so* can connect independent clauses only.

He did not have much money, *nor* did he know how to get any.

The student glanced anxiously at the clock, *for* only twenty minutes remained in the exam period.

Yusha worked two shifts on Thursday, *so* she can take Friday off.

Correlative conjunctions (*both ... and, either ... or, just as ... so, neither ...*

nor, not only … but [also], whether … or) also join equivalent words or word groups. See 27b for more information on the principle of equivalency or balance in the use of correlative conjunctions.

> *Both* W.H. Auden *and* William Carlos Williams wrote poems about Bruegel's *Fall of Icarus*.

> Jeff *not only* applied for a summer job *but also* volunteered to work at the community centre.

Subordinating conjunctions introduce dependent clauses and signal the relationship between the dependent clause and another clause, usually an independent clause. For instance, in the following sentence the subordinating conjunction *while* signals a time relationship, letting us know that the two events in the sentence happen simultaneously.

> Sweat ran down my face *while* I frantically searched for my child.

Following are some of the most common subordinating conjunctions:

after	before	since	unless
although	even though	so that	until
as	if	than	when
as if	in order that	that	where
because	once	though	while

> *Unless* sales improve dramatically, the company will soon be bankrupt.

> My grandmother began travelling *after* she sold her house.

Conjunctive adverbs connect one independent clause (or sentence) to another. As their name suggests, conjunctive adverbs can be considered both adverbs and conjunctions because they modify the second clause in addition to expressing the connection in meaning between it and the preceding clause. Like many other adverbs and unlike other conjunctions, they can be moved to different positions in a clause without changing or disrupting the meaning of the clause. Look at the following sentences:

> The cider tasted bitter; *however,* each of us drank a tall glass of it.

> The cider tasted bitter; each of us, *however,* drank a tall glass of it.

> The cider tasted bitter. Each of us drank a tall glass of it, *however.*

Commonly used conjunctive adverbs including the following:

also	besides	finally
anyway	certainly	futhermore

however	moreover	similarly
incidentally	namely	still
indeed	nevertheless	then
instead	next	therefore
likewise	now	thus
meanwhile	otherwise	undoubtedly

Independent clauses connected by a conjunctive adverb must be separated by a semicolon or a period, not just a comma (see 21c1).

> Carmen grabbed the ball and ran down the street; *consequently,* the stickball game came to an abrupt end.

> Some think the CBC is a Canadian jewel; others, *however,* consider it over-funded.

Exercise 14.5

Identify and underline the coordinating, correlative, and subordinating conjunctions and the conjunctive adverbs in each of the following sentences.

EXAMPLE
David used his sleeping bag <u>even though</u> the cabin was furnished with sheets <u>and</u> blankets.

1. When we arrived at the pond, we saw many children playing there.

2. Pokey is an outside cat; nevertheless, she greets me at the front door each night as I arrive home.

3. The colt walked calmly, for he seemed to know he would win the race.

4. The shops along the waterfront were open, but business was slow.

5. The Tetraults were forced to buy a new house because radon had rendered their old house uninhabitable.

6. The office manager found imperfections not only in everything I did but also in the work every other employee did.

7. I did not know whether to laugh or cry after I realized my mistake.

8. Exhausted workers operated the pumps until their arms ached.

9. Although I live in a big city, my neighbourhood has enough trees and raccoons to make me feel as if I live in the suburbs.

10. Neither Henry nor Rachel could understand the invitation; therefore, they did not respond to it.

8. Recognizing interjections

Interjections are words that express surprise or emotion: *oh, ouch, ah, hey.* Interjections often stand alone, as fragments, and even when they are included in a sentence, they are not related grammatically to the rest of the sentence. They are used mostly in speaking; in writing they are used mostly in dialogue.

> *"Bravo! Encore!"* The watching crowd cheered as the performers began to leave the stage.

> We tiptoed cautiously through the dark basement until—*oh, no!*—we saw what lay under the pile of discarded clothing in the corner.

Recognizing the parts of a sentence

While the parts of speech system helps us to understand the grammar of sentences, a sentence is not just made up of individual words. Every sentence has a grammatical pattern or structure, and the parts of speech are simply the categories of words used to create this structure.

Look again at the word *book.* In 14b we saw that *book* can function as various parts of speech—as a noun, an adjective, and a verb.

> NOUN
> A book is always a welcome gift.

> ADJECTIVE
> Henry has more book knowledge than wisdom.

> VERB
> May I book a flight to Winnipeg?

Notice that *book* has exactly the same form for each part of speech; it would be impossible to recognize its meaning outside the context of a particular sentence. In fact, even in a sentence a word that can be categorized as a certain part of speech can function in more than one way.

> SUBJECT
> This book looks great!

> DIRECT OBJECT
> I need a certain book.

Book acts as a noun in both of these sentences, yet in the first it serves as the subject of the verb *looks,* and in the second it serves as the direct object of the verb *need*. Knowing the word's part of speech tells only part of the story; we have to recognize the part it plays in the pattern or structure of the sentence.

Most English sentences follow one of five basic patterns: (1) subject/ verb, (2) subject/verb/subject complement, (3) subject/verb/direct object, (4) subject/verb/indirect object/direct object, and (5) subject/verb/direct object/object complement. For example:

       S   V
1. Babies cry.

       S   V   SC
2. Babies seem fragile.

       S   V   DO
3. Babies drink milk.

       S   V   IO   DO
4. Babies give grandparents pleasure.

       S   V   DO   OC
5. Parents consider babysitters essential.

This section examines the essential parts of a sentence—subjects, predicates, objects, complements, phrases, and clauses—and provides practice in using them to construct sentences of various kinds.

1. Recognizing subjects

As explained in 14a, almost every sentence has a stated subject, which identifies whom or what the sentence is about. The **simple subject** consists of one or more nouns or pronouns; the **complete subject** consists of the simple subject with all its modifiers. Depending on the kinds of modifiers, subjects can be as plain as one word or far more complex. The following examples show the complete subjects in italics, with the simple subjects labelled *ss*:

    ss
Baseball is a summer game.

           ss
Sailing over the fence, the ball crashed through Mr. Wilson's window.

    ss
Stadiums with real grass are hard to find these days.

    ss
Those who sit in the bleachers have the most fun.

A **compound subject** contains two or more nouns or pronouns joined by a coordinating conjunction (*and, but, or*) or a correlative conjunction (*both ... and, either ... or, neither ... nor, not only ... but also*).

> *Carter and Alomar* destroy pitchers.
> *Both he and Alomar* destroy pitchers.

In imperative sentences, which express requests or commands, the subject *you* is implied but not stated.

> *(You)* Keep your eye on the ball.

In English sentences the simple subject usually comes before the predicate, or verb, but not always. Sometimes writers reverse this order for effect.

> Up to the plate stepped *Casey*.

In questions, the subject usually appears between the auxiliary verb and the main verb.

> Did *Casey* save the game?

In sentences beginning with *there* or *here* followed by a form of the verb *be* (*is, are, was, were, have been, will be,* and so on), the subject always follows the verb. *There* and *here* are never the subject.

> Here is the sad *ending* of the poem.

Exercise 14.6

Identify the complete subject and the simple subject in each of the following sentences. Underline the complete subject once and the simple subject twice.

EXAMPLE
A fresh, moist breeze kicked up at just the right time.

1. The writing of Lee Maracle has received much critical acclaim.
2. A sixty-centimetre snowfall on April 13 was most unexpected.
3. Decisions about courses and majors should be the students'.
4. Anyone who knows Gabriel seems to like him.
5. Some women worried about osteoporosis take calcium supplements.

2. Recognizing predicates

In addition to a subject, every sentence has a predicate that asserts or asks something about the subject or tells the subject to do something (as explained in 14a). The "hinge" or key word of most predicates is a verb. As we saw in 14b1, a verb can include auxiliary verbs (as in this sentence, where *can* is an auxiliary and *include* is the main verb). The **simple predicate** of a sentence is the main verb and any auxiliaries; the **complete predicate** also includes any modifiers of the verb and any objects or complements and their modifiers. In the following examples, the complete predicates are italicized and the simple predicates are labelled *sp:*

Several of my friends and I *have become interested in literature of the Holocaust.*

She *originally comes from Moose Jaw, Saskatchewan.*

Both of us *are planning to major in history.*

A **compound predicate** contains two or more verbs that have the same subject and are usually joined by a coordinating or correlative conjunction.

> The student *shut the book, put it back on the shelf, and sighed.*
>
> The Old Order Mennonites *neither drive cars nor use electricity.*

On the basis of how they function in predicates, verbs can be divided into three categories: linking, transitive, and intransitive.

Linking verbs

A **linking verb** links, or joins, the subject with a **subject complement**, a word or word group that identifies or describes the subject. If it identifies the subject, the complement is a noun or pronoun (and is sometimes called a **predicate noun**). If it describes the subject, the complement is an adjective (and is sometimes called a **predicate adjective**). In the following two sentences, for example, *an investment banker* is a predicate noun and *rich* is a predicate adjective:

Christine is an investment banker.

She is rich.

The forms of *be,* when used as main verbs rather than as auxiliary verbs, are linking verbs (like *are* in this sentence). Other verbs, such as *appear, become, feel, grow, look, make, seem, smell,* and *sound,* can also function as linking verbs, depending on the sense of the sentence.

> Our mayor's famed contentiousness has become tedious.

> His political rivals seem pleased.

Transitive and intransitive verbs

If a verb is not a linking verb, it is either transitive or intransitive. A **transitive verb** expresses action that is directed toward a noun or pronoun, called the **direct object** of the verb.

> I will analyze three poems.

A direct object answers the question *what?* or *whom?* about the transitive verb. In the preceding example sentence, the subject and verb alone do not express a complete thought: *what* will I analyze? The direct object completes the thought.

A direct object may be followed by an **object complement**, a word or words that identifies or describes the direct object.

> I consider Dennis Lee's poetry delightful.

> His books and records have made Lee a celebrity.

A transitive verb may also be followed by an **indirect object**, which tells to whom or to what, or for whom or for what, the verb's action is done. You might say that the indirect object is the recipient of the direct object.

> *Jelly Belly* has given many children considerable pleasure.

> Canada owes Dennis Lee something.

An **intransitive verb** expresses action that is not directed toward an object or is directed toward an object that is not mentioned. Therefore, an intransitive verb does not have a direct object.

> The Blue Jays persevered.

$$\overline{\quad} S \overline{\quad}\overline{\quad} V \overline{\quad}$$
Their fans watched hopefully.

In the preceding sentences, the action of the verb *persevered* has no object (it makes no sense to ask *persevered what?* or *persevered whom?*), and the action of the verb *watched* is directed toward an object that is implied but not expressed.

Some verbs that express action can be only transitive or intransitive, but most such verbs can be used both ways, with or without a direct object.

$$\overline{\qquad\qquad} S \overline{\qquad\qquad}\overline{\quad} V \overline{\quad}\overline{\quad} DO \overline{\qquad}$$
The premier from Alberta opened the discussions.

$$\overline{\quad} S \overline{\quad}\overline{\quad} V \overline{\quad}$$
The door opened silently.

Exercise 14.7

Identify and underline the predicate in each of the following sentences. Then identify each verb as linking, transitive, or intransitive. Finally, identify all subject and object complements and all direct and indirect objects.

EXAMPLE

$$\overline{\qquad} V \overline{\qquad}\overline{\quad} DO \overline{\quad}\overline{\quad} OC \overline{\quad}$$
We considered city life unbearable.

1. Manitoba is dry in the summer.
2. The committee appointed Kayla chair.
3. The real victims become the taxpayers.
4. The price of apples will rise again.
5. Advertisers promise uncritical consumers the world.

3. Recognizing and using phrases

A **phrase** is a group of words that lacks either a subject or a predicate or both. Phrases function in useful ways to add information to a sentence or shape it effectively. Look at the following sentence:

The new law will restrict smoking *in most public places.*

The basic subject and predicate of this sentence is simply *the new law will restrict smoking;* additional information is provided by the prepositional phrase *in most public places.* The phrase functions in the sentence as an adverb, telling *where* smoking will be restricted. This section will discuss the various kinds of phrases: noun, verb, prepositional, verbal, absolute, and appositive.

Noun phrases

Made up of a noun and all its modifiers, a **noun phrase** can function in a sentence as a subject, object, or complement.

┌──────── SUBJECT ────────┐
Delicious, gooey peanut butter is surprisingly healthful.

┌ OBJECT ┐
Dieters prefer *green salad.*

┌COMPLEMENT┐
A tuna sandwich is *a popular lunch.*

Verb phrases

A main verb and its auxiliary verbs make up a **verb phrase**, which functions in a sentence in only one way: as a predicate.

François *had been depressed* for some time.

His problem *might have been caused* by tension between his parents.

Prepositional phrases

A **prepositional phrase** includes a preposition, a noun or pronoun called the **object of the preposition**, and any modifiers of the object. Prepositional phrases function as either adjectives or adverbs.

ADJECTIVE   Our house *in Whitehorse* was a cabin.

ADVERB   *From Lake Kawagama* you can clearly see the northern lights.

Exercise 14.8

Combine each of the following pairs of sentences into one sentence by making the second sentence into one or more prepositional phrases.

EXAMPLE
The Greeks won a tremendous victory. They were fighting the Persians.

The Greeks won a tremendous victory *over the Persians.*

1. Socrates was condemned. His fellow citizens made up the jury that condemned him.

2. Socrates faced death. He had no fear.

3. The playwright Aristophanes wrote a comedy. Its subject was Socrates.

4. Everyone thought Socrates was crazy. Only a few followers disagreed.

5. Today Socrates is honoured. He founded Western philosophy.

Verbal phrases

Verbals are verb forms that do not function as verbs in sentences. Instead, they function as nouns, adjectives, and adverbs. There are three kinds of verbals: participles, gerunds, and infinitives.

The **present participle** is the -ing form of a verb: *dreaming, being, seeing.* The **past participle** of most verbs ends in -ed: *dreamed, watched.* But some verbs have an irregular past participle: *been, seen, hidden, gone.* (See 16b for a list of irregular past participles.) Participles function as *adjectives* in sentences.

The child's cries disturbed his *sleeping* parents.

The cryptographers deciphered the *hidden* meaning in the message.

The **gerund** has the same form as the present participle but functions in sentences as a *noun.*

SUBJECT   *Writing* takes practice.

OBJECT   More than anything, my sister loves *canoeing.*

The **infinitive** is the *to* form of a verb: *to dream, to be, to see.* An infinitive can function in a sentence as a noun, adjective, or adverb.

NOUN   She wanted *to write.*

ADJECTIVE   They had no more time *to waste.*

ADVERB   The corporation was ready *to expand.*

A verbal can never stand alone as the verb of a sentence because it is a **nonfinite** (or "unfinished") **verb.** Take the present participle *barking,* for instance. *The terrier barking* is not a sentence; to make it a sentence you need to change the verbal to a verb by using one or more auxiliaries: *The terrier is barking* or *The terrier had been barking.* The verb phrases *is barking* and *had been barking* are **finite verbs,** which do not need any other auxiliary to function as verbs in a sentence.

Verbal phrases are made up of a verbal and any modifiers, objects, or complements. Let us turn now to examine the forms and functions of the various kinds of verbal phrases.

Participial phrases

Participial phrases consist of a present participle or past participle with any modifiers, objects, or complements. Participial phrases always function as adjectives in sentences.

Thrilled with his performance, Elvis awaited the scores.

The couple *standing proudly* in the front row are Stojko's parents.

Notice that many participial phrases may appear in different places in a sentence, as long as it is clear which word they modify (see Chapter 23). Decisions about where to place participial phrases must usually be made within the larger context of a piece of writing; the choice often depends on the rhythm or emphasis the writer wants to achieve.

Fearing that I would be left alone, I quickly followed the group.

I followed the group, *fearing that I would be left alone.*

Gerund phrases

Gerund phrases consist of a gerund with any modifiers, objects, or complements: *hoping for a victory, critical thinking.* In sentences, gerund phrases function as nouns—as a subject, a subject complement, a direct object, an indirect object, or an object of a preposition.

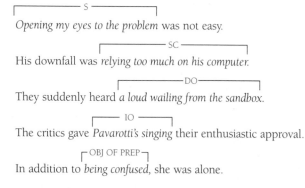

Opening my eyes to the problem was not easy.

His downfall was *relying too much on his computer.*

They suddenly heard *a loud wailing from the sandbox.*

The critics gave *Pavarotti's singing* their enthusiastic approval.

In addition to *being confused,* she was alone.

Infinitive phrases

Infinitive phrases consist of an infinitive with any modifiers, objects, or complements: *to be happy, to see a show tonight.* They can function as nouns, adjectives, or adverbs.

```
         ┌──── NOUN/SC ────┐
My goal is to complete a triathlon.
```

```
                    ┌──── ADJECTIVE ────┐
A party would be a good way to end the term.
```

```
┌──── ADVERB ────┐
To perfect a draft, always proofread carefully.
```

Notice that infinitive phrases used as adverbs, as in the last example above, may appear in different places in a sentence as long as it is clear which word they modify (see Chapter 23). For example, *To perfect a draft* could be moved to the end of its sentence. As with participial phrases, the placement should depend on the effect it creates within the larger context of the piece of writing.

Exercise 14.9

Identify each participial phrase, gerund phrase, and infinitive phrase in the following sentences, and specify which part of speech it functions as in the sentence.

EXAMPLE

```
┌──── PARTICIPIAL-ADJ ────┐
Pacing the hall with impatience, I wished my friends would arrive.
```

1. Buying her first Saab was the happiest moment in Terry's life.
2. After four years of careful saving, he got his computer.
3. The solution was to warn Georgina: unless she worked to improve her behaviour, she could not continue to attend our school.
4. Raised in Alberta, I spent plenty of time exploring nature.
5. Sitting by the window and listening to the wind blowing through the trees, I feel happy and lucky to be alive.

Absolute phrases

An **absolute phrase** consists of a noun or pronoun and a participle, together with any objects or modifiers. It modifies an entire sentence rather than a particular word. Absolutes may appear almost anywhere in a sentence and are always set off from the rest of the sentence with punctuation, usually commas. (See Chapter 34.)

I jumped onto my bike and took off, *tires screeching in protest.*

My fears laid to rest, I climbed into the plane for my first solo flight.

Appositive phrases
A noun phrase that renames the noun or pronoun that immediately precedes it is called an **appositive phrase.**

Alice Munro, *the celebrated writer,* will appear on campus tonight.

That's my sister, *the skinny kid in tights.*

Exercise 14.10

Read the following sentences, and identify and label all of the prepostional, verbal, absolute, and appositive phrases. Notice that one kind of phrase may appear within another kind.

EXAMPLE

┌──── ABSOLUTE ────┐
His voice breaking, Ed thanked us for the award.

1. Approaching the rope, I suddenly fell into the icy pond.
2. To listen to k.d. lang is sheer delight.
3. The figure outlined against the sky seemed unable to move.
4. Floating on my back, I ignored my practice requirements.
5. Naomi stood still, her fingers clutching the fence.
6. Lorenzo, a sensitive child, was filled with a mixture of awe and excitement.
7. Shocked into silence, they kept their gaze fixed on the odd creature.
8. Basking in the sunlight, I had been lost somewhere in a reminiscence of golden birch trees.
9. Susan, the leader of the group, was reluctant to give up any authority.
10. Despite Ernie's complaints, Bert's favourite form of recreation is taking a nap.

Using phrases to shape and expand sentences
Phrases provide valuable tools for shaping or expanding sentences. Not only do they bring in additional information, but they can help you to emphasize certain parts of a sentence and de-emphasize others. In this way they help to distinguish the main idea of the sentence from the extra details. Look, for instance, at the following sentence:

Jupiter crashed through the tomato vines with the remains of a felt hat in his mouth.

– JOHN CHEEVER, "The Country Husband"

Cheever might have expressed this sentence in many other ways. For instance:

Jupiter crashed through the tomato vines. He had the remains of a felt hat in his mouth.

Crashing through the tomato vines, Jupiter held the remains of a felt hat in his mouth.

In the first possibility, turning some of the prepositional phrases into a second sentence separates the statement into two parts and thus weakens or at least changes the impact it has on readers—perhaps because we see the crash and the torn hat at some chronological distance from each other. In the second possibility, turning the verb of the original sentence into a participle puts greater emphasis on what was in the dog's mouth than on his crash through the vines and thus describes a slightly different scene.

As you write sentences, you should be alert to how you can use phrases to present your ideas and bits of information in particular ways. This consideration is especially important when you are revising. As you read over a draft, consider each sentence individually to see if phrases could help you add necessary detail, make your point clearer, or emphasize one idea instead of another.

Following are some examples of how some student writers used various kinds of phrases to shape and expand particular sentences.

NOUN PHRASE

That car will never win the race.

That battered, valveless, bent-up bone-shaker will never win the race.

PARTICIPIAL PHRASE

The subway was anything but inviting. It was overheated and packed with commuters.

Overheated and packed with commuters, the subway was anything but inviting.

ABSOLUTE PHRASE

The dictator's long period of absolute rule was over, and he stepped into his limousine and disappeared.

> *His long period of absolute rule over,* the dictator stepped into his limousine and disappeared.

Positioning phrases

As noted earlier, many phrases can be placed at the beginning, in the middle, or at the end of a sentence, as the following examples illustrate:

Calling on every ounce of energy, Jo sprinted toward the finish line.

Jo, *calling on every ounce of energy,* sprinted toward the finish line.

Jo sprinted toward the finish line, *calling on every ounce of energy.*

The phrase in these examples is a participial phrase that modifies *Jo.* While changing the placement of the phrase does not alter the basic meaning of the sentence, it does affect rhythm and emphasis, most notably in the third example by changing the important concluding words of the sentence.

Prepositional, infinitive, and absolute phrases can also occupy more than one sentence position. There are no absolute guidelines for placement, but always (1) check to see that the phrase clearly modifies any word it should modify (see Chapter 23), and (2) read the sentence in the context of the surrounding sentences to see which placement seems most effective (see 28b).

Exercise 14.11

Use a participial, infinitive, gerund, absolute, or appositive phrase to combine each of the following pairs of sentences into one sentence.

EXAMPLE
He complained constantly. This habit irritated his co-workers.
His constant complaining irritated his co-workers.

1. Anita Best gave a concert at the university. She is a folklorist and performer.

2. We waited to go through customs. Our passports were clutched in our hands.

3. She visited an old friend in New Brunswick. This trip lifted her spirits.

4. Michael had his ear pierced. He did this because it annoyed his parents.

5. The protesters were carrying their banners. They headed down the street.

4. Recognizing and using clauses

A **clause** is a group of words containing a subject and a predicate. There are two kinds of clauses: independent and dependent. **Independent clauses** (also known as **main clauses**) can stand alone as complete sentences.

The window is open.

The batter swung at the ball.

Independent clauses may be joined with a coordinating conjunction and a comma. For more on joining independent clauses, see 14b7.

The window is open, *so* we'd better be quiet.

The batter swung at the ball, *and* the umpire called her out.

Like independent clauses, **dependent clauses** (also known as **subordinate clauses**) contain a subject and a predicate. They cannot stand alone as complete sentences, however, for they begin with a subordinating word—a subordinating conjunction (see 14b7) or a relative pronoun (see 14b3). The subordinating word connects the dependent clause to an independent clause. Each of the following sentences, for instance, consists of one brief independent clause.

The window is open.

The room feels cool.

You might choose to combine these two independent clauses with a comma and coordinating conjunction: *The window is open, and the room feels cool.* But you could also combine the two clauses by turning one into a dependent clause.

Because the window is open, the room feels cool.

In this combination the subordinating conjunction *because* transforms the independent clause *the window is open* into a dependent clause. In doing so, it indicates a causal relationship between the two clauses.

Dependent clauses function in sentences as nouns, adjectives, or adverbs.

Noun clauses

Noun clauses can function as subjects, direct objects, subject complement, or objects of prepositions. Thus they are always contained within another clause rather than simply attached to it, as adjective and adverb clauses are. They usually begin with a relative pronoun (*that, which, what,* *who, whom, whose, whatever, whoever, whomever, whichever)* or with *when, where, whether, why* or *how.*

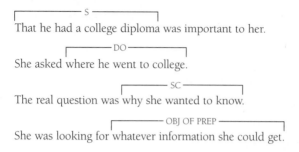

That he had a college diploma was important to her. [S]

She asked where he went to college. [DO]

The real question was why she wanted to know. [SC]

She was looking for whatever information she could get. [OBJ OF PREP]

Notice that in each of these sentences the noun clause is an integral part of the independent clause that makes up the sentence; for example, in the second sentence the independent clause is not just *She asked* but *She asked where he went to college.*

Adjective clauses

Adjective clauses modify nouns and pronouns in another clause. Usually, they follow immediately after the words they modify. Most adjective clauses begin with the relative pronouns *who, whom, whose, that,* or *which.* Some begin with *when, where,* or *why.*

Zoe's decision, *which astonished everyone,* was to have a baby.

Aren't babies devious little creatures *who cry a great deal?*

All parents experience moments *when they feel that way.*

Sometimes the relative pronoun introducing an adjective clause may be deleted, as in the following example:

That is one book [that] I intend to read.

Adverb clauses

Adverb clauses modify verbs, adjectives, or other adverbs. They always begin with a subordinating conjunction (see 14b7). Like adverbs, they usually tell why, when, where, how, under what conditions, or to what extent.

We hiked *where there were few other hikers.*

My backpack felt heavier *than it ever had.*

I climbed as swiftly *as I could under the weight of my backpack.*

Like adverbs, adverb clauses can usually be placed in different positions in a sentence without affecting the meaning.

If you look up from the highway, you will see Hollyburn Mountain.

You will see Hollyburn Mountain *if you look up from the highway.*

Exercise 14.12

Identify the independent and dependent clauses and any subordinating conjunctions and relative pronouns in each of the following sentences.

EXAMPLE

┌─────── DEPENDENT CLAUSE ───────┐

If I were going on a really long hike, I would carry a lightweight stove. [*If* is a subordinating conjunction.]

1. The aid workers who went to Somalia saw unspeakable things.

2. As a potential customer entered the store, Tony nervously attempted to retreat to the safety of the back room.

3. The names they called my grandmother still haunt me.

4. When she was deemed old enough to understand, she was told the truth, and she finally knew why her father had left home.

5. Though most of my grandfather's farm was wooded, there were also great expanses of green lawns and quiet, trickling streams.

6. Abe and Sasha decided to make a chocolate cream pie, which was Timothy's favourite.

7. When they asked him to accompany them, he became very excited, but he also felt some trepidation.

8. Public speaking was easier than she had expected.

9. After she finished the painting, Hongxing cleaned the brushes.

10. I could see that he was very tired, but I had to ask him a few questions.

Using clauses to shape and expand sentences

Like phrases, clauses are an important means of shaping sentences in particular ways or expanding sentences into more varied or interesting ones.

For example, look at the following sentences, each of which consists of one independent clause expressing one idea:

Sarah's parents disliked her boyfriend. She was determined to marry him.

Now look at how clauses can be used to combine these ideas in one sentence.

1. Although her parents disliked her boyfriend, Sarah was determined to marry him.
2. Sarah's parents disliked her boyfriend, whom she was determined to marry.
3. Sarah's parents disliked her boyfriend, but she was determined to marry him.

In sentence 1, putting the information about the parents' dislike of the boyfriend into a dependent adverb clause gives less emphasis to that idea and more emphasis to the idea expressed in the subject and predicate—Sarah's determination to marry him. In sentence 2, on the other hand, the idea of Sarah's determination is de-emphasized by being placed in a dependent adjective clause. Finally, in sentence 3, the two ideas are given equal emphasis by being expressed in two independent clauses connected by the coordinating conjunction *but*.

As you write sentences, and especially when you are revising a draft, pay attention to how you can use clauses to add details or emphasis to your ideas and information. Following are some examples of how student writers used various kinds of clauses to shape and expand particular sentences.

NOUN CLAUSE

Charles later learned the truth.
Charles later learned *what Vinnie had known for years.*

ADJECTIVE CLAUSE

Everything was swept away.
Everything *that he valued most in life* was swept away.
My childhood seemed entirely happy. I grew up on a large farm.
My childhood, *which was spent on a large farm*, seemed entirely happy.

ADVERB CLAUSE

The children loved the snow, and they rolled and played in it.
Because they loved the snow, the children rolled and played in it.

Positioning clauses

Like many phrases, most *adverb* clauses can be placed at the beginning, in the middle, or at the end of a sentence.

> *If nothing goes wrong,* the furniture will be delivered tomorrow.
>
> The furniture, *if nothing goes wrong,* will be delivered tomorrow.
>
> The furniture will be delivered tomorrow *if nothing goes wrong.*

Changing the position of the adverb clause *if nothing goes wrong* does not affect the basic meaning of the sentence, but it affects the rhythm and the emphasis by highlighting or downplaying the possibility that something could go wrong. For more information about positioning clauses within sentences, see 23a and 28b.

Exercise 14.13

Examine a piece of writing you've completed recently, and identify independent and dependent clauses, subordinating conjunctions, and relative pronouns. Do you notice many dependent clauses? Would the essay be improved if dependent clauses were used more frequently?

Classifying sentences

Like words, sentences can be classified in several different ways: grammatically, functionally, or rhetorically. Grammatical classification groups sentences according to how many and what types of clauses they contain. Functional classification groups them according to whether they make a statement, ask a question, issue a command, or express an exclamation. Rhetorical classification groups them according to where in the sentence the main idea is located. Understanding these methods of classification can help you analyze and assess your sentences as you write and revise.

1. Classifying sentences grammatically

Grammatically, sentences fall into one of the following types: *simple sentences, compound sentences, complex sentences,* and *compound-complex sentences.* You have already seen most of these types in the section on clauses.

Simple sentences

A **simple sentence** consists of one independent clause and no dependent clause. The subject or the predicate of the independent clause, or both, may be compound.

> The trailer is surrounded by a wooden deck.
>
> My friend and I started a penny collection for the food bank.
>
> At the restaurant, the owner and her assistant prepare the food, serve the food, and clear the tables.

Compound sentences

A **compound sentence** consists of two or more independent clauses and no dependent clause. The clauses may be joined by a comma and a coordinating conjunction, by a comma and a correlative conjunction, or by a semicolon. (See Chapters 21, 26, 34, and 35.)

> Occasionally, a car goes up the dirt trail, and dust flies everywhere.
>
> Not only are the adults unable to relax there, but their conflicting interests create even more tension among them.
>
> George is obsessed with soccer; he eats, breathes, and lives the game.

Complex sentences

A **complex sentence** consists of one independent clause with at least one dependent clause.

> ┌──────────────── DEPENDENT CLAUSE ────────────────
> I am surprised that so many children at my son's day-care regularly turn neu-
> ────────────────────────┐
> tral objects into weapons.

> ┌────── DEPENDENT CLAUSE ──────┐
> People who support the Parti Québécois don't necessarily support sovereignty.

> ┌── DEPENDENT CLAUSE ──┐
> As I awaited my interview, I sat with other nervous candidates.

Notice that when a dependent clause comes before the independent clause, as in the last example above, it is usually set off with a comma (see 34a).

Compound-complex sentences

A **compound-complex sentence** consists of two or more independent clauses and at least one dependent clause.

```
┌─ IND CL ─┐ ┌──── IND CL ────┐ ┌──────── DEP CL ────────┐
```
We liked Joe, for he was a kind man who was nice to everyone.
```
┌──────────── IND CL ────────────┐      ┌──────── IND CL ────────┐
```
Sister Lucy tried her best to help Martin, but he was an undisciplined boy
```
┌──────────── DEP CL ────────────┐
```
who drove many teachers to despair.

2. Classifying sentences functionally

In terms of function, sentences can be classified as **declarative** (making a statement), **interrogative** (asking a question), **imperative** (giving a command), or **exclamatory** (expressing strong feeling).

DECLARATIVE   Jennika plays cello for the symphony orchestra.

INTERROGATIVE   Has she performed in Europe?

IMPERATIVE   Get me a ticket for her next performance.

EXCLAMATORY   What a talented musician she is!

3. Classifying sentences rhetorically

In addition to permitting functional and grammatical classifications, some sentences can be classified rhetorically as either cumulative or periodic sentences. Such a classification is important because the two patterns create very different rhythms and emphases. Learning to identify them takes you well on the way toward incorporating such sentences in your own writing.

Cumulative sentences begin with the subject and predicate containing the main thought and then build on this foundation with a series of phrases or clauses. When they are constructed skilfully, cumulative sentences create a strong rhythm and make for easy, often exciting, reading. Look at the following examples (the second example includes two cumulative sentences):

> He stood before her, proud in his black bowler hat, his long white silk scarf knotted loosely and flowing down over his shiny black leather jacket.

> I could still feel the way I'd moved with the horse, the ripple of muscle through both the striving bodies, uniting as one. I could still feel the irons round my feet, the calves of my legs gripping, the balance, the nearness to my head of the stretching brown neck, the mane blowing in my mouth, my hands on the reins.

> — DICK FRANCIS

In contrast, **periodic sentences** save the subject and verb of the independent clause until the end, building toward them and making the reader wait for the full meaning or significance to emerge.

> Pulling my tie off and flinging it haphazardly onto the sofa, stretching and sighing with the ease of homecoming, listening to the familiar silences of the place, I felt—as usual—the welcoming peace unlock the gritting tensions of my outside world.

> Though we long for the easy answer, the simple solution, the quick rationalization, only the harsh truth shall set us free.

Although cumulative sentences are more common in most modern prose than are periodic sentences, the ability to construct both will give you stylistic options that will strengthen your writing. For more information on such sentence types, see 28c.

Exercise 14.14

The following sentence is from an essay by Erika Ritter. Try rewriting the sentence as a series of short sentences. Then try combining these short sentences in your own way.

> Working out is, as we know, distasteful, disheartening, and curiously lonely work, carried out in overheated, overpriced, and overcrowded studios traditionally located over stores with windows full of chic clothes that are still too skinny for you to get into, despite the fact that you've been working out four times a week for almost a year now, with other people's sweaty elbows flapping in your face and other people's white-leather Reeboks whacking up against the bridge of your nose as you lie on the floor performing painful leg raises, going for the burn while you dream almost deliriously of going for the Aspirin.
>
> — ERIKA RITTER, "Working Out Reworked"

Taking inventories: sentences

Examine a piece of writing you have done recently and identify your sentences as simple, compound, complex, or compound-complex. In addition, note any sentences that could be classified as cumulative or periodic or as imperative, interrogative, or exclamatory. Does your examination turn up a variety of sentence structures or do you tend to use one or two sentence types repeatedly? How might you vary sentence structure?

15

Understanding Pronoun Case

The grammatical term *case* may be unfamiliar to you (since it comes, like many such terms, from Latin), but the concept it represents is one you will recognize immediately. Take a look, for example, at the first-person pronouns in the following excerpt.

> *I* want a wife who will care for *me* when I am sick and sympathize with *my* pain … *I* want a wife who will keep *my* clothes clean, ironed, mended, replaced when need be, and who will see to it that *my* personal things are kept in their proper place …
>
> — Judy Brady, "I Want a Wife"

Most of us know intuitively when to use *I*, when to use *me*, and when to use *my*. Our choices reflect differences in **case**, the form a noun or pronoun takes to indicate its function in a sentence. The italicized words in the excerpt show the singular first-person pronoun in three different cases: the subjective case *(I)*, the objective case *(me)*, and the possessive case *(my)*. Pronouns functioning as subjects are in the subjective case; those functioning as objects are in the objective case; and those functioning as possessives are in the possessive case.

Nouns and indefinite pronouns have the same form whether they function as subjects or objects, but they have a separate possessive case. It is usually formed by adding 's to a singular noun or an indefinite pronoun *(the cat's meow, nobody's fool)* or an apostrophe to a plural noun *(the players' strike)*. See Chapter 37 for additional discussion and examples of the possessive case of nouns and indefinite pronouns.

This chapter focuses on the following pronoun case forms:

SUBJECTIVE

I/we   you   he/she/it   they   who/whoever

OBJECTIVE

me/us   you   him/her/it   them   whom/whomever

POSSESSIVE

my   your   his/her/its   their   whose
mine   yours   his/her/its   theirs

Using the subjective case

A pronoun should be in the **subjective case** when it is a subject of a clause, a subject complement, or an appositive renaming a subject or subject complement. (See 14b and 14c.)

SUBJECT OF AN INDEPENDENT CLAUSE

They could either fight or face certain death with the lions.

We felt that Rico was enthusiastic and wanted to learn the material.

My brother and *I* adored our grandparents.

Who wrote *In the Skin of a Lion*?

SUBJECT OF A DEPENDENT CLAUSE

Before *she* discovered the new migraine drug, *she* suffered almost daily.

Jason did not seem like the type of person *who* would plagiarize.

Our group appealed to *whoever* was willing to listen.

SUBJECT COMPLEMENT

Even though pronouns used as subject complements should, grammatically, be in the subjective case, many people often use the objective case, especially in conversation: "Who's there? It's *me*." To many speakers of English, "it's me" sounds not only acceptable but preferable to "it's I." Nevertheless, you should use the subjective case for all formal writing.

The first person to see Monty after the awards was *she*.

The players invited for a second auction were Kwan and *I*.

It is *he* who brings life and spirit to the class.

If you find the subjective case for a subject complement stilted or awkward, try rewriting the sentence using the pronoun as the subject.

She was the first person to see Monty after the awards.

APPOSITIVE RENAMING A SUBJECT

Three students—Peter, Etovre, and *she*—wrote on the report.

APPOSITIVE RENAMING A SUBJECT COMPLEMENT

The finalists were two dark horses, Ali and *I*.

15b

Using the objective case

A pronoun should be in the **objective case** when it functions as a direct or indirect object (of a verb or verbal), a subject of an infinitive, an object of a preposition, or an appositive renaming an object. (See 14b3 and 14c3.)

OBJECT OF A VERB

The professor surprised *them* with a quiz. [direct object of *surprised*]

The weather report gave *us* hope. [indirect object of *gave*]

Trudeau was a prime minister *whom* many Canadians adored. [direct object of *adored*]

OBJECT OF A VERBAL

The Parisians were wonderful about helping *me*, and I ended the year speaking fluently. [object of gerund]

Wishing *her* luck, the coach stepped back to watch the performance. [object of participle]

Leonard offered to show *him* around town. [object of infinitive]

SUBJECT OF AN INFINITIVE

The objective case is also used in sentences like the following, where the pronoun is preceded by a verb and followed by an infinitive. Even though the pronoun in such constructions is called the subject of the infinitive, it is in the objective case.

Writing helps *me* to know myself better.

The student campaigners convinced his wife and *him* to vote in favour of the school board.

The trip led *us* to appreciate the weather in Winnipeg.

OBJECT OF A PREPOSITION

As Paul entered the room, a strange feeling came over *me*.

Alice planned a surprise party for *them*.

APPOSITIVE RENAMING AN OBJECT

We selected two managers, Joan and *her*, to attend the seminar.

Using the possessive case

A pronoun should be in the **possessive case** when it shows possession or ownership. Notice that there are two forms of possessive pronouns: adjective forms, which are used before nouns or gerunds (*my, your, his, her, its, our, their, whose*), and noun forms, which take the place of a noun (*mine, yours, his, hers, its, ours, theirs, whose*). (See Chapter 37.)

ADJECTIVE FORMS

Many of Spielberg's movies put viewers on the edge of *their* seats.

Whose car are you driving?

The sound of *his* hammering echoed through the corridor.

When a pronoun precedes a verb form ending in -ing, as in the preceding example, you need to decide whether the verb form is a gerund or a present participle to determine whether to use the possessive or the objective case of the pronoun. Gerunds always function as nouns, and if the verb form is a gerund, the pronoun modifies it and must be in the possessive case. Present participles function as adjectives, and if the verb form is a participle, it modifies the pronoun, which should be in the objective case.

Usually you can tell from the context of the sentence whether an -ing verb form is a gerund or a participle. In the example sentence, for instance, you can tell that *hammering* is a gerund and the pronoun should be *his* because it was the sound of *hammering*, not the sound of *him*, that was echoing through the corridor. In some sentences like this, however, you could use either an objective or a possessive pronoun, depending on the exact meaning you intend. Look at these two sentences:

I remember *his* singing.

I remember *him* singing.

In the first example, the memory is of *singing*, which is a gerund, modified by the possessive pronoun *his*. In the second example, the memory is of *him*, which functions as a direct object of *remember* and thus is in the objective case; *singing* is a present participle modifying *him*.

NOUN FORMS

The responsibility is *hers*.

"He's *mine*!" declared the child, clutching his Barney.

Whose did she borrow?

Exercise 15.1

Examine three or four paragraphs from a favourite piece of writing (possibly one of your own), and identify each pronoun used as subjective, objective, or possessive. Note the function of each pronoun.

Using *who*, *whoever*, *whom*, and *whomever*

One of the most common problems with pronoun case is deciding whether to use *who* or *whom*. In speech and even in some informal writing, *whom* has become a rarely used word. Even when traditional grammar requires *whom*, many people use *who* instead. Nevertheless, in formal written English, which includes most of the writing you do at college or university, the case of the pronoun should properly reflect its grammatical function. *Who* and *whoever* are the subjective case forms and should be used when the pronoun is a subject or subject complement. *Whom* and *whomever* are the objective case forms and should be used when the pronoun is a direct or indirect object or the object of a preposition.

Most writers find that two particular situations can lead to confusion with *who* and *whom*: when they begin a question and when they introduce a dependent clause. In a dependent clause, you may also have to choose between *whoever* and *whomever*. (See 14c4.)

1. Beginning a question with *who* or *whom*

You can determine whether to use *who* or *whom* at the beginning of a question by answering the question using a personal pronoun. If the answer is in the subjective case, use *who*; if the answer is in the objective case, use *whom*.

> *Who* saw Madonna on Letterman? [*She* saw Madonna on Letterman. *She* is subjective; thus *who* is correct.]
>
> *Whom* did you visit? [I visited *them*. *Them* is objective; thus *whom* is correct.]
>
> *Whom* are you voting for? [I am voting for *her*. *Her* is objective; thus *whom* is correct.]

Notice that even if the *who/whom* clause is interrupted by the main subject and verb of the sentence—for example, *did you say* or *does she think*—answering the question using a personal pronoun will still tell you the right case to use.

> *Who* does he think can best narrate such a story? [He thinks *she* can best narrate such a story. *She* is subjective; thus *who* is correct.]

2. Beginning a dependent clause with *who*, *whoever*, *whom*, or *whomever*

The case of a pronoun in a dependent clause is determined by its function in the clause, no matter how that clause functions in the sentence. If the pronoun acts as a subject in the clause, use *who* or *whoever.* If the pronoun acts as an object, use *whom* or *whomever.* (See 14c4.)

> The new president was not *whom* she had expected. [*Whom* is the object of the verb *had expected* in the clause *whom she had expected.* Though the clause as a whole is the complement of the subject *president*, the pronoun should be in the objective case.]
>
> The supply teacher's work schedule changed from week to week, depending on *whoever* needed time off. [*Whoever* is the subject of the clause *whoever needed time off.* Though the clause as a whole is the object of the preposition *on*, the pronoun should be in the subjective case.]
>
> Richard feels like a knight *who* is headed for great adventure. [*Who* is the subject of the clause *who is headed for great adventure.*]
>
> *Whomever* the party suspected of disloyalty was executed. [*Whomever* is the object of the verb *suspected* in the clause *Whomever the party suspected of disloyalty.* Though the clause as a whole is the subject of the sentence, the pronoun should be in the objective case.]

If you are not sure which case to use, try separating out the dependent clause from the rest of the sentence and looking at it in isolation. Rewrite the clause as a new sentence with a personal pronoun instead of *who(ever)* or *whom(ever).* If the pronoun is in the subjective case, use *who* or *whoever* in the original clause; if it is in the objective case, use *whom* or *whomever.*

> Anyone can hypnotize a person (*who/whom*) wants to be hypnotized. [Separate out the clause *who/whom wants to be hypnotized.* Substituting a personal pronoun gives you *he wants to be hypnotized. He* is subjective case; therefore: Anyone can hypnotize a person *who* wants to be hypnotized.]
>
> The minister grimaced at (*whoever/whomever*) made any noise. [Separate out the clause *whoever/whomever made any noise.* Substituting a personal pronoun gives you *they made any noise. They* is subjective case; therefore: The minister grimaced at *whoever* made any noise.]
>
> The minister smiled at (*whoever/whomever*) she greeted. [Separate out the clause *she greeted whoever/whomever.* Substituting a personal pronoun gives you *she greeted them. Them* is objective case; therefore: The minister smiled at *whomever* she greeted.]

If the dependent clause is interrupted by an expression such as *he thinks* or *she says*, delete the expression when you separate out the clause.

> The minister grimaced at *(whoever/whomever)* she thought made any noise. [Separate out the clause *whoever/whomever made any noise*, deleting the interrupting expression *she thought*. Substituting a personal pronoun gives you *they made any noise. They* is subjective case; therefore: The minister grimaced at *whoever* she thought made any noise.]

Exercise 15.2

Insert *who, whoever, whom,* or *whomever* correctly in the blank in each of the following sentences.

EXAMPLE
She is someone <u>who</u> will go far.

1. _____ shall I say is calling?
2. _____ the voters choose faces an almost impossible challenge.
3. The manager promised to reward _____ sold the most cars.
4. Professor Quiñones asked _____ we wanted to collaborate with.
5. _____ will the new tax law benefit most?

15e

Using the correct case in compound structures

Most problems with case of personal pronouns occur when the pronoun is part of a compound subject, complement, or object. Each part of a compound structure should be in the same case as it would if used alone: pronouns in compound subjects and subject complements should be in the subjective case; pronouns in compound objects should be in the objective case.

SUBJECTS
Mrs. Wentzel and *I* simply could not exist in the same classroom.
When Anne and *he* were first married, they lived in Moncton.

SUBJECT COMPLEMENTS

The winners of the competition were *Renata* and *he*.

The next two speakers will be *Philip* and *she*.

OBJECTS OF VERBS

Red Deer College accepted *Geli* and *me*. [direct object]

Dalhousie offered *Bob* and *her* a scholarship. [indirect object]

OBJECTS OF PREPOSITIONS

This morning saw yet another conflict between *my sister* and *me*.

My aunt put me in the room once shared by *my uncle* and *her*.

If you are unsure whether to use the subjective or the objective case in a compound structure, make each part of the compound into a separate sentence.

> Come to the lecture with my roommate and (*I/me*). [Separating the compound structure gives you *come to the lecture with my roommate* and *come to the lecture with me*; thus: Come to the lecture with my roommate and *me*.]

15f

Using the correct case in appositives

The case of a pronoun that is part of an appositive is determined by the word that the appositive renames. If the word functions as a subject or subject complement, the pronoun should be in the subjective case; if if functions as an object, the pronoun should be in the objective case.

> Three students—Victor, Dorota, and *he*—were asked to leave the room. [*Students* is the subject of the sentence, so the pronoun in the appositive *Victor, Dorota, and he* should be in the subjective case.]

> The poker game that night produced two big winners, my mother and *me*. [*Winners* is the direct object of the verb *produced*, so the pronoun in the appositive *my mother and me* should be in the objective case.]

Using the correct case in elliptical constructions

Elliptical constructions are those in which some words are understood but left out. In comparisons with *than* or *as*, we often leave words unsaid: *I see Elizabeth more often than [I see] her sister.* When sentences with such constructions end in a pronoun, the pronoun should be in the case it would be in if the construction were complete.

> His brother has always been more athletic than *he* [is].

In some constructions like this, the case of the pronoun depends on the meaning intended.

ELLIPTICAL	Willie likes Lily more than *she.*
COMPLETE	Willie likes Lily more than *she* [likes Lily].
ELLIPTICAL	Willie likes Lily more than *her.*
COMPLETE	Willie likes Lily more than [he likes] *her.*

As these examples demonstrate, use the subjective case if the pronoun is actually the subject of an omitted verb; use the objective case if it is an object of an omitted verb.

Using *we* and *us* correctly before a noun

When the first-person plural pronoun is used with a noun, the case of the pronoun depends on the way the noun functions in the sentence. If the noun functions as a subject, the pronoun should be in the subjective case (*we*); if the noun functions as an object, the pronoun should be in the objective case (*us*).

> *We* NDP supporters never give up hope. [*NDP supporters* is the subject.]
> The NDP depends on *us* supporters. [*Supporters* is the object of a preposition.]

If you are unsure about which case to use, recasting the sentence without the noun will give you the answer. Use whichever pronoun would be correct if the noun were omitted: *We never give up hope. The NDP depends on us.*

Exercise 15.3

Choose the appropriate pronoun from the pair in parentheses in each of the following sentences.

EXAMPLE
The fear of (them/_their_) taking advantage of him never entered his mind.

1. The relationship between (they/them) and their brother was often strained.

2. When I was young, I had a friend (who/whom) I idolized.

3. This love for children probably began because there were three children younger than (I/me) in my family.

4. I thought the only candidates left in the race were (she/her) and Chrétien.

5. I am getting more and more interested in (him/his) accompanying me on the trip.

6. When Carol and (she/her) first met, they despised each other.

7. The two people closest to me, (he/him) and my mother, expected me to return home after graduation.

8. E.N.G. appeals to (whoever/whomever) is interested in intrigue, suspense, joy, pain, grief, and romance.

9. Later (we/us) "rejects" were taken to watch the taping of the show.

10. The only mother and father (who/whom) they know are the people (who/whom) raised them and took care of them.

Taking inventory: pronoun case

Research shows that one of the most overused words in any language is the word for *I*. Whenever you write about your own experience or your own opinions, you probably rely to some degree on first-person pronouns, singular and plural. Write two or three paragraphs about a personal experience—your first time travelling on your own or a time when you experienced a feeling of loss or defeat. When you are finished, underline all the personal pronouns you used, and label each one for case. Do you find any patterns? If you find that you rely heavily on any one case— that half your sentences begin with *I*, for example—decide whether your writing seems at all monotonous as a result. If so, try revising, paying attention to pronoun case. See, in other words, whether revising some sentences by changing *I* to *me* (or vice versa) brings greater variety of your writing. If you keep a writing log, you might enter your work into it, noting what you have learned about your use of pronoun case.

16

Using Verbs

When used skilfully, verbs are the heartbeat of prose, moving it along, enlivening it, carrying its action. Verbs are extremely flexible and can change form to mark grammatical agreement with the subject (see Chapter 17) or to indicate *tense, voice,* or *mood.*

| CHANGE IN TENSE | The runner *skims* around the track. [present tense] |
| The runner *skimmed* around the track. [past tense] |

| CHANGE IN VOICE | She *savours* every step. [active voice] |
| Every step *is savoured.* [passive voice] |

| CHANGE IN MOOD | She *is* completely content. [indicative] |
| If she *were* not content, she would not be smiling. [subjunctive] |

This chapter explores in detail the way verbs work, with attention to form, tense, voice, and mood.

VERB FORMS

Except for *be,* all English verbs have five forms.

BASE FORM	PAST TENSE	PAST PARTICIPLE	PRESENT PARTICIPLE	-S FORM
talk	talked	talked	talking	talks
adore	adored	adored	adoring	adores
jog	jogged	jogged	jogging	jogs

The **base form** is the one listed in the dictionary. For all verbs except *be,* it is the form used to indicate action that takes place (or a condition that exists) in the present when the subject is a plural noun or the pronoun *I, you, we,* or *they.*

> In summer, many people *think* about dieting.
>
> They *refuse* desserts and *avoid* fatty foods.

The **past tense** indicates action that took place (or a condition that existed) in the past. The past tense of most verbs is formed by adding -*ed* or -*d* to the base form. Some verbs, however, have an irregular past-tense form, as is explained in 16b. *Be* has two past-tense forms, *was* and *were.*

> The Globe *served* as the playhouse for many of Shakespeare's works.
>
> In 1613 it *caught* fire and *burned* to the ground.

The **past participle** usually has the same form as the past tense. As with the past tense, some verbs have irregular forms for the past participle (see 16b). The past participle cannot function alone as the predicate of a clause or sentence. To function as a predicate, it must be used with a form of the auxiliary verb *have* or *be.* In addition, the past participle can function as an adjective, modifying a noun or pronoun. (See 16e.)

> She *had accomplished* the impossible.
>
> The doctors *have asked* for my cooperation.
>
> No one *was injured* in the explosion.
>
> *Standardized* tests usually require *sharpened* pencils.

The **present participle** is constructed by adding -*ing* to the base form. Like the past participle, it cannot function alone as a predicate but must be used with one or more auxiliary verbs. A present participle used with the auxiliary *be* is called the progressive form of a verb and indicates continuing action. The present participle can also function as an adjective, like the past participle, or as a noun, called a gerund. (See 14c.)

> Several hundred students *are competing* in the race.
>
> He tried to comfort the *crying* child.
>
> Philosophy emphasizes the value of *thinking.*

Except for *be* and *have,* the **-s form** consists of the base form plus -*s* or -*es.* This form indicates the present tense when the subject is third-person singular. All singular nouns, the pronouns *he, she,* and *it,* and many indefinite pronouns (such as *everyone* and *someone*) are third-person singular.

> The natural garden *offers* an alternative to the traditional manicured one.

She usually *takes* the shortcut across campus.

No one *believes* his story.

It is very important to note that the *-s* form occurs *only* in the third-person singular.

	SINGULAR	PLURAL
FIRST PERSON	I wish	we wish
SECOND PERSON	you wish	you wish
THIRD PERSON	he/she/it wishes	they wish
	Sam wishes	children wish
	someone wishes	

Forms of be

Be has three different forms in the present tense and, as mentioned earlier, two forms in the past tense.

PRESENT TENSE

	SINGULAR	PLURAL
FIRST PERSON	I *am*	we *are*
SECOND PERSON	you *are*	you *are*
THIRD PERSON	he/she/it is	they *are*
	Sam *is*	children *are*
	someone *is*	some *are*

PAST TENSE

	SINGULAR	PLURAL
FIRST PERSON	I *was*	we *were*
SECOND PERSON	you *were*	you *were*
THIRD PERSON	he/she/it was	they *were*
	Sam *was*	children *were*
	someone *was*	some *were*

Using auxiliary verbs

Sometimes called helping verbs, **auxiliary verbs** are used with a base form, present participle, or past participle to create verb phrases. The base form or participle in a verb phrase is called the main verb. The most commonly used auxiliaries include forms of *have, be,* and *do,* which are used to indicate a completed action or condition (see 16c and 16d), to indicate the passive voice, to indicate a continuing action or condition, to add emphasis, to ask questions, and to make negative statements. *Will* and *shall* are auxiliaries used to show future time; unlike most auxiliaries, they never change form.

> Dennis *has worked* late all month.
>
> I *am working* hard.
>
> She *has been warned* several times.
>
> We *do respect* your viewpoint.
>
> *Do* you *know* the answer?
>
> He *does* not *like* wearing a tie.
>
> They *will explain* the procedure.

Modal auxiliaries—*can, could, might, may, must, ought to, should, would*—show possibility, necessity, obligation, and so on.

> On a clear day, you *can see* Mount Baker from Vancouver. [possibility]
>
> I *must try* harder. [necessity]
>
> She *should visit* her parents more often. [obligation]

16b

Using regular and irregular verbs

A verb is **regular** when its past tense and past participle are formed by adding *-ed* or *-d* to the base form:

BASE FORM	PAST TENSE	PARTICIPLE
love	loved	loved
support	supported	supported

The past tense and past participle of regular verbs sometimes cause difficulty for writers, because some verbs double the final consonant or change final *y* to *i* before adding *-ed*. (See 33d.)

A verb is **irregular** when it does not follow the *-ed* or *-d* pattern. The past tense and past participle of irregular verbs are most often formed by changing an internal vowel: *begin, began, begun.* In some verbs like this, *-en* or -n is also added to the past participle: *break, broke, broken.* Other verbs change form more radically: *go, went, gone.* Still others do not change at all: *hurt, hurt, hurt.* If you are uncertain about the correct verb form, consult your dictionary, which lists any irregular past tense and past participle forms under the entry for the base form.

You probably know most irregular verb forms intuitively, but you may want to take the time now to memorize any that cause you difficulty. Here are some of the most common irregular verbs:

BASE FORM	PAST TENSE	PAST PARTICIPLE
arise	arose	arisen
be	was/were	been
bear	bore	borne/born
beat	beat	beaten
become	became	become
begin	began	begun
bite	bit	bitten
blow	blew	blown
break	broke	broken
bring	brought	brought
build	built	built
burn	burned/burnt	burned/burnt
burst	burst	burst
buy	bought	bought
catch	caught	caught
choose	chose	chosen
come	came	come
cost	cost	cost
cut	cut	cut
dig	dug	dug
dive	dived/dove	dived
do	did	done
draw	drew	drawn
drink	drank	drunk
drive	drove	driven
eat	ate	eaten
fall	fell	fallen
feel	felt	felt
fight	fought	fought
find	found	found
fly	flew	flown

BASE FORM	PAST TENSE	PAST PARTICIPLE
forget	forgot	forgotten/forgot
freeze	froze	frozen
get	got	gotten/got
give	gave	given
go	went	gone
grow	grew	grown
hang[1]	hung	hung
have	had	had
hear	heard	heard
hide	hid	hidden
hit	hit	hit
keep	kept	kept
know	knew	known
lay	laid	laid
lead	led	led
leave	left	left
lend	lent	lent
let	let	let
lie (recline)[2]	lay	lain
lose	lost	lost
make	made	made
mean	meant	meant
meet	met	met
pay	paid	paid
prove	proved	proved/proven
put	put	put
read	read	read
ride	rode	ridden
ring	rang	rung
rise	rose	risen
run	ran	run
say	said	said
see	saw	seen
send	sent	sent
set	set	set
shake	shook	shaken

---

[1] *Hang* meaning "execute by hanging" is irregular: hang, hanged, hanged.

[2] *Lie* meaning "tell a falsehood" is regular: *lie, lied, lied.*

BASE FORM	PAST TENSE	PAST PARTICIPLE
shine (give light)[3]	shone	shone
shoot	shot	shot
show	showed	showed/shown
shrink	shrank	shrunk
sing	sang	sung
sink	sank	sunk
sit	sat	sat
sleep	slept	slept
speak	spoke	spoken
spend	spent	spent
spread	spread	spread
spring	sprang/sprung	sprung
stand	stood	stood
steal	stole	stolen
strike	struck	struck/stricken
swim	swam	swum
swing	swung	swung
take	took	taken
teach	taught	taught
tear	tore	torn
tell	told	told
think	thought	thought
throw	threw	thrown
wake	woke/waked	waked/woken/woke
wear	wore	worn
win	won	won
wind	wound	wound
write	wrote	written

---

[3] *Shine* meaning "polish" is regular: *shine, shined, shined.*

Using *lie* and *lay, rise* and *raise*

Two pairs of verbs—*lie* and *lay,* and *rise* and raise—cause problems for many writers because the two verbs in each pair have similar-sounding forms and somewhat related meanings. In each pair one of the verbs is transitive, meaning that it takes a direct object; the other is intransitive, meaning that it does not take an object. The best way to avoid confusing the two is to memorize their forms and meanings. All of these verbs except *raise* are irregular. Their forms are as follows:

BASE FORM	PAST TENSE	PAST PARTICIPLE	PRESENT PARTICIPLE	-S FORM
lie	lay	lain	lying	lies
lay	laid	laid	laying	lays
rise	rose	risen	rising	rising
raise	raised	raised	raising	raises

Lie is intransitive and means "recline" or "be situated." *Lay* is transitive and means "put" or "place." This pair is especially confusing because *lay* is also the past-tense form of *lie*.

INTRANSITIVE   He *lay* on the floor unable to move.

TRANSITIVE   I *laid* the package on the counter.

Rise is intransitive and means "get up" and "go up." *Raise* is transitive and means "lift" or "cause to go up."

INTRANSITIVE   He *rose* from the bed and left the room.

TRANSITIVE   He *raised* himself to a sitting position.

INTRANSITIVE   The price of coffee is *rising*.

TRANSITIVE   The store is *raising* the price of coffee.

Exercise 16.1

Choose the appropriate verb form from the pair in parentheses in each of the following sentences:

1. Sometimes she just (*lies/lays*) and stares at the ceiling.

2. I (*lay/laid*) my books down just as the telephone rang.

3. The doctor asked the patient to (*lie/lay*) on his side for an injection.

4. He used whatever was (*lying/laying*) around the house.

5. The Bank of Canada is planning to (*rise/raise*) interest rates.

6. When the temperature (*rises/raises*), the relative humidity usually declines.

7. We (*rose/raised*) every morning at six and went jogging.

VERB TENSES

Tenses are the forms of a verb that show when the action or condition expressed by the verb takes place or exists. We characteristically think of time in terms of present, past, and future, and the three *simple tenses* are the present tense, the past tense, and the future tense.

PRESENT TENSE	I jump
PAST TENSE	I jumped
FUTURE TENSE	I will jump

More complex aspects of time relationships, such as ongoing or completed actions or conditions, are expressed through *progressive, perfect,* and *perfect progressive forms* of the simple tenses. Such terminology sounds complicated in the abstract, but, in fact, you use all of these forms in everyday speech. Here are all the tense forms of one verb, *ask.*

SIMPLE PRESENT	she *asks*
SIMPLE PAST	she *asked*
SIMPLE FUTURE	she *will ask*
PRESENT PERFECT	she *has asked*
PAST PERFECT	she *had asked*
FUTURE PERFECT	she *will have asked*
PRESENT PROGRESSIVE	she *is asking*
PAST PROGRESSIVE	she *was asking*
FUTURE PROGRESSIVE	she *will be asking*
PRESENT PERFECT PROGRESSIVE	she *has been asking*
PAST PERFECT PROGRESSIVE	she *had been asking*
FUTURE PERFECT PROGRESSIVE	she *will have been asking*

The simple tenses locate an action or condition only within the three basic time frames of present, past, and future. The perfect form of each tense expresses the idea of a *completed* action or condition in the present, past, or future, and the progressive form expresses the idea of a *continuing* action or condition. Finally, the perfect progressive form expresses the idea of an action or condition continuing up to a point of completion. The next section describes in greater detail how each of the forms of each tense is used.

16d

Using the present tense forms

The **simple present** indicates actions or conditions occurring at the time of speaking or writing, as well as those occurring habitually and those considered to be general truths or scientific facts. In addition, with appropriate expressions of time, the simple present can be used to indicate a scheduled event in the future.

> He now *lives* in Brandon.
>
> They *are* very angry about the decision.
>
> I *eat* breakfast every day at 8:00 a.m.
>
> Love *conquers* all.
>
> Water *freezes* at 0°C.
>
> The Charter of Rights *guarantees* certain rights to all citizens.
>
> Residents of Greenland *endure* bitter cold for most of the year.
>
> Grandpa *arrives* tomorrow.

The simple present is also used in discussing literary and artistic works created in the past that exist in our experience as timeless. For example, these literary characters in *Emma*, created by Jane Austen almost two hundred years ago, exist in our present time as well.

> Mr. Knightley *is* the only person who sees Emma as she really *is* and he *reveals* her faults to her.

The **present progressive** indicates actions or conditions that are ongoing or continuous in the present.

> The children *are playing* in the back yard this afternoon.
>
> The defence attorney *is asking* for a retrial.

The present progressive is typically used to describe an action that is happening at the moment of speaking, in contrast to the simple present, which more often indicates habitual actions.

> PRESENT PROGRESSIVE   You *are driving* too fast.
>
> SIMPLE PRESENT   I always *drive* carefully.

With an appropriate expression of time, the present progressive can also be used to indicate a scheduled event in the future.

We *are having* friends over for dinner tomorrow night.

The **present perfect** indicates actions or conditions begun in the past and either completed at some unspecified time in the past or continuing into the present.

> My father *has told* me many stories of his childhood in Antigonish.
>
> Uncontrolled logging *has destroyed* many forests.
>
> Citizen groups *have tried* to reverse the decision.

The **present perfect progressive** indicates that an ongoing action or condition begun in the past is very likely to continue into the present.

> For many years medical professionals *have been warning* us about the effects of smoking.
>
> Since I *have been taking* vitamins regularly, I have no colds.
>
> Provincial drug plans *have been covering* fewer and fewer prescription costs over the past several years.

Using the past tense forms

The **simple past** indicates actions or conditions that occurred at a specific time and do not extend into the present.

> She *felt* better as soon as her exams were over.
>
> Germany *invaded* Poland on September 1, 1939.
>
> We *moved* to this city only last year.

The **past progressive** indicates continuing actions or conditions in the past, often with specified limits.

> Lenin *was living* in exile in Zurich when the czar was overthrown.
>
> By the 1970s many North Americans *were buying* smaller cars.
>
> I *was visiting* a pecan orchard when I got a craving for a piece of pie.

The **past perfect** indicates actions or conditions that were completed by a specific time in the past or before some other past action or condition occurred.

> By the 4th century Christianity *had become* the state religion.

She *had asked* the instructor for help before she turned to me.

Homesteaders found that speculators *had* already *taken* the best land.

The **past perfect progressive** indicates continuous actions or conditions in the past that began before a specific time in the past or before some other past action or condition began.

They *had been living* beyond their means for years before they went bankrupt.

When they returned to Venice, the Polos *had been travelling* for almost twenty-five years.

Hannah *had been planning* an academic career, but she returned to Lethbridge to run the family business.

16f

Using the future tense forms

The **simple future** indicates actions or conditions that have yet to begin.

The exhibition *will come* to Saskatoon in September.

I *shall graduate* the year after next.

Generation X-ers *will find* it difficult to earn as much as their parents did.

The **future progressive** indicates continuing actions or conditions in the future.

The loans *will be coming* due in the next two years.

A team of international observers *will be monitoring* the elections.

The **future perfect** indicates actions or conditions that will be completed by or before some specific time in the future.

They *will have exhausted* all their resources before the new year arrives.

In ten years the original investment *will have doubled*.

Finally, the **future perfect progressive** indicates continuing actions or conditions that will be completed by some specified time in the future.

By the time the session ends, the negotiators *will have been working* for ten hours without a break.

Satwinder *will have been playing* the piano for five years this June.

Exercise 16.2

Complete each of the following sentences by filling in the blank with an appropriate form of the verb listed in parentheses. Since more than one form will sometimes be possible, be prepared to provide reasons for your choices.

1. In spite of the poor turnout in today's referendum, local officials _____ (expect) the new transit plans to go ahead.

2. Ever since the first nuclear power plants were built, opponents _____ (predict) disaster.

3. Thousands of Irish peasants _____ (emigrate) to North America after the potato famine of the 1840s.

4. The newspaper _____ (arrive) late every day this week.

5. The committee _____ (meet) again next week.

6. Jessica Emed was photographed while she _____ (ride) in a limousine.

7. By eleven o'clock this morning, stock prices _____ (fall) fifteen points.

8. By the time a child born today enters Grade 1, he or she _____ (watch) thousands of television commercials.

9. In "The Road Not Taken" the man _____ (come) to a fork in the road.

10. The supply of a product _____ (rise) when the demand is great.

Using verb tenses in sequences

Because tense is crucial to our understanding of when actions or conditions occur and because time relationships can be very complex, careful and accurate use of tenses is important to clear writing. Even the simplest narrative describes actions that take place at different times; using particular tenses for particular actions allows readers to follow such time changes readily.

The relationship between the tense of the verb in the independent clause of a sentence and the tense of a verb in a dependent clause or a verbal is called the **sequence of tenses**. In general, the verb in a dependent clause may be in any tense form required for your meaning. The only limitation is that the relationship between the forms in the independent and dependent clauses make sense. For example, all of the following make sense and are acceptable grammatically:

She *lent* him the money because she *is* a generous woman. [past/present]

> She *lent* him the money because she *loved* him. [past/past]
>
> She *lent* him the money because he *will invest* it wisely. [past/future]

Even though in general you can use almost any sequence of tenses, in a particular sentence the tense of the verb in the dependent clause may be limited by the meaning. For example, it makes no sense to say *She lent him the money because she will love him* or *She lent him the money because he had invested it wisely.*

Different forms of an infinitive are used to indicate the time relationship between the action expressed by the infinitive and that expressed by the verb in the predicate. The **present infinitive**, consisting of *to* plus the base form, indicates action occurring at the same time as or later than the action of the predicate verb.

> I *wanted to swim* in the ocean last summer. [The wanting and the swimming occurred at the same time in the past.]
>
> I *expect to swim* in the ocean next summer. [The expecting is present; the swimming is in the future.]

The **perfect infinitive**, consisting of *to have* plus the past participle, indicates action occurring *before* the action of the predicate verb.

> She *seems to have lost* her self-confidence. [The loss of self-confidence took place before the "seeming."]
>
> He *was reported to have left* his fortune to AIDS research. [The leaving of the fortune took place before the reporting.]

Similarly, different kinds of participles are used to indicate the time relationship between the action expressed by the participle and that expressed by the verb in the predicate. The **present participle** indicates action occurring at the same time as that of the verb.

> *Seeking* to relieve traffic congestion, the police *established* several detours. [Both the seeking and the establishment of the detours occurred simultaneously in the past.]

The **present perfect participle** indicates action occurring before that of the predicate verb. The present perfect participle consists of *having* plus the past participle: *having sent, having walked.*

> *Having won* the election, he *is planning* new legislation. [He began planning after he won the election.]

The **past participle** can indicate action occurring either before or at the same time as that of the predicate verb.

> *Flown* by an expert pilot, the passengers *felt* completely secure. [The flying and the feeling were simultaneous.]
>
> *Flown* to Clayoquot Sound, the children *joined* their parents in protest. [The flying occurred before the joining.]

Exercise 16.3

Look at one or two pages of an essay or report you've written recently. Identify all the verbs used and name their tenses. Write a short paragraph explaining choices of tense. Take special note of any shifts in tense.

VOICE

Voice is the feature of transitive verbs that tells whether the subject is acting (*he questions us*) or being acted upon (*he is questioned*). When the subject is acting, the verb is in the **active voice**; when the subject is being acted upon, the verb is in the **passive voice**. The passive voice is formed, as in this sentence, by using the appropriate form of the auxiliary verb *be* followed by the past participle of the main verb.

	ACTIVE VOICE	PASSIVE VOICE
PRESENT	He *questions* us.	He *is questioned*.
PAST	He *questioned* us.	He *was questioned*.
FUTURE	He *will question* us.	He *will be questioned*.
PRESENT PERFECT	He *has questioned* us.	He *has been questioned*.
PAST PERFECT	He *had questioned* us.	He *had been questioned*.
FUTURE PERFECT	He *will have questioned* us.	He *will have been questioned*.

Most contemporary writers use the active voice as much as possible because it makes prose more *active*, more lively. To say that "the mail was opened" (passive voice) does not give the sense of action or immediacy that "Cheryl opened the mail" (active voice) does. In the passive construction, the mail is just there—being opened, by no one or nothing in particular. Even adding "by Cheryl" does not do much to enliven the passive version. When passive-voice verbs pile up in a writing passage, that passage will generally be harder to understand and remember. For instance, readers indicate they *remember* passages as being in the active voice even if the version they read used the passive voice.

The most problematic use of the passive voice occurs when writers seek to avoid taking responsibility for what they have written. A university president who announces that "it is recommended that student fees be raised by 15 percent" skirts a number of pressing questions: recommended by whom? raised by whom?

In spite of such questionable uses, however, the passive voice can work to good advantage in some situations. Much scientific writing uses the passive voice effectively to highlight the object or phenomenon being studied rather than the person or persons doing the studying. Look at the following example, from an essay describing brain surgery:

> A curved incision was made behind the hairline so it would be concealed when the hair grew back. It extended almost from ear to ear. Plastic clips were applied to the cut edges of the scalp to arrest bleeding. The scalp was folded back to the level of the eyebrows. Incisions were made in the muscle of the right temple, and three sets of holes were drilled near the temple and the top of the head because the tumor had to be approached from directly in front. Th drill, powered by nitrogen, was replaced with a fluted steel blade, and the holes were connected. The incised piece of skull was pried loose and held out of the way by a large sponge.
>
> – ROY C. SELBY, JR., "A Delicate Operation"

Reporters often use the passive voice when they want to protect the confidentiality of their sources, as in the familiar phrase "It is reported that …," or when the performer of an action is unknown or less important than the recipient of the action, as in "Karla Homolka was sentenced today after a trial behind closed doors." In the following excerpt from *The Globe and Mail*, a reporter uses passive voice to focus on people seeking refugee status rather than on the Canadian government.

> Many people who have been refused refugee status during the past sixteen months will be allowed to apply again after relaxed criteria, the federal government says. About 10,000 people have been deprived refugee status during that period.

Writers, then, must decide for themselves when the passive voice is appropriate and when it is not. If you find that you overuse the passive, you may want to practise shifting your sentences to active voice. To do so, convert the subject of the verb into a direct or indirect object, and make the performer of the action into the subject.

PASSIVE   The test administrator *was told* to give the student an electric shock each time a wrong answer *was given*.

ACTIVE   Researchers *told* the test administrator to give the student an electric shock each time he or she *gave* a wrong answer.

PASSIVE   I *was awakened* at seven by the telephone.

ACTIVE   The telephone *awakened* me at seven.

See 20c and 29b for further discussion of voice.

Exercise 16.4

Convert each of the following sentences from active to passive voice or from passive to active, and note the differences in emphasis and rhythm these changes make.

EXAMPLE
Machiavelli advises the prince to gain the friendship of the people.

The prince *is advised* by Machiavelli to gain the friendship of the people.

1. Flannery O'Connor employs the images of both a boxcar and a swinging bridge to show the inconsistencies between Mrs. Turpin's classification of people and God's classification of people.
2. Huge pine trees were uprooted by the storm.
3. Marianne avoided such things as elevators, subways, and closets.
4. For months the baby kangaroo is protected, fed, and taught how to survive by its mother.
5. The lawns and rooftops of the neighbourhood were covered with the first snow of winter.

Exercise 16.5

Look at several essays you have written recently or pieces of writing by others that you particularly like, and find five examples each of the active voice and the passive voice. Convert each of the examples to the other voice, and note the difference in emphasis and rhythm the changes make.

MOOD

The **mood** of a verb indicates the attitude of the speaker or writer toward what he or she is saying or writing. Different moods are used to express a fact or inquiry (indicative mood), a command or request (imperative mood), or a wish, requirement, or condition contrary to fact (subjunctive mood).

INDICATIVE   I *ate* the plums.

IMPERATIVE   *Eat* the plums.

SUBJUNCTIVE   If I *were to eat* the plums, I would be sick.

The most frequently used mood is the **indicative mood**, the one used for stating facts or opinions or asking questions.

The Frisbees *soar* through the air.

Campbell *lost* the 1993 election.

Where *are* you *going*?

The **imperative mood** is used for giving commands or making requests. It always uses the base form of the verb and almost always omits the subject, (*you*).

Look at the girl with the orange spiked hair.

Take the appropriate wrench, and *loosen* the plug counterclockwise.

You *sit* down at once!

Help!

The **subjunctive mood** expresses wishes, conditions that are contrary to fact, requests, or demands. It is used primarily in dependent clauses beginning with *that* or *if*.

Using the subjunctive

The present tense of the subjunctive uses the base form of the verb. The past tense of the subjunctive is the same as the past tense of the indicative mood except for the verb *be*, which uses *were* for all subjects.

PRESENT

The professor demanded that she *arrive* as early as possible.

It is important that children *be* psychologically ready for a new sibling.

PAST

He spent money as if he *had* infinite credit.

If the store *were* better located, it would attract more customers.

Because the subjunctive can create a rather formal tone, many speakers today have a tendency to substitute the indicative in informal situations. Nevertheless, formal writing still requires the use of the subjunctive in the following kinds of dependent clauses:

INDICATIVE   If I *was* a better typist, I would type my own papers.

SUBJUNCTIVE   If I *were* a better typist, I would type my own papers.

1. Those expressing a wish

I wish I *were* with you right now.

He wished that his mother *were* not reluctant to quit smoking.

2. Those beginning with if and expressing a condition that does not exist

If all provincial governments *were to* lower taxes on cigarettes, smuggling would certainly decrease.

If no one *were allowed* to ignore the rules, language would cease to develop.

3. Those beginning with as if and as though

He cautiously started down the trail as if he *were walking* on thin ice.

At her seventieth birthday party, Mrs. Greenberg danced as though she *were* twenty.

4. Those beginning with that and expressing a demand, request, requirement, or suggestion

It is required that each student *raise* some money for school trips.

Dad advised that neither of us *do* anything too hastily.

The job demands that the employee *be* in good physical condition.

Exercise 16.6

Choose the appropriate verb form in each of the following sentences:

1. I saw how carefully he moved, as if he (was/were) caring for an infant.

2. Her stepsisters treated Cinderella as though she (was/were) a servant.

3. Hamlet wishes that he (was/were) not responsible for avenging his murdered father.

4. Freud recommended that an analyst (use/uses) dreams as a means of studying the human personality.

5. If more money (was/were) available, the university would be able to offer more scholarships.

6. It is necessary that the manager (know/knows) how to do any job in the store.

Reading with an eye for verbs

Read the following paragraph carefully, noting the way the author uses verbs to create a scene from the past.

> This facility for seeing the wrong thing, asking the wrong question, already a barrier between acquaintanceship and friendship, made my relations with my brother difficult. I resented having chores to do—washing dishes, making beds, both his and mine, cleaning the house—meanwhile his only duty was to protect the family name by staying out of trouble. I resented having my telephone callers interrogated, my letters scanned, my visitors judged, while he was free to socialize with people of his own choosing. I resented the late hours he was permitted to keep while I was forced to spend my evenings practising the ko-to, producing music that bored me to tears and put my father in mind of his ancestors, never far out of reach. I resented my brother's freedom to choose from among the girls he knew while I could meet only those men selected by my father, always architects, always older, always pained by courtship conducted before the boss.
>
> – NEIL BISSOONDATH, "The Cage"

Taking inventory: verbs

Write a few paragraphs about a past event in your life—a visit, a ceremony, a job, anything you remember that you wish to write about. Describe it as a past event, using past-tense verbs. Then rewrite your description in the present tense, as if the event were taking place right now. Study the two versions, and write down any observations you can make about the effectiveness of each approach.

17

Maintaining Agreement

In ordinary language, **agreement** refers to an accord or a correspondence between ideas or actions; you reach an *agreement* with your boss about salary; the major powers negotiate an *agreement* about nuclear arms. This ordinary meaning of *agreement* covers its grammatical use as well. When subjects and verbs or pronouns and antecedents match each other in person, in number, and in gender, we say that they "agree." This chapter explores the conventions governing such agreement.

SUBJECT–VERB AGREEMENT

A verb must agree with its subject in number (singular or plural) and in person (first, second, or third).

> *Neil Bissoondath comes* from Trinidad. [third-person singular]
> *We* always *wear* rubber gloves in the lab. [first-person plural]
> *Whales* are mammals. [third-person plural]

In practice, only very few subject-verb constructions cause confusion, so we will look at those constructions in greater detail.

Making verbs agree with third-person singular subjects

English once used a complex system of verb endings to reflect the person, number, and gender of the subject. Over the centuries, however, most such endings have disappeared from use. Today the main kinds of subjects requiring a special verb form are third-person singular subjects: singular nouns and third-person singular pronouns. To make a present-tense verb agree with a third-person singular subject, we normally add -s or -es to the base form.

A vegetarian diet *lowers* the risk of heart disease.

He *wishes* to go to China next summer.

The only two verbs that do not follow this -s or -es pattern for third-person singular subjects in the present tense are *have* and *be*. *Have* changes to *has; be* has different forms for both the first and third persons and for both the present and past tense. (See 16b.)

Notice that although an -s or -es ending indicates a plural noun, the same kind of ending indicates a "singular" verb form. If the subject is a *plural* noun, the verb form does *not* take the -s or -es.

A car *needs* regular maintenance.

Cars *need* regular maintenance.

Making the subject and verb agree

When the simple subject of a sentence or clause is separated from the verb by other words, such as a prepositional phrase, be careful to make the verb agree with the subject and not with another noun that is closer to the verb.

A *vase* of flowers *makes* a room attractive.

Many *books* on the bestseller list *have* little literary value.

Many writers forget to maintain agreement when a plural noun falls between a singular subject and the verb, as in the first example above, or when a singular noun falls between a plural subject and the verb, as in the second example. In the first sentence, notice that the single subject is *vase*, not *flowers*, which is the object of the preposition *of*. In the second sentence, the simple subject is *books*, not *list*, which is the object of the preposition *on*.

Also be careful when a simple subject is followed by a phrase beginning with *as well as, along with, together with, in addition to,* or a similar expression. Make the verb agree with the simple subject, not with a noun in the intervening phrase.

The *prime minister*, along with many MPs, *supports* the new legislation.

A *passenger*, as well as the driver, *was injured* in the accident.

Some writers think it awkward to use a singular verb form when the complete subject, including the intervening phrase, expresses a plural idea. If a sentence like this strikes you as awkward, revise it by making the subject plural and using a plural verb form (see 17c).

> The prime minister and many MPs *support* the new legislation.
>
> The driver and a passenger *were injured* in the accident.

If you know that you have problems with subject-verb agreement when the simple subject and the verb are separated by other words, proofread each of your sentences to identify the simple subject and the verb. Then mentally delete the intervening words, if any, to make sure that the subject and verb agree in number and person.

Making verbs agree with compound subjects

Two or more subjects joined by *and* generally require a plural verb form.

> Tony and his friends *commute* every day from Kamloops.
>
> Reducing, reusing, and recycling *are* environmental values.

When subjects joined by *and* are considered a single unit or refer to a single person or thing, they take a singular verb form.

> Drinking and driving *remains* a major cause of highway fatalities.
>
> Bagels and cream cheese *is* Dorah's idea of a great breakfast.
>
> His closest friend and political ally *was* his brother.

If the word *each* or *every* precedes singular subjects joined by *and*, the verb form is singular.

> Each boy and girl *chooses* one gift to take home.
>
> Every city, town, and hamlet *has* a Main Street.

For compound subjects whose parts are joined by *or* or *nor*, the verb agrees in number and person with the part of the subject closest to the verb.

> Laws or convention *governs* most of our everyday decisions.
>
> Neither my brother nor my parents *plan* to vote.
>
> Either Jean or you *were* at fault.

Either you or I *am* wrong.

To avoid awkwardness with compound subjects made up of both singular and plural parts, place the plural part closest to the verb.

AWKWARD   Either the pigs or the cow *tramples* down my rhubarb every year.

REVISED   Either the cow or the pigs *trample* down my rhubarb every year.

Making verbs agree with collective-noun subjects

Collective nouns, such as *family, team, audience, group, jury, crowd, band, class, flock,* and *committee,* are singular in form but refer to a group of individual persons or things. When used as subjects, collective nouns can take either singular or plural verb forms, depending on the context. When they refer to a group as a single unit, they take a singular verb form.

The team wearing red and black *controls* the ball.

Waving banners frenetically, the crowd *screams* its support.

When they refer to the individual members of a collective, however, they take a plural verb form.

The family of lions *scatter* when Gabe approaches.

The committee *have* not agreed on many points.

The meaning of a sentence as a whole is your guide to whether the collective noun refers to a unit or to the separate parts of a unit.

After deliberating, the jury *reports* its verdict. [as a single unit]

The jury still *disagree* on a number of counts. [as separate individuals]

Making verbs agree with indefinite-pronoun subjects

Indefinite pronouns can pose difficulties with subject-verb agreement because they do not refer to specific persons or things, because some of them can be either singular or plural, and because some of them (*everybody, everyone, everything)* sound plural but are grammatically singular.

The following indefinite pronouns are singular in meaning and thus take singular verb forms:

another	everyone	nothing
anybody	everything	one
anyone	much	other
anything	neither	somebody
each	nobody	someone
either	no one	something

> Of the two jobs, neither *holds* much appeal.
>
> Each of the plays *depicts* a hero undone by a tragic flaw.

Indefinite pronouns that take plural verb forms include *both, few, many, others,* and *several.*

> Though many apply, few *are* chosen.
>
> Both *require* careful attention.

Several indefinite pronouns—*all, any, enough, more, most, none, some*—can be singular or plural, depending on the noun they refer to.

SINGULAR   All of the cake *was* eaten.

PLURAL   All of the candidates *promise* to improve the schools.

17f

Making verbs agree with relative-pronoun subjects

When the relative pronouns *who, which,* or *that* act as the subject of a dependent clause, the verb in the clause should agree in number with the antecedent of the pronoun.

> Fear is an ingredient that *goes* into creating stereotypes. [*That* refers to *ingredient*; hence the singular verb form *goes*.]
>
> Guilt, jealousy, and fear are ingredients that *go* into creating stereotypes. [*That* refers to *ingredients*; hence the plural form *go*.]

When the phrase *one of the* precedes the relative pronoun, you have to be especially careful to determine whether the pronoun refers to the word *one* or to another word. Look at the following sentence:

Alex is one of the *employees* who always *work* overtime.

In this sentence a number of employees always work overtime, and Alex is among them. Thus *who* refers to *employees*, and the verb form is plural. Now look at the following sentence:

Alex is the only *one* of the employees who always *works* overtime.

In this sentence only one employee always works overtime, and that employee is Alex. Thus *one* and not *employees* is the antecedent of *who*, and the verb form is singular.

Making linking verbs agree with their subjects, not complements

A linking verb should agree with its subject, which precedes it, not with the subject complement, which follows it (see 14c2).

> The signings of three key treaties *are* the topic of my talk. [The subject is *signings*.]
>
> Nero Wolfe's passion *was* orchids. [The subject is *passion*.]

Making verbs agree with subjects that are plural in form but singular in meaning

Some nouns that seem plural in form (such as *athletics, mathematics, measles, politics, statistics*) are usually singular in meaning and take singular verb forms.

> Mathematics *is* not always an exact science.
>
> Measles still *strikes* many Canadians.

Some of these nouns may be either singular or plural.

Statistics *is* a course I really dread.

The statistics in that study *are* highly questionable.

In the first sentence above, *statistics* refers to a single course of study; hence it takes a singular verb form. In the second sentence, *statistics* refers to a number of individual figures; hence it takes a plural verb form.

When the subject is the title of a book, film, or other work of art, the verb form is singular even if the title is plural in form.

Sons and Lovers was left to the mercy of critics, many of whom did not fully comprehend it.

Similarly, a word referred to as a word requires a singular verb form even if the word itself is plural.

Scruples has always sounded funny to me.

Steroids is a little word that packs a big punch in the world of sports.

17i

Making verbs agree with subjects that follow them

In English, the subject usually precedes the verb, so check carefully for subject-verb agreement when this order is inverted, or reversed. Make the verb agree with the subject, not with a noun that happens to precede it. Writers often invert word order to ask questions or to emphasize the subject.

Is a shark a vertebrate? [The subject is *shark*.]

Beside the tracks *stand* silos filled with grain. [The subject is *silos*.]

Another common inversion of subject-verb order occurs in sentences beginning with *there* followed by a form of *be (is, are, was, were)*. *There* is never the subject of such constructions; usually it has no meaning and serves only as an introductory word, or expletive (see 29a1).

There *are* five basic positions in classical ballet. [The subject is *positions*.]

Exercise 17.1

Choose the appropriate verb to establish subject–verb agreement in the following sentences:

1. Every cheque and money order (*cost/costs*) $1.75.

2. Talking and getting up from my seat (*was/were*) my crime.

3. If rhythm and blues (*is/are*) your kind of music, check out that new club on Yorkville Avenue.

4. His generosity and his recognized success in business (*make/makes*) him popular in the community.

5. *The vapours* (*was/were*) a Victorian term for hypochondria.

6. Neither the lighting on the painting nor the wall it is hanging on (*display/displays*) it well.

7. Child abuse is far more commonplace than anyone (*care/cares*) to admit.

8. Most of the voters (*support/supports*) a reduction in nuclear weapons.

9. Each of the players (*is/are*) dealt five cards to start the game.

10. Either his phony smile or his bragging (*seem/seems*) to fool many people.

11. The team (*need/needs*) time to learn to cooperate with one another.

12. Her grandmother is the only one of her relatives who still (*cycle/cycles*) to work.

13. The situation is not entirely hopeless, for some (*do/does*) see the light.

14. *Our Tapes* (*was/were*) one of Fitzgerald's earlier titles for *Tender Is the Night*.

15. Sweden was one of the few European countries that (*was/were*) neutral in 1943.

16. Politics (*has/have*) been defined as the art of the possible.

17. The short-term effect of the company's expansion (*was/were*) lower dividends.

18. Mumps (*cause/causes*) swelling of the salivary glands.

19. In the foreground (*is/are*) two women playing musical instruments and singing.

20. Dr. Pangloss believes that everything that (*happen/happens*) is for the best.

PRONOUN–ANTECEDENT AGREEMENT

Most pronouns function in sentences as replacements for nouns or other pronouns, known as their **antecedents.** Like a verb with its subject, a pronoun must agree with its antecedent in person and number. In addition, a third-person singular pronoun must agree with its antecedent in *gender*— masculine, feminine, or neuter. (See 14b3.)

Angry, *Mr. Blanchard* called in to say *he* was sick. [third-person singular, masculine]

The *workers* elected a representative to voice *their* common complaints. [third-person plural]

As with subject-verb agreement, only a few kinds of pronoun-antecedent constructions cause problems in practice, so we will look at those constructions in greater detail.

Making pronouns agree with compound antecedents

A compound antecedent whose parts are joined by *and* requires a plural pronoun.

> With great excitement, the children and I began *our* search for the perfect house.
>
> Keith, Molly, and Javiar hid behind the teacher's chair, and nobody saw them.

When a compound antecedent is preceded by *each* or *every*, however, it takes a singular pronoun.

> Every plant and animal has *its* own ecological niche.

A compound antecedent that refers to a single person or thing also takes a singular pronoun.

> The producer and director invested all of *her* savings in the film.

With a compound antecedent whose parts are joined by *or* or *nor*, the pronoun agrees with the nearest antecedent.

> Neither the players nor the owners will change *their* tactics.

> For us to win the meet, Marianne or Moberley must win *her* next dive.

This kind of sentence, however, may be awkward if the parts of the antecedent are of different genders. Consider, for example, the following sentence:

> AWKWARD   For us to win the meet, Tim or Moberley must win *her* next dive.

Such a sentence can be revised in a number of ways to eliminate the awkwardness.

REVISED   For us to win the meet, Tim or Moberley must win *his or her* next dive.

REVISED   For us to win the meet, Tim must win *his* next dive, or Moberley must win *hers.*

With compound antecedents containing both singular and plural parts, the sentence may sound awkward unless a plural part comes last.

AWKWARD   Neither the vice-presidents nor the president would disclose *her* income for 1994.

REVISED   Neither the president nor the vice-presidents would disclose *their* incomes for 1994.

Making pronouns agree with collective-noun antecedents

When a collective-noun antecedent (*herd, team, committee, audience,* for example) refers to a single unit, it requires a singular pronoun.

The audience fixed *its* attention on centre stage.

Finally, our team scored *its* first victory.

When such an antecedent refers to the individual parts of the unit, however, it requires a plural pronoun.

The staff divided the leftovers among *themselves.*

The director chose this cast because *they* had experience in the roles.

Remember that collective nouns referring to single units require not only singular pronouns but also singular verb forms. Collective nouns referring to separate individuals in a unit, on the other hand, require plural pronouns and plural verb forms.

Each generation *has its* own slang. [*generation* as single unit]

My generation *have* sold *their* souls for money. [*generation* as separate individuals]

17l

Making pronouns agree with indefinite-pronoun antecedents

A pronoun whose antecedent is an indefinite pronoun should agree with it in number. Indefinite pronouns may be always singular (as with *one*) or plural (as with *many*), or their number may depend on their context. (See 17e for a list.)

> One of the ballerinas lost *her* balance. [singular]
>
> Many in the audience jumped to *their* feet. [plural]
>
> All of the music was familiar to *its* listeners. [singular meaning for *all*]
>
> All of the principal dancers took *their* bows. [plural meaning for *all*]

17m

Avoiding sexism with pronouns

One somewhat complicated problem in pronoun-antecedent agreement involves a pronoun referring to a singular antecedent that may be either male or female. Look at the following passage:

> … the Country Club pool was small. One diving board, no spinning top. But its size seemed to me to be a measure of its exclusiveness. *Whoever* had laid out plans for the Country Club was an entrepreneur with an eye for the one beautiful, rolling and wooded piece of land outside Ames. *He* must have known immediately that such an acreage had to be saved; *he* had a true aristocrat's instinct and converted it into a private preserve.
>
> – SUSAN ALLEN TOTH, "Swimming Pools"

Notice that although the author apparently does not know who laid out the plans for the Country Club, she uses the pronoun *he* to refer to this person. In traditional English grammar, writers used masculine pronouns, known as the **generic *he***, in such cases. In recent decades, however, many people have pointed out that such wording ignores or even excludes females—and thus should be avoided.

There are several ways of avoiding the generic *he*. Consider, for example, the following sentence:

> Every citizen should know *his* rights under the law.

Now look at three ways to express the same idea without the *he*.

1. Every citizen should know *his or her* rights under the law.
2. All citizens should know *their* rights under the law.
3. Everyone should have some knowledge of basic legal rights.

As these examples show, you have three basic options: (1) using both masculine and feminine pronouns—*he or she, his or her*, and so forth; (2) revising into the plural; and (3) revising the sentence altogether.

When the antecedent is an indefinite pronoun (*anybody, both, each, few, neither, none, somebody;* see 14b3 for a more complete list), some people avoid the generic *he* by using a plural pronoun. For example:

Everyone had *their* own theory about Marcia's resignation.

You will probably hear—and perhaps use—such sentences in conversation, but you should be careful about using them in writing, for many readers do find the construction jarring. See 19c5 and 30a2 for more discussion of how to avoid sexist language.

Exercise 17.2

Revise the following paragraph to create subject-verb and pronoun-antecedent agreement and to eliminate the generic *he*.

> By this time, most of us has heard from one source or another that an excess of salt in our diets are damaging to our health. Why, then, does recent statistics indicate that North Americans are consuming as much salt as ever? First of all, few of us is aware of how much salt the average person consumes unnecessarily each day. Second, once we acquire a taste for salt, food begins to taste bland without it. Third, and perhaps most important, almost nobody realize what salt does to their bodies and why they should cut down on the excess. The North American has to shake his salt habit.

Reading with an eye for pronouns

Following is a paragraph from "The Tyranny of the Clock," George Woodcock's essay on how mechanical clocks have changed people's lives. Read the paragraph with an eye for pronouns. Does the exclusive use of the masculine pronoun seem odd to you when the author is obviously talking about human beings in general? Revise the paragraph to eliminate the use of the masculine pronouns to refer to both men and women.

Nor does the financial imposition of regularity tend, in the long run, to greater efficiency. Indeed, the quality of product is usually much poorer, because the employer, regarding time as a commodity which he has to pay for, forces the operative to maintain such a speed that his work must necessarily be skimped. Quantity rather than quality becomes the criterion, the enjoyment is taken out of the work itself, and the worker in his turn becomes a "clock-watcher," concerned only with when he will be able to escape to the scanty and monotonous leisure of industrial society, in which he "kills time" by cramming in as much time-scheduled and mechanical enjoyment of cinema, radio, and newspaper as his wage packet and tiredness will allow.

– GEORGE WOODCOCK, "The Tyranny of the Clock"

Taking inventory: agreement

Write a descriptive paragraph about a person you know—another student, a member of your family, a friend, a mentor, whomever. Analyze your draft for agreement—between subjects and verbs, of course, but especially between pronouns and their antecedents.

Using Adjectives and Adverbs

As words that describe other words, adjectives and adverbs can add liveliness and colour to writing, helping writers to *show* rather than just tell. Adjectives and adverbs can help readers visualize objects, scenes, or even abstractions. See, for instance, how much Gretel Ehrlich relies on adjectives and adverbs in the following description of the cowboy.

> In our *hellbent* earnestness to romanticize the cowboy we've *ironically* disesteemed his *true* character ... Instead of the *macho, trigger-happy* man our culture has *perversely* wanted him to be, the cowboy is *more apt* to be *convivial, quirky,* and *softhearted* ...
>
> — GRETEL EHRLICH, "About Men"

Ehrlich could have said simply, "We have misrepresented the cowboy. He is not really so macho." But adjectives such as *convivial* and *soft-hearted* create a vivid image of the cowboy; adverbs such as *ironically* and *perversely* evoke a definite impression of Ehrlich's own attitude to her subject.

Adjectives are particularly useful for conveying concrete and sensory details in physical descriptions. Look, for example, at the adjectives Farley Mowat uses in describing the false idea most people have of the Canadian North.

> The North, this Arctic of the mind, this *frigid* concept of a *flat* and *formless* void of ice and snow congealed beneath the *impenetrable* blackness of the polar night, is pure illusion. Behind it lies a *lost* world obscured in drifts of *literary* drivel, obliterated by blizzards of bravado and buried under an *icy* weight of *obsessive* misconceptions.
>
> — FARLEY MOWAT, "The Nature of the North"

Adverbs can also make writing vivid or add emphasis to a point. In the following sentence, the qualifications provided by the adverbs carry the central idea:

> After three years of torture, the man was found guilty—*legally, officially,* but *unjustly* found guilty.

The three adverbs build up to culminate in an accusation: the verdict is not a just one.

But if adjectives and adverbs can create many dramatic effects in writing, they can also betray a writer who uses them inappropriately. Like any other part of a sentence, they must follow certain rules and conventions. This chapter discusses some of these rules and conventions and common problems that writers have with adjectives and adverbs.

Distinguishing adjectives from adverbs

Although adjectives and adverbs both modify other words, they each modify different parts of speech. **Adjectives** modify nouns and pronouns, answering the questions *which? how many?* and *what kind?* Many adjectives are formed by adding the suffixes *-able, -ful, -ish, -less,* or *-y* to nouns and verbs.

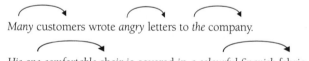

> Many customers wrote *angry* letters to *the* company.

> His *one comfortable* chair is covered in *a colourful Spanish* fabric.

Participles and infinitives can also function as adjectives. (See 14c3.)

> The *perplexed* clerk looked at me with a *questioning* expression.

> Sandra could not decide what job *to take.*

Although adjectives usually precede the noun or pronoun they modify, they sometimes follow it instead. An adjective can also appear after a linking verb, as a subject complement that modifies the subject of the sentence or clause (see 14c2 and 18b).

> Butler found the Victorian family *stifling.*

Chocolate is *irresistible* to Lee.

For information about when to capitalize adjectives, see 40b. For information about when to use commas between adjectives preceding a noun, see 34d.

Adverbs modify verbs, adjectives, and other adverbs; they answer the questions *how? when? where?* or *to what extent?* Many adverbs are formed by adding *-ly* to adjectives.

The speaker smiled *nervously*. [modifies the verb *smiled*]

She was *almost* ready. [modifies the adjective *ready*]

The audience had arrived *rather* early. [modifies the adjective *early*]

Adverbs can modify an entire clause:

Fortunately, the rain had ended before the wedding.

Infinitives can function as adverbs. (See 14c3.)

Gabriel went *to meet* his sister. [modifies the verb *went*]

While adjectives usually are closely tied to the words they modify, adverbs that modify verbs or clauses can often move easily from one position in a sentence to another.

Connor *gleefully* tore open his presents.

Connor tore open his presents *gleefully*.

Gleefully, Connor tore open his presents.

Since adjectives and adverbs both act as modifiers, often have similar forms, and can sometimes occupy the same positions in sentences, sometimes the only way of recognizing an adjective or an adverb is to identify its function in the sentence. Remember: adjectives modify *nouns* and *pronouns*; adverbs modify *verbs, adjectives,* and other *adverbs.*

Exercise 18.1

Read the following paragraph with an eye for the adjectives and adverbs. Identify each one, and determine which word each modifies:

There is something slightly inhuman and robotic about the reporters who deliver the news to us on television. As a class they do not represent humanity. TV news people are never ugly. They are never old and seldom middle-aged. They are rarely overweight or bald and they do not wear striking or ungainly clothing. They are never unhappy or ill at ease. They are, without exception, middle class: no national TV reporter speaks with a regional or working class accent, or for that matter a Rosedale honk or a Westmount whine. Whatever eccentricities they may have are suppressed.

— ROBERT FULFORD, "The Grand Illusion"

18b

Using adjectives after linking verbs

Be careful to use adjectives, not the corresponding -ly adverbs, after linking verbs. The most frequently used linking verbs are forms of *be,* but they also include sensory verbs such as *look, appear, seem, sound, feel, smell,* and *taste* and verbs of becoming such as *become, grow, prove,* and *turn.* (See 14c2.) When they function as linking verbs, they are always followed by adjectives (or nouns). Most of these verbs, however, can also be used to express action. When they express action, they can be followed by adverbs.

> The dog looked *hungry.* [linking verb with adjective]
>
> The dog looked *hungrily* at the steak. [action verb with adverb]

18c

Using adverbs to modify verbs, adjectives, and adverbs

Be careful to use adverbs, not adjectives, to modify verbs, adjectives, and other adverbs.

| NOT | His writing style is *excessive* formal. |
| BUT | His writing style is *excessively formal.* |

Good *and* well, bad *and* badly

The modifiers *good, well, bad,* and *badly* cause problems for some writers because the distinctions between *good* and *well* and between *bad* and *badly* are often not observed in conversation and because *well* can function as either an adjective or an adverb.

Good and *bad* are adjectives, and can be used after a linking verb. Do not use them to modify a verb, an adjective, or an adverb; use *well* or *badly* instead.

Marcia looks *good* in black.

He felt *bad* about missing his father's retirement party.

| NOT | He plays the trumpet *good* and the trombone not *bad*. |
| BUT | He plays the trumpet *well* and the trombone not *badly*. |

Badly is an adverb and can be used to modify a verb, an adjective, or another adverb. Do not use it after a linking verb; use *bad* instead.

In her first recital, the soprano sang *badly*.

| NOT | The clams tasted *badly*. |
| BUT | The clams tasted *bad*. |

Well can be either an adjective (meaning "in good health") or an adverb.

| ADJECTIVE | After a week of rest Julio felt *well* again. |
| ADVERB | He cooks *well* enough to be a chef. |

Real *and* really

Be careful also to observe the distinction between *real* and *really*. In conversation and informal writing, the adjective *real* is often used in place of the adverb *really*, but in formal and academic writing, use the adverb form.

| INFORMAL | Most Canadians were *real* shocked by the report. |
| FORMAL | Most Canadians were *really* shocked by the report. |

18d

Using comparatives and superlatives

In addition to their simple or positive form, many adjectives and adverbs have two other forms, the **comparative** and **superlative**, that are used for making comparisons.

POSITIVE	COMPARATIVE	SUPERLATIVE
large	larger	largest
early	earlier	earliest
careful	more careful	most careful
happily	more happily	most happily

Canada is *larger* than the United States.

He promised to be *more careful* with his money.

They are the *most happily* married couple I know.

As these examples suggest, the comparative and superlative of most short (one-syllable and some two-syllable) adjectives are usually formed by adding the endings -er and -est. *More* and *most* are also used with short adjectives, however, and can sometimes create a more formal tone. The only way to form the comparative and superlative of longer adjectives—three syllables or more—and of most adverbs is by using *more* and *most*. If you are not sure whether an adjective or adverb has -er and -est forms, consult the dictionary entry for the simple form, where the -er and -est forms are usually listed if they exist.

1. Recognizing irregular forms

Some adjectives and adverbs have irregular comparative and superlative forms. Here is a list of them:

POSITIVE	COMPARATIVE	SUPERLATIVE
Adjectives		
good	better	best
well	better	best
bad	worse	worst
ill	worse	worst
little (quantity)	less	least
many	more	most
some	more	most
much	more	most
Adverbs		
well	better	best
ill	worse	worst
badly	worse	worst

2. Distinguishing between comparatives and superlatives

The comparative form of an adjective or adverb is used to compare two things. The superlative form is used to compare three or more things.

Rome is a much *older* city than Montreal.

Damascus is one of the *oldest* cities in the world.

In conversation, you will often hear the superlative form used even when only two things are being compared: *Of those two suits, the black one is the most becoming.* However, the comparative form is correct: *Of those two suits, the black one is the more becoming.*

Exercise 18.2

Choose three of the following numbered words, and write a brief passage that uses the simple, comparative, and superlative forms of each one.

EXAMPLE
frisky   friskier   friskiest

George adopted a small, *frisky* puppy named Brutus. Quickly, Brutus became even *friskier,* chasing neighbours and jumping on children. He was at his *friskiest* the day Aunt Rosa came to visit.

1. loudly   2. well (adverb) 3. wholesome   4. some   5. little
6. rare   7. good   8. thirsty   9. heavily 10. sarcastically

Using nouns as modifiers

Sometimes a noun can function as an adjective by modifying another noun, as in the following examples:

chicken soup	control centre	atom bomb	law school
money supply	space station	day care	rye bread

In familiar terms such as those listed above, we have no trouble under-standing the meaning. In fact, a phrase like *chicken soup* is the most succinct and direct way of expressing the idea of soup made from chicken. If the noun modifiers pile up, however, they can obscure meaning and should thus be revised.

AWKWARD   The 1994 Toronto café shooting left everyone feeling vul-nerable.

REVISED   The 1994 shooting in a Toronto café left everyone feeling vul-nerable.

Reading with an eye for adjectives and adverbs

Find some examples of adjectives and adverbs that you consider noteworthy. You might look anywhere—in essays, short stories, newspaper or magazine articles, your own journal. Copy down five examples, and comment in writing on why they impress you as so effective. What do they add to the larger piece of writing? What would be lost if they were removed? Compare your excerpts to those chosen by other students and discuss your choices.

Taking inventory: adjectives and adverbs

Think of something you can observe or examine closely, and take a few minutes to study it. In a paragraph or two, describe your subject for someone who has never seen it. Identify all the adjectives and adverbs in your description, and list two possible synonyms for each one. Would changing any of these modifiers strengthen your description? Are there any places where you could make it more specific or vivid by adding an adjective or adverb? Do you see any adjectives or adverbs that are not really necessary or that do not create exactly the image you intend? Revise the description with such considerations in mind.

PART FIVE

Making Sentence-Level Choices: Conventions

Maintaining Clear Pronoun Reference

Recognizing Shifts

Identifying Comma Splices and Fused Sentences

Recognizing Sentence Fragments

Recognizing Misplaced, Disruptive, and Dangling Modifiers

Maintaining Consistent and Complete Grammatical Structures

Maintaining Clear Pronoun Reference

Readers are more likely to understand your writing when your pronouns refer clearly to their antecedents. Clear pronoun reference can help avoid unnecessary repetition and move a passage along easily, as in the following paragraph:

> Sam did not say that *he* had pictured *himself* lately working in a bank, a business college graduate. *He* saw *himself* in a three-piece suit in the teller's cage. *He* would have grown a mustache. Some tellers became bank managers. It had just recently occurred to *him* that bank managers did not come into the world ready-made. They were something else first.
>
> – ALICE MUNRO, *The Progress of Love*

If you read the paragraph again, repeating *Sam* in place of every *he* and *him,* you can see how useful these pronouns are. But look what happens when another man is added to the story:

> Sam did not say that *he* had pictured *himself* lately working in a bank, nor did Ted, a business-college graduate. *He* saw *himself* in a three-piece suit …

In this instance, the reference for the first *he* is clear, because it follows *Sam.* But what about the second *he,* and *himself*—do they refer to Sam, or to Ted?

This chapter will alert you to ways of avoiding problems of pronoun reference in your writing.

19a

Matching pronouns to their appropriate antecedents

If more than one possible antecedent for a personal pronoun appears in a sentence or passage, a pronoun must refer unambiguously to only *one* of them.

AMBIGUOUS	The meeting between Bowman and Sonny makes *him* compare *his* own unsatisfying domestic life with one that is emotionally secure and involved.
CLEAR	The meeting between Bowman and Sonny makes *Bowman* compare *his* own unsatisfying domestic life with one that is emotionally secure and involved.
CLEAR	Meeting Sonny makes *Bowman* compare *his* own unsatisfying domestic life with one that is emotionally secure and involved.
CLEAR	After meeting Sonny, whose domestic life is emotionally secure and involved, *Bowman* finds *his* own domestic life unsatisfying.

In the ambiguous sentence, readers cannot tell whether Bowman or Sonny is the antecedent of *him* and *his*. All three revisions make the reference clear. The first does so by replacing a pronoun *(him)* with a noun *(Bowman)*, but it requires repeating the noun. The second alternative eliminates one of the pronouns, and the third recasts the sentence altogether.

If you are reporting what someone else said, check carefully for clear pronoun reference. In the sentence *Karen told Talia she should be ready soon,* readers cannot be sure which of the two people should be ready because *she* does not clearly relate to one or the other. Such a sentence can be revised by quoting directly to make clear who is saying what, or it can be reworded to eliminate the ambiguity.

Karen told Talia to be ready soon.

Karen told Talia, "I should be ready soon."

Karen told Talia, "You should be ready soon."

Keeping pronouns and antecedents close together

If a pronoun is too far from its antecedent, readers will have trouble making the connection between the two. Maintaining clear reference calls for keeping pronouns and their antecedents in close proximity.

CONFUSING The right-to-life coalition believes that a zygote, an egg at the moment of fertilization, is as deserving of protection as is the born human being, and thus that abortion is as much murder as is the killing of a child. The coalition's focus is on what *it* will become, a conscious being with reasoning power, a sense of self, and the capacity to communicate, as much as on what *it* is now.

CLEAR The right-to-life coalition believes that a *zygote,* an egg at the moment of fertilization, is as deserving of protection as is the born human being, and thus that abortion is as much murder as is the killing of a child. The coalition's focus is on what *the zygote* will become, a conscious being with reasoning power, a sense of self, and the capacity to communicate, as much as on what *it* is now.

Recognizing troublesome pronoun references

Matching a pronoun to one specific antecedent and keeping pronouns and antecedents close together will take you a long way toward establishing clear pronoun reference. A few pronouns, however, cause particular problems for writers. The sections that follow provide practice in checking to see that these pronouns are used clearly and properly.

1. Checking for vague and ambiguous use of *it, this, that,* and *which*

Writers are often tempted to use *it, this, that,* or *which* as a kind of shortcut, a quick and easy way of referring to something mentioned earlier. But such shortcuts can often cause confusion. Make sure that these pronouns refer clearly to a specific antecedent.

VAGUE	The Engineering Society sponsored a charity drive last week, and students responded enthusiastically. *It* really surprised us. [What does *it* refer to—the fact that the Engineering Society sponsored a charity drive, that students responded enthusiastically, or perhaps both?]
CLEAR	The Engineering Society sponsored a charity drive last week, and students responded enthusiastically. *The response* really surprised us.
VAGUE	The art of rhetoric was created in the ancient world in response to the economic and political need for a fair method of property redistribution. Corax devised the first known system for *this*. [For what, exactly—creating rhetoric? redistribution property?]
CLEAR	Rhetoric was created in the ancient world out of the economic and political need for a fair method of property redistribution. Corax devised the first *such method* known.
AMBIGUOUS	I am taking a course in Romantic poetry, *which* has been the bane of our existence. [What does *which* refer to—the course or the poetry?]
CLEAR	I am taking a course in Romantic poetry, *a kind of literature* that has been the bane of my existence.
CLEAR	I am taking a course in Romantic poetry, *a class* that has been the bane of my existence.

If *that* or *which* opens a clause that refers to a specific noun, put *that* or *which* directly after the noun, if possible.

AMBIGUOUS	We worked all night on the brochure for the campaign *that* we designed. [Does *that* refer to the brochure or the campaign?]
CLEAR	We worked all night on the brochure *that* we designed for the campaign.

2. Checking for appropriate use of *who, which,* and *that*

Be careful to use the relative pronouns *who, which,* and *that* appropriately. *Who* refers primarily to people or to animals with names. *Which* refers to animals or to things, and *that* refers to animals, things, and anonymous persons or people treated collectively. (See 34c for information about the use of commas with clauses beginning with *who, which,* and *that*.)

Northrop Frye, *who* won many awards for his writing, taught at the University of Toronto.

The whale, *which* has only one baby a year, is subject to extinction because it does not reproduce quickly.

People *that* support animal rights oppose laboratory experimentation with animals.

People *who* support animal rights oppose laboratory experimentation with animals.

3. Checking for indefinite use of *you* and *they*

In conversation, we frequently use *you* and *they* in an indefinite sense, as in such expressions as *you never know* and *on television they said*. In academic and professional writing, however, such constructions are inappropriate. Be careful to use *you* only to mean "you, the reader," and *they* only to refer to a clear antecedent.

> INAPPROPRIATE Television commercials try to make *you* buy without thinking.
>
> REVISED Television commercials try to make *viewers* buy without thinking.
>
> INAPPROPRIATE In France *they* allow dogs in most restaurants.
>
> REVISED Most restaurants in France allow dogs.

4. Checking to see that antecedents are nouns or pronouns, not adjectives or possessives

In conversation, a pronoun often refers to an antecedent that is an adjective or the possessive form of a noun. In writing, an antecedent must always be a noun or pronoun in the subjective case.

> INAPPROPRIATE In Welty's story, *she* characterizes Bowman as a man unaware of his own isolation.
>
> REVISED In her story, Welty characterizes Bowman as a man unaware of his own isolation.
>
> REVISED In Welty's story, Bowman is characterized as a man unaware of his own isolation.

5. Checking for sexist pronoun usage

Remember to avoid using masculine pronouns to refer to antecedents that include or may include both males and females. For example, the sentence *Every lawyer values his client's testimony* implies that only men are lawyers. Such a sentence can be revised in several ways: by eliminating the pronoun, by using both masculine and feminine pronouns, or by shifting to the plural. A more complete discussion of nonsexist pronoun usage can be found in 17m.

Every lawyer values *a* client's testimony.

Every lawyer values *his or her* client's testimony.

All lawyers value *their* clients' testimonies.

Exercise 19.1

Revise the following sentences to establish clear and appropriate pronoun reference, and to eliminate any sexist pronoun usage. Most of the sentences can be revised in more than one way.

EXAMPLE
It says in the newspaper to expect rain today.

The newspaper says to expect rain today.

1. On the highway they charge very high prices for gasoline.

2. In Canada, you often hear about the influence of pharmaceutical companies on physicians.

3. They said on the radio that somebody had won the lottery.

4. A friend of mine recently had a conversation with a new parent that changed his view of child rearing.

5. She dropped off a friend which had gone to the party with her.

6. Not only was the chair delivered three weeks late, but the store told me this was normal.

7. I take care not to get too bundled up in the winter because it will be too hot when you are indoors.

8. The company had a policy prohibiting smoking, which many employees resented.

9. I called as soon as the catalogue arrived, but they were already sold out of the leather moccasins.

10. Is it true that a lawyer can count on making his fortune within ten years of graduation?

Taking inventory: pronoun reference

Write a paragraph or two describing two favourite aunts—or two other people of the same sex. Then analyze your use of pronouns. Have you used any pronouns that do not refer clearly and directly to the correct antecedent? Any whose antecedents could be ambiguous? Using the guidelines shown in this chapter, revise as necessary.

(20) Recognizing Shifts

A **shift** in writing is, most simply, an abrupt change of some sort that results in inconsistency. Consider, for example, this passage from Erika Ritter's "Bicycles":

> Just the other day, there was a piece in the paper about a bicycle that went berserk in a shopping centre, smashing two display windows before it was subdued. And did you hear about the recent sighting of a whole herd of riderless bicycles, all rolling soundlessly across a park in the night?
>
> It all kind of gets you to thinking. I mean, do *you* know where your tenspeed is tonight?

Now replace the last sentence with this one: *If one ponders the information, one might query, are you aware of where your bi-pedal vehicle is located this evening?* As readers, we would be jolted and no doubt confused by such a shift in tone, from informality to exaggerated formality.

Such a shift, because it is so blatant, is hard to miss. This chapter will help you to recognize shifts that are more subtle and will offer strategies for revising to eliminate them. These include shifts in the tense, mood, and voice of verbs; in the person and number of pronouns; from direct to indirect discourse; and in tone and diction.

(20a)

Recognizing shifts in tense

If the verbs in a sentence or passage refer to actions occurring at different times, they may require different tenses: *Mac <u>started</u> the kennel because he <u>had</u> always <u>loved</u> dogs.* Be careful, however, not to change tenses unnecessarily or in a way that does not make sense. Look, for instance, at this sentence: *Pongo <u>yowled</u> until his owner <u>looks</u> up.* The shift in tenses from past to present confuses readers, who are left to guess which tense is the correct one.

INCONSISTENT   A very few countries *produce* most of the world's illegal drugs, but drug addiction *affected* many more countries.

REVISED   A very few countries *produce* most of the world's illegal drugs, but drug addiction *affects* many more countries.

INCONSISTENT   Some people never really *settle* down to a book. Instead, they *limited* themselves to newspapers and magazines, since these *required* less commitment.

REVISED   Some people never really *settle* down to a book. Instead, they *limit* themselves to newspapers and magazines, since these *require* less commitment.

See Chapter 16 for a complete discussion of verb tense.

Recognizing shifts in mood

Be careful not to shift from one mood to another without reason. The mood of a verb can be indicative (He <u>closes</u> the door), imperative (<u>Close</u> the door), or subjunctive (If the door <u>were closed</u>, ...). (See Chapter 16 for a discussion of mood.)

INCONSISTENT   *Keep* your eye on the ball, and you *should bend* your knees. [shift from imperative to indicative]

REVISED   *Keep* your eye on the ball, and *bend* your knees.

INCONSISTENT   The counsellor asked that Mei *tutor* the Chinese children in English and that she *teaches* them some Canadian games as well. [shift from subjunctive to indicative]

REVISED   The counsellor asked that Mei *tutor* the Chinese children in English and that she *teach* them some Canadian games as well.

20c

Recognizing shifts in voice

Do not shift unnecessarily between the active voice (She <u>sold</u> the furniture) and the passive voice (The furniture <u>was sold</u>). Sometimes a shift in voice is perfectly justified. In the sentence I <u>am known</u> for being unpredictable and adventurous, but I <u>consider</u> myself a practical person, the shift from passive (am known) to active (consider) allows the writer to keep the emphasis on the subject I. Making both verbs active (People <u>know</u> me as an unpredictable and *adventurous person, but I* <u>consider</u> *myself a practical person*) changes the focus of the sentence. Often, however, shifts in voice merely confuse readers. (See Chapter 16.)

INCONSISTENT   After we *finished* decorating the house, it *was photographed* by us.

REVISED   After we *finished* decorating the house, we *photographed* it.

INCONSISTENT   Four children *approached* him, and he *was asked* to buy a raffle ticket.

REVISED   Four children *approached* him and *asked* him to buy a raffle ticket.

Recognizing shifts in person and number

Do not shift unnecessarily between first person (*I, we*), second person (*you*), and third person (*he, she, it, one,* or *they*) or between singular and plural. Such shifts in person and number create confusion.

INCONSISTENT   *One* can do well in college if *you* budget *your* time carefully.

REVISED   *One* can do well in college if *one* budgets *one's* time carefully.

REVISED   *You* can do well in college if *you* budget *your* time carefully.

INCONSISTENT   *Nurses* are paid much less than doctors, even though *a nurse* has the primary responsibility for daily care of patients.

REVISED   *Nurses* are paid much less than doctors, even though *nurses* have the primary responsibility for daily care of patients.

Many shifts in number are actually problems with pronoun-antecedent agreement (see 15j–15m).

INCONSISTENT   I have difficulty seeing another *person's* position, especially if *their* opinion contradicts mine.

REVISED   I have difficulty seeing another *person's* position, especially if *his or her* opinion contradicts mine.

REVISED   I have difficulty seeing other *people's* positions, especially if *their* opinions contradict mine.

Recognizing shifts between direct and indirect discourse

When you quote someone's exact words, setting them off in quotation marks, you are using **direct discourse**. On the other hand, when you summarize or report what someone has said (rather than quote the exact words), you are using **indirect discourse**.

DIRECT	My textbook defines *memorandum* as a "piece of written communication used within an organization."
INDIRECT	My textbook says that a memorandum is a written document that is used by organizations internally.

Do not shift between direct and indirect discourse in the same sentence. Use *either* direct or indirect discourse throughout.

INCONSISTENT	Chief Seattle said that one nation *followed* another like the waves of the sea and therefore "regret is useless."
REVISED	Chief Seattle said that "nation follows nation, like the waves of the sea" and that therefore "regret is useless."
REVISED	Chief Seattle said that one nation followed another like the waves of the sea and that therefore regret was useless.

20f

Recognizing shifts in tone and diction

Tone in writing refers to the way the writer's attitude toward the topic and/or audience comes across to the audience. (See 2d and 2e.) Tone is closely related to **diction**, or word choice—not only the choice of individual words but the overall level of formality, technicality, or other effects created by the individual words. Within a sentence, a paragraph, or an entire piece of writing, be careful not to change your tone or level of diction unless you have a reason for doing so. (See Chapter 30 for a complete discussion of diction and tone.)

Tone
When they are used for emphasis or humour, shifts in tone can be

effective. Mark Twain was a master of such shifts. In the following passage, he presents a mock graduation address, "Advice to Youth," beginning with a serious tone and then shifting at the beginning of the second paragraph to characteristic humour:

> Being told I would be expected to talk here, I inquired what sort of a talk I ought to make. They said it should be something suitable to you—something didactic, instructive, or something in the nature of good advice. Very well. I have a few things in my mind which I have often longed to say for the instruction of the young; for it is in one's tender early years that such things will best take root and be most enduring and most valuable. First, then, I will say to you, my young friends—and I say it beseechingly, urgingly—
>
> Always obey your parents, when they are present. This is the best policy in the long run, because if you don't they will make you. Most parents think they know better than you do, and you can generally make more by humoring that superstition than you can by acting on your own better judgment.
>
> – MARK TWAIN, "Advice to Youth"

Twain opens with a flowery, slightly pompous tone with references to the "instruction of the young" and "one's tender early years." With the adverbs *beseechingly, urgingly,* he seems about to launch into a stereotypically high-flown "leaders of tomorrow" commencement speech. Abruptly, however, he overturns readers' expectations in the second paragraph, to deliver his subversive advice in brisk, plain language. The only "formal" phrase in this paragraph, *humoring that superstition,* only highlights and contributes to the informal comic tone.

Unintended shifts in tone, on the other hand, confuse readers and leave them wondering what the writer's real attitude is. In the following passage, notice how the tone shifts in the last sentence:

> The question of child care forces a society to make profound decisions about its economic values. Can most families with young children actually live adequately on only one salary? If some people had their way, women would still be stuck in the kitchen baking cookies for the kiddies and waiting for hubby to bring home the bacon, except that with only one income the family would be lucky to afford hot dogs.

The first two sentences of this passage set a serious, formal tone, discussing child care in fairly general, abstract terms, but in the third sentence the writer shifts suddenly to a sarcastic attack. Readers cannot tell whether the writer is presenting an analysis of the child-care issue or an argument about it. See how the passage was revised to make the tone consistent.

The question of child care forces a society to make profound decisions about its economic values. Can most families with young children actually live adequately on only one salary? Some people believe that women with young children should not work outside the home, but many such women are forced to do so for financial reasons.

Diction

Like shifts in tone, inappropriate shifts in level of diction can confuse readers. In general, diction may be classified as technical *(Araucaria araucama instead of monkey puzzle tree)*, informal or colloquial *(Give me a ring if there's anything I can do)*, formal *(Please inform me if I can be of further assistance)*, or slang *(He thinks he's cool, but he's just another skater)*. In the following sentences, the diction shifts from formal to highly informal, giving an odd, disjointed feeling to the passage:

INCONSISTENT	Their law enabled illegal aliens who had entered the country before 1982 and resided there continuously to obtain legal status and citizenship. But folks who'd gone home since the beginning of 1982 were in deep trouble.
REVISED	Their law enabled illegal aliens who had entered the country before 1982 and resided there continuously to obtain legal status and citizenship. But aliens who had left the country since the beginning of 1982 were not eligible.

Reading with an eye for shifts

Read the following passages carefully, noting any shifts in tone and diction. Then revise them for consistency.

1. Lately, I have been bugged because there are not enough cashiers on each shift. We cashiers attempt to ring the customer's orders through quickly and efficiently, but sometimes we make a few mistakes, and the customers get mad that we are messing up their bills. Some people are very mean and sarcastic toward us, and, of course, we cannot protest. Repressing my feelings is the most frustrating thing about this job. The customers complain about high prices, too, something over which we have no control. In short, it is difficult to work in such a high-pressure atmosphere. Cashiering is a hard job; we deserve more respect than we normally get.

2. In *The Great Gatsby*, the rich and poor alike can harbour malevolence. For instance, Myrtle Wilson is unkind to her husband primarily because he is poor. To Myrtle, the rich are better people, so she becomes a rich man's mistress. Her lover, Tom Buchanan, is filthy rich, but he beats her up. There must be a message here!

Taking inventory: writing shifts

Locate a piece of writing you have done recently and examine it for the various types of shifts discussed in this chapter. This is a good exercise to do in groups of three or four students, because it is often easier to find shifts in other people's writing than in one's own. If shifts are found in your writing, revise for consistency.

21

Identifying Comma Splices and Fused Sentences

The terms *comma splice* and *fused sentence* grow out of metaphors based on the words *splice* and *fuse*. In grammatical terms, a **comma splice** occurs when two independent clauses are joined with only a comma; a **fused sentence**, when two independent clauses are joined with no punctuation or connecting word between them.

SPLICE   It was already spring, the tulips were in bloom.

FUSED   It was already spring the tulips were in bloom.

Comma splices and fused sentences can be problematical, for though both are considered "errors," we do find them in literary and journalistic writing. Like many other structures we commonly identify as "errors," each can be used to powerful effect.

E.M. Foster, for instance, is a careful stylist who sometimes deviates from the "correct" to create special effects. Look, for example, at the following passage from his essay about the 1937 Paris Exhibition:

> … For the Soviet Pavilion … is trying to dodge money and to wipe away the film of coins and notes which keeps forming on the human retina. One of the evils of money is that it tempts us to look at it rather than at the things that it buys. They are dimmed because of the metal and the paper through which we receive them. That is the fundamental deceitfulness of riches, which kept worrying Christ. That is the treachery of the purse, the wallet and the bank-balance, even from the capitalist point of view. *They were invented as a convenience to the flesh, they have become a chain for the spirit.*
>
> – E.M. FORSTER, "The Last Parade"

Forster uses a common splice in the last sentence to emphasize parallel ideas; any conjunction, even *and*, would change the causal relationship he wishes to show. The effect is to stop us in our tracks as readers. Because the grammar is unexpected, it attracts just the attention that Forster wants for his statement.

In your academic and professional writing, you will probably not wish to focus attention on sentences in this particular way, for your teachers are (perhaps unfortunately) more alert to errors than to unexpected grammatical turns. This chapter aims to help you learn to recognize comma splices and fused sentences in your own writing and provides five methods of revising to eliminate them.

Five methods of eliminating splices and fused sentences

21a Revise by separating the clauses into two sentences.

21b Revise by linking the clauses with a semicolon.

21c Revise by linking the clauses with a comma and a coordinating conjunction.

21d Revise by recasting the two clauses as *one* independent clause.

21e Revise by recasting one of the independent clauses as a dependent clause.

As a writer, you must decide which method to use in revising—or avoiding—comma splices and fused sentences. The choice requires looking at the sentences before and after the ones you are revising to see how a particular method will affect the rhythm of the passage, and perhaps reading the passage aloud to see how the revision will sound.

21a

Separating the clauses into two sentences

The simplest way to revise comma splices or fused sentences is to separate them into two sentences.

COMMA SPLICE   Thomas Kuhn contrasts "normal science" with "revolutionary science," he says normal science is based on past achievements in a particular field.

FUSED SENTENCE   Thomas Kuhn contrasts "normal science" with "revolutionary science" he says normal science is based on past achievements in a particular field.

REVISED   Thomas Kuhn contrasts "normal science" with "revolutionary science." He says normal science is based on past achievements in a particular field.

Although this method may be the simplest, it is not always the most appropriate. In the preceding example, choosing to divide the two independent clauses into two separate sentences makes good sentence sense: the combined sentences contain twenty-one words, and dividing them into sentences contain twenty-one words, and dividing them into two sentences of eight and thirteen words adds emphasis to both. If the two spliced or fused clauses are very short, however, dividing them into two separate sentences may not succeed so well.

COMMA SPLICE   Thomas Kuhn writes about revolutions in science, his work has been very influential.

FUSED SENTENCE   Thomas Kuhn writes about revolutions in science his work has been very influential.

REVISED   Thomas Kuhn writes about revolutions in science. His work has been very influential.

Here the two short sentences in a row, both opening with the subject, sound abrupt and overly terse, and some other method of revision would probably be preferable. (See Chapter 28.)

Linking the clauses with a semicolon

If the ideas in the two independent clauses in a comma splice or fused sentence are closely related and you want to give them equal emphasis, link them with a semicolon.

COMMA SPLICE   This photograph is not at all realistic, it uses dreamlike images to convey its message.

FUSED SENTENCE   This photograph is not at all realistic it uses dreamlike images to convey its message.

REVISED   This photograph is not all realistic; it uses dreamlike images to convey its message.

In the preceding example, the second independent clause elaborates on and gives a reason for the statement in the first independent clause: it offers evidence that the photograph is not at all realistic. Because the two independent clauses are closely related and of equal importance, linking them with a semicolon represents a sound choice.

Linking the clauses with a comma and a coordinating conjunction

For comma splices and fused sentences in which the two clauses are fairly closely related and equally important, another alternative for revision is to use a comma and a coordinating conjunction: *and, but, or, nor, for, so,* or *yet.* Using a coordinating conjunction helps to indicate what kind of link exists between the ideas in the two clauses. For instance, *but* and *yet* signal opposition or contrast *(I am strong, but she is stronger); for* and *so* signal cause-effect relationships *(The cabin was bitterly cold, so we built a fire).*

COMMA SPLICE	Windows were opened to the warm night air, furnaces were turned off for the season.
FUSED SENTENCE	Windows were opened to the warm night air furnaces were turned off for the season.
REVISED	Windows were opened to the warm night air, *and* furnaces were turned off for the season.

In the preceding example, two acts simply occur in conjunction with each other; thus *and* is an appropriate conjunction to link the two clauses.

See 26a for more information about using coordinating conjunctions to write more varied and interesting sentences.

Distinguishing between coordinating conjunctions and conjunctive adverbs or transitional phrases

The seven coordinating conjunctions can be used with a comma alone to link independent clauses. Do not confuse them with conjunctive adverbs (words like *however, therefore, moreover, then, also)* or with transitional phrases *(in fact, in contrast, in addition).* (See 14b7.) Such words and phrases, even if preceded by a comma, are not enough to link independent clauses grammatically; they must be used with a semicolon, a period, or a coordinating conjunction. In fact, the inappropriate use of conjunctive adverbs and transitional phrases is responsible for many comma splices and fused sentences.

COMMA SPLICE	Some countries have very high birth rates, therefore most of the citizens are young.
FUSED SENTENCE	Some countries have very high birth rates therefore most of their citizens are young.

REVISED	Some countries have very high birth rates. Therefore, most of their citizens are young.
REVISED	Some countries have very high birth rates; therefore, most of their citizens are young.
REVISED	Some countries have very high birth rates; most of their citizens, therefore, are young.
REVISED	Some countries have very high birth rates, and therefore most of their citizens are young.

As you can see from the preceding example, any of the three methods discussed thus far in this chapter can be used to revise a comma splice or fused sentence that uses a conjunctive adverb or transitional phrase inappropriately. The context of the passage can help you decide which method to choose. Notice that conjunctive adverbs and transitional phrases, unlike coordinating conjunctions, can appear in positions other than between independent clauses. These words and expressions are usually set off from the rest of the clause by commas (see 34a).

Recasting the two clauses as a single independent clause

Sometimes two independent clauses that are spliced or fused together can be reduced to a single independent clause that gets the point across in fewer words.

COMMA SPLICE	High school and university prepare students for later life, they do so in different ways.
FUSED SENTENCE	High school and university prepare students for later life they do so in different ways.
REVISED	High school and university prepare students for later life in different ways.

The revision deletes *they do so*, three words that simply repeat what has been said in the first independent clause. Deleting these three words reduces the sentence to a single independent clause that is more direct and succinct than the original version. (See 25b for more information about ways to avoid needless repetition.)

Recasting one of the independent clauses as a dependent clause

Another option for revising two splices or fused independent clauses is to convert one of them to a dependent clause.

This method is most appropriate when the meaning or effect of one clause is dependent on the other or when one is less important than the other.

COMMA SPLICE	Rosalyn Yalow won the Nobel Prize for Medicine, some magazines wrote about her skill as a homemaker.
FUSED SENTENCE	Rosalyn Yalow won the Nobel Prize for Medicine some magazines wrote about her skill as a homemaker.
REVISED	*When* Rosalyn Yalow won the Nobel Prize for Medicine, some magazines wrote about her skill as a homemaker.

In the preceding example, the first clause stands in contrast to the second one; in contrast to Yalow's achievement (she won a Nobel Prize) is the press coverage she sometimes received (on her skill as a homemaker). In the revision, the writer chose to emphasize the second clause and to make the first one into a dependent clause by adding the subordinate conjunction *when*. (For a review of subordinating conjunctions, see 14b7.)

COMMA SPLICE	The Arts and Crafts movement called for simplicity, it reacted against Victorian clutter.
FUSED SENTENCE	The Arts and Crafts movement called for simplicity it reacted against Victorian clutter.
REVISED	The Arts and Crafts movement, *which* reacted against Victorian clutter, called for simplicity.

In this example, both clauses discuss related aspects of the Arts and Crafts movement. In the revision, the writer chose to emphasize the first clause, the one describing what the movement advocated, and to make the second clause, the one describing what it reacted against, into a dependent clause by adding the relative pronoun *which*. (For a review of relative pronouns, see 14b3.)

Notice that dependent clauses must often be set off from the rest of the sentence with commas. For information about the use of commas with dependent clauses, see Chapter 34.

See 26a2 and 26b2 for more information about using dependent clauses to write more varied and effective sentences.

Exercise 21.1

Combine each of the following pairs of sentences into one sentence, using one of the five methods presented in this chapter for revising comma splices and fused sentences. Use each method at least once. In some sentences, you may have to add, delete, or change words.

EXAMPLE

The rain subsided.

The players returned to the field.

The rain subsided, *and* the players returned to the field.

As soon as the rain subsided, the players returned to the field.

1. Yashmin called for volunteers to raise money for the symphony.
   Four people stood up as a result.

2. The mother eagle called twice.
   The young eagle finally answered.

3. Jim grew beautiful tulips.
   He had less success with strawberries.

4. The Soviet Union expelled Solzhenitsyn in 1974.
   He returned to Russia in 1994.

5. The music lifted her spirits.
   She stopped sighing and began singing.

Exercise 21.2

Revise the following paragraph, eliminating the comma splices and fused sentences by using any of the methods discussed in this chapter. Then revise the paragraph again, this time eliminating each comma splice and fused sentence by a *different* method. Decide which paragraph is more effective and why. Finally, compare the revision you prefer with the revisions of several other students, and discuss the ways in which the versions differ in meaning.

Gardening can be very satisfying, it is also hard work people who just see the pretty flowers may not realize this. My mother spends long hours every spring tilling up the soil, she moves many wheelbarrows of disgusting cow manure and chicken droppings, in fact, the whole early part of gardening is nauseating. The whole garden area has to be rototilled every year, this process is not much like the advertisements showing people walking quietly behind the Rototiller, on the contrary, my father has to fight that machine every inch of the way, sweating so much he looks like Hulk Hogan after a hard bout. Then the planting all must be done by hand, my back aches, my hands get raw, my skin gets sunburned. All my clothes get filthy whenever I go near that garden my mother always asks me to help, though. When harvest time comes the effort is *almost* worth it, however, there are always all those extra zucchinis I have to try to give away at school everybody else is trying to give away zucchinis, too. We also have tomatoes, squash, beans, and lettuce, there is always more than we need and we feel bad wasting it wouldn't you like this nice five-pound bag of cucumbers?

Reading with an eye for prose style

Comma splices and fused sentences are sometimes used to create special effects. In the following passage, see how Anne Cameron uses comma splices to create momentum and build to a climax:

> Golden eagles sit in every tree and watch them watch us, although there are bird experts who will tell you in all seriousness that there are NO golden eagles here. Bald eagles are common, ospreys abound, we have herons and mergansers and kingfishers, we have logging with percherons and belgians, we have park land and nature trails, we have enough oddballs, weirdos, and loons to satisfy anybody.

In the second sentence, six independent clauses are spliced together with commas. The effect: a rush of details from the rather oddball birds to the oddball people, and finally to the *loons*, a word that can apply to either birds or people.

Look through some pieces of writing to find some comma splices and fused sentences. Copy down one or two, including enough of the surrounding text to show context, and comment in writing on the effect they create.

Taking inventory: comma splices and fused sentences

Go through the last two or three pieces you have written, checking for comma splices and fused sentences. If you find any, revise them using one of the methods discussed in this chapter. Comment in writing on your chosen methods.

22

Recognizing Sentence Fragments

Sentence fragments are groups of words punctuated as sentences but lacking some element grammatically necessary to a sentence, usually either a subject or a finite verb. We see them sometimes in literary works, used to add dramatic emphasis, to speed up rhythm, or to create realistic dialogue. Notice the effect that is achieved with sentence fragments in the following example:

> My father never saw Paris. *Never read Yeats. Never stayed out with the boys drinking too much. Never flew to New York on a whim. Nor turned over in bed and slept in, rather than report to work. Never knew a reckless love.* What did he hope for? What did he want?
>
> — MORDECAI RICHLER, "My Father's Life"

Richler's stringing together of sentence fragments gives a momentum to his prose. Notice how the fragments add emphasis to the repeated word *never*, and thus to Richler's portrayal of his father.

Although you will find sentence fragments in literature, hear them in conversation, and see them everywhere in advertising, they are usually considered "errors" in academic prose. This chapter will help you recognize and revise sentence fragments.

Two methods of eliminating fragments

In general, a fragment can be revised by combining it with an independent clause or by turning it into an independent clause.

FRAGMENT	The beaver dam holding back the shallow pond.
REVISED	I was startled at the sight of the beaver dam holding back the shallow pond. [combined with independent clause *I was startled*]

REVISED   The beaver dam was holding back the shallow pond. [turned into independent clause by adding *was* to participle *holding*, making verb finite]

Revising phrase fragments

Phrases, groups of words lacking either a subject, a finite verb, or both, appear frequently as fragments. Most common are verbal phrases, prepositional phrases, noun phrases, and appositive phrases.

Verbal-phrase fragments

A verbal phrase includes a gerund, an infinitive, a present participle, or a past participle, together with any objects or modifiers (see 14c3). To revise, combine them with an independent clause or turn them into two separate sentences.

FRAGMENT   Vivian stayed out of school for three months after Julia was born. *To get some rest and to take care of her.*

REVISED   Vivian stayed out of school for three months after Julia was born to get some rest and to take care of her. [combined with independent clause]

REVISED   Vivian stayed out of school for three months after Julia was born. She did so to get some rest and to take care of her. [turned into complete sentence]

Prepositional-phrase fragments

A prepositional phrase consists of a preposition, its object, and any modifiers of the object (see 14c3). Like verbal-phrase fragments, prepositional-phrase fragments contain neither subjects nor finite verbs. Usually you can best revise them by simply joining them to the independent clause containing the word they modify.

FRAGMENT   Several civic groups are sponsoring public debates. *With discussions afterward.*

REVISED   Several civic groups are sponsoring public debates with discussions afterward.

Noun-phrase fragments

A noun phrase consists of a noun together with any adjectives, phrases, or clauses that modify it (see 14c3). Noun-phrase fragments contain a subject but no finite verb, and they frequently appear before fragments containing a verb but no subject. You can best revise such fragments by combining them into one sentence containing both a subject *and* a verb.

FRAGMENT   *His editorial making a plea for good day-care facilities for all children who need day care. Pointed out that reliable day care is available only to some children.*

REVISED   In his editorial making a plea for good day-care facilities for all children who need day care, he pointed out that reliable day care is available only to some children.

REVISED   His editorial making a plea for good day-care facilities for all children who need day care pointed out that reliable day care is available only to some children.

Appositive-phrase fragments

An appositive phrase is a noun phrase that renames or describes another noun (see 14c3). You can revise appositive-phrase fragments by joining them to the independent clause containing the noun to which the appositive phrase refers.

FRAGMENT   One of our country's most cherished dreams seems to be in danger. *The dream of a good education for every child.*

REVISED   One of our country's most cherished dreams, the dream of a good education for every child, seems to be in danger.

REVISED   One of our country's dreams seems to be in danger: the dream of a good education for every child. [In this revision, the use of the colon creates greater emphasis.]

Revising compound-predicate fragments

A compound predicate consists of two or more verbs, along with their modifiers and objects, that have the same subject (see 14c2). Compound-predicate fragments occur when one of these verbs is punctuated as a separate sentence without a subject. These fragments usually begin with the conjunction that connects the parts of the compound. You can revise them by attaching them to the independent clause that contains the rest of the predicate.

FRAGMENT   The miser put some of the money in the bank. *But hid most of it under his mattress.*

REVISED   The miser put some of the money in the bank but hid most of
               it under his mattress.

Revising dependent-clause fragments

Unlike phrases, dependent clauses contain both a subject and a finite verb.
Because they *depend* upon an independent clause to complete their meaning, however, they cannot stand alone as grammatically complete sentences
(see 14c4). Such clauses usually begin with a subordinating conjunction—
such as *after, even though, if*—or a relative pronoun—such as *who, which, that.*
(See 14b3 and 14b7 for lists of relative pronouns and subordinating conjunctions.) You can usually revise dependent clause fragments (1) by combining the dependent clause with the independent clause that precedes or
follows it, or (2) by deleting the subordinating word to create an independent clause.

FRAGMENT   *If all the people who signed up for the lecture stay home to watch
              the hockey game instead.* The lecture hall will be empty.

REVISED   If all the people who signed up for the lecture stay home to
              watch the hockey game instead, the lecture hall will be empty.

FRAGMENT   The plane landed at Heathrow. *Which is one of the world's largest
              airports.*

REVISED   The plane landed at Heathrow, which is one of the world's
              largest airports.

FRAGMENT   Injuries in automobile accidents occur in two ways. *When an
              occupant is hurt by something inside the car, or when an occupant
              is thrown from the car.*

REVISED   Injuries in automobile accidents occur in two ways: when an
              occupant is hurt by something inside the car, or an occupant
              is thrown from the car.

REVISED   Injuries in automobile accidents occur in two ways. An occu-
              pant is hurt by something inside the car, or an occupant is
              thrown from the car.

Exercise 22.1

Identify all of the sentence fragments in the following items, and explain why each
is grammatically incomplete. Then revise each one in at least two ways.

EXAMPLE

Controlling my temper. That has been one of my goals this year.

Controlling my temper has been one of my goals this year.

One of my goals this year has been controlling my temper.

1. When Rick was in Grade 5. His parents often left him with his sister.

2. The protagonist comes to a decision. To leave her parents and move to the Yukon.

3. Fear, one of the basic emotions people have experienced throughout time.

4. Many MPs opposed the bill. Because of its restrictions on mining and oil drilling.

5. I plan to buy a computer. Which will help me organize my finances and my calendar.

6. Forster stopped writing novels after *A Passage to India*. One of the greatest novels of the 20th century.

7. This battery never runs out of water. Eliminating the possibility of ruined clothing from battery acid.

8. I loved Paul Shapiro's *The Lotus Eaters*. And thought it deserved to win more awards.

9. The chair appointed five members. Who drew up a set of guidelines.

10. One might say that rebellion is normal. Because the younger generation often rejects the ways of its elders.

Reading with an eye for fragments

Each of the following paragraphs includes a sentence fragment. Read each paragraph, identify the fragment, and then decide what effect each writer wished to achieve by using a fragment rather than a complete sentence.

> I was looking through binoculars at a pair of whistling swans. Whistling swans! It is impossible to say how excited I was to see whistling swans in Daleville, Virginia. The two were a pair, mated for life, migrating north and west from the Atlantic coast to the high arctic. They had paused to feed at Daleville Pond. I had flushed them, and now they were flying and circling the pond. I crouched in the reeds so they would not be afraid to come back to the water.
>
> — ANNIE DILLARD, "Lenses"

> The building of the ark was a monstrous undertaking—and once the keel frame had been laid and the ribs of the ark itself set in place, it was obvious how vast its size would be: the largest structure ever built in the whole

district. The workmen were now in awe of it, as though they were building a temple, and this produced a thoroughly satisfying atmosphere of *"no more questions asked—no more questions needed."* Noah was able, now, to stare each workman squarely in the eye and dare him with a look to challenge the grandeur of the project. As if the grandeur of the ark was its whole justification.

— Timothy Findley, *Not Wanted on the Voyage*

Taking inventory: sentence fragments

Read through several of your own pieces of writing to see whether they include any sentence fragments. Check each group of words punctuated as a sentence to be sure that it contains the three elements listed at the beginning of this chapter: (1) a subject, (2) a finite verb, and (3) unless the sentence is a question, at least one clause that does not begin with a subordinating word. If you find any groups of words that lack any of these elements, revise them to form complete sentences.

23

Recognizing Misplaced, Disruptive, and Dangling Modifiers

Adjectives, adverbs, and the various kinds of phrases and clauses used as adjectives and adverbs enrich writing by making it more concrete, vivid, and memorable. To be effective, however, these **modifiers** must be carefully placed and must refer clearly to another word or words in the sentence. If modifiers seem to modify words they are not meant to, if they disrupt the continuity of a grammatical structure or of the sentence as a whole, or if they are not clearly attached to any other word in the sentence, the results can be ambiguous, confusing, or even nonsensical.

Problems with modifiers are common even in the work of professional writers. This chapter will examine three types of problem modifiers—misplaced, disruptive, and dangling—and suggest ways of revising them.

Revising misplaced modifiers

Misplaced modifiers are words, phrases, and clauses that cause ambiguity or confusion because they are not placed closely enough to the words they modify or because they could modify the words either before or after them.

1. Misplaced words and phrases

In the sentence *Softly I could hear the tumbleweeds rustling in the wind,* the adverb *softly* seems to modify *could hear.* Yet the writer obviously meant it to modify *rustling.* Such confusion can be avoided by placing a modifier close to the word or words it really refers to.

I could hear the tumbleweeds *softly* rustling in the wind.

I could hear the tumbleweeds rustling *softly* in the wind.

Be especially careful with the placement of **limiting modifiers** like *almost, even, hardly, just, merely, nearly, only, scarcely,* and *simply.* In general, these modifiers should be placed right before the words they modify, because putting them in other positions may produce not just ambiguity but a completely different meaning. Consider the following set of sentences:

AMBIGUOUS   The court only hears civil cases on Tuesday.

CLEAR   The court hears *only* civil cases on Tuesday.

CLEAR   The court hears civil cases *only* on Tuesday.

In the first sentence, placing *only* before the verb makes the meaning ambiguous. Does the writer mean that civil cases are the only kind of cases heard on Tuesdays, or that it is the only day on which civil cases are heard? The second and third sentences each express one of these meanings clearly.

Phrases also should ordinarily be placed close to the words they modify. The most common type of phrase modifier, the prepositional phrase, usually appears right after the word it modifies. In the following sentences, note how misplaced prepositional phrases cause confusion.

MISPLACED   The runners stood ignoring the crowd in their lanes. [This sentence implies that the crowd were in the lanes.]

REVISED   The runners *stood in their lanes* ignoring the crowd.

MISPLACED   She will be teaching a seminar this term on teenage suicide at a nearby high school. [The suicide was not at the school.]

REVISED   She will be teaching *a seminar on teenage suicide* this term at a nearby high school.

Participial phrases usually appear right before or right after the words they modify. In the following sentences, notice how misplacing these phrases can lead to confusion.

MISPLACED   The host pointed out the tapestry to the guests mounted on the wall. [This sentence implies that the guests were mounted on the wall.]

REVISED   The host pointed out *the tapestry mounted on the wall* to the guests.

REVISED   The host pointed out to the guests *the tapestry mounted on the wall.*

MISPLACED   Billowing from every window, we saw clouds of smoke.

[People cannot billow from windows.]

REVISED   We saw *clouds of smoke billowing from every window.*

Exercise 23.1

Revise each of the following sentences by moving any misplaced modifying words and phrases so that they clearly modify the words they are intended to.

EXAMPLE
The law only allowed food and medicine to be sold on Sundays.
The law allowed *only food and medicine* to be sold on Sundays.

1. Slick and professional, the audience applauded the comedian's routine.
2. Enthusiastically, I heard my friends talk about their great weekend while I tried to finish my assignment.
3. The city almost spent $5 million on the new stadium that opened last year.
4. On the day in question, the patient was not normally able to breathe.
5. The reporter barely submitted his story ahead of deadline.
6. He sat very quietly rolling his eyes in his chair.
7. I went through the process of taxiing and taking off in my mind.
8. Vernon made an agreement to pay back the loan with his father.
9. The bank offered flood insurance to the homeowners underwritten by the federal government.
10. Revolving out of control, the maintenance worker shut down the turbine.

2. Misplaced clauses

While you have more flexibility in the placement of dependent clauses than of modifying words and phrases, you should still try whenever possible to place them close to whatever you wish them to modify. If you do not, unintended meanings can result.

MISPLACED   The man carrying a baby *who was quoting Cicero* startled us. [Surely the baby wasn't quoting Cicero.]

REVISED   The *man who was quoting Cicero* and carrying a baby startled us.

MISPLACED   David told his coach he planned get out of swimming after he lost the semifinal race. [The sentence implies that David planned to lose the race.]

REVISED   *After he lost the semifinal race,* David told his coach that he planned to get out of swimming.

3. Squinting modifiers

If a modifier can refer to *either* the word(s) before it *or* the word(s) after it, it is called a **squinting modifier**. For example:

SQUINTING   Students who practise writing *often* will improve their grades.

The modifier *often* might describe either *practise* or *will improve*. That is, the sentence might have either of the following meanings:

REVISED   Students who *often practise* writing will improve their grades.

REVISED   Students who practise writing will *often improve* their grades.

If a sentence can be read more than one way because of your placement of a modifying word, phrase, or clause, move the modifier to a position where it clearly relates to only a single term.

Revising disruptive modifiers

Whereas misplaced modifiers confuse readers by appearing to modify the wrong word(s), **disruptive modifiers** cause problems because they interrupt the connections between parts of a grammatical structure or a sentence, making it hard for readers to follow the progress of the thought. Be careful not to place modifiers in such a way that they disrupt the normal grammatical flow of a sentence.

1. Modifiers splitting an infinitive

In general, do not split an infinitive by placing a modifier between the *to* and the verb. Doing so makes it hard for readers to recognize that the two go together.

DISRUPTIVE   Hitler expected the British to fairly quickly surrender.

REVISED   Hitler expected the British *to surrender* fairly quickly.

In some cases, however, a modifier sounds awkward in any position other than between the parts of the infinitive.

She hopes this year *to* almost exactly *equal* her last year's income.

To avoid a split infinitive, it may be best to reword the sentence to eliminate the infinitive altogether.

> She hopes that this year she will earn almost exactly as much as she did last year.

2. Modifiers between the parts of a verb phrase

A verb phrase consists of a main verb together with one or more auxiliary verbs: *had studied, will be moving* (see 14c3). Modifiers consisting of one or even two or three adverbs can often appear between parts of a verb phrase without causing awkwardness: *He had very seldom actually fired a gun in the line of duty.* In general, however, do not interrupt a verb phrase with modifiers that are phrases or clauses.

DISRUPTIVE   Vegetables will, if they are cooked too long, lose most of their nutritional value.

REVISED   Vegetables *will lose* most of their nutritional value if they are cooked too long.

REVISED   If they are cooked too long, vegetables *will lose* most of their nutritional value.

3. Modifiers between a subject and verb

Adjective phrases and clauses often appear between a subject and verb: *The books that the librarians had decided were no longer useful were discarded.* In general, however, do not use an adverb clause or phrase in this position, because it disrupts the natural progression from subject to verb that readers expect.

DISRUPTIVE   The books, because the librarians had decided they were no longer useful, were discarded.

REVISED   The *books were discarded* because the librarians had decided they were no longer useful.

REVISED   Because the librarians had decided the books were no longer useful, *they were discarded.*

4. Modifiers between a verb and an object or subject complement

In general, do not place an adverb phrase or clause between a verb and a direct object complement, because readers expect the object or complement to follow directly after the verb.

DISRUPTIVE	He bought with his first paycheque a secondhand car.
REVISED	He *bought a secondhand car* with his first paycheque.
REVISED	With his first paycheque he *bought a secondhand car*.

Revising dangling modifiers

Dangling modifiers are words (usually adverbs), phrases (prepositional or participial), and elliptical clauses (clauses from which a word or words have been left out) that modify nothing in particular in the rest of a sentence. They often seem to modify something that is suggested or implied but does not exist grammatically in the sentence. Such modifiers are called dangling because they hang loosely from the rest of the sentence, attached to no specific element. They frequently appear at the beginnings or ends of sentences.

To revise dangling modifiers, you can change the subject of the main clause so that the modifier clearly refers to it, or you can change the dangling modifier itself into a phrase or a nonelliptical clause that clearly modifies an existing part of the sentence.

1. Dangling words and phrases

DANGLING	Satisfactorily, Martin was confined to the dugout for a week. [There is no indication of who found the confinement satisfactory.]
REVISED	*To the umpires' satisfaction*, Martin was confined to the dugout for a week.
DANGLING	Growing up in Montreal, good bagels were never hard to find. [*Growing up in Montreal* does not refer specifically to anything in the sentence, though it seems to refer to some person or persons.]
REVISED	*Growing up in Montreal*, I never had trouble finding good bagels.
REVISED	*Because I grew up in Montreal*, good bagels were never hard to find.
REVISED	*For those who grow up in Montreal*, good bagels are not hard to find.
DANGLING	As a young boy, his grandmother told stories of her years as a country schoolteacher. [His grandmother was never a young boy.]

REVISED   *As a young boy, he* heard his grandmother tell stories of her years as a country schoolteacher.

REVISED   *When he was a young boy,* his grandmother told stories of her years as a country schoolteacher.

DANGLING   In thumbing through the magazine, my eyes automatically noticed the perfume ads. [Eyes cannot thumb through magazines.]

REVISED   *In thumbing through the magazine, I automatically* noticed the perfume ads.

REVISED   *As I was thumbing through the magazine,* my eyes automatically noticed the perfume ads.

Exercise 23.2

Revise each of the following sentences to correct the dangling words or phrases.

EXAMPLE
Having spent the last six summers on my grandparents' farm, my return was expected this summer.

Having spent the last six summers on my grandparents' farm, *I was expected* to return this summer.

1. Looking at the statistics on employment, more Canadian women are working full time.

2. Given the sharp increase in their employment, day care is needed.

3. To support themselves and their children, full-time work is sought by many single mothers.

4. Job retraining is often achieved by going back to school.

5. Based on surveys, many women are not going to work only for financial reasons.

2. Dangling elliptical clauses

DANGLING   Where still seen, tourists find cobblestone streets a picturesque spectacle. [Is it the tourists who are still seen?]

REVISED   *Where cobblestone streets are still seen,* tourists find them a picturesque spectacle.

REVISED   Tourists find cobblestone streets, *where still seen,* a picturesque spectacle.

DANGLING   Although a reserved and private man, everyone who met him seemed to like him. [The elliptical clause cannot refer to *every-one*.]

REVISED   *Although he was a reserved and private man*, everyone who met him seemed to like him.

REVISED   *Although a reserved and private man*, he seemed to be liked by everyone who met him.

Exercise 23.3

Revise each of the following sentences to correct any dangling elliptical clauses.

EXAMPLE
While cycling through southern France, the music on my Walkman entertained me.

While cycling through southern France, I was entertained by the music on my Walkman.

1. However unhappy, my part-time job is something I have to put up with.

2. While leading a performance at Roy Thomson Hall, the baton fell out of the conductor's hand.

3. A waiter's job can become very stressful when faced with a busy restaurant full of hungry people.

4. Dreams are somewhat like a jigsaw puzzle; if put together in the correct order, organization and coherence become obvious.

5. No matter how costly, my family insists on a university education.

Exercise 23.4

Revise the following passage to eliminate any misplaced, disruptive, or dangling modifiers.

One day last December, before going to class, a blizzard forced the administration to, for the first time anyone could remember, announce that all classes would be until further notice suspended. After leaving the residence the first thing that we noticed was the silence. The snow that had been falling all night steadily covered the ground. Being the last day of the semester, we weren't very worried about classes, so we "arranged," with another residence, a snowball fight. While building up a stock of good snowballs near Lord Hall, our jackets began to get oppressively warm. Eventually, we peeled down to shirt sleeves, ready for a fight. The central lawn became the battleground for the great Stoke–Lord Snowball Fight, where the Stoke Hall people finally set up their forts. Our piles of snowballs almost reached the tops of our forts, which were well-packed and handy to be picked up and thrown. At last both sides were ready, and the first snowball flew through the air from the "Stoke stack." The bombardment was for a while fierce and deadly. I learned that when throwing a snowball, the standing position is very risky, getting a hard one in the mouth. Finally, having almost thrown all of our snowballs, the Stoke charge was met and resisted. The timing was measured with great accuracy, being sure not to countercharge until we saw that Stoke was low on snowballs. Then we all ran toward the enemy carrying three or four snowballs each and routed them.

Taking inventory: modification

Choose two or three pages of a draft you have written recently, and examine them for clear and effective modification. Can you identify any misplaced, disruptive, or dangling modifiers? Then, exchange papers with another student, and examine his or her draft to identify problems with modifiers, while he or she examines yours. Using the guidelines in his chapter, work together to revise both drafts.

Maintaining Consistent and Complete Grammatical Structures

About twenty years ago, a writing researcher named Mina Shaughnessy demonstrated that many student sentences found by instructors simply to be "wrong" fell largely into two categories: (1) unsuccessful attempts to combine sentence structures that did not fit together grammatically or sensibly and (2) sentences missing some element necessary to complete meaning. In fact, many writers who produce problem sentences do so in an attempt to use complex and sophisticated structures. What look like "errors," then, may be stepping stones on a writer's way to greater stylistic maturity. This chapter will provide practice in recognizing such mixed or incomplete structures and, more important, in revising or building on them.

24a

Making grammatical patterns consistent

Mixed construction results from beginning a sentence with one grammatical pattern and then switching to another one. In informal speech, we are all familiar with the kind of "sentence" that starts out one way and ends in another, as in the following example:

MIXED   The fact that I get up at 5 a.m. every day, which explains why I'm always tired in the evenings.

The speaker starts out with a subject (*fact*) followed by a dependent clause (*that I get up at 5 a.m. every day*). This structure should lead into a predicate to complete the independent clause begun by *The fact*, but instead the speaker shifts to another dependent clause *(which explains why I'm always tired in the evenings)*. Thus the independent clause is never completed, and what results is a fragment. In writing, this fragment could be revised into a complete sentence in at least two ways:

REVISED   The fact that I get up at 5 a.m. every day explains why I'm always tired in the evenings. [Deleting *which* changes the second dependent clause into a predicate.]

REVISED   I get up at 5 a.m. every day, which explains why I'm always tired in the evenings. [Deleting *The fact that* makes the first dependent clause into an independent clause.]

Although most listeners would have little difficulty in following the speaker's intended meaning, failure to maintain consistent grammatical patterns often leads to confusion, especially in writing. Recognizing and revising mixed sentences call for very careful proofreading, and especially for noting the relationship between subject and predicate or between clauses. Here is another example of a mixed sentence:

MIXED   Because hope was the only thing left when Pandora finally closed up the mythical box explains why we never lose hope no matter haw bad life gets. [The adverb clause beginning with *Because is* followed not by an independent clause but by a predicate beginning with *explains*, which lacks a subject.]

REVISED   Because hope was the only thing left when Pandora finally closed up the mythical box, we never lose hope no matter how bad life gets. [Deleting *explains why* changes the original predicate into an independent clause to which the adverb clause can be attached.]

Matching subjects and predicates

Another kind of mixed sentence occurs when a subject and predicate do not fit together grammatically or do not make sense together. Such a mismatch, sometimes called **faulty predication**, often appears in sentences with the verb *be*, in which the subject complement that follows the verb does not grammatically or sensibly rename the subject. In many cases, faulty predication results from using forms of *be* in sentences in which another verb would be stronger and more appropriate.

FAULTY   A characteristic that I admire is a person who is generous.

This sentence says that a person is a kind of characteristic. To make its subject and predicate consistent, you could change either the subject or the complement to make them both refer to either persons or characteristics, or you could rewrite the sentence to change the verb.

REVISED   *A characteristic* that I admire is *generosity.*

REVISED   *A kind of person* that I admire is *one who is generous.*

REVISED   I *admire* a person who is generous.

The verb *be* also leads to faulty predication when it is used before an adverb clause opening with *when* or *where.*

FAULTY   A stereotype is when someone characterizes a group unfairly.

Although you will often hear constructions like this in conversation, an adverb clause cannot function as a subject complement in academic or other formal writing. To revise this sentence, you can change the complement to a noun that will grammatically match the subject *stereotype,* or you can rewrite the sentence to change the verb.

REVISED   *A stereotype* is an unfair *characterization* of a group.

REVISED   *A stereotype characterizes* a group unfairly.

REVISED   *When someone characterizes a group unfairly*, he or she *creates* a stereotype.

Using *the reason (that) ... is because* construction, which causes inconsistency between the subject and the subject complement, is another form of faulty predication.

FAULTY   The reason I like to play soccer is because it provides aerobic exercise.

REVISED   I like to play soccer *because it provides aerobic exercise.* [Deleting *the reason (that)* leaves an independent clause to which the *because* clause can be attached.]

REVISED   *The reason* I like to play soccer *is that* it provides aerobic exercise. [Changing *because* to *that* makes the adverb clause into a noun clause that can function as a subject complement.]

Faulty predication also occurs with verbs other than *be,* as the following examples illustrate:

FAULTY   The rules of the corporation expect employees to be properly dressed. [*Rules* cannot expect anything.]

REVISED	As its rules state, the corporation expects employees to be properly dressed.
REVISED	The rules of the corporation require that employees be properly dressed.
FAULTY	The popularity of underground comics began to appear in many stores throughout the country. [*Popularity* cannot appear in stores.]
REVISED	The popularity of underground comics began to be obvious to owners of many stores throughout the country.
REVISED	Increasing numbers of underground comics began to appear in many stores throughout the country.

Using elliptical structures carefully

Sometimes writers can avoid repetition and gain emphasis by using **elliptical structures**, in which they omit certain words or phrases in compound structures, as the following sentences demonstrate (omitted words are in brackets):

We are wise in mind but [we are] weak in body.

A person without an education, or [without] the desire for one, is an unlucky person indeed.

His hair was red, his skin [was] fair, and his body [was] strong.

These sentences are clear and effective because the omitted words match those in the other part of the compound.

In the following sentence, however, the omitted verb does not match the one that occurs in the first part of the compound, and so the sentence is incomplete. Therefore, the sentence must be revised to include both verbs.

| INCOMPLETE | His skills *are* underdeveloped, and his performance only average. |
| REVISED | His skills *are* underdeveloped, and his performance *is* only average. |

Checking comparisons for completeness, consistency, and clarity

As you revise and proofread your writing, check comparative structures closely, remembering that when you compare two or more things, the comparison must be *complete, logically consistent,* and *clear.* (See Chapter 18 for further discussion of comparative and superlative forms of adjectives and adverbs.)

Complete comparisons

INCOMPLETE   A person who drives drunk is more dangerous. [More dangerous than what?]

REVISED   A person who drives drunk is more dangerous *than one who drives carelessly.*

Logically consistent comparisons

ILLOGICAL   Woodberry's biography is better researched than Fields. [This sentence compares *biography*, a book, to *Fields*, a person.]

REVISED   Woodberry's biography is better researched than *the one by* Fields.

REVISED   Woodberry's biography is better researched than *Fields's is.*

Clear comparisons

UNCLEAR   Ted always felt more affection for his brother than his sister. [Did Ted feel more affection for this brother than his sister did or more affection for his brother than he felt for his sister?]

REVISED   Ted always felt more affection for his brother than *he did for* his sister.

REVISED   Ted always felt more affection for his brother than his sister *did.*

Taking inventory: mixed or incomplete structures

Read over two or three pages of an essay or report you have drafted recently, checking for any mixed sentences and incomplete or missing structures. Then exchange papers with another student, and check his or her piece of writing for these structural problems, while he or she checks yours. Work together to revise both drafts.

PART SIX

Making Sentence-Level Choices: Style

Constructing Effective Sentences

Creating Coordinate and Subordinate Structures

Creating and Maintaining Parallel Structures

Varying Sentence Lengths and Structures

Creating Memorable Prose

25

Constructing Effective Sentences

The philosopher, critic, and poet Kenneth Burke defines *form* in writing as "the arousal and fulfillment of desire." Burke's definition is odd but compelling; it invites us to see an **effective sentence** as one that creates or appeals to certain expectations and then either fulfils those expectations or—as is sometimes the case—startles or amuses readers by *not* fulfilling them. Look at the following sentence:

> I sometimes think of the reader as a cat, endlessly fastidious, capable, by turns, of mordant indifference and riveted attention, luxurious, recumbent, and ever poised.
>
> — PATRICIA HAMPL, "Memory and Imagination"

This sentence fulfils expectations by following up on the image of the reader as cat with cat imagery ("endlessly fastidious," "luxurious"), thus linking the picture of the reader with one of a cat. In addition, the sentence is structured so as to pull its readers along, saving its most powerful image for the end, closing with the image of the catlike reader "ever poised."

The writer of the following sentence, on the other hand, surprises readers by *breaking* expectations:

> He was tall, dark, and loathsome.

In this sentence, the writer plays on readers' expectations of the trio *tall, dark,* and *handsome*—only to undercut those expectations.

You may want to try using such an element of surprise as one way to create effective sentences. The rest of this chapter, however, will focus on two basic devices writers use to create effective sentences by fulfilling rather than breaking expectations: *emphasis* and *conciseness*.

Emphasizing main ideas

Effective sentences put the spotlight on main ideas, thus letting readers know which elements of the sentence are most important. We call this spotlighting or significant words and ideas **emphasis**. Careful control of the emphasis in each sentence will make your writing both easier and more enjoyable to read. This section focuses on the ways you can emphasize main ideas by putting them in opening and closing positions and by arranging them in climactic order.

1. Using opening and closing positions for emphasis

When you read a sentence, what are you most likely to remember? Other things being equal, you remember the end. This is the part of the sentence that should move the writing forward by providing new information, as it does in the following example:

> To protect her skin, *she took plenty of sun-block lotion.*

A less emphatic but still important position in a sentence is the opening, which hooks up the new sentence with what has come before.

> When Rosita went to the beach, she was anxious not to get a sunburn.
> *To protect her skin*, she took plenty of sun-block lotion.

In this example, *To protect her skin* connects the new sentence to *anxious not to get a sunburn* in the sentence before. The second sentence would lose emphasis if the key words, *plenty of sun-block lotion,* were buried in the middle, as in the following version:

> To protect her skin, *she took plenty of sun-block lotion,* and she also planned to stay under a beach umbrella most of the time.

Placing relatively unimportant information in the memorable closing position of a sentence undercuts proper emphasis or gives more emphasis to the closing words than you may intend:

> She contributed $500 000 to the campaign last month.

Revised to gain emphasis, the sentence reads:

Last month she contributed $500 000 to the campaign.

To emphasize the amount of the contribution even more, the sentence could be reworded this way:

Last month she gave the campaign committee $500 000.

2. Using climactic order

Presenting ideas in **climactic order** means sequencing them in order of increasing importance, power, or drama—building to climax. The following sentences show climactic order at work:

Dissidents risk social rejection, forced relocation, long imprisonment, and almost certain death.

CanLit, in one sense, does not exist; it is a dream, a folly, a vast bureaucratic phantasmagoria fueled by government gold.

– JOHN METCALF, "What Ever Happened to CanLit?"

Each of the preceding examples derives much of its power from the sequencing of its details. If the sentence concluded with "long imprisonment" rather than "almost certain death," it would not make such an emphatic statement; similarly, the second example saves its most dramatic item for last, making its point forcefully. The following sentence includes a series that fails to achieve strong emphasis by not sequencing verbs in order of increasing power:

UNEMPHATIC   Soap operas assault our eyes, damage our brain cells, and offend our ears.

REVISED   Soap operas offend our ears, assault our eyes, and damage our brain cells.

3. Checking for emphatic sentences

As you revise a draft, make sure that each sentence emphasizes the ideas you *want* emphasized. First, identify the word or words you want to receive special emphasis, and underline them. If those words are buried in the middle of the sentence or blurred in some way, revise the sentence to change their position, remembering that the end position is generally most emphatic.

Next, note any sentences that include a series of three or more words, phrases, or clauses. Check to see whether the items in the serious could be arranged in climactic order and, if so, whether they are. If they could be but are not, decide whether the sentence would be stronger with climactic order, and rearrange if necessary.

Notice how the sentence below can be revised using these two steps:

For a whole complex of claimed "reasons," we in the Student Association have for years been saddled with the burdens, which we're tired of, of low budgets, no real legislative power, and a depressing room to meet in.

The main point the writer wants to emphasize, that the Student Association is tired of being saddled with poor conditions and no power, is obscured by unemphatic placement in the middle of the sentence. A revision of it might look like this:

We in the Student Association are tired of being saddled, whatever the claimed "reasons," with a depressing room to meet in, low budgets, and no real legislative power.

Exercise 25.1

Revise each of the following sentences to highlight what you take to be the main or most important ideas.

EXAMPLE
Environmental groups continue to fight industrial polluters through the highest courts of the land, through political lobbying, through local advertising.

Environmental groups continue to fight industrial polluters through local advertising, through political lobbying, through the highest courts of the land.

1. All seagoing vessels, whether outrigger canoes, giant aircraft carriers, or run-of-the-mill cargo ships, must be designed according to certain specifications.

2. Also notable is the image of chrysanthemums throughout the story.

3. I feel that living in residence was easier to adjust to than living in my condominium.

4. The CBC offers decent music programming, this country's best hope for a national culture, and excellent public affairs programming.

5. Victorian women were warned that if they smoked they would become sterile, grow a moustache, die young, contract tuberculosis, or have trouble breathing.

Being concise

In general, effective sentences are as **concise** as possible. There are exceptions: on some occasions, writers want—or need—to hammer home a point or create a certain effect by using what in other situations might look like unnecessary repetition, or redundancy. In *The Elements of Style*, E.B. White uses such repetition to good effect when he says, "There is no satisfactory explanation of style, no infallible guide to good writing, ... no key that unlocks the door, no inflexible rule by which the young writer may shape his [or her] course." So as White's advice both suggests and illustrates, every writer must decide individually when "redundancy" is worthwhile and when it is not. More often than not, however, making a point in the fewest possible words is a hallmark of effective prose. Look at the following sentence:

> It is not a mistake—nor is it incorrect—to say that the characteristics of repetition, redundancy, and saying the same thing over and over again that typify most or much or at least a great deal of writing in the modern world of today should be eliminated or done away with by every means available to the person or persons who teach these writers.

Why write that whey you could instead write the following?

> Instructors should use all means of decreasing redundancy in their students' writing.

This example demonstrates how radical a change can be wrought by snipping away at the underbrush of *unnecessary* words and phrases in a sentence. Doing so involves several kinds of changes: deleting unnecessarily repetitive words, deleting or replacing "buzzwords," replacing wordy phrases with one-word equivalents, and simplifying grammatical structures.

1. Deleting unnecessarily repetitive words

Some of the most common unnecessary words are parts of redundant phrases, in which only one word of the phrase is necessary to the meaning. Such phrases include *few in number, large in size, combine together, continue on, end result, repeat again, red in colour,* and *free gift.* Redundancy can also result from unnecessary repetition of information that can be found elsewhere in the sentence.

REDUNDANT	*Physical aerobic exercise* is her hobby.
REVISED	*Aerobic exercise* is her hobby.
REDUNDANT	Delia sold houses at a *large 600-home* development.
REVISED	Delia sold houses at a *600-home* development.
REDUNDANT	*"Contemporary* antiques" *made recently* have been showing up more and more at auctions.
REVISED	*"Contemporary* antiques" have been showing up more and more at auctions.
REVISED	"Antiques" *made recently* have been showing up more and more at auctions.

2. Deleting or replacing buzzwords

In addition to unnecessarily repetitive words, you should note another class of unnecessary words, called **buzzwords** because, while they *sound* as if they mean something, they are only "vibrating" or "buzzing" without contributing any real meaning. Common buzzword nouns include the following: *angle, area, point, aspect, case, nature, character, element, factor, field, sort, kind, situation, scope, type, thing,* and so on. The other important class of buzzwords consists of adjectives and adverbs used as all-purpose modifiers: *absolutely, definitely, really, very, quite, literally, great, awfully, fine, weird, major, central, important,* and so on. Because buzzwords tend to make your writing dull as well as wordy, use them very sparingly. When you cannot simply delete them, take the time to think of a more specific term that says exactly what you mean.

WORDY	I found that *the area of encyclopedia sales* did not offer the *sort of thing* I was looking for *in the marketing field*.
REVISED	I found that *encyclopedia sales* did not offer the *varied marketing experience* I was looking for.
WORDY	She found the apartment *quite nice in most ways,* and although she was nervous about *the situation of* living *alone* the friendly neighbours were *the major factor in her decision* to stay.
REVISED	She found the apartment *bright and spacious,* and although she was nervous about *living alone,* the friendly neighbours *made her decide* to stay.

3. Replacing wordy phrases

Writers sometimes fall back on wordy, overused phrases, as they do on buzzwords, rather than taking time to think of a single word that will convey meaning more forcefully. Usually, such roundabout "filler" expressions only clutter up a page and put up barriers to comprehension. Here are some of the most common filler phrases and their more concise counterparts.

at the present time	now/today
at that point in time	then
in the event that	if
it is believed by many	many believe
form a consensus of opinion	agree
exhibit a tendency to	tend to
inform as to the fact that	tell

WORDY   I see no reason at this point in time why we should not rely, as has often been the case in the past, on the good offices of the mayor.

REVISED   We should rely now, as we have in the past, on the help of the mayor.

Jargon, including corporate, bureaucratic, academic, and scientific jargon, is often the cause of wordiness. Examples of jargon include: *facilitate, viable, ambulate.*

4. Simplifying grammatical structures

Using the simplest grammatical structures possible to express your meaning will tighten and strengthen your sentences considerably. In the following sentence, for example, notice how conciseness results from reducing an adjective clause to an appositive phrase, deleting a grammatically unnecessary *to be,* and reducing an adverb phrase to a one-word adverb.

WORDY   Janice, *who was only the second woman to be hired by the Sebringville Fire Department,* had to handle the gender issue *in a careful way.*

REVISED   Janice, *only the second woman hired by the Sebringville Fire Department,* had to handle the gender issue *carefully.*

In the following example, reducing an adverb clause to an elliptical form and combining two sentences by using a compound predicate produces one concise sentence.

WORDY   When he was questioned about his previous job, he seemed nervous. He also tried to change the subject.

REVISED   When questioned about his previous job, he seemed nervous and tried to change the subject.

Other ways to achieve conciseness by simplifying grammatical structures include using strong verbs and nouns, avoiding expletive constructions (those beginning with *there* or *it* followed by a form of *be*), and using the active rather than the passive voice. All of these methods are discussed in detail in Chapter 29.

5. Checking for conciseness

When you revise a draft, work on making each sentence as concise and powerful as possible. To do so, underline any unnecessarily repetitive words or buzzwords that you can find. Then go back over each sentence, seeking out overused phrases and other official-sounding but unnecessarily wordy language. Finally, look for grammatical structures that could be simplified. When you have identified the words and phrases that do not add directly to your meaning, rephrase or delete them until you have tightened up each sentence. In the following sentence, note how the writer has trimmed unnecessary words and phrases to produce a much shorter but a much more pithy and effective sentence:

> The child's constant and continual use of the vulgar expressions with obscene meanings indicated to her pre-elementary supervisory group that she was rather deficient in terms of her ability to interact in an efficient manner with peers in her potential interaction group.

> The child's constant use of "four-letter words" told the day-care workers that she might have trouble getting along with other four-year-olds.

Exercise 25.2

Revise each of the following sentences to make it clear and concise by eliminating unnecessary words and phrases.

EXAMPLE
Let me fill you in on the main points of the overall picture here.

Let me summarize.

1. Managers, if they are to be effective, must have a full understanding of how a variety of types of systems work.

2. The purpose of this report is to describe for its readers the employment opportunities open to people who have received a university education.

3. One of the major problems that is faced at this point in time is that there is world hunger.

4. After I stopped the practice of exercising regularly, I became ten pounds heavier in weight in a relatively short amount of time.

5. It frequently happens that a child can be scolded a numerous amount of times for doing something wrong, and he or she will persist in performing the forbidden act.

6. The way in which one goes about checking the engine is to listen for rattling or pinging noises.

7. A situation of quality, deep-powder snow symbolizes a goal that is not easily attainable by skiers and that they can achieve only in rare cases.

8. It is Randall's approach that exposes the injustices with which the Canadian woman is confronted.

9. Humans are very socially oriented beings; this statement is substantiated by the fact that a person left completely alone in a room with adequate food and water would eventually die from the lack of social interaction. However, the opposite end of the social interaction concept relates to the idea that the case of two people forced to be together all of the time is not healthy either.

10. Sweeping and mopping half a restaurant after running around waiting on tables for five or six hours is enough to give occasion for an exhaustive collapse.

Exercise 25.3

Read over Andrea Imada's essay in 4j, paying attention to the sentences. Then choose a paragraph and evaluate its sentences in terms of emphasis and conciseness. Try to find a paragraph that you think might be made more emphatic or more concise, and revise accordingly.

Reading with an eye for sentence style

Here are some sentences from "Memory and Imagination," Patricia Hampl's essay about memoir writing. (You will recognize the example sentence from the opening of this chapter.) Each sentence makes a powerful emphatic statement. Read each one, and decide how Hampl achieves such uncommonly strong emphasis. Then choose one to use as a model for writing a sentence of your own.

EXAMPLE
I sometimes think of the reader as a cat, endlessly fastidious, capable, by turns, of mordant indifference and riveted attention, luxurious, recumbent, and ever poised.

I sometimes think of television as a shrew, incessantly noisy, demanding attention at all times to its advertising and mindless programming, insistently shrill, forever heckling.

1. We wish to talk to each other about life and death, about love, despair, loss, and innocence.

2. The heart, the guardian of intuition with its secret, often fearful intentions, is the boss.

3. I am forced to admit that memoir is not a matter of transcription, that memory itself is not a warehouse of finished stories, not a static gallery of framed pictures.

Taking inventory: sentence effectiveness

Study two or three paragraphs you have written recently to determine how emphatic and effectively concise each sentence is. Using the suggestions in this chapter, revise your paragraphs, making each sentence as emphatic and concise as possible.

26

Creating Coordinate and Subordinate Structures

Creating effective sentences calls on a writer to direct the arrangement and flow of verbal passages just as the conductor of an orchestra does with musical passages. Such effective orchestration often involves creating sentences that use *coordinate* and *subordinate* structures. **Coordinate structures** give equal importance to two or more words, phrases, or clauses, often linking them together with coordinating conjunctions like *and* or *but*. In the following sentence, linking the two clauses with *but* gives them equal significance:

> Freud's theories cannot be proved by laboratory experiment, but their "rightness" can be sensed in myths and legends.

Subordinate structures create different levels of significance, stressing some ideas by expressing them in independent clauses or in key nouns or verbs and subordinating others by putting them into dependent clauses, phrases, or single words. In the following sentence, beginning the first clause with *although* subordinates the idea in that clause to the one in the second clause.

> Although Freud's theories cannot be proved by laboratory experiment, their "rightness" can be sensed in myths and legends.

Learning to use different kinds of coordinate and subordinate structures will increase your sentence repertoire and allow you to write varied, interesting, and effective sentences. Look, for instance, at the following sentences:

> Jean-Paul went through the new part of the library to the old.
>
> He walked around for a while.
>
> Then he went to the periodical section.
>
> He started looking at the *Gazette* on microfilm.

We could choose to combine these sentences in several ways:

Using coordination

Jean-Paul went through the new part of the library to the old, and he walked around for a while; then he went to the periodical section and started looking at the *Gazette* on microfilm.

Using subordination

After going through the new part of the library to the old and walking around for a while, Jean-Paul went to the periodical section, where he started looking at the *Gazette* on microfilm.

Of course, these sentences could be combined in a number of other ways as well, but these two will serve to illustrate how coordinate structures differ from subordinate structures. In the example that uses coordination, the four actions of going through the new part of the library to the old, walking around, going to the periodical section, and looking at the *Gazette* are all given the same emphasis or importance by being placed in three independent clauses, the last of which has a compound predicate. The second combination gives a different emphasis to the sentence, suggesting that Jean-Paul's destination, the periodical section, is most important. The action of his going there is expressed in an independent clause, whereas the other three actions are given less emphasis by being placed in a prepositional phrase (with compound gerund-phrase objects) and a dependent clause.

In addition to indicating emphasis, coordination and subordination can be used to create special, sometimes dramatic effects in writing. As a writer, you must often decide whether to use coordination, subordination, both, or neither, depending on which structure provides the emphasis and effect you want to achieve. This chapter will furnish you with some guidelines for using these structures appropriately.

Using coordination to relate equal ideas

What can you say about the following passage?

It was my birthday today, and I took cupcakes to school, and I wore a birthday crown, and we ate cupcakes, and we sang "Happy Birthday," and I sat in the middle, and I'm 6 years old.

We realize early on that the writer is a child—or someone writing from a child's point of view. Because the passage mentions cupcakes and school and a crown, we make this assumption even before we find out, in the last clause, that the writer is 6 years old. But the *style* of this passage, as well as its content, helps identify the writer. We get a clue from the seven short independent clauses strung together like beads with the coordinating conjunction *and,* a style typical of young writers who are learning to sequence events in a story. Note that aside from the clue "I'm 6 years old" at the very end of the sentence (generally an emphatic spot), we are given no grammatical signals to tell us how these clauses rank in importance. Were the cupcakes most significant to the writer? the birthday crown? We cannot tell, because the coordinate structure makes all the clauses grammatical equals.

Not all coordination must be so monotonous, however. When used well, coordinate structures relate separate but equal elements, making clear the emphasis given to different ideas. The precise relationship is stated in the element that links the ideas, usually a coordinating conjunction *(and, but, for, nor, or, so, yet)* or a semicolon. In the following paragraph on the Canadian economy, coordinating conjunctions and a semicolon are used effectively to show relationships between points.

> In 1946, 35 per cent of Canada's manufacturing was foreign controlled, *but* this rose to 50 per cent by 1953, *and* 56 per cent by 1957; in mining and smelting the increases during the same years rose from 38 per cent to 57 per cent to 70 per cent. Thus, in the course of a decade, the productive cornerstones of Canada's economy ceased to be Canadian *and* became foreign dominated.
>
> — WALLACE CLEMENT, "Uneven Development: A Mature Branch-Plant Society"

1. Using coordination for special effect

Coordination can also be used to create special effects. The formal name for the conspicuous use of conjunctions to join words, phrases, or clauses is **polysyndeton**, from Greek *poly-* ("many") and *syndeton* ("connectives"). Following are some examples:

> Satan pursues his way. And swims, or sinks, or wades, or creeps, or flies.
>
> — JOHN MILTON, *Paradise Lost*

Here the use of coordination piles up images of movement, giving the impression that Satan can use *any* kind of movement and cannot be stopped.

> He [the writer] must teach himself that the basest of all things is to be afraid;

and, teaching himself that, forget it forever, leaving no room in his workshop for anything but the old verities and truths of the heart, the old universal truths lacking which any story is ephemeral and doomed—*love and honor and pity and pride and compassion and sacrifice.*

— WILLIAM FAULKNER, Nobel Prize Acceptance Speech

Here the repetition of the coordinating conjunction *and* creates a solemn rhythm, almost like the tolling of a bell.

Are you familiar with the Deer Valley Inn? It is an exclusive hotel in northern Ontario—three hundred dollars a night gets you the deluxe suite with private jacuzzi *and* silky satin sheets. There's a cordless phone in every room *and* a remote control for every device imaginable—television, VCR, CD player, central air conditioning, *and* sauna. You see gold-encrusted dowagers in the opulent lobby, *and* only gold American Express cards, *and* more gold on the bathroom fixtures, and young golden-haired beauties clinging onto middle-aged Armani arms.

The use of *and* in this paragraph results in a catalogue of detail. By stringing together images in this way, the author conveys a sense of overwhelming indulgence and extravagance.

2. Revising for more effective coordination

As you revise, consider the relative importance of the different ideas within each sentence. How many coordinate structures can you identify in the draft? If you find few, see whether any ideas or elements should be linked in some way. If you find that you depend primarily on coordination rather than subordination to link ideas, does the draft sound jerky or unnatural? Should any of the coordinate structures be deleted or changed to subordinate ones?

You can answer this last question by taking the following steps. Underline all of the coordinating conjunctions (*and, but, for, nor, or, so, yet*) or semicolons. Now look on either side of each conjunction, and ask yourself two questions. First, does the conjunction link words, phrases, or clauses that really need to be related? Second, are the words, phrases, or clauses linked by the conjunction *equally important* ideas? If the answer to either of these questions is no, revise the sentence to eliminate the coordinate structure or to substitute a subordinate one. Notice how the following passage can be analyzed and revised.

Part of the problem is that spring term is a heavy term for me, <u>and</u> I have five courses, <u>but</u> part of the problem is that I just promised too much to too many people, <u>so</u> I have to do a lot of other library work too. In addition, I had to begin wearing that back brace, <u>and</u> it's making my skin sore, <u>and</u> each night I have to come home <u>and</u> take it off, <u>and</u> that takes time, <u>or</u> I have to go out to the library.

This passage depends too heavily on coordination, which obscures the ways in which the ideas in the sentences relate to one another. Rewritten, with more subordinate structures and with the first sentence separated into two sentences with the coordinating conjunction *but* replaced by the conjunctive adverb *through,* the passage reads more clearly.

Part of the problem is that spring term is a heavy term for me, with five courses. Part of the problem, though, is that I just promised too much to too many people, so I have to do a lot of other work, especially in the library at night. In addition, I had to begin wearing that back brace, which makes my skin sore, and when I come home each night, I have to spend time taking it off.

If you think you are using too many coordinating conjunctions in your own writing, turn to 26b for advice about using subordination.

In addition to checking for excessive and insufficient coordination, check to see that the relationship between coordinated elements of a sentence is clear and makes sense. Look at the following sentence:

Watching television is a good way to spend some leisure time and makes viewers apathetic.

The relationship of the ideas here is confusing. What does being a good way to spend leisure time have to do with making viewers apathetic? This sentence might be revised in either of the following ways:

Watching television is a good way to spend some leisure time, but excessive watching makes viewers apathetic and indifferent to their real lives.

Although watching television is a good way to spend some leisure time, excessive watching makes viewers apathetic and indifferent to their real lives.

Notice that the revisions not only signal a contrast by using *but* or *although,* but also add information to explain *apathetic.*

Exercise 26.1

Many of the ideas in the following passage are related in ways that are not made clear. Revise the passage by using coordinate structures, where appropriate, to clarify the relationships between equally important ideas.

We came to the Friday Candlelight Dinner. We had a wonderful meal. We got a tour from Bud that we both found quite moving. We came away with very good memories of Pioneer Village. We came away with very good memories of the people we had met there, all of whom seemed to go out of their way to be pleasant. On Monday, a Visa slip came for me in the mail. It indicated that I would be charged $48.00 despite my cancellation of two of the reservations. I called to ask if this bill was a mistake. I engaged in a conversation with Sophie that was deeply disturbing. She told me then that the Candlelight Dinner had a 48-hour cancellation policy. She told me that both Dori and I had been charged the full $48.00 for the dinner. She refused to consider any argument. I argued that I had never been told about the policy. I said that if I had known about it, I could have brought two other friends on Friday. That way the meals would not have been wasted. I was told repeatedly that this was the policy. I was told that I should have known the policy. I was told that she had been too busy to tell me the policy when I called Thursday to cancel the reservations. It was, to tell the truth, like a scene from Kafka.

Exercise 26.2

Using the principles of coordination to signal equal importance or to create special emphasis, combine and revise the following twelve short sentences into several longer and more effective ones. Add or delete words if you need to. Then compare your new sentences with those of two or three other students, and discuss the different effects created by combining the short sentences in different ways.

The bull-riding arena was fairly crowded.
The crowd made no impression on me.
I had made a decision.
It was now time to prove myself.
I was scared.
I walked to the entry window.
I laid my money on the counter.
The clerk held up a Stetson hat filled with slips of paper.
I reached in.
I picked one.
The slip held the number of the bull I was to ride.
I headed toward the stock corral.

Using subordination to distinguish main ideas

Subordination provides the means of distinguishing major points from minor points or bringing in supporting context or details. If, for instance, you put your main idea in an independent clause, you might then put any lesser ideas in dependent clauses, phrases, or even single words. Look, for instance, at the following sentence by Maya Angelou, which shows the subordinated point in italics:

> Mrs. Viola Cullinan was a plump woman *who lived in a three-bedroom house somewhere behind the post office.*
>
> — MAYA ANGELOU, "My Name Is Margaret"

In this sentence, the dependent clause adds information about Mrs. Cullinan. While the information is important, it is grammatically subordinate to the independent clause, which carries the main idea: *Mrs. Viola Cullinan was a plump woman.*

Notice that the choice of what to subordinate rests with the writer and depends on the intended meaning. Angelou might have given the same basic information differently: *Mrs. Viola Cullinan, a plump woman, lived in a three-bedroom house somewhere behind the post office.* Subordinating the information about Mrs. Cullinan's size to that about her house would have resulted in a slightly different meaning, of course. As a writer, you must think carefully about where you want your emphasis to be and subordinate accordingly.

Besides adding information, subordination also helps establish logical relationships among the facts in a sentence. These relationships are often specified by the subordinating conjunctions introducing many dependent clauses—words such as *after, because,* or *so* (see 14b7 for a complete list). Subordination can be used to combine short sentences in ways that signal logical relationships. For example:

SEPARATE SENTENCES

Todd tried to explain the frying process.

I was mesmerized by the blast of heat.

The heat billowed from the vat of grease.

COMBINED SENTENCE

While Todd tried to explain the frying process, I was mesmerized by the blast of heat *that* billowed from the vat of grease.

Depending on what grammatical structures you use to subordinate, you can call attention to a less important element of a sentence in various ways, as the following series demonstrates:

The Parks Council report was persuasively written. It contained five typed pages. [no subordination]

The Parks Council report, *which contained five typed pages*, was persuasively written. [clause]

The Parks Council report, *containing five typed pages*, was persuasively written. [participial phrase]

The *five-page* Parks Council report was persuasively written. [single-word modifier]

The Parks Council report, *five typed pages*, was persuasively written. (appositive]

Exercise 26.3

Combine each of the following sets of sentences into one sentence that uses subordination to signal the relationships among ideas. Compare your new sentences with those of a few other students, and discuss any differences in effect created by using different combinations, subordinating conjunctions, and subordinating structures.

EXAMPLE

I was looking over my books.

I noticed that *Love in the Time of Cholera* was missing.

This book is a favourite of my roommate's.

While I was looking over my books, I noticed that *Love in the Time of Cholera*, one of my roommate's favourite books, was missing.

1. I entered the hospital room.
   I was shocked.
   Tubes and life-support machines filled the room.

2. Entwhistle and Townshend met Roger Daltrey.
   Roger Daltrey played guitar and sang.

They formed a group called the High Numbers.

3. We had dug a 25 m ditch.
   My boss would pour gravel into the ditch.
   I would level the gravel with a shovel.

4. *Obasan* was written by Joy Kogawa.
   It is an important book.
   It examines the situation of Japanese Canadians during the Second World War.

5. The scenery there is beautiful.
   The mountains have caps of snow.
   The lakes are deep and full of fish.
   The pastures are green.
   It is an ideal spot to spend spring break.

Exercise 26.4

Revise the following paragraph, subordinating the less important ideas to the more important where appropriate.

> I stayed with my friend Louise. She owns a huge mangy wolf. It is actually a seven-eights wolf cross. The poor creature is allergic to everything. It looks like a shabby, moth-eaten exhibit of a stuffed wolf in a third-rate museum. Louise and Bill feed it rice and raw potatoes. It slavers all over everything. It snaps up the pieces of potato. It never goes out of the house. It sleeps on the beds. They are covered with animal hair. It makes no sounds. It just looks at you with those sunken, wild eyes. It is not dangerous or ferocious. It is just completely miserable. This animal should never have been born. It's trying to tell you that with every twitch.

1. Using subordination for special effect

Carefully used subordination can create powerful effects. In the following passage Hugh MacLennan piles up dependent clauses, each beginning with the subordinating conjunction "that," to emphasize the idea that the two Canadian "solitudes" in fact share a great deal.

> Then, even as the two race-legends woke again remembering ancient enmities, there woke with them also the felt knowledge that together they had fought and survived one great war they had never made, and that now they had entered another; that for nearly a hundred years the nation had been spread out on the top half of the continent over the powerhouse of the United States and still was there; that even if the legends were like oil and alcohol in the same bottle, the bottle had not broken yet. And, almost grudgingly, out

of the instinct to do what was necessary, the country took the first irrevocable steps towards becoming herself, knowing against her will that she was not unique but like all the others, alone with history, with science, and the future.

– HUGH MACLENNAN, *Two Solitudes*

A dependent clause can also be used to create an ironic effect if it somehow undercuts the independent clause. Stephen Leacock uses this technique in a humorous essay on hunting, "Roughing It in the Bush," in which the hunters are neither "roughing it" nor "in the bush." The narrator indicates under what conditions he and his companions might partake of the illegal alcohol they've brought with them:

But we are hardly likely to touch it,—*unless we hit a cold snap, or a wet spell* ...

Since the season is autumn, likely to be cold or wet, this dependent clause creates irony—and makes us laugh. Now look at a student writer's use of the same technique:

Never eat fattening foods—*unless you are hungry.*

2. Revising for more effective subordination

When you are revising a draft, it is a good idea to give some attention to the way you use subordination, especially if you tend to use too many short sentences or coordinate structures. Begin by figuring out which of your ideas are most important. Take a page of your draft and underline the main ideas. You may find it useful to underline major ideas twice, lesser ones once. If the ideas marked as *most* important do not appear in independent clauses, revise the page so that they do. Subordinate the less important ideas by putting them in dependent clauses or phrases. If ideas are of equal importance, turn back to 26a2 for advice.

Study the following passage from an essay about Edgar Allan Poe's "William Wilson," a strange tale about a young man who meets his double. Notice how the paragraph can be revised in order to connect and order its ideas more effectively.

In the following years at the academy, <u>the two William Wilsons shared a bizarre relationship</u>. <u>The second Wilson established himself as equal to the first</u>. He was equal both in the classroom and on the playground. The first Wilson was used to feeling superior to his schoolmates, so <u>he was quite disturbed at the thought of having an equal</u>. He was especially disturbed that this equal had the same name and birthdate.

This passage depends heavily on simple sentences and use of simple coordination. Underlining the most important ideas gives the writer an idea of what might be subordinated to them, and the revision changes three of the less important ideas into prepositional phrases, an adjective clause, and an appositive phrase (shown here in italics).

> In the following years at the academy, the two William Wilsons shared a bizarre relationship. The second Wilson established himself as equal to the first, *both in the classroom and on the playground*. The first Wilson, *who was used to feeling superior to his schoolmates*, was quite disturbed at the thought of having an equal, *especially one with the same name and birthdate*.

In addition to checking for places where subordination might be more effective than coordination or separate sentences, you need to make sure that you have not used subordination inappropriately. **Excessive subordination** occurs when too many subordinating structures, usually dependent clauses, are strung together, so that readers have trouble keeping track of the main idea expressed in the independent clause. Look, for example, at the following sentence:

> Philip II sent the Spanish Armada to conquer England, which was ruled by Elizabeth, who had executed Mary because she was plotting to overthrow Elizabeth, who was a Protestant, whereas Mary and Philip were Roman Catholics.

The long string of subordinate clauses at the end of this sentence makes the relationship of the ideas very hard to follow and also makes it hard for readers to remember the idea in the independent clause at the beginning. Notice how changing one of the dependent clauses to the independent clause of a new sentence and reducing two others to appositive phrases makes the relationship of ideas clearer:

> Philip II sent the Spanish Armada to conquer England, which was ruled by Elizabeth. She had executed Mary, a Roman Catholic like Philip, because Mary was plotting to overthrow Elizabeth, a Protestant.

Reading with an eye for coordination and subordination

Turn to the first draft of Andrea Imada's essay in 3i. Read it over with special attention to the use of coordination and subordination. Do you notice any patterns—is there some of each? more of one than the other? Analyze one paragraph, identifying the coordinate and subordinate phrases and clauses. Do they make their points with clear emphasis? If not, revise the paragraphs following the advice given in 26a2 and 26b2.

Taking inventory: subordination

Choose two paragraphs from one of your current drafts, and analyze them for use of subordination. How many dependent clauses do you find? How do they function in the sentences—as nouns, adjectives, or adverbs? Are the ideas in the dependent clauses those that *should* be subordinate to the ones in the independent clauses? On the basis of this analysis, revise the passage to use subordination effectively.

27

Creating and Maintaining Parallel Structures

Parallel grammatical structures form many of our most familiar phrases: *sink or swim, live and let live, shape up or ship out.* These clichés demonstrate **parallelism**, expressing corresponding elements in the same grammatical form. Parallelism also characterizes some of the most elegant passages in our language. Look, for example, at how E.B. White uses balanced structures to describe the enchantment of watching a bareback circus rider practising her act.

> The enchantment grew *not out of something that happened* or was performed *but out of something that seemed* to go round and around and around with the girl, attending her, a steady gleam in the shape of a circle—a ring *of ambition, of happiness, of youth.*
>
> – E.B. WHITE, "The Ring of Time"

This description uses the power of parallelism to create its special rhythms. Just as the young woman goes "round and around and around," balanced easily on her horse, so the sentence circles rhythmically too, balanced by a series of parallel phrases and clauses. Read the sentence aloud, and you will hear the effect of those parallel structures, rocking gently back and forth much as does the horse in the ring.

This chapter will give you the opportunity to practise parallelism and help you to create pleasing rhythmic effects in your own writing.

27a

Using parallel structures in a series

All items in a series should be in parallel form—all nouns, all prepositional phrases, all adverb clauses, and so on. Parallel structure makes the series clear and easy to follow, bringing both grace and coherence.

> The quarterhorse *skipped, pranced,* and absolutely *sashayed* onto the track. [verbs]

> Three subjects guaranteed to cause a fight are *politics, religion,* and *money.* [nouns]

> A cloud *of critics, of compilers, of commentators,* darkened the face of learning, and the decline *of genius* was soon followed by the corruption *of taste.* [prepositional phrases]
>
> — EDWARD GIBBON, *The Decline and Fall of the Roman Empire*

> As more and more anti-smoking laws are passed, we see legions of potential nonsmokers *munching Nicorette, gnawing peppermints, chewing pencils, knitting sweaters,* or *practising self-hypnotism.* [participial phrases]

> *Pushing a pen or pencil, pounding a typewriter,* or *manipulating a word processor* just does not appeal to me. [gerund phrases]

When parallel elements are *not* presented in parallel grammatical form, the result can be awkward and even difficult to follow.

NONPARALLEL   The duties of the job included baby-sitting, housecleaning, and the preparation of the meals.

PARALLEL   The duties of the job included *baby-sitting, housecleaning,* and *preparing the meals.*

Lists

Items in a list should also be parallel in structure. Note the lack of parallelism in the following list:

> Please observe the following regulations when using the library coffee service:
>
> 1. Coffee *to be made* only by library staff.
> 2. Coffee service *to be closed* at 4 p.m.
> 3. Doughnuts *to be kept* in cabinet.
> 4. No faculty members *should handle* coffee materials.

The fourth item on the list is not parallel with the others because it contains a finite verb rather than an infinitive, and thus is a full sentence, not a phrase. Rewritten to maintain parallelism, this item could read:

> 4. Coffee materials *not to be handled* by faulty members.

A formal outline should also be parallel in form (see 12b2).

Using two of the example sentences above as models to imitate, write two sentences of your own that include a series of parallel phrases.

Using parallel structures with pairs

One common use of parallel structures occurs in the pairing of two ideas. If the ideas in a pair are parallel in thought, they should be parallel in grammatical structure. Parallel structures are especially appropriate when two ideas are being compared or contrasted.

> History became popular, and historians became alarmed.
>
> — WILL DURANT

> It's easier to drive a new pickup truck than an old luxury car.

When two clauses in a sentence express compared or contrasted ideas in exactly or almost exactly parallel structures, they produce a **balanced sentence**, one with two parts that "mirror" each other. Balanced sentences create an especially forceful impression.

> People must eliminate pollution, or pollution will eliminate people.

> There is much in your book that is original and valuable—but what is original is not valuable, and what is valuable is not original.
>
> — SAMUEL JOHNSON

With coordinating conjunctions

In general, use the same grammatical structure on both sides of any of the coordinating conjunctions—*and, but, or, nor, for, so.* (See 14b7 for more information about coordinating conjunctions.) The more nearly parallel the two structures are, the stronger the connection of ideas will be.

> The group performed *whenever anyone would listen* and *wherever anyone would pay.*

When elements connected by a coordinating conjunction are not parallel in form, the relationship of the elements can be hard to see.

> NONPARALLEL   Medical surveys suggest that North Americans *are dieting more* but *still consume too much fat.*

REVISED
Medical surveys suggest that North Americans *are dieting more* but *are still consuming too much fat.*

With correlative conjunctions

Use the same structure after both parts of a correlative conjunction—*either ... or; both ... and; neither ... nor; not only ... but also.* (See 14b7 for more information about correlative conjunctions.)

This report is directed not only *to my supervisor*, but also *to my co-workers*.

NONPARALLEL
I wanted not only *to go away to school* but also *to New Brunswick.*

REVISED
I wanted not only *to go away to school* but also *to live in New Brunswick.*

Including all necessary words in parallel constructions

In addition to making parallel elements grammatically similar, be careful to include any other necessary words—prepositions, relative pronouns, and so on.

NONPARALLEL
We considered moving to a small town in Quebec or a suburb of Montreal.

PARALLEL
We considered moving *to a small town in Quebec* or *to a suburb of Montreal.*

NONPARALLEL
High on our list was Pointe Claire, a residential community and which is less than a half-hour from Montreal.

PARALLEL
High on our list was Pointe Claire, *which is a residential community* and *which is less than a half-hour from Montreal.*

Using parallel structures for emphasis and special effect

Parallel structures can help a writer emphasize the most important ideas in a sentence. Look at the following sentence:

> The dancers wore costumes that were exquisitely perfect in every detail, and they filed onto the stage with their arms akimbo and their toes pointed.

The meaning of this sentence is clear, but what seems to be the most important idea, the exquisitely perfect costumes, is buried in a dependent clause in the middle of the sentence. This idea can be emphasized by making it the last in a series of parallel absolute phrases arranged in climactic order:

> The dancers filed onto the stage, arms akimbo, toes pointed, costumes exquisitely perfect in every detail.

See 25a for more information about emphasis within a sentence.

Besides emphasizing main ideas, parallel structures can create a number of different stylistic effects. One of these is orderliness, a sense of steady or building rhythm, as in the following sentence:

> Most police work is concerned with scared people who have been bitten by dogs, frantic people whose children have run away from home, old people who have no one to talk to, and impatient people whose first response to any situation is to "call the cops."

Note here how the repetition of the parallel phrases *scared people ... frantic people ... old people ... impatient people* builds a rhythm or beat that leads us to expect more of the same. Parallel elements thus work to create and fulfil reader expectations.

> At work, he may have time to gulp down a cup of coffee if the dining halls are running smoothly, if all the workers show up, and if the boss is not asking questions.

This sentence creates an impression of somewhat desperate activity as it piles up the three parallel *if* clauses.

Exercise 27.2

Revise the following sentences to make effective use of parallel clauses. Change or add words if need be.

EXAMPLE
Where we eat, how we eat, what we eat, and what are our reasons for eating—these are major questions for many people in the 90s.

Where we eat, how we eat, what we eat, and *why we eat*—these are major questions for many people in the 90s.

1. I will always remember how the girls dressed in green plaid skirts and the boys wearing green plaid ties.

2. There are three ways to apply Ninhydrin to the area to be examined: it may be applied with a brush; it may be sprayed on with a spray gun; or you can dip the object in the solution.

3. No longer are women required to play supporting roles behind their male leads; they do not have to play empty-headed debutantes whose only attributes are superficial, either.

4. There are two types of wallflowers: the male wallflower is known as the nerd, and the female, who is known as the skeeve.

5. Paulo was off to university and life in residence; John, on the other hand, was remaining at home and attending the local community college.

Taking inventory: parallelism

Choose four or five paragraphs from a draft you have recently written. Read through them carefully, noting any series of words, phrases, or clauses. Determine whether these series are in parallel form, and if not, revise them for parallelism. Then reread the paragraphs, looking for places where parallel structures would add emphasis or clarity to your writing, and revise those places using such structures.

28

Varying Sentence Lengths and Structures

Unanimity in anything can become tiresome. In sentence structure, sameness can result in dull, listless prose. If, for example, after some revision work, you find an essay somehow boring, it could be that the problem is uniformity of sentence length. Counting the words in your sentences, you may discover that the sentences are virtually all the same length—perhaps twenty-two to twenty-five words long. You can add life to your essay simply by carving some sentences into shorter ones and combining others into longer ones, thus creating new rhythms.

This chapter will examine how to use the traditional foe of boring sentences—variety in lengths, in openings, and in grammatical, functional, and rhetorical patterns.

Varying sentence lengths

Varying sentence lengths not only makes prose more readable and interesting but also creates a pleasing rhythmic effect. Once you begin to pay attention to sentence length, varying it for specific effects can be very satisfying.

1. Using short sentences

Very short sentences can be very powerful. Study the following famous short sentences, and see if you agree that each owes much of its power to its brevity:

Nice guys finish last.

Crime doesn't pay.

Let them eat cake.

The following passage from a speech by Chief Sitting Bull illustrates how effective a series of short sentences and other short structures can be:

> What treaty that the whites have kept has the red man broken? Not one. What treaty that the white men ever made with us have they kept? Not one. When I was a boy the Sioux owned the world; the sun rose and set on their land; they sent ten thousand men to battle. Where are the warriors today? Who slew them? Where are our lands? Who owns them?
>
> — SITTING BULL, *Touch the Earth*

Notice how Sitting Bull's short questions, clauses, and fragments build a rhythm that gives power to his words. Repeated short sentences, if used with awareness of their effect, can go far beyond monotony into rhythmic beat and cadenced dignity.

2. Using long sentences

Long sentences are particularly useful for presenting a set of complex, interlocking ideas or for building up momentum. The following paragraph, detailing some of the events at the Chernobyl atomic power station in 1986, shows how long sentences can be used effectively, especially when they are not used exclusively.

> When the power reached 200 MW, plant supervisors decided to proceed with the test. Two more pumps were connected to the reactor shortly after 1:00 a.m. to provide enough pumps to support the experiment. However, because the reactor was running at lower power than originally planned, this resulted in too much cooling water flowing through the core, which in turn caused the steam pressure and the water level in the steam separators to drop. In order to prevent the reactor being shut down automatically when these parameters fell below a critical point, the operators blocked signals from pressure and water-level sensors, thereby disabling a key part of the emergency shutdown system.
>
> — COLIN NORMAN, "Chernobyl: Errors and Design Flaws"

Notice that the three long sentences each indicate complexities that short sentences could not adequately reflect.

3. Alternating short and long sentences

Although series of short and long sentences can be effective in individual situations, frequent alternation in sentence length characterizes much memorable writing. Notice the difference between these two passages, one of which contains sentences of fairly uniform length and the other of which varies sentence length.

UNIFORM LENGTHS

The house is a fixer-upper, of course. For the past two days, I've been fixing things. It seems like the past two decades. I've been crawling about in the basement, which is dirt-floored, trying to learn to fix copper plumbing. The people renting the house last winter froze and burst the pipes. As a result, I have to put in all new stuff, learning as I go. With 1.5 metre headroom, it's a real joy to be playing with torch and hot solder down there. I climb around oozing soilpipes from another era. I crouch Quasimodo-like, measuring, cutting, crouching, slouching, until my back is permanently bent. I have been picking spiders out of my beard, and my clothes are indescribable.

VARIED LENGTHS

The house is a fixer-upper, of course, and so for the past two days (it seems like the past two decades), I've been fixing things, crawling about in the basement—dirt-floored, naturally—trying to learn to fix copper plumbing. What a nightmare! The people renting the house last winter froze and burst the pipes, and so I have to put in all new stuff. I'm learning as I go. With 1.5 metre headroom, it's a real joy to be playing with torch and hot solder down there, climbing around oozing soilpipes from another era, crouching Quasimodo-like, measuring, cutting, crouching, slouching. My back is permanently bent. My beard is full of spiders. My clothes are indescribable.

See the next section (28a4) for an analysis of this passage.

4. Checking for varied sentence lengths

As you revise a draft, begin by looking at the lengths of your sentences. If they do not seem to vary enough in length, begin revising them so that they do. Do not, however, change sentence lengths arbitrarily. Rather, balance them so they most effectively convey your meaning. For example, if two or more short sentences in a row express closely related ideas, ask yourself if you could make the relationship between these ideas clearer or more precise by using coordination or subordination to combine them into a single, longer sentence. (See Chapter 26 for more information about coordination and subordination.) You may discover, on the other hand, that a long sentence contains two or three important ideas that would be more emphatic if each was expressed in a short sentence of its own.

Look back at the passage in 28a3 to see how this kind of revision can bring life to prose that suffers from uniform sentence lengths. In the second version, the writer uses coordination and subordination to combine the first four sentences of the first version into one long sentence that connects the main ideas of *a fixer-upper,* doing the fixing, and crawling about the basement. After this long sentence, he then adds a very short exclamatory sentence that both sums up the ideas in the first sentence and points ahead to the rest of the passage. Next, he combines two closely related ideas, about burst pipes and the installation of new ones, into one sentence of medium length, changing the participial phrase, *learning as I go* into a separate short sentence. The next three sentences of the original version, all dealing with the ordeal of working in the basement, are combined into one long sentence. Finally, a dependent clause and the two short clauses of a compound sentence are separated into three short parallel sentences (see Chapter 27), which give a blunt, hammering effect to the writer's expression of his complaints.

Varying sentence openings

In making prose readable and interesting, varying sentence openings is just as important as varying sentence lengths. For instance, when each sentence begins with the subject of an independent clause, a passage may seem to lurch or jerk along:

> *The way* football and basketball are played is as interesting as the players. *Football* is a game of precision. *Each play* is diagrammed to accomplish a certain goal. *A coach* designs the plays as an engineer would design a bridge. *Basketball* is a game of availability. *A basketball game* looks like a track meet. *The team* that drops of exhaustion first loses. *Basketball players* are also often compared to artists. *The players' moves and slam dunks* are their masterpieces.

Varying sentence openings can prevent this jerky effect. This section will focus on three ways of varying openings—using transitional expressions; using prepositional, verbal, and absolute phrases; and using dependent clauses.

1. Using transitional expressions

Note the ways in which opening transitions bring variety and clarity to this passage:

My life, I now realize, falls into three disproportionate parts. *Till the age of eight* I lived in the typical joint family, indistinguishable from my twenty cousins, indistinguishable, in fact, from an eternity of Bengali Brahmin girls. *From eight till twenty-one* we lived as a single family, enjoying for a time wealth and confidence. *And since twenty-one* I have lived in the West. Each phase required a repudiation of all previous avatars; an almost total rebirth.

— BHARATI MUKHERJEE, "Intimations"

Here the transitional words establish chronology and help carry us along smoothly through the paragraph. Other groups of transitional expressions that establish a sequence include *on the one hand ... on the other hand* and *on the left ... straight ahead ... on the right.*

Single-word transitional expressions that can be used to vary sentence openings include these:

ADVERBS	suddenly, fortunately, surprisingly
COORDINATING CONJUNCTIONS	and, but, or, nor, for, so, yet
CONJUNCTIVE ADVERBS	however, nevertheless, therefore, hence

Be careful to check that any such sentence opening suits the occasion and signals the appropriate chronological, spatial, or logical relationship with the preceding sentence. (See 6c5 for a discussion and list of transitional expressions.)

2. Using phrases

Prepositional, verbal, and absolute phrases can also provide variety in sentence openers.

Prepositional phrases

At each desk, a computer printout gives the necessary data.

From a few scraps of wood in the Middle Ages to a precisely carved, electrified instrument in the 1990s, the guitar has gone through uncounted changes.

Verbal phrases

Dressed in jeans and a dark-blue chamois shirt, a young woman appeared at the door.

To qualify for flight-training, one must be in good physical condition and pass a written test.

Absolute phrases

Our hopes for snow shattered, we started home.
Baton raised in a salute, the maestro readied the orchestra.

3. Using dependent clauses

Dependent clauses are another way to open a sentence.

While the boss sat on his tractor, I was down in a ditch pounding in stakes and levelling out the bottom.
What she wrote is difficult to explain.

4. Checking for varied sentence openings

As you revise, especially if you think your writing may be choppy, look carefully at your sentence openings. Underline the subject of each sentence. If most of your sentences begin with the subject, revise some of them by opening with transitional expressions, phrases, or dependent clauses.

Look at the following passage, which uses only subject openings, and then see how varying the sentence openings makes the passage easier to read.

FIRST DRAFT

<u>Most marathon runners</u> find that running with another person is helpful. <u>They</u> must not be afraid to pass this person, though, in order to run as well as possible. <u>Runners</u> must realize furthermore that even if they do not win the race, they achieve a victory by pushing their bodies to finish.

REVISED

Most marathon runners find that running with another person is helpful. In order to run as well as possible, though, *they* must not be afraid to pass this person. Furthermore, *runners* must realize that even if they do not win the race, they achieve victory by pushing their bodies to finish.

Exercise 28.1

Go back to the paragraph comparing football and basketball in 28b. Using transitional expressions, phrases, and/or dependent clauses, revise the paragraph to vary its sentence openings and thus to make the passage smoother and more coherent.

Varying sentence types

In addition to using different lengths and openings, you can help to vary your sentence structures by using different *types* of sentences. Sentences can be classified in three different ways: grammatically, functionally, and rhetorically (see 14d).

Grammatical types

Grammatically, sentences fall into four categories—**simple, compound, complex,** and **compound-complex**—based on the number of independent and dependent clauses they contain. Varying your sentences among these grammatical types will go a long way toward creating readable, effective prose. (See 14d1 for an explanation and examples of each type.)

Functional types

Functional types of sentences include **declarative** (making a statement), **interrogative** (asking a question), **imperative** (giving a command), and **exclamatory** (expressing strong feeling). (See 14d2.) Most sentences in essays are declarative, but occasionally you may want to include a command, a question, or even an exclamation of some kind if such sentence types are appropriate for your purpose. Note how they are used in these examples:

> Coal-burning plants undoubtedly harm the environment in various ways; among others, they contribute to acid rain. *But consider the alternatives.*

> We kept pressing on into the park. *And why? Why would sixteen exhausted people try to backpack sixty kilometres?* At this point, I was not at all sure.

> *Divorcés! They were everywhere!* Sometimes he felt like a new member of an enormous club, the Divorcés of Canada, that he had never before even heard of.

Rhetorical types

Two rhetorical sentence types, periodic and cumulative, spotlight sentence endings and beginnings and can be especially helpful in achieving sentence variety.

Periodic sentences postpone the main idea (usually in an independent clause) until the very end of the sentence. Effectively written periodic sentences are especially useful for building tension or building toward a climactic or surprise ending. At their best, they keep us alert by forcing us to hold information suspended, until the end. (See 14d3 for more discussion.)

> Early one morning, under the arc of a lamp, carefully, silently, in smock and leather gloves, old Doctor Manza grafted a cat's head onto a chicken's trunk.
> — Dylan Thomas

> Onie Stickland, Simeon Spencer, Uncle Art, and the rest of our friends and neighbours who were usually so ready, not to say eager, to keep us informed of everything that happened in Burgeo, spoke not a word to us about the whale.
> — Farley Mowat, *A Whale for the Killing*

> Even though large tracts of Europe and many old and famous states have fallen or may fall into the grasp of the Gestapo and all the odious apparatus of Nazi rule, we shall not flag or fail.
> — Winston Churchill

Note in each example how the writer holds back the main idea, thus using the end of the sentence to shock, surprise, or inspire.

Look at the following sentence and its revision to see how periodic order can provide emphasis.

> The nations of the world have no alternative but coexistence because another world war would be unwinnable and because total destruction would certainly occur.

PERIODIC

> Because another world war would be unwinnable and because total destruction would certainly occur, the nations of the world have no alternative but coexistence.

Nothing is wrong with the first sentence, which conveys the information clearly. But to put greater emphasis on the idea in the independent clause of the sentence—no alternative but coexistence—the writer chose to revise using the periodic pattern.

Cumulative sentences, which begin with an independent clause and then add details in phrases and other clauses, are the dominant rhetorical pattern today, far more common than periodic sentences. They are useful when you want to provide both immediate understanding of the main idea and a great deal of supporting detail. Note how the writers of the following sentences use the cumulative pattern not only to add important detail to the independent clause but also to end with a strong word or image:

He was sitting, rocking, in the frightful day room, his face and eyes closed, a picture of regression.

— OLIVER SACKS, "The Autist Artist"

Four steps past the turnstiles everybody is already backed up haunch to paunch for the climb up the ramp and the stairs to the surface, a great funnel of flesh, wool, felt, leather, rubber and steaming alumicrom, with the blood squeezing through everybody's old sclerotic arteries in hopped-up spurts from too much coffee and the effort of surfacing from the subway at the rush hour.

— TOM WOLFE

Exercise 28.2

Revise the following sentences into periodic form.

1. The members of the team entered the shell house one by one, tired and weary, at four o'clock on a cold, damp morning in Hamilton, Ontario.

2. I became the best salesperson in our store once I mastered the problems that I had encountered at the beginning and once I had become thoroughly familiar with the stock.

1. Checking for varied sentence types

As you revise, check to see that you have varied your sentence types sufficiently. Begin by noting the grammatical types you have used, marking each of your sentences as simple, compound, complex, or compound-complex. If any one or two patterns overwhelmingly predominate, combine, divide, and otherwise revise sentences until you have a wide range of types in your draft.

Next, note any sentences that are commands, questions, or exclamations. Decide whether these sentences are appropriate in context, and if not, delete or revise them.

To check for rhetorical sentence types, underline the independent clause(s) in each sentence. If a sentence opens with an independent clause and then builds with a series of modifying details, label it cumulative. If a sentence opens with a series of subordinating clauses or phrases and holds the independent clause until the end, label it periodic. (Many sentences will be neither.) Now consider whether each type is being used as effectively as possible. For each periodic sentence, see if you have used suspense to best advantage and built up to a climax. For each cumulative sentence, see if you have established your main point at the beginning and if the information in the rest of the sentence develops this point clearly and grammatically.

Finally, look at the balance of all sentence types. If your writing is like most people's, you will have few periodic sentences; few imperative, interrogative, or exclamatory sentences; and few compound-complex sentences. Be aware of this information as you revise, but do not revise arbitrarily to include more of a specific type. Revise only when the content calls for it— if, for instance, a sentence contains a surprise, a periodic structure will help emphasize that surprise.

Study how the sentences in the following passage are identified and then revised:

FIRST DRAFT

The purpose of speech is most often to persuade. [simple] It is seldom to generate understanding or to stimulate thoughtful response. [simple] Speeches on television take advantage of this fact. [simple] A televised speech gives viewers the time only to receive information, to respond emotionally to it, to "feel" it. [simple/cumulative] Viewers can simply enjoy or deplore its impact. [simple] Unlike a televised speech, a written speech can be read, reread, and analyzed. [simple] The reader can thoroughly process and analyze it. [simple] For this reason, I prefer to read and study a speech, not watch and instantly swallow it. [simple] This preference is limited to speeches that may be of great importance to me. [simple]

REVISED

The purpose of speech is most often not to generate understanding or to stimulate thoughtful response; rather, its purpose is merely to persuade. [compound] A televised speech takes advantage of this merely persuasive purpose by giving viewers time only to receive information, to respond emotionally to it, to "feel" or simply enjoy or deplore it. [simple/cumulative] Unlike a televised speech, a written speech can be read and reread, thoroughly analyzed and processed. [simple/periodic] For this reason, I prefer to read and study, not watch and instantly "swallow" any speech that may be of great importance to me. [complex]

Exercise 28.3

Following is an introductory paragraph from an essay. Analyze the paragraph carefully, noting for each sentence the length, the kind of opening, and the grammatical and rhetorical type. Then revise the paragraph to add variety in sentence lengths, sentence openings, and sentence types.

> When we arrived at the accident scene, I could tell that the injuries were not minor. I walked up to the car nearest me to check the injuries of the people inside. I looked through the driver's window and saw the woman's

body entangled in the steering wheel. I told dispatch, via two-way radio, to send medics "code red, lights and siren." I then went to see how the passenger in the car was. The passenger appeared to be in shock and had a broken leg. The officer walked over and checked the other vehicle. The driver of the other vehicle was drunk and had received no injuries at all.

Reading with an eye for sentence variety

Read the following paragraph, paying careful attention to the way the author varies its sentences—in length, opening, and types (grammatical, functional, and rhetorical).

> Creatures like José are not supposed to exist. Autistic child-artists like "Nadia" were not supposed to exist. Are they indeed so rare, or are they overlooked? Nigel Dennis, in a brilliant essay on Nadia in the *New York Review of Books* (4 May 1978), wonders how many of the world's "Nadias" may be dismissed or overlooked, their remarkable productions crumpled up and consigned to the trash can, or simply, like José, treated without thought, as an odd talent, isolated, irrelevant, of no interest. But the autistic artist or (to be less lofty) the autistic imagination is by no means rare. I have seen a dozen examples of it in as many years, and this without making any particular effort to find them.
>
> — Oliver Sacks, "The Autist Artist"

Taking inventory: sentence variety

Choose several paragraphs of an essay you have recently written, and examine them very carefully for variety of sentence structure. For each sentence, note the length, the kind of opening, and the grammatical, functional, and rhetorical type. Then revise the paragraphs to achieve as wide a range of variation as possible in these qualities. Read the original and revised versions aloud (better still, read them to another student), noting the differences in rhythm and impact.

29

Creating Memorable Prose

How many times have you read something so striking that you wanted immediately to share it with a friend? And how many times have you remembered the exact words of something you have read or heard? All of us recognize, and can even quote, certain passages from literature or history—the opening of *A Tale of Two Cities,* perhaps, or passages from famous speeches. It makes sense to examine some of the elements that make pieces such as these so memorable. Consider, for instance, these lines from some of Sir Winston Churchill's speeches:

> Victory at all costs, victory in spite of all terror, victory however long and hard the road may be; for without victory there is no survival.

> From Stettin in the Baltic to Trieste in the Adriatic an iron curtain has descended across the Continent.

> The inherent vice of capitalism is the unequal sharing of blessings; the inherent virtue of socialism is the equal sharing of miseries.

What strategies did Churchill use to make these lines memorable? First would be his use of *repetition:* in sentence 1, the repetition of the word *victory* creates a powerful rhythm. Second might be his use of *inverted word order:* saving the subject until the second part of sentence 2 adds dramatic emphasis to his sentence. Third would be his use of *antithesis,* seen in sentence 3 in the two parallel clauses that accentuate the contrast of capitalism and socialism.

Each of these strategies and devices can be used to good effect by all writers. This chapter will examine each one and offer practice to help you use them in your work.

29a

Choosing strong verbs

The greatest writers in any language are those with a genius for choosing the precise words that will arrest and hold a reader's attention. In your own writing, you can help to gain this attention by using precise nouns and adjectives instead of vague, catchall "buzzwords" (see 25b2). Perhaps even more important, however, you can use strong, precise verbs instead of weak, catchall verbs and instead of nouns.

1. Using strong, precise verbs

Verbs serve as the real workhorses of our language. Take a look, for instance, at the strong, precise verbs in the following passage:

> Entirely out of control, the human technomachine *guzzles* and *lurches* and *vomits* and *rips* its random crazy course over the face of the once-blue planet, as though some *filthy* barbaric fist were drunkenly *swiping* with a gigantic paint roller across an ancient tapestry.
>
> – JOHN A. LIVINGSTON, *The Fallacy of Wildlife Conservation*

Using precise verbs, Livingston describes—graphically—human violation of nature.

Some of the most common verbs in English—especially *be, do,* and *have*—carry little or no sense of specific action, and many writers tend to use them where a more precise verb would be clearer and more effective. Look at how the following sentences are strengthened by replacing forms of *be, do,* and *have* with more precise verbs:

WEAK	Constant viewing of television violence *is* harmful to children's emotional development.
REVISED	Constant viewing of television violence *skews* children's emotional development.
WEAK	In front of the hotel, an artist would *do* your portrait on a framed sheet of glass.
REVISED	In front of the hotel, an artist would *etch* your portrait on a framed sheet of glass.
WEAK	We *had* exams in April.
REVISED	We *suffered* through exams in April.

The verb *be* is essential to writing. In general, however, if forms of *be* (*is, are, was, were, has been,* and so on) account for more than about a third of the verbs in a piece of writing, the writing may well seem static and flat.

Expletives

One verb construction to watch out for is the **expletive**, which begins with *there* or *it* followed by a form of *be.* Expletives can be effective ways of introducing something with emphasis, but too many writers overuse them, writing sentences that needlessly bury action in a noun, verbal, or dependent clause. Notice how the following sentences are strengthened by deleting the expletive:

WEAK	*There are* many people who fear success because they believe they do not deserve it.
REVISED	Many people *fear* success because they believe they do not deserve it.
WEAK	*It is* necessary for a political candidate today to perform well on television.
REVISED	A political candidate today *must perform* well on television.

2. Changing nouns to verbs

Much modern writing tends to express action by using nouns that are formed from verbs, a process called **nominalization**. Although nominalization can help make prose clearer and more concise—for example, using *abolition* instead of *the process of abolishing*—it can also produce the opposite effect, making a sentence unnecessarily wordy and hard to read. Nominalization reduces the *active* quality of a sentence, burying the action in an abstract noun and forcing the writer to use weak, generalized verbs and too many prepositional phrases. Too often, writers use nominalizations not to make a complex process easier to talk about but to make an idea *sound* more complex and abstract than it really is. Bureaucratic writing especially tends to use excessive nominalization in this way.

You can decide when to use a nominalized form and when to use the verb from which it derives by asking one question: which is most readily understandable? Take a look at the following sentence, for example:

> The firm is now engaged in an assessment of its procedures for the development of new products.

This sentence scarcely impresses itself on our memories, and it sounds pretentious and stuffy as well. In contrast, note the more easily understood and forceful version:

The firm is now assessing its procedures for developing new products.

3. Checking your verbs and nouns

To revise a draft for stronger verbs, first circle all the verbs, and look to see whether you are relying too much on *be, do,* and *have.* If so, try to substitute more specific verbs whenever possible. Next, circle every noun whose meaning could be expressed by a verb. Try rewriting the sentence using the verb instead of the noun, adjusting any words necessary to keep the meaning you intended. Finally, underline all expletives, omitting any that are not used to create special emphasis. Study how the following passage is revised:

WEAK

Last February, when I (made) the decision to (buy) a house, I (opened) a separate chequing (and savings) account in order to (give) (attention) more easily to my household expenses. (There (is) a credit union policy that for every chequing account there (must be) a matching savings account: thus the dormant savings account.) This new chequing account (was) where the (deposit) of the (inheritance) from my grandmother (occurred) along with any other (accumulation) of money from outside sources.

REVISED

Last February, when I decided to buy a house, I opened a separate chequing (and savings) account to deal more easily with household expenses. (Credit union policy demands a matching savings account for every chequing account; thus the dormant savings account.) Into this new chequing account I deposited the inheritance from my grandmother, along with any other money I accumulated from outside sources.

Exercise 29.1

Revise the following paragraph to eliminate weak verbs and unnecessary nominalizations and expletives.

There has long been resistance to the proposition that the effectiveness of methods and teachers must be measured in terms of the results secured. Those responsible for evaluating teachers have exalted procedures in teaching and have seldom examined the products, that is, the efficiency of the teacher as indicated by what his or her pupils can do following instruction. However, we are beginning to see an increasing number of bold proposals founded on the assumption that the Canadian public has expectations of results from schooling. As public support of education increases, there will be greater insistence on judging a teacher in the light of his or her ability to enhance the learning of pupils.

Choosing between active and passive voice

In addition to choosing strong, precise verbs, you can help to make your prose memorable by varying those verbs appropriately between active and passive voice. Look at the following paragraph:

> I remember as a child the death of a farmer. He fell from a tree and was not expected to live. He asked simply to die at home, a wish that was granted without question. He called his daughters into the bedroom and spoke with each one of them alone for a few moments. He arranged his affairs quietly, though he was in great pain, and distributed his belongings and his land, none of which was to be split until his wife should follow him in death. He also asked each of his children to share in the work, duties, and tasks that he had carried on until the time of the accident. He asked his friends to visit him once more, to bid goodbye to them. Although I was a small child at the time, he did not exclude me or my siblings. We were allowed to share in the preparations of the family just as we were permitted to grieve with them until he died ...
>
> — ELISABETH KÜBLER-ROSS, "On the Fear of Death"

In this paragraph, Kübler-Ross uses both active and passive voice, but you will notice she uses active voice especially to describe the actions of the farmer himself—what he does, what he chooses. She tends to use passive voice to describe the actions of others, whose identities are less important: the farmer *was not expected to live;* his wish to die at home *was granted without question;* none of his belongings *was to be split* until the death of his wife; and so on.

To make your own writing memorable, try to use the active voice unless you have a good reason to use the passive.

As the Kübler-Ross passage indicates, the passive can be used effectively in certain situations: when the performer is unknown, or less important than the recipient of the action (or, in some cases, unwilling to be identified).

See Chapter 16 for further discussion of voice.

Exercise 29.2

Look at the following sentences, in which some of the verbs are active and some passive. Then rewrite each sentence in the other voice, and decide which version you find preferable and why.

EXAMPLE

You are hereby relieved of your duties by me.

I hereby relieve you of your duties.

1. In Gower's research, it was found that pythons often dwell in trees and live near rivers.

2. They started shooting pool, and before Marie knew it, she owed the kid ten dollars.

3. When I was 8, my father's crazy dreams uprooted our family from Saskatoon to the Northwest Territories.

4. For me, living in a dorm was more easily adjusted to than living in an apartment.

5. Canadian artists often have been ignored in Canada until they are recognized in the United States.

29c

Creating special effects

Rhetorical devices such as repetition, antithesis, and alteration of word order can create special effects, animating your prose and often making it more memorable.

1. Using repetition

Carefully used, repetition of sounds, words, phrases, or other grammatical constructions serves as a powerful stylistic device. Orators in particular have long known its power. Here is a famous use of repetition, from one of Sir Winston Churchill's addresses to the British people during World War II:

> We shall not flag or fail, we shall go on to the end. We shall fight in France, we shall fight on the seas and oceans, we shall fight with growing confidence and growing strength in the air, we shall defend our island, whatever the cost may be; we shall fight on the beaches, … we shall fight in the fields and in the streets, … we shall never surrender.
>
> — WINSTON CHURCHILL

The constant hammering *we shall*, accompanied by the repetition of *f* sounds (*flag, fail, fight, France, confidence, defend, fields*) make this passage especially compelling.

A less daunting example of effective repetition is found in the following piece of student writing.

> Pepperoni and sausage, mushrooms and olives, onions and anchovies, peppers and tomatoes, and cheese and cheese and cheese: we ate it all. We ate, and ate, and ate, and ate. And when we couldn't possibly eat another bite, ... then we ate some more.

Be careful to use repetition only for a deliberate purpose. See 25b for a discussion of how unnecessary repetition can lead to wordiness.

2. Using antithesis

Another special effect that can contribute to memorable writing is **antithesis**, the use of parallel structures to highlight a contrast or opposition. Like other uses of parallelism (see Chapter 27), antithesis provides a pleasing rhythm that calls readers' attention to the contrast, often in a startling or amusing way. For example:

> Love is an ideal thing, money a real thing.

> The congregation didn't think much of the new preacher, and what the new preacher thought of the congregation she didn't wish to say.

You can often use antithesis effectively when you are developing a paragraph by the alternating method of comparison and contrast (see 3e3 and 6d). By using parallel form to express the differences between two things or ideas or between two aspects of the same thing or idea, antithesis helps to clarify points of contrast. Look at the following paragraph, in which each sentence is an example of antithesis:

> Yesterday's scholars admired and emulated the world's great thinkers; today's students admire and emulate the world's top business moguls. The pursuit of wealth, not the pursuit of knowledge, is of the most interest to many of them.

3. Using altered word order

Altering the usual word order of a sentence can make for memorable writing by creating surprise or putting emphasis on a particular word or phrase. The word order in English is usually subject-verb-object/complement (if any). An alteration in that order may put the verb before the subject or put the object or complement before the subject and verb. Look at the following example:

| NORMAL | Two dead birds plummeted out of the tree. |
| INVERTED | Out of the tree plummeted two dead birds. |

The inverted word order of the second version makes for a more dramatic sentence by putting the emphasis on *two dead birds* at the end of the sentence.

As with any unusual sentence pattern, altered word order should be used sparingly. But as the following examples illustrate, this technique can indeed create special effects:

Into this grey lake plopped the thought, I know this man, don't I?

— DORIS LESSING

In a hole in the ground there lived a hobbit.

— J.R.R. TOLKIEN

The bulk of her estate she left to the Humane Society.

Good-looking he was not; wealthy he was not; but brilliant—he was.

Exercise 29.3

After studying the examples above, look at an essay you have recently written, and find a sentence that might be more effective with altered word order. Experiment with the word order, reading the results aloud and comparing differences in effect.

Reading with an eye for memorable prose

The following piece of writing is by Twila Krown, a student at the University of British Columbia. Twila wrote this piece in response to an assignment to evoke an emotion by using a situated description. When you read the essay, you will be able to identify many of the strategies for memorable writing discussed in this chapter.

I am in the passenger's seat of my mother's car. She is driving slowly, silently. We pass that restaurant—Dixie Lee Chicken. My grandmother used to take me there. Mom asks for a cigarette. I hate her noxious habit, so in insolence I make her ask twice. As I reach behind her seat for the grey purse, containing her "smokes" and a ton of other stuff, I see those old pictures. My ancestors: my grandmother's parents. The pictures were framed behind glass with dried roses by my grandmother before I was an idea. For two days, these portraits have been in the car. Yesterday, the heat must have been stifling; it must have been killing them. Now my great-grandparents stare blankly up at me through a milky sheet of wax, embalmed by the rose oil that has melted and spread over them in the back of this makeshift hearse.

Mom left the pictures in the sun. She was the undertaker. She gives me a sharp nudge with her elbow to remind me of the task. Now I have it in my hand, a flammable bundle of dead leaves wrapped in white paper. I pass her the damned cigarette and the car lighter pops out immediately. She must have this timed.

I watch the smoke from her cigarette wind upward in a curly stream and suck out of the tiny crack above the window. I imagine that my grandmother's smoky essence swirled up and diffused the same way, leaving what is here, near my left foot, in the gold cardboard box from the crematorium: ashes. Dust, like the film on the dashboard of the car from dirt roads and neglect. I can feel it dropping out of the stagnant air and settling on my skin. You can write in it: clean me.

Ashes should be in that box, but I have looked in, and I have seen that my grandmother has been reduced to nothing finer than a few hundred fragments of dense pinkened bone. This is the reality of losing the woman who had been the bond of love between my mother and me. My grandmother, like pleasant soft plaster that we could lean on from either side, our impressions coming close but the two of us never really touching. Now the cast has hardened and shattered and my mother and I have stumbled into one another. Here we sit, awkwardly composed in a small car full of cigarette smoke and exhaled sorrow. We are heading toward the cemetery. Today we will bury the past and move on to the uncertain future, hoping to find that something more than similar features makes us mother and daughter.

Taking inventory: memorable prose

One way of working with strategies for making your prose more memorable is to *imitate* the writing of a favourite author. Select an author, and read and reread passages of his or her work, trying to get a feel for its rhythms, structures, and special effects. See if you can identify the elements that contribute to its distinctive style. Then write a paragraph or more in the style of your chosen author. When you've completed a draft, write about your success in imitating the elements of style you admire.

Following are a paragraph by the well-known author Margaret Atwood and one by student Lara Dal Monte, written in imitation. Atwood's paragraph is from her essay "Writing the Male Character"; Lara attempts something on "writing the female character." The third paragraph below is Lara's commentary on her own imitation.

"Why do men feel threatened by women?" I asked a male friend of mine. (I love that wonderful rhetorical device, "a male friend of mine." It's often used by female journalists when they want to say something particularly bitchy but don't want to be held responsible for it themselves. It also lets people know that you *do* have male friends, that you aren't one of those fire-breathing mythical monsters, The Radical Feminists, who walk around with little pairs of scissors and kick men in the shins if they open doors for you. "A male friend of mine" also gives—let us admit it—a certain weight to the opinions expressed.) So this male friend of mine, who does by the way exist, conveniently entered into the following dialogue. "I mean," I said, "men are bigger, most of the time, they can run faster, strangle better, and they have on the average a lot more money and power." "They're afraid women will laugh at them," he said. "Undercut their world view." Then I asked some women students in a quickie poetry seminar I was giving, "Why do women feel threatened by men?" "They're afraid of being killed," they said.

– MARGARET ATWOOD, "Writing the Male Character"

While men and women are indeed different, women are not all the same. Despite what you might see on afternoon television (not that I am ever to be found in front of one of those devious, dangerous, mind-numbing contraptions—except of course when a good cooking show or hair depilatory advertisement is on), we women are not a homogeneous assembly of man-hungry debutantes or over-the-hill matrons planning the quintessential Groundhog Day Ball. Granted, one or two of us may be, but no single gender could possibly claim more than, say, twelve Erica Kaine wanna-be's. (For those among us who spend our afternoons rereading back copies of Ms magazine, Erica is the ultimate soap opera diva.) Nor are we all perky housewives with a deep-seated hatred for less than sparkling toilet bowls, or an unquenchable curiosity about the latest technological breakthrough in feminine hygiene products. We are somewhat more diverse than that. In fact, women can be as strange and wonderful and—yes, I am going to say it—they can be as despicable and ignorant and messy as men. That is the horror and the majesty of life rolled into one unpalatable bundt cake: we are in this together, for better or worse, and we better start picking our allies based on their individual strengths and weaknesses, not based on whether or not they pee standing up.

– LARA DAL MONTE

The main elements of Atwood's writing that I was trying to emulate were her obviously sharp wit and the intimacy she creates between herself and her audience. I don't think I copied her wit, but I never believed that I could; I think she is an incredibly smart, funny, and sharp woman … I tried to create intimacy by using parenthetical statements like she does. These explanations and elaborations in her writing seem to pull the audience close to her, as if she is inviting them to lean in towards her so that she can share a secret with them. She also uses ellipses, and they create a stream-of-consciousness feeling. It seems as though she is spouting out words as they enter her mind without any editing. This contributes to the conspiratorial mood of this essay. My greatest limitation in this exercise is that I don't have access to Atwood's cache of literary, cultural, and etymological allusions (mine is still developing).

– LARA DAL MONTE

Selecting Effective Words

Considering Diction

Enriching Vocabulary

Using Dictionaries

Working on Spelling

30

Considering Diction

In writing of someone you work with, you might choose one or more of the following words: *accomplice, ally, associate, buddy, cohort, collaborator, colleague, comrade, co-worker, mate, partner, sidekick.* The choice you make is a matter of **diction**, which derives from the Latin word for "say" and means literally how you say or express something. Good diction, or choosing words well, involves many issues discussed elsewhere in this book, such as being concise (see 25b), using parallel structures (see Chapter 27), choosing strong, precise verbs (see 29a), using dictionaries (see Chapter 32), and strengthening vocabulary (see Chapter 31). This chapter will give you some guidance about other aspects of good diction: writing for common ground, using the appropriate register, choosing words with suitable denotations and connotations, balancing general and abstract words with specific and concrete ones, and using figurative language.

Writing for common ground

Language has power. It can praise, delight, inspire. It can also hurt, offend, destroy. Language that insults or offends any group of readers at the very least prevents many readers from identifying with you and damages your credibility as a writer.

In many instances, avoiding such language is simple enough. We can safely assume, for instance, that no readers respond well to being referred to disparagingly—for example, as "slobs" or "nerds." But other cases are more subtle and perhaps surprising. One student found that members of a group he had been referring to as *senior citizens* were irritated by that label. Similarly, a recent survey of people with physical disabilities reported that most of them resented euphemisms like *differently abled* and *physically challenged* because they saw these terms as trivializing their difficulties.

Because language usage changes constantly and people's preferences vary widely, few absolute guidelines exist that will respect differences and build common ground in every instance. Two general rules, however, can help: watching for words that carry stereotypes and unintended assumptions, and considering carefully the sensitivities and preferences of others.

1. Watching for stereotypes and other assumptions

Children like to play; citizens of Canada value freedom; people who do not finish high school fare less well in the job market than those who graduate. These broad statements all contain **stereotypes**, standardized or fixed ideas about a group. To some extent, we all think in terms of stereotypes, and sometimes they can be helpful in making a generalization. Stereotyping any individual on the basis of generalizations about a group can be dangerous, however, for it can lead to inaccurate and even hurtful conclusions.

Stereotyping becomes especially evident in language, in the words we choose to refer to or describe others. Stereotyped language can and often does break the links between writers and readers—or between speakers and listeners.

In an article in *The New Yorker* magazine, an executive who worked to find jobs for teenagers pointed up additional dangers of language that stereotypes others.

> When I hear the word *dropout*, I have this image in my mind of a kid sitting across from me in the subway car: he's smoking a cigarette; he has a radio the size of a grand piano, and he keeps turning up the volume; his legs are stretched out so nobody can pass; he is staring at me with a look I can only describe as hate. I know that's not fair or accurate because I've hired many of them. Still, I can't help thinking of that kid on the subway.

Note the ways in which the executive admits he stereotypes people on the basis of a label: *dropouts* are apparently all young and male—and all rude, noisy, and hostile. Like all stereotypes, his is the result of a stock response built up and maintained by many things in his experience—songs, books, movies, television shows, and news reports, as well as personal encounters with some individuals who have dropped out of school. The mass media are particularly powerful in creating stereotypes. But as the executive recognizes and points out, they are often not accurate or fair.

Very often based on half-truths, misunderstandings, and hand-me-down prejudices, stereotypes can lead to intolerance, irrational bias, and bigotry. Even apparently positive or neutral ones can hurt, for they inevitably ignore the uniqueness of an individual. As writers, we need to check carefully to make sure that our language doesn't stereotype any group *or* individual. Other kinds of unstated assumptions that enter into our thinking and writing destroy common ground by ignoring differences between others and ourselves. For example, a student whose paper for a religion seminar uses *we* to refer to Christians and *they* to refer to members of other religions had better be sure that all the class members and the instructor are Christian, or some of them may well feel left out of this discussion.

On the other hand, stereotypes and other assumptions often lead writers to mention a group affiliation unnecessarily when it has no relation to the point under consideration, as in *a woman bus driver* or *a Jewish doctor*. Decisions about whether to generalize about a group or whether to describe an individual as a member of a group are often very difficult for writers. The following sections invite you to think about how your language can build—rather than destroy—common ground.

2. Considering assumptions about gender

The feminist movement of the last three decades has done much to demonstrate how powerfully and often invisibly gender-related elements of language affect the ways we think and behave. We now know, for instance, that many young women at one time were discouraged from pursuing careers in medicine or engineering at least partially because our language, following stereotyped assumptions about gender roles in society, always referred to hypothetical doctors or engineers as *he* (and then labelled any woman who worked as a doctor as a *woman doctor*, as if to say, "She's an exception; doctors are normally male"). Equally problematic is the traditional use of *man* and *mankind* to refer to people of both sexes and the use of *he, him, his*, and *himself* to refer to people of unknown sex, as in "a lawyer must pass the bar exam before he can begin to practise." Such usage ignores half the human race—or at least seems to assume that the other half is more important. Similarly, labels like *male nurse* or *male secretary* may offend by reflecting stereotyped assumptions about proper roles for males.

Revising sexist language

Sexist language—those words and phrases that stereotype or ignore members of either sex or that unnecessarily call attention to gender—can usually be revised fairly easily. Here are some alternatives to the use of masculine pronouns to refer to persons of unknown sex.

- Use plural forms:
  Lawyers must pass the bar exam before *they* can begin to practise.
- Use *he or she, him or her,* and so on:

A lawyer must pass the bar exam before *he or she* can begin to practise.

- Eliminate the pronouns:
  A lawyer must pass the bar exam before beginning to practise. (For more discussion of nonsexist pronouns, see 17m).

3. Considering assumptions about race and ethnicity

As we all know only too well, generalizations about racial and ethnic groups can result in especially harmful stereotyping. Such assumptions can be seen in statements that suggest, for instance, that all Asians excel in math and science, or that Germans are all efficiency experts. Negative stereotypes, of course, are even more damaging. Writers should watch for any language that ignores differences among individual members of a race or ethnic group.

Using preferred terms

For writers, avoiding stereotypes and other assumptions based on race or ethnicity is only a first step. Beyond that lies the task of attempting to refer to any group in terms that its members actually desire. Doing so is sometimes not an easy task, for preferences change and even vary widely.

The word *coloured,* for example, was once widely used in North America to refer to people of African ancestry (in fact, it still appears in the name of the NAACP, the National Association for the Advancement of Colored People). By the 1950s, the preferred term had become *Negro;* in the 1960s, however, *black* came to be preferred by most, though certainly not all, members of that community. Then, toward the end of the 1980s, some leaders of the American black community urged that *black* in turn be replaced by *African American.* One such leader, the Reverend Jesse Jackson, argued that *African American* has "cultural integrity" because it designates "some land base, some historical cultural base," whereas *black* is a "baseless" designation.

Similarly, the word *Oriental,* which not too long ago was commonly used to refer to people of East Asian decent, is now often considered offensive; the terms *Asian* or *East Asian* are preferred. Many of those once referred to as *Indians* prefer to be called *native Canadians* or *First Nations People*, and people once referred to as *Eskimos* are now called *Inuit.*

Ethnic terminology may seem to change quickly. The best advice to the writer is to consider words carefully, to listen for the way members of groups refer to themselves (or ask for their preferences), and to check any term you're unsure of in a current dictionary. The 1991 edition of the *Random House Webster's College Dictionary* includes particularly helpful usage notes about racial and ethnic designations.

4. Considering other kinds of difference

Gender, race, and ethnicity are among the most frequent challenges for a writer seeking to find common ground with readers, but you will face many others as well. The following section discusses some of them.

Age

Mention age if it is relevant, but be aware that age-related terms can carry derogatory connotations (*matronly, well-preserved,* and so on). Although describing Mr. Fry as "elderly but still active" may sound polite to you, chances are that Mr. Fry would prefer being called "an active 78-year-old"—or just "a 78-year-old," which eliminates the unstated assumption of surprise that he would be active "at his age."

Class

Because you may not usually think about class as consciously as you do about age or race, for example, you should take special care to examine your words for stereotypes or assumptions about class. Their potential to offend was shown in a *New York Times* column entitled "Young, Privileged, and Unemployed," written by a young woman who had lost her high-paying professional job. Unable to find other "meaningful work," the author wrote, she and others like her had been forced to accept "absurd" jobs like cleaning houses and baby-sitting.

The column provoked a number of angry letters to the *Times,* like this one: "So the young and privileged are learning what we of the working classes have always understood too well: there is no entitlement in life. We have always taken the jobs you label 'absurd.' Our mothers are the women who clean your mothers' houses ..." Thus did the writer destroy common ground with her readers by assuming that cleaning houses is an "absurd" way to make a living and that educational or social standing entitles people to more "meaningful" occupations.

Physical ability or health

The most important question to ask yourself when writing about a person with a serious illness or other physical disability is whether to mention the disability at all if it is not in some respect relevant to what you are discussing. If you do refer to a disability, consider whether the words you use carry negative connotations. You might choose, for example, to say someone *uses a wheelchair* rather than to say he or she *is confined to* one, language that is grammatically passive and connotes physical passivity as well. Similarly, you might note a subtle but meaningful difference between calling someone *a person with AIDS*, rather than *an AIDS victim*. Mentioning the person first and the disability second, as in referring to *a child with diabetes* rather than *a diabetic child* or *a diabetic*, is always a good idea. On the other hand, the survey of people with disabilities that was mentioned earlier shows that you sometimes need to be careful not to minimize a disability.

Sexual orientation

Partly because sexual orientation was a topic "erased" from most public discourse until recent decades, the stereotypes and assumptions that surround it are particularly deep-seated and, often, unconscious. Writers who wish to build common ground, therefore, should not generally assume that readers all share any one sexual orientation—that everyone is attracted to the opposite sex, for example.

As with any label, reference to sexual orientation should be governed by context. Someone writing about Svend Robinson's economic views would probably have no reason to refer to his sexual orientation. On the other hand, a writer concerned with diversity in government might find it important to note that Robinson is one of the few legislators to have made his homosexuality public.

Religion

Religious stereotypes are very often inaccurate and unfair. Roman Catholics hold a wide spectrum of views on abortion, for example, Muslim women do not all wear veils, and many Baptists are not fundamentalists. In fact, not all people believe in or practise a religion at all, so be careful of such assumptions. As in other cases, do not use religious labels without considering their relevance to your point, and make every effort to get them right—for example, *Reformed* churches but *Reform* synagogues.

Exercise 30.1

One good way to start thinking about differences and common ground is to look around the classroom and try to describe them in writing. Like you, generations of college students have found themselves in classes filled with people both like them and different from them. Here is Eudora Welty, describing her first year (1926) at Mississippi State College for Women.

> There I landed in a world to itself, and indeed it was all new to me. It was surging with twelve hundred girls. They came from every nook and corner of the state, from the Delta, the piney woods, the Gulf Coast, the black prairie, the red clay hills, and Jackson—as the capital city and the only sizeable town, a region to itself. All were clearly differentiated sections, at that time, and though we were all put into uniforms of navy blue so as to unify us, it could

have been told by the girls' accents, by their bearings, the way they came into the classroom and the way they ate, where they'd grown up. This was my first chance to learn what the body of us were like and what differences in background, persuasion of mind, and resources of character there were among Mississippians—at that, among only half of us, for we were all white. I missed the significance of both what was in, and what was out of, our well-enclosed but vibrantly alive society.

— EUDORA WELTY, *One Writer's Beginnings*

Take time now to examine where you've come from—your age, ethnicity, religion, and so on. Then do the same for one or more of your classmates. Write a paragraph about the differences *and* the common ground you see. Finally, study your paragraph for any assumptions your language reveals.

Using the appropriate register

Sensitivity to an audience means not only writing for common ground but also making a number of other decisions about word choice. **Register**—or level of diction—is another matter for the writer to consider when he or she is thinking about how to make writing respectful of and appropriate to particular audiences. While the *formal register* is the one most often appropriate and useful for academic writing, you should be able to recognize and use other registers as well.

1. Familiar register

Familiar register represents a very close relationship between writer and topic and between writer and audience—it is the language you probably use to talk to yourself or to those you are closest to. It is the register found in diaries, journals, and personal letters; writers sometimes use it in essays, stories, plays, and novels to create a sense of intimacy between themselves and readers or between characters. Among the characteristics of familiar register are the frequent use of the first person (*I*) and first names, a lack of explicitly stated context (because the audience does not need it), and the use of sentence fragments, contractions, slang, colloquial language, regionalisms, dialect, and other grammatical constructions that disregard the "rules."

You will seldom, if ever, be called on to write in familiar register in academic writing. You should, however, learn to recognize it as a reader. The following example is a letter from the English writer Virginia Stephen responding to a marriage proposal from her future husband, Leonard Woolf:

My dear Leonard,

   I am rushing for a train so I can only send a line in answer. There isn't anything really for me to say, except that I should like to go on as before; and that you should leave me free, and that I should be honest. As to faults, I expect mine are just as bad—less noble perhaps. But of course they are not really the question. I have decided to keep this completely secret, except for Vanessa; and I have made her promise not to tell Clive. I told Adrian that you had come up about a job which was promised you. So keep this up if he asks.

   I am very sorry to be the cause of so much rush and worry. I am just off to Firle.

Yrs.

VS

Notice that Stephen assumes Woolf will know what her "line" is "in answer" to, what "this" is, and who Vanessa, Clive, and Adrian are. She uses a contraction (*isn't*) and abbreviations (*Yrs.*, her initials), as well as the colloquial expression *keep this up* to mean "pretend that this story is true." Because she was a professional writer living in a different time and a different culture, your familiar register is probably less formal than hers, but you can see that she is writing to a very intimate audience (of one) on a very intimate topic.

2. Informal register

Informal register assumes a fairly close but not extremely close relationship or familiarity between the writer and the audience and topic. It may use colloquial language or slang as well as contractions and other grammatical constructions that are not considered appropriate in more formal writing. The language of most conversation and of much popular media, it is often found in short stories and novels as well, especially in dialogue. Some of your classes, particularly if you take journalism, communications, or creative writing, may call on you to use informal register. Here is an example:

> They've changed! Weight trainers are no longer the freshly primed Charles Atlas impersonators who attempted to conquer the world by kicking sand in the faces of skinnier men. In fact—are you sitting down?—many of them are women.
>
> – JILL DAVEY, "Pumping Iron—à la Femme"

Davey is obviously closely involved with her topic, although the involvement is not as close as that of Virginia Stephen with Leonard Woolf's marriage proposal. Nor is she as intimately related to her audience, but her use of a contraction, an exclamation, a mid-sentence question, and, of course, humour, all create an informal tone of easy familiarity.

3. Formal register

Formal register is the language found in most academic, business, and professional writing and in serious nonfiction books and magazine articles. Because most of the writing you will do in college or university and probably throughout your life should be in formal register, study carefully the following list of its characteristics:

1. Emotional distance between the writer and the audience: your stance should be friendly and courteous but not chummy or intimate.

2. Emotional distance between the writer and the topic: though you may know the topic very well and have strong feelings about it, your stance toward it should be as objective as possible.

3. No colloquial language or slang.

4. Careful attention to the conventions of edited Canadian English, the grammatical "rules" like those presented in this book.

5. Attention to the logical relationships among words and ideas: phrases and sentences should be carefully structured, not just tossed out.

Here is an example of formal register:

> It is well documented that men are more likely than women to abuse alcohol (Eland, 1982). Data from both the United States and Canada indicate that there are about three men who are problem drinkers for every one woman. The groundwork for this gender difference may be laid very early; research shows that even among adolescents, males report more use of all drugs except cigarettes (Kandel, 1980). These findings certainly fit the gender stereotypes about drinking; when people think of a skid row alcoholic they usually think of a man, and the image of a temperance advocate is inevitably female.
>
> – HILARY M. LIPS, *Sex and Gender: An Introduction*

Note the tone of objectivity Lips tries to create and her appeal to published authority. Her sentences are straightforward and she uses some of the conventional language of academic writing, stating for example that the tendency she writes about is "well documented" and that her claim is supported by what the "data … indicate."

4. Ceremonial register

For some solemn occasions, speakers or writers move beyond formal language to **ceremonial register**, the language of ceremony or ritual. You can recognize ceremonial register by its very careful attention to rhythm or cadence, to the sound of words, and to building toward a climax, a powerful dominant impression. If you are ever asked to make a statement at a funeral, to present a very important award, or to address a group on a very important occasion, you may want to use ceremonial register. Here is an example:

> Was it only yesterday that men sailed around the moon ... And is it tomorrow they will stand upon its barren surface? You and I marvel that man should brave so far and so fast ... Yet, if they have travelled far then I have travelled farther ... and if they have travelled fast, then I faster ... for I was born a thousand years ago ... born in a culture of bows and arrows. But within the span of half a life I was flung across the ages to the culture of the atom bomb ... and from bows and arrows to atom bombs is a distance far beyond a flight to the moon.
>
> — CHIEF DAN GEORGE

5. Register in technical writing

One special kind of language frequently found in formal register is the technical discourse used in particular fields that have created special vocabularies or given common words special meaning. Business people talk about *greenmail* and *upside movement,* biologists about *nucleotides* and *immunodestruction,* and baseball fans about *fielder's choices* and *suicide bunts.* Such terms are understood by other specialist, but they can be very confusing to those outside the field. You need, then, to judge any use of technical language very carefully, making sure that your intended audience will understand your terms and replacing or defining those that they will not. Technical language can be divided into two overlapping categories: neologisms and jargon.

Neologisms

New words that have not yet found their way into dictionaries, **neologisms** can be very helpful to writers, especially in the sciences and applied disciplines, where new things and concepts appear every day and need names. Terms like *byte, thermosiphon, deconstruct,* and *neutrino,* for example, could not be easily replaced except by a much longer and more complex explanation. Some neologisms, however, do not meet a real need. Words like *deaccess* and *prioritization* could be easily replaced by existing words or phrases that general readers would understand.

Jargon

Jargon is the special vocabulary of a trade or profession, enabling members to speak and write concisely to one another. Thus, jargon should be reserved as much as possible for a specific technical audience. Here is an example of jargon used inappropriately in writing addressed to general readers:

JARGON   The VDTs were down at the newspaper office last week, so we had to do the page makeup on dummies and use a wheel to crop the pictures.

Notice that the following revision eliminates some of the jargon terms and defines others:

REVISED   The video display terminals were not working at the newspaper office last week, so we had to arrange the type for each page on a large cardboard sheet and use a wheel, a kind of circular slide rule, to figure out the size and shape of the pictures.

6. Pompous language, euphemisms, and doublespeak

In addition to avoiding inappropriate use of technical language, be alert to three other kinds of language sometimes found in formal register that can make for ineffective tone: pompous language, euphemisms, and doublespeak.

Pompous language is unnecessarily formal for the purpose, audience, or topic. Hence it often gives writing an insincere or unintentionally humorous tone, making the writer's idea seem less significant or believable rather than more so.

POMPOUS   Pursuant to the recent memorandum issued August 9, 1979, because of petroleum supply exigencies, it is incumbent upon us all to endeavour to make maximal utilization of telephonic communication in lieu of personal visitation.

REVISED   As of August 9, 1979, shortages of petroleum require us to try to use the telephone as much as possible rather than make personal visits.

Euphemisms are terms designed to make an unpleasant idea more attractive or acceptable. *Your position is being eliminated* seeks to soften the blow of being fired or laid off; the British call this *being declared redundant,* while Canadians refer to it as *being made surplus.* Other euphemisms include *pass on* for *die* and *sanitation engineer* for *garbage collector.*

While euphemisms can appeal to an audience by showing that the writer is considering their feelings, they can also sound pompous or suggest a wishy-washy, timid, or evasive attitude. Moreover, when they are used to protect the speaker or writer rather than the audience, they cross the line into doublespeak. Therefore, use euphemisms with great care.

Based on the terms "doublethink" and "newspeak," from George Orwell's novel *1984*, **doublespeak** is the use of language to hide or distort the truth in the interest of the speaker or writer. The extensive use of such language by public officials led the National Council of Teachers of English in the United States and the Canadian Council of Teachers of English in Canada to form committees to alert citizens to such verbal sleight of hand to promote honesty and clarity in public language use. These committees draw our attention to the following kind of language use: A consumer affairs minister proposed a surcharge on grave markers and called the surcharge not a new tax, but a "mandatory contribution" (*The Ottawa Citizen*, 5 December 1991). As writers—and as readers—we should be aware of the dangers of misleading language.

Exercise 30.1

Write a paragraph about something you might want to do at school—change your major, spend a year abroad, take a semester off, or something else. Use familiar register, assuming your audience to be someone close—parents, spouse, good friend. Then rewrite your paragraph to address your academic adviser, using formal register. Finally, work with another student to identify the elements that create familiar or formal register.

Being alert to denotation and connotation

Think of a stone tossed into a pool, and imagine the ripples spreading out from it, circle by circle. Or think of a note struck clear and clean, and the multiple vibrations that echo from it. In such images you can capture the distinction between **denotation**, the general meaning of a word, and **connotation**, the ripples, vibrations, associations that accompany the word. As a writer, you want to choose words that are both denotatively and connotatively appropriate.

Words with similar denotations may have connotations that vary widely. The words *maxim, epigram, proverb, saw, saying,* and *motto,* for instance, all carry roughly the same denotation. Because of their different connotations, however, *proverb* would be the appropriate word to use in reference to a saying from the Bible; *saw* in reference to the kind of wisdom handed down to us anonymously; *epigram* in reference to something written by Oscar Wilde. *Dirt* and *soil* have roughly the same denotative meaning, and their connotations are close enough to allow us to use them interchangeably in most cases. *Pushy* and *assertive* also have much the same denotative meaning, but in this case their connotations suggest different attitudes on the part of the speaker or writer, one neutral or positive, the other negative.

Mistakes in denotation are bound to occur as we try out new words. A person who writes "The party managed to diverge my thoughts from the hard work ahead" is confusing *divert* and *diverge* but is on the way to learning to use both. To avoid mistakes in denotation, pay careful attention to the way words are used in context, and check your dictionary whenever you are unsure of meaning.

Although words with the wrong connotations for your intended meaning may not be as obvious as those with wrong denotations, take equal care to avoid them. Good writers and readers are sensitive to the power of connotation for a number of reasons. In the first place, we do not want to be misunderstood: calling someone *skinny* rather than *slender*, for instance, might be taken as an insult or joke when such a meaning was unintended. And because connotation plays an important part in the language of politics and advertising (to name only the two most obvious fields), being alert to connotation and its power can help us read and listen more critically.

Many words carry fairly general connotations, evoking similar associational responses in most listeners or readers. But connotations can be personal or distinctive to a particular audience as well. If you ever got violently ill right after eating some particular dish as a child, you know the power of personal connotation. The mere mention of, say, peanut butter cookies carries powerful negative connotations. Whenever you write for a particular audience, try to be aware of the connotations your language will hold for that person or group of people.

Exercise 30.2

The contractor who advertises "We don't build *houses*, we build *homes*" counts on the positive connotations of *home* to boost sales. *New* and *improved* apparently have such powerful connotations that advertisers rely on them regularly. Look through a magazine you read frequently, and find three or four especially effective uses of connotation—either negative or positive—in advertisements. Bring these advertisements to class for discussion.

Exercise 30.3

Study the italicized words in each of the following passages, and decide what each word's connotations contribute to your understanding of the passage. Think of a synonym for each word, and see if you can decide what difference your word would make to the effect of the passage.

1. Tivadar was *flushed* with *pleasure* and *excitement* at the applause and not at all expecting it when I *lashed out* with my fist and sent him *sprawling* backward on the cobbles.

   – GEORGE BABORI, "Coming of Age in Putnok"

2. If boxing is a sport, it is the most *tragic* of all sports because, more than any human activity, it *consumes* the very excellence it *displays*: Its very *drama* is this consumption.

   – JOYCE CAROL OATES, "On Boxing"

3. I had to *forsake* the *aristocratic* habit of eating in restaurants and join the other *bums* knocking on doors to ask for *handouts*.

   – AL PURDY, "The Iron Road"

4. The air *held* a *keenness* that made her nose *twitch*. The harvesting of the corn and cotton, peanuts and squash, made each day a golden *surprise* that caused excited *little tremors* to run up her jaw.

   – ALICE WALKER, "The Flowers"

Balancing general and specific diction

Good writers move their prose along and help readers follow the meaning by balancing **general words**—those that refer to groups or classes of things—with **specific words**—those that refer to individual things. One kind of general words, **abstractions**, are words or phrases that refer to qualities or ideas, things we cannot perceive through our five senses. Specific words are often **concrete words**; they name things we can see, hear, touch, taste, or smell. Most often, we cannot draw a clear-cut line between general or abstract words on the one hand and specific or concrete ones on the other. Instead, most words and phrases fall somewhere on a continuum between these two extremes:

GENERAL	LESS GENERAL	SPECIFIC	MORE SPECIFIC
book	dictionary	unabridged dictionary	my 1988 edition of *Webster's Dictionary*
furniture	bed	antique bed	1840 curly maple bedstead of my grandmother's

ABSTRACT	LESS ABSTRACT	CONCRETE	MORE CONCRETE
culture	art	painting	Van Gogh's *Starry Night*
winter	cold weather	icicles	forty-centimetre icicle hanging from the eaves of the residence

Because passages that contain mostly general terms or abstractions demand that readers supply most of the specific examples or concrete details, such writing is often hard to read. Taken to extremes, it is dull or boring. But writing that is full of specifics can also be tedious and hard to follow if the main point is not made clearly or is lost amid a flood of extraneous details. Strong writing must usually both provide readers with a general idea of "big picture" and tie that idea down with specific examples or concrete details.

In the following passage, for instance, the author might have simply made a main general statement—*For the woman it is now an ordeal to be asked her age*—or described the aging process in detail. Instead she does both.

> For the woman it is now an ordeal to be asked her age. There is a fine tracery of lines around her eyes, a furrow in her brow even when she smiles. The bloom is off her cheeks. Around the age of 50 she will buy her last box of sanitary pads. The body's production of estrogen and progesterone, which govern menstruation (and also help to protect her from heart attack and the effects of stress) will have ceased almost completely. She may suffer palpitations, suddenly break into a sweat; her moods may shift abruptly. She looks in the mirror and asks, "Am I still a woman?"
>
> – JUDY STOFFMAN, "The Way of All Flesh"

Here are two student writers balancing general statements with illustrative specific details.

GENERAL   My neighbour is a nuisance.

SPECIFIC   My next-door neighbour is a nuisance, poking and prying into my life, constantly watching me as I enter and leave my house, complaining about the noise when I am having a good time, and telling my parents whenever she sees me kissing my date.

GENERAL   Northern British Columbia has an unusual climate.

SPECIFIC   Few places in Canada display the wild climatic variations of northern British Columbia: at one moment, the sky may be clear blue and the air balmy; at another, a driving rain may drown the landscape.

Exercise 30.4

The following passage is from Joan Didion's essay "In Bed." Read it carefully, and discuss with another student the balance of abstract and concrete and of general and specific diction.

> Migraine is something more than the fancy of a neurotic imagination. It is an essentially hereditary complex of symptoms, the most frequently noted but by no means the most unpleasant of which is a vascular headache of blinding severity, suffered by a surprising number of women, a fair number of men (Thomas Jefferson had migraine, and so did Ulysses S. Grant, the day he accepted Lee's surrender), and by some unfortunate children as young as two years old. (I had my first when I was eight. It came on during a fire drill at the Columbia School in Colorado Springs, Colorado. I was taken first home and then to the infirmary at Peterson Field, where my father was stationed. The Air Corps doctor prescribed an enema.) Almost anything can trigger a specific attack of migraine: stress, allergy, fatigue, an abrupt change in barometric pressure, a contretemps over a parking ticket. A flashing light. A fire drill. One inherits, of course, only the predisposition. In other words I spent yesterday in bed with a headache not merely because of my bad attitudes, unpleasant tempers and wrongthink, but because both my grandmothers had migraine, my father has migraine and my mother has migraine.
>
> — JOAN DIDION, "In Bed"

Using figurative language

Figurative language paints pictures in our minds, allows us to "see" a point and hence understand more readily and clearly. Economists trying to explain the magnitude of the national deficit use figurative language when they tell us how many times a chain of $100 000 bills would have to circle the globe to equal it; scientists describing the way genetic data are transmitted use figurative language when they liken the data to a messenger that carries bits of information from one generation of cells to another. Far from being a mere "decoration" of writing, figurative language plays a crucial role in helping us follow the writer's meaning, quickly and easily. Particularly helpful in building an appealing tone are figures that compare one thing to another—similes, metaphors, and analogies. Other figures include personification, hyperbole, litotes, irony, and allusion.

1. Similes

Similes make explicit the comparison between two things by using the terms *like, as,* or *as if:*

> To this day, Claire and I are just waiting to be taken aside by Irene for a hushed devotional talking-to about the lines of cosmetic products she represents and stockpiles in her garage like so many thousand unwanted, non-give-away-able kittens. "Honey, my elbows were like *pine bark* before I tried this stuff."
>
> — DOUGLAS COUPLAND, *Generation X*

> We were all brothers and sisters alike, born in a long three-storey wooden house, a house as humped and crusty as a loaf of homemade bread, as warm and clean inside as the white of the loaf.
>
> — FÉLIX LECLERC, "The Family House"

> Her eyes have grown bigger than her face; they're like black caves.
>
> — Janette Turner Hospital

2. Metaphors

Metaphors are *implicit comparisons,* omitting the *like, as,* or *as if* of similes.

> The giant trunks of the trees have grown so close together that the forest is both a prison and a fort.
>
> — HIMANI BANNERJI, "The Sound Barrier: Translating Ourselves in Language and Experience"

> Famine had been weighing for some time past with an iron hand on the hapless people and its terrible grasp was daily closing more tightly upon them.
>
> — J.L. LEPROHAN, "The Manor House of De Villerai"

3. Analogies

Analogies compare similar features of two dissimilar things and are often extended to several sentences or paragraphs in length. The following sentence, for example, uses an analogy to help us understand the rapid growth of the computer industry:

> If the aircraft industry had evolved as spectacularly as the computer industry over the past twenty-five years, a Boeing 767 would cost $500 today, and it would circle the globe in twenty minutes on nineteen litres of fuel.

The analogy in the next passage helps us "see" an abstract point.

> Our lives are plays, and we are the actors playing the parts. The scenes are set, and each of us takes on a role—followers, leaders, manipulators. Manipulators, who coax and coerce people into doing what the manipulators want, are often the playwrights in our lives.

Before you use an analogy, though, make sure that the two things you are comparing have enough points of similarity so that the comparison is justified and will convince readers. For further discussion of analogies, see 5f3.

4. Clichés and mixed metaphors

Just as effective use of figurative language can create the tone or impression that the writer wants to create, so *ineffective* figures of speech can create the *wrong* impression by boring, irritating, or unintentionally amusing readers. Among the most common kinds of ineffective figurative language are clichés and mixed metaphors.

Cliché comes from the French word for "stereotype," a metal plate cast from a page of type and used, before photographic printing processes, to produce multiple copies of a book or page without having to reset the type. So a **cliché** in language is an expression stamped out in duplicate to avoid the trouble of "resetting" the thought. Many clichés, like *busy as a bee* or *youth is the springtime of life*, are similes or metaphors.

By definition, we use clichés all the time, especially in speech, and many serve us quite usefully as familiar shorthand for familiar ideas. But you should use them with caution in your writing for good reason: if your audience recognizes that you are using stereotyped, paint-by-numbers language, they are likely to conclude that what you are saying is not very new or interesting—or perhaps even true. The person who tells you that you look "pretty as a picture" uses a clichéd simile that may well sound false or insincere. Compare it with a more original compliment a grandmother once paid to her grandchildren: "You all look as pretty as brand-new red shoes."

How can you check for clichés? While one person's trite phrase may be completely new to another, one general rule will serve you well: if you can predict exactly what the upcoming word(s) in a phrase will be, it stands a very good chance of being a cliché.

Mixed metaphors are comparisons that are not consistent. Instead of creating a clear and dominant impression, they confuse the reader by pulling against one another, often in unintentionally funny ways, as in the announcement by a government official that "we must not drag our dirty linen through the eye of the public."

Here is a mixed metaphor revised for consistency.

MIXED   The lectures were like brilliant comets streaking through the night sky, drenching the listeners with a blizzard of insight.

REVISED   The lectures were like brilliant comets streaking through the night sky, dazzling listeners with flashes of insight.

5. Personification

Personification gives human qualities to animals, inanimate objects, or ideas, making them more vivid or understandable.

[Television] … stays in one corner of the room like a horrible electronic gossip.

– JONATHAN MILLER

The wind was a circus master brandishing a whip, and the snow a mad graceful dancer, pirouetting or sinking to the ground as he commanded.

– GABRIELLE ROY, *The Tin Flute*

6. Hyperbole

Hyperbole, or **overstatement**, deliberately exaggerates to create special emphasis or a humorous tone.

Under certain emotional circumstances, I can stand the spasms of a rich violin, but the concert piece and all wind instruments bore me in small doses and flay me in large doses.

– VLADIMIR NABOKOV

Jiggins is dead. He was, of course, a pioneer, but the fact that he dumb-belled himself to death at an early age does not prevent a whole generation of young men from following in his path.

– STEPHEN LEACOCK, "How to Live to Be 200"

7. Litotes

Like hyperbole, **litotes** (or **understatement**) depends on a gap between statement and fact. But while hyperbole is loud and noisy, litotes turns the volume down to a whisper. Understatement can help create a very solemn tone, as it does when the hero of Ernest Hemingway's *A Farewell to Arms*, having lost his wife and baby in childbirth, quietly "left the hospital and walked back to the hotel in the rain." It can also create dark humour, as when Jonathan Swift remarks in *A Tale of a Tub*, "Last week I saw a woman flayed, and you will hardly believe how much it altered her appearance for the worse." Understatement can be effective in other ways as well. In their first article on DNA, Watson and Crick were reporting that they had discovered what they felt was the secret of life. Yet they carefully closed the article with understatement, creating a tone of quiet confidence: "It has not escaped our notice that the specific pairing we have postulated immediately suggests a possible copying mechanism for the genetic material."

8. Irony

Irony, language that suggests a meaning that contrasts with or undercuts the literal meaning of the words, can result in a lighthearted, spoofing tone or a serious and bitter one. In probably the most famous piece of sustained irony in English literature, Jonathan Swift's "A Modest Proposal," Swift solemnly recommends the sale and consumption of children, a proposal intended to reveal the poverty and inhuman conditions in Ireland that were condoned by its British rulers at the time. The following "definition" of *writing principles* provides an example of more lighthearted irony.

> Write hurriedly, preferably when tired. Have no plans; write down items as they occur to you ... Hand in your manuscript the moment it is finished.
>
> — AMBROSE BIERCE

Irony can work well to gain an audience's attention and set a definite tone, but only if the audience can be expected to recognize and appreciate the irony. (See 38d for a discussion of ways you can use quotation marks to convey irony.)

9. Allusion

Allusions, indirect reference to cultural works, people, or events, can bring an entire world of associations to the minds of readers who recognize them. If, for instance, you tell a friend in a letter that you have to return to your herculean task of writing a research essay, you are expecting that your reader will understand, by your allusion to the Labours of Hercules in classical mythology, how big a job you think the essay is.

You can draw allusions from history, from literature, from the Bible, from common wisdom, or from current events. Many current popular songs are full of allusions. Remember, however, that allusions work to create effective tone only if your audience recognizes them.

Exercise 30.5

Identify the similes and metaphors in the following passages, and discuss with another student how each contributes to an understanding of the passage in which it appears.

1. Suddenly I am shaken with despair. Fleeting images circle aimlessly like germ-ridden mosquitoes in my mental jungle.

    – HUBERT AQUIN, *Prochain Épisode*

2. Where a satirist like Pope destroys his victims with flashes of lighting ... Jane Austen often roasted her victims over a fire so slow and nicely judged that the thick-skinned feel no discomfort on their behalf but only a gentle tickling.

    – WILLIAM GOLDING, *A Moving Target*

3. He has had no tangible evidence yet that his body, as the poet Rilke said, enfolds old age and death as the fruit enfolds a stone.

    – JUDY STOFFMAN, "The Way of All Flesh"

4. I was watching everyone else and didn't see the waitress standing quietly by. Her voice was deep and soft like water moving in a cavern.

    – WILLIAM LEAST HEAT-MOON, "In the Land of 'Coke-Cola' "

Exercise 30.6

Read through a magazine, an essay, or a story and find some examples of personification, hyperbole, litotes, irony, and allusion. Bring these examples to class for discussion.

Taking inventory: diction

Look again at Twila Krown's essay near the end of Chapter 29. What are the effects of her various decisions about diction—her choice of concrete over abstract terms, for example, or her use of metaphor? Once you have identified various devices of diction in Twila's essay and considered their effects, try to find similar devices in samples of your own writing. Revise one of your own essays, attending to these matters of diction.

31

Enriching Vocabulary

Vocabulary comes from a Latin term for "name" (*vocabulum*), which in turn comes from the Latin verb for "call." Thus, our vocabulary "calls forth" or names things in our worlds. This connection between vocabulary and calling into being is what led the philosopher Ludwig Wittgenstein to declare that "the limits of my language are the limits of my world." You can recognize what he means easily enough by remembering a time in your life when you learned the name of something new. Before that time, this thing did not exist for you; yet curiously enough, once you know its name, you begin to recognize it all around you. Such is the power of vocabulary in enriching our lives.

If you grew up speaking English, your English vocabulary is already extensive. At its largest, it includes all those words whose meanings you either recognize or can deduce from context. This, your **processing vocabulary**, allows you to interpret the meanings of many passages whose words you might not actively use yourself. Your **producing vocabulary** is more limited, comprising those words you actually use in writing and/or speaking.

Part of what it means to mature intellectually is to broaden your mental horizons by learning how to name more things more accurately. Doing so involves consciously strengthening the bridges between your processing vocabulary and your producing vocabulary by using more of the words you recognize and can interpret in context. To accomplish this goal, you must investigate your own language and the language of others.

31a

Charting the history of English

Try to imagine a world without language. In fact, you probably cannot do so, for language is perhaps the most ancient heritage of the human race. Because language brings us together and indeed allows us to name and structure our experience of the world, it is well worth understanding how this heritage originated and has changed over the centuries.

English has always been a hybrid language, what Daniel Defoe called "your Roman-Saxon-Danish-Norman English." Where did this hybrid come from, and how did it evolve? English, like one-third of all languages in the world, descends from Indo-European, a language spoken by a group of seminomadic peoples who almost certainly had domestic animals, worked leather, wove wool, and planted crops. Where they lived is the subject of great controversy; their home may have been in some part of north-central Europe. Scholars began to argue for Indo-European, the language of these people, as a "Common source" and to try to identify its features when they noted more and more striking resemblances between words in a number of languages:

English	Latin	French	Greek	German	Dutch	Swedish	Danish
three	*tres*	*trois*	*treis*	*drei*	*drie*	*tre*	*tre*

An Indo-European language of the Germanic family was brought to Britain by the Germanic invasions following 449. This early language, called Anglo-Saxon or Old English, was further influenced by Latin and Greek when Christianity was reintroduced into England beginning in 597, was later shaped by the Viking invasions beginning in the late 700s, and was transformed after the Norman Conquest (1066) by French.

While the English vernacular continued to evolve in the centuries after the Conquest, however, Latin and French remained the languages of the learned—of the church and court. (Indeed, lectures at Oxford University were delivered in Latin well into the 19th century.) It was Chaucer, through his decision in the late 1300s to write *The Canterbury Tales* not in Latin or French but in the language of the people, who helped establish English as the political, legal, and literary language of Britain. And with the advent of printing in the mid-1400s, that language became more accessible and more standardized.

One brief example will give you an idea of how much English had evolved up to this time. Here are three versions of a biblical passage:

ANGLO-SAXON GOSPELS, AROUND 1000 C.E.

And eft hē ongan hī æt þǣre sæ lǣran. And him wæs mycel męnegu tō gegaderod, swā þæt hē on scip ēode, and on bǣre sǣ wæs; and eall sēo męnegu ymbe þē sæ wæs on lande.

WYCLIFFE BIBLE, ABOUT 1380

And eft Jhesus bigan to teche at the see; and myche puple was gaderid to hym, so that he wente in to a boot, and sat in the see, and al the puple was aboute the see on the loond.

KING JAMES VERSION, 1611

And he began to teach by the seaside: and there was gathered unto him a great multitude, so that he entered into a ship, and sat in the sea: and the whole multitude was by the sea on the land.

Note that in the Old English text, only a few words—*and, he, him, waes, lande, sae*—look familiar. By the time of Chaucer, however, many words are recognizable. And by the time of the Renaissance, the language is easily readable by us.

In the last four hundred years, the extension of British and, later, North American political and cultural influence has made English the second most widely spoken language in the world. Continued borrowings from many languages have given it the world's largest vocabulary.

31b

Recognizing word roots

As its name suggests, a **root** is a word from which other words grow, usually through the addition of prefixes or suffixes. From the Latin roots *-dic-* or *-dict-* ("speak"), for instance, grows a whole range of words in English: *contradict, dictate, dictator, diction, edict, predict*, and others. From the Greek root *-chrono-* ("time") come our words *chronology, chronometer, synchronize,* and so on.

Here are some other Latin (marked L) and Greek (marked G) roots. Recognizing them will help you recognize networks of words in the language.

ROOT	MEANING	EXAMPLES
-audi- (L)	to hear	audience, audio, auditorium
-bene- (L)	good, well	benevolent, benefit, benefactor
-bio- (G)	life	biography, biosphere, biopsy

ROOT	MEANING	EXAMPLES
-duc(t)- (L)	to lead or to make	ductile, reduce, reproduce
-gen- (G)	race, kind	genealogy, gene
-geo- (G)	earth	geography, geometry
-graph- (G)	to write	graphic, photography, pictograph
-jur-, -jus- (L)	law	justice, jurisdiction
-log(o)- (G)	word, thought	biology, logical, logocentric
-luc- (L)	light	lucid, translucent
-manu- (L)	hand	manufacture, manual, manipulate
-mit-, -mis- (L)	to send	permit, transmission, intermittent
-path- (G)	feel, suffer	empathy, pathetic
-phil- (G)	love	philosopher, bibliophile
-photo- (G)	light	photography, telephoto
-port- (L)	to carry	transport, portable
-psych- (G)	soul	psychology, psychopath
-scrib-, -script- (L)	to write	inscribe, manuscript, descriptive
-sent, -sens- (L)	to feel	sensation, resent
-tele- (G)	far away	telegraph, telepathy
-tend- (L)	to stretch	extend, tendency
-terr- (L)	earth	inter, territorial
-therm- (G)	heat	thermonuclear, thermostat
-vac- (L)	empty	vacuole, evacuation
-vid-, -vis- (L)	to see	video, envision, visit

Exercise 31.1

Using the list of roots above, try to figure out the meaning of each of the following words. Working with another student, write a potential definition for each one, and then compare your dictionary's definition with yours.

1. terrestrial
2. scriptorium
3. geothermal
4. lucent
5. beneficent
6. audiology
7. vacuous
8. pathogenic
9. juridical
10. graphology

31c

Recognizing prefixes and suffixes

Prefixes and suffixes—most of them words themselves, originally—are groups of letters added to words or to word roots to create new words. These word additions account for much of the flexibility of English, often allowing dozens of words to be built on one root.

1. Prefixes

Prefix appropriately demonstrates its own meaning: it is made up of a prefix (-*pre*-) and root (-*fix*-) and means literally "fasten before." Fastened to the beginnings of words or roots, prefixes modify and extend meanings. Recognizing common prefixes can often help you decipher the meaning of otherwise unfamiliar words.

Prefixes of negation or opposition

PREFIX	MEANING	EXAMPLES
a-, an-	without, not	ahistorical, anemia
anti-	against	antibody, antiphonal
contra-	against	contravene, contramand
de-	from, take away from	demerit, declaw
dis-	apart, away	disappear, discharge
il-, -im-, in-, ir-	not	illegal, immature, indistinct, irreverent
mal-	wrong	malevolent, malpractice
mis-	wrong, bad	misapply, misanthrope
non-	not	nonentity, nonsense
un-	not	unbreakable, unable

Prefixes of quantity

PREFIX	MEANING	EXAMPLES
bi-	two	bipolar, bilateral
milli-	thousand	millimetre, milligram

mono-	one, single	monotone, monologue
omni-	all	omniscient, omnipotent
semi-	half	semicolon, semiconductor
tri-	three	tripod, trimester
uni-	one	unitary, univocal

Prefixes of time and space

PREFIX	MEANING	EXAMPLES
ante-	before	antedate, antebellum
circum-	around	circumlocution, circumnavigate
co-, col-, com-, con-, cor-	with	coequal, collaborate, commiserate, contact, correspond
e-, ex-	out of	emit, extort, expunge
hyper-	over, more than	hypersonic, hypersensitive
hypo-	under, less than	hypodermic, hypoglycemia
inter-	between	intervene, international
mega-	enlarge, large	megalomania, megaphone
micro-	tiny	micrometer, microscopic
neo-	recent	neologism, neophyte
post-	after	postwar, postscript
pre-	before	previous, prepublication
pro-	before, onward	project, propel
re-	again, back	review, recreate
sub-	under, beneath	subhuman, submarine
super-	over, above	supercargo, superimpose
syn-	at the same time	synonym, synchronize
trans-	across, over	transport, transition

Exercise 31.2

Using the list of prefixes above and the list of roots in 31b, try to figure out the meaning of each of the following words. Working with another student, write a potential definition for each one, and then compare your dictionary's definition with yours.

1.	remit	6.	superscript
2.	subterranean	7.	deport
3.	translucent	8.	neologism
4.	monograph	9.	inaudible
5.	distend	10.	apathetic

---

2. Suffixes

Attached to the ends of words and word roots, **suffixes** modify and extend meanings, many times by altering the grammatical function or part of speech of the original word. Suffixes can, for example, turn the verb *create* into a noun, an adjective, or an adverb.

VERB	*create*
NOUNS	*creator* / *creation* / *creativity* / *creature*
ADJECTIVE	*creative*
ADVERB	*creatively*

Noun suffixes

SUFFIX	MEANING	EXAMPLES
-acy	state or quality	democracy, privacy
-al	act of	rebuttal, refusal
-ance, -ence	state or quality of	maintenance, eminence
-dom	place or state of being	freedom, thralldom
-er, -or	one who	trainer, investor
-ism	doctrine or belief characteristic of	liberalism, Taoism
-ist	one who	organist, physicist
-ity	quality of	veracity, opacity
-ment	condition of	payment, argument
-ness	state of being	watchfulness, cleanliness
-ship	position held	professorship, fellowship
-sion, -tion	state of being or action	digression, transition

Verb suffixes

SUFFIX	MEANING	EXAMPLES
-ate	cause to be	concentrate, regulate
-en	cause to be or become	enliven, blacken
-ify, -fy	make or cause to be	unify, terrify, amplify
-ize	cause to become	magnetize, civilize

Adjective suffixes

SUFFIX	MEANING	EXAMPLES
-able, -ible	capable of being	assumable, edible
-al	pertaining to	regional, political
-esque	reminiscent of	picturesque, statuesque
-ful	having a notable quality	colourful, sorrowful
-ic	pertaining to	poetic, mythic
-ish	having the quality of	prudish, clownish
-ious, -ous	of or characterized by	famous, nutritious
-ive	having the nature of	festive, creative, massive
-less	without	endless, senseless

Exercise 31.3

Using the list of suffixes above, work with another student to figure out the meaning of each of the following words. (Use your dictionary if necessary.) Then choose two of the words, and use each one in a sentence.

1. contemplative
2. fanciful
3. impairment
4. liquefy
5. barrenness
6. defiance
7. defiantly
8. redden
9. standardize
10. satirist

Extending your vocabulary

Making good use of prefixes or suffixes will increase the power of your vocabulary, but other methods will extend your vocabulary further. These methods include analyzing word contexts, becoming an active reader, and becoming a collector of words.

1. Analyzing word contexts

If you have ever run into a person you knew but simply could not place—until you remembered the place where you normally saw the person—you know firsthand the importance of context in helping you identify people and things. The same principle holds true for words. So if a word is at first unfamiliar to you, look carefully at its context, paying attention to all the clues that context can give; often you will be able to deduce the meaning.

For instance, if the word *accoutrements* is unfamiliar in the sentence *We stopped at a camping supply store to pick up last-minute accoutrements,* you can figure out its meaning from its context: *the camping supply store* and *last-minute* suggest strongly that *equipment* or some similar word fits the bill. And that is what *accoutrements* means.

Sometimes, as in the following sentence, the context will include examples of unfamiliar words:

> The troop leader quickly removed all *incendiary* materials—matches, gas lanterns, and firecrackers.

Sometimes, however, deciphering the meaning of a word calls on your greatest detective powers. The following example, for instance, demands very careful attention to context:

> Interpretive frameworks at their most radical become reflexive, arguing that the observer's own understanding of any phenomenon must arise through a complex interaction between the process of observing and the characteristics of the thing being observed.

This is not an easy sentence to read, because much of the diction is general and abstract. *Interpretive frameworks* suggests structures that interpret information or data. *Radical* interpretive frameworks is more problematic. Although *radical* refers back to Latin *radix* ("root"), the usual meaning of *radical* today is "extreme." So the most extreme forms of interpretive frameworks become reflexive. What might that mean? A reflex is a response, like the knee-jerk reflex, so *reflexive* probably has to do with response. The sentence structure tells us that *become reflexive* here means that an observer's understanding arises through an interaction between observing and what is observed. Perhaps that interaction is the response that *reflexive* seems to refer to. Our provisional understanding of this sentence, then, might be paraphrased as "extreme forms of interpretation depend on an interaction of observer and observed." When you encounter such passages, your best strategy is to continue reading, looking for additional contextual clues to meaning.

2. Becoming an active reader

As processors of information, we can read words alone, or we can read meanings. To read meanings means filling in blanks, making connections, leaping ahead, asking questions, taking mental notes. Active readers flex their mental muscles while reading; they exercise their own understanding and thereby stretch to greater knowledge. Here are some tips for extending your vocabulary through active reading:

- Make a habit of paraphrasing or summarizing unfamiliar words or phrases. Then check the dictionary to see how accurate your paraphrase is.

- Practise naming the opposites of words. If you see *abbreviation*, for instance, try supplying its opposite—*enlargement, elaboration*, etc.

- Challenge authors by trying to come up with a better word or words than the ones they used.

- Read aloud to yourself from time to time, noting any words whose pronunciation you are unsure of. Check them out in the dictionary.

3. Becoming a collector of words

You are already a collector of words in one sense: you probably add words to your vocabulary on a fairly regular basis. All you need to do now is make that activity more conscientious and systematic. Begin by choosing a writer you admire and reading for as long as it takes to identify several words you like but would not use in speaking or writing. Your collection has started. Now analyze these words for what you like about them—for pronunciation, meaning, and usage. Next, try the words out on your friends and instructors.

Taking inventory: vocabulary

Read over a piece of writing you are working on or have recently completed. Underline any words you think could be improved on, and then come up with several possible substitutes. Bring them and your piece of writing to class for discussion.

32

Using Dictionaries

One aim of a dictionary is to fix a standard of the language, so that users of it can know once and for all what is "right" and what is "wrong." Before the advent of the printing press, English spelling in particular was far from fixed, and with good reason; few people had occasion to write words down. Even later, the author we designate as Shakespeare is known to have spelled his own name in several different ways. The 18th century, however, writers such as Alexander Pope urged a codification of the language, which they felt had reached perfection. Enter Samuel Johnson, whose *English Dictionary* (1755) established an authoritative right and wrong for a long time.

But a second and competing aim of an English dictionary was articulated forcefully about 100 years after Johnson: to record a full inventory of the language as it is used, without trying to prescribe "right" and "wrong." These dual aims persist in our dictionaries today and may in fact influence your choice of what dictionary to use on which occasion. This chapter will map the territory covered by dictionaries and provide you with a means of choosing the dictionaries you want to work with.

Exploring the dictionary

A good dictionary packs a lot of information into a relatively small space. Take a look, for instance, at this entry in the *Concise Oxford Dictionary,* New Edition.

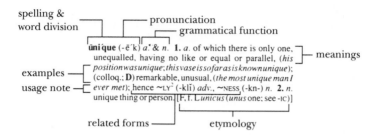

In fact, a dictionary entry may contain a dozen or more kinds of information about a word, the most common of which are listed below. The first six normally appear in all entries, the others only where they are necessary or relevant.

1. *Spelling*, including alternative spellings if they exist

2. *Word division*, with bars and/or dots separating syllables and showing where a word may be divided at the end of a line

3. *Pronunciation*, including alternative pronunciations

4. *Grammatical functions* and *irregular forms*, including plurals of nouns, principal parts of verbs, and comparative and superlative forms of adjectives and adverbs

5. *Etymology*, the languages and words that the word comes from

6. *Meanings*, in order of either development or frequency of use

7. *Examples* of the word in the context of a phrase or sentence

8. *Usage labels and notes* (see explanation below)

9. *Field labels*, including that a word has a specialized meaning in a particular field of knowledge or activity

10. *Synonyms* and *antonyms*

11. *Related words* and their grammatical functions

12. *Idioms,* phrases in which the word appears and their meanings

Usage labels and notes

For some words, many dictionaries include a kind of usage labelling, intended to let readers know that some or all meanings of the word are not considered appropriate in certain contexts. You can generally find such labels identified at the beginning of the dictionary. Here are some of the labels the *Concise Oxford* uses.

1. *Colloquial:* not used in formal discourse, but widely used and entirely acceptable in informal circumstances

2. *Slang:* used only in certain circumstances

3. *Derogatory:* used only contemptuously

4. *Archaic:* used only in old-fashioned (or religious or legal) speech or writing

5. *Jocular:* used only in humorous or playful style

In addition to labels, dictionaries sometimes include markings indicating usage in greater detail. In the *Concise Oxford* entry for *unique,* notice that the "D" tags the colloquial meaning of the word as *disputed.*

Exercise 32.1

Look up the spelling, syllable division, and pronunciation of the following words in your dictionary. Note any variants in spelling and/or pronunciation.

1. process (noun)   5. whippet   8. hurrah
2. heinous   6. crayfish   9. greasy
3. exigency   7. macabre   10. theatre
4. schedule

Exercise 32.2

Look up the etymology of the following words in your dictionary.

1. rhetoric   5. apple   8. tortilla
2. student   6. sex   9. cinema
3. curry (noun)   7. okra   10. video
4. whine

Exercise 32.3

Use your dictionary to find synonyms (and antonyms) for the following words.

1. coerce   4. odious
2. prevaricate   5. awesome
3. parameter

Distinguishing among dictionaries

Since the time of Samuel Johnson's 1755 dictionary, the number and kinds of English-language dictionaries have multiplied many times over. While they all share the name *dictionary*, these numerous volumes differ considerably from one another. You may most often use an easily portable paperback dictionary, but you should be familiar with larger abridged and unabridged dictionaries as well.

1. Abridged dictionaries

Abridged or "abbreviated" **dictionaries** are the ones most often used by college and university writers. Though they are not as complete as unabridged dictionaries, they are more affordable and more portable than their larger cousins. These are among the most helpful abridged dictionaries.

Concise Oxford Dictionary

Gage Canadian Dictionary

Funk and Wagnalls Standard College Dictionary

The Random House College Dictionary

Webster's New Collegiate Dictionary

Webster's New World Dictionary

Houghton Mifflin Canadian Dictionary of the English Language

Here is the *Gage Dictionary* entry for *unique*. Notice that it provides a note discussing the usage of this word.

> **u·nique** (yü nēk′) *adj.* **1** having no like or equal; being the only one of its kind. **2** *Informal,* rare; unusual. [< F < L *unicu*] —**u·nique′ly**, *adv.* —**u·nique′ness,** *n.*
>
> ☛ *Usage.* In formal English **unique** means 'being one of a kind,' and so it cannot be compared or qualified; something is either unique or not. In informal English **unique** is sometimes used with **more** or **most** and more often with a qualifier like **quite, rather,** or **really;** *Her clothes are rather unique.* This usage should be avoided in careful speech and writing.

2. Unabridged dictionaries

Unabridged, or "unabbreviated," **dictionaries** are the royalty of their species—the most complete, richly detailed, and thoroughly presented dictionaries of English. Whereas good abridged dictionaries may include

200 000 items, unabridged dictionaries far more than double that figure. Because they are large and often multivolume—and hence expensive—you may not own an unabridged dictionary, but you will want and need to consult one on occasion in your library. Among the leading unabridged dictionaries are the *Oxford English Dictionary* and *Webster's Third New International Dictionary of the English Language.*

The Oxford English Dictionary II. 20 volumes. New York: Oxford UP, 1933, 1972, 1976, 1989. The grandparent of unabridged dictionaries in English, *The Oxford English Dictionary* (known as the *OED*) began in Britain in the 19th century as an attempt to give a full history of each English word, recording its entry into the language and illustrating the development of its various meanings with dated quotations in chronological order. Volunteers all over the world contributed quotations to the editors at Oxford University, and the first edition of the dictionary was published piecemeal over a period of more than forty years. The *OED* lists more than half a million words and is unparalleled in its historical account of changes in word meanings and spellings. A compact edition of the *OED II* was published in 1991 and is kept up to date on CD-ROM (the book itself costs about $350); a two-volume *New Shorter Oxford* (this one priced at about $165) appeared in 1993.

Here is the original *OED*'s entry for *unique*. Notice that in addition to the meanings given in the two abridged dictionaries, it lists several obsolete and specialized meanings for *unique* as an adjective; it also includes meanings and examples for *unique* as a noun, a use that is apparently too rare to find space in the abridged dictionaries. Compared with these, the *OED* also provides more detailed etymological information and uses a different system of phonetic symbols for pronunciation. Finally, notice that the related forms *uniquely* and *uniqueness* are not included because they have their own entries.

Unique (yŭnī·k), *a.* and *sb.* Also 7 unick(e, 7–8 unio. [a. F. *unique* (+ *unic* masc.), ad. L. *ūnic-us* (whence also Sp., Pg., It. *unico*) single, sole, alone of its kind, f. *ūnus* one. In early use also directly ad. L. *ūnicus*, and stressed on the first syllable.]

Regarded by Todd (1818) as 'an affected and useless term of modern times '.

A. *adj.* **1.** Of which there is only one ; one and no other ; single, sole, solitary.

1602 DOLMAN *La Primaud. Fr. Acad.* (1618) III. 639 Engendring one eternitie, and by an alone vnique action never disturbed, his linage full of understanding. *c* **1645** HOWELL *Lett.* II. xliv, He hath lost..his unic Son in the very flower of his age. **1677** GALE *Crt. Gentiles* IV. I. ii. 53 Divines, who make..right Reason the unic Criterion or Rule of moral Virtue. **1818** TODD, *Unique, adj.,..sole ;..* without another of the same kind known to exist. **1861** PALEY *Æschylus, Prometh.* (ed. 2) 39 The student will notice the unique example of στιχομυθία. **1873** HAMERTON *Intell. Life* III. iii. 87 A man

..who made Latin scholarship his unique intellectual purpose. **1882** FARRAR *Early Chr.* II. 476 St. John instantly leaves the subject..to which he has made this unique and passing allusion.

2. That is or forms the only one of its kind ; having no like or equal ; standing alone in comparison with others, freq. by reason of superior excellence ; unequalled, unparalleled, unrivalled.

In this sense readopted from French at the end of the 18th c. and regarded as a foreign word down to the middle of the 19th, from which date it has been in very common use, with a tendency to take the wider meaning of 'uncommon, unusual, remarkable '.

The usage in the comparative and superlative, and with advs. as *absolutely, most, quite, thoroughly, totally,* etc., has been objected to as tautological.

1618 W. BARCLAY *Well at King-horne* A vij, This is a soueraigne and vnicke remedie for that disease in Women. **1794** R. J. SULIVAN *View Nat.* I. 3 A concentrated, and an unique aggregation of almost all the wonders of the natural world. **1809** R. K. PORTER *Trav. Sk. Russia & Sweden* (1813) I. xxv. 285 As it was thoroughly *unique*, I cannot forbear presenting you with so singular a curiosity. **1842** J. P. COLLIER *Armin's Nest Ninn.* Introd., A relic.. not only *unique* in itself, but unprecedented in its kind. **1866** LIDDON *Bamp. Lect.* v. (1867) 368 [Christ's] relationship to the Father..is absolutely unique. **1871** B. TAYLOR *Faust* (1875) II. ii. i. 84 A thing so totally unique The great collectors would go far to seek. **1885** *Harper's Mag.* April 703/1 When these summer guests found themselves defrauded of their uniquest recreations.

   b. Of persons. **1808** FOSTER *Contrib. Eclectic Rev.* (1844) I. 233 [Sir T. More] is a person so *unique* in the records of statesmen, that [etc.]. **1871** BLACKIE *Four Phases* 15 Such a unique mortal.. no man can describe. **1885** MABEL COLLINS *Prettiest Woman* xi, He believed this woman whom he loved to be unique.

   c. *absol.* with *the* : (see quots.). **1767** *Phil. Trans.* LVIII. 26 All these are examples of the *unique*; that is, of quantities in a state that is..exclusive of all others. **1849** C. BRONTE *Shirley* xxiii, She felt that Rose Yorke was a peculiar child—one of the unique.

† 3. Formed or consisting of one or a single thing. *Obs.*—[1] *a* **1631** DONNE *Lett.* (1651) 163 A Mathematique point, which is the most indivisible and unique thing which art can present.

B. *sb.* **1.** A thing of which there is only one example, copy, or specimen ; esp., in early use, a coin or medal of this class. **1714** R. THORESBY *Diary* 23 June, My Lord showed me some unics and other valuable curiosities. **1730** A. GORDON *Maffei's Amphith.* 47 It ..may be an Unic, for what we know as yet. **1774** *Gentl. Mag.* XLIV. 8 A coin, which I have reason to think is a Unic. **1826** DISRAELI *V. Grey* II. viii, Mr. Vivian Grey had promised his Lordship, who was a collector of medals, an unique which had never yet been heard of. **1872** O. W. HOLMES *Poet Breakf.-t.* iii. 89 A unique, sir, and there is a pleasure in exclusive possession.

† b. Something of which only one is possessed by a person or persons. *Obs. rare.* **1783** H. WALPOLE *Let. to C'tess Upper Ossory* 20 June, Lady Pembroke having lent them a servant besides their own unique. **1806** SURR *Winter in Lond.* III. 170 This Belcher girdle was not old ; but being an *unique*, it had been..constantly in use.

2. A thing, fact, or circumstance which by reason of exceptional or special qualities stands alone and is without equal or parallel in its kind. **1768** *Phil. Trans.* LVIII. 215 When I presented this map to the Academy..it was looked upon as an Unique. **1781** *Gentl. Mag.* LI. 280/2 The dedication [of a volume of Sermons] being an *unique* in its kind. **1794** PALEY *Evid.* II. ix. iii. ad fin., The propagation of Christianity..is an *unique* in the history of the species. **1835** *Tait's Mag* II. 651 It is.. an *unique* in English biography. **1838** DE QUINCEY *Lamb* Wks. 1858 IX. 156 Of Lamb's writings..some were so memorably beautiful as to be uniques in their class. **1844** *N. Brit. Rev.* I. 124 A conflict, that stands out from all shadow of parallelism—a wild originality—a terrible unique.

   b. A person of this class. **1758** *Case of Authors Stated* 14 He presumes, that he, this *Unic*, must therefore appear in the same stupendous Magnitude to every body else. **1782** COWPER *Let.* Nov., Wks. (1876) 121 He is a man much to my taste, and quite an unique in this country. **1802** MRS. E. PARSONS *Myst. Visit* IV. 145, I trust that he though very good, is not an unique. **1813** *Examiner* 22 Feb. 122/2 Those..charms of manner, which constitute an *unique*. **1866** ALGER *Solit. Nat. & Man* II. 65 The peculiar endowment in which he so far surpasses others as to be an insulated unique.

Webster's Third New International Dictionary of the English Language. Springfield, MA: Merriam, 1986. Containing more entries than any dictionary besides the *OED*—more than 450 000 in all—this one-volume work stirred considerable controversy at its publication because of its tendency to *describe* rather than to *prescribe* usage. In all, the editors collected 6 165 000 examples of recorded usage, on which they drew for their Usage Notes. *Webster's Third* lists meanings in order of their entry into the language and quotes from over 14 000 different authors to provide illustrations of words in context.

Here are the *Webster's Third* entries for *unique* as an adjective and as a noun. Notice that the adjective entry simply lists the meaning "unusual, notable" and examples of the use of *most unique*, without discussing the controversy over this usage. In addition, notice that at the end of the entry, the notation **syn** refers the reader to the entries for *single* and *strange*, where the shades of meaning that distinguish *unique* from its synonyms are explained. The phonetic symbols differ slightly from those in either the *OED* or the abridged dictionaries.

¹**unique** \yü'nēk, '≠,≠\ *adj, sometimes* -ER/-EST [F, fr. L *unicus* sole, single, unique, fr. *unus* one + -*icus* -ic — more at ONE] **1 a :** being the only one **:** SOLE ⟨earning money whose ~ object could be nothing but Cyril's welfare —Arnold Bennett⟩ ⟨has thus preserved the original and often ~ records —G.B. Parks⟩ ⟨you are a miracle, a wonder, a mystery . . . one single ~ and inimitable living thing —J.C.Powys⟩ **b** *of a book* **:** known to exist in no other copy **2 :** being without a like or equal **:** single in kind or excellence **:** UNEQUALED ⟨they stand alone, ~, objects of supreme interest —A.B.Osborne⟩ ⟨as historian he knows that events, like persons, are ~ —J.M. Barzun⟩ ⟨remains singularly himself, a ~ lyrist of the first water —I.L.Salomon⟩ ⟨an almost ~ experience —Havelock Ellis⟩ ⟨tendencies present in our contemporary world which make our own times somewhat ~~—M.B.Smith⟩ ⟨story of his life is considerably more ~ than most autobiographies —Dorothy C. Fisher⟩ ⟨the more we study him, the less ~ he seems —Harry Levin⟩ — sometimes used with *to* ⟨the problem of what to do with surplus women is by no means ~ to our own society — Ralph Linton⟩ or *with* ⟨by no means ~ with the song sparrow —*Nature Mag.*⟩ **3 :** UNUSUAL, NOTABLE ⟨possessed ~ ability in the raising of funds —C.F.Thwing⟩ ⟨the wife of a career diplomat has a ~ opportunity to observe the world political scene —Ray Pierre⟩ ⟨a frankness ~ in literature —David Daiches⟩ ⟨~ peace and privacy —R.W.Hatch⟩ ⟨cheap, nourishing, and a ~ dining experience —T.H.Fielding⟩ ⟨the most ~ characteristic of that environment —R.A.Billington⟩ ⟨she's the most ~ person I ever met —Arthur Miller⟩ ⟨the most ~ theater in town —*advt*⟩ **4 :** capable of being performed in only one way ⟨the factorization of a number into its prime factors is ~⟩ **syn** see SINGLE, STRANGE
²**unique** \"\ *n* -S **:** something (as a specimen, thing, circumstance, or person) that is unique **:** the only one of its kind ⟨mistaking the ~ for the typical —W.J.Reilly⟩ ⟨the zest of the collector for possession of a ~ —Roy Bedichek⟩ ⟨a display of glass, including undercoated ~s —*Danish Foreign Office Jour.*⟩ ⟨the phoenix, the ~ of birds —Thomas De Quincey⟩

Exercise 32.4

Compare two of the entries on *unique* in this chapter for their advice on how to use the word correctly. Then write a paragraph in which you summarize their differences of opinion.

Exercise 32.5

Look up the following words in at least one abridged and one unabridged dictionary, and compare the entries. Record any differences or disagreements you find, and bring this record to class for discussion.

1. dogmatism
2. alienate
3. discriminate
4. hopefully
5. humanism

Exercise 32.6

Look up one of the following words in the *OED*, and write a paragraph describing any changes in meaning it has undergone since its entry into English.

1. lie (verb)
2. cheerful
3. machine
4. ornament (noun)
5. vulgar
6. humour (noun)
7. quaint
8. honest
9. testify
10. romance

32c

Consulting specialized dictionaries

The dictionaries you have just surveyed will provide you with an enormous amount of information. Sometimes, however, you will need to turn to additional sources for more specialized information. Such sources are available in dictionaries of usage, of synonyms, of slang, and of particular subjects (such as philosophy, mathematics, and biography).

1. Dictionaries of Usage

As the entries for *unique* in 32a and 32b demonstrate, dictionaries sometimes are unable to provide agreed-upon answers to questions of usage. More often than not, questions of usage are not reducible to any simple, easy right or wrong; most of them are very complex and relate not only to linguistic concerns but to social, educational, economic, and regional matters as well. In cases where usage is disputed or where you feel unsure of your own usage, you may wish to consult a specialized dictionary of usage. The most widely used such work, primarily concerned with British usage, is H.W. Fowler's *Dictionary of Modern English Usage*, which was published in 1926 and revised by Sir Ernest Gowers in 1965. Here is Fowler's discussion of *unique*.

unique. A watertight definition or paraphrase of the word, securing it against confusion with all synonyms that might be suggested, is difficult to frame. In the first place, it is applicable only to what is in some respect the sole existing specimen, the precise like of which may be sought in vain. That gives a clean line of division between it and the many adjectives for which it is often ignorantly substituted—*remarkable, exceptional, fabulous, rare, marvellous,* and the like. In the qualities represented by those epithets there are degrees; but uniqueness is a matter of yes or no only; no unique thing is more or less unique than another unique thing, as a rare thing may be rarer or less rare than another rare thing. The adverbs that *u.* can tolerate are e.g. *quite, almost, nearly, really, surely, perhaps, absolutely,* or *in some respects*; and it is nonsense to call anything *more, most, very, somewhat, rather,* or *comparatively u.* Such nonsense, however, is often written:

What made Laker's achievement all the more unique was. . . . | *I am now at one of* the most unique *writers' colonies imaginable.* | *I have just come across the production of a boy aged seven which is, in my experience,* somewhat unique. | *Sir, I venture to send you a copy of* a rather unique *inscription on a tombstone.* | *A* very unique *child, thought I.*

But, secondly, there is another set of synonyms—*sole, single, peculiar to,* etc.—from which *u.* is divided not by a clear difference of meaning, but by an idiomatic limitation (in English though not in French) of the contexts to which it is suited. It will be admitted that we improve the two following sentences if we change *u.* in the first into *sole,* and in the second into *peculiar*: *In the always delicate and difficult domain of diplomatic relations the Foreign Minister must be* the unique *medium of communication with foreign Powers.* | *He relates Christianity to other religions, and notes what is* unique *to the former and what is common to all of them.* Unique *so used is a* GALLICISM.

Exercise 32.7

Look up *unique* in William and Mary Morris's *Harper Dictionary of Contemporary Usage,* Second Edition. Compare its entry with the one printed above from Fowler. Then write a brief description of how these works agree and disagree on the usage of *unique.*

2. Dictionaries of synonyms

All writers are sometimes stuck for just the right word, and at such times, a dictionary of synonyms or a thesaurus can help. These works follow each entry with a list of words whose meanings are similar to the meaning of the entry. A useful source for students is *Webster's New Dictionary of Synonyms,* which includes the following entry for *unique:*

> **unique** 1 *single, sole, lone, solitary, separate, particular
> *Ana* *only, alone
> 2 singular, *strange, peculiar, eccentric, erratic, odd, queer, quaint, outlandish, curious
> *Ana* *exceptional: uncommon, rare, *infrequent

The entry indicates, by way of asterisks, that further information on synonyms for *unique* may be found by looking up several other words (the abbreviation *Ana.* marks analogous words). Checking these entries carefully should help you decide which, if any, of these synonyms would be appropriate in a particular sentence.

A **thesaurus**, which comes from a word meaning "treasury" or "storehouse," provides lists of antonyms as well as synonyms for many words. Two are particularly helpful: *Webster's Collegiate Thesaurus* and *The New Roget's Thesaurus of the English Language in Dictionary Form*.

Remember, however, to use dictionaries of synonyms and thesauruses very carefully, because very rarely in English are two words so close in meaning that they can be use interchangeably.

Exercise 32.8

Look up the entry for *strange* in *Webster's New Dictionary of Synonyms*. Read it carefully, and then write a brief summary of what the entry has to say about the relationship of *unique* to *strange*. Then look up *strange* in *The New Roget's Thesaurus*, and compare that entry with the one in *Webster's*.

3. Dictionaries of etymology, regional English, and slang

On some occasions, you may want or need to find out all you can about the origins of a word, to find out about a term used only in one area of the country, or to see whether a term is considered to be slang or not. The following specialized dictionaries can help out:

> *The Oxford Dictionary of English,* ed. C.T. Onions, 1966.
>
> *A Dictionary of Canadianisms on Historical Principles,* ed. Walter Avis et al., 1967.
>
> *Dictionary of Slang and Unconventional Usage,* 7th edition, ed. Eric Partridge, 1970.
>
> *Dictionary of American Slang,* ed. Harold Wentworth and Stuart Berg Flexner, 1978.

Exercise 32.9

Look up the following words in several specialized dictionaries, and find out as much as you can about their meanings, origins, and uses.

1. tip
2. scam

3. jazz
4. whammy

4. Subject dictionaries

Special subject dictionaries can help us understand specialized or technical vocabulary and provide a rough map of any field. Such dictionaries exist for music, classical literature, biography, mathematics, philosophy, geography, religion, and many other fields. Suppose, for instance, that you find the word *unique* used in a math textbook in a way that puzzles you. Check a source such as the *Mathematics Dictionary*, 4th edition (ed. Glen James and Robert C. James. New York: Van Nostrand Reinhold Co., 1976). There you will find the following entry:

> **U-NIQUE′,** *adj.* Leading to one and only one result; consisting of one, and only one. The product of two integers is unique; the square root of an integer is not unless the integer is 0.
>
> **unique factorization.** See DOMAIN—integral domain, FUNDAMENTAL—fundamental theorem of arithmetic, IRREDUCIBLE—irreducible polynomial.

You will find more on special subject dictionaries in Chapter 11.

Reading with attention to words

Choose a writer whose work you admire, and read that author's work for at least thirty minutes, jotting down six or seven words that you would not ordinarily have thought to use in such a situation. Do a little dictionary investigative work on these words, and bring your results to class for discussion.

Taking inventory: words

Look back through the last several pieces you have written, looking for two or three words you have used that interest you but that you know very little about. Then look up those words in at least one abridged and one unabridged dictionary and in any specialized dictionary that might give you further information. On the basis of what you have learned, check the way you have used these words in your essay. How accurately and appropriately have you used them? What synonyms could you have appropriately substituted? Do this exercise with another student to further expand your vocabulary.

33

Working on Spelling

The evolution of the English language from the tongue of Germanic tribes to a hybrid of Anglo-Saxon, Scandinavian, and Norman French, with a multitude of other languages represented as well, makes English spelling a complex system. For example, English includes at least eleven different ways of representing the *sh* sound: *sh*oe, *s*ugar, o*c*ean, i*ss*ue, na*ti*on, *sch*ist, suspi*c*ion, con*sc*ious, nau*se*ous, man*si*on, and fu*chs*ia.

In spite of this complexity, modern linguists have demonstrated that English spelling is much more regular than is commonly thought and that this regularity relates not only to sound–letter connections but also to our stored visual memory of related words. We know that *president* is not spelled "presadent," for example, because we recognize its relation to *preside*.

The good news, then, is simply this: careful attention to your own spelling patterns and attention to some fairly straightforward guidelines of English spelling can help you avoid spelling errors. This chapter will introduce you to these guidelines and help you begin your analysis.

Attending to the most commonly misspelled words

A study of spelling errors in the research for this book revealed a fairly small number of persistently misspelled words. A list of the fifty most common misspellings appears below. You may want to look over it carefully and compare it with words you have trouble spelling correctly (see 33f for ways to establish your own spelling inventory).

1. their/there/they're
2. too/to
3. a lot
4. noticeable
5. received/e/es
6. lose
7. you're/your
8. an/and
9. develop/s
10. definitely
11. than/then
12. believe/d/s
13. occurred
14. affect/s
15. cannot
16. separate
17. success
18. through
19. until
20. where
21. successful/ly
22. truly
23. argument/s
24. experience/s
25. environment
26. exercise/s/ing
27. necessary
28. sense
29. therefore
30. accept/ed
31. heroes
32. professor
33. whether
34. without
35. business/es
36. dependent
37. every day
38. may be
39. occasion/s
40. occurrences
41. woman
42. all right
43. apparent/ly
44. categories
45. final/ly
46. immediate/ly
47. roommate/s
48. against
49. before
50. beginning

Exercise 33.1

Choose the correct spelling from the pair of words in the parentheses in each of the sentences below. After checking your answers, compare your misspellings with the list of fifty words most frequently misspelled. Enter the words you misspelled in your spelling log.

1. (*Their/There/They're*) going to put (*their/there/they're*) new stereo system over (*their/there/they're*) in the corner.

2. My little brother wants (*to/too*) go swimming (*to/too*).

3. The (*begining/beginning*) of spring term is (*a lot/alot*) earlier this year than last.

4. The rise in temperature isn't (*noticable/noticeable*) (*until/untill*) the humidity rises.

5. The accident (*occured/occurred*) (*before/befour*) I could step aside.

6. We couldn't (*beleive/believe*) the national champions were expected to (*loose/lose*) the playoffs.

7. In making your major life decisions, (*your/you're*) (*definately/definitely*) on (*your/you're*) own.

8. Nothing (*affects/effects*) (*success/sucess*) more (*than/then*) self-confidence or (*its/it's*) absence.

9. We (*received/recieved*) our notice (*threw/through*) the mail.

10. The group hopes to (*develop/develope*) a (*trully/truly*) (*succesful/successful*) fast-food franchise.

11. We cannot easily (*separate/seperate*) fact and opinion.

12. Local (*busineses/businesses*) are (*dependant/dependent*) on a strong tourist trade.

13. (*Heroes/Heros*) are (*necesary/necessary*) to every culture's mythology.

14. The (*professor/profesor*) agreed to (*accept/except*) our essays on Friday.

15. Our top speaker qualified for three (*catagories/categories*) in the (*final/finel*) competition.

16. The plane to Halifax (*may be/maybe*) late; (*therefore/therfore*), we don't need to leave for the airport (*imediately/immediately*).

17. A (*woman's/women's*) place is now wherever she wants it to be.

18. Police report (*occurences/occurrences*) of more and more burglaries (*every day/everyday*).

19. (*Its/It's*) not (*all right/alright*) to forego common sense.

20. (*Aparently/Apparently*), the shipment of books never arrived.

Recognizing homonyms

Of the words most often misspelled by college and university students, the largest number are **homonyms**—words that sound alike but have different spellings and meanings. English has many homonyms, but a relatively small number of them—seven pairs or trios—cause student writers frequent trouble. If you tend to confuse any of these words, now is a good time to stop and study them, looking for some twist of memory to help you remember the differences.

their [possessive form of *they*]
there [in that place]
they're [contraction of *they are*]

to [in the direction of]
too [in addition; excessive]
two [number between one and three]

your [possessive form of *you*]
you're [contraction of *you are*]

affect [to have an influence]
effect [noun: result]
        [verb: to cause to happen]

accept [to take or receive]
except [to leave out]

who's [contraction of *who is* or *who has*]
whose [possessive form of *who*]

its [possessive form of *it*]
it's [contraction of *it is* or *it has*]

For your easy reference, here is a list of other homonyms and of other words that are frequently confused because they sound *nearly* alike:

Homonyms and frequently confused words

advice [suggestion]
advise [to suggest (to)]

allude [to refer]
elude [to avoid or escape]

allusion [reference]
illusion [false idea or appearance]

altar [sacred platform or table]
alter [to change]

are [form of *be*]
our [belonging to us]

bare [uncovered]
bear [animal; to carry or endure]

board [piece of lumber]
bored [uninterested]

brake [device for stopping]
break [to fragment]

buy [to purchase]
by [near; beside; through]

capital [principal city]
capitol [legislative building]

cite [to refer to]
sight [seeing; something seen]
site [location]

coarse [rough or crude]
course [plan of study; path]

complement [something that
    completes; to make complete]
compliment [praise; to praise]

conscience [feeling of right and
    wrong]
conscious [mentally aware]

council [leadership group]
counsel [advice; to advise]

dairy [source of milk]
diary [journal]

desert [dry area; to abandon]
dessert [sweet course of a meal]

device [something planned or
    invented]
devise (to plan or invent]

die [to expire]
dye [colour; to colour]

elicit [to draw forth]
illicit [illegal]

eminent [distinguished]
immanent [inherent]
imminent [expected in the immediate
    future]

fair [just or right; light in complex-
    ion; exposition]
fare [price of transportation; to go
    through an experience

forth [forward; out into view]
fourth [between third and fifth]

gorilla [ape]
guerrilla [irregular soldier]

hear [to perceive with the ears]
here [in this place]

heard [past tense of *hear*]
herd [group of animals]

hoarse [sounding rough or harsh]
horse [animal]

know [to understand]
no [opposite of *yes*]

lead [a metal; to go before]
led [past tense of *lead*]

loose [not tight; not confined]
lose [to misplace; to fail to win]

meat [flesh used as food]
meet [to encounter]

passed [went by; received passing
    grade]
past [beyond; events that have
    already occurred]

patience [quality of being patient]
patients [persons under medical care]

peace [absence of war]
piece [part]

personal [private or individual]
personnel [employees]

plain [simple, not fancy; flat land]
plane [airplane; tool; flat surface]

presence [condition of being]
presents [gifts; gives]

principal [most important; head of a
    school]
principle [fundamental truth]

rain [precipitation]
rein [strap to control a horse]
reign [period of rule]

right [correct; opposite of left]
rite [ceremony]
write [to produce words on a surface]

road [street or highway]
rode [past tense of *ride*]

scene [setting; view]
seen [past participle of *see*]

sense [feeling; intelligence]
since [from the time that; because]

stationary [unmoving]
stationery [writing paper]

than [as compared with]
then [at that time; therefore]

threw [past tense of *throw*]
thorough [complete]
through [in one side of and out the
    other; by means of]

waist [part of the body]
waste [to squander]

weak [feeble]
week [seven days]

wear [to put onto the body]
were [past tense of *be*]
where [in what place]

which [what; that]
witch [woman with supernatural
    power]

Exercise 33.2

Choose the appropriate word in parentheses to fill each blank in the following paragraph.

If _____ (*your/you're*) looking for summer fun, _____ (*accept/except*) the friendly _____ (*advice/advise*) of thousands of happy adventurers: spend three _____ (*weaks/weeks*) kayaking _____ (*threw/thorough/through*) the inside passage _____ (*to/too/two*) Alaska. For ten years, Outings, Inc., has _____ (*lead/led*) groups of novice kayakers _____ (*passed/past*) some of the most breathtaking scenery in North America. _____ (*Their/There/They're*) goal is simple: to give participants the time of _____ (*their/there/they're*) lives. As one of the last year's adventurers said, "_____ (*Its/It's*) a trip I will remember vividly, one that _____ (*affected/effected*) me powerfully."

1. Recognizing words with more than one form

One special group of homonyms appearing in the list of words most often misspelled by writers are words written sometimes as one word and other times as two words. The correct spelling depends on the meaning. Note the differences illustrated here:

Of course, they did not wear *everyday* clothes *every day* of the year.

Ideally, children *always* love their parents—in *all ways.*

By the time we were *all ready* for the game to begin, the coach's patience was *already* exhausted.

We *may be* on time for the meeting, or *maybe* we won't.

Nobody was surprised when the police announced that they had found *no body* at the scene of the crime.

A lot and *all right* are always written as two words.

2. Recognizing Canadian, British, and American spellings

Spelling varies slightly among English-speaking countries. What is considered correct in Canada, for example, may be considered incorrect in the United States, and vice versa. Canadian spelling reflects both British and American practices, and varies according to regional preferences.

Although research has suggested that the simpler, phonetic American spellings are beginning to edge out British spellings in Canada, some Canadian spelling still shows a preference for the British: we find, for example, *catalogue* rather than *catalog, cheque* rather than *check.* If you have trouble remembering the preferred spellings of words or whether, for instance, a verb ends in *-ise* or *-ize,* consult a dictionary, such as the *Gage Canadian Dictionary,* designed to meet the needs of Canadian users. It will list preferred and variant spellings.

Linking spelling and pronunciation

The best way to link spelling and pronunciation is to learn to "pronounce" words mentally as they look, every letter and syllable included (so that, for example, you hear the *b* at the end of *crumb*) and to enunciate them slowly and clearly when you are trying to spell them.

1. Noting unpronounced letters or syllables

Learning to "see" words with unpronounced letters or syllables will help you remember to spell them correctly. Here are some of the most frequently misspelled words of this kind, with their unpronounced letters or syllables italicized:

condem*n*	*fo*reign	mus*c*le
diff*e*rent	gov*e*rnment	sep*a*rate (adjective)
drasti*cal*ly	int*e*rest	Wed*nes*day
Feb*r*uary	mar*ri*age	

2. Noting unstressed vowels

In English words, *a, i,* and *e* can often sound alike if they are in syllables that are not stressed. Hearing the word *definite,* for instance, gives us few clues as to whether the vowels in the second and third syllables should be *i*'s or *a*'s. In this case, remembering how the related word *finite* looks or sounds helps us know that the *i*'s are correct. If you are puzzled about how to spell a word containing unstressed vowels, first try to think of a related word that would give you a clue to the correct spelling. Then check your dictionary.

33d

Taking advantage of spelling rules

Fortunately, English spelling does follow some general rules that can be of enormous help to writers. This section focuses on those rules closely related to commonly misspelled words.

1. Remembering "i before e"

Most of you probably memorized the *"i before e"* rule long ago. Here is a slightly expanded version:

i before *e* except after *c*
or when pronounced *ay*
as in *neighbour* or *weigh*
or in *weird* exceptions like *either*

i BEFORE e

achieve	experience	piece
believe	friend	relieve
brief	field	thief
chief		

EXCEPT AFTER c

ceiling	deceive	perceive
conceive	receive	

OR WHEN PRONOUNCED "AY"

neighbour	weigh	eighth

OR IN WEIRD EXCEPTIONS

either	leisure	height
weird	seize	caffeine
neither	foreign	

2. Adding prefixes

Prefixes are verbal elements placed at the *beginning* of words to add to or qualify their meaning. The prefix *re-*, for example, adds repetition to the meaning of a word: *reappear* means "appear again." (See 31c for more information about prefixes.) Prefixes do not change the spelling of the words they are added to, even when the last letter of the prefix and the first letter of the word it is added to are the same. In such cases, keep both letters:

dis- + service = disservice

over- + rate = overrate

Some prefixes require the use of hyphens. For a discussion of such usage, see 43c. If you are in doubt about whether to hyphenate a word beginning with a prefix, always check your dictionary.

3. Adding suffixes

Suffixes are verbal elements placed at the *end* of words in order to form related words. For example, we can build on the basic word *short* to get the following words:

short*age*   short*en*   short*er*   short*ly*   short*ness*

This section will provide guidance to spelling words with suffixes.

Dropping the final e

For words ending in an unpronounced *e* (*receive, lose, definite*), you must decide whether or not to drop the *e* when adding a suffix. In general, if the suffix starts with a vowel, *drop* the *e*.

explore + -ation = exploration
imagine + -able = imaginable
future + -ism = futurism
exercise + -ing = exercising
continue + -ous = continuous
productive + -ity = productivity

EXCEPTIONS

- To distinguish homonyms or potentially confusing words

  dye + -ing = dyeing (not *dying*)
  singe + -ing = singeing (not *singing*)

- To clarify pronunciation

  be + -ing = being (not *bing*)
  shoe + -ing = shoeing (not *shoing*)

- To keep the sound of *c* or *g* soft

notice + -able = noticeable
marriage + -able = marriageable
salvage + -able = salvageable
courage + -ous = courageous
peace + -able = peaceable

Keeping the final e
If the suffix starts with a consonant, *keep* the *e*.

force + -ful = forceful
excite + -ment = excitement
state + -ly = stately
same + -ness = sameness

EXCEPTIONS

argue + -ment = argument
true = -ly = truly
whole + ly = wholly
nine + -th = ninth

Exercise 33.3

Combine each of the following words and suffixes, dropping the unpronounced *e* when necessary.

1. future + -ism
2. whole + ly
3. argue + ment
4. lone + -ly
5. malice + -ious
6. dye + -ing
7. hope + ful
8. continue + -ous
9. exercise + -ing
10. outrage + ous

Using -ally
Use *-ally* if the base word ends in *ic*.

drastic + -ally = drastically
basic + -ally = basically
characteristic + -ally = characteristically
dramatic + -ally = dramatically

Using -ly
Use *-ly* if the base word does not end in *ic*.

apparent + -ly = apparently

certain + -ly   = certainly
conscious + -ly = consciously
quick + ly = quickly
supposed + -ly = supposedly

EXCEPTION
public + -ly = publicly

Exercise 33.4

Insert either -*ally* or -*ly* in the blank in each of the following words.

1. tragic _____
2. fatal _____
3. realistic _____
4. final _____
5. apparent _____

Using -cede, -ceed, *and* -sede

Almost all words ending in the sound pronounced "seed" use the spelling -*cede*. Use -*sede* with only one word: supersede. Use -*ceed* with only three words: exceed, proceed, succeed. Use -*cede* with all other words ending in the "seed" sound:

accede	intercede	recede
concede	precede	secede

Words ending in consonant and y

For words ending in *y*, you must sometimes change the *y* to *i* when you add a suffix. In general, if the *y* is preceded by a consonant, *change* the *y*.

bounty + -ful = bountiful
try + -ed = tried
silly + -er = sillier
breezy + -ness = breeziness
busy + -ily = busily

EXCEPTIONS
*   Keep the *y* before the suffix -*ing*.

dry + -ing = drying
liquefy + -ing = liquefying
carry + -ing = carrying

- Keep the *y* in some one-syllable base words.

  shy + -er = shyer
  dry + -ly = dryly
  wry + -ness = wryness

- Keep the *y* if the base word is a proper name.

  Tolstoy + -esque = Tolstoyesque

Words ending in vowel and **y**
If the *y* is preceded by a vowel, keep the *y*.

joy + -ous = joyous
play + -ful = playful
employ + -ment = employment
buoy + -ed = buoyed

EXCEPTIONS
day + ly = daily
gay + ly = gaily

Exercise 33.5

Combine each of the following words and suffixes, changing the final *y* to *i* when necessary.

1. lonely + -er
2. carry + -ing
3. defy + -ance
4. study + -s
5. supply + -ed
6. duty + -ful
7. likely + -hood
8. obey + -ed
9. rainy + -est
10. coy + -ly

Doubling the final consonant
When a word ends in a consonant, the consonant is sometimes doubled when a suffix is added. If the word ends in consonant-vowel-consonant, the suffix begins with a vowel, and the word contains only one syllable or ends in an accented syllable, double the final consonant.

stop + -ing = stopping
slap + -ed = slapped
hot + -est = hottest
run + -er = runner
begin + -ing = beginning
occur + -ence = occurrence
refer + -ing = referring

EXCEPTION

Double the final *l* even in words that do not end in an accented syllable.

counsel + or = counsellor
travel + ed = travelled
label + ing = labelling

DO NOT DOUBLE THE CONSONANT

- If it is preceded by more than one vowel or by another consonant

bait + -ing = baiting
sleep + -ing = sleeping
fight + -er = fighter
start + -ed = started

- If the suffix begins with a consonant

ship + -ment = shipment
fit + -ness = fitness

- If the word is not accented on the last syllable

benefit + -ing = benefiting
fasten + -er = fastener

- If the accent shifts from the last to the first syllable when the suffix is added.

infer + -ence = inference
prefer + -ence = preference

If the last letter of the word and the first letter of the suffix are the same, keep both letters:

mortal + -ly = mortally
room + mate = roommate
rotten + -ness = rottenness
usual + -ly = usually

Exercise 33.6

Combine each of the following words and suffixes, doubling the final consonant when necessary.

1. occur + -ed
2. fast + -est
3. skip + -er
4. refer + -ence
5. commit + -ment
6. regret + -able
7. submit + -ed
8. drastic + -ally
9. benefit + -ed
10. quarrel + -ing

33e

Making words plural

Making singular nouns into plurals calls for using several different spelling guidelines.

Adding -s
For most words, add -s.

pencil, pencils   computer, computers

Adding -es
For words ending in *s, ch, sh, x,* or *z,* add *-es.*

Jones, Joneses   church, churches
bus, buses   flash, flashes
fox, foxes   buzz, buzzes

For words ending in *o,* add *-es* if the *o* is preceded by a consonant.

potato, potatoes   veto, vetoes
hero, heroes

EXCEPTIONS
memo, memos   piano, pianos
pro, pros   solo, solos

Add *-s* if the *o* is preceded by a vowel.

rodeo, rodeos   patio, patios
zoo, zoos   curio, curios

Words ending in f or fe
For some words ending in *f* or *fe,* change *f* to *v* and add *-s* or *-es.*

calf, calves   shelf, shelves
half, halves   elf, elves
self, selves   leaf, leaves
life, lives   hoof, hooves
wife, wives   knife, knives

Words ending in y
For words ending in *y, change* y to *i* and add *-es* if the *y* is preceded by a consonant.

| theory, theories | huckleberry, huckleberries |
| eighty, eighties | sky, skies |

EXCEPTIONS

- Proper names

  Henry, Henrys

- Keep the y and -s if the y is preceded by a vowel.

| guy, guys | attorney, attorneys |
| delay, delays | alloy, alloys |

Irregular plurals

For irregular plurals and nouns that have the same form in the singular and plural, memorize those you do not already know.

man, men	medium, media	deer, deer
woman, women	locus, loci	sheep, sheep
child, children	alga, algae	moose, moose
foot, feet	basis, bases	series, series
tooth, teeth	phenomenon, phenomena	species, species
bacterium, bacteria		

Compound words

For compound nouns written as one word, make the last part of the compound plural.

| briefcase, briefcases | bookshelf, bookshelves |
| mailbox, mailboxes | grandchild, grandchildren |

For compound nouns written as separate words or hyphenated, make the most important part of the compound plural.

brother-in-law, brothers-in-law	sergeant major, sergeants major
lieutenant-governor, lieutenant-	leap year, leap years
governors	bus stop, bus stops

Exercise 33.7

Form the plural of each of the following words.

1. tomato	5. dish	9. radio
2. hoof	6. stepchild	10. phenomenon
3. volunteer	7. turkey	11. spoof
4. baby	8. kilometre per hour	12. beach

13. yourself   14. golf club   15. rose

Taking a personal spelling inventory

This chapter has surveyed general spelling rules and guidelines. You need now to tailor this advice to your own spelling patterns and problems. Begin by examining a large and varied sample of your prose.

1. Identifying troublesome words and patterns

You can begin your inventory by looking through several essays you have written and making a list of every word misspelled. Whenever possible, identify the guideline in this chapter that deals with the misspellings. Here is the beginning of one student's personal spelling inventory:

WORD	MISSPELLING	GUIDELINE
their	there	homonyms
receiving	recieving	"*i* before *e*"
hastiest	hastyest	suffix with final *y*
beginning	begining	double consonants
affect	effect	homonyms
sharing	shareing	unpronounced final *e*
environment	enviroment	unpronounced letters
theories	theorys	plural for words ending in *y*
successful	succeful	double consonants
dissatisfied	disatisfied	prefix

2. Using a spell checker

If you write on a computer, you may be able to use a *spell checker* to identify misspelled words. Those who use this feature, however, know that it provides only limited help. It will not, for instance, pick up homonym problems—*you're* may be the wrong spelling in the context of the essay, but the spell checker will recognize it only as a correct possible spelling.

3. Annotating your dictionary

Author John Irving recommends making a mark and listing the date when-ever you look up a word in the dictionary. If you follow this advice, you will be able to identify words you are looking up frequently—and take steps to learn the correct spelling once and for all. You may also find that some or most of these words follow a similar pattern.

4. Building on memory cues

You can learn to use memory cues, or **mnemonic devices** (named for the Greek goddess of memory, Mnemosyne), to help with words whose spelling tends to trip you up. Here are some memory cues one student devised to go along with her personal spelling inventory:

WORD	MISSPELLING	CUE
environment	enviroment	There's *iron* in our environment.
all right	alright	I wouldn't write *alwrong,* would I?
a lot	alot	I wouldn't write *alittle,* would I?
government	goverment	Government should serve those it *governs.*
separate	seperate	*Separate* rates two a's.
definitely	definately	There is a *finite* number of ways to spell *definitely.*

Reading for spelling

Readers store the visual memory of words in their minds and can often spell them correctly by "seeing" them. You can make use of this fact by attending to the spelling of new or unfamiliar words as you read, making a conscious mental note of how the word looks correctly spelled. Many writers, in fact, jot down new words as they read and later concentrate on learning the meaning—and spelling— of them.

Taking inventory: spelling

If you are keeping a writing log, devote a section of it to a personal spelling inven-tory. Choose a sample of your recent writing, and identify every misspelling. If you have any drafts on disk, use a spell checker, and ask an instructor or several friends who are good spellers to help you. Then, following the format presented in 33f1, enter the word, your misspelling, and the guideline or pattern that relates to it. For persistent misspellings, create a memory cue (see 33f4), and enter it in the log along with the correct spelling of the word.

PART EIGHT

Using Conventional Punctuation

Using Commas

Using Semicolons

Using End Punctuation

Using Apostrophes

Using Quotation Marks

Using Other Punctuation Marks

34

Using Commas

The word *comma* comes from the Greek *komma*, meaning "cut" or "segment." A clause, for example, is a segment of a sentence, and is often set off with a comma. In English, the comma is the most frequently used punctuation mark, serving to separate words and word groups.

Although the comma appears everywhere in modern writing, reducing this punctuation mark to hard and fast rules is very difficult, for several reasons. First, the comma can play a number of different roles in a sentence, making general rules hard to come by. More important, many decisions about commas relate to matters of purpose, rhythm, and style. As a result, comma conventions can and do differ from one English-speaking country to another, and even from one professional writer to another.

Getting full control of comma usage in your own writing presents a special challenge to you, one that involves not only learning some rules but practising the use of commas in writing and concentrating on the stylistic decisions you must learn to make as a writer. This chapter presents an opportunity for you to accomplish both these goals.

Using commas after introductory elements

A comma usually follows an introductory word, expression, phrase, or clause. Introductory elements that are followed by commas include adverbs (see 14b5); conjunctive adverbs (see 14b7); transitional expressions (see 6c5); participles, infinitives, and prepositional, participial, infinitive, and absolute phrases (see 14c3); and adverb clauses (see 14c4).

> *Slowly*, she became conscious of her predicament. [adverb]
>
> *Nevertheless*, the hours of a typist are flexible. [conjunctive adverb]
>
> *In fact*, only you can decide. [transitional expression]

Frustrated, he wondered whether he should change careers. [participle]

In his review, Timothy Findley said that the main character in George Payerle's *Unknown Soldier* was "thoroughly unforgettable." [prepositional phrase]

Sporting a pair of specially made running shoes, Dimitri prepared for the race. [participial phrase]

To win the contest, Paul needed luck. [infinitive phrase]

Pens poised in anticipation, the students waited for the test to be distributed. [absolute phrase]

Since her mind was not receiving enough stimulation, she had to resort to her imagination. [adverb clause]

For certain kinds of introductory elements—adverbs, infinitives, prepositional and infinitive phrases, and adverb clauses—some writers omit the comma if the element is short and does not seem to require a pause after it. Try to use your ear to decide if a comma is needed in such cases; if in doubt, put in the comma.

At the racetrack Henry lost nearly his entire paycheque.

If the introductory element is followed by inverted word order, with the verb preceding the subject, do not use a comma.

From directly behind my seat came huge clouds of cigar smoke.

Exercise 34.1

Place a comma after the introductory element in any of the following sentences where the comma is needed. Some of the sentences do not require a comma.

1. In one of his most famous poems Frost asks why people need walls.
2. Unfortunately the door to the kennel had been left open.
3. Unable to make such a decision alone I asked my brother for help.
4. If you follow instructions carefully you will be able to install your software.
5. Therefore answering the seemingly simple question is very difficult.
6. With the 5th century came the fall of the Roman Empire.
7. Their bags packed they waited for the taxi to the airport.
8. To become an Olympic competitor an athlete must train for year.
9. Like other disciplines psychology draws general principles from specific observations.
10. Founded by Alexander the Great Alexandria became a great centre of learning.

Using commas in compound sentences

A comma usually precedes a coordinating conjunction (*and, but, or, for, nor, so, or yet*) that joins two independent clauses in a compound sentence.

> The title may sound important, but *administrative clerk* is only a euphemism for *photocopier*.
>
> The climbers will reach the summit today, or they must turn back.
>
> The show started at last, and the crowd grew quiet.
>
> I was often bullied in school, for I was the smallest in my class.

You may want to use a semicolon rather than a comma when the clauses are long and complex or contain other punctuation.

> All over the suburbs in duplexes and fourplexes, families would be enjoying cold suppers in the open air on their balconies; but the Calverts' apartment had none.
>
> — HUGH HOOD, "Flying a Red Kite"

If the clauses are very brief, on the other hand, you can often omit the comma before *and* or *or*.

> She saw her chance and she took it.

Always use the comma if there is any chance the sentence will be misread without it.

> CONFUSED　　The game ended in victory and pandemonium erupted on the court.
>
> REVISED　　The game ended in victory, and pandemonium erupted on the court.

Be careful not to use *only* a comma between independent clauses; doing so is considered a serious grammatical error, called a comma splice. Either use a coordinating conjunction after the comma or use a semicolon. (See Chapter 21 for further discussion of comma splices.)

> COMMA　　Do not thank "luck" for your new job, give yourself the credit
> SPLICE　　you deserve.
>
> REVISED　　Do not thank "luck" for your new job, *but* give yourself the credit you deserve.

REVISED Do not thank "luck" for your new job; give yourself the credit you deserve.

Exercise 34.2

Choose a piece of writing you are working on or have recently completed. Read through it, looking for coordinating conjunctions: *and, but, or, nor, for, so, yet.* Then examine the words before each coordinating conjunction. Do they function as a complete sentence, with a subject and a predicate? Do the words following each conjunction function as a complete sentence? If the answer to both these questions is yes, the two groups of words form a compound sentence: two independent clauses joined with a coordinating conjunction. Make sure each conjunction is preceded *(not followed)* by a comma.

Using commas to set off nonrestrictive elements

Nonrestrictive elements of a sentence—clauses, phrases, and appositives that do not limit or "restrict" the meaning of the words they modify or refer to—are set off from the rest of the sentence with commas. **Restrictive** elements *do* limit meaning and are *not* set off with commas. Look at the following examples:

RESTRICTIVE Drivers who have been convicted of drunken driving should lose their licences.

NONRESTRICTIVE The two drivers involved in the accident, who have been convicted of drunken driving, should lose their licences.

In the first sentence, the clause *who have been convicted of drunken driving* is essential to the meaning of the sentence because it limits the word it modifies, *Drivers*, to only those drivers who have been convicted of drunken driving. Therefore, it is not set off by commas. In the second sentence, the same clause is not essential to the meaning because it does not limit what it modifies, *The two drivers involved in the accident*, but merely provides additional information about these drivers. Therefore, it *is* set off with commas.

Notice how using or not using commas to set off such an element can change the meaning of a sentence:

The bus drivers *rejecting the management offer* remained on strike.

The bus drivers, *rejecting the management offer*, remained on strike.

506 34c , USING COMMAS

In the first sentence, not using commas to set off the participial phrase *rejecting the management offer* makes the phrase restrictive, limiting the meaning of *The bus drivers*. This sentence says that only some of the total group of bus drivers, the ones who rejected the offer, remained on strike, implying that other drivers went back to work. In the second sentence, using the commas around the participial phrase makes it nonrestrictive, implying that *The bus drivers* refers to all of the drivers and that all of them remained on strike.

To decide whether a sentence element is restrictive or nonrestrictive, mentally delete the element, and then decide whether the deletion changes the meaning of the rest of the sentence or makes it unclear. If it does, the element is probably restrictive and should not be set off with commas; if it does not, the element is probably nonrestrictive and requires commas.

Sentence elements that may be nonrestrictive and require commas to set them off include adjective and adverb clauses; participial, infinitive, and prepositional phrases; and appositive phrases.

1. Using commas with adjective and adverb clauses

Adjective clauses begin with *who, whom, whose, which, that, when, where,* or *why.* (See 14c4.) Adverb clauses begin with subordinating conjunctions like *because, although,* or *before.* (See 14b7 and 14c4). Adverb clauses are usually essential to the meaning of the sentence; do not set them off with commas unless they precede the independent clause (see 34a) or begin with *although, even though, while, whereas,* or another conjunction expressing the idea of contrast.

NONRESTRICTIVE CLAUSES

The giddy tourists, *who were just the beginning of the summer's influx,* crowded out of the bus and filled the small courtyard. [The central statement of this sentence is that the tourists left the bus and filled the courtyard; the adjective clause merely provides additional information and therefore should be set off with commas.]

I borrowed the necessary books from the Dana Porter Library, *which is the tall square building on centre campus.* [The adjective clause gives additional information not necessary to complete the meaning of the independent clause and therefore is set off with commas.]

The park soon became a popular gathering place, *although some nearby residents complained about the noise.* [The adverb clause expresses the idea of contrast; therefore it is set off with a comma.]

RESTRICTIVE CLAUSES

Our children are ashamed of the dingy cities *where we got our start.* [The information in the adjective clause is essential to the meaning of the sentence and therefore should not be set off with commas.]

> – BHARATI MUKHERJEE, "The Lady from Lucknow"

There is a story *that one day she didn't make it.* [The adjective clause beginning with *that* is necessary to the meaning of the sentence and is not set off with commas.]

> – HARRY BRUCE, "Toronto Islands in Winter"

An adjective clause that begins with *that* is always restrictive and is not set off with commas. An adjective clause beginning with *which* may be either restrictive or nonrestrictive; however, some writers prefer to use *which* only for nonrestrictive clauses.

2. Using commas with participial, infinitive, and prepositional phrases

Participial phrases may be either restrictive or nonrestrictive. Infinitive and prepositional phrases are usually restrictive but sometimes are not essential to the meaning of a sentence and are therefore set off with commas.

NONRESTRICTIVE PHRASES

Tamar, amazed, stared at the strange vehicle. [The participle does not limit the meaning of *Tamar.*]

Income tax, *introduced as a temporary measure after the war*, has now become the focus of government and citizen alike. [The participle phrase does not limit the meaning of *Income tax* or change the central meaning of the sentence.]

Her long-term goal, *to become a child psychologist*, would require great financial discipline. [The infinitive phrase does not limit the meaning of *Her long-term goal.*]

The beluga whale, *despite its great size*, is threatened by pollution of the oceans. [The prepositional phrase does not limit the meaning of *The beluga whale.*]

RESTRICTIVE PHRASES

A penny *saved* is a penny *earned.* [Without the participles, the sentence has a very different meaning.]

Wood *cut from living trees* does not burn as well as dead wood. [The participial phrase is essential to the meaning.]

His ability *to make decisions quickly* made him a valuable employee. [The infinitive phrase restricts the meaning of *ability.*]

The wire *for the antenna* is the last one to be connected. [The prepositional phrase restricts the meaning of *wire.*]

3. Using commas with appositive phrases

An appositive phrase is a noun or noun substitute, together with its modifiers, that renames the noun immediately preceding it. When the appositive phrase is not essential to identify the noun it follows, it is set off with commas.

NONRESTRICTIVE APPOSITIVES

Ms. Baker, *my high-school chemistry teacher*, inspired my love of science. [Ms. Baker's name identifies her; the appositive simply provides extra information.]

Beethoven's opera, *Fidelio*, includes the famous "Prisoners' Chorus." [*Fidelio* is nonrestrictive because Beethoven wrote only one opera, so the name is not essential.]

RESTRICTIVE APPOSITIVES

The cartoonist *Lynn Johnston* takes her material from family situations. [The appositive identifies *The cartoonist* as a specific cartoonist.]

Mozart's opera *The Marriage of Figaro* was considered revolutionary in the 18th century. [The appositive is restrictive because Mozart wrote more than one opera.]

Exercise 34.3

Use commas to set off nonrestrictive clauses, phrases, and appositives in any of the following sentences that contain such elements. Some of the sentences do not contain nonrestrictive elements.

1. Anyone who is 14 years old faces strong peer pressure every day.

2. Embalming is a technique that preserves a cadaver for viewing.

3. I would feel right at home in the city dump which bears a striking resemblance to my bedroom.

4. The first one is the power wire which is usually red; the second is the ground wire which is usually black.

5. Most noteworthy is Aristarchus who showed that the sun is larger than the earth and proposed a heliocentric model for the solar system.

6. Seymour Segal one of Canada's most gifted painters will be visiting Toronto this week.

7. Sociology which encompasses most of the other social sciences is the study of human social behaviour.

8. An important 19th-century sociologist was Karl Marx who believed that his role as a social thinker was to change the world.

9. About two-thirds of the Swiss speak a German dialect while most of the rest speak French.

10. Britain and France agreed to come to each other's aid if one of them was attacked.

Using commas to separate items in a series

A comma is used after each item in a series of three or more words, phrases, or clauses.

> From the past and from our ancestors we have inherited a language harmonious to the ear, ceremonies edifying to attend, and traditions to be observed and continued.
>
> — BASIL JOHNSTON, *Ojibway Ceremonies*

> Every now and then I get up and walk over to the counter, peer into the yellow tub, watch, pretend to watch, and then sit down again.
>
> — CAMIE KIM, "They Speak Quickly"

You may often see a series with no comma after the next-to-last item, particularly in newspaper writing, as in *The day was cold, dark and dreary.* Occasionally, however, omitting the comma can cause confusion, and you will never be wrong to include it.

When the items in a series are long and complex or when they contain commas of their own, use semicolons rather than commas to separate them (see 35b).

Coordinate adjectives, those that relate equally to the noun they modify, should be separated by commas. In the sentence *They are sincere, inquisitive, talented researchers*, the three adjectives are coordinate: they each modify *researchers* and are therefore separated by commas. Here are some other examples of coordinate adjectives.

The *long, twisting, muddy* road led to a shack in the woods.

His *bizarre, outrageous* sense of humour endeared him to his friends.

In a sentence like *The cracked bathroom mirror reflected his face*, however, *cracked* and *bathroom* are not coordinate because *bathroom mirror* is the equivalent of a single word, which is modified by *cracked*. Hence they are *not* separated by commas.

Byron carried an *elegant pocket* watch.

Outdated black nylon furniture sat in dusty silence on the porch.

You can determine whether adjectives are coordinate by inserting the conjunction *and* between them. If the sentence makes sense with the *and*, the adjectives are coordinate and should be separated by commas.

> They are sincere *and* talented *and* inquisitive researchers. [The sentence makes sense with the inserted *and*'s, so the adjectives *sincere, talented*, and *inquisitive* should be separated by commas.]
>
> Byron carried an elegant *and* pocket watch. [In this instance, the sentence does not make sense with the *and*, so the adjectives *elegant* and *pocket* should not be separated by a comma.]

Exercise 34.4

Revise those of the following sentences that require commas to set off words, phrases, or clauses in a series. Some of the sentences do not require commas.

1. They found employment in truck driving farming and mining.

2. The social sciences included economics psychology political science anthropology and sociology.

3. Members plant tend and harvest corn.

4. The daddy-long-legs' orange body resembled a coloured dot amidst eight black legs.

5. A prestigious car a large house and membership in an exclusive club are taken as signs of success.

6. Superficial observation does not provide accurate insight into people's lives—how they feel what they believe in how they respond to others.

7. What is impossible today may soon become reality: travelling to other planets colonizing the moon maybe even reaching out to distant galaxies.

8. I timidly offered to help a loud overbearing lavishly dressed customer.

9. Ellen is an accomplished freelance writer.

10. These armchair quarterbacks insist on reviewing every play judging every move and telling everyone within earshot what is wrong with the team.

Using commas to set off parenthetical and transitional expressions, contrasting elements, interjections, direct address, and tag questions

Use commas to set off parenthetical and transitional expressions, elements expressing a contrast with what precedes them, mild interjections, words directly addressing readers, and tag questions.

Parenthetical and transitional expressions

Parenthetical expressions are relatively unimportant comments by the writer or pieces of supplementary information. Transitional expressions include conjunctive adverbs like *however* and *furthermore* (see 14b7) and other words and phrases used to express conjunctions between clauses, sentences, or paragraphs. (For a full list, see 6c5.)

Some studies, *incidentally*, have shown that chocolate, *of all things*, helps to prevent tooth decay.

Ceiling fans, are, *moreover*, less expensive than air conditioners.

Many people do not realize that ozone is produced by dry cleaning, *for example*.

Contrasting elements

On official business it was she, *not my father,* one would usually hear on the phone or in stores …

       — RICHARD RODRIGUEZ, "Aria: A Memoir of a Bilingual Childhood"

The story is narrated objectively at first, *subjectively toward the end.*

Interjections

My God, who wouldn't want a wife?

       — JUDY BRADY, "I Want a Wife"

We had hiked for, *say*, twelve kilometres before stopping to rest.

Stronger interjections are followed by exclamation points (see 36c).

Direct address

Gentlemen, those who have gone before you have bequeathed you a splendid inheritance.

— EARL OF MINTO

Kids, it's time to bathe the cat.

Tag questions
Tag questions "echo" the statement preceding them.

The homeless are our fellow citizens, *are they not?*
Ottawa is not the capital of Ontario, *is it?*

Exercise 34.5

Revise each of the following sentences, using commas to set off parenthetical and transitional expressions, contrasting elements, interjections, words used in direct address, and tag questions.

1. One must consider the society as a whole not its individual components to understand a particular culture.
2. Sophie in fact has supported her children alone for the past eight years.
3. Her friends did not know about her illness did they?
4. Fictions about race not the facts influence human relations.
5. We found therefore that we had more tomatoes than we could use.
6. We must act quickly to stop this threat to our health and safety.
7. Oh I do not know how to do anything but farm.
8. And now customers follow along as I demonstrate the latest in notebook computers.
9. Regional accents have shown few signs of weakening surprisingly enough.
10. This is imported pâté not chopped liver.

Using commas in dates, addresses, titles, and numbers

Commas are used according to established rules within dates, addresses and place names, and numbers. Commas are also used to separate personal and professional titles from the name preceding them.

Dates

For dates, use a comma between the day of the week and the month, between the day of the month and the year, and between the year and the rest of the sentence, if any.

> The British North America Act was signed on *March 29, 1867*, and became effective on *July 1, 1867*.

Do not use a comma with dates in inverted order or with dates consisting only of the month and the year.

> 11 October 1994

> Some still remember the invocation of the War Measures Act in *October 1970*.

Addresses and place names

In addresses and place names, use a comma after each part, including the province if no postal code is given. In addresses that include the postal code, do not use a comma either before or after it.

> Forward my mail to the Department of English, University of Waterloo, Waterloo, Ontario N2L 3G1 until further notice.

> Hull, Quebec, was the site of one of the important meetings on the Meech Lake Accord.

Titles

Use commas to set off a title such as *Jr., M.D.*, and so on from the name preceding it and from the rest of the sentence.

> James Siddens, *Ph.D.*, recently joined the faculty as the new dean of the Schools of Arts and Sciences.

> Martin Luther King, *Jr.*, was one of the country's greatest orators.

Numbers

In numbers of five digits or more, a comma is frequently used between each group of three digits, starting from the right.

> Give me *10,000* reasons, and then I'll change my mind.

Do not use a comma within street numbers or postal codes.

My parents live at *11311* Hilliards Road, Corner Brook, Newfoundland *A2H 7E7*.

The comma is optional within numbers of four digits, except for years, where it is never used.

The Engineering Faculty has an enrolment of *1,789* (or *1789*) this semester.

The French Revolution began in *1789*.

The adoption of the metric system has meant that Canadian writers now often insert spaces instead of commas in numbers of five digits or more. The space is optional within numbers of four digits.

At least *25 000* eager fans crowded the stadium.

Using commas with quotations

Commas are used to set off quotations from words used to introduce or explain the quotations. A comma following a quotation goes *inside* the closing quotation mark.

"No one becomes depraved all at once," wrote Juvenal.

A German proverb warns, "Go to law for a sheep, and lose your cow."

"Nothing has really happened," said Virginia Woolf, "until it has been recorded."

When a quotation followed by explanatory words is a question or an exclamation, do not use a comma after the question mark or exclamation point.

"What's a thousand dollars?" asks Groucho Marx in *Coconuts*. "Mere chicken feed. A poultry matter."

"Out, damned spot!" cried Lady Macbeth.

Do not use a comma when a quotation is introduced by *that* or when the rest of the sentence includes more than the words used to introduce or explain the quotation.

The writer of Ecclesiastes concludes that "all is vanity."

People who say "Have a nice day" irritate me.

Do not use a comma before an indirect quotation, one that does not include the speaker's exact words.

> Pierre Trudeau declared that the state should stay out of the nation's bedrooms.
>
> Virginia Woolf said that a woman needs money and her own room in order to write fiction.

Using commas to facilitate understanding

Sometimes a comma, though not required, can make a sentence much easier to read or understand.

CONFUSING	The members of the dance troupe strutted in in matching tuxedos and top hats.
REVISED	The members of the dance troupe strutted in, in matching tuxedos and top hats.
CONFUSING	Still liquids are necessary to sustain life.
REVISED	Still, liquids are necessary to sustain life.

Exercise 34.6

Revised the following paragraph by inserting commas where necessary. Be prepared to explain why you added each comma.

> It doesn't mean it will never mean that as a defensive forward he stops craving the glory and excitement of scoring goals. It is only in the last few years that Gainey has not gone home in the summer intent on returning to Montreal a more complete player practising several times a week working on his shooting and puck-handling using the summer as a breathing space as time to deprogram himself from his defensive run to redirect his mind to new and broader roles to play. In the 1976 Canada Cup with linemates who play a quicker less defensive style Gainey discovered he could successfully play a more offensive role. When the tournament ended he returned to our training camp and recalls now that he scored nine goals in nine exhibition games (it was actually four—to a defensive player it only *seemed* like nine). When the season began however old habits old instincts returned and gradually he scored less and less ending the year with fourteen goals.
>
>   – KEN DRYDEN, *The Game*

Exercise 34.7

In the following passage, Northrop Frye tells about questions his students ask about literature. Read the passage aloud, listening for Frye's use of commas. Then read it again, mentally deleting the commas and noting how their absence affects meaning and rhythm.

> For the past twenty-five years I have been teaching and studying English literature in a university. As in any other job, certain questions stick in one's mind, not because people keep asking them, but because they're the questions inspired by the very fact of being in such a place. What good is the study of literature? Does it help us to think more clearly, or feel more sensitively, or live a better life than we could without it? What is the function of the teacher and scholar, or of the person who calls himself, as I do, a literary critic?
>
> — NORTHROP FRYE, "The Motive for Metaphor"

34i

Checking for unnecessary commas

Just like insufficient use, excessive use of commas can spoil what may otherwise be a fine sentence or passage. This section will help you avoid using commas unnecessarily.

1. Omitting commas around restrictive phrases and clauses

Do not use commas to set off restrictive elements, which limit or restrict the meaning of the words they modify or refer to (see 34c).

UNNECESSARY	I don't let my children watch TV shows, that are violent.
REVISED	I don't let my children watch TV shows that are violent. [restrictive adjective clause]
UNNECESSARY	The decision, to stop the flow of irrigation water, is long overdue.
REVISED	The decision to stop the flow of irrigation water is long overdue. [restrictive infinitive phrase]
UNNECESSARY	My only defence, against my allergies, is to stay indoors.
REVISED	My only defence against my allergies is to stay indoors. [restrictive prepositional phrase]
UNNECESSARY	The writer, Evelyn Lau, will speak on campus this fall.

REVISED	The writer Evelyn Lau will speak on campus this fall. [restrictive appositive phrase]

2. Omitting commas between subjects and verbs, verbs and objects or complements, and prepositions and objects

Do not use a comma between a subject and its verb, a verb and its object or complement, or a preposition and its object. This general rule holds true even if the subject, object, or complement is a long phrase or clause.

UNNECESSARY	*Watching movies on my VCR late at night, has become* an important way for me to relax. [comma between subject and verb]
REVISED	Watching movies on my VCR late at night has become an important way for me to relax.
UNNECESSARY	Parents *must decide, how much TV their children may watch.* [comma between verb and object]
REVISED	Parents must decide how much TV their children may watch.
UNNECESSARY	*The winner of, the trophy* stepped forward. [comma between preposition and object]
REVISED	The winner of the trophy stepped forward.

3. Omitting commas in compound constructions

Do not use a comma before or after coordinating conjunctions joining the two parts of a compound construction.

UNNECESSARY	*Better working conditions, and higher pay* were the goals of the union. [compound subject]
REVISED	Better working conditions and higher pay were the goals of the union.
UNNECESSARY	Paul *trained as a teacher and, worked as a taxi driver.*
REVISED	Paul trained as a teacher and worked as a taxi driver.

4. Omitting commas before the first item or after the last item in a series

Do not use a comma before the first item or after the last item in a series, unless another rule requires a comma

UNNECESSARY	By operating her business as a sole proprietorship, the owner was able to avoid, *the costs of incorporating, securing a corporate name, maintaining certain records, and filing certain papers.*

REVISED   By operating her business as a sole proprietorship, the owner was able to avoid the costs of incorporating, securing a corporate name, maintaining certain records, and filing certain papers.

UNNECESSARY   The swimmer took slow, powerful, strokes.

REVISED   The swimmer took slow, powerful strokes.

Reading with an eye for commas

The following excerpt from a poem by Louis Dudek uses commas to create rhythm and guide readers. Read the poem aloud, listening especially to the effect of those commas at the end of lines 1 and 6. Then read it again as if those commas were omitted, noting the difference. Discuss your observations with another student.

> Coming suddenly to the sea in my twenty-eighth year,
> to the mother of all things that breathe, of mussels and whales,
> I could not see anything but sand at first
> and burning bits of mother-of-pearl.
> But this was the sea, terrible as a torch
> which the winter sun had lit,
> flaming in the blue and salt sea-air
> under my twenty-eight year infant eyes.
>
> — LOUIS DUDEK, "Coming Suddenly to the Sea"

Taking inventories: commas

Study the way Alice Walker uses commas in the following description of a scene from her childhood. Write a paragraph about some scene from your life, perhaps beginning as she has: "It is a _____ day in _____." Try imitating the structure of her second sentence, using commas as she does. Then examine your own use of commas: read your paragraph aloud, listening for the rhythm of your description.

> It is a bright summer day in 1947. My father, a fat, funny man with beautiful eyes and a subversive wit, is trying to decide which of his eight children he will take with him to the country fair. My mother, of course, will not go. She is knocked out from getting most of us ready: I hold my neck stiff against the pressure of her knuckles as she hastily completes the braiding and then beribboning of my hair ... Whirling happily in my starchy frock, showing off my biscuit-polished patent-leather shoes and lavender socks, tossing my head in a way that makes my ribbons bounce, I stand, hands on hips, before my father. "Take me, Daddy," I say with assurance; "I'm the prettiest!"
>
> — ALICE WALKER, *In Search of Our Mothers' Gardens*

35

Using Semicolons

In classical Greek, groups of words comparable to what we call sentences were set off and called *colons*. A semicolon, therefore, is literally half a colon, or half a sentence divided by the punctuation mark we call a **semicolon**. Semicolons have the effect of creating a pause stronger than that of a comma but not as strong as the full pause of a period. Their primary uses are to link coordinate independent clauses and to separate items in a series.

Using semicolons to link independent clauses

You can join independent clauses in several ways: with a comma and a coordinating conjunction (see 34b), with a colon (see 39d), with a dash (see 39c), or with a semicolon. Semicolons provide writers with subtle ways of signalling closely related clauses: the second clause often restates an idea expressed in the first; it sometimes exemplifies or presents a contrast to the first. As a writer, you must choose when and where to use semicolons to signal such relationships. Note, for instance, the way semicolons are used in the following examples:

> A voice is a gift; it should be cherished and used, to utter fully human speech if possible.
>
> — MARGARET ATWOOD, "The Writer's Responsibility"

> The power of science for good and evil has troubled other minds than ours. We are not fumbling here with a new dilemma; our subject and our fears are as old as the tool-making civilizations.
>
> — JACOB BRONOWSKI, "The Creative Mind"

In the first sentence, Atwood uses a semicolon to lead to a clause that elaborates on the statement made in the first clause. She might have joined the two clauses with the coordinating conjunction *and*, but such a link would be somewhat misleading, for *and* tells readers to expect more information, not an elaboration. She might also have used a period to separate the two clauses into two sentences, but then the two ideas would not be so clearly linked. In the second example, the semicolon links two contrasting clauses; the logical connection between the two clauses is far more subtle and more immediate than it would be had Bronowski instead used the coordinating conjunction *for*.

The sentences above are compound sentences containing only two independent clauses, but semicolons can also join independent clauses in compound-complex sentences and in compound sentences containing more than two independent clauses.

> The Good Souls will, doubtless, gain their reward in Heaven; on this earth, certainly, theirs is what is technically known as a rough deal.

> On Mother's Day, Good Souls conscientiously wear carnations; on St. Patrick's Day, they faithfully don boutonnieres of shamrocks; on Columbus Day, they carefully pin on miniature Italian flags.

> — DOROTHY PARKER, "Good Souls"

A semicolon can also be used to link independent clauses joined by conjunctive adverbs like *therefore, however*, and *indeed* or transitional expressions like *in fact, in addition*, or *for example*. (See 14b7 and 6c5 for lists of conjunctive adverbs and transitional expressions.)

> The West German economy recovered quickly from the devastation of World War II; indeed, the recovery was labelled the "economic miracle."

Note that conjunctive adverbs can change position in a sentence:

> Fine diamonds are colourless; some, however, have a yellowish tint.

> Fine diamonds are colourless; some have a yellowish tint, however.

If two independent clauses joined by a coordinating conjunction contain commas, use a semicolon instead of a comma before the conjunction. The semicolon makes such a sentence easier to read.

> Until quite recently, however, all were voices crying in the wilderness; for few Canadians were interested enough in their speech to undertake the gigantic task of finding out about it.

> — WALTER S. AVIS, "Canadian Spoken Here"

Exercise 35.1

Revise each of the following sentences by adding a semicolon to link independent clauses.

EXAMPLE

The exam begins in two hours please be on time.

The exam begins in two hours; please be on time.

1. If you are preoccupied, your game will suffer an opportunity for a relaxing afternoon will turn into a frustrating experience.

2. City life offers many advantages, however, in many ways, life in a small town is much more pleasant.

3. *Newspeak* greatly reduced people's vocabulary they could no longer understand philosophical and scientific works.

4. Physical education forms an important part of a school's program nevertheless, few students and instructors clearly recognize its value.

5. Physical education provides students with exercise moreover, games and sports provide a chance for them to mingle outside of the classroom.

6. Voltaire was concerned about the political implications of his scepticism he warned his friends not to discuss atheism in front of the servants.

7. Oil, electricity, and solar power are popular sources of energy for heating homes in Ontario the most popular, however, is natural gas.

8. My high school was excessively competitive virtually everyone went on to university, many to the top schools in the country.

9. Chaim was once notorious for his flashy clothes today, however, he is more conservative.

10. Propaganda is defined as the spread of ideas to further a cause therefore, propaganda and advertisement are synonymous terms.

Using semicolons to separate items in a series

Ordinarily, commas separate items in a series (see 34d). But when the items themselves contain commas or other punctuation, using semicolons will make the sentence clearer and easier to read.

There is, too, another point of view about life on the family farm which, since it comes from ex-farm people themselves, can't be ignored or brushed away. For these people the good memories are by far outweighed by the bad: the unrelenting, unbelievably hard physical labor; the continual poverty; the struggle to acquire amenities of living that urban people took for granted— all-weather roads, telephones, electricity and the labor-saving devices like washing machines that come with it; the lack of freedom in that wherever there was livestock it was impossible ever to leave the farm for more than 12 hours at a time, year after year, and there were no days off; the threadbareness of lives lived without food for the soul—without music or art or poetry or the theater; the stifling of dreams and ambitions that had nothing to do with farming; the omnipresent, eternal worry about money and the threat of foreclosure.

                                          – SHARON BUTALA, "Time, Space and Light"

Note that a semicolon never introduces a series (see 35d).

Exercise 35.2

Using one of the example sentences in 35a or 35b as a model, write a sentence of your own that uses semicolons to separate items in a complex series.

35c

Checking for overused semicolons

If semicolons are used too often, they distract readers in the same way unnecessary repetition does, by calling attention to themselves instead of to what the writer is saying. In addition, sentence upon sentence punctuated with semicolons will sound monotonous and jerky.

OVERUSED   Like many people in public life, he spoke with confidence; perhaps he even spoke with arrogance; yet I noted a certain anxiety; it touched and puzzled me; he seemed too eager to demonstrate his control of a situation and his command of the necessary data.

REVISED   Like many people in public life, he spoke with confidence, perhaps even with arrogance; yet I noted a certain anxiety that touched and puzzled me. He seemed too eager to demonstrate his control of a situation and his command of the necessary data.

Checking for misused semicolons

A comma, not a semicolon, should separate an independent clause from a dependent clause or a phrase.

MISUSED   For centuries, the Inuit of Labrador maintained their way of life; which included hunting, fishing, and trapping.

REVISED   For centuries, the Inuit of Labrador maintained their way of life, which included hunting, fishing, and trapping.

A colon, not a semicolon, should introduce a series.

MISUSED   The tour includes visits to the following art museums; the Prado, in Madrid; the Louvre, in Paris; and the Rijksmuseum, in Amsterdam.

REVISED   The tour includes visits to the following art museums: the Prado, in Madrid; the Louvre, in Paris; and the Rijksmuseum, in Amsterdam.

35e

Using semicolons with quotation marks

Ordinarily, a semicolon goes *outside* closing quotation marks.

Jackson's most famous story is "The Lottery"; it is a horrifying allegory about the power of tradition and the search for scapegoats.

Exercise 35.3

In the reading you are currently doing, find two passages that use semicolons particularly effectively. Then use them as models for sentences of your own.

Reading with an eye for semicolons

In the following paragraph, Annie Dillard describes a solar eclipse in elaborate detail, using semicolons to separate each part of her description. Read the paragraph with attention to the use of semicolons. What different effect would the paragraph have if Dillard had used periods instead of semicolons? Imagine also if she had used commas and coordinating conjunctions. What is the effect of all the semicolons?

> You see the wide world swaddled in darkness; you see a vast breadth of hilly land, and an enormous, distant, blackened valley; you see towns' lights, a river's path, and blurred portions of your hat and scarf; you see your husband's face looking like an early black-and-white film; and you see a sprawl of black sky and blue sky together, with unfamiliar stars in it, some barely visible bands of cloud, and over there, a small white ring. The ring is as small as one goose in a flock of migrating geese—if you happen to notice a flock of migrating geese. It is one 360th part of the visible sky. The sun we see is less than half the diameter of a dime held at arm's length.
>
> — ANNIE DILLARD, "Solar Eclipse"

Taking inventory: semicolons

Think of something you might take five or ten minutes to observe—a football game, a brewing storm, an ant awkwardly carrying a crumb—and write a paragraph describing your observations point by point and using semicolons to separate each point, as Annie Dillard does in the paragraph above. When you have finished, look at the way you used semicolons. Discuss your use of semicolons with another student. Are there places where a period or a comma and a coordinating conjunction would better serve your meaning? Revise appropriately.

36

Using End Punctuation

When you end a sentence with a well-chosen period, question mark, or exclamation point, you allow your readers a certain satisfaction: they have reached the end of one unit of thought and can pause and take a mental breath before moving on to the next one. As a writer, you are most often guided by meaning in your choice of end punctuation. Sometimes, however, you can use end punctuation for special effect. Look, for instance, at the way end punctuation guides readers in the following three sentences:

Am I tired.

Am I tired?

Am I tired!

In these brief examples, the end punctuation tells us how to read each sentence: the first one as a dry, matter-of-fact statement; the second as a puzzled or perhaps ironic query; the last as a note of exasperation. This chapter will explain how you can use these three kinds of end punctuation.

Using periods

Use a period to close sentences that make statements or give mild commands.

> The two cyclists ride slowly across Beach Avenue, drinking popcorn from their bags.
>
> – GEORGE PAYERLE, *Unknown Soldier*

> Never use a foreign phrase, a scientific word or a jargon word if you can think of an everyday English equivalent.
>
> – GEORGE ORWELL, "Politics and the English Language"

A period also closes indirect questions, which report rather than ask questions.

> I asked how old the child was.
>
> We all wonder who will win the election.
>
> Many parents ask if autism is an inherited disorder.

Periods are also used with most abbreviations:

Mr.	A.M./a.m.	B.C.	Dr.	D.D.S.
Ms.	P.M./p.m.	A.D.	Ph.D.	R.N.
Mrs.	Jr.	ibid.	M.D.	M. Ed.

Note: Ms. is not actually an abbreviation, but it is used with a period for consistency with other titles.

Some abbreviations do not require periods. Among them are the capital-letter abbreviations of province and territory names used with postal codes, such as SK and NF (although note that the traditional abbreviations of province names such as Sask. or Nfld. do call for periods); abbreviations of familiar businesses, organizations, and government agencies (*CBC, YWCA, RCMP*); and groups of initials that are pronounced as words (*CIDA, CUPE, UNICEF*).

If you are not sure whether a particular abbreviation should include periods, check the term in a dictionary. (See Chapter 41 for more information about abbreviations.)

Using question marks

A question mark closes sentences that ask direct questions.

> If women's professional sports can thrive in Europe, why not in Canada?
>
> What, then, is conveyed about science and technology in the press?
>
> — DOROTHY NELKIN, *Selling Science*

Question marks do not close *indirect* questions, which report rather than ask questions. Indirect questions close with a period (see 36a).

Do not use a comma or a period after a question mark that ends a direct quotation.

> "What do I do now?" my mind kept repeating.

My mind kept repeating, "What do I do now?"

Polite requests phrased as questions can be followed by periods rather than question marks.

Would you please close the door.

Question marks appear between questions in a series even when the questions do not form separate sentences:

I often confronted a dilemma: should I go to practice? finish my homework? spend time with my friends?

A question mark in parentheses can be used to indicate that a writer is unsure about a date, figure, or word.

The house has a total of 465 square metres (?).

Quintilian died in A.D. 95 (?).

The meeting is on Oleonga (?) Street.

Using exclamation points

Exclamation points close sentences that show surprise or strong emotion: emphatic statements, interjections, and emphatic commands.

Look out!

Help!

When times are bad they'll be back. I remember the Depression. Oh, boy!
— MORDECAI RICHLER, "My Father's Life"

Use exclamation points very sparingly because they can distract your readers by suggesting an exaggerated sense of urgency. Do not, for instance, use exclamation points with mild interjections or to suggest sarcasm or criticism. In general, try to create emphasis through diction (see Chapter 30) and sentence structure (see 25a) rather than exclamation points.

Do not use a comma or a period after an exclamation mark that ends a direct quotation.

"We shall next be told," exclaims Seneca, "that the first shoemaker was a philosopher!"
— THOMAS BABINGTON MACAULAY, "Francis Bacon"

Reading with an eye for end punctuation

Read the following passage and consider the author's use of end punctuation. Then read it again, and experiment with changing some of the end punctuation. What would be the effect of deleting the exclamation point from the quote by Cicero? What would be the effect of changing Cicero's question to a statement? Discuss your observations with another student.

> To be admired and praised, especially by the young, is an autumnal pleasure enjoyed by the lucky ones (who are not always the most deserving). "What is more charming," Cicero observes in his famous essay *De Senectute*, "than old age surrounded by the enthusiasm of youth! ... Attentions which seem trivial and conventional are marks of honor—the morning call, being sought after, precedence, having people rise for you, being escorted to and from the forum ... What pleasures of the body can be compared to the pre-rogatives of influence?" But there are also pleasures of the body, or the mind, that are enjoyed by a great number of older persons.
>
> – MALCOLM COWLEY, *The View from 80*

Taking inventory: end punctuation

Look through a draft you have written recently, noting end punctuation carefully. How many of your sentences end with periods? How many with question marks? Have you used any exclamation points, and if so, are they actually called for? Then read through the essay again, seeing if you can find any sentences that might be better phrased as questions. If you find that all or almost all of your sentences end with periods, see if changing one or more to questions or exclamations proves effective. If you keep a writing log, you might copy some of this work into it for future study.

37

Using Apostrophes

As a mark of the possessive case, the punctuation mark we call the apostrophe has an interesting history. In Old English, the endings of nouns changed depending on their grammatical function—a noun used as a subject, for example, had a different ending from the same noun used as a direct object. By the 14th century, Middle English had dropped most of this complicated system except for possessive and plural endings: *Haroldes* (or *Haroldis* or *Haroldys*) *sword* was still used to mean "the sword of Harold." Then, in the 16th century, scholars concluded that the ending *-es* and its variant forms were actually contractions of *his*. Believing that *Haroldes sword* meant "Harold his sword," they began using an apostrophe instead of the *e*: *Harold's sword*.

Even though this theory was later discredited, the possessive ending retained the apostrophe because it was a useful way to distinguish between possessive and plural forms in writing. Today, we use the apostrophe primarily to signal possessive case, contraction and other omissions of words and letters, and certain plural forms. This chapter presents the conventions governing its use.

Using apostrophes to signal possessive case

The possessive case denotes ownership or possession of one thing by another (see Chapter 15). The apostrophe is used to form the possessive case of nouns and indefinite pronouns—*Helena's report, nobody's fault.*

1. Forming the possessive case of singular nouns and indefinite pronouns

Add an apostrophe and *-s* to form the possessive of most singular nouns and indefinite pronouns, including those singular nouns that end in -s.

> His *coach's* advice helped Antonio win the race.
>
> *Stephen Leacock's* short stories tell about the lives of Canadians with humour and wit.
>
> The reading list included *Keats's* poem.
>
> *Anyone's* guess is as good as mine.

Apostrophes are *not* used with the possessive forms of *personal* pronouns: *yours, his, hers, its, ours, theirs.*

2. Forming the possessive case of plural nouns

For plural nouns not ending in -s, add an apostrophe and -s as with singular nouns.

> The *women's* caucus will include representatives from ten cities.
>
> The *children's* first Christmas was spent in Wales.

For plural nouns ending in -s, add only the apostrophe.

> The *clowns'* costumes were bright green and orange.
>
> *Fifty dollars'* worth of groceries filled only two shopping bags.

3. Forming the possessive case of compound words

For compound words, make the last word in the group possessive.

> The *Member of Parliament's* speech was televised.
>
> Her *daughter-in-law's* birthday falls in July.
>
> His *in-laws'* disapproval dampened his enthusiasm for the new house.

4. Forming the possessive case with two or more nouns

To signal individual possession by two or more owners, make each noun possessive.

> There are great differences between my *mother's* and my *father's* tastes.

To signal joint possession, make only the last noun possessive.

> *Wayne and Shuster's* entertainment career spanned more than forty years.

37b

Using apostrophes to signal contractions and other omissions

Contractions are combinations of two words that are formed by leaving out certain letters, which are indicated by apostrophes. Note the use of apostrophe in the following commonly contracted forms:

it is	it's	would not	wouldn't
was not	wasn't	do not	don't
I am	I'm	does not	doesn't
he is, he has	he's	will not	won't
you will	you'll	let us	let's
I would	I'd	who is, who has	who's
he would	he'd	cannot	can't

Contractions are common in conversation and informal writing. Most academic work, however, calls for greater formality. Check with your instructor about the appropriateness of contractions in your formal writing.

Do not confuse the possessive pronoun *its* with the contraction *it's*. *Its* is the possessive form of *it*. *It's* is a contraction for *it is*.

This disease is unusual; *its* symptoms vary from person to person.

It's a difficult disease to diagnose.

(See 33b for other commonly confused pairs of possessive pronouns and contractions—*their/they're, whose/who's,* and *your/you're.*)

An apostrophe is also used to signal omission of letters or numbers in other common phrases:

ten of the clock	rock and roll	class of 1989
ten o'clock	rock 'n' roll	class of '89

In addition, writers can use an apostrophe to signal omitted letters in approximating the sound of spoken English or some specific dialect of spoken English. Note the way Mark Twain uses the apostrophe to form contractions in the following passage, in which Huckleberry Finn tells Jim about King Henry the Eighth:

S'pose people left money laying around where he was—what did he do? He collared it. S'pose he contracted to do a thing, and you paid him, and didn't set down there and see that he done it—what did he do? He always done the other thing. S'pose he opened his mouth—what then? If he didn't shut it up powerful quick he'd lose a lie every time. That's the kind of a bug Henry was; and if we'd 'a' had him along 'stead of our Kings he'd 'a' fooled that town a heap worse than ours done.

> – MARK TWAIN, *The Adventures of Huckleberry Finn*

Exercise 37.1

Go through the Twain passage in 37b, writing out the full form in place of each contraction. Then read the two versions aloud, and note how much more the one with contractions sounds like spoken English.

37c

Using apostrophes to form the plural of numbers, letters, symbols, and words used as terms

An apostrophe and -s are usually used to form the plural of numbers, letters, symbols, and words referred to as terms.

> Several Cessna *150*'s sat on the ground.
>
> The gymnasts need *8*'s and *9*'s to qualify for the finals.
>
> Ideally, all swimmers should know the *ABC*'s of lifesaving.
>
> The computer prints *e*'s whenever there is an error in the program.
>
> I marked special passages with a series of three ***'s.
>
> The five *Shakespeare*'s in the essay were spelled five different ways.

Note that numbers, letters, and words referred to as terms are usually italicized; but the plural ending is not, as in the examples above.

Like some other plurals, the plural of years can be written with or without the apostrophe (*1990*'s or *1990s*). Whichever style you follow, be consistent.

Taking inventory: apostrophes

As a tool for presenting contractions and omitted letters, apostrophes play a larger role in informal writing than in formal writing. One thing that many students need to learn is to write with few or no contractions, a task that requires some effort because we all use contractions in conversation. To get an idea of the difference between spoken and written language, try transcribing a "paragraph" or so of your own spoken words. Make a point of using apostrophes whenever you use a contraction or otherwise omit a letter. Look over your paragraph to see how many apostrophes you used, and then revise the piece to make it more formal, eliminating all or most apostrophes.

38 Using Quotation Marks

"By necessity, by proclivity,—and by delight, we all quote," wrote Ralph Waldo Emerson. Quotation marks, which tell readers that certain words were spoken or written by someone other than the writer, have been a convention of written English since before the time of the printing press. As printing techniques evolved and became standardized, quotation marks came to signal not only direct quotations but also certain titles, definitions, and words used ironically or invented by the writer. This chapter presents the conventions governing their use.

Using quotation marks to signal direct quotation

In written North American English, double quotation marks signal a direct quotation.

> "Imagery," Laurence Perrine states, "may be defined as the representation through language of sense experience."
>
> He smiled and said, "Son, this is one incident that I will never forget."

Single quotation marks enclose a quotation within a quotation. Open and close the passage your are quoting with double quotation marks, and change any quotation marks that appear *within* the quotation to single quotation marks.

> In "The Uses of the Blues," James Baldwin says, "The title 'The Uses of the Blues' does not refer to music; I don't know anything about music."

Do not use quotation marks for *indirect* discourse, which does not quote the speaker's or writer's exact words.

The father smiled and said that he would never forget the incident.

1. Quoting longer passages

If the passage you wish to quote exceeds four typewritten or handwritten lines, set it off from the rest of the text by starting it on a new line and indenting it ten spaces from the left margin. Double-space above and below the quotation, and double-space the quotation itself. This format, known as **block quotation**, does not require quotation marks.

> Michael Asch identifies the Dene people as
>
> > an aboriginal nation whose homeland encompasses an area of over 460,000 square miles in Western Canada's sub-Arctic and Arctic regions. The term Dene itself means "people" in a number of their own languages, and is used extensively today as a term of self-designation by members of the nation. The nation is made up of a large number of regional groupings, some of whom speak different but often mutually understandable languages.
> >
> > – MICHAEL ASCH, "Contemporary Native Life: Images and Realities"

2. Quoting poetry

The same general rules apply to quoting poetry as to quoting prose. If the quotation is brief (fewer than four lines), include it within your text, enclosed in double quotation marks. Separate the lines of the poem with slashes, each preceded and followed by a space.

> Writing about the "Birth of Sound," Michael Ondaatje recalls, "At night the most private of a dog's long body groan. / It comes with his last stretch / in the dark corridor outside our room."

If the poetic quotation is longer, set it off from the text with double spacing, and indent each line ten spaces from the left margin.

> The duke in Robert Browning's "My Last Duchess" is clearly a jealous, vain person, whose arrogance is illustrated through his statement:
>
> > She thanked men—good! but thanked
> > Somehow—I know not how—as if she ranked
> > My gift of a nine-hundred-years-old name
> > With anybody's gift.

When you quote poetry, take care to follow the indentation, spacing, capitalization, punctuation, and other features of the original passage.

Using quotation marks to signal dialogue

When you write dialogue or quote a conversation, enclose the words of each speaker in quotation marks, and mark each shift in speaker by beginning a new paragraph, no matter how brief the quoted remark may be.

> "You are the only visitor who has come our way today," said Chapdelaine, "and I suppose you have seen no one either. I felt pretty certain you would be here this evening."
>
> "Naturally ... I would not let New Year's Day go by without paying you a visit. But, besides that, I have news to tell."
>
> "News?"
>
> Under the questioning eyes of the household he did not raise his eyes.
>
> "By your face I am afraid you have bad news."
>
> "Yes."
>
> With a start of fear the mother half rose. "Not about the boys?"
>
>   – LOUIS HÉMON, *Maria Chapdelaine*

Beginning a new paragraph with each change in speaker helps readers follow the dialogue.

Using quotation marks to signal titles and definitions

Quotation marks are used to enclose the titles of short poems, short stories, articles, essays, songs, sections of books, and episodes of television and radio programs.

> Matthew Arnold moves from calmness to sadness in "Dover Beach." [poem]
>
> In "The Shadow of Captain Bligh" Hugh MacLennan seems to suggest that artists today cannot have any real effect on the way we live. [short story]
>
> In "Don't Pay the Language No Mind, Honey," William Grieder uses informal language effectively. [essay]
>
> A recent *Maclean's* article on athletes is called "The Riches of Sport." [article]
>
> To distract the children, we began singing "She'll Be Coming 'Round the Mountain" and "The Green Grass Grows All Around." [songs]

Throughout the chapter "Our Two Cultures," Patricia Smart uses examples from Canadian literature to highlight the history of the French and English in this country. [section of a book]

In tonight's episode, "Murder Most Foul," Jessica matches wits with a psychopath. [television episode]

Use italics rather than quotation marks for the titles of longer works, such as books and magazines (see 42a).

Definitions of words or phrases are sometimes set off with quotation marks:

The French phrase *idée fixe* means literally "fixed idea."

Oxymoronic means "self-contradictory."

38d

Using quotation marks to signal irony and coinages

One way of showing readers that you are using a word or a phrase ironically is to enclose it in quotation marks.

During that rehearsal, I really was "lucky" enough to break a leg. [The quotation marks around the word *lucky* suggest ironically that the narrator was anything but lucky, although "break a leg" is the good-luck call of the theatre.]

Quotation marks are also used to enclose words or phrases coined by the writer.

Your whole first paragraph or first page may have to be guillotined in any case after your piece is finished: it is a kind of "forebirth." [The word *forebirth* was coined by the writer.]

— JACQUES BARZUN, "A Writer's Discipline"

Exercise 38.1

Revise each of the following sentences, using quotation marks appropriately to signal titles, definitions, irony, or coinages.

1. Nursery Rhyme, a poem by Anne Wilkinson, recounts the death of a small child.

2. In Flannery O'Connor's short story Revelation, colours symbolize passion, violence, sadness, and even God.

3. The little that is known about gorillas certainly makes you want to know a great deal more, writes Alan Moorehead in an essay called A Most Forgiving Ape.

4. The fun of surgery begins before the operation ever takes place.

5. I will evaluate an article entitled The Greying of the Campuses.

6. The Dream of Little Raven, a Chippewa tale in *Indian Legends of Canada*, reflects on a child's experience of loss and grief.

7. Tolkien refers to this sudden, joyous turn as a eucatastrophe, a word he invented to mean the consolidation of the happy ending.

8. Pink Floyd's song Time depicts the impact of technology on society.

9. My dictionary defines *isolation* as the quality or state of being alone.

10. This review will examine a TV episode entitled 48 Hours on Gang Street.

38e

Checking for misused quotation marks

Use quotation marks only when there is a reason for them; do not use them just to emphasize particular words or phrases, as in the following sentence:

MISUSED   "Some of the boys," not including Travis, of course, would take "stingers" off wasps and bees and then put the insects "down" others' shirts.

REVISED   Some of the boys, not including Travis, of course, would take stingers off wasps and bees and then put the insects down others' shirts.

Do not use quotation marks around slang or colloquial language that you think is inappropriate for formal register (see 30b3); they create the impression that you are apologizing for using such language. In general, try to express your ideas in formal language. If you have a good reason to use a slang or colloquial term, use it without quotation marks.

MISUSED   After their thirty-five kilometre hike, the campers were "wiped out" and ready to "hit the sack."

REVISED   After their thirty-five kilometre hike, the campers were exhausted and ready to go to bed.

Even though you enclose many titles in quotation marks to refer to them in writing, do not use them with the titles of your own essays.

Exercise 38.2

According to Lewis Thomas, "The most objectionable misuse of quotation marks, but one which illustrates the dangers of misuse in ordinary prose, is seen in advertising." What is the effect of quotation marks in the following advertisements?

On a movie marquee: Coming "Attractions"

At a supermarket: "Fresh" Asparagus

Using quotation marks with other punctuation

1. Periods and commas go inside quotation marks.

"I've been female all my life," she said, "but old only recently."

2. Colons and semicolons go outside quotation marks.

Everything is dark, and "a visionary light settles in her eyes"; this vision, this light, is her salvation.

I felt only one emotion after finishing "Eveline": pity.

3. Question marks, exclamation points, and dashes go inside quotation marks if they are part of the quotation.

PART OF QUOTATION

Gently shake the injured person while asking, "Are you all right?"

"Jump!" one of the firefighters shouted.

"Watch out—watch out for—" Marie began nervously.

NOT PART OF QUOTATION

Is Hawthorne expressing his subconscious thoughts in "My Kinsman, Major Molineux"?

What a shame that Terry Fox was not able to complete his "Marathon of Hope"!

4. Footnote numbers go outside quotation marks.

Tragedy is defined by Aristotle as "an imitation of an action that is serious and of a certain magnitude."[1]

For more information on footnotes and for examples of quotation marks used with bibliographical references, see Chapter 13.

Reading with an eye for quotation marks

Read the following passage from an essay by Joan Didion about the painter Georgia O'Keeffe, paying particular attention to the use of quotation marks. What effect is created by Didion's use of quotation marks around the words *Hardness, crustiness,* and *crusty*? How do the quotations by O'Keeffe help to support Didion's description of her?

> "Hardness" has not been in our century a quality much admired in women, nor in the past twenty years has it even been in official favor for men. When hardness surfaces in the very old we tend to transform it into "crustiness" or eccentricity, some tonic pepperiness to be indulged at a distance. On the evidence of her work and what she has said about it, Georgia O'Keeffe is neither "crusty" nor eccentric. She is simply hard, a straight shooter, a woman clean of received wisdom and open to what she sees. This is a woman who could early on dismiss most of her contemporaries as "dreamy," and would later single out one she liked as "a very poor painter." (And then add, apparently by way of softening the judgment: "I guess he wasn't a painter at all. He had no courage and I believe that to create one's own world in any of the arts takes courage.") This is a woman who in 1939 could advise her admirers that they were missing her point, that their appreciation of her famous flowers was merely sentimental. "When I paint a red hill," she observed coolly in the catalogue for an exhibition that year, "you say it is too bad that I don't always paint flowers. A flower touches almost everyone's heart. A red hill doesn't touch everyone's heart."
>
> – JOAN DIDION, "Georgia O'Keeffe"

Taking inventory: quotation marks

Choose a topic that is currently of interest to students on your campus, and interview one of your friends about it for ten or fifteen minutes. On the basis of your notes from the interview, write two or three paragraphs about your friend's views on the topic, using as many direct quotations as possible. Then look at what you have written to see how closely you followed the conventions for quotation marks that have been explained in this chapter. Discuss your observations with another student.

39

Using Other Punctuation Marks

Parentheses, brackets, dashes, colons, slashes, and ellipses are marks that allow writers to punctuate sentences so that readers can best understand their meaning. Following is an excerpt that demonstrates the use of some of these punctuation marks.

> The postmodern seems to worry people … even people who rather enjoy it. For instance, they worry about the digital sampling music computer, the most postmodern musical instrument yet invented, because it can manipulate and reproduce any sound it has encoded. In so doing—and here is where people really get worried—the "sampler" encodes the tried and true (read: romantic, capitalist) distinction between original and copy, just as the modernist collage form in the visual arts had done before it.
>
> — LINDA HUTCHEON, "Canada's 'Post': Sampling Today's Fiction"

Here Hutcheon uses ellipses, parentheses, and dashes to create rhythm and build momentum in her sentences. This chapter will guide you in deciding when you can use such marks of punctuation to signal relationships among sentence parts, to create particular rhythms, and to help readers follow your thoughts.

Using parentheses

Parentheses can be used to add information that is of minor or secondary importance—information that clarifies, comments on, or illustrates what precedes it. Parentheses are also used around numbers or letters that precede items in a list.

Adding information

When the bear peeks through where the window used to be (the heavy ice pane having melted and fallen in), the mother of the blind boy is telling him to shoot it with a bow and arrow.

– AISA QUPIQRUALUK, "Lumaaq"

For years now, I have resisted the pressure to buy a personal computer. I am not mesmerized by technology, nor am I a technophobe (as proof, I have two VCRs and love my stereo system).

– DAVID SUZUKI, "Resisting the Revolution"

Lanoue is a Bren-gunner with the first battalion of *Le Régiment du Saint-Laurent*. (The author uses fictitious regimental names as well as real ones.)

– GILBERT DROLET, "Loin de toi et du pays"

As the second and third examples above demonstrate, a period may be placed either inside or outside a closing parenthesis, depending on whether the material inside the parentheses is a complete sentence. A comma, on the other hand, is always placed *outside* a closing parenthesis (and never before an opening one).

Topics include sales of real estate (Chapter 8), sales of goods (Chapters 8 to 10), loans and security documents (Chapter 11), and guarantees (Chapter 12).

– HAROLD STERLING, *Business Law for Business People*

If the material in parentheses is a question or an exclamation, use a question mark or exclamation mark inside the closing parenthesis.

Before this chat is over, he will learn that Canadians use *hood* for his *bonnet, muffler* for *silencer, bumper* for *fender,* and (egad, sir!) *fender* for *wing.*

– WALTER S. AVIS, "Canadian Spoken Here"

As a writer, you can punctuate supplemental information in three ways: with commas, with parentheses, or with dashes. The distinction is partially one of how interruptive the information is and partially one of personal style. In general, use commas when the material is least interruptive (see 34c and e), parentheses when it is more interruptive, and dashes when it is the most interruptive (see 39c). One other consideration is whether the material to be added ends in an exclamation point or question mark (as does the preceding Avis example); if so, you can use *only* parentheses or dashes.

Use parentheses judiciously, because they break up the flow of a sentence or passage, forcing readers to hold the original train of thought in their minds while considering a secondary one. To decide whether to use parentheses, read the sentence or passage aloud, or have someone read it aloud to you. Decide whether the parentheses make it harder to follow; if so, try to revise to eliminate them.

Enclosing numbers or letters in a list

Three topics are discussed: (1) fetal brain implants, (2) sex determination before conception, and (3) genetic profiles of test-tube babies.

– FRED D. WHITE, Science and the Human Spirit

According to Hiller, the British conquest had three major impacts on Quebec society: (1) it created resentments and antagonisms on the part of Quebec toward the British, which have never been obliterated; (2) it resulted in English control over Quebec's economic and political institutions; and (3) it impelled French Canadians to turn to the Church in order to insulate themselves from the institutions of the British, and at the same time preserve and maintain their own cultural and social institutions.

– SUBHAS RAMCHARAN, Social Problems & Issues:
A Canadian Perspective

Using brackets

Brackets are used to set off parenthetical elements in material within parentheses and set off explanatory words or comments inserted into a quotation. If your typewriter does not include keys for brackets, draw them in by hand.

Setting off material within parentheses

Eventually the investigation had to examine the major agencies (including the previously sacrosanct American Central Intelligence Agency [CIA]) that were conducting covert operations.

Adding material to quotations

In the following sentence, the bracketed word replaces the word *he* in the original quotation.

Turner writes, "[Hawthorne] is known as Oberon and has shown himself closely akin to the Oberon in 'The Devil in Manuscript.'"

In the following passage, the bracketed material summarizes a longer passage of the original that has not been quoted.

Meanwhile, James Purdie, former art critic for *The Globe and Mail*, has announced, "Alex Colville is dangerously close to God. He has made life supreme. [In his work] life has triumphed over time and that must mean that somewhere, somehow, it will find a way to triumph over death."

— HARRY BRUCE, "'The Most Important Realist Painter of the Western World'"

In the quotation in the following sentence, the artist Gauguin's name is misspelled. The bracketed word *sic*, which means "thus," tells readers that the person being quoted made the mistake—not the writer.

One admirer wrote, "She was the most striking woman I'd ever seen—a sort of wonderful combination of Mia Farrow and one of Gaugin's [sic] Polynesian nymphs."

Using dashes

Pairs of dashes allow you to interpret the normal word order of a sentence to insert additional explanation or information. Compared with parentheses or commas, dashes bring special emphasis to the added material.

Interrupting the normal word order

On the 16th of August, about a month from now, I will have—if I live—my sixtieth birthday.

— TIMOTHY FINDLEY, *The Telling of Lies*

Emphasizing parenthetical or explanatory elements

I feel that if you remove the initial gut response from reading—the delight or excitement or simply the enjoyment of being told a story—and try to concentrate on the meaning or the shape or the "message" first, you might as well give up.

— MARGARET ATWOOD, *Survival*

Single dashes are used to mark a sudden shift in tone, to introduce a summary or explanation of what has come before, or to indicate hesitation in speech.

Emphasizing a sudden change in tone

When they intend to change the individual, arbitrarily deciding to make him the same as everyone else—then I claim the right to be different.
— EDGAR ROUSSEL, "Letter from Prison"

If you are truly serious about preparing your child for the future, don't teach him to subtract—teach him to deduct.
— FRAN LEBOWITZ, "Parental Guidance"

Introducing a summary or explanation

As it turned out, the electron, rather than being a charged, solid entity, was a cross between pure energy and matter—a matter-wave, or quantum of radiation.
— FRED D. WHITE, Science and the Human Spirit

Indicating hesitation or awkwardness in speech

As the officer approached the car, the driver stammered, "What—what have I done?"

The difference between a single dash and a colon is a subtle one. In general, dashes are much less formal than colons. In fact, you should use dashes sparingly, if at all, in most of your academic writing.

Using colons

Colons are used to introduce a sentence that is an explanation, example, or appositive of what precedes it; to introduce a series, list, or quotation; and to separate elements such as hours, minutes, and seconds; biblical chapter numbers; titles and subtitles; and parts of bibliographical references.

Introducing an explanation, example, or appositive

And we are all on our own when it comes to keeping those lines open to ourselves: your notebook will never help me, nor mine you.
— JOAN DIDION, "On Keeping a Notebook"

Three red bulls—sluggish bestial creatures with white faces and morose bloodshot eyes—made me long to get away from the village. But I could not: there was no boat.

— EMILY CARR, *Klee Wyck*

Introducing a series, list, or quotation

The patient package insert issue is of interest to three professional groups: physicians, pharmacists, and lawyers.

In "The Ecstasy of Rita Joe," Ryga uses understatement in his poignant closing line to capture the painful experience of Rita Joe in the city: "the cement made her feet hurt."

Separating elements according to standard use

HOURS, MINUTES, AND SECONDS

4:59 p.m.   2:15:06

BIBLICAL CHAPTERS AND VERSES

Deuteronomy 17:2–7

I Chronicles 3:3–5

TITLES AND SUBTITLES

"Planetary Rhetoric: Public Discourse on the Environment"

Critical Discourse: A Survival of Literary Theorists

PARTS OF BIBLIOGRAPHICAL REFERENCES

Scarborough: Nelson Canada [The colon separates the place of publication from the publisher.]

Maclean's, February 26, 1994: 24 [The colon separates the year of publication from the page number.]

Checking for incorrect colons

Except when it is used to separate the standard elements discussed in the preceding section, a colon should be used only at the end of an independent clause.

Do not put a colon between verb and object or complement, or between preposition and object. Avoid putting colons after such expressions as *such as, especially*, or *including*.

MISUSED	Some of these effects include: reddening of the eyes, an increase in heartbeat, dryness of the mouth, and irritation of the throat.
REVISED	Some of these effects include reddening of the eyes, an increase in heartbeat, dryness of the mouth, and irritation of the throat.
MISUSED	The artificial heart can cause complications, especially: blood clots, brain seizures, and strokes.
REVISED	The artificial heart can cause complications, especially blood clots, brain seizures, and strokes.
MISUSED	Every year, in the name of science, thousands of animals are exposed to: severe pain, physical and behavioural stress, extreme heat and cold, electric shock, starvation, and mutilation.
REVISED	Every year, in the name of science, thousands of animals are exposed to severe pain, physical and behavioural stress, extreme heat and cold, electric shock, starvation, and mutilation.
MISUSED	In poetry, additional power may come from devices such as: simile, metaphor, and alliteration.
REVISED	In poetry, additional power may come from devices such as simile, metaphor, and alliteration.

Using slashes

Slashes are used to mark line divisions in poetry quoted within text (see 38a2), to separate two alternative terms, and to separate the parts of fractions. When used to separate lines of poetry, the slash should be surrounded by space.

Marking line divisions in poetry

In "Sonnet 29," the persona states, "For thy sweet love rememb'red such wealth brings, / That then I scorn to change my state with kings."

Separating alternatives

Bunyan's famous work is the age-old tale of the sinner/pilgrim's arduous journey towards salvation.

Separating parts of fractions

Over the last thirty years, the average yield of Canadian farms increased by only 2 1/2 percent.

Using ellipses

Ellipses are three equally spaced dots used to indicate that something has been omitted form a quoted passage. They can also be used to signal hesitation, in the same way that a dash can (see 39c).

Indicating omissions

Just as you should be very careful to use quotation marks around any material that you quote directly from a source, so you should use ellipses to indicate that you have left out part of a quotation that appears to be a complete sentence. Look at the following example:

ORIGINAL TEXT

The quasi-official division of the population into three economic classes called high-, middle-, and low-income groups rather misses the point, because as a class indicator the amount of money is not as important as the source.

– Paul Fussell, "Notes on Class"

WITH ELLIPSES

As Paul Fussell argues, "The quasi-official division of the population into three economic classes ... rather misses the point...."

In this example, the ellipses are used to indicate two different omissions—one in the middle of the sentence and one at the end of the sentence. When you omit the last part of a quoted sentence, you may add a period before the ellipses—for a total of four dots. Be sure a complete sentence comes before and after the four points. If your quotation ends with a source documentation (such as a page number, a name, or a title), follow these steps:

1. Use three ellipsis points but no period after the quotation.

2. Add the closing quotation mark, closed up to the third ellipsis point.

3. Add the source documentation in parentheses.

4. Use a period to indicate the end of the sentence.

Hawthorne writes, "My friend whom I shall call Oberon—it was a name of fancy and friendship between him and me ..." (575).

Indicating a pause or hesitation

He says there's heaps of jobs. You pick them off the trees ... like orchids.
— Mavis Gallant, "The Ice Wagon Going Down the Street"

Because of her creativity with her flowers, even my memories of poverty are seen through a screen of blooms—sunflowers, petunias, roses, dahlias, forsythia, spirea, delphiniums, verbena ... and on and on.
— Alice Walker, *In Search of Our Mothers' Gardens*

Exercise 39.1

The following sentences use the punctuation marks presented in this chapter very effectively. Read the sentences carefully; then choose one, and use it as a model for writing a sentence of your own, making sure to use the punctuation marks in the same way in your sentence.

1. It was inevitable: the scent of bitter almonds always reminded him of the fate of unrequited love.
— Gabriel Garcia Marquez, *Love in the Time of Cholera*

2. The obsession with local concerns and interests is a great obstacle to the growth of Canadian identity than either the size of the land (twenty times that of France) or the lack of population.
— Claude Juben, "A Mosaic of Provinces"

3. If the person seems nice after this many encounters, then he is to be trusted ... or is he?
— Richard Gossage and Melvin Gunton, "Peopleproofing Your Child"

4. Simigak was the chief of the Etidliajuk area—I've heard he was the tallest man in Seekooseelak—and he was in charge.
— Peter Pitseolak, "The First Religious Time"

5. My political action, or my theory—insomuch as I can be said to have one—can be expressed very simply: create counter-weights.
— Pierre Elliott Trudeau, "Checks and Balances"

Reading with an eye for punctuation

Although Emily Dickinson's poems are characteristically punctuated with dashes, the first editor of her work systematically eliminated them. Here is a brief Dickinson poem—with her original dashes restored. Read it twice, first ignoring the dashes and then using them to guide your reading. What effect does the final dash have? Finally, try composing a four-line poem that uses dashes to guide reading and meaning.

> Much Madness is divinest Sense—
> To a discerning Eye—
> Much Sense—the starkest Madness—
> 'Tis the Majority
> In this, as All, prevail—
> Assent—and you are sane—
> Demur—you're straightway dangerous—
> And handled with a Chain—
> — EMILY DICKINSON

Taking inventory: punctuation

Look through a draft you have recently written or are working on, and check your use of parentheses, brackets, dashes, colons, slashes, and ellipses. Have you followed the conventions presented in this chapter? If not, revise accordingly. Then read through the draft again, looking especially at all the parentheses and dashes. Are there too many? Check the material in parentheses to see if it could use more emphasis and thus be set off instead with dashes. Then check any material in dashes to see if it could do with less emphasis and thus be punctuated with commas or parentheses. If you keep a writing log, enter some examples of this work in your log.

Using Conventional Mechanics

Using Capitals

Using Abbreviations and Numbers

Using Italics

Using Hyphens

40

Using Capitals

AT ONE TIME, ALL LETTERS WERE WRITTEN AS CAPITALS, LIKE THIS. By the time that movable type was invented, a new system had evolved, and printers used a capital letter only for the first letter of any word they felt was particularly important. Today, the conventions of capitalization are fairly well standardized. This chapter presents those conventions.

40a

Using capitals for the first word of sentence or of a line of poetry

Capitalize the first word of sentence.

> Family photos bring great pleasure.
> May I take your picture?
> Smile, and say cheese!

If you are quoting a full sentence, set off that sentence, too, with an initial capital letter.

> Everyone was asking the question, "What will I do after I graduate?"

Capitalization of a sentence following a colon is optional.

> Gould cites the work of Darwin: The [or the] theory of natural selection incorporates the principle of evolutionary ties between all animals.

A sentence that is set off within another sentence by dashes or parentheses should not be capitalized. Note, however, that a sentence within parentheses that stands by itself *is* capitalized.

A simpler model, however, was proposed in 1514 by a Polish priest, Nicholas Copernicus. (At first, perhaps for fear of being branded a heretic by his church, Copernicus circulated his model anonymously.) His idea was that the sun was stationary at the center and that the earth and the planets moved in circular orbits around the sun.

— STEPHEN HAWKING, "Our Picture of the Universe"

The first word of each line in a poem is also usually capitalized.

Hidden in wonder and snow, or sudden with summer,
This land stares at the sun in a huge silence
Endlessly repeating something we cannot hear.
Inarticulate, arctic,
Not written on by history, empty as paper,
It leans away from the world with songs in its lakes
Older than love, and lost in the miles.

— F.R. SCOTT, "Laurentian Shield"

Some poets do *not* capitalize each line, however. When citing lines from a poem that has unconventional capitalization, copy them exactly as they appear in their original form.

My mother sends a postcard
from Tobago. I am there again,
sun in my life. I continue
to make humming noises
in my sleep.
        — CYRIL DABYDEEN, "Legends"

Using capitals for proper nouns and proper adjectives

Capitalize **proper nouns** (those naming specific persons, places, and things) and **proper adjectives** formed from them. In general, do not capitalize **common nouns** (those naming general classes of people, places, and things) unless they start a sentence. When used as part of a proper noun, however, many common nouns are capitalized.

PROPER	COMMON
Alfred Hitchcock, Hitchcockian	a director, directorial
Brazil, Brazilian	a nation
Peace Bridge	a bridge

Following are some categories of words that are commonly capitalized:

NAMES OF INDIVIDUALS

Sir Wilfrid Laurier	Moberley Luger
Bette Davis	Anthony Paré
Emma Laroque	Frederick G. Banting
Aristotelian logic	Petrarchan sonnet form

NAMES OF GEOGRAPHICAL AREAS

Asia	Pacific Ocean
Nepal	Painted Desert
St. John's	Lake Huron
the Dead Sea	St. Catherine Street

STRUCTURES AND MONUMENTS

Saddle Dome	Brock Monument
Lions Gate Bridge	CN Tower

SHIPS, TRAINS, AIRCRAFT, AND SPACECRAFT

S.S. *Titanic*	*Concorde*
Queen Elizabeth	*Pioneer II*

INSTITUTIONS AND ORGANIZATIONS

National Research Council	Kiwanis Club
University of New Brunswick	Canadian Labour Congress
Centennial School	New Democratic Party

HISTORICAL EVENTS, ERAS, AND CALENDAR ITEMS

Riel Rebellion	Saturday
Great Depression	July
Confederation	Remembrance Day

RELIGIONS AND RELIGIOUS SUBJECTS

Buddhism, Buddhists	Allah
Catholicism, Catholics	Jesus Christ
Hinduism, Hindus	God
Islam, Moslems or Muslims	the Bible
Judaism, Jews	the Koran

RACES, NATIONALITIES, AND LANGUAGES

Haitian	Portuguese
Inuit	Chinese
Slavic	Japanese
Arab	Latin

TRADE NAMES

Reeboks	Huggies
Kleenex	Levi's
Chanel	Roots

1. Using capitals for titles of individuals

Capitalize titles used before a proper name, but not those used alone or following a proper name.

Hon. Mme. Justice Bertha Wilson	Bertha Wilson, the justice
Hon. Royce Frith	Royce Frith, the senator
Professor Siân Echard	Siân Echard, the professor
Doctor Edward Davies	Edward Davies, the doctor

When they are used without a name attached, most titles are not capitalized. The only exceptions are titles of some very powerful officials—for example, many writers capitalize the term *Prime Minister* when it refers to the Prime Minister of Canada.

2. Using capitals for specific academic institutions and courses

Capitalize specific schools, departments, or courses, but not the common nouns or names of general subject areas.

University of Alberta (*but* an Alberta university)
History Department (*but* a history major)
Political Science 100 (*but* political science for nonmajors)

Using capitals for titles of works

Capitalize most words in titles of books, articles, stories, essays, plays, poems, documents, films, paintings, and musical compositions. Articles *(a, an, the)*, prepositions, conjunctions, and (often) the *to* of an infinitive are not capitalized unless they are the first or last words in a title or subtitle.

A Jest of God	"Fire and Ice"
"Revelation"	Magna Carta
"Shooting an Elephant"	*Animal Dreams*
Our Town	*The Tin Flute*

Remember to capitalize the titles of your own compositions.

Using capitals for the pronoun *I* and the interjection *O*

Always capitalize the pronoun *I* and the interjection *O*. Be careful, however, to distinguish between the interjection *O* and *oh*. *O* is an older form that is usually used for direct address in ceremonial register (see 30b4). It is always capitalized, whereas *oh* is not unless it begins a sentence.

> I took her advice, and oh, how I regretted it!
>
> Grant us peace, O Lord.

Checking for unnecessary capitals

1. With compass directions, unless the word designates a specific geographical place

> Jean-Guy headed west this year, planning to fish for salmon up at Stuart Island. Next year, he hopes to go to the North and try his luck at dog-sledding.

2. With family relationships, unless the word is used as part of the name or as a substitute for the name

My nieces, Jamie and Marianne, both are lifeguards.

We all agreed that Father had every right to be grumpy.

The train on which Uncle Charlie arrived spewed out thick black smoke, foreshadowing a disastrous visit.

3. With medical and scientific terms, except for proper nouns that are part of the term

scarlet fever	deoxyribonucleic acid
Kaposi's sarcoma	Wassermann test
insectivore	homo sapiens

Exercise 40.1

Capitalize words as needed in the following sentences.

EXAMPLE

t.s. eliot, who wrote *the waste land,* worked as an editor at faber and faber.

T.S. Eliot, who wrote *The Waste Land,* worked as an editor at Faber and Faber.

1. the town where i was raised had a war monument in the centre of main street.

2. eating at a restaurant, whether it be a fast-food, chinese, or italian place, is always a treat.

3. his car skidded right into the rear of a toyota van.

4. the council of trent was convened to draw up the catholic response to the protestant reformation.

5. In the *odyssey,* three members of odysseus's crew go ashore and lose their memories by eating the lotus plant.

6. i wondered if my new lee jeans were faded enough and if i could possibly scuff up my new nikes just a little more before i arrived for spring term.

7. in a speech accepting an award for the musical score for the film the high and the mighty, dimitri tiomkin began by thanking beethoven, brahms, wagner, and strauss.

8. in this essay i will be citing the works of vladimir nabokov, in particular his novels *pnin* and *lolita* and his story "the vane sisters."

9. the intersection of king and queen streets was mobbed on new year's eve.

10. few music lovers can resist the music of george gershwin. (*rhapsody in blue* and *porgy and bess* are two personal favourites.)

Reading with an eye for capitalization

The following poem uses capitalization in an unconventional way. Read it over a few times, at least once aloud. What effect does the capitalization have on your understanding and recitation of the poem? Why do you think the poet chose to use capitals as she did?

> A little Madness in the Spring
> Is wholesome even for the King,
> But God be with the Clown—
> Who ponders this tremendous scene—
> This whole Experiment of Green—
> As if it were his own!
> — EMILY DICKINSON

Taking inventory: capital letters

Read over something you have written recently with an eye for capitalization. Have you capitalized all proper nouns and adjectives? Have you used capitals properly with dashes and parentheses? Have you capitalized sentences following colons, and if so, have you done so consistently? If you keep a writing log, enter notes and examples of any problems you have with capital letters.

41

Using Abbreviations and Numbers

Abbreviations and numerals serve to speed up prose and to allow readers to process information most efficiently. As with other elements, there are certain conventions for using abbreviations and numerals, especially in formal or academic work. This chapter will explain these conventions to help you as a writer use abbreviations and numbers appropriately and correctly.*

ABBREVIATIONS

41a

Abbreviating personal and professional titles

When they are used before or after a name, most personal and professional titles and academic degrees are regularly abbreviated, even in academic writing.

Ms. Marika Anthony-Shaw   St. Matthew
Mr. Richard Guenette   Paul Irvin, M.D.
Dr. Nancy Carlman   Jamie Barlow Kayes, Ph.D.

---

* For rules on using abbreviations and numbers in a particular discipline, you might ask your instructor what style manual you should consult. In general, the *MLA Handbook for Writers of Research Papers* is usually followed in the humanities; the *Publication Manual of the American Psychological Association*, in the social sciences; and the *CBE Style Manual*, in the natural sciences.

Less common titles, including religious, military, academic, and government titles, may be abbreviated when they appear before a full name. If they appear before only a surname, the title should be spelled out. In academic writing, such titles should always be spelled out.

Rev. Paul Newel	the Reverend Paul Newel
Col. Oliver Wickham	Colonel Wickham
Prof. Linda Johnson	Professor Johnson

Never abbreviate personal or professional titles used alone.

MISUSED   She was a rigorous *prof.*, and we worked hard.

REVISED   She was a rigorous *professor,* and we worked hard.

Use either a title or an academic degree, but not both.

MISUSED   Dr. Jack Gray, Ph.D.

REVISED   Dr. Jack Gray

REVISED   Jack Gray, Ph.D.

Using abbreviations with numerals

The following abbreviations are always acceptable, as long as they are used with numerals.

399 B.C. ("before Christ"; follows the date)

399 B.C.E. ("before the common era"; used in lieu of B.C.)

A.D. 49 (*anno Domini*, Latin for "year of our Lord"; precedes the date)

49 C.E. ("common era"; in lieu of A.D. but follows the date)

11:15 a.m. (*ante meridiem*, Latin for "before noon")

9:00 p.m. (*post meridiem*, Latin for "after noon")

2700 r.p.m. (revolutions per minute)

212°F (Fahrenheit scale)

24°C (Celsius or Centigrade scale)

Abbreviations for some units of measurements (*km, cc, mL, cm*) are frequently used in scientific and technical writing—but again, only with a numeral (see 41d).

41c

Using acronyms and initial abbreviations

Abbreviations that can be pronounced as words are called **acronyms**: CUSO, for example, is the acronym for the Canadian University Services Overseas. **Initial abbreviations** are those pronounced as separate initials: CBC for Canadian Broadcasting Corporation, for instance. Many of the most common abbreviations of these types come from business, government, and science: IBM, SSHRC, DNA, UNICEF, AIDS.

As long as you can be sure your readers will understand them, you can use such abbreviations in much of your academic writing. You have to use them carefully and according to convention, however. If you are using a term only once or twice in a paper, you should spell it out, but when you need to use a term repeatedly, abbreviating it will serve as a convenience for you and your readers alike.

If you need to use an abbreviation your readers may not know, you can do so as long as you first "define" it for them. Spell out the full term at the first use, and give the abbreviation in parentheses. After that, you can use the abbreviation by itself.

> The Comprehensive Test Ban (CTB) Treaty was first proposed in the 1950s. For those nations signing it, the CTB would bring to a halt all nuclear weapons testing.

41d

Checking for inappropriate abbreviations

Abbreviations exist to facilitate reading and writing, but they are not appropriate in all writing contexts. The following guidelines will help you to use some common abbreviations in the writing you do for your courses.

Company names

It is acceptable to use such abbreviations as *Inc., Co.,* and *Corp.* and the ampersand symbol (&) if they are part of a company's official name. You should not, however, use these abbreviated forms in most other contexts.

> One company—Jones, Forrest & Co.—had sales of over $27 billion and a net income of just over $650 million in 1981 alone.

Reference information

Though it is conventional to abbreviate such words as *chapter* (ch.) or *page* (p.) in endnotes or source citations, it is not acceptable to do so in the body of your essay.

INAPPROPRIATE   In his preface to the 1851 *ed.* of *Twice-Told Tales*, Hawthorne states that the stories are not autobiographical.

REVISED   In his preface to the 1851 *edition* of *Twice-Told Tales*, Hawthorne states that the stories are not autobiographical.

Latin abbreviations

In general, avoid the following abbreviations except when citing sources or making parenthetical remarks.

c.f.   compare *(confer)*

e.g.   for example *(exempli gratia)*

et al.   and others *(et alii)*

etc.   and so forth *(et cetera)*

i.e.   that is *(id est)*

N.B.   note well *(nota bene)*

INAPPROPRIATE   Many firms now have policies to help working parents—e.g., flexible hours, parental leave, day care.

REVISED   Many firms now have policies to help working parents—*for example,* flexible hours, parental leave, day care.

Geographical places

Place names can be abbreviated in informal correspondence or in reference notes, but they should always be written out within sentences.

INAPPROPRIATE   Tired of life in the West, we set off for Charlottetown, *PEI.*

REVISED   Tired of life in the West, we set off for Charlottetown, *Prince Edward Island.*

One common exception is *U.S.,* which is acceptable used as an adjective, though not as a noun.

UNACCEPTABLE   As an exchange student, I spent a summer in the *U.S.*

ACCEPTABLE   The *U.S. delegation* negotiated the treaty with success.

Symbols

Symbols such as ¢ @ # % + and = should not be used in the body of a paper, though they are commonly used in graphs and tables. One common exception is the dollar sign ($), which is acceptable to use with figures.

INAPPROPRIATE Less than *50%* of those who applied were accepted.

REVISED Less than *50 percent* of those who applied were accepted.

Units of measurement

Except for scientific and technical writing, most units of measurement should not be abbreviated in the body of a paper.

INAPPROPRIATE The ball sailed 30 *m* over the left-field fence.

REVISED The ball sailed 30 *metres* over the left-field fence.

NUMBERS

Spelling out numbers of one or two words

If a number can be written as one or two words, spell it out.

The victim's screams were heard by *thirty-eight* people, none of whom called the police.

Six days later, people arrested the assailant.

41f

Using figures for numbers longer than two words

Numbers that cannot be written in one or two words should be stated in figures.

Did you know that a baseball is wrapped in 159 metres of blue-grey wool yarn and is held together by 216 red stitches?

If one of several numbers in the same sentence needs to be expressed in figures, they all should be expressed that way.

INCONSISTENT A complete audio system can range from one hundred dollars to $2500; however, a reliable system can be purchased for approximately five hundred dollars.

CONSISTENT   A complete audio system can range in cost from $100 to $2500; however, a reliable system can be purchased for approximately $500.

Spelling out numbers that begin sentences

When a sentence begins with a number, spell out the number or rewrite the sentence.

INAPPROPRIATE   2020 square metres, with 16 rooms, the house cost $1 million to build.

HARD TO READ   Two thousand and twenty square metres, with sixteen rooms, the house cost $1 million to build.

REVISED   The 16-room house measured 2020 square metres and cost $1 million to build.

Using figures according to convention

ADDRESSES

23 Spruce Street; 175 W. Fifth Avenue, Flin Flon, Manitoba R8A 0Z2

DATES

September 17, 1951, 411 B.C.E., 1865
Spell out dates that do not include the year: *June sixth.*
Spell out decades: *the fifties.*

DECIMALS, FRACTIONS, AND PERCENTAGES

65.34, $8\frac{1}{2}$, 77% (or 77 percent)

DIVISIONS OF BOOKS AND PLAYS

Volume 5, pages 81–85 (*not* 81–5)
Act III, Scene ii (or Act 3, Scene 2), lines 3–9

SPECIFIC AMOUNTS OF MONEY

$7348, $1.46 trillion
Spell out dollars or cents of two or three words: *fifty cents.*

SCORES AND STATISTICS

an 8–3 Expos victory, an average age of 22
a mean of 53, a ratio of 3 to 1

TIME OF DAY

6:00 a.m., 5:45 p.m., eight o'clock
Without a.m. or p.m., spell out time: *five in the morning.*
With the word *o'clock*, spell out time: *four o'clock* (*not* 4 o'clock).

Taking inventory: abbreviations and numbers

Look over an essay or two that you have written, noting all the places where you use abbreviations and numbers. Check your usage for both correctness and consistency. If you discover anything you have done wrong, make a note of it (in your writing log, if you are keeping one) so that you will do it correctly the next time.

42

Using Italics

After the invention of printing, most type-carvers produced type that printed letters with the vertical strokes straight up and down, as in this sentence; today such type is called *roman*. Early Italian type designers, however, came to specialize in a slanted type, *like this*, known today as *italic*. Italics are used to set off words and phrases for special consideration or emphasis. As with other formal devices in writing, italic usage is governed by conventions, which this chapter presents.

If you have a word processor and printer, you may be able to print italic type. Otherwise, you can indicate italics by <u>underlining</u> the words you wish to treat in that way.

42a

Using italics for titles

In general, italics are used to signal the titles of long or complete works; shorter works or sections of works are set off with quotation marks. Use italics for the following kinds of words:

BOOKS

A Tale of Two Cities
The Handmaid's Tale

CHOREOGRAPHIC WORKS

Robert Desrosier's *Brass Fountain*
Brian Macdonald's *Double Quartet*

FILMS

Exotica
Black Orpheus

JOURNALS

New England Journal of Medicine
English Studies in Canada

LONG MUSICAL WORKS

Bach's *The Well-Tempered Clavier*
The Grateful Dead's *American Beauty*

LONG POEMS

The Odyssey
Hiawatha

MAGAZINES

Maclean's
Saturday Night

NEWSPAPERS

The London Free Press
Cape Breton Post

PAMPHLETS

Thomas Paine's *Common Sense*

PAINTINGS AND SCULPTURE

Christopher Pratt's *Cottage*
Georgia O'Keeffe's *Black Iris*

PLAYS

Blowin' on Bowen
She Stoops to Conquer

TELEVISION AND RADIO PROGRAMS

Seinfeld
Morningside

A couple of exceptions are worth noting. Sacred books, such as the Bible or the Koran, and public documents, such as the Free Trade Agreement or the Magna Carta, should *not* be italicized. Some style manuals require that, with magazines and newspapers, an initial *the* is neither italicized nor capitalized, even if it is part of the official name.

Using italics for words, letters, and numbers referred to as words

Italicize words, letters, or numbers referred to as words.

> Words like *romantic, plastic, values, human, dead, sentimental, natural, vitality,* as used in art criticism, are strictly meaningless, in the sense that they not only do not point to any discoverable object, but are hardly ever expected to do so by the reader.
>
> — GEORGE ORWELL, "Politics and the English Language"

> The first four orbitals are represented by the letters *s, p, d,* and *f,* in lieu of numerical values.

> On the back of his jersey was the famous *99*.

Italics are also sometimes used to signal a word that is being defined.

> Learning to play the flute depends mostly on *embouchure*—the way in which the lips are positioned over the mouthpiece.

Using italics for foreign words and phrases

Italicize words and phrases from other languages unless they are so frequently used by English speakers that they have come to be considered a part of English. The French word "bourgeois" or the Italian "pasta," for instance, do not need to be italicized. If you are in doubt about whether or not to italicize a particular word, most dictionaries offer guidelines.

> At last one of the phantom sleighs gliding along the street would come to a stop, and with gawky haste Mr. Burness in his fox-furred *shapka* would make for our door.
>
> — VLADIMIR NABOKOV, *Speak, Memory*

Note, in addition, that Latin genus and species names are always signaled by italics.

> The caterpillars of *Hapalia*, when attacked by the wasp *Apanteles machaeralis,* drop suddenly from their leaves and suspend themselves in air by a silken thread.
>
> — STEPHEN JAY GOULD, "Nonmoral Nature"

Using italics for the names of vehicles

Italicize names of specific aircraft, spacecraft, ships, and trains. Do not italicize types and classes, such as "Learjet," "space shuttle," or "airbus."

AIRCRAFT AND SPACECRAFT

Challenger
Pioneer VII

SHIPS

the *Santa Maria*
the *Queen Elizabeth*

TRAINS

the *Orient Express*
the *Montrealer*

Using italics for special emphasis

Just as vocal stress can add emphasis in spoken language, so italics can help create emphasis in writing.

> Among conservationists the quality of life concept is very often expressed in terms of *environmental* quality.
>
> — JOHN A. LIVINGSTON, *The Fallacy of Wildlife Conservation*

I am one of those unambitious lawyers who never address a jury, or in any way draw down public applause; but, in the cool tranquility of a snug retreat, do a snug business among rich men's bonds, and mortgages, and title-deeds. All who know me, consider me an eminently *safe* man.

— HERMAN MELVILLE, "Bartleby, the Scrivener"

Although italic emphasis is useful on occasion, especially in informal writing, it is best to use it sparingly. It is usually better to create emphasis with sentence structure and word choice.

Exercise 42.1

In each of the following sentences, underline any words that should be italicized and circle any italicized words that should not be.

EXAMPLE
Many people thought The Lotus Eaters was a superb film.
Many people thought *The Lotus Eaters* was a superb film.

1. Hawthorne's story *My Kinsman, Major Molineux* bears a striking resemblance to Shakespeare's play A Midsummer Night's Dream.

2. When people think about the word business, they may associate it with people and companies that care about nothing but making money.

3. Montreal offers a great blend of cultures and styles, a *potpourri* of people.

4. The word *veterinary* comes from the Latin *veterinarius,* meaning *of beasts of burden.*

5. Niko Tinbergen's essay *The Bee-Hunters of Hulsherst* is a diary of the experiments performed by the author on *Philanthus triangulum,* the *bee-killer wasp.*

6. Flying the Glamorous Glennis, a plane named for his wife, Chuck Yeager was the first pilot to fly faster than the speed of sound.

7. The Globe and Mail provides extensive reporting on financial affairs.

8. The Waste Land is a long and difficult but ultimately rewarding poem.

9. If you have seen only a reproduction of Picasso's Guernica, you can scarcely imagine the impact the original painting makes.

10. My grandparents remember the sinking of the Titanic.

Reading with an eye for italics

The following passage about Outremont, an affluent area of Montreal, uses italics in several different ways—for emphasis, for a foreign phrase, and for a title. Read the passage carefully, particularly noting the effects created by the italics. How would it differ without any italic emphasis? What other words or phrases might Richler have chosen to emphasize?

Outremont, our heart's desire, was amazing. Kids our own age there didn't hang out at the corner store or poolroom, they had their very own quarters. *Basement playrooms, Ping-Pong tables.* There were heated towel racks in the bathrooms. In each kitchen, a Mixmaster. No icebox, but a refrigerator. I had a school friend up there whose mother wore *pince-nez,* and had hired a maid to answer the door, and even the telephone.

We would ring the house again and again, crowding round the receiver, stifling giggles, if only to hear the maid chirp, "This is the Feigelbaum residence."

But on St. Urbain, our fathers worked as cutters or pressers or scrap dealers and drifted into cold-water flats, sitting down to supper in their freckled Penman's long winter underwear, clipping their nails at the table. Mothers organized bazaars, proceeds for the Jewish National Fund, and jockeyed for position on the ladies' auxiliary of the Talmud Torah or the Folkshule, both parochial schools. Visiting aunts charged into the parlor, armed with raffle books, ten cents a ticket. Win an RCA Victor radio. Win a three-volume *History of the Jews*, slipcover case included.

— MORDECAI RICHLER, "St. Urbain Street Then and Now"

43

Using Hyphens

The **hyphen** is a small horizontal line used to divide words at the end of a line and to link words or word parts (such as *hand-me-down* or *bye-bye*). As such, it serves purposes both mechanical and rhetorical. Its mechanical ones are fairly straightforward, with simple rules that tell us when and where to divide a word at the end of a line. The rhetorical ones, however, are somewhat more complicated, for though they are governed in some cases by rules, they are, in other cases, defined by the needs of readers. Stewart Beach points out the rhetorical usefulness of a hyphen nicely in his comments about one experience he recalled having as a reader:

> I came across a word I thought was a series of typos for *collaborators*. Reading it again, I realized the word was *colaborers*. But a hyphen would have [prevented] all the confusion.
>
> – STEWART BEACH

Indeed, had the word included a hyphen—*co-laborers*—its meaning would have been instantly clear. Sometimes the dictionary will tell you where to hyphenate a word. Other times, you will be putting together words in ways not listed in a dictionary, and you will have to decide whether or not to add a hyphen. This chapter will help you with the decisions and the rules that go along with using hyphens.

Using hyphens to divide words at the end of a line

Hyphens are used at the end of a line to break a word that will be completed on the next line. It is best not to have to divide words in this way, but sometimes you must. When you do, the main thing to remember is to break words between syllables. The word *metaphor*, for instance, is made up of three syllables (*met-a-phor*), and you could break it after either the *t* or the *a*. All dictionaries show syllable breaks, and so the best advice for dividing words correctly is simply to look them up. In addition, you should follow certain other conventions, including the following:

- *Never divide one-syllable words*, even relatively long words such as *draught* or *through*.

- *Divide compound words only between the parts*. Words such as *headache* or *mother-in-law* should be broken between their parts (*head-ache*) or at their hyphens (*mother-in-law*).

- *Divide words with prefixes or suffixes between the parts*. The word *disappearance*, then, might be broken after its prefix (*dis-appearance*) or before its suffix (*disappear-ance*). Prefixed words that include hyphens, such as *self-righteous*, should be divided at the hyphen.

- *Never divide abbreviations, contractions, or figures*. Though such "words" as *NATO, didn't*, and *250* do have audible syllables, it is not permissible to divide them in writing.

- *Leave at least two letters when dividing a word*. Words such as *acorn* (*a-corn*) or *scratchy* (*scratch-y*), therefore, cannot be divided at all, and a word such as *Canadiana* (*Ca-na-di-a-na*) cannot be broken after the second *n*.

43b

Using hyphens with compound words

Compound words are words such as *rowboat* or *up-to-date* that are made up of more than one word. Compound words are written as one word, as separate words, or with hyphens.

ONE WORD   *grandmother, textbook, extraterrestrial*

SEPARATE WORDS *high school, parking meter, hard disk*

WITH HYPHENS   *city-state, great-grandmother, ex-husband*

It is difficult, maybe even impossible, to know when a particular compound word is one word, separate words, or hyphenated. Even compounds that begin with the same word are treated every which way—*blueberry, blue-collar,* and *blue cheese*, for instance. In general, then, you should always consult the dictionary to find out how to spell compounds. There are, in addition, some conventions that can guide you in using hyphens with compound words.

1. Hyphenating compound modifiers

Often you will use compound modifiers that are not listed in a dictionary. The guiding principle then is to hyphenate most compound adjectives that precede a noun but not to hyphenate ones that follow a noun.

> a *hard-nosed boss*, a *two-to-one* decision
>
> My boss is extremely *hard nosed*.
>
> The decision against the plan was *two to one*.

In general, the reason for hyphenating such compound modifiers is to facilitate reading. Notice, for example, how the hyphen affects your understanding of the following two sentences.

> The designers used potted palms as *living room* dividers.
>
> The designers used potted palms as *living-room* dividers.

In the first sentence, the word *living* seems to modify *room dividers;* in the second, the hyphen makes clear that it is part of a compound adjective. Compound adjectives that are commonly used and thus likely to be easily understood by your readers, however, do not always need to be hyphenated—*income tax reform* or *first class mail* would never be misunderstood, for example.

Two more instances of compound modifiers that are never hyphenated include those with an adverb ending in *-ly* and those with comparative or superlative forms.

> a *radically different* approach
>
> *more extensive* coverage, the *most stimulating* group

A series of compound words in a sentence that share the same base word can be shortened by the use of suspended hyphens.

> I taught 2-, 3-, and 4-*year-olds.*

2. Hyphenating specially coined compounds

You may sometimes coin your own original compounds, usually for descriptive reasons. Such **coined compounds** should always be hyphenated.

> Unfortunately, nature is very much a *now-you-see-it, now-you-don't* affair.
>
> — ANNIE DILLARD, "Sight into Insight"

The ... problem with a *no-first-use* policy is that it might paradoxically increase the chances of nuclear war.

      – CHARLES KRAUTHAMMER, "In Defense of Deterrence"

3. Hyphenating fractions and compound numbers

To write out fractions, use a hyphen to join the numerator and denominator.

> one-seventh
>
> seven-sixteenths

Use hyphens to spell out whole numbers from twenty-one to ninety-nine, both when they stand alone and when they are part of larger numbers. (Note that such larger numbers can usually be written as numerals.)

> thirty-seven
>
> three hundred fifty-four thousand

Using hyphens with prefixes and suffixes

Most words with prefixes or suffixes are written as one word, without hyphens: *antiwar, misinform, understand.* Only in the following cases do you need a hyphen with prefixed or suffixed words:

CAPITALIZED BASE WORDS

post-World War II, pro-Liberal

FIGURES

pre-1960, post-1945

WITH ALL-, EX-, SELF-, AND -ELECT

all-inclusive, ex-wife, self-possessed, mayor-elect

Note, however, that *selfish* is written without a hyphen because *self* acts as a root, not a prefix.

BEFORE COMPOUND WORDS

pre-high school, pro-democracy

TO AVOID CONFUSION WITH HOMONYMS

Re-cover means to "cover again"; the hyphen distinguishes it from *recover,* meaning "get well."

Exercise 43.1

Using the dictionary and this chapter, insert hyphens as needed in the following items. Circle the number of any item that is correct as it stands.

1. deionization
2. pre World War II
3. two and four-cylinder motorcycles
4. happily married couple
5. a come up and see me sometime gaze
6. self important
7. premier elect
8. seven hundred thirty three
9. a hard working farmer
10. a politician who is quick witted

Reading with an eye for hyphenation

The following paragraph about semi-professional baseball uses many hyphens. Read it carefully, and note how the hyphens make the paragraph easier to read. Why is it necessary to hyphenate *junior-college* in the last sentence?

> All semi-pro leagues, it should be understood, are self-sustaining, and have no farm affiliation or other connection with the twenty-six major-league clubs, or with the seventeen leagues and hundred and fifty-two teams (ranging from Rookie League at the lowest level, to Class A and Summer Class A, up to the AAA designation at the highest) that make up the National Association—the minors, that is. There is no central body or semi-pro teams, and semi-pro players are not included among the six hundred and fifty major-leaguers, the twenty-five hundred-odd minor-leaguers, plus all the managers, coaches, presidents, commissioners, front-office people, and

scouts, who, taken together, constitute the great tent called organized ball. (A much diminished tent, at that; back in 1949, the minors included fifty-nine leagues, about four hundred and forty-eight teams, and perhaps ten thousand players.) Also outside the tent, but perhaps within its shade, are five college leagues, ranging across the country from Cape Cod to Alaska, where the most promising freshman, sophomore, and junior-college ballplayers may compete against each other in the summertime without losing their amateur status ...

– ROGER ANGELL, "In the Country"

Taking inventory: hyphenation

Look carefully at an assignment you are working on, particularly noting your use of hyphens. Have you broken words at the ends of lines correctly? Have you followed the conventions governing use of hyphens in compound words, with prefixes and suffixes, with fractions and numbers? If you find you are misusing hyphens or are unsure about how to use them in certain situations, check those instances against the advice in this chapter. If you are keeping a writing log, make an entry in it about anything with hyphens that confused you.

PART TEN

For Multilingual Writers: Understanding the Nuances of English

44

Understanding Nouns and Noun Phrases

If you spoke another language when you first started learning English, you may have felt sometimes as though you were repeating the struggles of early childhood in trying to make yourself understood. Nevertheless, as a speaker of another language you had, and continue to have, a major advantage in acquiring a command of English: since all human languages are built on the same foundation, there is a great deal in your first language that you will encounter once again as you progress in English. For example, you are probably familiar with the way sentences are built up out of two primary components—nouns and verbs. This chapter will focus on some of the ways English nouns differ from those in some other languages.

44a

Distinguishing count and noncount nouns

The nouns *tree* and *grass* differ not only in meaning but in the way they are used in sentences.

	The hill was covered with trees.
	The hill was covered with grass.
BUT NOT	The hill was covered with grasses.

| | I can count twenty trees in this picture. |
| BUT NOT | I can count twenty grasses in this picture. |

	Whitman regarded even one tree as a miracle.
	He regarded even one blade of grass as a miracle.
BUT NOT	Whitman regarded even one grass as a miracle.

Tree is a **count** noun and *grass* a **noncount** (or **mass**) noun. These terms do not mean that grass cannot be counted, but only that English grammar requires that if we count grass, we express it indirectly: *one blade of grass, two blades of grass,* not *one grass, two grasses.*

Count nouns usually have singular and plural forms: *tree, trees.* Noncount nouns usually have only a singular form: *grass.*

Count nouns convey the image of a distinct individual or entity or a group of distinct individuals or entities: *a doctor, a tiger, a book, a mountain, a tree; doctors, tigers, books, mountains, trees.* Noncount nouns convey the image of an indeterminate mass without distinctly separate components: *milk, ice, clay, blood, grass.* But often much the same reality can be represented either in the sharp focus of a count noun or through the hazy lens of a noncount noun.

COUNT	NONCOUNT
people (plural of *person*)	humanity
tables, chairs, beds	furniture
letters	mail
pebbles	gravel
beans	rice
oats (plural only)	wheat

Abstract nouns are likely to be noncount, but not always.

COUNT	NONCOUNT
suggestions	advice (NOT advices)
facts	information (NOT informations)

Some words can be either count or noncount, the choice of grammatical form depending on meaning.

COUNT	Before there were video games, children would spend hours playing with *marbles.*
NONCOUNT	The floor of the palace was made of *marble.*

Some general patterns for using count and noncount nouns

• Use a count noun to refer to a living animal, but a noncount noun to the food derived from that animal.

COUNT	The *chickens* in the yard were making a racket.
NONCOUNT	I prefer *chicken* to beef.

- Things that come in different varieties are noncount, but we can make those nouns plural to talk about those varieties.

NONCOUNT   We like *wine* with dinner.

COUNT   The *wines* of California are often as good as those of France.

- Abstract nouns that are noncount can often be made count to shift attention from the concept in general to specific instances of it.

COUNT   *Kindness* is never wasted.

COUNT   I appreciate all your *kindnesses* to me in the past.

When you learn a noun in English, you need to learn whether it is count, noncount, or both. Most dictionaries do not supply this information; one that does is the *Oxford Advanced Learner's Dictionary*. Most important, pay attention to how a word is used when you hear or read it. If it has a plural form, then it can be used as a count noun; if it occurs in the singular without a determiner (see 44c), it is noncount.

Maintaining singular and plural

Look at this sentence, which might appear in a traffic report:

All four bridges into the city are crowded with cars right now.

There are three count nouns in this sentence; one is singular (*city*), and two are plural (*bridges, cars*). If you speak a language with nouns that generally have no distinct plural forms (for example, Chinese, Japanese, or Korean), you might be tempted to argue that no information would be lost if the sentence were rendered as *All four bridge into the city are crowded with car right now*. After all, the numeral *four* indicates that *bridge* is plural, and obviously there would have to be more than one car if the bridges are crowded. But each language makes its own demands, and English requires that every time you use a count noun, you ask yourself whether you are talking about one item or more than one, and that you choose a singular or a plural form accordingly. It does not matter whether that information is unimportant or obvious or has already been supplied; it must be stated explicitly again and again.

Since noncount nouns have no plural forms and are not used directly with numerals, they can be quantified only with a preceding phrase: *one litre of milk, three kilograms of rice, four heads of lettuce, five blades of grass, several bits of information.* Note that the noun itself remains singular.

Using determiners

A noun together with all its modifiers constitutes a **noun phrase**, and the noun around which the modifiers cluster is called the **head**. For example, in *My adventurous sister is leaving for New Zealand tomorrow,* the noun phrase *my adventurous sister* consists of two modifiers (*my* and *adventurous*) and the head *sister.* See Chapter 23 for discussion of placing modifiers. Chapter 18 discusses adjectives and adverbs.

Both *my* and *adventurous* may be called adjectives, but *my* is a very different kind of adjective from *adventurous,* distinguished from most adjectives by several characteristics.

It is more like a pronoun, belonging to the same set of forms as *mine, me,* and *I.* It almost always comes at the beginning of the noun phrase; though you can say *my brilliant, adventurous sister,* you cannot put *brilliant* or any other adjective before *my.* In the example sentence, you cannot omit the word *my; adventurous sister* or *brilliant, adventurous sister* are not acceptable noun phrases in English. You might substitute another word for *my* (*our adventurous sister, this adventurous sister*), but the words that can be substituted are very limited in number; most adjectives would not qualify.

Words like *my, our,* and *this* are **determiners.** They are among the most common and important words in the English language. Using them appropriately can go a long way toward enabling you to write smooth, comprehensible English.

Unlike other adjectives, determiners do not describe the noun head; instead they identify or quantify it. They include the following:

1. *a/an, the*

2. *this, these, that, those*

3. *my, our, your, his, her, its, their;* possessive nouns and noun phrases (*Sheila's, my friend's*)

4. *whose, which, what*

5. *all, both, each, every, some, any, either, no, neither, many, much, (a) few, (a) little, several,* and *enough*

6. the numerals *one, two,* etc.

Some of these are treated in more detail in 44d.

Being careful to use determiners with singular count nouns

Every noun phrase with a singular count noun head must begin with a determiner.

| NOT | adventurous sister |
| BUT | *my* adventurous sister |

NOT	big, bad wolf
BUT	*the* big, bad wolf
OR	*a* big, bad wolf

NOT	old neighbourhood
BUT	*that* old neighbourhood
OR	*an* old neighbourhood

If there is no reason to use a more specific determiner, use an indefinite article: *a big, bad wolf; an old neighbourhood.*

Notice that every noun phrase need not begin with a determiner, only those whose head is a singular count noun. Noncount and plural count nouns sometimes have determiners, sometimes not: *This grass is green* and *Grass is green* are both acceptable, though different in meaning, as are *These trees are green* and *Trees are green.* You cannot say *Tree is green,* however; say instead *This tree is green, Every tree is green,* or at least *A tree is green.*

Remembering which determiners go with which types of noun

1. Use *this* or *that* with singular count or noncount: *this book, that milk.*

2. Use *these, (a) few, many, both,* or *several* with plural count: *these books, those plans, a few ideas, many students, both hands, several trees.*

3. Use *(a) little* or *much* with noncount: *a little milk, much affection.*

4. Use *some* or *enough* with noncount or plural count: *some milk, some books; enough trouble, enough problems.*

5. Use *a, an, every,* or *each* with singular count: *a book, every child, each word.*

Working with articles

The definite article *the* and the indefinite articles *a/an* are challenging to multilingual speakers. Many languages have nothing directly comparable to them, and languages that do have articles may differ from English in the details of their use.

Why do articles play such a dominant role in English when some other languages manage quite well without them? Part of the answer is that many other languages can move words around in a sentence with much greater freedom than English can, and what these languages accomplish with variations in word order English does with articles. Both techniques serve to orchestrate the interaction between writer and reader (or speaker and listener), and to keep the reader alert to the flow of information.

Consider this example: *If you have ever read a book or seen a movie about Helen Keller, you will remember the electrifying moment when she first learns to "read," when she first realizes that the symbols traced in her palm contain meanings.* The sentence uses indefinite articles at the beginning (*a book* and *a movie about Helen Keller*). If the writer had used *the* instead of *a*, she would have told readers that she expected them to recognize which book and movie she meant. That might have been appropriate if the book and movie had been mentioned earlier, or if everyone could be expected to know that there was only one book and movie about Helen Keller. But in fact the writer is less demanding of her readers and does not assume they've read a book or seen a movie about Helen Keller. When the sentence shifts to definite articles (*the electrifying moment, the symbols*), the reader is drawn closer to the writer, who is essentially saying that if they have read such a book or seen such a movie, she and they share the same memories, and if not, that she's giving enough information to help them recognize the memories she has.

That is an example of what articles contribute to meaning. This section will discuss the meaning conveyed by definite articles and indefinite articles and by the absence of an article.

1. The definite article

The definite article *the* is used with nouns whose identity is known or is about to be made known to readers. The necessary information for identification can come from any of the following sources:

From the noun phrase itself

the canals *of Amsterdam*
the *new* restaurant *on Oak Street*
the earthquake *that devastated Mexico City in 1985*

In these examples, the information needed by the reader to make the appropriate identification is in italics.

From elsewhere in the text

Last Saturday *a fire* that started in *a restaurant* spread to a neighbouring dry-goods store. *The store* was saved, although *the merchandise* suffered water damage. It was reported that there were suspicious similarities to *a fire* that had broken out nearby two days earlier.

The second mention of the word *store* is preceded by *the,* which directs our attention to the information in the previous sentence, where the store is identified. *The* before *merchandise* similarly directs us to look for identifying information; in this case we cannot find another occurrence of the same word, but we can infer that since a dry-goods store carries merchandise, it must be the merchandise of that store that is being referred to. Notice also that when a noun is repeated, the second mention does not always call for *the.* The noun *fire* occurs twice with *a,* since the second fire was not the same as the first.

From context or general knowledge

. A professor speaking to a student in her office: "Please shut *the door* when you leave."

The professor is referring to the door to her office and expects the student to understand that.

The pope is expected to visit Africa in October.

The reader knows which pope is being spoken of on the basis of general knowledge: there is only one living pope.

In the above cases the use of an indefinite article rather than a definite article would convey a different meaning. However, in some cases *the* is always required:

• Before the word *same (the same person)*

- Usually before an ordinal number *(the third little pig)*
- Before a superlative *(the best choice)*

2. The indefinite article

Unlike the definite article, which can appear with any kind of noun, the indefinite article *a/an* occurs only with singular count nouns. *A* is used before a consonant sound: *a car, a tree. An* is used before a vowel sound: *an uncle, an apple.* Pay attention to sounds rather than to spelling: *a house, an hour.*

A/an tells readers they do not have enough information to identify the noun. The writer may or may not have a particular thing in mind, but in either case will use *a/an* if the reader lacks the information necessary for identification. Compare the following two sentences:

I need *a* new *parka* for the winter.

I saw *a parka* that I liked at Holt Renfrew, but it wasn't heavy enough.

The parka in the first sentence is hypothetical rather than actual. Since it is indefinite to the writer, it clearly is indefinite to the reader, and is used with *a*, not *the*. The second sentence refers to a very specific actual parka, but since the writer cannot expect the reader to know which one it is, it is used with *a* rather than *the*.

If you want to speak of an indefinite quantity, rather than just one indefinite thing, use the determiner *some* with a noncount noun or a plural count noun.

I need *some* more *salt* for this stew.

I saw *some plates* that I liked at Gump's, but they didn't match those I already have.

3. The zero article

If a noun appears without *the, a/an,* or any other determiner (even if it is preceded by other adjectives), it is said to have a **zero article.** The zero article is used with noncount and plural count nouns: *cheese, hot tea, crackers, ripe apples* (but not *cracker* or *ripe apple*).

Use the zero article to make generalizations.

In this world nothing is certain but *death* and *taxes.*

— Benjamin Franklin

The zero article with *death* and *taxes* indicates that Franklin refers not to a particular death or specific taxes but to death and taxes in general.

Here English differs from many other languages that also have articles—Greek or Spanish or German, for example—and that would use the definite article to make generalizations. In English, a sentence like *The snakes are dangerous* can only refer to particular, identifiable snakes, not snakes in general.

It is sometimes possible to make general statements with *the* or *a/an* and singular count nouns.

> *First-year college students* are confronted with a wealth of new experiences.
>
> *A first-year student* is confronted with a wealth of new experiences.
>
> *The first-year student* is confronted with a wealth of new experiences.

These sentences all make the same general statement, but the last two are more vivid than the first. The second focuses on a hypothetical student taken at random, and the third sentence, which is characteristic only of formal written style, projects the image of a typical student as representative of the whole class.

44e

Arranging modifiers

Some modifiers can precede the noun head and others can follow; you need to learn what can go where. Modifiers that follow the noun head are usually phrases or clauses (*the tiles on the wall; the tiles that we bought last summer*). Modifiers that precede the head fall into two groups: cases where a specific position for a word is obligatory, and cases where a certain position may be preferred but is not obligatory.

Obligatory modifier positions

- Put determiners at the very beginning of the noun phrase: *these old-fashioned tiles*. *All* or *both* must precede, and numerals must follow, any other determiners: *all these tiles, these six tiles.*

- Put noun modifiers directly before the noun head: *these kitchen tiles.* (See 18e.)

- Put all other adjectives between determiners and noun modifiers: *these old-fashioned kitchen tiles.* If there are two or more of these adjectives, their order is variable, but there are strong preferences, described below.

Preferred modifier positions

- In general, put subjective adjectives (those that show the writer's attitude) before objective adjectives (those that merely describe): *these beautiful old-fashioned kitchen tiles.*

Preferred positions among objective adjectives

- Those that indicate size generally come early: *these beautiful large old-fashioned kitchen tiles.*

- Those that indicate colour generally come late: these beautiful large old-fashioned blue kitchen tiles.

- Those derived from proper nouns or from nouns that refer to materials generally come after colour terms and right before noun modifiers: *these beautiful large old-fashioned blue Portuguese ceramic kitchen tiles.*

- All other objective adjectives go in the middle. Series of adjectives for which a preferred order does not exist are separated by commas: *these beautiful large decorative, heat-resistant, old-fashioned blue Portuguese ceramic kitchen tiles.*

It goes without saying that the interminable noun phrase presented as an illustration in the preceding paragraph is a monstrosity that would be out of place in almost any conceivable kind of writing. You should always budget your use of adjectives.

Exercise 44.1

Each of the following sentences contains an error. Rewrite each sentence correctly.

1. At an end of the 18th century, England and France were at war.
2. Napoleon, the French ruler, invaded Egypt with much soldiers.
3. His ultimate goal was India, which England had conquered many year before.
4. At Rosetta, near the Nile, some French soldiers were building fort.
5. They found a black large stone—the Rosetta Stone.

Exercise 44.2

Insert articles as necessary in the following passage from *The Silent Language*, by Edward T. Hall.

Hollywood is famous for hiring _____ various experts to teach

_____ people technically what most of us learn informally. _____ case in point is _____ story about _____ children of one movie couple who noticed _____ new child in _____ neighbourhood climbing _____ tree. _____ children immediately wanted to be given _____ name of his instructor in _____ tree climbing.

Understanding Verbs and Verb Phrases

Verbs can be called the heartbeat of prose in every language, but in English the metaphor is especially meaningful. With rare exceptions, you cannot deprive an English sentence of its verb without killing it. If you speak Russian or Arabic, you might wonder what is wrong with a sentence like *My teacher very intelligent*. But unlike sentences in those and many other languages, English sentences must have a verb (for example, *My teacher impresses me as very intelligent*), and if no other verb is chosen, a form of the verb *be* must be used: *My teacher is very intelligent*.

45a

Forming verb phrases

Verb phrases have strict rules of order. See how verb phrases can be built up out of the main verb and one or more auxiliaries (see 16a):

> My cat *drinks* milk.
>
> My cat *is drinking* milk.
>
> My cat *has been drinking* milk.
>
> My cat *may have been drinking* milk.

If you try to rearrange the words in any of these sentences, you will find that most alternatives are impossible. You cannot say *My cat drinking is milk* or *My cat been has drinking milk* or *My cat have may been drinking milk*. The only permissible rearrangement is to move the first auxiliary to the beginning of the sentence in order to form a question.

> *Has* my cat *been drinking* milk?

A review of auxiliary and main verbs

In *My cat may have been drinking milk*, the main verb *drinking* is preceded by three auxiliaries: *may, have,* and *been.*

- *May* is a modal, which must be followed by the base form *(have).*
- *Have* indicates that the tense is perfect, and it must be followed by a past participle *(been).*
- *Been* (or any other form of *be*), when it is followed by a present participle (such as *drinking*), indicates that the tense is progressive.
- A form of *be* can also represent passive voice, but then the following verb form must be a past participle, as in *My cat may have been bitten by a dog.*

The main verb (MV) can be preceded by as many as four auxiliaries in sequence; however, more than three are very rare. They must be in the following order: modal + perfect *have* + progressive *be* + passive *be.*

PERF PASS   MV
Sonya *has been invited* to stay with a family in Prague.

PERF PROG   MV
She *has been taking* an intensive course in Czech.

MOD PROG   MV
She *must be looking* forward to her trip eagerly.

Only one modal is permitted in a verb phrase.

MOD MV
Sonya *can speak* a little Czech already.

MOD PROG   MV
She *will be studying* for three more months.

MOD MOD MV
BUT NOT   She *will can speak* Czech much better soon.

To convey the intended meaning of the last sentence, you would need to use other words: *She will be able to speak Czech much better soon.* Every time you use an auxiliary, you should be careful to put the next word in the appropriate form. Study the following pairs of example sentences; in each case, the second sentence adds an auxiliary to the first.

MODAL + BASE FORM

Alice *reads* Latin.

Alice *can read* Latin.

Paul *has* been studying.

Paul *might have* been studying.

Notice that even though sentence 1 requires *-s* at the end of the main verb *read*, sentence 2, with the modal *can*, leaves *read* in the base form. In sentence 4, the modal *might* is also followed by the base form *have*.

In many other languages the equivalent of a modal like *can* or *must* is followed by the infinitive. Be careful not to substitute an infinitive + *to* for the base form. Do not say *Alice <u>can to read Latin.</u>*

PERFECT *HAVE* + PAST PARTICIPLE

Everyone *went* home.

Everyone *has gone* home.

They *will be* working all day.

They *have been* working all day.

In sentence 2, the auxiliary *has* transforms the following verb into its past participle *gone* (not *has went* or *has go*). In sentence 4, where *have* has replaced the modal *will* of sentence 3, the following auxiliary *be* has become the past participle *been*.

PROGRESSIVE *BE* + PRESENT PARTICIPLE

The children *study* history in school.

The children *are studying* history in school.

A progressive form of the verb is signalled by two elements, a form of the auxiliary *be* (*are* in the second sentence) and the ending *-ing* attached to the next word. Be sure to include both elements.

NOT	The children studying in school.
OR	The children are study in school.
BUT	The children are studying in school.

PASSIVE *BE* + PAST PARTICIPLE

People *speak* Tagalog in the Philippines.

Tagalog *is spoken* in the Philippines.

Notice that the difference between progressive *be* and passive *be* is that the following word ends in the -*ing* of the present participle with the progressive, but with the passive the following word never ends in -*ing* and instead becomes the past participle.

If the first auxiliary in a verb phrase is *be* or *have,* it must show either present or past tense, and it must agree with the subject.

Zoe and Gabe *are* studying music.

Lisa *is* studying music.

Zoe and Gabe *were* taught by a famous violinist.

Lisa *was* taught by a famous violinist.

Zoe and Gabe *have* played in an orchestra.

Lisa *has* played in an orchestra.

Notice that although a modal auxiliary may also show present or past tense (for example, *can* or *could*), it never changes form to agree with the subject.

NOT   Zoe and Gabe cans play two instruments.

BUT   They *can* play two instruments.

NOT   Lisa cans play two instruments.

BUT   She *can* play two instruments.

Using present and past tenses

Every English sentence must have at least one **finite verb** or verb phrase, one that is not an infinitive, a gerund, or a participle without any auxiliaries. Furthermore, every finite verb or verb phrase must have a tense.

In some languages, such as Chinese and Vietnamese, the verb form never changes regardless of when the action of the verb takes place, and the time of the action is simply indicated by other expressions such as *yesterday, last year,* or *next week.* In English, the time of the action must be clearly indicated by the tense form of each and every finite verb, even if the time is obvious or there are other indications of time in the sentence. Therefore, if you write a sentence like *During the Cultural Revolution millions of young people cannot go to school and are sent to the countryside,* you must change the finite verb phrases *can*(*not*) *go* and *are sent* to the past tense.

During the Cultural Revolution millions of young people could not go to school and were sent to the countryside.

In some languages, words end in either a vowel or a single consonant, not in one consonant followed by another (Spanish, for example). If you speak such a language, remember to add the *-s* of the present tense third person singular or the *-ed* of the past tense. If you have such problems, go over your writing carefully to check whether you have added the appropriate ending to every finite verb.

NOT   Last night I call my aunt who live in Montreal.

BUT   Last night I called my aunt who lives in Montreal.

Understanding perfect and progressive verb phrases

The perfect and progressive auxiliaries combine with the present or past tense, or with modals, to form complex verb phrases with special meanings. In particular you should learn to recognize sentences in which the perfect or the progressive must be used and distinguish them from sentences in which a simple tense is used.

1. Distinguishing the simple present and the present perfect

Imagine writing the following sentence:

My sister *drives* a bus.

The simple present *(drives)* merely tells us about her current occupation. But if you were to add the phrase *for three years,* it would be incorrect to say My sister <u>*drives*</u> a bus *for three years.* You need to set up a time frame that encompasses the past and the present, and therefore you should use the present perfect or the present perfect progressive.

My sister *has driven* a bus for three years.

My sister *has been driving* a bus for three years.

2. Distinguishing the simple past and the present perfect

Consider this sentence:

> Since she started working, she *has bought* a new car and a VCR.

The clause introduced by *since* sets up a time frame that runs from past to present, and requires the present perfect *(has bought)*. Furthermore, the sentence does not say exactly when she bought the car or the VCR, and that indefiniteness also calls for the perfect. It would be less correct to say *Since she started working, she <u>bought</u> a new car and a VCR*. But what if you should go on to say when she bought the car?

> She *bought* the car two years ago.

It would be incorrect to say *She <u>has bought</u> the car two years ago* because the perfect is incompatible with definite expressions of time. In this case, use the sample past *(bought)* rather than the present perfect *(has bought)*.

3. Distinguishing the simple present and the present progressive

Return to the sentence *My sister <u>drives</u> a bus*. You might continue *But she <u>is taking</u> a vacation now*. Many languages, such as French and German, use the simple present *(drives, takes)* for both types of sentence. In English, it would be incorrect to say *But she <u>takes</u> a vacation now,* although you might say *But she <u>takes</u> a vacation every year.*

When an action is in progress at the present moment, use the present progressive. Use the simple present for actions that frequently occur during a period of time that might include the present moment (though such an assertion makes no claim that the action is taking place right now).

4. Distinguishing the simple past and the past progressive

Finally, consider this sentence:

> My sister *spent* the summer in Italy.

You might be tempted into using the past progressive here instead of the simple past, since spending the summer involves a continuous stretch of time of some duration, and duration and continuousness are typically associated with the progressive. As a result, you might write *My sister <u>was spending</u> the summer on a farm.*

But English speakers use the past progressive infrequently, and would be unlikely to use it in this case except to convey actions that are simultaneous with other past actions. For example:

My sister *was spending* the summer on a farm when she *met* her future husband.

Use the past progressive to focus on duration, continuousness, and simultaneousness, to call attention to past action that went on at the same time as something else.

Distinguishing stative and dynamic verbs

Consider the following two sentences:

Karen *resembles* her mother.

Jorge *knows* the answer.

It would sound strange to say *Karen is resembling her mother* or *Jorge is knowing the answer. Resemble* and *know* are called stative verbs, and they are rarely used with progressive forms. They can be contrasted with the majority of verbs in English, those which are called dynamic verbs and which can be used in the progressive without restriction. **Dynamic verbs** tell us about something that is happening, most typically about an action that someone or something is deliberately performing. **Stative verbs** tell us instead that someone or something is in a state that is unchanging, at least for a while. Dynamic verbs tell us about doing, while stative verbs tell us about being or having; the sentences about Karen and Jorge are equivalent to the following:

Karen is like her mother. [resemble = be]

Jorge has the answer in his mind. [know = have]

Many verbs have more than one meaning, and some of these verbs are stative with one meaning and dynamic with another. For example:

Lynne *has* the answer.

Jason *is having* a good time at the party.

Have is stative in the first sentence but dynamic in the second.

In addition to *be, have, resemble,* and *know,* verbs that are stative, at least for some of their meanings, include designations of mental states like *believe, hate, like, love, think,* and *understand,* and of other states like *belong, cost, mean, need, own,* and *weigh.*

One group of verbs calls for special attention. Imagine the following dialogue:

Helen: Listen. Do you hear anything?

Paul: O.K., I'm *listening.* Yes, I *hear* something in the hall. It *sounds* peculiar.

Listen, hear, and *sound* all have to do with sense perceptions. Yet *listen* can be used in the progressive, whereas *hear* and *sound* cannot. *Listen* indicates that Paul is deliberately doing something, whereas *hear* and *sound* refer to an experience over which Paul has no control. In other words, *hear* and *sound* are stative rather than dynamic verbs because they do not indicate voluntary action. Paul is the subject of *hear,* while the experience itself is the subject of *sound.*

With verbs of vision, *see* corresponds to *hear,* and *look* to both *listen* and *sound: I'm looking. I see something. It looks peculiar.*

But other verbs of sense perception, like *smell, taste,* and *feel,* use the same word in all three functions: *Have you tasted the soup? I'm tasting it now. I taste something strange. It tastes sour.*

One final caution: Even though stative verbs are not usually used with the *-ing* forms of the progressive aspect, they occur freely with *-ing* in nonfinite participles and gerunds. For example: *Seeing is believing.*

45e

Using modals

Consider the following passage :

… your college course work will call on you to do much reading, writing, research, talking, listening, and note-taking. And as you probably have already realized, you will not—or need not—always carry out all these activities in solitude. Far from it. Instead, you can be part of a broad conversation that includes all the texts you read. …

This passage contains four modal auxiliaries: *will, will not, need not,* and *can.* These modals tell the reader what the writer judges to be the options available—in this case, in college work. The passage begins with *will,* which makes a firm prediction of what the reader is to expect. It continues with a firm negative prediction (*will not*), but immediately revises it to a more tentative forecast (*need not*), and finally opens up a new vista of possibilities for the reader (*can*).

The most commonly used modals

The nine basic modal auxiliaries are *can, could, will, would, shall, should, may, might,* and *must.* There are a few others as well, in particular *ought to,* which is close in meaning to *should,* and occasionally the verb *need,* which can also be a modal.

1. Using modals to refer to the past

The nine basic modals fall into the pairs *can/could, will/would, shall/should, may/might,* as well as the loner *must.* In earlier English the second member of each pair was the past tense of the first. To a very limited degree, the second form still functions as a past tense, especially in the case of *could.*

> Ingrid *can* ski.
> Ingrid *could* ski when she was five.

But for the most part, in present-day English all nine modals typically refer to present or future time. This means that when you want to use a modal to refer to the past, you follow the modal with a perfect auxiliary.

> If you have a fever, you *should* see a doctor.
> If you had a fever, you *should have seen* a doctor.

In the case of *must,* refer to the past by using the modal substitute *had to.*

> You *must* renew your visa by the end of this week.
> You *had to* renew your visa by the end of last week.

2. Using modals to make requests or to give instructions

The way modals contribute to human interaction is most evident in requests and instructions. Imagine making the following request of a flight attendant:

> *Will* you bring me a pillow?

You have expressed your request in a demanding manner, and the flight attendant might resent it. A more polite request:

> *Can* you bring me a pillow?

This statement acknowledges that fulfilling the request may not be possible.

Another way of softening the request is to use the past form of *will*, and the most discreet choice is the past form of *can*.

Would you bring me a pillow?

Could you bring me a pillow?

Using the past of modals is considered more polite than using their present forms because it makes any statement or question less assertive.

Now imagine that each of the following instructions is given by different professors to their classes:

1. You *can* submit your term paper on a floppy disk.

2. You *may* submit your term paper on a floppy disk.

3. You *should* submit your term paper on a floppy disk.

4. You *must* submit your term paper on a floppy disk.

5. You *will* submit your term paper on a floppy disk.

Instructions 1 and 2 give permission to submit the paper on disk, but do not require it; of these, 2 is more formal. Instruction 3 adds a strong recommendation; 4 allows no alternative; and 5 implies, "Don't even think of doing otherwise."

3. Using modals to reveal doubt and certainty

Modals tell the reader how confident the writer is about the likelihood that what is being asserted is true. Look at the following two sets of sentences, the first set about the present and the second about the future. Each set starts with a tentative suggestion and ends with full assurance.

Please sit down; you *might* be tired.

Please sit down; you *may* be tired.

Please sit down; you *must* be tired.

Don't lie on the grass; you *might* get Lyme disease.

Don't lie on the grass; you *may* get Lyme disease.

Don't lie on the grass; you *will* get Lyme disease.

The second set of sentences illustrates why the modal *will* (or *shall* in some varieties of English) is regarded as the marker of the future tense. It makes a prediction about what lies ahead and suppresses any sense of uncertainty.

Using participial adjectives

Many verbs refer to feelings that some situation, person, or thing produces in someone's mind—for example, *bore, confuse, excite, fascinate, frighten, interest*. With most such verbs, the subject produces the feeling and the object has the feeling. For example: *The dinosaur display frightened the little boy*. This idea can be expressed in the passive as *The little boy was frightened by the dinosaur display*.

The past participle that is part of the passive formation can be used as an ordinary adjective. In such a case, it will describe the person having the feeling:

> The *frightened* boy started to cry.

The same verb can form an adjective with the present participle. Then the adjective will describe the thing (or person) causing the feeling:

> The *frightening* dinosaur display gave him nightmares.

Be careful not to confuse the two types of adjectives. Do not write, for example, *I am interesting in African literature*. This idea should be expressed instead in one of these ways:

> African literature *interests* me.
>
> I am *interested* in African literature.
>
> African literature is *interesting*.

You might find the following sentences helpful as a guide to using participial adjectives:

> Anything can be *interesting*.
>
> Only someone with a mind can be *interested*.

Notice that the words *anything* and *interesting* end in the same letters, as do *mind* and *interested*.

Exercise 45.1

Each of the following sentences contains an error. Rewrite each sentence correctly.

1. The Rosetta Stone was cover with inscriptions in two ancient languages,

Greek and Egyptian.

2. Ancient Egyptian writing called hieroglyphics.

3. In the 18th century no one can read hieroglyphics.

4. Very soon after its discovery, the French have made copies of the stone.

5. They sent these copies to scholars who were interesting in hieroglyphics.

Exercise 45.2

Rewrite the following passage, adapted from "In a Jumbled Drawer" by Stephen Jay Gould, adding appropriate auxiliaries and verb endings where necessary.

As my son ____grow____, I ___monitor___ the changing fashions in kiddie culture

for words expressing deep admiration—what I ____call____ "cool" in my day,

and my father ___designate___ "swell." The half-life ____seem____ to be about six

months, as "excellent" (with curious lingering emphasis on the first syllable)

____give____ way to "bad" (extended, like a sheep bleat, long enough to turn

into its opposite), to "wicked," to "rad" (short for radical). The latest incum-

bent— "awesome"— ___possess___ more staying power, and ____reign____ for at

least two years.

46

Understanding Prepositions and Prepositional Phrases

All languages have nouns and verbs, but not all have prepositions. See, for instance, how the sentence *I went from Yokohama to Nagoya by car* might be rendered in Japanese:

Yokohama	kara	Nagoya	made	kuruma	de	ikimashita.
Yokohama	from	Nagoya	to	car	by	I went

Directly below each Japanese word is its English equivalent. As you can see, both Japanese and English have words that show the relationship of a noun to the rest of the sentence (*kara* for "from," *made* for "to," *de* for "by"), but in Japanese (as well as in some other languages) they are not **prepositions**, that is, words placed before noun objects, but **postpositions**, words placed after such nouns.

English differs in various ways from other languages in the way prepositions are used. Think about whether prepositions are used differently in your native language; if so, you may need to pay special attention to the way you use prepositions in English.

Using prepositions idiomatically

Even if you usually know where to use prepositions, you may have difficulty from time to time knowing which preposition to use. Each of the most common prepositions, whether in English or in other languages, has a wide range of different applications, and this range never coincides exactly from one language to another. See, for example, how English speakers use *in* and *on*.

The peaches are *in* the refrigerator.

The peaches are *on* the table.

Is that a diamond ring *on* your finger?

If you speak Spanish, you would use one preposition (*en*) in all these sentences, which might lead you to say in English *Is that a diamond ring *in* your finger?*

There is no easy solution to the challenge of using English prepositions idiomatically, but there are some strategies that can make it less formidable:

Strategies for using prepositions idiomatically

1. Keep in mind typical examples of the most basic sense of each preposition. For example:

   IN   The peaches are *in* the refrigerator.
         There are still some pickles *in* the jar.

   Here the object of the preposition *in* is a container that encloses something.

   ON   The peaches are *on* the table.
         The book you are looking for is *on* the top shelf.

   Here the object of the preposition *on* is a horizontal surface that supports something with which it is in direct contact.

2. Add to these examples others that show some similarities and some differences in meaning. For example:

   IN   You shouldn't drive *in* a snowstorm.

   Here there is no container, but like a container the falling snow surrounds and seems to enclose the driver.

   ON   Is that a diamond ring *on* your finger?

   A finger is not a horizontal surface, but like such a surface it can support a ring with which it is in contact.

3. Use your imagination to create mental images that can help you remember figurative uses of prepositions. For example:

   IN   Michael is *in* love.

   Imagine a warm bath in which Michael is immersed (or a raging tor-rent, if you prefer to visualize love that way).

ON   I've just read a book *on* computer science.

Imagine a shelf labelled COMPUTER SCIENCE on which the book you have read is located.

4. Try to learn uses of prepositions not in isolation, but as part of a system. For example, in identifying the location of a place or an event, the three prepositions *in, on,* and *at* can be used.

The preposition *at* specifies the exact point in space or time.

AT   There will be a meeting tomorrow *at* 9:30 a.m. *at* 160 Main Street.

Expanses of space or time within which a place is located or an event takes place are treated as containers, and so require *in.*

IN   I arrived *in* Canada *in* January.

Instead of *in* or *at, on* must be used in two cases: with the names of streets (but not the exact address), and with days of the week or month.

ON   I visited the airlines office, which is *on* University Avenue, *on* Wednesday.

ON   I'll be moving from my apartment *on* Park Road *on* September 30.

You might remember to use *on* in these cases if you picture in your mind the base of a building in direct contact with the pavement of a street and a 365-day appointment calendar with a date printed on the surface of each page.

46b

Using two-word verbs

Compare these two sentences:

The balloon rose off the ground.
The plane took off.

In the first sentence, the word *off* is a preposition that introduces the prepositional phrase *off the ground.* In the second sentence, on the other hand, *off* does not function as a preposition and does not introduce a prepositional phrase. Instead, it combines with *took* to form a two-word verb with its own special meaning. Such a verb is called a **phrasal verb**, and the word *off*, when used in this way, is called an **adverbial particle**. Many prepositions, as well as several other words (for example, *back* and *away*), can function as adverbial particles to form phrasal verbs.

In the first sentence, in which *off* is part of a prepositional phrase, it is possible to put other phrases between the verb and the preposition. You can say, for example:

> The balloon *rose off the ground* without difficulty.
>
> OR   The balloon *rose* without difficulty *off the ground*.

But you cannot insert such phrases in sentence 2, where *off* is not a preposition. You can say, for example:

> The plane *took off* without difficulty.
>
> BUT NOT   The plane *took* without difficulty *off*.

The verb + particle combination that makes up a phrasal verb is a tightly knit entity that usually cannot be torn apart. However, there is one major exception.

Many phrasal verbs are transitive, meaning that they take a direct object (see 14c). Take, for example, the verb + particle combination *pick up;* in the following sentence, it takes the noun phrase *my baggage* as its direct object:

> I *picked up my baggage* at the terminal.

Like any other phrasal verb, it cannot easily be split apart. English speakers would never say I <u>*picked* at the terminal *up my baggage*</u>. Yet nothing prevents the direct object from being moved between the verb and the participle. The following sentence is perfectly normal:

> I *picked my baggage up* at the terminal.

Furthermore, if a personal pronoun is used as the direct object, it must separate the verb from its particle:

> I *picked it up* at the terminal.

In fact, it would be unacceptable for the pronoun to follow the particle, as in I *picked up it at the terminal*.

Phrasal verbs are extremely common in English. Some of them are slang (*cop out,* "fail to take responsibility"), and others, though appropriate in most conversation, are much less so in formal writing (*mess up,* "spoil").

But many phrasal verbs are normal both in speech and in most varieties of formal written English. For example, an essay by Lewis Thomas includes two phrasal verbs: "... you got all the writer intended to *parcel out* and now you have to *move along*."

Thomas also uses a two-word verb of a different type: "It is almost always a greater pleasure to *come across* a semicolon than a period." *Come across* does not operate like a phrasal verb. For one thing, you can insert an additional phrase between *come* and *across: to come suddenly and unexpectedly across a semicolon* is acceptable if a bit unwieldy. On the other hand, the object that follows *across* cannot be moved between it and *come;* you would never say *to come a semicolon across. Come across* seems to consist of the verb *come* followed by the preposition *across,* which introduces the prepositional phrase *across a semicolon.* Yet *to come across a semicolon* is different from a normal verb + prepositional phrase, such as *to rise off the ground.* If you know the typical meanings of *rise* and *off,* you can interpret *to rise off the ground.* Not so with *to come across a semicolon;* the combination *come + across* has a special meaning ("find by chance") which could not be determined from the typical meanings of *come* and *across.* Therefore *come across* must be considered a two-word verb, but one that has much more in common with verbs followed by prepositions than with phrasal verbs. Such verbs as *come across* are called **prepositional verbs.**

Prepositional verbs include such idiomatic two-word verbs as *run into,* meaning "meet by chance," *take after,* meaning "resemble" (usually a parent or other older relative), *get over,* meaning "recover from," and *count on,* meaning "trust." They also include verb + preposition combinations in which the meaning is predictable, but the specific preposition that is required is less predictable, and must be learned together with the verb (for example, *depend on, look at, listen to, approve of*). There are also **phrasal-prepositional verbs,** which are verb + adverbial particle + preposition sequences (for example, *put up with, look forward to, give up on, get away with*).

Every comprehensive dictionary includes information about the various adverbial particles and prepositions that a verb can combine with, but only some dictionaries distinguish verb + particle from verb + preposition.

Exercise 46.1

Each of the following sentences contains a two-word verb. In some, the verb is used correctly; in some, incorrectly. Identify the two-word verb in each case, indicate whether it is a phrasal or prepositional verb, and rewrite any incorrect sentences correctly.

1. Shortly after the French invasion of Egypt, the British struck at Napoleon back.

2. By 1801, the French forces in Egypt were compelled to give up.

3. As part of the treaty of surrender, the French were required to turn the Rosetta Stone over to the British.

4. The British took back it to England.

5. The Rosetta Stone is now in the British Museum, where millions of visitors have looked at it.

47

Forming Clauses and Sentences

Just as the living body is made up of cells, so most messages that we communicate are made up of sentences. But cells vary in nature from one living thing to another, and sentences are not formed in the same way in every language.

Expressing subjects explicitly

English sentences consist of a subject and a predicate. This simple statement defines a gulf separating English from many other languages. Recall the Japanese sentence used at the beginning of Chapter 46: *Yokohama kara Nagoya made kuruma de ikimashita,* presented as the equivalent of "I went from Yokohama to Nagoya by car," with *ikimashita* translated as "I went." But *ikimashita* can also be rendered as "we went," "you went," "she went," "he went," or "they went." The subject is actually unexpressed but is understood from the context.

Many other languages leave out the subject when it can easily be inferred. Not English. With only limited exceptions, English demands that an explicit subject accompany an explicit predicate in every sentence. Though *Went from Yokohama to Nagoya by car* is possible on a postcard to a friend, in most varieties of spoken and written English the extra effort of explicitly stating who went is not simply an option but an obligation.

In fact every subordinate clause must have an explicit subject.

NOT   They flew to London on the Concorde because was fast.

BUT   They flew to London on the Concorde because *it* was fast.

English even requires a kind of "dummy" subject to fill the subject position in the following sentences:

It is raining.

There is a strong wind.

Speakers of some other languages might be inclined to say: *Is raining* or *Has a strong wind.* In English, however, *it* and *there* are indispensable.

Expressing objects explicitly

Transitive verbs typically require that objects also be explicitly stated, and in some cases even other items of information as well (see 16c). For example, it is not enough to tell someone *Give!* even if it is clear what is to be given to whom. You must say *Give it to me* or *Give her the passport* or some other such sentence. Similarly, saying *Put!* or *Put it!* is insufficient when you mean *Put it on the table.*

Using English word order

You should not move subjects, verbs, or objects out of their normal positions in the sentence. In the following sentence, each element is in its appropriate place:

SUBJECT VERB OBJECT ADVERB
Omar reads books voraciously.

If you speak Turkish, Korean, or Japanese, in which the verb must come last, you may have to make a special effort never to write such a sentence as *Omar books voraciously reads,* which is not acceptable in English.

If you speak Russian, which permits a great deal of freedom in word order, you must remember never to interchange the position of subject and object (*Books reads Omar voraciously* is not acceptable English) and to avoid separating the verb from its object (*Omar reads voraciously books*). See 14c and 23b.

47d

Recognizing the sentence nucleus

This chapter began with an analogy between living cells and sentences. In English this analogy can be carried further. Just as a cell contains a nucleus that determines the essential nature of that cell, so an English sentence also contains a nucleus. Consider this brief dialogue:

A: Have Bulgaria and Brazil reached the finals in the World Cup?
B: Brazil has. Bulgaria hasn't.
A: Did Bulgaria lose to Italy?
B: Yes, it did.

When B says *Brazil has,* the combination of the subject + the auxiliary stands for the whole sentence *Brazil has reached the finals in the World Cup.* That combination can be called the **sentence nucleus.** Notice that B could not have left out more or less than those two elements; if B had said *Brazil* or *Brazil has reached,* the response would have been unacceptable English. The nucleus must be intact to represent the whole sentence.

The sentence nucleus serves many purposes, including the formation of negative statements and questions:

1. To form a negative statement, add *not* directly after the nucleus, either as a separate word or contracted with the auxiliary (*Bulgaria has not* or *Bulgaria hasn't*).

2. Form questions by reversing the order of the nucleus to auxiliary + subject, as in <u>*Have Bulgaria and Brazil*</u> *reached the finals in the World Cup?*

Notice that in B's second reply, *it did* stands for *Bulgaria lost to Italy.* In the full sentence, the verb *lost* has no auxiliary. In such a case, use the auxiliary *do* to form a nucleus with the subject, with *do* taking the tense form (in this case, the past tense form *did*) from the main verb.

Remember that *do* is used as an auxiliary only when no other auxiliaries are present. Note also that when it is used and the nucleus is followed by the rest of the sentence, the main verb appears in the base form.

NOT   Did Bulgaria lost to Italy?

BUT   Did Bulgaria lose to Italy?

Using noun clauses, infinitives, and gerunds

Consider once again the analogy between the sentence and a cell of the living body. In one important respect, the analogy does not hold. Body tissues are made up of cells, but they are not cells themselves; sentences, on the other hand, are frequently built up (with some adjustments) out of smaller sentences, which are called **clauses.**

1. Using noun clauses

Examine the following sentence:

> In my last year in high school, my adviser urged that I apply to several colleges.

This is built up out of two sentences, one of them (B) embedded in the other (A):

A.   In my last year in high school, my adviser urged B.
B.   I (should) apply to several colleges.

When these are combined as in the first sentence above, sentence B becomes a noun clause introduced by *that* and takes on the role of object of the verb *urged* in sentence A. Now look at the following sentence:

> It made a big difference that she wrote a strong letter of recommendation.

Here the two component sentences are C and D:

C.   D made a big difference.
D.   She wrote a strong letter of recommendation.

In this case the noun clause formed from sentence D functions as the subject of sentence C, so that the combination reads as follows:

> That she wrote a strong letter of recommendation made a big difference.

This is an acceptable sentence, but somewhat top-heavy. Usually when a lengthy noun clause is the subject of the sentence, it is moved to the end. When that is done, the result is *Made a big difference that she wrote a strong letter of recommendation.* If you speak Italian or Spanish or Portuguese, you might see nothing wrong with such a sentence. In English, however, the subject position must be filled. The "dummy" element *it* comes to the rescue and sets things right, converting the preceding example to *It made a big difference that she wrote a strong letter of recommendation.*

2. Using infinitives and gerunds

As you can see, when you construct a larger sentence out of smaller ones in English, the architecture can get complicated. In fact, you have more choices still. Not only can you use noun clauses; you can also use infinitives and gerunds. Some languages, such as Greek, do very well with just noun clauses; French and a great many other languages employ infinitives but have no equivalent to gerunds. When to use one or the other may be a challenge to multilingual writers. Though there is no simple explanation that will make it an easy task, here are some hints that will help you know when to use an infinitive or a gerund.

See how the two sentences considered above can also be stated.

In my last year in high school, my adviser urged that I apply to several colleges.

In my last year in high school, my adviser urged *me to apply* to several colleges.

It made a big difference that she wrote a strong letter of recommendation.

Her writing a strong letter of recommendation made a big difference.

In the first pair, the verb in the noun clause *that I apply to several colleges* has been changed to an infinitive (*to apply*), and the subject *I* has been put into the objective case (*me*). In the second, the verb in the noun clause *that she wrote a strong letter of recommendation* has been transformed into a gerund (*writing*), and the subject *she* has become the possessive *her.*

Why was an infinitive chosen for the first and a gerund for the second? In general, **infinitives** tend to represent intentions, desires, or expectations, while **gerunds** tend to represent facts. The gerund in the second pair calls attention to the fact that a letter was actually written; the infinitive in the first pair conveys the message that the act of applying was something desired, not an accomplished fact.

The distinction between fact and intention is not a rule but only a tendency, and it can be superseded by other rules. For instance, only a gerund, never an infinitive, can be directly preceded by a preposition. For this reason sentences like the one below must be changed as shown:

CHANGE   This fruit is all right for to eat.

TO   This fruit is all right *to eat.*

OR   This fruit is all right *for eating*.

OR   This fruit is all right *for us to eat*.

The association of fact with gerunds and of intention with infinitives can help you know in the majority of cases whether to use an infinitive or a gerund when another verb immediately precedes. Consider the following examples:

Gerunds

Marion *enjoys going* to the theatre.

We *resumed working* after our coffee break.

Caitlin *appreciated getting* chocolates from Sean.

In all of these cases the second verb is a gerund, and the gerund indicates that the action or event that it expresses actually has happened. Verbs like *enjoy, resume,* and *appreciate* can be followed only by gerunds, not by infinitives. In fact, even when these verbs do not convey clear facts, the verb that comes second must still be a gerund:

Caitlin *would appreciate getting* chocolates from Sean, but he hardly knows she exists.

Infinitives

Scott *expected to get* a good job after graduation.

Last year, Tina *decided to become* a math major.

The strikers have *agreed to go* back to work.

Here it is irrelevant whether the actions or events referred to by the infinitives did or did not materialize; at the moment indicated by the verbs *expect, decide,* and *agree,* those actions or events were merely intentions. These three verbs, as well as many others that specify intentions (or negative intentions, like *refuse*), must always be followed by an infinitive, never a gerund.

A few verbs can be followed by either an infinitive or a gerund; with some, such as *begin* or *continue,* the choice makes little difference in meaning, but with a handful of others, the difference in meaning is striking.

Using an infinitive to state an intention

Ivan was working as a medical technician, but he *stopped to study* English.

The infinitive indicates that Ivan intended to study English when he left his job. We are not told whether he actually did study English or not.

Using a gerund to state a fact

Ivan *stopped studying* English when he left Canada.

The gerund indicates that Ivan actually did study English, but later stopped.

Checking when to use a gerund or an infinitive

A full list of verbs that can be followed by an infinitive and verbs that can be followed by a gerund can be found in the *Index to Modern English*, by Thomas Lee Crowell, Jr. (McGraw-Hill, 1964).

47f

Using adjective clauses

Adjective clauses can be a challenge to multilingual writers. Look at the following sentence and then see what can go wrong:

The company *Mario's uncle invested in* went bankrupt.

The subject is a noun phrase in which the noun *company* is modified by the article *the* and the adjective clause *Mario's uncle invested in*. The sentence as a whole says that a certain company went bankrupt, and the adjective clause identifies the company more specifically by saying that Mario's uncle had invested in it.

One way of seeing how the adjective clause fits into the sentence is to rewrite it like this: *The company (Mario's uncle had invested in it) went bankrupt.* This is not a normal English sentence, but it helps to demonstrate a process that leads to the sentence we started with. The steps are:

1. Change the personal pronoun *it* to the relative pronoun *which: The company (Mario's uncle had invested in which) went bankrupt.* That still is not acceptable English.

2. Either move the whole prepositional phrase *in which* to the beginning of the adjective clause, or just move the relative pronoun: *The company in which Mario's uncle had invested went bankrupt* or *The company which Mario's uncle had invested in went bankrupt.* Both of these are good English sentences, the former somewhat more formal than the latter.

3. If no preposition precedes, substitute *that* for *which* or leave out the relative pronoun entirely. *The company that Mario's uncle had invested in went bankrupt* or *The company Mario's uncle had invested in went bankrupt.* Both of these are good English sentences, not highly formal but still acceptable in much formal writing.

Speakers of some languages find adjective clauses difficult in different ways. Following are some guidelines that might help.

If you speak Korean, Japanese, or Chinese
If you speak Korean, Japanese, or Chinese, the fact that the adjective clause does not precede the noun that it modifies may be disconcerting, both because that is the position of such clauses in the East Asian languages and because other modifiers, such as determiners and adjectives, do precede the noun in English.

If you speak Farsi, Arabic, or Hebrew
If you speak Farsi, Arabic, or Hebrew, you may expect the adjective clause to follow the noun as it does in English, but you might need to remind yourself to change the personal pronoun (*it*) to a relative pronoun (*which* or *that*) and then to move the relative pronoun to the beginning of the clause. You may mistakenly put a relative pronoun at the beginning but keep the personal pronoun, thus producing incorrect sentences such as *The company that Yossi's uncle invested in it went bankrupt.*

If you speak a European or Latin American language
If you are a speaker of some European or Latin American languages, you are probably acquainted with adjective clauses very much like those of English, but you may have difficulty accepting the possibility that a relative pronoun that is the object of a preposition can be moved to the beginning of the clause while leaving the preposition stranded. You might, therefore, move the preposition as well even when the relative pronoun is *that,* or you might drop the preposition altogether, generating such incorrect sentences as *The company in that Carmen's uncle invested went bankrupt* or *The company that Carmen's uncle invested went bankrupt.*

Finally, the fact that the relative pronoun can sometimes be omitted may lead to the mistaken notion that it can be omitted in all cases. Remember that you cannot omit a relative pronoun that is the subject of a verb.

NOT   Everyone invested in that company lost a great deal.

BUT   Everyone who invested in that company lost a great deal.

Understanding conditional sentences

English pays special attention to whether or not something is a fact, or to the degree of confidence we have in the truth or likelihood of an assertion. It is no surprise, therefore, that English distinguishes on this basis among many different types of **conditional sentences,** that is, sentences that focus on questions of truth and that are introduced by *if* or its equivalent. The following examples illustrate a range of different conditional sentences. Each of these sentences makes different assumptions about the likelihood that what is stated in the *if*-clause is true, and then draws the corresponding conclusion in the main clause.

> If you *practise* (or *have practised*) writing frequently, you *know* (or *have learned*) what your chief problems are.

This sentence assumes that what is stated in the *if*-clause may very well be true; the alternatives in parentheses indicate that any tense that is appropriate in a simple sentence may be used in both the *if*-clause and the main clause.

> If you *practise* writing for the rest of this term, you *will* (or *may*) *get* a firmer grasp of the process.

This sentence makes a prediction about the future and again assumes that what is stated may very well turn out to be true. Only the main clause uses the future tense (*will get*) or some other modal that can indicate future time (*may get*). The *if*-clause must use the present tense, even though it too refers to the future.

> If you *practised* (or *were to practise*) writing every single day, it *would* eventually *seem* much easier to you.

This sentence casts some doubt on the likelihood that what is stated will be put into effect. In the *if*-clause, the verb is either past (actually past subjunctive—see 16h) or *were to* + the base form, though it refers to future time. The main clause has *would* + the base form of the main verb.

> If you *practised* writing on Mars, you *would find* no one to show your work to.

This sentence contemplates an impossibility at present or in the foreseeable future. As with the preceding sentence, the past subjunctive is used in the *if*-clause, although past time is not being referred to, and *would* + the base form is used in the main clause.

> If you *had practised* writing in ancient Egypt, you *would have used* hiero-glyphics.

This sentence shifts the impossibility back to the past; obviously you are not going to find yourself in ancient Egypt. But since past forms have already been used in the preceding two sentences, this one demands a form that is "more past": the past perfect in the *if*-clause, and *would* + the perfect form of the main verb in the main clause.

And so, with a feeling of gratitude that you do not have to write in hieroglyphics, you should approach the challenge of writing in English with confidence.

Exercise 47.1

Revise the following sentences as necessary. Not all sentences contain an error.

1. The scholar who deciphered finally hieroglyphics was Jean-François Champollion.

2. Champollion enjoyed to study the languages of the Middle East.

3. By comparing the Greek and Egyptian inscriptions on the Rosetta Stone, he made a great deal of progress in understanding hieroglyphics.

4. Was of great importance that he knew Coptic, a later form of the Egyptian language.

5. In 1822 Champollion wrote a paper which he presented his decipherment of hieroglyphics in it.

6. If the Rosetta Stone was not discovered, it would have been much more difficult to decipher hieroglyphics.

Exercise 47.2

In his nonsense poem "The Walrus and the Carpenter," Lewis Carroll uses conditional sentences for humorous effect. Look back at the five sentence types in 47g. What sentence type is used in the following two stanzas?

> The Walrus and the Carpenter
>   Were walking close at hand:
> They wept like anything to see
>   Such quantities of sand.

"If this were only cleared away,"
    They said, "it *would* be grand."

"If seven maids with seven mops
    Swept it for half a year,
Do you suppose," the Walrus said,
    "That they could get it clear?"
"I doubt it," said the Carpenter,
    And shed a bitter tear.

Glossaries

Glossary of Grammatical Terms

Glossary of Usage

Glossary of Grammatical Terms

absolute phrase See *phrase*.

abstract noun See *noun*.

acronym A word formed from the first letters of several words, such as RADAR for *radio detecting and ranging*.

active voice See *voice*.

adjective A word that modifies, quantifies, identifies, or describes a word or words acting as a noun. An attributive adjective precedes and a **predicative** adjective follows the noun or pronoun that it modifies (*a good book, the book is good*). Of the overlapping types of adjectives, **descriptive adjectives** identify a quality that is *common,* such as a type, colour, or weight (*research paper, yellow paper, heavy paper*) or *proper,* derived from a proper noun (*English history, Jacobean drama,* Homeric *epic*). **Demonstrative adjectives** (*this, that, these,* and *those*) point out words acting as nouns (*this paper, those papers*). **Indefinite adjectives** define the specificity of the words they modify (*some research, any research, such research*). **Relative adjectives** qualify words bound directly to a modifying clause (*I know which research is yours*). **Interrogative adjectives** ask questions about the words they modify (*Whose research us finished? What research is she doing? Which research is in progress?*). **Limiting** adjectives are the articles *a, an,* and *the.* Numerical adjectives modify words with *cardinal* or *ordinal* numbers (*two girls in their tenth year*). **Participial adjectives** are verbs that act as adjectives (*a waiting car, a damaged package*). **Possessive adjectives** include *my, yours, his, her, its, one's, our, your, their* (*her research, our research*) as well as proper possessives formed by adding an -'s to a proper noun (*Einstein's research, Italy's coastline*). See 14b4, 18a, 18b, and 18d.

adjective clause See *clause.*

adjective forms Changes in an adjective from the **positive** (simply *tall, good*) to **comparative** (comparing two—taller, better) or the **superlative** (comparing more than two—*tallest, best*). Short regular adjectives (*tall*) just add -*er* and -*est,* but irregular adjectives (*good*) do not follow this pattern. Most longer adjectives form the comparative by adding *more* or *less* (*more beautiful, less beautiful*) and the superlative by adding *most* and *least* (*most beautiful, least beautiful*). Some adjectives (*only, forty*) do not change form.

adverb A word that qualifies, modifies, limits, or defines a verb, an adjective, another adverb, or a clause, frequently answering the questions *where?, when?, how?, why?, to what extent?,* or *under what conditions?* Adverbs derived from adjectives and nouns commonly end in the suffix -*ly. She will <u>soon</u> travel <u>south</u> and <u>probably</u> visit her <u>very</u> favourite sister.* See also *conjunction.* See 14b5, 18c, and 18d.

adverb clause See *clause.*

adverb forms Changes in an adverb from the **positive** (simply *eagerly*) to the **comparative** (comparing two—*more eagerly*) or the **superlative** (comparing more than two—*most eagerly*). The forms of some adverbs and adjectives are identical (*fast, faster, fastest; little, less, least*). Most adverbs, however, add *more* or *less* in the comparative and *most* or *least* in the superlative (*quickly, more quickly, most quickly*).

adverbial particle The word that, when combined with a verb, forms a **phrasal verb.** *The plane took <u>off</u> smoothly.* See 46b.

agreement The correspondence of a pronoun with its antecedent in person, number, and gender, or of a verb with its subject in person and number and gender, or of a verb with its subject in person and number. *Tina sings, and her fans go wild; the band members play and the crowd goes wild.* See also *antecedent, gender, number, person.* See Chapter 17.

antecedent A specific noun that a pronoun replaces and to which it refers. The two must agree in person, number, and gender. *<u>Gene Kelly</u> moved <u>his</u> feet as no one else has.* The antecedent can sometimes follow the pronoun that refers to it. *Moving <u>his</u> feet as no one else has, <u>Gene Kelly</u> was a singular dancer.* See 14b3, 19a, and 19b.

appositive One noun or noun phrase that parallels another, illuminating it with additional information. *Marcia, <u>a person I've always respected</u>, has advised me not to continue. The cruelest month, <u>April</u>, is my favourite.* See 14c3 and 34c3.

article A, *an*, or *the*, the most common adjectives. *A* is used before consonants, *an* before vowels. Both are **indefinite** and do not specifically identify the nouns they modify. <u>*A*</u> *strange feeling came over me as* <u>*an*</u> *awful spectre arose. The* is **definite** or specific. <u>*The*</u> *awful figure of my long-lost grandfather stood before me.* A noun is said to have a **zero article** if it appears without *the, a, an,* or any other determiner. *I prayed for rain.* See 44d3.

auxiliary verb A verb that combines with the base form or with the present or past participle of a main verb to form a verb phrase and to determine tense. The **primary** auxiliaries (*do, have, be*) have different forms and make verb phrases that are reasonably straightforward in terms of tense and mood (*I* <u>*did*</u> *think; I* <u>*had*</u> *thought; I* <u>*am*</u> *thinking*). **Modal** auxiliaries such as *can, may, shall, will, could, might, should, would,* and *ought [to]* have only one form and show possibility, necessity, obligation, ability, capability, and so on. Some modals form uncomplicated verb phrases (*I shall [will] think*), but others achieve subtle variations in tense and mood (*I* <u>*should have*</u> *agreed with you* <u>*had*</u> *I not known better*). See 14b1 and 16a.

cardinal number A simple number that answers the question *how many?*— *seven, one hundred fifty.* Distinguished from *ordinal number.*

case The form of a noun or pronoun that reflects its grammatical role in a sentence. Nouns and indefinite pronouns can be **subjective, possessive,** or **objective,** but they change form only in the possessive case. *The* <u>*dog*</u> (subjective) *barked. The* <u>*dog's*</u> (possessive) *tail wagged. The mail carrier called the* <u>*dog*</u> (objective). The personal pronouns *I, he, she, we,* and *they,* as well as the relative or interrogative pronoun *who,* change form in all three cases. <u>*We*</u> (subjective) *will take the train to Windsor.* <u>*Our*</u> (possessive) *trip will last a week. Dr. Baker will meet* <u>*us*</u> (objective) *at the station.* See also *person; pronoun.* See Chapter 15.

clause A word cluster containing a subject and a predicate. An **independent** clause can stand alone as a sentence. *The car hit the tree.* A **dependent clause,** as the name suggests, is subordinate to an independent clause, linked to it by a subordinating conjunction or a relative pronoun. The dependent clause can function as an adjective, an adverb, or a noun. *The car hit the tree* <u>*that stood at the edge of the road*</u> (adjective clause). *The car,* <u>*when it went out of control,*</u> *hit the tree* (adverb clause). *The car hit* <u>*what grew at the side of the road*</u> (noun clause). See also *nonrestrictive element, restrictive element.* See 14c4.

collective noun See *noun.*

comma splice An error resulting from joining two independent clauses with only a comma. See Chapter 21 for ways of revising comma splices.

common noun See *noun.*

comparative See *adjective forms, adverb forms.*

complement A word or group of words completing the predicate in a sentence. A **subject complement** follows a linking verb and renames or describes the subject. It can be a **predicate noun** (*Anorexia is an illness*) or a **predicate adjective** (*Karen Carpenter was anorexic*). An object complement renames or describes a direct object (*We considered him a hero and his behaviour heroic*). See 14c2.

complete predicate See *predicate.*

complete subject See *subject.*

complex sentence See *sentence.*

compound adjective A combination of words (or whatever parts of speech) that function as a single adjectival unit (*blue-green sea, ten-storey building, get-tough policy, supply side economics, north by northwest journey*). Most, but not all, compound adjectives use hyphens to separate their individual elements.

compound-complex sentence See *sentence.*

compound noun A combination of words forming a unit that can function as a single noun (*go-getter, in law, oil well, southeast*).

compound predicate See *predicate.*

compound sentence See *sentence.*

compound subject See *subject.*

concrete noun See *noun.*

conditional sentence A sentence, often introduced by *if*, that concerns a question of truth (*If you practise, you will get better*). See 47g.

conjunction A word or words that join words, phrases, clauses, or sentences. A *coordinating conjunction* (such as *and, but, or,* or *yet*) joins elements that are grammatically comparable (*Marx and Engels wrote* [two nouns]; *Marx writing one essay, but Engels writing the other* [two independent phrases]; *Marx wrote one essay, yet Engels wrote the other* [two independent clauses]). **Correlative conjunctions** (such as *both, and; either, or;* or *not only, but* [*also*] are used in pairs to connect elements that are grammatically equivalent (*neither Marx nor Engels; not only Marx, but also Engels*). A **subordinating conjunction** (such as *although, because, before, if, that, when, where,* or *why*) introduces a dependent clause, which it subordinates to an independent clause. *Marx wrote at the British Museum, where he did most of his work. Before his association with Marx, Engels was already a social theorist.* A **conjunctive adverb** (such as *consequently, moreover,* or *then*) modifies one independent clause following another independent clause. A conjunctive adverb often generally follows a semicolon or colon and precedes a comma. *Thoreau lived simply at Walden; however, he regularly joined his aunt for tea in Concord.* See 14b7 and 21c.

coordination The grammatical equality of two or more sentence elements. When elements are coordinate, they seem to express equally significant ideas. *She wanted both to stay and to go.* See also *subordination.* See 26a.

coordinating conjunction See *conjunction.*

correlative conjunction See *conjunction.*

count noun See *noun.*

dandling modifier A word, phrase, or clause that fails to modify the sentence element that it logically ought to. *Studying Freud, the subject of artistic creativity became complicated* (incorrect; the subject of artistic creativity was not studying Freud). *Studying Freud, the class appreciated the complicated nature of artistic creativity* (correct; the class was studying Freud). See 23c.

declension See *case, inflection, number, person.*

degree See *adjective forms, adverb forms.*

demonstrative adjective See *adjective.*

demonstrative pronoun See *pronoun.*

denotation The literal meaning of a term, as opposed to its **connotation** or associations. See 30c.

dependent clause See *clause.*

descriptive adjective See *adjective.*

determiner See *article.*

direct address A construction that uses a noun or pronoun naming whoever is spoken to. *Hey, Jack. You, get moving.*

direct discourse   Quotation that reproduces a speaker's words exactly, using quotation marks. *Nellie McClung often said, "The world has suffered long from too much masculinity, and not enough humanity."* See 38a and 38b.

direct object   A noun or pronoun receiving the action of a **transitive verb** in an **active** construction. *McKellan recited Shakespearean <u>soliloquies</u>.* See also *indirect object*. See 14c2.

double comparative   The incorrect use of a comparative to modify another comparative *(more better; less longer)*. See also *adjective forms, adverb forms*.

double superlative   The incorrect use of a superlative to modify another superlative *(<u>most</u> <u>unkindest</u> cut; <u>least profoundest</u> thought)*. See also *adjective forms, adverb forms*.

dynamic verb   See *verb*.

expletive   A construction that introduces a sentence with *there* or *it* and a form of *be*. *<u>There are</u> good reasons for having a physical exam. <u>It is</u> a good idea to see your doctor once a year.*

finite verb   A verb that can join a subject to form an independent clause without adding any auxiliary verb. *I <u>breathe</u>.* See 14c3, 16d, 16e, 16f, and 16g.

fused sentence   An error in which two main clauses are run together without a coordinating conjunction or suitable punctuation. Also known as a *run-on* sentence. See Chapter 21.

future   See *tense*.

gender   The classification of a noun or pronoun as masculine, feminine, or neuter—*god, he* (masculine); *goddess, she* (feminine); *godliness, it* (neuter). To avoid sexist language, use words that can refer equally to members of either sex, as in *police officer* rather than *policeman* or *policewoman*.

gerund   A verbal identical in form to the present participle but functioning as a **noun**. *<u>Studying</u> is a bore* (gerund subject). *I enjoy <u>studying</u>* (gerund object). See 14c3.

gerund phrase   See *phrase*.

head   The noun around which modifiers cluster. See 44c.

helping verb   An auxiliary verb. See *auxiliary verb*.

imperative mood   The form of a verb expressing a command or urging an action. An imperative may or may not have a stated subject. _Leave_. You _be quiet_. _Do come_ in. _Let's go_.

inconsistent structure The joining of two or more logically and grammatically incompatible elements in a single sentence.

indefinite adjective See _adjective_.

indefinite pronoun See _pronoun_.

independent clause See _clause_.

indicative mood The form of a verb expressing a fact, questioning a fact, or voicing an opinion or probability. _Molly _eats_ pancakes on Sundays. _Does_ she _make_ them herself?_ See also _mood_.

indirect discourse A paraphrased quotation that does not repeat another's words verbatim and hence is not enclosed in quotation marks. _Juan said that, if elected, he would not run._

indirect object A noun or pronoun identifying to or for whom or what a transitive verb's action is performed. The indirect object almost always precedes the direct object; it is usually the personal recipient of verbs of giving, showing, telling, and the like. _I handed _the dean_ my application and told _him_ that I needed financial aid._ See also _direct object_. See 14c2.

indirect question A sentence pattern in which a question is the basis of a subordinate clause. _Everyone wonders _why young people continue to take up smoking_._ (The question, phrased directly, is "Why do young people continue to take up smoking?")

infinitive The base form of a verb (_go, run, hit_), usually preceded by _to_ (_to go, to run, to hit_). The _to_ form is a verbal that can serve as a noun, adverb, or, occasionally, an adjective. _To go_ would be unthinkable (noun, subject). _I do not wish _to go_ (noun, object). _I shall go _to beg, to borrow_, or _to steal_ (adverbs). _I'd like my sandwich _to go_ (adjective). An infinitive can be active (_to hit_) or passive (_to be hit_). Further, the infinitive has two tenses, present (_to [be] hit_) and perfect (_to have [been] hit_). Frequently an infinitive is preceded not by _to_ but by a **modal auxiliary,** such as _can, may, must_, or _would_, or by the **primary auxiliary** _do_ (_I can _go_, I did _go_). An infinitive may be modified or take objects or complements as an **infinitive phrase.** See _phrase_. See 14b1, 14c3, and 16a.

inflection Changes in word forms to indicate person, number, gender, and case in pronouns; number, gender, and case in nouns; comparative and superlative forms in adjectives and adverbs; and person, tense, voice, and mood in verbs.

intensifier A modifier that increases the emphasis of the word or words that it modifies. *I should very much like to go. I'm so happy.* Despite their name, intensifiers are stylistically weak; they are best avoided in formal writing.

intensive pronoun See *pronoun.*

interjection A grammatically independent word or group of words that is usually an exclamation of surprise, shock, dismay, or the like. *Help! We're losing control. My word, what do you think you're doing?*

interrogative adjective See *adjective.*

interrogative pronoun See *pronoun.*

intransitive verb A verb that does not need a direct object to complete its meaning. *The children raced up the path.* See also *verb.* See 14c2.

irregular verb A verb with a past tense and past participle that does not follow the usual -*ed* or -*d* pattern. Irregular verbs may be *strong*, with a vowel change in the past and a past participle ending in -*n* or -*en* (*see, saw, seen*), or *weak*, with other abnormalities (*go, went, gone; get, got, got/gotten*). See also *regular verb.* See 16b.

limiting adjective See *adjective.*

linking verb A linking verb joins a subject with a subject complement or complements. Common linking verbs are *appear, be, become, feel,* and *seem. The argument appeared sound. It was an exercise in logic.* See also *verb.* See 14c2.

main clause An independent clause. See *clause.*

mass noun See *noun.*

misplaced modifier A word, phrase, or clause confusingly positioned so that it fails to apply clearly to the expression intended. *With a credit card, the traveller paid for the motel room and opened the door. The traveller paid for the motel room and opened the door with a credit card.* Unless the writer intended to indicate that the traveller broke into a room already paid for, *with a credit card* should follow *paid* or *room.* See 23a.

modal auxiliaries See *auxiliary verb.*

modifier A word, phrase, or clause that acts as an adjective or an adverb and qualifies the meaning of another word, phrase, or clause. See also *adjective, adverb, clause, phrase.*

mood The form of a verb used to indicate whether an action or a state is a possible fact or to ask a question (*indicative*), to give a command (*imperative*), or to express a wish or condition contrary to fact (*subjunctive*). In other words, mood reflects the writer or speaker's attitude toward the idea expressed in the verb. *The sea is turbulent* (indicative). *Be still, ye seas* (imperative). *Would that sea were calm* (subjunctive). See also *imperative mood, indicative mood, subjunctive mood.* See Chapter 16.

nominal A word, phrase, or clause that acts as a noun.

noncount noun See *noun.*

nonfinite verb See *verbal.*

nonrestrictive element A word, phrase, or clause that modifies but does not limit or change the essential meaning of a sentence element. A nonrestrictive element is set off from the rest of the sentence with commas, dashes, or parentheses. *Quantum physics, a difficult subject, is fascinating. He addressed, acerbically, the failure of the system.* See also *restrictive element.* See 34c.

noun A noun names a person, place, tangible object, concept, quality, action, or the like. Nouns serve as subjects, objects, complements, and appositives. Most nouns form the plural with the addition of *-s* or *-es* and the possessive with the addition of *'s* (see *number, case*). **Common nouns** name one (*rock, child, box*) or more (*rocks, children, boxes*) in a class or general group. **Proper nouns** begin with capital letters and name specifics such as a particular person, place, religion, time period, holiday, movement, or thing (*Achebe, Caesar, Saskatchewan, CN Tower, Elizabethan Age, July, Rosicrucianism, Ramadan*). Some proper nouns can form plurals (*Adamses, Caesars*). **Abstract nouns** name intangible qualities, concepts, actions, or states (*virtue, peace, violence, evil, health, haste, time, inertia*). Some abstract nouns may be common or proper, depending on the sense that the writer wishes to communicate. Many abstract nouns have plural forms (*virtues, evils*), and as plurals they become increasingly *concrete.* **Concrete nouns** name people, places, or things and may be common or proper. In addition, **collective nouns** name coherent groups. In its singular form, a collective noun names a body or group of related elements; in its plural form, it names several such bodies or groups (*pride, prides* [of lions]; *family, families; Senate, Senates*). **Count nouns** name people, places, and things that can be counted (*one woman, two women; one park, three parks; one tree, four trees; one Smith,* *five Smiths*). **Mass nouns** (or **noncount nouns**) name concrete things that are not usually counted, although their plural forms are common (*sand, sands* [of Waikiki]; *rain,* [summer] *rains*). See 14b2.

noun clause See *clause.*

noun phrase See *phrase.*

number The form of a noun, pronoun, demonstrative adjective, or verb that indicates whether it is singular or plural: *oak* is singular, *oaks* plural; *I* and *me* are singular, *we* and *us* plural; *he buys* is singular, *they buy* plural; *this book* is singular, *these books* plural. See 14b1, 14b2, Chapter 16 introduction, and 17a.

object A word or words, acting as a noun or pronoun, influenced by a transitive verb, a verbal, or a preposition. See also *direct object, indirect object, object of a preposition.* See 14c2.

object complement See *complement.*

objective case See *case.*

object of a preposition A noun or pronoun connected to a sentence by a preposition, thus completing a **prepositional phrase.** *Johnson went to Pembroke College at Oxford. Thank you for coming.* See 14b6 and 14c3.

ordinal number The form of a number that expresses order or sequence (*first, seventeenth, twenty-third, two hundredth*). See also *cardinal number.*

participial adjective See *adjective.*

participial phrase See *phrase.*

participle A verb with properties of both an adjective and a verb. Like an adjective, a participle can modify a noun or pronoun; like a verb, it has present and past tenses and can take an object. The **present** participle usually ends in *-ing*, the **past** participle in *-ed, -d, -en*, or an irregular form. Without any auxiliary verbs, the present participle is active, the past participle passive. *Reeling, Spinks hit the canvas. The torn page was a clue.* See 14c3. With auxiliary verbs, present participles form the progressive tenses (I *am making,* I *was making,* I *will be making,* I *have been making,* I *had been making,* I *will have been making*). Similarly, past participles form the perfect tenses (I *have made,* I *had made,* I *will have made*). Further, past participles, with auxiliary verbs, are used to form the passive voice (I *am beaten,* I *was beaten*). These compound tenses are known as verb phrases. See also *adjective, phrase, tense, verbal, voice.*

parts of speech The eight grammatical categories into which words can be grouped depending on how they function in a sentence. Many words act as different parts of speech in different sentences. The parts of speech are *adjectives, adverbs, conjunctions, interjections, nouns, prepositions, pronouns,* and *verbs.* See 14b.

passive voice See *voice.*

past participle See *participle.*

past perfect tense See *tense.*

past tense See *tense.*

perfect tenses See *participle, tense, verb.*

person The relation between a subject and its corresponding verb, indicating whether the subject is speaking about itself (first person *I* or *we*), being spoken to (second person *you*), or being spoken about (third person *he, she, it,* or *they*). *Be* has several forms depending on the person (*am, is,* and *are* in the present tense plus *was* and *were* in the past). Other verbs change form in the present tense with a third-person singular subject (*I fall, you fall, she falls, we fall, they fall*). See 14b1, Chapter 16 and 17a. **Personal pronouns** also change form as subjects, objects, and possessives. See 14b3.

personal pronoun See *pronoun.*

phrasal-prepositional verb The combination of verb, adverbial particle, and preposition, in that order, e.g., *put up with.* See 46b.

phrasal verb The combination of a verb and a preposition to carry its own special meaning (*blow away, take off, pick up,* etc). See 46b. See also *adverbial particle.*

phrase A group of words that functions as a single unit but lacks a subject, a finite verb in a predicate, or both. Phrases can be grouped not only by the parts of speech that govern or introduce them but also by their grammatical functions as adjectives, adverbs, nouns, or verbs. An **absolute phrase** modifies an entire sentence and thus is grammatically divorced from the sentence. It uses a noun or pronoun as its subject and a participle (possibly implied) or participial phrase as its predicate. *The party being over, everyone left. The party over, everyone left* (participle implied). A **gerund phrase** serves as a noun, acting as a subject, a complement, or an object. It is built around a gerund, the -ing form of a verb acting as a noun. *Exercising regularly and sensibly is a key to good health* (subject). *I dislike exercising regularly and sensibly* (direct object). *I am bored with exercising regularly and sensibly* (object of a preposition). An **infinite phrase** may serve as an adjective, an adverb, or a noun and is governed by an infinitive. *The Pacific Coast is the place to be* (adjective). *She went to pay her taxes* (adverb). *To be young again is all I want* (noun). A **noun phrase,** including a noun and its modifiers, may serve as a subject, a complement, or an object. *A long, rough road* (subject) *crossed the barren desert* (object). *A raccoon is a resourceful animal* (complement). A **participial phrase** is governed by a present or past participle and functions as an adjective. *Breaking his leg, he stumbled. Having broken his leg, he stumbled.* A **prepositional phrase** is introduced by a preposition and may act as an adjective, an adverb, or a noun. *The gas in the laboratory is leaking* (adjective). *The firefighters went to the lab to check* (adverb). *Out of season is the least crowded time* (noun). A **verb phrase** is composed of a main verb and one or more auxiliaries, acting as a single verb in the sentence predicate. *I should have come to the review session.* See 14c3.

positive degree See *adjective forms, adverb forms.*

possessive adjective See *adjective, case.*

possessive case See *case.*

postposition In Japanese and in some other languages, any word placed after a noun to show the relationship of that noun to the rest of the sentence. A postposition's grammatical function corresponds to that of the preposition in English. See 46.

predicate The actual or implied finite verb and related words in a sentence. The predicate expresses what the subject does, experiences, or is. A **simple predicate** is a verb or a verb phrase that reflects on the subject. *For years the Young People's Theatre has been a cultural centre in Toronto.* A **compound predicate** has more than one simple predicate. *The athletes swam, cycled, and ran in the triathlon competition.* A **complete predicate** includes the simple predicate and any associated modifiers and objects. *I gave Sarah an engagement ring.* See 14c2.

predicate adjective See *complement.*

predicate noun See *complement.*

prefix An addition (often derived from a Latin preposition or negative) to the beginning of a root word to alter its meaning (*preview, undress*). See 31c1.

preposition A part of speech that indicates the position of a noun or pronoun in space or time and links it to other sentence elements. *He was at the* *top of the ladder before the other contestants had climbed to the fourth rung.* See *phrases.* See 14b6.

prepositional verb A two-word verb (such as *come across*) whose meaning depends entirely on the combination of the two words. See 46b.

present participle See *participle.*

present perfect See *participle, tense, verb, verbal.*

present progressive See *participle, tense, verb, verbal.*

present tense See *tense, verb.*

progressive forms See *participle, tense, verb.*

pronoun A single-word noun substitute that refers to an actual or logical antecedent. **Demonstrative pronouns** *(this, that, these,* and *those)* point out particular nouns. *This is the article I read. Those are the books I bought.* **Indefinite pronouns** do not refer to specific nouns and include *any, each, everybody, everyone, some,* and similar words. *Never in the field of human conflict was so much owed by so many to so few.* Some indefinite pronouns have a possessive case. *Everyone's best interests will be served by this research.* **Intensive pronouns** *(myself, yourself, himself, herself, oneself, itself, ourselves, yourselves, themselves)* emphasize their antecedent nouns or personal pronouns, agreeing with them in person, number, and gender. *She herself knew that we ourselves were blameless. The fire did not damage the house itself.* **Interrogative pronouns** *(who, which,* and *what)* ask questions. *Which one would you like? What is going on?* **Personal pronouns** *(I, you, he, she, it, we, you,* and *they)* observe number, gender, and case as they refer to particular people or things. *He knew what was his and also what was best for him.* See also *case, gender, number.* **Reciprocal pronouns** *(each other, one another)* refer to the individuals included in a plural antecedent. *Holmes and Frazier fought each other. The candidates debated one another. Each other* is preferred in sentences involving two subjects, and *one another* in those involving more than two subjects. **Reflexive pronouns,** identical in form to intensive pronouns, refer back to the subject of the sentence or clause. *I washed myself* (direct object). *I gave myself a pat on the back* (indirect object). **Relative pronouns** *(who, whom, which, that, what, whoever, whomever, whichever,* and *whatever)* connect a dependent clause to a sentence. *I wonder who will win the prize.* See 14b3.

proper adjective See *adjective.*

proper noun See *noun.*

reciprocal pronoun See *pronoun.*

reflexive pronoun See *pronoun.*

regular verb A verb with a past tense and past participle ending in *-d* or *-ed* (*care, cared, cared; look, looked, looked*). See also *irregular verb.* See 16b.

relative adjective See *adjective.*

relative pronoun See *pronoun.*

restrictive element A word, phrase, or clause that limits the essential meaning of the sentence element it modifies. The restrictive element is not set off from the element that it modifies with commas, dashes, or parentheses. *The tree that I hit was an oak. The oak at the side of the road was a hazard.* See also *nonrestrictive element.* See 34c and 34i1.

run-on sentence See *comma splice, fused sentence.*

sentence The grammatically complete expression of an idea. In writing, a sentence begins with a capital letter and ends with a period, a question mark, or an exclamation point. A sentence may be **declarative** and make a statement (*The sun rose.*), **interrogative** and ask a question (*Did the sun rise?*), **exclamatory** and indicate surprise or other strong emotion (*How beautiful the dawn is!*), or **imperative** and express a command (*Get up earlier tomorrow.*). Besides having these functions, sentences are classified grammatically. A **simple** sentence is a single independent clause without dependent clauses. *I left the house.* Its subject, predicate, or both may be compound. *Sears and Roebuck founded a mail-order house and a chain of stores.* A **compound** sentence contains two or more independent clauses linked with a coordinating conjunction, a correlative conjunction, or a semicolon. *I did not wish to go, but she did. I did not wish to go; she did.* A **complex** sentence contains an independent clause and one or more dependent clauses. *After he had cleaned up the kitchen, Tom fell asleep in front of the television.* A **compound-complex** sentence contains at least two independent clauses and one or more dependent clauses. *We had hoped to go climbing, but the trip was postponed because she sprained her ankle.* See also *clause.* See 14a and 14b.

sentence fragment An apparent sentence that fails to communicate a complete thought, usually because it lacks a subject or a finite verb. Often fragments are dependent clauses, introduced by a subordinating word but punctuated as sentences. Fragments should be revised to be complete sentences in formal writing. See Chapter 22 for ways of correcting sentence fragments.

sentence nucleus The combination of subject plus auxiliary to stand for a complete sentence, as in a response to a question. *Alex did.* See 47d.

simple predicate See *predicate.*

simple sentence See *sentence.*

simple subject See *subject.*

simple tense See *tense.*

split infinitive The often awkward intrusion of an adverb between *to* and the base form of the verb in an infinitive constructions (*to boldly go* rather than *to go boldly*). See 23b1.

squinting modifier A misplaced word, phrase, or clause that could refer equally, but with different meanings, to words preceding or following it. *Playing poker often is dangerous.* The position of *often* fails to indicate whether frequent poker playing is dangerous or whether poker playing is often dangerous. See 23a3.

stative verb See *verb.*

subject The noun, pronoun, and related words that indicate who or what a sentence is about. A **simple** subject is a single noun or pronoun. *Owls are nocturnal birds.* A **complete** subject is the simple subject and its modifiers. *The timid grey mouse fled from the owl.* (*Mouse* is the simple subject; *the timid grey mouse* the complete subject.) Further, a subject may be **compound:** *The mouse and the owl heard the fox.*

subject complement See *complement.*

subjective case See *case.*

subjunctive mood The form of a verb used to express a wish, a request, or a condition that does not exist. The *contrary-to-fact subjunctive* using *were* is the most common. *If I were premier, I would change things.* The dependent *that* clause expressing a command, demand, necessity, request, requirement, or suggestion is also common. *I asked that he come.* The subjunctive also survives in many time-honoured expressions. *Be that as it may. Suffice it to say that I have had enough.* See 16h.

subordinate clause A dependent clause. See *clause.*

subordinating conjunction See *conjunction.*

subordination The grammatical dependence of one sentence element on another. _Because the counselling didn't seem to be helping_, she decided to find _another therapist._ When one element is subordinate or dependent on another, instead of being equal to it, the subordinate element seems less significant, and the independent element seems more significant. See also _clause, coordination._ See 26b.

substantive A word, phrase, or clause that serves a noun.

suffix An addition to the end of a word that alters the word's meaning or part of speech—as in _migrate_ (verb) and _migration_ (noun) or _late_ (adjective or adverb) and _lateness_ (noun). See 31c2.

superlative See _adjective forms, adverb forms._

syntax The agreement of words in a sentence in order to reveal the relation of each to the whole and each to the other.

tense The verb forms that indicate the time at which an action takes place or a condition exists. The times expressed by tense are basically present, past, and future. Verbs have **simple** _(I love)_, **perfect** _(I have loved)_, **progressive** _(I am loving)_, and **perfect progressive** _(I have been loving)_ forms that show tense and, used in sequences, show the time relationships of actions and events. See 16d, 16e, 16f, and 16g.

transitive verb A verb that directs action toward a direct object and may express action done to or for an indirect object. A transitive verb may be in the active or passive voice. _The artist gave me the sketch._ See also _verb._ See 14c2.

verb A word or group of words, essential to a sentence, that expresses what action the subject takes or receives, what the subject is, or what the subject's state of being is. Verbs change form to show tense, number, voice, and mood. A **transitive** verb takes an object or has passive forms. _Edison invented the incandescent bulb. The incandescent bulb was invented by Edison._ An **intransitive** verb does not take an object. _The bulb glowed._ **Linking** verbs join a subject and its complement. _Edison was pleased._ Depending on its use in a sentence, a verb may sometimes belong to all three groups. _Evans grew oranges_ (transitive). _The oranges grew well_ (intransitive). _The oranges grew ripe_ (linking). See also _auxiliary verb, irregular verb, mood, person, regular verb, tense, verbal, voice._ See 14b1 and Chapter 16. **Dynamic** verbs tell something about what is happening, usually about an action that someone is performing. **Stative** verbs tell us that someone or something is in an unchanging state. See 45d.

verbal A **gerund, participle**, or **infinitive** serving as a noun, an adjective, or an adverb. *Running is excellent exercise* (gerund/noun). *A running athlete is an exhilarating sight* (participle/adjective). *We went to the track to run* (infinitive/adverb). See also *gerund, infinitive, participle*. See 14c3.

verbal phrase A phrase using a gerund, a participle, or an infinitive. See *phrase*.

verb phrase A main verb and its auxiliary verbs. A verb phrase can act only as a predicate in a sentence. *She should have won the first race*. See *phrase*.

voice The form of a transitive verb that indicates whether the subject is acting or being acted on. When a verb is **active,** the subject is the doer or agent. *Parker played the saxophone fantastically.* When a verb is **passive**, the subject and verb are transposed. Then the grammatical subject receives the action of the verb, action taken by the object of a preposition. *The saxophone was played fantastically by Parker.* The passive voice is formed with the appropriate tense of the verb *be* and the past participle of the transitive verb. See also *verb*. See Chapter 16.

zero article See *article*.

Glossary of Usage

This glossary provides usage guidelines for some commonly confused words and phrases. Conventions of usage might be called the "good manners" of discourse. Just as our notions of good manners vary from culture to culture and time to time, so do conventions of usage. The word *ain't*, for instance, now considered bad manners in formal discourse, was once widely used by the most proper British speakers, and is still used normally in some spoken North American dialects. So usage matters, like other choices you must make in writing, depend on what your purpose is and what is appropriate for a particular audience at a particular time. Matters of usage, especially those that are controversial or that seem to be changing, are treated in the body of this textbook. In addition, this glossary provides you, in brief form, with a guide to generally accepted usage in college and university writing and with a guide for distinguishing between words whose meanings are similar or that are easily confused. For fuller discussion of these matters, you may want to consult one of the usage guides listed in 32c.

a, an Use *a* with a word that begins with a consonant (*a forest, a book*), with a sounded *h* (*a hemisphere*), or with another consonant sound such as "you" or "wh" (*a euphoric moment, a one-sided match*). Use *an* with a word that begins with a vowel (*an umbrella*), with a silent *h* (*an honour*), or with a vowel sound (*an X ray*).

accept, except The verb *accept* means "receive" or "agree to." *Melanie will accept the job offer.* Used as a preposition, *except* means "aside from" or "excluding." *All the plaintiffs except Mr. Sneath decided to accept the settlement offered by the defendant.*

advice, advise The noun *advice* means an "opinion" or "suggestion"; the verb *advise* means "offer or provide advice." *Charlotte's mother advised her to become a doctor, but Charlotte, who intended to become a dancer, ignored the advice.*

affect, effect As a verb, *affect* means "influence" or "move the emotions of." *Effect* is a noun meaning "result", or, less commonly, a verb meaning "bring about." *A nuclear war would have far-reaching <u>effects</u>. Many people are deeply <u>affected</u> by this realization, and some join groups aimed at <u>effecting</u> arms reduction.*

aggravate Colloquially, *aggravate* means "irritate" or "annoy," but this usage should be avoided in formal writing. The formal meaning of *aggravate* is "make worse." *Having another mouth to feed <u>aggravated</u> their poverty.*

all ready, already *All ready* means "fully prepared." *Already* means "previously." *We were <u>all ready</u> for Lucy's party when we learned that she had <u>already</u> left.*

all right *All right* is always two words, not one.

all together, altogether *All together* means "all in a group" or "gathered in one place." *Altogether* means "completely," "in all," or "everything considered." *When the students were <u>all together</u> in the room, it was <u>altogether</u> filled.*

allude, elude *Allude* means "refer indirectly." *Elude* means "avoid" or "escape from." *The candidate frequently <u>alluded</u> to his immigrant grandparents who had come here to <u>elude</u> political oppression.*

allusion, illusion An *allusion* indirectly refers to something, as when a writer mentions or hints at a well-known event, person, story, quotation, or other information, assuming that the reader will recognize it (*a literary <u>allusion</u>*). An *illusion* is a false or misleading appearance (*an optical <u>illusion</u>*).

a lot *A lot* is not one word but two. Do not use *a lot* in formal writing to express "a large amount" or "a large number."

already See *all ready, already.*

alright See *all right.*

altogether See *all together, altogether.*

among, between In referring to two things or people, use *between*. In referring to three or more things or people, use *among*. *The relationship <u>between</u> the twins is different from that <u>among</u> the other three children.*

amount, number Use *amount* for quantities that you cannot count (singular nouns such as water, light, or power). Use *number* for quantities that you can count (usually plural nouns such as objects or people). *A small <u>number</u> of volunteers cleared a large <u>amount</u> of brush within a few hours.*

an See *a, an.*

and/or *And/or* should be avoided except in business or legal writing, where it is a short way of saying that one or both of two items apply. In other formal writing, take time and space to write out *X, Y, or both* rather than *X and/or Y.* If you mean *and* or *or,* use that word.

any body, anybody, any one, anyone *Anybody* is an indefinite pronoun, as is *anyone.* Although <u>anyone</u> could enjoy carving wood, not just <u>anybody</u> could make a sculpture like that. *Any body* is two words, an adjective and the noun it modifies. <u>*Any body*</u> *of water has its own distinctive ecology. Any one is allowed to buy only two sale items at* <u>*any one*</u> *time.*

anyplace, anywhere In formal writing, use *anywhere,* not *anyplace. She walked for an hour, not going* <u>*anywhere*</u> *in particular.*

anyway, anyways Use *anyway,* not *anyways,* in writing.

anywhere See *any place, any where.*

apt, liable, likely *Likely to* means "probably will," and *apt to* means "inclines or tends to," but either word will do in many instances. *During an argument, he is* <u>*apt*</u> *to yell while she is* <u>*likely*</u> *to slam doors. Liable to* is a more negative phrase that means "in danger of." *That dog is* <u>*liable*</u> *to dig up my garden. Liable* is also a legal term meaning "obligated" or "responsible for." *The dog's owners are* <u>*liable*</u> *for any damage that he causes.*

as Avoid using *as* for *because* or *when* in sentences where its meaning is not clear. For example, does *Carl left town* <u>*as*</u> *his father was arriving* mean *at the same time as his father was arriving* or *because his father was arriving?*

as, as if, like These expressions are used when making comparative statements. Use *as* when comparing two qualities that people or objects possess. *The box is* <u>*as*</u> *wide* <u>*as*</u> *it is long.* Also use *as* to identify equivalent terms in a description. *Françoise served as a moderator at the town meeting.* Use *like* to indicate similarity but not equivalency: *Hugo,* <u>*like*</u> *Mei, was a detailed observer.* In such instances, *like* acts as a preposition, followed by a noun or noun phrase, while *as* may act either as a preposition or as a conjunction introducing a clause. *The dog howled like a wolf, just* <u>*as if*</u> *she were a wild animal.*

assure, ensure, insure *Assure* means "convince" or "promise," and its direct object is usually a person or persons. *The candidate* <u>*assured*</u> *the voters he would not raise taxes. Ensure* and *insure* both mean "make certain," but *insure* is usually used in the specialized sense of protection against financial loss. *When the city began water rationing to* <u>*ensure*</u> *that the supply would last, the Browns* *found that they could no longer afford to* <u>insure</u> *their car wash business.*

as to *As to* should not be used as a substitute for *about. Phoebe was unsure* <u>about</u> (not <u>as to</u>) *Bruce's intentions.*

at, where See *where.*

awful, awfully The formal meanings of *awful* and *awfully* are "awe-inspiring" and "in an awe-inspiring way," respectively. Colloquial speech often dilutes *awful* to mean "bad" (*I had an* <u>awful</u> *day*) and *awfully* to mean "very" (*It was* <u>awfully</u> *cold*). In formal writing, avoid these casual usages.

awhile, a while The adverb *awhile* can be used to modify a verb. *A while,* however, is an article and a noun and can be the object of a preposition such as *for, in,* or *after. We drove* <u>awhile</u> *and then stopped for a* <u>while</u>.

bad, badly *Bad* is an adjective, used to modify a subject or an object or to follow a linking verb such as *be, feel,* or *seem. Badly* is an adverb, used to modify a verb. *The guests felt* <u>bad</u> *because the dinner was so* <u>badly</u> *prepared.*

because of, due to Both phrases are used to describe the relationship between a cause and an effect. Use *due to* when the effect (a noun) is stated first and followed by the verb *be. His illness was* <u>due to</u> *malnutrition.* (*Illness,* a noun, is the effect.) Use *because of,* not *due to,* when the effect is a clause, not a noun. *He was sick* <u>because of</u> *malnutrition.* (*He was sick,* a clause, is the effect.)

being as, being that These expressions are used colloquially as substitutes for *because;* avoid them in formal writing. <u>Because</u> (not <u>being as</u>) *Romeo killed Tybalt, he was banished to Padua.*

beside, besides *Beside,* a preposition, means "next to." *Besides* is either a preposition meaning "other than" or "in addition to" or an adverb meaning "moreover." *No one* <u>besides</u> *Francesca knows whether the tree is still growing* <u>beside</u> *the house.*

between See *among, between.*

breath, breathe *Breath* is the noun, and *breathe* is the verb. "<u>Breathe</u>," *said the dentist, so June took a large* <u>breath</u> *of laughing gas.*

bring, take *Bring* is comparable to *come; take* is comparable to *go.* Use *bring* when an object is moved from a farther place to a nearer one; use *take* when the opposite is true. *Please* <u>take</u> *my prescription to the pharmacist, and* <u>bring</u> *my medicine back to me.*

but, yet Use these words separately, not together. *He is strong-minded but* (not *but yet*) *gentle.*

but that, but what Avoid using these as substitutes for *that* in expressions of doubt. *Hercule Poirot never doubted that* (not *but that*) *he would solve the case.*

can, may *Can* refers to ability and *may* to possibility or permission to do something. *Since I can ski the slalom well, I may win the race. May* (not *can*) *I leave early to practise?*

can't, couldn't These are the contractions for *cannot* and *could not*. Avoid them, like other contractions, in formal writing. *If I couldn't complete it during the break, I certainly can't now.*

can't hardly, can't scarcely Both *hardly* and *scarcely* are negatives; therefore, the expressions *can't hardly* and *can't scarcely* are redundant double negatives. *Tim is claustrophobic and can* (not *can't*) *hardly breathe in elevators.*

can't help but This expression is wordy and redundant. Use the more formal *I cannot but go* or the less formal *I can't help going* instead of *I can't help but go.*

can't scarcely See *can't hardly, can't scarcely.*

censor, censure *Censor* means to remove material that is considered offensive for political, moral, personal, or other reasons. *Censure* means "formally reprimand." *The board of professional ethics censured the newspaper for censoring negative letters to the editor.*

centre around This idiom rarely if ever appears in formal writing. Use *centre on* instead. *Their research centres on the disease-resistant hybrid varieties.*

compare to, compare with *Compare to* means "describe one thing as similar to another." *Hillary compared the noise to the roar of a waterfall. Compare with* is the more general activity of noting similarities and differences between objects or people. *The detective compared the latest photograph with the old one, noting how the man's appearance had changed.*

complement, compliment *Complement* means "go well with" or "enhance." *Compliment* means "praise." *Several guests complimented Julie on her marmalade, which complemented the warm, buttered scones.*

comprise, compose *Comprise* means "contain" (the whole *comprises* the parts). *Compose* means "make up" (the parts *compose* the whole). *The class comprises twenty students. Twenty students compose the class.*

conscience, conscious *Conscience,* a noun, means "a sense of right and wrong." *Conscious,* an adjective, means "awake" or "aware." *After the argument, Lisa was <u>conscious</u> of her troubled <u>conscience</u>.*

consensus of opinion Use *consensus* instead of this redundant phrase. *The family <u>consensus</u> was to sell the old house.*

consequently, subsequently *Consequently* means "as a result" or "therefore." *Subsequently* just means "afterward." *Roger lost his job, and <u>subsequently</u> I lost mine. <u>Consequently</u>, I was unable to pay my rent.*

continual, conscious *Continual* describes an activity that is repeated at regular or frequent intervals. *Continuous* describes either an activity that is ongoing without interruption or an object that is connected without break. *The damage done by <u>continuous</u> erosion was increased by the <u>continual</u> storms.*

couple of *Couple of* is used informally to mean either "two" or "a few." Avoid it in formal writing, and say specifically what you mean.

could of See *have, of.*

criteria, criterion *Criterion* means "a standard of judgment" or "a necessary qualification." *Criteria* is the plural form. *Many people believe that performance record is the best <u>criterion</u> for choosing the next prime minister of Canada.*

data *Data* is the plural form of the Latin word *datum,* meaning "a fact" or "a result collected during research." Although colloquially *data* is used as either singular or plural, in formal writing it should be treated as plural. *These <u>data</u> indicate that fewer people smoke today than ten years ago.*

different from, different than *Different from* is generally preferred in formal writing although both phrases are used widely. *Her lab results were no <u>different from</u> his.*

differ from, differ with *Differ from* means "be unlike" in identity, appearance, or actions. *Differ with* means "disagree with" in opinion or belief. *Mr. Binns <u>differs with</u> Ms. White over the importance of class discussion. Therefore, the way Mr. Binns conducts his class <u>differs from</u> the way she conducts hers.*

discreet, discrete *Discreet* means "tactful" or "prudent." *Discrete means "distinct" or "separate." The dean's <u>discreet</u> encouragement brought representatives of all the <u>discrete</u> factions to the meeting.*

disinterested, uninterested *Disinterested* means "unbiased" or "impartial." *It was difficult to find <u>disinterested</u> people for the jury. Uninterested means "not interested" or "indifferent." Cecile was <u>uninterested</u> in the outcome of the trial.*

distinct, distinctive *Distinct* means "separate" or "well defined." *The experiment involved separating the liquid into its five <u>distinct</u> elements. Distinctive* means "distinguishing from others" or "characteristic." *Even from a distance, everyone recognized Greg's <u>distinctive</u> way of walking.*

doesn't, don't *Doesn't* is the contraction for *does not* and should be used with *he, she, it,* and singular nouns. *Don't* is the contraction for *do not* and should be used with *I, you, we, they,* and the plural nouns. In formal writing, however, avoid these and all other contractions.

due to See *because of, due to.*

effect See *affect, effect.*

elicit, illicit The verb *elicit* means "to draw out" or "evoke." The adjective *illicit* means "illegal." *The police tried to <u>elicit</u> from the criminal the names of others involved in his <u>illicit</u> activities.*

elude See *allude, elude.*

emigrate from, immigrate to, migrate *Emigrate from* means "move away from one's country." *Immigrate to* means "move to a foreign country and settle there." *My mother's family <u>emigrated</u> from Poland in 1920. They <u>immigrated</u> to Canada. Emigration* and *immigration* are generally permanent actions; *migration* suggests movement that is temporary or seasonal and either *to* or *from* a place. *Every winter, whales off the Pacific coast <u>migrate</u> south from Alaska toward warmer water.*

ensure See *assure, ensure, insure.*

enthused, enthusiastic *Enthused* is used colloquially to mean "enthusiastic about." Avoid it in formal writing. *The students remained <u>enthusiastic</u> despite the rain and the mud that threatened to flood the excavation.*

equally as good Replace this redundant phrase with either *equally good* or *as good as. The two tennis players were <u>equally good</u>, each <u>as good</u> as the other.*

especially, specially *Especially* means "very" or "particularly." *Specially* means "for a special reason or purpose." *The audience <u>especially</u> enjoyed the new composition, <u>specially</u> written for the holiday.*

every day, everyday *Everyday* is an adjective used to describe something as ordinary or common. *Every day* is an adjective modifying a noun, specifying which particular day. *I ride the subway every day even though pushing and shoving are <u>everyday</u> occurrences.*

every one, everyone   *Everyone* is a indefinite pronoun. *Every one* is a noun modified by an adjective, referring to each member of a group. *Because he began the assignment after _everyone_ else, David knew that he could not finish _every one_ of the sections.*

except   See *accept, except.*

explicit, implicit   *Explicit* means "directly or openly expressed." *Implicit* means "indirectly expressed or implied." *The _explicit_ message of the ad urged consumers to buy the product while the _implicit_ message promised popularity.*

farther, further   *Farther* refers to physical distance. *How much _farther_ is it to Munich? Further* refers to time or degree. *I want to avoid _further_ delays and _further_ misunderstandings.*

fewer, less   Use *fewer* with objects or people that can be counted (plural nouns). Use *less* with amounts that cannot be counted (singular nouns). *The world would be safer with _fewer_ bombs and _less_ hostility.*

finalize   *Finalize* is a pretentious way of saying "end" or "make final." *We _closed_ (not _finalized_) the deal.*

firstly, secondly, thirdly   These are old-fashioned and unwieldy words for introducing a series of points. Use *first, second,* and *third* instead.

flaunt, flout   *Flaunt* means "show off." *Flout* means "mock" or "scorn." *The teens _flouted_ convention by _flaunting_ their multi-coloured wigs.*

former, latter   *Former* refers to the first and *latter* to the second of two things previously introduced. *Anna and Kim are both excellent athletes; the _former_ plays tennis, and the _latter_ has won several marathons.* See also *later, latter.*

further   See *farther, further.*

good, well   *Good* is an adjective and should not be used as a substitute for the adverb *well. Gabriel is a _good_ host who cooks quite _well_.*

good and   *Good and* is colloquial for "very"; avoid it in formal writing. *After Peter lost his sister's camera, he was _very_ (not _good and_) sorry.*

half a, a half, a half a   Both *half a* and *a half* are standard. A *half a* is wordy. *She ate _half a_ (or _a half_ but not _a half a_) sandwich.*

hanged, hung   Of these two past forms of the verb *hang,* only *hanged* refers to executions while *hung* is used for all other meanings. *The old woman _hung_ her head as she passed the tree where the murderer was _hanged_.*

hardly See *can't hardly, can't scarcely.*

has got to, has to These colloquial phrases for "must" should be avoided in formal writing. *She must* (not *has to*) *be intelligent.*

have, of *Have,* not *of,* should follow *could, would, should,* or *might. We should have* (not *of*) *invited them.*

herself, himself, myself, yourself Do not use these reflexive pronouns as subjects or as objects in a prepositional phrase. *Tamara went with me* (not *myself*) *to see the pottery show.*

himself See *herself, himself, myself, yourself.*

his/her See *he/she, his/her.*

hopefully *Hopefully* is widely misused to mean "it is hoped," but its correct meaning is "with hope." *Sam watched the roulette wheel hopefully,* not *Hopefully, Sam will win.*

hung See *hanged, hung.*

if, whether Use *whether* or *whether* or *not* to express an alternative. *She was considering whether or not to buy the new software.* Reserve *if* for the subjunctive case. *If it should rain tomorrow, our tai chi class will meet in the gym.*

illicit See *elicit, illicit.*

illusion See *allusion, illusion.*

immigrate to See *emigrate from, immigrate to, migrate.*

impact As a noun, *impact* means "a forceful collision." As a verb, it means "pack together." *Because they were impacted, Jason's wisdom teeth needed to be removed.* Avoid the colloquial use of *impact* as a weak and vague word meaning "to affect." *Population control may reduce* (not *impact*) *world hunger.*

implicit See *explicit, implicit.*

imply, infer To *imply* is to suggest. To *infer* is to make an educated guess. Speakers and writers *imply;* listeners and readers *infer. Beth and Peter's letter implied that they were planning a very small wedding; we inferred that we would not be invited.*

incident, instance, incidence *Incident* refers to a specific occurrence. It should not be confused with *instance,* which is an overused, though correct, word for "example" or "case." *The violent incident was just one instance of John's* *personality disorder. Incidence* usually refers to a rate of effect or occurrence. *A high incidence of birth defects followed the nuclear mishap.*

incredible, incredulous *Incredible* means "unbelievable." *Incredulous* means "not believing." *When townspeople attributed the <u>incredible</u> events in their town to the presence of a UFO, Marina was <u>incredulous</u>.*

infer See *imply, infer.*

inside, inside of, outside, outside of Drop *of* after the prepositions *inside* and *outside*. *The class regularly met <u>outside</u>* (not <u>*of*</u>) *the building.*

instance See *incident, instance.*

insure See *assure, ensure, insure.*

interact with, interface with *Interface with* is computer jargon for "discuss" or "communicate." *Interact with* is a vague phrase meaning "doing something that somehow involves another person." Avoid these colloquial expressions.

irregardless, regardless *Regardless* is the correct word because *irregardless* is a double negative.

is when, is where These vague and faulty shortcuts should be avoided in definitions. *Schizophrenia is a psychotic condition <u>in which</u>* (not <u>*when*</u> or <u>*where*</u>) *a person withdraws from reality.*

its, it's *Its* is a possessive pronoun, even though it does not have an apostrophe. *It's* is a contraction for *it is*; avoid *it's* and other contractions in formal writing. *<u>It's</u>* (more formally, <u>*it is*</u>) *important to begin each observation just before the rat has <u>its</u> dinner.*

kind, sort, type As singular nouns, *kind, sort,* and *type* should be modified by *this* and followed by singular nouns. The plural forms, *kinds, sorts,* and *types* should be modified by *these* and followed by plural nouns. Write *this kind of dress* or *these kinds of dresses,* not *these kind of dress.* Use such phrases to classify or categorize, but leave them out otherwise.

kind of, sort of Avoid using these colloquial expression as substitutes for "rather" or "somewhat." *Laura was somewhat* (not <u>*kind of*</u>) *tired after painting for several hours in the studio.*

later, latter *Later* means "more late" or "after sometime." *Later* refers to the second of two items mentioned and can be used to avoid repeating a subject twice. *Jackson and Chad won all their early matches, but the <u>latter</u> was injured <u>later</u> in the season.* See also *former, latter.*

latter See *former, latter* and *later, latter.*

lay, lie *Lay* means "place" or "put." Its forms are *lay, laid, laying, laid,* and *laid.* It generally has a direct object, specifying what has been placed. *She laid her books on the desk. Lie* means "recline" or "be positioned," and does not take a direct object. Its forms are *lie, lay, lain, lying. She lay awake until two, worrying about the exam.*

leave, let *Leave* means "go away" or "depart." *Let* means "allow." The expressions *leave alone* and *let alone,* however, are generally considered interchangeable. *Let me leave now, and leave* (or *let*) *me alone from now on!*

lend, loan In formal writing, use *loan* as a noun, and *lend* as a verb. *Please lend me your pen so that I may fill out this application for a loan.*

less See *fewer, less.*

let See *leave, let.*

liable See *apt, liable, likely.*

lie See *lay, lie.*

like See *as, as if, like.*

like, such as Both *like* and *such as* may be used in a statement giving an example or a series of examples. *Like* means "similar to"; use *like* when comparing the subject mentioned to the examples. *A hurricane, like a flood or any other major disaster, may strain a region's emergency resources.* Use *such as* when the examples represent a general category of things or people. *Such as* is often a graceful alternative to *for example. A destructive hurricane, such as Gilbert in 1988, may drastically alter an area's economy.*

likely See *apt, liable, likely.*

literally *Literally* means "actually" or "exactly as it is written" and may be used to stress the truth of a statement that might otherwise be understood as figurative. *Literally* should not be used as an intensifier in a figurative statement. *Sarah was literally at the edge of her seat* may be accurate, but *Sarah was so hungry that she could literally eat a horse* is not.

loan See *lend, loan.*

loose, lose *Lose* is a verb meaning "misplace." *Loose,* as an adjective, means "not securely attached." *Sew on that loose button before you lose it.*

lots, lots of These informal expressions, meaning "much" or "many," should be avoided in formal writing.

man, mankind In the past, *man* and *mankind* were used to represent all human beings, but many people now consider these terms sexist because they do not mention women. Replace such words with *people, humans, humankind, men and women,* or simple all-encompassing phrases. Replace occupational terms ending with -*man* with gender-free phrasing such as *fire fighter* for *fireman, letter carrier* for *mailman,* and *minister* or *cleric* for *clergyman.*

may See *can, may.*

may be, maybe *May be* is a verb phrase. *Maybe,* the adverb means "perhaps." *He may be the prime minister today, but maybe he will lose the next election.*

media *Media,* the plural form of *medium, takes a plural verb. The media are* (not *is*) *going to cover the council meeting.*

might of See *have, of.*

migrate See *emigrate from, immigrate to, migrate.*

moral, morale A *moral* is a succinct lesson. *The unstated moral of the story is that generosity eventually is rewarded. Morale* is the spirit or mood of an individual or a group of people. *Office morale was low.*

myself See *herself, himself, myself, yourself.*

nor, or Use *either* with *or* and *neither* with *nor. Jeanette hopes to study abroad either next year or the year after. Neither her mother nor her father is very encouraging.*

number See *amount, number.*

of See *have.*

off of Use *off* rather than *off of. The spaghetti slipped off* (not *of*) *the plate.*

O.K., OK, okay All are acceptable spellings, but do not use the term in formal writing. Replace it with more exact language. *The performance was unpolished but enthusiastic* (not *O.K.*).

on, upon *Upon* is an old-fashioned and overly formal substitute for *on. My grade will depend on* (not *upon*) *how well I do on my final examination.*

on account of Use this substitute for *because of* sparingly or not at all. See also *because of, due to.*

or See *nor, or.*

outside, outside of See *inside, inside of, outside, outside of.*

owing to the fact that Avoid this and other unnecessarily wordy expressions for *because.*

per Use the Latin *per* only in standard technical phrases such as *kilometres per hour.* Otherwise, find English equivalents. *As mentioned in* (not <u>*as per*</u>) *the latest report, our town's average food expenses every week* (not <u>*per week*</u>) *are $40* <u>*per capita*</u>.

percent, percentage words identify a number as a fraction of 100. Because they show exact statistics, these terms should not be used casually to mean "portion," "amount," or "number." *Last year, 80* <u>*percent*</u> *of the club's members were female.* Use *percent* after a figure. In formal writing, spell out *percent* rather than using its symbol (%). *Percentage*, a noun, is not used with a specific number. *A large* <u>*percentage*</u> *of sales representatives are single.*

plenty *Plenty* means "enough" or "a great abundance." *Many immigrants consider Canada a land of* <u>*plenty*</u>. In formal writing, avoid its colloquial usage, meaning "very." *He was* <u>*very*</u> (not <u>*plenty*</u>) *tired.*

plus *Plus,* a preposition meaning "in addition to," is often used in the context of money. *My inheritance is enough to cover my debts* <u>*plus*</u> *yours.* Avoid using *plus* as a transitional adverb meaning "besides," "moreover," or "in addition." *That dress does not fit me.* <u>*Besides*</u> (not <u>*plus*</u>), *it is the wrong colour.*

precede, proceed Both verbs, *precede* means "come before," and *proceed* means "continue" or "go forward," as in the related word *procession. Despite the storm that* <u>*preceded*</u> *the hallway flooding, we* <u>*proceeded*</u> *to class.*

pretty Avoid using *pretty* in formal writing as a substitute for *rather, somewhat,* or *quite. Bill was* <u>*quite*</u> (not <u>*pretty*</u>) *disagreeable.*

principal, principle These words are unrelated but are often confused because of their similar spellings. *Principal,* as a noun, refers to a head official or an amount of money loaned or invested. When used as an adjective, it means "most significant." The word meaning "a fundamental law, belief, or standard" is *principle. When Albert was sent to the* <u>*principal*</u> *he defended himself with the* <u>*principle*</u> *of free speech.*

proceed See *precede, proceed.*

quotation, quote *Quote* is a verb, and *quotation* is a noun. In colloquial usage, *quote* is sometimes used as a short form of *quotation.* In formal writing, however, use *quotation* as the noun form. *He* <u>*quoted*</u> *the prime minister, and the* <u>*quotation*</u> *was preserved in history books.*

raise, rise *Raise* means "lift" or "move upward." In the case of children, it means "bring up" or "rear." As a transitive verb, it takes a direct object— someone raises something. *The guests raised their glasses in good cheer.* *Rise* means "go upward." It is not followed by a direct object; something rises by itself. *She saw the steam rise from the pan just as the soup bubbled into a boil.*

rarely ever In formal writing, use *rarely* by itself, or use *hardly ever.* *When we were poor, we rarely went to the movies.*

real, really The adjective *real* means "true" or "not artificial." The adverb *really,* in informal usage, means "very" or "extremely." Do not substitute *real* for *really.* *The old man walked really* (not *real*) *slowly.* In formal writing, avoid using *really* altogether. *The old man walked very* (not *really*) *slowly.*

reason is because This expression mixes *the reason is that* and *because.* Use one or the other but not both together. In general, use the less wordy *because* unless you want to give a statement the air of an explanation. *The reason the copier stopped is that* (not *is because*) *the paper jammed.*

regardless See *irregardless, regardless.*

respectfully, respectively *Respectfully* means "with respect." *Respectively* means "in the order given." *The brothers, respectively a juggler and an acrobat, respectfully greeted the audience.*

rise See *raise, rise.*

scarcely See *can't hardly, can't scarcely.*

secondly See *firstly, secondly, thirdly.*

shall, will Today *shall* is used much more in British English than in North American English. *Shall* is used in, for example, polite questions in the first person (*"Shall we buy it?" "Shall I call a taxi?"*) *Will* is used in most other cases involving the future tense.

should of See *have, of.*

since *Since* has two meanings. The first meaning shows the passage of time (*I have not eaten since Tuesday*); the second and more informal meaning is "because" (*Since you are in a bad mood, I will go away*). Be careful not to write sentences in which *since* is ambiguous in meaning. *Since I broke my leg, I have been doing nothing but sleeping.* (*Since* here could mean either "because" or "ever since." In order to avoid such problems some writers prefer not to use *since* to mean "because.")

so, so . . . that   In formal writing, avoid using *so* by itself as an intensifier, meaning "very." Instead, follow *so* with *that* to show how the intensified condition leads to a result. *Aaron was <u>so</u> tired <u>that</u> he fell asleep at the wheel of his car.*

some body, somebody, some one, someone   *Somebody* is an indefinite pronoun, as is *someone*. *When <u>somebody</u> comes walking down the hall, I always hope that it is <u>someone</u> I know. Some body* is two words, an adjective modifying a noun, while *some one* is two adjectives or a pronoun modified by an adjective. *In dealing with <u>some body</u> like the senate, arrange to meet consistently <u>some one</u> person who can represent the group.*

someplace, somewhere   *Someplace* is informal for *somewhere;* use the latter in formal writing.

some time, sometime, sometimes   *Some time* means "a length of time." *Please leave me <u>some time</u> to use the computer. Sometime* means "at some indefinite later time." *<u>Sometime</u> I will take you to Pender Island. Sometimes* means "occasionally." *<u>Sometimes</u> I see him on my way to class.*

somewhere   See *someplace, somewhere.*

sort of   See *kind of, sort of.*

so that   See *so, so that.*

specially   See *especially, specially.*

stationary, stationery   *Stationary* is an adjective meaning "standing still." *Stationery* is a noun meaning "writing paper or materials." *When the bus was <u>stationary</u> at the light, Karen took out her <u>stationery</u> and wrote a quick note to a friend.*

subsequently   See *consequently, subsequently.*

such as   See *like, such as.*

supposed to, used to   Both of these expressions require the final *-d* indicating past tense. *He is <u>supposed</u> to bring his calculator to class.*

sure, surely   Avoid using *sure* as an intensifier in formal writing. Replace this colloquial expression with "certainly" or "without a doubt," or use the adverb *surely,* which means "it must be so." *Surely* is often used to express a hope-for situation. *<u>Surely</u> Carlos will go to a doctor.* It is also used persuasively. *We cannot go on a picnic. <u>Surely</u> it will rain.*

take   See *bring, take.*

than, then Use the conjunction *than* in comparative statements. *The cat was bigger than the dog.* Use the adverb *then* when referring to a sequence of events or emotions. *Jim finished university, and then he joined CUSO.*

that, which *That,* always followed by a restrictive clause, singles out the object being described. *The trip that you took to Japan was expensive.* ("That you took to Japan" singles out the specific trip.) *Which* may be followed by either a restrictive or a nonrestrictive clause but often is used only with the latter. The *which* clause may simply add more information about a noun or noun clause, and it is set off by commas. *The book, which is on the table, is a good one.* (This *which* clause simply adds extra, nonessential information about the book—its location. In contrast, *The book that is on the table is a good one* specifies or singles out the book on the table as opposed to the book on the chair or the book in some other particular place.)

their, there, they're *Their* is a pronoun, the possessive form of *they.* *The gardeners held onto their hats as the helicopter flew over.* *There* refers to a place. *There, birds sing even at night.* *There* also is used with the verb *be* in expletive construction *(there is, there are).* *There is only a short line at the cafeteria right now.* *They're* is a contraction of *they* and *are* and, like all contractions, it should be avoided in formal writing. *They're* (more formally, *they are*) *living in Japan.*

then See *than, then.*

thirdly See *firstly, secondly, thirdly.*

'til, till, until *Till* and *until* are both acceptable in formal writing, but some writers prefer the full word *until.* The older form *'til,* like all contractions, should be avoided in formal writing.

to, too, two *To* is a preposition, generally showing direction or nearness. *Stan flew to Capetown.* Avoid using *to* after *where.* *Where are you flying* (not *flying to*)? *Too* means "also." *I am flying there too.* *Two* is the number. *We too are going to the meeting in two hours.*

to, where See *where.*

toward, towards *Toward* is generally preferred, but either word is acceptable.

try and, try to *Try and* is colloquial for *try to;* use *try to* in formal writing. *Try to have an expressive face.*

two See *to, too, two.*

type See *kind, sort, type.*

uninterested See *disinterested, uninterested.*

unique *Unique* means "the one and only." It describes an absolute state and therefore should not be used with adjectives that suggest degree, such as *very* or *most. Martha's hands are* <u>*unique*</u> (not <u>*very unique*</u>).

until See *'til, till, until.*

upon See *on, upon.*

used to See *supposed to, used to.*

very Avoid using *very* to intensify a weak adjective or adverb; instead, replace both words with one stronger, more precise, and more colourful word. Instead of *very nice,* for example, use *kind, warm, sensitive, endearing,* or *friendly,* depending on your precise meaning. Replace *very interesting* with a word such as *curious, fascinating, insightful, lively, provocative,* or *absorbing.*

way, ways When referring to distances, use *way,* not *ways. The Trivia Bowl championships were a long* <u>*way*</u> (not *ways*) *off.*

well See *good, well.*

when, where See *is when, is where.*

where Use *where* alone, not with prepositions such as *at* or *to.* <u>Where</u> *are you going?* (not <u>*Where*</u> *are you going* <u>*to?*</u>) <u>Where</u> *do you shop?* (not <u>*Where*</u> *do you shop* <u>*at?*</u>)

whether See *if, whether.*

which See *that, which.*

which, who When referring to ideas or things, use *which.* When referring to people, use *who,* not *which. My aunt,* <u>*who*</u> *was irritated, pushed on the door,* <u>*which*</u> *was still stuck.*

who, whom Use *who* if the following clause begins with a verb. *Monica,* <u>*who*</u> *smokes incessantly, is my godmother.* (*Who* is followed by the verb *smokes.*) *Monica,* <u>*who*</u> *is my godmother, smokes incessantly.* (*Who* is followed by the verb *is.*) Use *whom* if the following clause begins with a pronoun. *I have heard that Monica,* <u>*whom*</u> *I have not seen for ten years, wears only purple.* (*Whom* is followed by the pronoun *I*). An exception occurs when a verbal phrase such as *I think* comes between *who* and the following clause. Ignore such a phrase as you decide which form to use. *Monica,* <u>*who*</u> *[I think] wears nothing but purple,* *is my godmother.* (Ignore *I think*; *who* is followed by the verb *wears.*)

who's, whose *Who's* is the contraction of *who* and *is.* Avoid *who's* and other contractions in formal writing. <u>*Who's*</u> (more formally, <u>*Who is*</u>) *in the garden? Whose* is a possessive form; it may be followed by the noun it modifies. <u>*Whose*</u> *sculpture is in the garden?* <u>*Whose*</u> *is on the patio?*

will See *shall, will.*

would of See *have, of.*

yet See *but, yet.*

your, you're *Your* shows possession. *Bring* <u>*your*</u> *sleeping bags along. You're* is the contraction of *you* and *are.* Avoid it and all other contractions in formal writing. <u>*You're*</u> (more formally, <u>*You are*</u>) *in the wrong room.*

yourself See *herself, himself, myself, yourself.*

Answers to Even-Numbered Exercises

To help you check your progress as you work, here are answers to some exercises in Chapters 14–43. Specifically, you will find answers to even-numbered items of those exercises with predictable answers. Exercises with many possible answers—those asking you to imitate a sentence or to revise a paragraph, for example—are not answered here.

ANSWERS TO EXERCISE 14.1

2. On October 4, 1922 the separate lines were consolidated into one system with a new board of directors, with Sir Henry Thornton as president, forming the new transcontinental Canadian National Railways.

4. The company is one of the world's major transportation and communication systems.

ANSWERS TO EXERCISE 14.2

2. ran, ran over (two-word verb)
4. can collect; might run; should finish
6. walked
8. will extend
10. smelled

ANSWERS TO EXERCISE 14.4

2. through; across; into
4. from; beyond; toward

ANSWERS TO EXERCISE 14.5

2. conj – nevertheless
4. coor – but

6. corr – not only/but also
8. sub/until
10. corr – neither/nor; conj – therefore

ANSWERS TO EXERCISE 14.6

The complete subject is set in italics; the simple subject is set in boldface.

2. A *sixty-centimetre* **snowfall** *on April 13*
4. **Anyone** *who knows Gabriel*

ANSWERS TO EXERCISE 14.7

2. pred. appointed Kayla chair; trans. appointed; d.o. Kayla; o.c. chair
4. pred. will rise again; intr. will rise

ANSWERS TO EXERCISE 14.8 (WILL VARY)

2. Without fear, Socrates faced death.
4. Except for a few of his followers, everyone thought Socrates was crazy.

ANSWERS TO EXERCISE 14.9

2. gerund – saving; n, object of prep
4. part – raised; adj, modifying "I"; part – exploring; adj, obj compl

ANSWERS TO EXERCISE 14.10

2. inf – To listen; prep – to k.d. lang
4. part – Floating; prep – on my back
6. app – a sensitive child; prep – with a mixture; prep – of awe and excitement
8. part – Basking; prep – in the sunlight; prep – in a reminiscence; prep – of golden birch trees
10. prep – Despite Ernie's complaints; prep – of recreation; gerund – taking a nap

ANSWERS TO EXERCISE 14.11 (WILL VARY)

2. Waiting to go through customs, we clutched our passports.
4. To annoy his parents, Michael had his ear pierced.

ANSWERS TO EXERCISE 14.12

2. dep – As a potential customer entered the store; sub conj – As; ind – Tony nervously attempted to retreat to the safety of the back room.
4. dep – When she was deemed old enough to understand; sub conj – When; ind – she was told the truth; ind – she knew why; dep – her father had left home
6. ind – Abe and Sasha decided to make a chocolate cream pie; dep – which was Timothy's favourite; rel – which

8. ind – Public speaking was easier; dep – than she had expected; sub conj – than.

10. ind – I could see; dep – that he was very tired; rel – that

ANSWERS TO EXERCISE 15.2

2. whoever: subject of *faces*
4. whom: object of preposition *with* [... *whom we wanted*]

ANSWERS TO EXERCISE 15.3

2. whom
4. she
6. she
8. whoever
10. whom, who

ANSWERS TO EXERCISE 16.1

2. laid
4. lying
6. rises

ANSWERS TO EXERCISE 16.2

2. have predicted/have been predicting—action begun in past continues
4. arrived/has arrived—started in past, may continue today
6. rode/was riding—past action, completed
8. will have watched—future action, completed by a certain time
10. rises—general truth

ANSWERS TO EXERCISE 16.4

2. The storm uprooted huge pine trees.
4. For months, the mother kangaroo protects, feeds, and teaches her baby to survive.

ANSWERS TO EXERCISE 16.6

2. were
4. use
6. know

ANSWERS TO EXERCISE 17.1

2. was
4. make

6. displays
8. support
10. seems
12. cycles
14. was
16. has
18. causes
20. happens

ANSWERS TO EXERCISE 19.1 (WILL VARY)

2. Canadians often hear about the influence of pharmaceutical companies on physicians.
4. After a recent conversation with a new parent, a friend of mine began to view child rearing differently.
6. The chair was delivered three weeks late, a practice that, according to the store management, is normal.
8. Many employees resented the company's policy prohibiting smoking.
10. Is it true that a lawyer can count on making his or her fortune within ten years of graduation?

ANSWERS TO EXERCISE 21.1 (WILL VARY)

2. The mother eagle called twice *before* the young eagle finally answered.
4. The Soviet Union expelled Solzhenitsyn in 1974; he eventually returned to Russia in 1994.

ANSWERS TO EXERCISE 22.1 (WILL VARY)

2. verbal-phrase fragment: The protagonist comes to a decision to leave her family and move to the Yukon. The protagonist decides to leave her family and move to the Yukon.
4. subordinate-clause fragment: Many MPs opposed the bill because of its restrictions on mining and oil drilling. The bill restricted mining and oil drilling, and many MPs opposed it.
6. appositive fragment: Forster stopped writing novels after *A Passage to India,* one of the greatest novels of the twentieth century. *A Passage to India,* ... century, was Forster's last novel.
8. compound-predicate fragment: I loved Paul Shapiro's *The Lotus Eaters* and though it deserved to win more awards. In my opinion, Paul Shapiro's *The Lotus Eaters,* a film I loved, deserved to win more awards.
10. subordinate-clause fragment: Because the younger generation often rejects the ways of its elders, one might say that rebellion is normal. The younger generation often ... elders, and so one might say that ...

ANSWERS TO EXERCISE 23.1 (WILL VARY)

2. I heard my friends talk enthusiastically about their great weekend while I tried to finish my assignment.
4. On the day in question, the patient was not able to breathe normally.
6. He sat in his chair very quietly, rolling his eyes.
8. Vernon made an agreement with his father to pay back the loan.
10. The maintenance worker shut down the turbine that was revolving out of control.

ANSWERS TO EXERCISE 23.2 (WILL VARY)

2. Given the sharp increase in their employment, many women need day-care for their children.
4. Many women go back to school for job retraining.

ANSWERS TO EXERCISE 23.3 (WILL VARY)

2. While leading a performance at Roy Thomson Hall, the conductor dropped the baton.
4. Dreams are somewhat like a jigsaw puzzle: if put together in the correct order, both dreams and puzzles have organization and coherence.

ANSWERS TO EXERCISE 25.1 (WILL VARY)

2. Also notable throughout the story is the image of chrysanthemums.
4. The CBC offers decent music programming, excellent public affairs programming, and this country's best hope for a national culture.

ANSWERS TO EXERCISE 25.2 (WILL VARY)

2. This report will describe employment opportunities for university graduates.
4. I put on ten pounds soon after I stopped exercising.
6. To check the engine, listen for rattling or pinging noises.
8. Randall exposes the injustices that confront Canadian women.
10. Waiting on tables for six hours, followed by mopping and sweeping half a restaurant, can lead to exhaustion.

ANSWERS TO EXERCISE 26.3 (WILL VARY)

2. When Entwhistle and Townshend met singer and guitarist Roger Daltrey, they formed a group called the High Numbers.
4. *Obasan*, an important book by Joy Kogawa, examines the situation of Japanese Canadians during the Second World War.

ANSWERS TO EXERCISE 27.2 (WILL VARY)

2. There are three ways to apply Ninhydrin to the area to be examined: by brushing, spraying, or dipping.
4. There are two types of wallflowers: the male nerd and the female skeeve.

ANSWERS TO EXERCISE 28.2 (WILL VARY)

2. Once I mastered the problems that I had encountered at the beginning and once I had become thoroughly familiar with the stock, I became the best salesperson in our store.

ANSWERS TO EXERCISE 29.2 (WILL VARY)

2. They started shooting pool, and before Marie knew it, ten dollars was owed to the kid. [Preference depends somewhat on the context. The passive voice is unclear about who owes the kid ten dollars. Is Marie alone? Are she and the kid the "they" of the sentence, or is someone else involved? The active is clearer but might be incorrect, if others besides Marie owe the kid money.]
4. I adjusted more easily to living in a dorm than to living in an apartment. [The active is preferred, since the passive adds nothing.]

ANSWERS TO EXERCISE 30.4 (WILL VARY)

2. *tragic*—distressing, alarming, disturbing; *consumes*—defeats, feeds on, erodes; *displays*—champions, thrives on, builds up, promotes; *drama*—excitement, tension, vitality
4. *held*—breathed; *keenness*—coolness, crispness; *twitch*—perk up; *surprise*—adventure, enterprise; *tremors*—chills; *run*—jet

ANSWERS TO EXERCISE 30.6 (WILL VARY)

2. – destroys his victims with flashes of lightning (metaphor)
   – roasted her victims over a fire (metaphor): both of these metaphors suggest the powerful effect that Pope's and Austen's words could have on the targets of their criticism or attacks; Pope's words were flashes of lightning, Austen's words made her victims feel as though they were being roasted over a fire.
4. – deep and soft like water moving in a cavern (simile): this simile compares the sound of her voice to water in a cavern

ANSWERS TO EXERCISE 31.2 (WILL VARY)

2. subterranean: beneath earth; of or relating to things under the surface of the earth
4. monograph: a single writing; a learned treatise on a small area of learning
6. superscript: to write over or above; a distinguishing symbol written immediately over or above and to the right of another character

8. neologism: recent word or thought; a word, usage, or expression that is often disapproved of because of its newness or barbarousness

10. apathetic: without feeling or not suffering; having or showing little or no feeling or emotion, having or showing little or no interest or concern

ANSWERS TO EXERCISE 32.2

2. student: from ME < L *studere,* to study

4. whine: from ME *whinen* < Indo-European *kwein,* to whiz, hiss, whistle

6. sex: from ME < L *sexus* < *secare,* to cut

8. tortilla: from Sp, diminutive of *torta,* cake

10. video: from L, I see < *videre,* to see

ANSWERS TO EXERCISE 32.5 (WILL VARY)

2. The *OED* lists to make strange or turn away from, to transfer ownership, and to change or alter something. *Webster's New World Dictionary* adds two slightly different meanings: to cause to be withdrawn from society, and to transfer affection.

4. The *OED* defines *hopefully* as an adverb: "In a hopeful manner; with a feeling of hope; with ground for hope, promisingly." *Webster's New World Dictionary* lists both adverb and adjective uses but notes that the adjectival use is "regarded by some as loose usage, but widely current."

ANSWERS TO EXERCISE 33.1

2. to; too

4. noticeable; until

6. believe; lose

8. affects; success; than; its

10. develop; truly; successful

12. businesses; dependent

14. professor; accept

16. may be; therefore; immediately

18. occurrences; every day

20. Apparently

ANSWERS TO EXERCISE 33.3

2. wholly

4. lonely

6. dyeing

8. continuous

10. outrageous

ANSWERS TO EXERCISE 33.4

2. fatally
4. finally

ANSWERS TO EXERCISE 33.5

2. carrying
4. studies
6. dutiful
8. obeyed
10. coyly

ANSWERS TO EXERCISE 33.6

2. fastest
4. reference
6. regrettable
8. drastically
10. quarrelling

ANSWERS TO EXERCISE 33.7

2. hooves
4. babies
6. stepchildren
8. kilometres per hour
10. phenomena
12. beaches
14. golf clubs

ANSWERS TO EXERCISE 34.1

2. Unfortunately,
4. If you follow instructions carefully,
6. no comma needed
8. no comma needed
10. Founded by Alexander the Great,

ANSWERS TO EXERCISE 34.3

2. no comma needed
4. … power wire, which is usually red; … the ground wire, which is usually black.

6. Seymour Segal, one of Canada's most gifted painters, . . .
8. . . . was Karl Marx, who believed that his role as a social thinker . . .
10. aid, if one of them . . .

ANSWERS TO EXERCISE 34.4

2. The social sciences include economics, psychology, political science, anthropology, and sociology.
4. no comma needed
6. Superficial observation does not provide accurate insight into people's lives—how they feel, what they believe in, how they respond to others.
8. I timidly offered to help a loud, overbearing, lavishly dressed customer.
10. These armchair quarterbacks insist on reviewing every play, judging every move, and telling everyone within earshot exactly what is wrong with the team.

ANSWERS TO EXERCISE 34.5

2. Sophie, in fact, has supported . . .
4. Fictions about race, not the facts, influence human relations.
6. no comma needed
8. And now, customers, follow along as I demonstrate the latest in notebook computers.
10. This is imported pâté, not chopped liver.

ANSWERS TO EXERCISE 35.1

2. City life offers many advantages; however, in many ways, life in a small town is much more pleasant.
4. Physical education forms an important part of a school's program; nevertheless, few students and instructors clearly recognize its value.
6. Voltaire was concerned about the political implications of his scepticism; he warned his friends not to discuss atheism in front of the servants.
8. My high school was excessively competitive; virtually everyone went on to university, many to the top schools in the country.
10. Propaganda is defined as the spread of ideas to further a cause; therefore, propaganda and advertisement are synonymous terms.

ANSWERS TO EXERCISE 38.1

2. In Flannery O'Connor's short story "Revelation," colours symbolize passion, violence, sadness, and even "God."
4. The "fun" of surgery begins before the operation ever takes place.
6. "The Dream of Little Raven," a Chippewa tale in *Indian Legends of Canada*, reflects on a child's experience of loss and grief.

8. Pink Floyd's song "Time" depicts the growth of technology and its impact on society.

10. This review will examine a TV episode entitled "48 Hours on Gang Street."

ANSWERS TO EXERCISE 40.1

2. Eating at a restaurant, whether it be a fast-food, Chinese, or Italian place, is always a treat.

4. The Council of Trent was convened to draw up the Catholic response to the Protestant Reformation.

6. I wondered if my new Lee jeans were faded enough and if I could possibly scuff up my new Nikes just a little more before I arrived for spring term.

8. In this essay I will be citing the works of Vladimir Nabokov, in particular his novels *Pnin* and *Lolita* and his story "The Vane Sisters."

10. Few music lovers can resist the music of George Gershwin. (*Rhapsody in Blue* and *Porgy and Bess* are two personal favourites.)

ANSWERS TO EXERCISE 42.1

2. When people think about the word *business,* they may associate it with people and companies that care about nothing but making money.

4. The word *veterinary* comes from the Latin *veterinarius,* meaning "of beasts of burden."

6. Flying the *Glamorous Glennis,* a plane named for his wife, Chuck Yeager was the first pilot to fly faster than the speed of sound.

8. *The Waste Land* is a long and difficult but ultimately rewarding poem.

10. My grandparents remember the sinking of the *Titanic.*

ANSWERS TO EXERCISE 43.1

2. pre–World War II

4. correct

6. self-important

8. seven hundred thirty-three

10. correct

ANSWERS TO EXERCISE 44.1

2. Napoleon, the French ruler, invaded Egypt with many soldiers.

4. At Rosetta, near the Nile, some French soldiers were building a fort.

ANSWERS TO EXERCISE 44.2

Hollywood is famous for hiring various experts to teach people technically what most of us learn informally. A case in point is the story about the children of one movie couple who noticed a new child in the neighbourhood climbing a tree. The children immediately wanted to be given the name of his instructor in tree climbing.

ANSWERS TO EXERCISE 45.1

2. Ancient Egyptian writing was called hieroglyphics.
4. Very soon after its discovery, the French made copies of the stone.

ANSWERS TO EXERCISE 45.2

As my son grows, I have monitored the changing fashions in kiddie culture for words expressing deep admiration—what I called "cool" in my day, and my father designated "swell." The half-life seems to be about six months, as "excellent" (with curious lingering emphasis on the first syllable) gave way to "bad" (extended, like a sheep bleat, long enough to turn into its opposite), to "wicked," to "rad" (short for radical). The latest incumbent— "awesome"— possesses more staying power, and has been reigning for at least two years.

ANSWERS TO EXERCISE 46.1

2. correct; give up (phrasal verb)
4. The British took it back to England.
   took back (phrasal verb)

ANSWERS TO EXERCISE 47.1

2. Champollion enjoyed studing the language of the Middle East.
4. It was of great importance that he knew Coptic, a later form of the Egyptian language.
6. If the Rosetta Stone had not been discovered, it would have been much more difficult to decipher hieroglyphics.

ANSWER TO EXERCISE 47.2

The third sentence type.

Copyright Acknowledgments

Index of Authors and Titles

Subject Index